Advance praise

'Decision analysis has evolved in recent years to be increasingly synthetic, and this text is an impressive achievement in bringing together the diverse ingredients. It is highly recommended as a timely, integrated and practical course book.'

DEREK W. BUNN, Professor of Decision Sciences, London Business School

'This text makes a valuable contribution to the literature in decision making. The explicit goal of the authors has been to help the reader to understand the multifaceted field and learn the essentials in practical decision support. There is a balanced coverage of both descriptive and normative models with a strong emphasis on the process. The discussion of the social aspects and methods of participation in decision support contributes to the understanding of the big picture of this important field. The comprehensive list of up-to-date references gives the interested reader easy access to current research in the area.'

RAIMO P. HÄMÄLÄINEN, Professor and Director of the Systems Analysis Laboratory, Helsinki University of Technology

'The authors lead us in an exciting waltz through descriptive, prescriptive and normative models for decision aid. Other authors have addressed all three approaches, but none has woven together such a tapestry in which each modelling approach informs and is informed by the other approaches. Between them, the authors bring together expertise from a wide range of disciplines ranging from quantitative analysis, information systems and cognitive psychology. The text is a must for those wishing to gain comprehensive understanding of the subtleties of decision science.'

THEO STEWART, Professor of Statistical Sciences, University of Cape Town

Decision Behaviour, Analysis and Support

Behavioural studies have shown that, while we humans may be the best decision makers on the planet, we are not quite as good as we think we are. We are regularly subject to biases, inconsistencies and irrationalities in our decision making. *Decision Behaviour, Analysis and Support* explores perspectives from many different disciplines in order to help decision makers to deliberate and make better decisions. It considers the use of computers and databases to support decisions, as well as aids to building analyses and some 'fast-and-frugal' tricks to facilitate more consistent decision making. In its exploration of decision support the book draws together results and observations from decision theory, behavioural and psychological studies, artificial intelligence and information systems, philosophy, operational research and organisational studies. This provides a valuable resource for managers with decision-making responsibilities and students from a range of disciplines, including management, engineering and information systems.

SIMON FRENCH is Professor of Information and Decision Sciences at Manchester Business School, the University of Manchester.

JOHN MAULE is Professor of Human Decision Making and Director of the Centre for Decision Research at Leeds University Business School, University of Leeds.

NADIA PAPAMICHAIL is Senior Lecturer in Information and Decision Systems at Manchester Business School, the University of Manchester.

Decision Behaviour, Analysis and Support

Simon French,
John Maule and
Nadia Papamichail

CAMBRIDGE
UNIVERSITY PRESS

CAMBRIDGE UNIVERSITY PRESS
Cambridge, New York, Melbourne, Madrid, Cape Town,
Singapore, São Paulo, Delhi, Mexico City

Cambridge University Press
The Edinburgh Building, Cambridge CB2 8RU, UK

Published in the United States of America by Cambridge University Press, New York

www.cambridge.org
Information on this title: www.cambridge.org/9780521709781

First published 2009

A catalogue record for this publication is available from the British Library

Library of Congress Cataloguing in Publication data
French, Simon, 1950–
Decision behaviour, analysis and support / Simon French, John Maule, Nadia Papamichail.
p. cm.
Includes bibliographical references and index.
ISBN 978-0-521-88334-4 (hardback) 1. Decision making. I. Maule, John.
II. Papamichail, Nadia. III. Title.
T57.95.F73 2009
658.4003–dc22
2009004683

ISBN 978-0-521-88334-4 Hardback
ISBN 978-0-521-70978-1 Paperback

To Judy, Beth and George

Contents

Figures

Tables

Case vignettes

Abbreviations and notation

Abbreviation/notation Meaning

a_i	The ith action in the action space $A = \{a_1, a_2, \ldots, a_m\}$
$a \succcurlyeq b$	The DM holds a to be at least as good as b
$a \succ b$	The DM strictly prefers a to b
$a \sim b$	The DM is indifferent between a and b
AHP	Analytic hierarchy process
AI	Artificial intelligence
ANN	Artificial neural network
CBA	Cost–benefit analysis
c_{ij}	The consequence of taking action a_i when the state of the world is θ_j
CSCW	Computer-supported cooperative work
DA	Decision analyst
DBMS	Database management system
DM	Decision maker
DSS	Decision support system
D2P	Decisioning for decision support
EBA	Elimination by aspects
EIS	Executive information system
ES	Expert system
$Eu[a]$	Expected utility of action a
GDSS	Group decision support system
GIS	Geographic information system
HCI	Human–computer interface
KB-DSS	Knowledge-based decision support system
KMS	Knowledge management system
MAU	Multi-attribute utility
MAVA	Multi-attribute value analysis
MCDAid	Multi-criteria decision aid
MCDM	Multi-criteria decision making
MIS	Management information system

MODM	Multi-objective decision making
NPV	Net present value
OR	Operational research
$P(\theta)$	Subjective probability representing a DM's likelihood for the state θ
SEU	Subjective expected utility
SMART	Simple multi-attribute rating technique
SQL	Structured query language
$u(\cdot)$	A utility function representing a DM's preferences in conditions of uncertainty
$v(\cdot)$	An (ordinal) value function representing a DM's preferences in conditions of certainty
wGDSS	Web-based group decision support system
θ_j	The jth possible state of the world lying in the state space, $\Theta = \{\theta_1, \theta_2, \ldots, \theta_n\}$

Preface

An article by Ian Ayres in the *Financial Times Magazine* of 1 September 2007 begins:

How can a mathematical formula outperform a wine connoisseur? Or predict how the US Supreme Court will vote more accurately than a panel of legal experts? The answer lies partly in the overconfidence of humans and partly in the fast improving powers of database analysis.

In many ways these sentences chart the course we shall be steering in exploring decision making: how we do it and how we could do it better. Many behavioural studies have shown that, while we humans may be the best decision makers on the planet, we are not as good as we think we are. We are subject to biases, inconsistencies and – dare we say it? – irrationalities in our decision making. We could do better. Therefore, it is not surprising, perhaps, that computers bringing advanced forecasting algorithms to bear on vast modern databases that bulge with fact upon fact are able to outperform even the best experts in highly structured forecasting tasks.

Of course, this is not to suggest that computers are more intelligent than humans (we designed and programmed them, after all!), just that they are more consistent, able to keep more facts 'in mind' and less likely to be distracted by some outlying fact that runs against the broad thrust of evidence or, worse, some personal pet theory. They are not prone to overconfidence. Experts tend not to notice their failures. They fail to moderate their future predictions with the humility of their past inaccuracies.

Nor shall we suggest that we should leave prediction and decision making to computers: far from it. We believe that if we support people properly, perhaps with computers or perhaps just with a paper and pencil, then we can improve their decision-making behaviour. Most importantly, we believe that the responsibility for decision making should be left with the human. We do not seek to supplant humans, only support them.

Moreover, our book is about decision making, not forecasting. Certainly, forecasting is central to good decision making. It is surely impossible to choose rationally if we cannot predict to some degree the possible consequences of our actions. We also need to consider and listen to our values, however. Decision making is about how much we care about the possible outcomes as well as how likely these are. Which do we prefer? Keeney in his seminal 1992 book *Value-focused Thinking* exhorts us to use values to drive our decision making. If we do not focus on our objectives and goals, can we really select a course of action to achieve them? Accordingly, much of our text focuses on how we might understand our values and use them to drive our decision making. Once we understand what we are trying to achieve, how do we combine that self-knowledge with our understanding of the world and our forecasts of what might result from our actions? In short, how do we balance our values and uncertainties?

All this assumes that we know what our options are. Sometimes they are obvious; but many times we face a mess of ill-comprehended issues without any idea of what we might do – and, yes, in decision science 'mess' is a technical term! Our opening quotation from Ayres misses perhaps the most difficult aspect of much decision making, and the one that computers, as yet at least, cannot address: novel situations. Another skill that we emphasise, therefore, is issue and problem formulation. We need to learn to understand the world and to think creatively about the different decisions we can take in response to it.

Our text, then, is about supporting decision makers. This is not a task that a single discipline can address alone. Certainly, artificial intelligence, cognitive science, economics, information systems, mathematics, management science, psychology, philosophy and many other disciplines all have much that is cogent to say about decision making. Alone, however, they do not say enough. Only when we draw on many complementary perspectives can we see how to support and improve decision making. Thus our text is multidisciplinary.

For the last six paragraphs we have been committing a failing that we attribute to many others: we have been talking about 'decisions' without acknowledging that there are many types of decision that occur in many contexts. While many texts focus on one type of decision, perhaps strategic or operational, ours is more catholic. We consider many different types of decision that occur in many different contexts, and we recognise that the type of support that each needs may vary from context to context. That and our multidisciplinarity are, we believe, the contribution that this text makes to the literature.

To be more precise, our objectives are:

- to demonstrate that decision making permeates the activities of individuals, groups, organisations and society and that the characteristics of the choices faced vary greatly from context to context;
- to introduce cognitive and behavioural theories of how people make judgements and take decisions and the 'errors and biases' that may be found in these activities;
- to introduce some of the normative theories of how people should make decisions;
- to show how prescriptive approaches to decision support and analysis draw together our behavioural understandings of human judgement with the imperatives of normative theories to help improve decision making;
- to outline how such prescriptive decision support may be embedded in information systems; and
- to provide a guide to a very wide range of literature offering valuable perspectives on analysing and supporting decision making, thus reflecting the multidisciplinary nature of our topic.

We have written for a varied audience. Some of the material has been used with undergraduates in business studies, computer science, economics, mathematics and operational research. Other parts have been used to teach Masters students in a similar variety of subjects. Some have been used with Master of Business Administration (MBA) students, and some to support executive education. Many sections have served at more than one level. Other parts of the text derive from our research. We hope, nonetheless, that we have woven all the sections into a coherent whole. One of the joys of working across disciplines is that usually our students, whatever their background, find some new idea, theory or procedure to intrigue them. We hope that you do too.

Our one little indulgence has been to begin the majority of sections with what we believe are relevant quotations. This is possibly a dangerous indulgence. French began his 1986 book *Decision Theory: An Introduction to the Mathematics of Rationality* with the quotation '"I used to be indecisive, but now I am not so sure." Boscoe Pertwee (18th-Century wit)' (Rees, 1978: 37). He had originally heard it on the long-running BBC radio quiz *Quote...Unquote* in the late 1970s. Some thirty years after that broadcast, the show's presenter, Nigel Rees, admitted on another series of the same programme that he had been conned. Someone had made up the quotation and the life of the eighteenth-century wit to whom it was attributed purely to hoodwink Rees. That he also hoodwinked French was an unintended, and probably unnoticed, side effect! So, if you spot some further mistakes in the quotations that we have used: laugh quietly to yourself and don't tell us!

Simon French
John Maule
Nadia Papamichail

Acknowledgements

We are grateful to many people for comments and advice on the ideas in this text. Many cohorts of students have studied from various sections of the text. Some sections date back to Simon's text on decision theory published in 1986, now long out of print. We are grateful to all who have struggled with and helped us improve the many opaque passages. In addition, many colleagues and research students have worked with us on many of the ideas in the text. We thank them all.

Our families too have had a major input, being supportive over several years as we worked on drafts and revisions. To them we owe the biggest 'thank you'.

Reason is, and only ought to be, the slave of the Passions.

David Hume

Introduction

1.1 Decisions, decisions, decisions!

I really do hate making decisions. Life is so full of them. This evening I was fed up, and I told Thomasina how I felt. 'There are always choices to be made,' I complained. 'Whether to eat the meat that has been put out or to try the new crunchy things they've bought. Whether to go out mouse or shrew hunting. Whether to sharpen my claws on the oak tree or sycamore tree. And so on. Decisions. Decisions. Decisions.'

'You need to rest and relax,' said Thomasina.

'How?' I demanded.

'Go and lie down somewhere,' said Thomasina.

'Where?' I asked.

'Underneath the willow tree,' she replied. 'Or on the window seat. On the sofa. Or underneath the garden bench.'

Dear old Thomasina. She means well. (Vernon Coleman)

We make decisions all the time: whether to take the lift or the stairs; whether to buy a new car; whether to contradict our boss's latest edict; and so on. Some decisions have so little impact on our lives that we take them without much, if any, thought. Others have much greater potential impacts, and we reflect and deliberate upon the alternatives before choosing one. Some decisions are personal, some professional. How do we make decisions? How should we make them? Are we naturally good decision makers (DMs)? Can we learn techniques to improve our decision making? Can we develop computer programmes – *decision support systems* (DSSs) – that embody such techniques? These questions are essentially the ones that we address in the following chapters. We focus on the more significant of our decisions: whether to have a tea or a coffee can safely be left to whim.

No two situations that call for a decision are ever identical. They differ because a decision changes both the world and the DM in some small way, and neither can ever go back to the previous status quo. There are many other ways in which decisions differ, however: the context of the problem, the abilities, skills and dispositions of the people involved and the social context in which they find themselves (see figure 1.1).

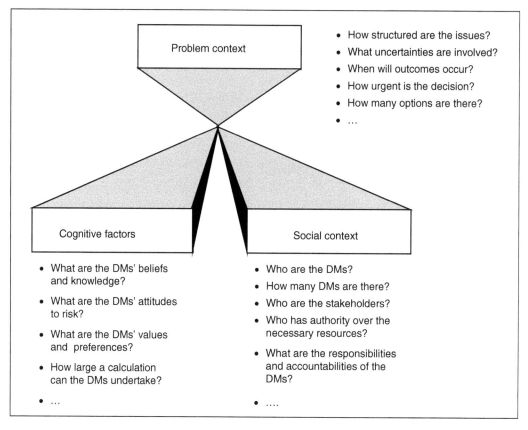

Figure 1.1   Factors that affect decision making
                     Source: Payne *et al.* (1993).

Our purpose in this chapter is to raise issues, introduce general ter
minologies and indicate topics that we cover in later chapters. We begin
by considering a broad categorisation that will give shape to much of our
discussion.

1.2 The strategy pyramid

You've got to be very careful if you don't know where you're going, because you might not get
there. (Yogi Berra)

Perhaps the most commonly discussed distinction between decisions is that
between strategic, tactical and operational decisions – the so-called *strategy
pyramid* (see figure 1.2). *Strategic* decisions set the goals for an organisation
or an individual. Mintzberg (1992) suggests that a strategy provides five P's:
a *plan* for future action; a *ploy* to achieve some end: a *pattern* of behaviour; a

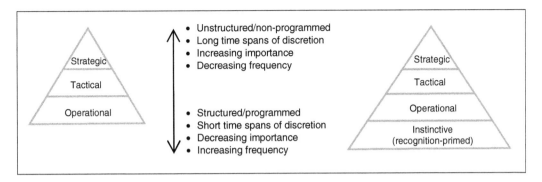

Figure 1.2   The strategy pyramid

position defined by goals and values; and a *perspective* on how to view the world. A strategy sets the direction and a broad framework in which more detailed decisions can be taken. *Tactical* and *operational* decisions fill in those details. Thus, a retail company might make a strategic decision to expand into a new region. It would then need to decide tactically in which towns and shopping malls it should establish itself and in what order it should open these. Operational decisions would develop and run the necessary supply chains, financial systems, staffing, etc. Similarly, a personal strategic decision might concern a career direction and be followed by operational and tactical decisions on where and for which company to work, how hard to strive for promotion, etc.

Simon (1960) notes that strategic decisions tend to be associated with *unstructured* or *non-programmed* problems. Seldom do DMs, such as a board of directors, come to a strategic issue with a straight choice between, say, various acquisitions. Rather, they first become aware that the company may need to grow. Through discussion, they formulate their objectives and the possible strategies they might follow. Only then do they have a strategic decision to make. In contrast, operational decisions are usually much more structured – for example, should an inventory level be increased to support a production plan or in what order should the production of various items be scheduled? Another concept, which correlates well with the unstructured/structured dimension, is that of the *time span of discretion* (Jacques, 1989). Roughly speaking, this relates to the length of time before the consequences of a decision have their full impact. The longer the time span of discretion the more unstructured and strategic the decision is likely to be.

The original 'three-level' strategy pyramid on the left of figure 1.2 misses an important type of decision. In many cases, DMs seem to match the current circumstances to something similar that has happened in the past and do roughly what they did then – or perhaps what they thought after the event they should have done. In such *recognition-primed* decision making (Klein, 1993) there is little or no comparison of options, just an instinctive choice of action. Therefore, we extend the strategy pyramid to include a fourth level. The term 'programmed' fits well with the idea of instinctive decision making based upon recognising that the current situation is familiar and that the action proven to be successful in the past is appropriate. Situations are rarely identical, however, so DMs often simulate how the usual action will play out in the new situation and what small modifications are necessary to increase its effectiveness. This form of decision making is common among experts who regularly make very similar kinds of decisions, such as surgeons deciding on how to suture a wound, bank managers deciding whether to extend a loan or fire chiefs deciding how to tackle a fire in a building.

Within the discipline of artificial intelligence (AI) much effort has been expended on developing knowledge-based decision support systems (KB-DSSs), which seek to 'automate' decision making. These tools operate at the lower levels of the strategy pyramid precisely because they need training – i.e. they need to be provided either with a set of rules that tells them how to recognise and react to different types of situations or they need data on how experienced DMs reacted in the past. One of AI's research objectives is to develop KB-DSSs that need less training and operate at the highest levels of the strategy pyramid. For the present, however, machines able to think strategically and creatively in unstructured, novel situations belong to the realm of science fiction; we discuss this topic further in chapter 5.

We note that the importance of a decision increases the further up the pyramid we go – i.e. the potential consequences of strategic decisions are much more significant than those of instinctive ones. Conversely, the frequency with which a decision – or, rather, type of decision – is faced increases towards the base: operational and instinctive decisions are much more common than strategic ones.

Jacques (1989) argues that the tasks and decision making undertaken by staff at different levels within an organisation may be characterised by the longest time span of discretion required by their roles. Jacques' theory is a mixture of the descriptive and normative – i.e. it includes observations of how organisations *are* structured and reflections on how they *should* be. In many empirical studies he has shown that the concept of the time span of discretion provides a useful explanatory tool. He goes further, however, and argues persuasively that organisations are best able to achieve their objectives when members of the organisation work at levels with time

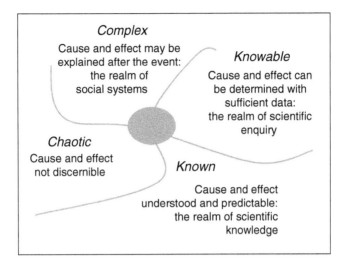

Figure 1.3   The cynefin model
Source: Snowden (2002).

spans of discretion within the limits of their ability to envisage the future. He terms such organisations *requisite*.

In his empirical studies, Jacques distinguishes four domains of activity:
- the *corporate strategic* domain, which sets the guiding values and vision and develops strategy to take the organisation towards these;
- the *general* domain, which develops an implementation plan for strategy;
- the *operational* domain, which organises the detailed delivery of the strategy; and
- the *hands-on work* domain, which delivers the work.

Note how these domains map onto the four levels (strategic, tactical, operational and instinctive) of the extended strategy pyramid (figure 1.2).

In the context of knowledge management, Snowden (2002) has argued for a further typology of decisions: the *cynefin*[1] model (figure 1.3). For decision contexts in the *known space*, cause and effect are fully understood. We know everything about the circumstances underpinning the choice, what the alternatives are and what consequences might arise from each. In the *knowable space* cause and effect relationships exist, but there are insufficient data immediately available to make immediate firm forecasts of the consequences of any action. In the *complex space* there are so many interacting causes and effects that predictions of system behaviours are

---

[1] *Cynefin* is Welsh for 'habitat', although it does not translate quite so simply into English: the word includes the cultural and social as well as the environmental aspects of habitat.

subject to considerable uncertainty. Indeed, the range of actions available may be very unclear. Typically, such complexity arises in social systems. In the *chaotic space* things happen beyond our experience and we cannot perceive any candidates for cause and effect.

Snowden suggests that decision making in the known space tends to consist of recognising patterns in the situation and responding with well-rehearsed actions: recognition-primed decision making. In the knowable space, there is more analysis than recognition, as the DMs learn from the available data about the precise circumstances faced. In statistical terms they need to fit general models to the particular data of the current situation. In the known and knowable spaces, situations are *repeatable*. Essentially identical[2] or extremely similar situations have occurred in the past and the DMs have learnt the underlying cause and effect relationships. Moreover, they have learnt what they would *like* to happen: experience has clarified their preferences and values so that they have clear objectives, often so clear that these are no longer explicitly articulated. Such repeatability is the bedrock of empirical science: see, for instance, our discussion of frequentism in the foundations of probability in section 8.2.

In the complex space the DMs' knowledge is poor: there is much less perceived structure. There are simply too many potential interactions. Situations are so different as to be unique. Analysis is still possible, but its style will be broader, with less emphasis on details. Decisions will be based more on judgement than objective data, and the emphasis will be on developing broad strategies that are flexible enough to accommodate changes as the situation evolves. Before making decisions there may be a need to pause and clarify objectives – i.e. for the DMs to reflect upon how their general preferences and values apply in the current context. Decision making in the chaotic space cannot be analytical because there is no concept of how to break things down into an analysis. The DMs will simply need to take some action and see what happens, probing until they can make some sort of sense of the situation, gradually drawing the context back into one of the other spaces.

Thus, in a sense, the structured/unstructured dimension of decision making curves around from the known to chaotic spaces in the cynefin model (see figure 1.4). Indeed, in many ways the cynefin model adds little to the earlier writings of Simon (1960, 1978) and others. What it does provide, however, is an intuitive representation of the ideas that focuses

---

[2] No two situations can be entirely identical, by virtue of their different location in space and/or time.

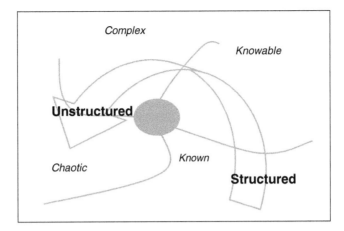

Figure 1.4   The cynefin model and the structured/unstructured dimension of decision
making
Note: Compare with figure 1.2.

attention on the knowledge and information available to the DMs. The
cynefin model also allows the dynamics of a sequence of decisions in a
changing environment to be represented usefully; in other words, as
knowledge and understanding of the situation changes, one moves into a
different quadrant of the model, suggesting the need for a different form of
decision making (see French and Niculae, 2005).

Note that there is much consistency here: the strategy pyramid, Simon's
structured/unstructured dimension, Jacques' concept of the time span of
discretion and Snowden's cynefin model essentially capture very similar
ideas.[3] Each offers a subtle alternative perspective, however, that informs
our understanding of the differences between decision contexts.

1.3 Rationalistic versus evolutionary strategic decision making

Most discussions of decision making assume that only senior executives make decisions or that
only senior executives' decisions matter. This is a dangerous mistake. (Peter Drucker)

It is tempting to think that decision making is nicely ordered. First one
makes strategic decisions to set context, values and direction; then it is
the turn of tactical decisions, to map in the details; operational decisions
to allocate resources and manage the work come next; and, finally, the

---

[3] Indeed, Snowden (2002; see also Snowden and Boone, 2007) also uses the ideas of cynefin to
discuss other issues, such as organisational culture and leadership, and in doing so captures
many of Jacques' views on these topics.

work itself is driven by almost unnoticed instinctive decision making. This chronologically ordered, logical perspective is, however, more often than not a complete fiction! Decision making is driven by events and developments in the external world as much as by some logical internal rationality. Thus, members of an organisation at any level may change what they do in order to gain some advantage, because the current situation has changed or is not as predicted. They might recognise some inefficiency or, more positively, the opportunities offered by some new technology. They might recognise a change in the behaviour of their customers and respond to that. Slowly a myriad of small changes at the operational or tactical levels can lead to quite significant changes at the strategic level: perceptions of values and strategic direction evolve. Such *emergent* strategic development is common in many – all? – organisations (Clarke, 2007; Mintzberg, 1987). Indeed, in our personal lives many major changes come about by events and happenstance rather than conscious decisions.

Our view is that both emergent and rationalistic decision making exist in all organisations. Strategy emerges and evolves in periods of 'calm'. Generally, all changes at different levels in the organisation are roughly, but not perfectly, aligned with an overall planned strategic direction; there is no careful, comprehensive analysis, however. Then some event or a growing awareness that some aspect of the organisation's business is not going as well as it might stimulates a period of reflection and deliberation on some or all parts of the strategy. At such times rationalistic thinking on strategy comes to the fore, decisions are made and a new strategy is adopted. Figure 1.5 illustrates this by 'funnels' of rational thinking

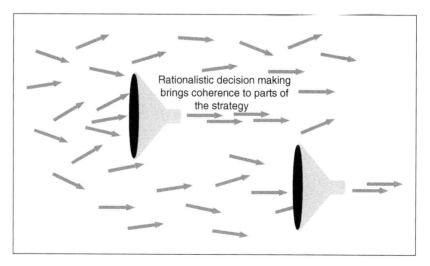

Rationalistic decision making brings coherence to parts of the strategy

Figure 1.5   The interplay between rationalistic and emergent strategic decision making

that bring coherence, aligning many, but seldom all, of an organisation's activities with a single direction. The funnels may operate at any level of the strategy pyramid and are not necessarily the same size, and some may be much larger, pulling most activities together and reflecting a major strategic deliberation.

In the following chapters our goal is to suggest how best to support these periods of rationalistic decision making. Nevertheless, while that is our emphasis, we are well aware that the context for such support will more often than not have been set by previous emergent strategy.

1.4 Players in a decision

If the people who make the decisions are the people who will also bear the consequences of those decisions, perhaps better decisions will result. (John Abram)

Notionally, the simplest decisions involve just one person: the DM. She[4] provides all the expert knowledge necessary, expresses her own judgements, performs her own analyses and makes her own decisions. In practice, however, this seldom happens. More often decisions are the responsibility of a group of DMs, such as a management board or a government department. They might involve others. They will probably work with accountants, scientists, engineers and other subject experts in order to acquire relevant information. Thus many will contribute to the process that leads to a choice and be a party to the decision making.

The *decision makers* are responsible for making the decision: they 'own the problem'. To be able to take and implement a decision, DMs need to hold the appropriate responsibility, authority and accountability.

- *Responsibility.* Individuals or groups are responsible for a decision if it is their task to see that the choice is made and implemented.
- *Authority.* Individuals or groups have the authority to take a decision if they have power over the resources needed to analyse and implement the choice.
- *Accountability.* Individuals or groups are accountable for a decision if they are the ones who take the credit or blame for the decision process and for the choice that is made, how it is implemented and the final outcome of that choice.

At various points in the decision process, responsibility may pass between different groups of DMs. When this happens, it is very important that

---

[4] We refer to an individual DM in the feminine and, shortly, the decision analyst (DA) in the masculine, creating a natural contrast in our language.

the appropriate authority and accountability are also passed across. When responsibility, authority and accountability do not pass between groups in a coherent fashion, there is an obvious danger that the decision-making process becomes dysfunctional.

The DMs are accountable to some, but not necessarily all, of the *stakeholders*. Stakeholders share, or perceive that they share, the impacts arising from a decision. They have a claim, therefore, that their perceptions and values should be taken into account – and in many cases they are. The DMs are stakeholders, if only by virtue of their accountabilities; but stakeholders are not necessarily DMs. The obvious stakeholders in a business are its shareholders or partners, but there are many others – e.g. employees, customers, unions, suppliers, local communities. In the public sector, the government and its agencies generally have many stakeholders, such as the public, industry, consumers or political parties; and accountability is correspondingly much broader.

Experts provide economic, marketing, scientific and other professional advice, which is used to formulate and understand the problem and assess the likelihood of the many eventualities that will affect the decision outcome. We often adopt the classical use of the term 'science' and use it to refer to a broad range of human knowledge. The knowledge that experts impart is used in the modelling and forecasting of outcomes of potential decisions. The DMs may have advisers who undoubtedly are experts in this sense, but they are unlikely to be the only experts involved. Other experts may advise some of the stakeholders, informing their perceptions and hence influencing the decision making.

Analysts develop and conduct the analyses, both quantitative and qualitative, that draw together the empirical evidence and expert advice to assess the likelihood of possible outcomes. They work with the DMs to clarify and elicit their uncertainties and values. They will also be concerned with a synthesis of the stakeholders' value judgements. These analyses are used to inform the DMs and guide them towards a balanced decision, reflecting the various expert and stakeholder inputs and the emphases that the DMs wish to give these. Whereas experts support decision making by providing information on the *content* of the decision, such as relevant economic data, the assessment of physical risks or whatever, analysts provide *process* skills, helping to structure the analysis and interpret the conclusions. For this reason, analysts are sometimes referred to as process experts.

Figure 1.6 offers a simplified representation of the interrelationship between experts, stakeholders, DMs and analysts. This separation of roles is, of course, very idealised. Some parties to a decision may take on several

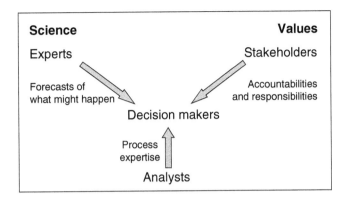

Figure 1.6   The players in a decision

roles. We have noted that DMs are necessarily stakeholders because of their accountabilities, but they may also be content experts and may conduct their own analyses. Similarly, experts may be stakeholders, and vice versa. Analysts may also be content experts and stakeholders, although there is a danger of bias entering the process if the analysts are too 'involved' in the decision itself. For this reason, it is common to arrange matters such that at least some of the team of analysts are dissociated from the issues (Eden and Radford, 1990).

Returning to the number of DMs involved, we consider four contexts for decision making: individual, group, organisation and societal. In the first and simplest case, a single DM is involved, obviating any need to consider issues such as communication, honesty or democratic choice. In the second, a group of individuals are jointly responsible for deciding upon a course of action. In the third, a legal entity – i.e. an organisation – takes the course of action, although the decision could be taken by an individual, such as the chief executive officer (CEO), or a group, such as a board of directors. Finally, society may 'take' decisions in some 'democratic' manner. Until chapter 11, we concentrate on issues relating to individual decision making, although we often refer to DMs in the plural when there is no risk of confusion.

1.5 Representation of decision problems

While we are free to choose our actions, we are not free to choose the consequences of our actions. (Stephen Covey)

How might a decision be represented – i.e. modelled? Here we sketch three ways that underpin much of our later discussion. For the moment,

Table 1.1 A decision table

		State			
		θ_1	θ_2	. . .	θ_n
	a_1	c_{11}	c_{12}	. . .	c_{1n}
	a_2	c_{21}	c_{22}	. . .	c_{2n}
Actions	.	.	.	. . .	.
	.	.	.	. . .	.
	.	.	.	. . .	.
	a_m	c_{m1}	c_{m2}	. . .	c_{mn}

however, our purpose is not so much to begin the process of modelling as to introduce particular concepts, terminology and notation.

Perhaps the simplest way of modelling a decision is via a *decision table* (see table 1.1). Generally, in a decision there are some things under the DM's control and some beyond it. The former define the *action space*, $A = \{a_1, a_2, \ldots, a_m\}$ – i.e. the set of options from which the DM may choose. The latter – exogenous factors – are referred to as *states of the world* or, simply, *states*. The *state space*, $\Theta = \{\theta_1, \theta_2, \ldots, \theta_n\}$, represents the range of possible futures that the DM believes might occur. The *consequence*, c_{ij} lying in some *consequence space*, C, that the DM receives is determined both by the chosen action a_i and the state of the world θ_j that pertains.

$$\text{action} \oplus \text{state} \rightarrow \text{consequence}$$

$$a_i \oplus \theta_j \rightarrow c_{ij}$$

If she knew the state that actually holds, which we call the *true state* (without venturing into philosophical questions of what 'truth' is), then she could predict the consequence of her choice with certainty. Let us give these symbols some substance through a trivial example (see table 1.2). A mother is planning the evening meal. She knows that her husband will be home, but does not know whether her son will be. She cannot reach her son on his mobile. She is planning a meal of steak. There are three steaks in the freezer, but her microwave is broken so she must defrost the number she needs now: two or three. Thus her choice is between defrosting two or three steaks: $A = \{\text{defrost two steaks, defrost three steaks}\}$. There are also two possible states: her son is staying in for dinner or going out: $\Theta = \{\text{son wants dinner, son does not want dinner}\}$. The consequences might be those described in table 1.2. The point to note is that, irrespective of

Table 1.2 The decision table for the family meal example

	State	
Action	Son is going out with his friends.	Son is staying in.
Defrost two steaks	Son goes out; mother and father have quiet meal together.	Mother has to replan and prepare meal; nice family dinner, though son feels he wasn't expected; two unused, but thawed, steaks.
Defrost three steaks	Son goes out; mother and father have quiet meal together; one steak is unused.	Pleasant family meal.

whether these consequences seem reasonable, the entries in table 1.2 are *descriptions*, not numbers. The symbols c_{ij} should *not* be interpreted as numerical variables.

Returning to the general format (table 1.1), the DM must choose a row in the face of an unknown choice of column. Note that there is a risk of anthropomorphising nature here. A classic paper in the field by Milnor (1954), entitled 'Games against nature', presents one approach for dealing with uncertainty in decision making in which the DM plays a strategy against a strategy 'chosen' by nature. There is an asymmetry, however: the DM *chooses* an action; the true state just *is*. There is no expression of free will on the part of nature. What we can see is that the state space Θ in a broad sense bounds the DM's uncertainty.

Our notation suggests that everything is finite: there are m actions, n states and $m \times n$ consequences – and one may take a philosophical stance that this is indeed so. One is never really faced with an infinite number of options. For instance, in an investment problem one can choose to invest sums only to the nearest £1, or perhaps £100. Thus there are only truly a finite number of options. When we come to explore some of the optimisation methods that are used in operational research (OR) and decision analysis, however, we find it advantageous to allow both the action and state spaces, and hence the consequence space, to become infinite. For instance, in an investment problem we may consider investing, say, £x, where x is any real number between 0 and 10,000.

In the late 1940s and early 1950s the decision table representation was much discussed, particularly among statisticians, economists and OR scientists. Three categories of problem were central to this discussion: decisions under certainty, decisions with risk and decisions with strict uncertainty.

Decisions under certainty. In these the DM either knows or learns the 'true' state before she has to make her choice. There is no uncertainty in her decision, therefore; she simply has to choose the option that brings her the best outcome. Of course, identifying which outcome she feels is best may not be trivial, requiring her to balance conflicting objectives; for example, safety cannot usually be maximised at the same time as profit. Moreover, if the numbers of actions or states is very large, the optimisation problem of identifying the best alternative can be mathematically difficult.

Decisions with risk. Although the DM does not know the true state for certain, she does have some knowledge, which makes some of the possible states seem to her to be more likely than others.

Decisions under strict uncertainty. Here the DM feels that she can say *nothing at all* about the true state. She is prepared to identify only what states may be possible.

We concentrate on the support of decisions under certainty and with risk, but for reasons given in French (1986) are almost silent on decisions under strict uncertainty. Essentially, the more one seeks to define the concept of strict uncertainty the more slippery and ill-defined it seems to become, leading to irrational prescriptions for decision making.

In the case of decisions under risk, the problem facing the DM is that she wishes to construct a ranking of the actions that reflects her preferences between the consequences taking into account her beliefs about the unknown state. We approach such problems via the *subjective expected utility* (SEU) model. In later chapters we discuss our reasons for doing this at some length. Here we simply note its form. Central to SEU analysis is the separation of the modelling of the DM's beliefs and preferences by, respectively,[5]

- a *subjective probability distribution*, $P(.)$, which represents her beliefs about the unknown state of the world; and
- a utility function, $u(.)$, which represents her preferences.

These obey the following three key properties, which together define the SEU model.

(1) The subjective probability distribution represents the DM's beliefs in the sense that

$$P(\theta) > P(\theta')$$

[5] If you are uncomfortable with mathematical symbolism, bear up. There is relatively little in this text, and you can manage to a large extent by focusing on the numerical examples. Skim-read the formal mathematics.

if and only if, after due reflection, she believes state θ to be more likely to occur than θ'.

(2) The utility function represents her preferences in the sense that

$$u(c) > u(c')$$

if and only if, after due reflection, she strictly prefers consequence c to consequence c'.

(3) The SEU model asserts that, to combine her beliefs and preferences coherently in order to rank the actions, the DM should form *expected utilities*:

$$Eu[a_i] = \sum_{j=1}^{n} P(\theta_j) u(c_{ij}) = P(\theta_1) u(c_{ij})$$
$$+ P(\theta_2) u(c_{i2}) + \ldots + P(\theta_n) u(c_{in})$$

Then she should rank a_i above a_k if and only if its expected utility is higher – i.e.

$$Eu[a_i] > Eu[a_k]$$

In the meal example, suppose that the mother believes that her son is 60 per cent likely to go out and, hence, 40 per cent likely to stay in. Suppose that, feeling that the best outcome is a pleasant family meal, and the worst a disgruntled son, she assigns[6] utilities as in table 1.3.

Note that this analysis is extremely simple; 'simplistic' or 'naïve' would be better words. Much of the rest of this book is about bringing sophistication into the way that this approach is used in real decision analyses. For our purposes here, however, it should serve to introduce the mechanics of SEU calculations.

We also note in passing that the SEU model has a long history of providing the model of *rational economic man*, a key concept in economic theory embodying a conception of perfect rationality. Rational economic man's behaviour is something of a contrast to that of most of us. We, it transpires, are seldom rational beings, at least in the sense that he is. Behavioural decision studies build on empirical observations to describe how people actually *do* make decisions. Such studies seek to understand real, not idealised, behaviour. The general finding is that people do not decide in accord with normative models, and, rather pejoratively, their departures from such rationality are dubbed 'biases'. Decision analysis starts from the premise that real decision makers would like their behaviour to

---

[6] Note that in chapter 8 we discuss how she might 'assign' these utilities.

Table 1.3 The decision table for the family meal example with probabilities and utilities

	State	
Action	Son is going out with his friends. *Probability:* 0.6	Son is staying in. *Probability:* 0.4
Defrost two steaks	Son goes out; mother and father have quiet meal together. *Utility:* 0.9	Mother has to re-plan and prepare meal; nice family dinner, though son is upset because he feels that he wasn't expected; two unused, but thawed, steaks. *Utility:* 0.0
Defrost three steaks	Son goes out; mother and father have quiet meal together; one steak is unused. *Utility:* 0.4	Pleasant family meal. *Utility:* 1.0

Then the expected utility of defrosting two steaks $= 0.6 \times 0.9 + 0.4 \times 0.0 = 0.54$. The expected utility of defrosting three steaks $= 0.6 \times 0.4 + 0.4 \times 1.0 = 0.64$. Thus, the expected utility would suggest that she should thaw three steaks.

conform to the ideals embodied in rationalistic – or, as we call them, normative – decision models, and that they need guidance to move from their instinctive but less rational ways of choosing to something rather better. We discuss decision theory and behavioural decision studies, but an understanding of decision analysis is our ultimate goal.

We now move onto two further representations of decision problems: *decision trees* and *influence diagrams*. We introduce these in the context of a research and development (R&D) decision, albeit a much simplified one.

Figure 1.7 presents a decision tree for a plant investment problem. A company is concerned with whether to invest in an R&D programme and, if that is successful, whether to invest further in a plant to bring the outcome of the programme to market. The initial decision is represented by the square to the left of the figure in which there are three possible courses of action:

- do not invest in the R&D programme;
- invest moderately in the R&D programme; or
- invest highly in the R&D programme.

If the company makes no investment, the decision making 'finishes'. This is indicated by the triangle. If they do invest in R&D,

- it may turn out poorly (a bad outcome),

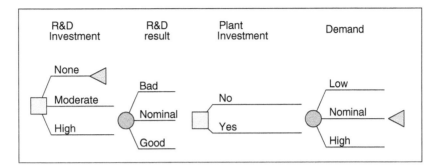

Figure 1.7   A decision tree for a plant investment problem

- about as expected (the nominal outcome), or
- better than expected (a good outcome).

This uncertainty is represented by the circle and three branches. The company then faces the decision as to whether to invest in improved plant, indicated by the square in the middle of the figure, and finally this investment may lead to low, nominal or high sales revenues, indicated by the circle and three branches to the right of the figure. The final triangle indicates that no further contingencies are considered within the decision tree model.

In summary, a decision tree lays out the sequence of decisions in a problem, together with the contingencies that may arise from taking a particular option. Very roughly, time flows from left to right across the diagram. Squares represent decision points; circles, chance points; and triangles, end points.

In drawing figure 1.7 we have used a 'non-standard' convention. For example, we have included just one R&D result node, on the understanding that it applies after *both* a moderate and a high investment. In 'traditional' decision trees this node would be duplicated, at the end of each investment branch. Similar remarks apply to the plant investment decision and the demand chance node. Some of our later examples use a full representation and you will see that they quickly become very bushy (see, for example, section 8.5).

Figure 1.8 provides an alternative perspective, using what is known as an *influence diagram*, on the same plant investment decisions. Again, squares are used to indicate decisions and circles or ellipse used to indicate uncertainties. The arrows do not indicate a flow of time from left to right, however, or the range of possibilities that might result from either a decision or chance. Rather, the arrows indicate dependencies that are reflected by the way the DM looks at the problem. For instance, the

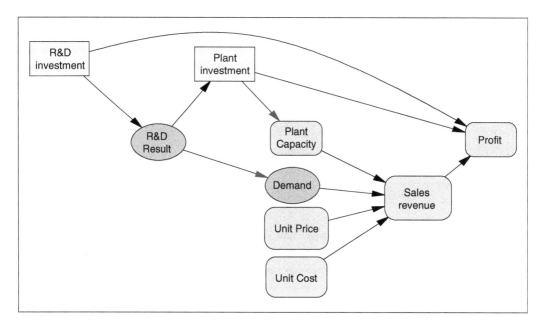

Figure 1.8   An influence diagram for the plant investment problem

sales revenue depends on the plant capacity, the demand, the unit price and the unit cost. Rounded rectangles indicate quantities that will be of concern to the DM, and the arrows represent influences between these – i.e. when the DM learns the R&D result this will affect her assessment of the likely demand: will the product be attractive? Equally, the absence of an arrow between nodes indicates that learning about one would not directly affect her beliefs about the other. In probabilistic terms, the arrows in influence diagrams represent conditional dependencies, and the absence of an arrow between a pair of nodes represents conditional independence.

An influence diagram can be used to represent the structure of a DM's knowledge – i.e. her beliefs – simply by avoiding the use of decision or value nodes. Such diagrams are usually referred to as *belief nets*, and are very common in the field of AI (Jensen, 1996, 2001; Oliver and Smith, 1990). We also note that the literature on influence diagrams and belief nets is relatively new, dating from the 1970s (Howard and Matheson, 2005a, 2005b), and that there is little consensus yet on the precise interpretation of arcs: one question, for example, is whether an arc implies any causality (Dawid, 2002; Howard, 1990; Lauritzen, 2004; Nadkarni and Shenoy, 2004; Pearl, 2000). A reader should take particular care therefore to take note of any individual author's definition of the concepts and notation.

Decision trees and influence diagrams provide complementary perspectives on a problem. A decision tree emphasises temporal contingencies between actions and possible events, whereas an influence diagram emphasises relationships between knowledge and beliefs, showing dependencies and independencies between beliefs. Decision trees have a disadvantage in that they can soon become so bushy that comprehending them becomes very difficult. Splitting the tree into sub-trees can mitigate this, but the difficulty remains. Influence diagrams, on the other hand, are more compact and can represent larger problems without challenging the DM's comprehension so much. They cannot easily represent *asymmetric decision problems*, however, in which a particular choice of action makes available different choices of action at subsequent decision nodes: see the airliner problem for an example (section 8.5). Unfortunately, asymmetric problems are the rule rather than the exception in practice.

As we shall see in chapter 8, the SEU ideas and methods carry across very simply into decision trees and influence diagrams. We should also note that there is seldom a need to choose between a decision table, decision tree, influence diagram or any other model of a problem, because few situations can be addressed with a single model. The world is typically complex: models are simplifications, so to appreciate the subtleties of a situation DMs often need a family of complementary models, each with its own informative perspective.

1.6 Some other terminology

A decision is a commitment to a course of action that is intended to produce a satisfying state of affairs. (Frank Yates, Elizabeth Veinott and Andrea Palatino)

We have not yet really defined a decision per se, although we have said much about the possible contexts and models. The definition above, from Yates *et al.* (2003), is typical of many, although it begs such questions as what is meant by 'intended' and what happens if all possible outcomes are far from satisfying – e.g. how would you prefer to be executed? Anglo-American writers tend to consider a decision as the selection of a course of action at given point in time. Some French writers, such as Roy (1996), see a decision as a process that changes one state of affairs into another. We tend to the Anglo-American view with its focus on a point of choice, although we recognise that any decision is embedded in a process that moves from discussion and deliberation through the selection of an alternative and onto implementation. Indeed, it is our purpose to support this process through the provision of appropriate decision analysis and DSS.

Some writers, like us, make no distinction between *choice* and *decision*; Allingham (2002) titles his book on decision theory *Choice Theory*. Others do make a distinction, however, requiring decisions to be preceded by rational deliberation, while choices are unthinking acts of selection. Thus one might argue that the DM would decide which car to hire, but choose a mint imperial from a bag of sweets. We avoid this distinction, because it is hard to maintain in the face of detailed examination. At the car hire firm, suppose the DM is offered the choice between black and blue, but otherwise identical, cars. She might choose blue automatically, because she likes blue more than black. There is certainly reason for her choice; but is there deliberation? On the other hand, in looking at the bag of sweets, she might see both mint imperials and toffees; and she might much prefer toffees. She might also have a dental crown, however, that is liable to become detached if she chews toffees. Balancing up the threat of a lost crown, discomfort and an expensive visit to the dentist with the additional enjoyment of a toffee over a mint imperial, after some heart-searching she selects a mint imperial. What if she had weighed things up on leaving the dentist last month and resolved never to eat another toffee? Then, when offered the bag of sweets, she selects the mint imperial without any reflection. Did she choose or did she decide? In part, this discussion raises the question of whether recognition-primed decision making is really decision making. For the reasons outlined above, we take it to be so, and move on.

Inference, also known as *induction*, is the process of learning from data. *Prediction*, or *forecasting*, is the process of building upon this learning to assess the likelihood of future events and the consequences of possible actions. Inference and prediction should preceed decision. The DM should learn from all the available data and forecast what is likely to happen if she should take each of the possible actions being considered, before committing to one of these actions. Inference, prediction and decision making are, therefore, intimately connected (French and Ríos Insua, 2000).

Risk is a much-used word in decision making; it is also one of the most ill-defined (Moore, 1983; Renn, 1998b; Vlek, 1996). Sometimes it is used just to indicate the hazardous event that might happen; sometimes it is used to describe the likelihood of it happening; sometimes it is used to quantify the magnitude of its potential impact on a variety of stakeholders; and sometimes some combination of all three. We eschew any technical definition, and tend to use the word in combinations that are well defined – e.g. 'decisions with risk'.

We should also recognise that words such as *theory* and *model* are far from unambiguous: they have subtly different meanings in different disciplines. Management models are qualitative, accounting models are quantitative and computer models are programmes. We tend to use words informally, relying on the context to provide the meaning (though see the further discussion in section 7.1).

Finally, it has recently been suggested by Howard (2004) that we need to standardise the language used by decision scientists. While it would be nice to have clear terminology used by all, thus reducing the potential for ambiguity, we do not believe that such a move can ever be successful. The concepts, theories and techniques of decision theory find much of their value in application, and that means that analysts need to communicate with DMs, stakeholders and experts. Communication generally, but particularly communication with clients, requires that the parties negotiate and agree a language. Since everybody makes decisions, all the participants in a decision analysis begin with their own terminology – albeit an everyday one; and it would be a very strong decision analyst who could completely impose his terminology over the everyday language of the others. Accordingly, we do not seek or claim to offer a standardised terminology.

1.7 Outline of the book

We begin in the next chapter with an introduction to behavioural studies of decision making. Here we learn that unguided human judgement and decision making are rather more fallible than we might think, and that all of us – and we do mean all of us! – could be rather better at decision making if we but paused and took advice. At many points during the rest of the book we return to behavioural issues and reflect upon their implications for supporting DMs. Chapter 3 introduces a broad outline for the process of supporting decision making. Here we discuss the interaction between three kinds of decision studies and analyses. Descriptive decision models are used by psychologists to describe and 'explain' the behaviours that we introduce in chapter 2. Descriptive or empirical decision science is about how we *do* make decisions. Normative models, on the other hand, have been used by philosophers, economists, management scientists and others to explore how we *should* make decisions. Supporting decision making requires us to draw on both types of model. Thus, in prescriptive decision analysis and support,[7] we need to be mindful of the behavioural characteristics of the DMs with whom we are working as we guide them towards the rationality of an appropriate normative theory.

---

[7] Beware: not all writers distinguish as clearly between 'normative' and 'prescriptive' as we do.

In chapter 4 we turn to information and knowledge management and the computer systems that provide access to basic data and knowledge on which to build our decision analyses. Then in chapters 5 to 10 we look at a range of decision support methods. We begin with AI methods, which are particularly suited to the hands-on domain, then consider OR techniques, which support decision making in the operational and general domains, before outlining the tools of decision analysis applicable to the corporate strategic domain. In each chapter we are careful to explore the behavioural reasons for providing support. What biases or dysfunctional behaviours are we trying to counter and what normative ideals are we trying to encourage?

Chapters 11, 12 and 13 discuss specific issues relating to group, organisational and societal decision making that were left implicit in earlier chapters. We also enter discussions on democracy, finding that democratic decision making is not as transparent a concept as one might think. Given that most decisions are made in groups, organisations and society, it may seem perverse that so much of the book is focused on individual decision making. It is our thesis, however, that decision making is essentially an individual activity. It involves intentionality, an expression of free will. Groups, from our perspective, are essentially social processes that draw together individual behaviours; so, to understand decision making in groups, we first need to understand individual decision making in depth.

In chapter 14 we return to a more general discussion of decision support systems, their design and their evaluation. Finally, in chapter 15, we offer some concluding thoughts on the process of decision support and future developments in decision science.

1.8 Background reading

This book draws together material from many literatures. Few other texts take such a multidisciplinary view (we note Kleindorfer *et al.*, 1993, Teale *et al.*, 2003, and von Winterfeldt and Edwards, 1986). Buchanan and O'Connell (2006) offer a history of decision making through the ages. The *Harvard Business Review* has published many key papers in the area (see, for example, *Harvard Business Review*, 2001, and Stewart, 2006). O'Brien and Dyson (2007) provide an introduction to strategic development that parallels and complements many of the themes in this text. Other background reading is cited as material is encountered in the following chapters.

Finally, Bazerman (2006), Gigerenzer (2002) and Hammond *et al.* (1998) are excellent texts for convincing you that there is a need to study decision making and seek to improve your choice behaviour.

1.9 Exercises and questions for discussion

(1) Before reading further, what do you think makes a good decision? How would you define rationality? Do you want your decision making to be rational?

(2) Give some examples from your own experience of strategic, tactical, operational, and instinctive decision making.

(3) What is the role of emotion in decision making?

(4) 'Good decisions have good outcomes.' Discuss.

(5) Write down up to three bad and three good decisions that you have made in your life. Compare the decisions and write down what was it that made each good or bad.

Behavioural decision studies

Everyone complains of his memory, no one of his judgement. (François de La Rochefoucauld)

2.1 Introduction

Behavioural or empirical decision science is concerned with how people actually make decisions – i.e. descriptive studies of human behaviour. In section 1.5 we briefly outlined SEU theory, a normative approach specifying how people *should* decide in the face of uncertainty if they wish to be rational. More broadly, there are many other normative theories that seek to encapsulate the essence of rational decision making, each doing so in a different context. We indicate more of what we mean by this in the next chapter, but the key point here is that each normative theory is based upon a number of simple axioms or assumptions that are generally plausible and that, their proponents argue, characterise rational decision behaviour. In this chapter we explore research investigating the extent to which people actually make decisions in ways that are compatible with a particular normative theory of risky decision making, based on the maximisation of SEU. We show that this normative theory rarely predicts human choice and that we need to develop a different set of theories, referred to as descriptive theories, if we are to predict and explain the ways in which people actually make decisions. Further, in this chapter we consider the extent to which differences between normative and descriptive theories indicate important limitations in human decision making, and suggest how knowledge of these limitations can be used for developing procedures to improve our decision making.

Our objectives in this chapter are thus:

- to introduce empirical studies of decision-making behaviour;
- to demonstrate that unguided human decision making is not as flawless as we might hope;
- to show how an understanding of these flaws not only indicates a strong need for decision support, but also provides important insights about the nature of the support that is needed; and

- to introduce theories and models that seek to explain observed decision-making behaviour.

The chapter begins by reviewing research investigating whether people choose according to the SEU model and its underlying axioms, showing how this body of work has given rise to an alternative theory, prospect theory, which we introduce in section 5. Then, in sections 6 and 7, we consider whether people are able to make *effective* judgements of risk and uncertainty. Finally, in section 8 we briefly review research on the effects of emotion on decision making.

2.2 Do people choose in accordance with the rational SEU model?

The average man's judgement is so poor, he runs a risk every time he uses it. (Edgar W. Howe)

A virtue of a normative decision theory is that it specifies in precise terms the elements that underpin rational decision making and how these should be combined. The SEU model suggests that, in risky situations, these elements are associated with the probability and utilities of outcomes. Researchers have usually tested the descriptive validity of the rational model by investigating how people choose from a set of gambles, since a gamble is an archetypal risky situation – i.e. it involves clearly specified probabilities and outcomes. Generally, the findings show that participants in research studies do not always choose the gamble with the highest subjective expected utility (Beach and Connolly, 2005; Tversky, 1967), suggesting that the SEU model is a poor descriptive model of how people actually make decisions. Indeed, if the model cannot predict choice behaviour in simple gambling situations in which the probabilities and utilities are the only information presented and very clearly specified, it seems highly unlikely that it can predict human decision making in more complex managerial and organisational settings in which information is often incomplete and vague.

How should we interpret this failure of SEU theory to predict how people make decisions? One approach has been to argue that the theory may predict human choice in some situations but not others – e.g. it predicts successfully across a long series of choices, but not when a single choice is being considered (Lopes, 1981). From this standpoint people might be considered to be particularly vulnerable when making one-off decisions, given that these are less likely to be based on the normative theory than repeated decisions.[1] A second approach has been to augment the theory to increase its ability to predict actual choice behaviour – e.g. adding an extra component to take account of the fact that people may have a utility for gambling (Diecidue *et al.*, 2004; Fishburn, 1980) or anticipated regret (Loomes and Sugden, 1982). Adding these components can indeed increase the extent to which the theory can predict choices between gambles, but, since they are not specified by the underlying axioms, we may question whether people ought to be influenced by them, if they wish to be rational. Also, there seems to be little agreement about what these added elements ought to be.

Simon (1960) argued that people have limited cognitive capacity and so are unable to carry out all the mental operations that are required by the SEU model – or, indeed, many other normative models. His view was that, instead, people use simpler decision strategies that involve processing less information, often in a much simpler way. One such strategy, *satisficing*, involves establishing a minimum standard for each attribute[2] of an action or outcome and then choosing the first alternative that meets these standards. For instance, according to many normative models, when purchasing a house a buyer should develop an overall evaluation of all houses that are available (and there are usually a lot of them!) in terms of how each performs on all the attributes that he or she feels are important (e.g. cost, closeness to work, 'atmosphere'), making sure that each attribute is weighted appropriately to take account of the importance he/she attaches to it. Not only does this suggest a lot of cognitive processing, evaluating and weighting attributes and then aggregating them into an overall evaluation of each available house, but there is also a substantial load placed on the memory, given that the buyer needs to remember all these overall evaluations in order to choose the best. In contrast to this, in satisficing the buyer considers each house in turn to see whether it meets the minimum standard set for each attribute. If a house fails to meet a standard it is immediately rejected (and any evaluations already undertaken can be forgotten). As soon as a house meets all the standards it is chosen; though, of course, it might be the case that an option, yet to be considered, might be better – the DM would never know.

Satisficing means that DMs choose the first option that is reasonable rather than the best. Since many people have limited time and resources

---

[1] It should be noted, however, that SEU theory explicitly seeks to include a valuation of the risk inherent in one-off decisions: see our discussion of risk attitude in section 8.4.

[2] We discuss and define *attributes* in more detail later (see section 7.3). For the present, an informal understanding is sufficient.

to make decisions this may be better than trying to implement the rational model, given the lower demands this strategy makes on mental and other resources. Indeed, Simon suggested that there are often regularities in the environment (e.g. redundancy between different pieces of information) such that it is often not necessary to process all the available information. In these situations satisficing may perform quite as well as the rational model. He called this phenomenon *bounded rationality*, since people are using bounded or rather simpler strategies yet maintaining decision accuracy at a comparable level to that derived from the rational model. Since Simon's seminal work, researchers have identified many other strategies that people adopt when making decisions (see, for example, Svenson, 1979) and have provided evidence showing that simpler strategies, often referred to as *fast-and-frugal* – or, in the vernacular, quick and dirty – heuristics, can indeed do quite as well as, and sometimes better than more complex ones (Gigerenzer *et al.*, 1999). We discuss some of these in section 3.8.

Taken together, these findings show that people rarely, if at all, make decisions according to the SEU model, and that this is due in large part to the cognitive demands of choosing in this way. This conclusion has provided one of the primary reasons for developing the kinds of decision aids discussed in later chapters. Many of these aids structure the decision process so that it follows the approach advocated by the rational model and, at the same time, provide support mechanisms that address the problems arising from limitations in human cognitive capacity.

2.3 The sure-thing axiom

He is no wise man that will quit a certainty for an uncertainty. (Samuel Johnson)

A second way of assessing whether the SEU model is descriptive of how people actually make decisions is to investigate whether they behave in accordance with the axioms of the model. When asked, most people agree that these axioms[3] are acceptable and are principles that should be followed when making decisions (MacCrimmon, 1968). Research has shown that people often behave in ways that violate these axioms, however, even when the implications of the axioms are explained to them in the context of their choice (Slovic and Tversky, 1974). In this section we outline some

---

[3] Strictly, we should not say *the* axioms underlying SEU theory, for there are many derivations of the SEU model from apparently different sets of axioms. All are fundamentally equivalent, however. French and Ríos Insua (2000: chap. 2) provide a survey of several derivations.

of the many studies that demonstrate these violations and consider the implications these have for decision-making effectiveness.

A key implication[4] of the SEU model is the *sure-thing axiom*. Stated simply, this demands that, if there are some outcomes that will occur regardless of which option is chosen, the nature of these common outcomes should not affect choice behaviour. Baron (2001: 235) provides an example: imagine choosing between two different lotteries with the same likelihoods of winning but with different prizes if you actually win (e.g. foreign holidays at different locations A and B). Should you lose, then each lottery has the identical consolation prize (e.g. a discount on the next holiday that you book). The sure-thing principle states that, since the outcome from losing is the same for both options then the exact nature of this outcome (e.g. whether it is a 5 per cent or a 10 per cent discount) should not affect your choice between the lotteries. In other words, if you prefer the lottery with a prize for foreign location A when the outcome from losing is a 5 per cent discount then you should also prefer the same lottery when the outcome from losing is a 10 per cent discount.

Although this axiom seems highly plausible, there are a number of high-profile violations that have had a significant impact on our understanding of human decision making. In particular, both Allais (1953) and Ellsberg (1961) asked people to choose between different pairs of gambles that included common outcomes and showed that varying the pay-offs associated with these common outcomes affected choice behaviour. We describe each of these in more detail in the next sections.

The Allais paradox

In 1952 Allais presented the problem given in table 2.1. Pause for a minute and think about which option you would choose in each of the two choices. A majority of individuals choose option A in the first choice and option D in the second. They argue that option A makes them 'rich' beyond their wildest dreams so why should they risk the small chance (1 per cent) in option B of receiving nothing. In the second choice, however, there is roughly the same high probability of their receiving

---

[4] As indicated in footnote 3, there are many derivations of the SEU model, and some of the axioms of one derivation may be implied by those of another. In section 3.3 we give a very simple derivation, but one that does not explicitly use the sure-thing axiom discussed here. As problem 1 at the end of this chapter shows, however, the sure-thing axiom is a necessary implication of the SEU model. It is therefore implicit in our – and any other – development of SEU.

Table 2.1 Allais' paradox

Choice 1: which of the following options would you choose?			
Option A	£1 000 000	for certain	
Option B	£5 000 000	with probability	0.10
	£1 000 000	with probability	0.89
	£0	with probability	0.01
Choice 2: which of the following options would you choose?			
Option C	£1 000 000	with probability	0.11
	£0	with probability	0.89
Option D:	£5 000 000	with probability	0.10
	£0	with probability	0.90

Table 2.2 Allais' paradox explicated in terms of a lottery

	Lottery ticket number		
	1	2–11	12–100
Option A	£1 000 000	£1 000 000	£1 000 000
Option B	£0	£5 000 000	£1 000 000
Option C	£1 000 000	£1 000 000	£0
Option D	£0	£5 000 000	£0

nothing whichever option they choose. So they select option D, which has the possibility of the larger prize.

Sensible and rational though these arguments sound, there are strong prima facie arguments why choosing A in the first choice is inconsistent with choosing D in the second. For instance, Savage (1972) offers the following argument. Consider the 'implementation' of the Allais paradox illustrated in table 2.2. Imagine 100 lottery tickets placed in a hat. One will be drawn at random and the prize in each option allocated as illustrated. In the first choice between options A and B, there is no difference in the outcome on tickets 12–100. The distinction between the options arises only on the outcomes when tickets 1–11 are drawn. Similarly, in the second choice between options C and D, there is no difference in the outcome on tickets 12–100. The distinction between the options arises only on the outcomes when tickets 1–11 are drawn. Moreover, the pattern of outcomes on tickets 1–11 for options A and B is the same as that for options C and D. So consistency would seem to suggest that, if one chooses

Table 2.3 Ellsberg's paradox

		30 balls	60 balls	
		Red	Black	Yellow
Choice 1	Option A	$100	$0	$0
	Option B	$0	$100	$0
Choice 2	Option C	$100	$0	$100
	Option D	$0	$100	$100

Source: Baron (2000: 269).

A in preference to B, then one should choose C in preference to D. Equally, if one chooses B in preference to A one should choose D in preference to C.

This argument based upon table 2.2 is a simple instance of the sure-thing axiom. Persuasive though this may be, many experiments with variations in the prizes and probabilities have been conducted, and they consistently demonstrate preferences for A over B and for D over C, even when participants have been exposed to arguments articulating the sure-thing principle (Slovic and Tversky, 1974; further discussions may be found in Allais and Hagen, 1979, and French and Xie, 1994).

The Ellsberg paradox

Ellsberg's paradox is particularly important, because it reveals another problematic aspect of human decision making. He presented people with an urn that contained ninety balls, of which thirty were known to be red and sixty were a mixture of black and yellow but in unknown proportions. Participants were told that one ball was to be drawn from the urn on two different occasions and replaced between drawings. They were asked to choose which option they wanted on each occasion. The pay-offs for the two choices are presented in table 2.3. In choice 1 most people preferred option A, but in choice 2 they preferred option D. The sure-thing principle states that people should ignore the pay-off associated with drawing a yellow ball, since it is identical when choosing between option A and option B and between option C and option D. Instead, they should base their decision on the outcomes associated with drawing a red or black ball. Since these are identical for both choice 1 and choice 2, participants' preferences should have been the same for each choice. A preference for A over B and D over C violates the principle.

Ellsberg's paradox introduces a further complexity over that illustrated by Allais'. Baron (2001) explains this by pointing out that, in choice 1, participants know that there is a 1/3 probability of winning $100 if they choose red, but they do not know the probability of winning this amount if they choose black (it might be as low as 0 or as high as 2/3). In contrast to this, in choice 2 participants know there is a 2/3 probability of winning $100 if they choose black, but do not know the probability of winning if they choose red (it may be as low as 1/3 or as high as 1). In each case participants prefer the option with a known rather than an unknown probability – a phenomenon called *ambiguity aversion*. Ambiguity aversion leads to a tendency to prefer alternatives with positive outcomes characterised by known probabilities over alternatives with positive outcomes having unknown probabilities. This can lead to violations of some of the principles underpinning rational decision making (for a further review, see, for example, Camerer and Weber, 1992). It also means that people will pay a premium to resolve ambiguity.

2.4 Invariance and framing

How little do they see what really is, who frame their hasty judgments upon that which seems. (Robert Southey)

Put simply, the invariance axiom states that choices should depend upon the primary characteristics of the situation – i.e. the underlying outcomes and uncertainties – and should remain invariant across logically equivalent versions of the decision options – e.g. be unaffected by trivial changes to the way the options are described (Arrow, 1982). There are two bodies of work, however, that show that people systematically violate this axiom:

- preference reversals concerned with how the DMs' judgement and decisions are elicited; and
- framing effects concerned with how people construct mental representations of decision problems.

Preference reversal

SEU theory assumes that DMs evaluate alternatives and then choose the one associated with the highest expected utility. This basic principle was challenged by Lichtenstein and Slovic (1971), however, in studies using paired gambles of different types. For example, consider the following two types of gamble.

Probability gamble: win $2.50 with 95%; or lose $0.75 with 5% probability.

Dollar gamble: win $8.50 with 40%; or lose $1.50 with 60%.

Probability gambles are associated with relatively high probabilities of winning small amounts, whereas dollar gambles are associated with low probabilities of winning relatively large amounts. When presented with each gamble separately and asked to evaluate them by stating the least amount they would accept to sell each gamble if they owned it, participants generally gave a higher value to the dollar gamble. When the two gambles were presented together and participants had to decide which to play, however, they often chose the probability gamble – i.e. the one they had given a lower value to! Not only is this reversal of preference inconsistent with the assumptions underlying SEU theory, but it also challenges our common-sense views that people always choose alternatives that are of higher value to them.

Although there are several different explanations for this inconsistency, there is strong support for one in particular: the *compatibility hypothesis*. This hypothesis states that the response mode used to reveal a preference – i.e. evaluation or choice – leads people to focus on aspects of the presented information that are compatible with that mode. In the gambling problem described above, people focus more on the value of the outcomes when setting a price (because valuation and price are 'compatible'), but focus more on probability when making a choice, since this is more salient when choosing between uncertain alternatives (Wedell and Bockenholt, 1998). Thus, how we ask people to reveal their preferences (choosing or evaluating) can affect which aspects of the information they focus on, which, in turn, can affect how they express their preferences for options.

Such inconsistencies have far-reaching effects when the preferences of the public are sought on policy issues (Lee-Jones *et al.*, 1995). For example, consider a situation in which the preferred action for reducing environmental pollution is being evaluated. Asking the public to evaluate options – e.g. by indicating the maximum amount they would be willing to pay for each pollution reduction option – may induce a very different preference ordering as compared with asking the same individuals to choose between these options (see Slovic, 1995, for a stimulating discussion of these and related issues). Not only do the different response modes reveal different preferences, but also it is not at all clear which mode should be used in situations in which public preferences are called upon to inform important societal decisions.

A series of more recent studies has revealed another important, related principle, the *evaluability hypothesis*, indicating that people often give different evaluations to options when they are evaluated separately as opposed to side by side (Hsee, 1996, 2000). It is suggested that some options are harder to evaluate in isolation because it is not always clear how good and bad attributes should be traded off. When evaluated side by side, however, it is easier to assess the relative importance of each attribute, and so this can lead to different information being used to make the evaluation.

Slovic (1995) has concluded that such preference reversals indicate that people do not have a set of internalised stable values that can be accessed and used in a consistent way. Instead, these findings suggest that people construct their values 'on the spot', and how they do this – e.g. choice versus evaluation; simultaneously or successively – crucially affects how these are expressed. This conclusion not only calls into question normative theory assumptions that people have stable values, but also highlights some of the difficulties that arise when trying to determine the preferences of DMs. Our view, explored in later chapters, is that individuals do not have all their values and preferences – nor, for that matter, their uncertainties – fully determined at the outset of a decision analysis. Rather, they construct many of them as they deliberate. Our role in prescriptive decision analysis is to provide a supportive framework that helps people evolve their values and preferences in ways that are consistent with a normative theory that reflects the rationality that they wish their judgements to exhibit.

Framing effects

Framing is concerned with the ways in which individuals build mental representations of decision problems and how these determine the choices that they make. Seminal work by Kahneman and Tversky has shown that framing the same decision situation in different, but logically identical, ways often leads to inconsistencies in choice behaviour. For example, read the following decision problem (taken from Tversky and Kahneman, 1981) and decide which option you would choose.

Imagine that the United States is preparing for the outbreak of an unusual Asian disease, which is expected to kill 600 people. Two alternative programmes to combat the disease have been proposed. Assume that exact scientific estimates of the consequences of the programmes are as follows:

(A1) if programme A is adopted, 200 people will be saved;
(B1) if programme B is adopted, there is a one-third probability that 600 people will be saved, and a two-thirds probability that no people will be saved.

If you went for A1, then you are in good company: the majority of people choose this option. In many trials, about 75 per cent of participants choose A1. Now consider the options presented in a different way, however.

(A2) if programme A is adopted, 400 people will die;
(B2) if programme B is adopted, there is a one-third probability that nobody will die and a two-thirds probability that 600 people will die.

Presented this way, the majority of people, again about 75 per cent of the participants, choose B2 despite the fact that the two situations are logically identical – e.g., if 200 of the 600 are saved, then 400 will die. First, note that this pattern of responses indicates a reversal in preference associated with the form in which the problem is presented, thus violating the invariance axiom. Second, note that A1 and B1 are framed positively in terms of saving life, whereas A2 and B2 are framed negatively in terms of deaths. Studies have found that, roughly speaking, framing an issue in positive terms leads to the avoidance of risk and a preference for certainty, whereas the behaviour is risk-taking when the issue is phrased negatively. It should be noted that the same effect has also been observed with lower-impact outcomes, such as monetary gains and losses.

Since the initial studies of Kahneman and Tversky there have been many replications of this framing effect, as well as other studies identifying some of the conditions that strengthen and weaken it (Kühberger, 1998; Levin *et al.*, 1998). In a recent review, Maule and Villejoubert (2007) identify 427 published articles referring explicitly to framing effects across such diverse disciplines as politics, psychology, marketing, health and medicine. In nearly all these cases, the basic effect, as described above, was replicated. In addition, this was evident in the decisions of organisations (e.g. investment choices) and of professionals making choices in their area of expertise (Hodgkinson *et al.*, 1999).

Together, these studies show that how a decision problem is presented – in this case, wording that highlights either the gains or the losses – affects how people frame or internally represent the problem, which in turn affects how they choose. Work in this area has two important implications for the issues addressed in this book. First, several studies have shown that the framing bias is reduced or even eliminated when people use elaborated forms of thinking to develop more complex and balanced decision frames (Maule, 1989; Sieck and Yates, 1997). These findings suggest that procedures designed to induce frame elaboration provide useful ways of eliminating bias and thereby improving the quality of decision making. This is one of the reasons that we spend so much time emphasising the role of issue and problem formulation in chapters 9 and 10. Second, in a series of articles, Kahneman and Tversky have used violations of invariance and other axioms similar to those described above to develop *prospect theory*. Not only has this theory been very successful in predicting how people actually make decisions, but it has also identified and explained a broad range of other violations of rational decision making. Prospect theory is currently the most influential descriptive theory of human decision making, and it is described in more detail next.

2.5 Prospect theory

The dread of evil is a much more forcible principle of human actions than the prospect of good. (John Locke)

Prospect theory is similar to SEU theory in that it assumes that choosing involves maximising the value of expected outcomes. There are two key differences, however. First, in prospect theory two stages in the decision-making process are posited:

- *editing*, which involves constructing a decision frame – i.e. a mental representation of the problem; and
- *evaluation*, in which these 'framed' options are evaluated so that the one with the greatest value can be chosen.

Second, the utilities and probabilities that underpin these expected outcomes are subject to cognitive distortions that can reduce the quality of the decision taken. We now outline each of these phases, along with some discussion of the cognitive distortions and their implications.

Editing

Editing is dependent upon a number of relatively simple thinking processes designed to build up a DM's mental representation of the problem in hand – i.e. the decision frame. While several editing operations have been posited (Kahneman and Tversky, 1979), perhaps the most important is coding. This operation is responsible for representing the value to the DM of the possible outcomes that may occur. These are represented as gains and losses from a reference point rather than as final states of wealth, as assumed by SEU theory. This apparently small change has important ramifications for our understanding of how people take decisions. One such ramification is that, as the reference point adopted changes, so the way outcomes are framed also changes. For example, consider the following problem.

Imagine you are part of a team planning how European governments should respond to the next major nuclear accident. You are considering two possible strategies to protect people. Strategy 1 is based on protecting people in their own homes by sealing windows, providing instructions to remain indoors, etc., whereas strategy 2 is based on evacuating people so that they are a safe distance from the plume of nuclear contamination. The risks associated with these two strategies are rather different. Strategy 2 is riskier in the short term given the threats associated with evacuating a large number of people – e.g. traffic accidents, stress-related heart attacks and the possibility of being in the open during the passage of the plume – but better in the long term, given that removing people from the situation leads to less exposure to nuclear contamination, thereby reducing long-term health threats from cancer and related illnesses.

When framing the value of the outcomes of each strategy, there are at least two different reference points that could be adopted. The first reference point is 'what life was like before the accident'. From this reference point, outcomes associated with both strategies are framed as losses; the accident makes everything worse than before regardless of what strategy we adopt. The second reference point is 'what life would be like if no protective action was taken'; from this reference point, outcomes associated with both strategies are framed as gains, each offering some gain over doing nothing.

Does it matter which reference point is adopted? Research by McNeil *et al.* (1982) in the medical domain suggests that it does. They asked people to choose between different medical treatments with broadly similar risk characteristics to those described in the nuclear accident problem above. They predicted and then showed that, when outcomes were framed as losses, short-term risks were particularly aversive as compared with a situation in which those same outcomes were framed as gains. Thus, in the nuclear accident problem described above, we would predict that evacuation, associated with the short-term risks, would be more likely to be chosen when the reference point adopted leads to outcomes framed as gains rather than losses – i.e. the second reference point.

Most DMs, including those who actually make nuclear protection decisions, are unaware that they use reference points, so they are likely to adopt one of these at random without realising how it can bias their choice of action. Similarly, it is argued that the change in wording in the two versions of the Asian disease problem presented earlier also led to the adoption of different reference points. Why should framing in terms of gains and losses change attitudes to risk, however? In order to answer this question we need to consider the second or evaluation phase of prospect theory.

Evaluation

Similar to SEU theory, evaluation of an alternative involves summing the products of the values and probabilities associated with each possible outcome. Specifically, prospect theory ranks alternatives according to

$$\Sigma_i \pi(p_i) v(c_i)$$

where p_i is the 'actual' subjective probability of the ith consequence, $\pi(p)$ is a decision-weighting function that adjusts the probability, increasing the influence of small probabilities and decreasing the influence of high ones, and $v(c_i)$ is the value of the ith consequence.

As indicated above, the values of outcomes are represented as gains and losses rather than final states of wealth. Figure 2.1 presents a typical value function describing how people value varying amounts of gain or loss. Put simply, gains are evaluated positively, but with each incremental gain have less value as the total gain increases. The concave shape of the value function in gains leads to people valuing a certain gain more than a probable gain with equal or greater expected value – i.e. they exhibit risk

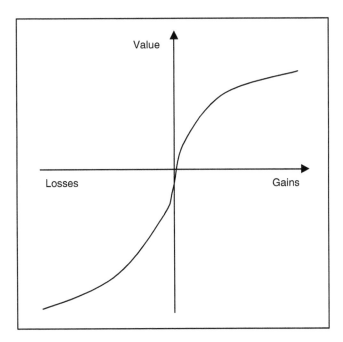

Figure 2.1   The form of the value function in prospect theory representing risk aversion for gains and risk proneness for losses

aversion.[5] Similarly, losses are evaluated negatively, but with each incremental loss having less negative value as the total loss increases. The convex shape of the value function in losses also means that people value a certain loss more than a probable loss with equal or greater expected value, but since this value is negative people prefer the risky option – i.e. they exhibit risk-seeking behaviour. A second important feature of the value function is that it is steeper in losses than in gains. This means that the impact of a loss is greater than a comparable gain and leads to loss aversion – i.e. people are overly sensitive to loss.

Prospect theory also predicts a cognitive distortion of probability, with the suggestion that the impact of a probability, referred to as a *decision weight* (π_p), is different from its numerical value. Figure 2.2 outlines the relationship between probabilities and their associated decision weights. The figure shows that small probabilities are overweighted. Thus, outcomes associated with small probabilities have a bigger impact on choice than they should. In addition, medium to high probabilities are underweighted, so outcomes associated with these probabilities have less of an impact on choice than they should. This pattern of weighting is found to occur regardless of whether people are given the probabilities or they have to estimate them for themselves.

A further feature of the probability-weighting function is that people are very sensitive to changes around the ends of the scale – i.e. 0 (impossibility) and 1 (certainty); in other words, changes in probability from 0.0 to 0.01 or 0.99 to 1.00 have a greater impact than changes from, say, 0.01 to 0.02 or 0.60 to 0.61. This effect ties in with the phenomenon of ambiguity aversion discussed earlier: people value certainty over uncertainty.

These cognitive distortions associated with value and probability combine together to predict a fourfold pattern of choice behaviour. Previously we identified two of these: risk aversion in gains and risk seeking in losses. This pattern occurs for medium to large probabilities only, however, with the pattern reversing (i.e. risk seeking in gains and risk aversion in losses) at small probabilities.

Overall, prospect theory has been used to explain many of the inconsistencies and violations of SEU theory, some of which have been described above, as well as making many new predictions about human decision making that have subsequently been supported by empirical research (Fox and See, 2003; Kahneman and Tversky, 2000).

---

[5] SEU models can also represent the same assumptions of decreasing marginal worth and risk aversion: see section 8.4.

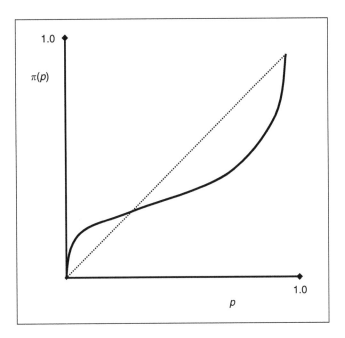

Figure 2.2   The form of the decision-weighting function, $\pi(p)$

2.6 Judgements of risk and probability

If an elderly, but distinguished scientist says that something is possible he is almost certainly right, but if he says that it is impossible, he is very probably wrong. (Arthur C. Clarke)

Many normative approaches to decision making, including SEU theory, advocate that people should take account of the likelihoods with which outcomes occur, without considering whether they can actually do this accurately or not. In this section we review evidence that shows that people are not good probability assessors, providing not just further reasons why intuitive decision making is sometimes suboptimal but also further issues to be addressed in prescriptive decision support. In section 8.6 we discuss how elicitation procedures may be developed to help DMs improve their assessments of probabilities.

The quality of human probability judgements can be assessed in two ways: their *coherence* and their *correspondence* (Hammond, 1996). Consider the following problem.

A health survey was conducted in a sample of adult males of all ages and occupations in British Columbia (Canada). Mr Smith was selected at random from the sample. Which of the following statements is more probable?

(A) Mr Smith has had one or more heart attacks.
(B) Mr Smith has had one or more heart attacks and is over fifty-five years old.

The majority of people choose option B (see, for example, Tversky and Kahneman, 1983). Choosing this is a mistake, however, called the *conjunction fallacy*, since A can be subdivided into those having heart attacks and over fifty-five years of age (i.e. option B) and those having heart attacks and under fifty-five years old. Thus, option A must either have the same probability (if nobody under fifty-five years old has had a heart attack) or greater (if some of those under fifty-five actually has had a heart attack as well).

Choosing B is a mistake, and we call it a failure of coherence because it violates a basic principle of probability theory: that if B is a subset of A then it cannot be more probable than A. Researchers have shown that people violate other principles of probability theory. Perhaps the most important of these is neglecting base rates. Consider the following.

A breast-cancer-screening procedure can detect 80 per cent of women with undiagnosed cancer of the breast and misclassifies only 5 per cent without cancer. It is estimated that the rate of cancer sufferers in women who are screened is thirty cases per 10,000. What is the probability that any particular woman who has a positive test actually has cancer? Give a value between 0 and 100 per cent.

Many people think that the probability is around 70 to 75 per cent, including a senior nurse one of us taught who was responsible for the breast-screening service in a large town. The true probability is about 5 per cent. The correct answer derives from a simple application of Bayes' theorem, which prescribes how probability judgements should be updated in the light of new data. This involves combining the information about the reliability of the test with the initial probability of having cancer in the first place, often referred to as the base rate.[6] Research indicates that experts often make errors similar to this when making judgements (see, for example, Casscells *et al.*, 1978, and Gigerenzer, 2002). These are just two of many examples of failures in coherence that together show that people often make inconsistent probability judgements (Kahneman *et al.*, 1982; Kahneman and Tversky, 2000).

A failure of correspondence is illustrated in a study reported by Lichtenstein *et al.* (1978), which asked research participants the following

---

[6] We provide an approximate application of Bayes theorem to this example in section 3.8.

question: is an adult male in the United States more likely to die from homicide or suicide? The majority of people judged that homicide was more likely despite the fact that government statistics at that time showed the opposite to be true. Here we have an error of correspondence because the judgement is not consistent with known facts.

There are other important examples of correspondence errors. Let us take another problem.

Consider the following three questions, indicate which answer you think is correct, (a) or (b), and then write down how probable it is that you are actually correct in terms of a percentage (i.e. 50 per cent if an equal chance that you are correct or not, 100 per cent if you are certain that you are correct).

> Is an absinthe
> (a)   a precious stone, or
> (b)   a liqueur?
> Which city in the United Kingdom is further east:
> (a)   Edinburgh, or
> (b)   Bristol?
> Which is longer:
> (a)   the Panama Canal, or
> (b)   the Suez Canal?

Many people, though perhaps not you, think that an absinthe is a precious stone. If you thought this then your answer is wrong. If you gave a probability of being correct of less than 100 per cent, however, then your judgement was good, in the sense that you realised that there was some chance that you could be wrong. If you were unsure about the knowledge underpinning a critical judgement then you would 'check your facts', and if this was not possible you might try to build in some contingency to take account of the uncertainty. When answering the second question many people in the United Kingdom choose Edinburgh and around 10 to 20 per cent of these, at least in our classes, judge the probability of being correct as 100 per cent. In fact, however, it is Bristol that is further east. So, for these individuals, not only is their decision wrong but also their judgement. Even for the apparently much more straightforward third question, people are overconfident in their answers – the Suez Canal is the longer, by the way.

Fischhoff *et al.* (1977) found that some 17 to 28 per cent of all judgements asserted with complete certainty in such almanac questions were actually wrong! They also found that people usually express higher degrees of confidence than they should – i.e. their judgements of the probability of being correct were significantly higher than their actual probability of being correct. This failure in correspondence occurs when the questions are difficult. With easy questions there is lack of correspondence in the opposite direction – i.e. underconfidence (for a recent review, see Griffin and Brenner, 2004). Overconfidence occurs in some expert groups, such as medics and financial analysts (Christensen-Szalanski and Bushyhead, 1981; Hilary and Menzly, 2006), but not others, such as weather forecasters (Murphy and Winkler, 1984). The situation is complex, however, and it is not easy to make generalisations across all contexts and professional groups (Glaser *et al.*, 2007). Overconfidence has been shown to affect the quality of decision making in many everyday situations, such as stock market investment (Barber and Odean, 2000).

These are just a few examples of the many studies demonstrating that people, including experts, regularly fall prey to violations in coherence and failures in correspondence when making probability judgements. These errors are likely to lead to poor decisions, given that they are made on the basis of inappropriate beliefs about the likelihood of outcomes (Gilovich *et al.*, 2002). In order to address these inaccuracies and help people make better judgements, we must first understand the thinking and reasoning processes that people use in these situations, where the potential error lies in these processes and how they can be corrected. Fortunately, there has been a very large body of research addressing these issues, and in the next section we briefly review this work.

2.7 Judgemental heuristics and biases

Reality is a cruel auditor. (Carl Weick)

The primary explanation for poor probability judgement is that people use 'heuristic' forms of thinking. These are simplifying or short cut forms of thinking that people adopt instead of following the formal rules of probability. (In recent years this form of thinking has been referred to as system 1 thinking, and contrasted with more analytical and systematic thinking based on sound rules, referred to as system 2 thinking: see Kahneman and Fredrick, 2002.) Critical to this approach are notions of attribute substitution and natural assessment. Attribute substitution can be explained as follows: when faced with a hard question requiring judgement, people often replace it with an easier one. Natural assessment means that the form of thinking adopted should be relatively automatic and frequently used in other situations. For example, in the second problem above, you were faced with the difficult problem of trying to take account of all the presented information when judging the probability that a woman had breast cancer, given a positive test. What many people do is to answer in terms of an easier question based on a simpler definition of how to calculate probability – one that takes account only of the detection rate and mis-classification rate and ignores the overall base rate that women have breast cancer in the first place and how this impacts on the judgement.

Tversky and Kahneman (1983) initially identified two heuristics: *representativeness* and *availability*. When people use representativeness they replace a difficult question concerning how probable some event is by an easier and more natural assessment in terms of the degree to which one thing resembles another. For example, consider the following.

Linda is thirty-one years old, single, outspoken and very bright. She majored in philosophy. As a student she was deeply concerned with issues of discrimination and social justice, and also participated in anti-nuclear demonstrations.
    Which of these statements is more probable?

(A) Linda is a bank teller.
(B) Linda is a bank teller and active in the feminist movement.

If you chose option B, you have followed the majority of people when given this problem. For reasons similar to those outlined above when discussing the first problem in section 2.6, however, option A must be more probable than B given that B is a subset of A. To explain this and similar errors from related problems, Tversky and Kahneman suggested that people use the representativeness heuristic. Faced with a somewhat difficult problem, people replace the difficult problem – i.e. assessing which statement is more probable – with an easier one – i.e. recognising the resemblance or match between the description of Linda and each of the options. They use this form of thinking because it is easier to implement and 'natural,' in the sense that we frequently use matching in other thinking situations, such as recognising people and objects in the world – something we do all our waking life. This heuristic is quite functional, in that it often returns a probability that is reasonably close to the true probability and does so quickly and without too much effort. Without it, people might be unable to make any kind of judgement at all, given that they have not been taught the principles of probability theory so do not know how to reason from this standpoint. Use of this heuristic, however, means that people often overlook relevant information, such as the need to take account of base rate information, and this can lead to errors of judgement.

People also use a second heuristic: availability. This involves replacing a difficult question concerning the likelihood of an event with an easier, more natural assessment in terms of the ease with which past occurrences of it happening can be brought to mind. For example, faced with a hard question about the probability of hackers attacking an organisation's computer facilities, senior managers may replace it with an easier question: how readily can they bring to mind examples of hackers attacking computer systems in the past? If it is relatively easy to bring an example of this to mind, they judge the probability of this occurring in their organisation as relatively high. If it is difficult to bring an instance to mind, the probability of it happening is judged to be relatively low. This form of thinking is natural, in that we readily and automatically evaluate the ease with which we can access information from our memories. It also has some face validity, in that, all other things being equal, those events that are more readily brought to mind tend to have occurred more often in the past, and are therefore more likely to occur in the future.

To illustrate this last point, imagine that there are two key threats to your organisation's success, which we will call As and Bs. In the past there have been many more As than Bs, so your memory for these events is as described schematically in figure 2.3(a). All other things being equal, it is more likely that event A will occur in the future (given that more of them have occurred in the past), and you will more readily bring to mind an example of event A given that there are more of them in memory. Thus, the ease with which you can retrieve previous examples is a good proxy for likelihood of occurrence in the future, and this is a somewhat simpler form of assessment. There are some events, however, that do not occur very often, but when they do they leave highly accessible memory traces by virtue of being dramatic, of personal significance or in some other way highly distinctive, as depicted in figure 2.3(b).

We would predict that if people use ease of retrieval of an event as a proxy for its probability of occurrence in the future, then they will over-predict the likelihood of event B. There is much research suggesting that people do use this heuristic and in doing so tend to overestimate the likelihood of highly 'available' risks. For example, earlier, we noted research by Lichtenstein *et al.* (1978) that showed that people incorrectly thought that dying from homicide was more likely than dying from suicide. We can explain this in terms of the availability heuristic. The media tend to report homicides more than suicides, so this will bias the number of events of each type we have in our memory (our major source of information for these kinds of events is the media). In addition, homicides tend to be more dramatic, and so they leave more distinctive memory traces that are more 'available', further increasing the bias. Thus, the errors may come about

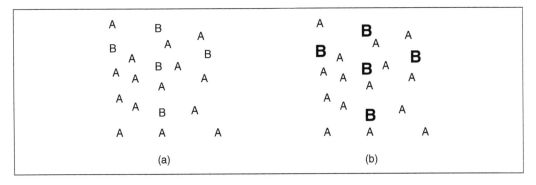

Figure 2.3   An illustration of the availability bias

Note: Suppose that the subject has to estimate the probability of events B in a population of As and Bs. If there is nothing to distinguish the impact of the events in the subject's memory, as in (a), then the ease with which he or she recalls Bs will reflect their probability. If, however, the Bs have more impact in his or her memory, as in (b), they will be easier to recall and hence their probability will be overestimated.

partly because our memories of events are biased by such factors as media reporting and partly by the fact that dramatic events are more 'available' in memory.

A further heuristic, the *affect* heuristic, draws on the natural tendency for events in the world to evoke emotional responses, either positive or negative, with the suggestion that these emotions can influence judgements. Finucane *et al.* (2003) show that judgements of the risks and benefits of particular items and events varied when they manipulated participants' emotional states, with positive states associated with lower risk and negative states associated with higher risk. Thus, a person faced with a 'difficult' judgement about the risks associated with a particular entity – e.g. nuclear power – may replace it with an 'easier' judgement based on a natural assessment of how it makes him or her feel. In this instance, negative feelings would induce higher risk judgements and positive feelings lower risk judgements.

The evidence briefly reviewed in this section shows that there are occasions when human judgements of risk and uncertainty are inaccurate in terms of both coherence and correspondence, and that this is due to the thinking processes that underpin these judgements. In addition, there is strong evidence to suggest that these forms of thinking are used regularly by busy managers and other professionals and have led to poor decision making that has impacted negatively on them and their organisations

(Hammond *et al.*, 1998; Roxburgh, 2003). Taken together, this body of work highlights the importance of developing procedures for supporting human judgements of risk and uncertainty, and the potential that this has for improving decision making.

2.8 Emotion

Men decide for more problems by hate, love, lust, rage, sorrow, joy, hope, fear, illusion, or some other inward emotion, than by reality, authority, any legal standard, judicial precedent or statute. (Marcus Tullius Cicero)

So far we have reviewed research that has focused on the cognitive or thinking processes that underlie human judgement and decision making, considering the extent to which these processes can lead people to act inconsistently with respect to SEU theory. In recent years, however, there have been three streams of research outlining how affect and emotion may also lead to inconsistency.

One stream of research has considered the general role that emotions play in decision making. For example, Zajonc (1980) proposed that affective reactions involving simple feelings of like and dislike precede cognitive evaluations. He suggested that we often delude ourselves by thinking that our decisions are based on a careful weighing up of the pros and cons when, in fact, they are based on these simple feelings. The weighing of pros and cons that people often report using are justifications constructed after they have chosen rather than the basis on which they actually make the choice. Although Zajonc's suggestions are likely to apply to some rather than all of our decisions, they are important in that they provide a way of explaining human decision making that is very different from that assumed in SEU theory. Allied to this is the affect heuristic described earlier, whereby people use the feelings elicited by a situation to determine their judgements of the risk involved, with negative feelings indicating relatively high risk and positive feelings relatively low risk.

A further suggestion regarding the role of affect in decision making has been outlined by Damasio and his co-workers (see, for example, Damasio, 2000). They reported research on people who have had accidents that damaged the emotional centres of their brains while leaving the intellectual centres intact. These individuals could readily complete quite complicated intellectual tasks but had great difficulty making decisions. The authors argued that this finding shows that emotions play a vital role in decision making by 'marking' possible future outcomes as positive and negative; without this emotional marking people are unable to commit to particular options and therefore find it very difficult to choose.

A second stream of research has investigated how a DM's emotional state can influence the thinking processes that underpin judgement and decision making. For example, there is strong evidence to suggest that positive emotional states induce broader, more creative thinking, whereas negative emotional states induce more focused analytical thinking (Schwarz and Clore, 1996) and promote a complete and correct use of structured decision protocols (Elsbach and Barr, 1999). This suggests that particular emotional states may be appropriate in some situations – e.g. a positive state is appropriate in situations that demand creativity in developing new and innovative options – but not in others – e.g. a positive state is inappropriate in situations that require a detailed analysis and evaluation of an already agreed set of alternatives. In addition, affect can influence risk attitudes such that people in positive emotional states are less likely to choose a risky option when the likelihood of a positive outcome is low, but more likely to choose it when the probability is high (Isen and Patrick, 1983). Moreover, Johnson and Tversky (1983) showed that people who have been induced into a good mood judge negative events to be some-what less likely to occur. These are just a few of the many studies showing that emotional states affect judgement and decision making (for reviews, see Finucane *et al.*, 2003, Schwarz, 2000, and Slovic *et al.*, 2004). To date, however, there has been little discussion of the implications of these findings in situations in which decisions are being supported by a DSS, structured analyses and other techniques.

Finally, a third stream of research, developed by Janis and Mann (1977), has focused on the impact of emotions associated with decisional conflict. Janis and Mann argue that conflict arises when people make important decisions, and that this can become quite acute when there is some risk of incurring large losses. The extent to which conflict can be resolved determines both the emotional state and decision strategy used. They identified five different patterns of decision making. The first of these, *vigilant decision making*, involves seven stages that are similar to those that prescriptive approaches seek to foster and support: see table 2.4.

Vigilant decision making involves recognising, analysing and resolving the conflicts that are present when evaluating current and potentially new courses of action in terms of the information available. Under these circumstances, the DM is thought to be aroused enough to mobilise sufficient cognitive resources to engage relatively deep levels of thinking that confront and resolve the conflicts, leading to a reasoned and effective decision. Sometimes, however, people use simpler strategies than this. One such strategy, *unconflicted adherence*, is employed when the incoming information does not conflict with the DM's present course of action, and

Table 2.4 The seven stages of vigilant decision making

1 Thorough canvassing of alternatives.
2 Survey the full range of objectives.
3 Carefully weigh the pros and cons of each alternative.
4 Search for new information to evaluate the alternatives.
5 Assimilate and take account of the new information.
6 Re-examine the positive and negative consequences of all alternatives, including those initially thought unacceptable
7 Make detailed plan for implementation or execute the course of action, making contingency plans where possible in case known risk materialises.

so she calmly maintains her present course of action. A second strategy, *unconflicted change*, is employed when the incoming information indicates that the current action is inadequate, but there is an obvious alternative that does not conflict with the available information. Under these circumstances, the DM calmly changes her course of action. While vigilant information processing is thought to be associated with good outcomes, these other two strategies may also be appropriate, though they do leave DMs exposed to threats that have not been fully recognised because of the paucity of the information processing engaged prior to choice.

Sometimes the conflicts cannot be resolved, however. When this occurs, not only are DMs unable to choose an option but they also experience unpleasant negative emotions because of their inability to cope with the situation. The pressures to make a choice and change the negative emotional state can together induce one of two suboptimal strategies. One of these, *defensive avoidance*, involves eliminating the conflict by bolstering – i.e. distorting information by accentuating positive aspects and/or downplaying negative aspects associated with an initially preferred course of action, and/or simply ignoring some of the conflicting information (see also the concept of bounded awareness; e.g. Bazerman and Chugh, 2006). While defensive avoidance eliminates the conflict and, in doing so, reduces the negative affect and resolves the choice, it does so at the cost of 'mentally cooking the books' – that is, distorting the information on which the decision is based. These distortions leave the decision maker exposed to those risks and threats that have been downplayed.

The second of the suboptimal strategies, *hypervigilance*, occurs under extreme conditions associated with panic, when the thinking strategies are so disrupted that people focus on just one action and implement it immediately without realising that there are other options and still some time left for evaluation. A failure to recognise the possibility of taking different actions and to use the time available for the evaluation of decision alternatives can lead the DM to take inappropriate action that in some cases may expose her to danger. The ideas underpinning Janis and Mann's theory are consistent with more recent research demonstrating that decision making can be heavily influenced by a need to manage and modify unpleasant emotions (see, for example, Luce *et al.*, 1997).

This brief review demonstrates the importance of understanding the interplay between emotion and cognition when describing how people make decisions. The cognitive factors are relatively well understood by those designing decision support and, as will be shown in later chapters, have provided important insights about the kinds of support systems that are required and how they should be implemented. Much less is understood about the implications of emotional factors for designing and implementing decision support, however.

2.9 Developing decision-thinking skills

Good judgement comes from experience. Experience comes from bad judgement. (Anonymous)

The earlier sections of this chapter have shown that human decision making is often underpinned by suboptimal thinking processes that are not in accordance with normative principles. Knowing this, and the ways in which these processes depart from normative principles, not only presents a powerful argument for the use of decision analysis and support but also provides important insights about which aspects of decision making need support and how this may be best achieved. Subsequent chapters of the book develop these points further. In recent years, however, researchers cataloguing these limitations have suggested a number of much simpler techniques focused directly on changing how people think. Put simply, an understanding of how people think and the associated errors and biases can provide a sound foundation for developing ways of helping people think more accurately. In this section, and later in section 3.8, we provide some examples of this work.

Taking an outside rather than an inside perspective

Making predictions about the likelihood of future outcomes on the basis of our past experience is a key facet of decision making. Indeed, these kinds of predictions play a crucial role in decision analysis (see chapter 8). In sections 6 and 7 above we showed that predictions about the future are often based on judgemental heuristics that are associated with errors and biases – e.g. optimism, which leads to an overestimation of the likelihood of positive outcomes and an underestimation of negative outcomes. Lovallo and Kahneman (2003) have argued that one important limitation underpinning these kinds of judgements is an overdependence on 'inside' rather than 'outside' thinking. Inside thinking focuses on the specific features and characteristics of the problem/situation in hand and uses these to make predictions about such aspects as its likelihood of success, profitability or time to completion. In contrast, outside thinking focuses on the outcomes of similar problems that have been completed in the past, considering where the current problem sits in terms of the distribution of these previous cases, and derives predictions from what might be expected given its position in the distribution of previous outcomes. Under inside thinking, people focus on the positive aspects of the situation, so they are overly optimistic. In contrast to this, outside thinking is based on previous outcomes, so it is not affected by this bias (or it is affected to a lesser degree)

To help facilitate outside thinking, Lovallo and Kahneman (2003) advocate using a five-step procedure. We present these steps and illustrate them in the context of predictions made by a pharmaceutical company about the profitability that might be expected from developing a new drug.

(1) Select a reference class: identify previous relevant/similar situations to the one that is currently being evaluated – e.g. previous instances in which similar drugs have been developed.

(2) Assess the distribution of outcomes: list the outcomes of these previous situations – e.g. how long the drugs took to develop, their actual profitability and other relevant output measures.

(3) Make an intuitive prediction about how the current situation compares with those in the reference class: use this to predict where in the distribution of past outcomes the current situation lies – e.g. in the past similar drugs have taken between four and eight years to come to market; this project is dealing with something quite difficult, so the estimate should be to the top end of the distribution, say around 7.5 years.

While the first three steps are sufficient to derive an outside prediction, Lovallo and Kahneman advocate two further steps to improve this forecast

(4) Assess the reliability of the prediction by deriving the likely correlation between this prediction and the actual outcome (i.e. a value between

0, indicating no correlation, and 1, indicating a perfect correlation). This may be derived from previous cases (i.e. how closely do previous predictions match actual outcomes? If high, then assume a correlation close to 1; if low, closer to 0) or by subjective comparisons with other forecasting situations (e.g. is this situation more like predicting tomorrow's weather, so nearer to 1, or next year's share price of a company during a period of economic turbulence, so nearer to 0?).

(5) Correct the intuitive estimate made in step 3 by the outputs from step 4, recognising that it is likely to be optimistic and so needs to be adjusted towards the mean of previous cases. The degree of adjustment depends upon the perceived reliability derived in step 4. In particular, the less the perceived reliability of the prediction the greater the regression towards the mean of previous cases.

The first step, involving the selection of the reference class of previous cases, is difficult, and there are no clear criteria to determine how this should be achieved. If an inappropriate set of previous cases is used then the resulting predictions may be no better, or even worse, than those derived from inside thinking. This procedure has considerable merit, however, given that it is focused on de-biasing known problems in human thinking.

Consider the opposite

Larrick (2004) discusses a second way of improving thinking that involves routinely asking oneself why initial judgements or views might be wrong. This counters a known bias in human thinking associated with a strong tendency to focus on information that supports initial views and to ignore information that would disconfirm such views. For example, in section 6 we discussed overconfidence, a strong tendency for people to hold views with higher degrees of confidence than is justified, and in some cases to be 100 per cent sure they are right when, in fact, they are wrong. Koriat *et al.* (1980) asked people to work through a series of general knowledge questions indicating which of two answers they thought was the correct one and then to judge the likelihood that their answer was correct. There were four different conditions, differentiated in terms of the activity that participants undertook between indicating which answer was correct and their likelihood judgement. Under condition 1, participants did nothing between the two activities (similar to you when completing the problem in section 6). Under the other three conditions, participants were asked to list reasons why their chosen answer *was* likely to be correct (condition 2); list reasons why their chosen answer *was* and *was not* likely to be correct (condition 3); and list reasons why their chosen answer *was not* likely to be correct (condition 4). Very similar levels of overconfidence were recorded for conditions 1 and 2, suggesting that even when not instructed to do so (i.e. condition 1) participants thought about reasons why their chosen alternative was correct when generating the likelihood judgements. The usual overconfidence effect disappeared in conditions 3 and 4, however, suggesting that instructing people to think about reasons why they might be wrong improves their judgement – i.e. improves correspondence.

There are other examples in which considering the opposite improves judgement by reducing the negative effects of known biases (see, for example, Arkes, 1991, Mussweiler and Pfeiffer, 2000, and Soll and Klayman, 2004). The advantage of this approach to thinking is that it is easy to implement: one simply needs to ensure that decision makers routinely write down reasons that both support and contradict the major assumptions underlying their judgements and decisions. Indeed, many organisations have structured decision procedures in this way – e.g. managing firearms incidents in the United Kingdom requires the completion of a structured log that involves documenting reasons for and against possible courses of action.

The rise of information and knowledge management techniques (discussed in chapter 4) has made ever more information accessible to decision makers. If this information is used simply to provide more reasons in support of initially preferred courses of action then these techniques may lead to even greater levels of overconfidence! Thus, counteracting this negative effect on judgement and decision making with techniques designed to consider the opposite is critical if the full potential of information and knowledge management techniques is to be realised.

2.10 Concluding remarks and further reading

From this brief review of behavioural research we may conclude that the thinking and reasoning processes underlying human decision making depart from normative principles and, therefore, are subject to error and bias. This conclusion, along with insights about why these errors and biases occur, provides not only a strong argument confirming the need for decision analysis and support but also insights into the kinds of support that are needed. For those readers wishing to learn more about this body of work, there are many fascinating introductions to this area of study (see, for example, Arkes and Hammond, 1986, Baron, 2001, Bazerman, 2006, Beach and Connolly, 2005, Gigerenzer, 2002, Gilovich *et al.*, 2002, Kahneman *et al.*, 1982, Newell *et al.*, 2007, Payne *et al.*, 1993, Slovic, 2001, Wright, 1984, Wright and Ayton, 1994, and Wright and Goodwin, 1998). Morse (2006) offers a neuro-scientific but accessible view of the underlying drivers of intuitive decision making.

Prospect theory (Bazerman, 2006; Edwards, 1996; Kahneman and Tversky, 1979, 2000; Levy, 2003; Mercer, 2005) has proved to be one of the most influential theories in behavioural decision research. Wakker (2004) has suggested that the decision weights may be decomposed into a component reflecting a DM's risk attitude and one related to her belief. Prospect theory is not the only one to address the reasons for differences between the ideals encapsulated by the SEU model and actual behaviour. There are several other models, classed variously as generalised, non-expected or non-linear utility models (Allais and Hagen, 1979; Edwards, 1992; Fishburn, 1988; Machina, 1991). Moreover, the differences between these models and the SEU model may not be as great as one first thinks: reframing of the decision context within the SEU perspective can also lead to very similar behaviours (Bordley and Hazen, 1992; French *et al.*, 1997; French and Xie, 1994).

The majority of behavioural studies have taken place in laboratories and have usually involved management or psychology students; it is natural, therefore, to ask whether similar biases occur in the real world. Though there is much less field research, there is, nonetheless, some support for prospect theory (see, for example, Hodgkinson *et al.*, 1999, and Kühberger *et al.*, 2002) and the use of judgemental heuristics (see, for example, Schwenk, 1985, and the special edition of *Harvard Business Review* published in January 2006). At several places in the text we noted studies among doctors and medical staff that indicate, worryingly, that medical decision making may be liable to such biases (for discussions of prescriptive decision analysis in the medical field, see Dowie, 1988, and Hunink, Glasziou, Siegel *et al.*, 2001).

2.11 Exercises and questions for discussion

(1) Consider a DM who chooses according to SEU theory.
  (a) Show that, in the choices posed by Allais (table 2.1), she will prefer A to B if and only if she prefers C to D.
  (b) Show that, in the choices posed by Ellsberg (table 2.3), she will prefer A to B if and only if she prefers C to D.
  (c) Show that in general she will obey the sure-thing axiom.

(2) Set yourself the task of predicting ten to twenty quantities, the values of which will become known in the next week or so: perhaps the price of a share at the close of business a week from now; or the temperature at a particular town, again a week from now. If you promise not to look up the answer, you might consider the length of a river or the height of a mountain. For each, give your best estimate of the value, and also give bounds so that you are 95 per cent sure that the value will lie between these bounds. For instance, if you are forecasting the temperature in central London at noon next Monday, you might believe that it will be 22°C and be 95 per cent sure that it will not be less than 18°C nor more than 27°C – i.e. you believe that there is no more than a one in twenty chance that it will lie outside these values. Note down all your predictions of all the quantities and the 95 per cent bounds that you put on these. Wait until the week is up and you can find the true values of all the quantities. Now compare these true values with your predictions. In how many cases do the true values lie outside your 95 per cent range? If more than 5 per cent do, your predictions were overconfident. Equally, if fewer than 5 per cent do, you were being too cautious.

(3) 'We will never fully understand managerial decision making without taking into account the effects of time pressure, stress and emotion.' Discuss.

Decision analysis and support

I can put two and two together, you know. Do not think that you are dealing with a man who has lost his grapes. (Tom Stoppard)

3.1 Introduction

Our discussions in the previous chapter should have given you pause for thought. Maybe we – and that 'we' includes you! – are not as good at making judgements and taking decisions as we thought. Few of us admit or even recognise our failings in this respect, however – and certainly not in the decision making that occupies our professional lives. To be fair, managers, politicians, doctors and other key DMs need to embody confidence in their judgements if their advice and leadership is to be followed. Being outwardly confident does not obviate the need to be inwardly reflective, however. We argue throughout this book that there are many ways of helping DMs to be more perceptive and reflective, and, in doing so, to improve the quality of their decision making. Here we begin the task of describing systems, processes and tools by which we can achieve this. Our objectives in this chapter are:

- to distinguish between normative theories, descriptive studies and prescriptive analysis;
- to set up the frameworks that are used in later chapters when outlining the processes of decision analysis and support;
- to indicate how rationality in decision making might be defined; and
- to define and categorise the decision support systems, software and tools that are used in these processes.

As we foreshadowed in section 1.7, we need to make a distinction between *normative* and *descriptive models*. Normative models suggest how people *should* make decisions; descriptive models describe how they actually *do*. Much of this book focuses on drawing these perspectives on decision making together to build *prescriptive* decision analysis and support. Prescriptive analyses guide DMs towards a decision by providing models that capture aspects of the issues before them and of their beliefs and value judgements, while at the same time reflecting some canons of rationality embodied in a normative theory. These models provide the DMs with informative perspectives on the issues, which bring them understanding; and through this understanding their judgements evolve and they reach a decision. In communicating with the DMs and in eliciting their beliefs and value judgements, however, an analyst needs to understand descriptive studies of how people do draw inferences and decide intuitively, because that is what they will do in answering his questions and understanding his reports (Svenson, 1998). Thus, both normative and descriptive models contribute to prescriptive analyses (figure 3.1).

We do not introduce and discuss normative theories of decision making in any great detail. In an ideal world we would: good decision support is built upon the twin pedestals of good understanding of descriptive and normative issues. Normative decision theory requires a deep knowledge of mathematical proof, however. It explores the relationships between a set of assumptions – or axioms – and a set of conclusions. Rather than require advanced mathematical skills, we intend to concentrate on introducing the broad ideas behind normative modelling; and we ask you to trust us later when we assert that the use of a particular method of decision analysis necessarily requires the adoption of a given set of assumptions. In the next section, however, we do venture into some mathematical detail of the simplest of normative theories, just to give an indication of their style and import. Readers who are uncomfortable with the symbolic presentation of assumptions and conclusions should still be able to understand the ideas from skimming the text. In section 3 we give a simple derivation of the SEU model indicating how it follows from a set of very plausible

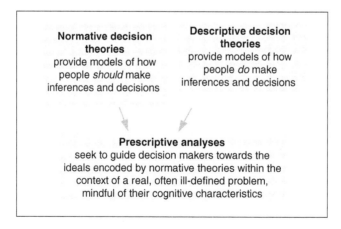

Figure 3.1   Prescriptive decision support

assumptions. The mathematical notation that we need to do this (though perhaps not the mathematical ideas themselves) is significantly more complex than that of section 2, and so we have structured the book and later discussion so that this axiomatic approach to the SEU model may be omitted at a first reading.

In sections 4, 5 and 6 we turn to a discussion of the process of prescriptive decision analysis. Section 7 introduces the concept of a decision support system and offers a categorisation of the different forms of decision support appropriate to different contexts. Finally, we close by indicating that we do not always need the structure of a DSS or a formal decision analysis to overcome the biases and other cognitive limitations indicated in the previous chapter. There are plenty of good heuristics that we can train ourselves to use to improve our judgements.

3.2 An introduction to normative modelling

Philosophy must be of some use and we must take it seriously: it must clear our thoughts and actions. (Frank Plumpton Ramsay)

Normative decision theories begin by making assumptions about the characteristics of rational decision making. They then explore the implications of these assumptions. In a very real sense, they seek to define operationally what is meant by rational decision making. Normative decision theories lie at the interface between philosophy, mathematics and economics. To give a flavour of such theories, in this section we discuss the assumptions underpinning the simplest of all models of rational preferences: weak orders and ordinal value functions. Then, in the next section, we sketch the development of the SEU model as a normative decision theory.

We focus in this section on decisions under certainty – i.e. we assume that each available action leads to an unambiguous consequence, and the DM has full knowledge of everything that she considers relevant to her problem. Our purpose, therefore, is to discuss and model a rational DM's preferences between the possible consequences. These preferences completely determine her choice of action, for we assume that a rational person will always choose an action that leads to a most preferred consequence; thus, for the present, we talk about her preferences between consequences and actions interchangeably. In modelling preference we must be careful to avoid dictating the actual preferences that a rational DM should hold. For instance, it would be wrong to demand that all rational people prefer tea to coffee. We do demand, however, that a rational person's preferences should be mutually compatible. For instance, if he or she prefers tea to coffee and, in turn, prefers coffee to hot chocolate, then surely he/she must prefer tea to hot chocolate. It is with this and similar requirements that we begin our study.

Let us introduce some notation. We write $a \succeq b$ to mean that the DM *weakly prefers a to b*. An alternative, perhaps more expressive interpretation is that she holds a to be *at least as good as b*. Operationally we take this to mean that, if offered the choice of a and b, she would not be disappointed if she were forced subsequently to take a. Let A be the set of objects over which the DM's preferences are expressed. We make two specific demands on the consistency that we expect of the rational use of $\succeq$.

First, we demand that $\succeq$ is *complete*: namely

Axiom WO1 (completeness):[1]
for all objects a, b in A, either $a \succeq b$ or $b \succeq a$.

Completeness may be restated as: there is no pair of objects a, b in A such that the DM holds neither a to be a least as good as b nor b to be at least as good as a. In other words, if we do not assume completeness there may be a pair of objects such that, if offered the choice between them, the DM would feel disappointment if she were subsequently forced to accept either one. In such a case it would appear that the act of choosing is more important to the DM than the receipt of the object of this choice. It may be true descriptively that people ascribe more value to the act of deciding than to the consequences of their decision, but it does not seem rational that they should do so. Certainly, when a decision has sufficient significance that a careful analysis seems merited, it is immaterial whether or not the DM enjoys her task. Her concern should be with the result of her decision making.

Second, we demand that her preferences are *transitive*: namely

Axiom WO2 (transitivity):
for all objects a, b, c in A, if $a \succeq b$ and $b \succeq c$, then $a \succeq c$.

The assumption of transitivity seems more than reasonable: surely if a is as good as b and b is as good as c, then a is as good as c, whatever a, b or c are. This cannot be justified other than by an appeal to self-evident good sense, however. In the case of strict preference (see below), a simple money pump argument suggests that transitivity should hold; for weak preferences,

---

[1] If you are uncomfortable with the notation and formality here, simply read the mathematics aloud, replacing $\succeq$ with 'is at least as good as', $\succ$ with 'strictly prefers' and $\sim$ with 'is indifferent to'. The statements will seem obvious. Indeed, you will probably convince yourself that mathematics is about making the blindingly obvious impenetrable!

though, there are no such motivating arguments. Moreover, behavioural studies have found that real DMs can exhibit intransitive preferences (Tversky, 1969).

There are two further preference orders related to weak preference: *indifference* and *strict preference*. We write $a \succ b$ to mean that the DM *strictly prefers a to b*; in other words, if she were offered a straight choice between a and b, she would be disappointed if she were forced subsequently to take b. We use the notation $a \sim b$ to mean that the DM is *indifferent* between a and b; in other words, she is equally happy to receive either a or b.

We demand that a rational DM uses the notions of weak preference, strict preference and indifference in a consistent fashion. Specifically,

Axiom WO3:
$a \succ b$ if and only if $a \succeq b$ and $b \nsucceq a$.

In other words, the DM strictly prefers a to b if and only if she considers a to be at least as good as b but not vice versa.

Axiom WO4:
$a \sim b$ if and only $a \succeq b$ and $b \nsucceq a$.

In other words, she holds a and b indifferent if she considers each to be at least as good as the other.

From the four axioms WO1 to WO4 some simple and totally unsurprising results follow. First, some properties of strict preference and indifference.

Theorem
(i)   Strict preference is asymmetric: for all objects a, b in A, $a \succ b$ implies $b \nsucc a$.
(ii) Strict preference is transitive: for all objects a, b, c in A, if $a \succ b$ and $b \succ c$, then $a \succ c$.
(iii) Indifference is reflexive: for all objects a in A, $a \sim a$.
(iv) Indifference is symmetric: for all objects a, b in A, $a \sim b$ implies $b \sim a$.
(v)   Indifference is transitive: for all objects a, b, c in A, if $a \sim b$ and $b \sim c$, then $a \sim c$.
(vi) Indifference and strict preference combine transitively: for all objects a, b, c in A, if $a \succ b$ and $b \sim c$, then $a \succ c$; and, if $a \sim b$ and $b \succ c$, then $a \succ c$.

Proof: see, for example, French (1986).

All these results seem sensible. Moreover, there is a *money pump* argument that gives normative weight to conclusion (ii) that strict preference is transitive. Consider the following example.[2]

An agency has three secretaries *a*, *b*, *c* on its books, and an employer has interviewed them all and (despite *our* better judgement) strictly prefers *a* to *b*, *b* to *c* and *c* to *a*. Suppose that, between the interviews and the appointment, *c* becomes unavailable. The employer's choice now being between *a* and *b*, she will pay the agency and employ *a*. Next the agency 'discovers' that *c* was not unavailable after all, but *b* has gone off after another job. The agency has *c*; the employer has selected *a*; but she strictly prefers *c* to *a*. The agency will not find it difficult to persuade her to swap *a* for *c* for a suitably small charge, say a penny. At this point the agency 'discovers' that *b* did not get the other job after all, but that *a* is no longer available having suddenly succumbed to a terrible cold. Since the employer strictly prefers *b* to *c*, she will need little persuasion to part with a further penny and swap *c* for *b*. Needless to say, there is a miraculous recovery on *a*'s part, but not before *c* has caught the cold while visiting *a*'s sick bed. Inevitably, the employer pays a further penny and swaps *b* for *a*. We leave the story as the cycle begins afresh, with the employer continually paying the agency three pence per cycle.

Clearly, the 'irrationality' of the employer holding intransitive strict preferences is allowing the agency to pump money endlessly into their coffers. Note that a similar argument would not work with weak preference, as there would be no imperative for the employer to swap one secretary for another.

Conclusion (v) above, that indifference is also transitive, highlights the distinction between normative and descriptive perspectives. Consider: no real person could discriminate between an air temperature and one $0.001°C$ higher. Thus, for any temperature $x°C$ we may assume that a DM is indifferent between being in a room at $x°C$ and one at $(x + 0.001)°C$; she simply would not be able to detect the difference. So, for her,

$$20°C \sim 20.001°C \sim 20.002°C \sim 20.003°C \sim \cdots \sim 100°C.$$

In other words, she is equally happy to be just comfortable as to be boiled alive! Obviously, this is nonsense; but this argument muddles a descriptive perspective with a normative one. Real decision makers are not blessed with infinite powers of discrimination, but we assume that the idealised ones in normative theories have such powers so that we can focus on rational choice per se, without being confused by human limitations. When we pull the normative perspective together with a descriptive one in

---

[2] Forget all aspects of employment and contract law!

a prescriptive analysis, then we need to address the behavioural realities of the actual DMs.

The similarity between weak preference $\succeq$ and the numerical ordering $\geq$ cannot have passed unnoticed; and there is much to be gained from exploiting this similarity. It allows us to model preferences numerically. We say that $v(.)$ is an (*ordinal*) *value function* representing the DM's preferences if $v(.)$ is a real-valued function on A such that

$$v(a) \geq v(b) \text{ if and only if } a \succeq b$$

We say that $v(.)$ *agrees with* or *represents* $\succeq$ *over A.*

Note that a value function[3] representation is very compact; to represent preferences over n objects, we need only n real numbers. Moreover, our great familiarity with real numbers means that we instinctively know the ordering of any two numbers, so we can also quickly perceive the ordering of the underlying alternatives. Analysis can become conceptually easier. For instance, most of us would find it simpler to identify a most preferred object by maximising a value function than by searching through the alternatives, even though the two tasks are essentially the same. Optimisation methods are central to much of decision analysis and OR (see chapter 6). In a variety of senses, one seeks to maximise a value function that represents an organisation's preferences. Simple optimisation methods are based upon the transitivity of numerical orderings. Consider the following maximisation algorithm. Suppose that a candidate solution with numerical value x_1 has been found and that this is bigger than all previous solutions. Now a better candidate solution x_2 is identified: $x_2 > x_1$. Because of transitivity, it is immediate that x_2 is also bigger than all previous solutions; there is no need to check this by comparing x_2 with each of them in turn.

Notwithstanding the advantages that a value function brings, we must be careful, because we are using only the ordering of real numbers in this representation; addition, subtraction, multiplication and division, for instance, have no part to play. Furthermore, the representation is not unique. Consider a set of preferences over five objects, $b \sim e \succ a \succ c \sim d$. These preferences may be represented by an ordinal value function as

$$v(b) = v(e) = 5 > v(a) = 3.5 > v(c) = v(d) = 1$$

---

[3] Generally, we make a distinction between *value functions*, which model preferences in circumstances in which there is no uncertainty, and *utility functions*, which model preferences in the presence of uncertainty and in doing so encode an attitude to risk: see section 8.4.

Instead of choosing 1, 3.5 and 5, we could have chosen any increasing sequence of numbers, such as -1, 0 and 29:

$$w(b) = w(e) = 29 > w(a) = 0 > w(c) = w(d) = -1$$

Comparing these two representations, we can see the danger of reading too much into the numerical representation. The mean of $v(.)$ over the five objects is quickly calculated as 3.1, which is less than $v(a) = 3.5$, whereas the mean of $w(.)$ is found to be 11.2, which is greater than $w(a) = 0$. So we cannot meaningfully say that a is worth more or less than the average. Similarly, $(v(a) - v(c)) > (v(b) - v(a))$ but $(w(a) - w(c)) < (w(b) - w(c))$, so we cannot ascribe a consistent meaning to value differences. It is meaningless to say that the increase in value of a over c is greater or less than that of b over a.

At least, these statements are meaningless under the assumptions made so far. It is important that during a decision analysis one communicates with the DMs in ways that are both meaningful in a cognitive sense – they need to understand the question – and also in the quantitative sense indicated here – otherwise false meaning may be taken from spurious numerical comparisons. It is tempting in any quantitative analysis to use *all* the numerical properties of a model even though only *some* of them correspond to the underlying judgements; and, if one succumbs to temptation, the resulting analysis will be flawed and possibly misleading. Meaningfulness is closely related to the *uniqueness* of the value function representation. In the example above, two different value functions were used to represent the same preferences. It can be shown that two ordinal value functions represent the same weak preference order if and only if they are related by a strictly increasing function: namely if and only if $v(a) = \phi(w(a))$ for all objects a, where the function ϕ is strictly increasing. We say that ordinal value functions are *unique up to strictly increasing transformations*.

We can now step back and see some of the advantages of the formal mathematical approach within normative studies.

- We can identify a set of fundamental assumptions on which our quantitative models are based. Here we have seen the assumptions that justify the use of an ordinal value function.
- We can see what mathematical operations are valid and meaningful within our quantitative model and which ones are not. Here we have seen that ordering (ranking) relationships are valid and meaningful, but, without further assumptions, averaging and taking differences are not.
- We can check that the algorithms that lie at the heart of decision analysis and decision support systems do reflect appropriate operations

related to the DMs' preferences and thus help her towards her most preferred solution. Here we have seen the validity of basic optimisation algorithms that rely on transitivity.

It is important to realise that, unless the mathematical assumptions of quantitative models are explored carefully and their 'good sense' confirmed, then the models may not help the DM to find a good solution to her problem.

3.3 An axiomatic development of the SEU model

We call rationality the distinction of man, when compared with other animals. (J. H. Newman)

Note: this section may be omitted at first (and subsequent!) readings. It is offered as a simple introduction to the axiomatic foundations of the SEU model. We do not give a full derivation; rather, we offer a sketch that, we hope, indicates how a set of plausible assumptions has the necessary implication that an idealised, rational DM should decide according to an SEU ranking.

Subjective probability[4]

The starting point is to assume that, given any two states or events,[5] A and B, that are not necessarily mutually exclusive, the DM has an inherent feeling of *relative likelihood* and so can say which of the following she believes:

A to be more likely than B;
A to be equally likely as B;
A to be less likely than B.

Note that we do not demand that the DM say how much more likely one event is than another, only that she rank them in order of her perception of their likelihood. Some writers, us included, feel that it is not necessary to define this intuitive ranking any further. We claim simply that anyone can meaningfully answer questions of the form 'Do you think it is more, less, or equally likely that it will snow tomorrow rather than rain?'.

---

[4] The reason that we use the adjective 'subjective' to describe probability here will become clear in section 8.2.

[5] Note that sometimes we talk of *states* and others of *events*. To a student of probability there is a serious distinction here; for our purposes there is little difference, however. When we are concerned with external happenings, then it seems more natural to talk in terms of 'events'; when we are concerned with decisions in which the external 'state of the world' is key, then 'state' seems a more natural terminology.

We use the following notation:

$A \succcurlyeq_\ell B$ – the DM believes A to be at least as likely to occur as B;
$A \succ_\ell B$ – the DM believes A to be strictly more likely than B to occur;
$A \sim_\ell B$ – the DM believes A and B to be equally likely to occur.

Thus we use a subscript 'ℓ' to distinguish the DM's judgements of relative likelihood, $\succcurlyeq_\ell$, from her preferences, $\succcurlyeq$. It is possible to make very reasonable assumptions about the consistency of the DM's judgements of relative likelihood that allow us to construct probabilities with the property

$$A \succcurlyeq_\ell B \Leftrightarrow P(A) \geq P(B)$$

These *normative* assumptions represent the consistency that the DM should aspire to. In practice, her unaided judgements of relative likelihood might well be subject to many of the inconsistencies discussed in chapter 2. There are three key assumptions – canons of rationality – that we believe the DM should wish her judgements to obey.

(1) For all events A, B and C, $A \succcurlyeq_\ell B$, $B \succcurlyeq_\ell C$ implies $A \succcurlyeq_\ell C$ – i.e., if she holds A to be at least as likely as B and B to be as least as likely as C, then she *should* hold A to be at least as likely as C – i.e. the relations should be transitive.

(2) If it matters to her, she can form a judgement between *any* two events.

(3) $\forall A, B, C$ with $A \cap C = \phi = B \cap C$,

$$A \succcurlyeq_\ell B \Leftrightarrow A \cup C \succcurlyeq_\ell B \cup C$$

i.e. under the assumption that neither A and C can happen together, nor B and C, if she holds A as likely as B then she should hold A or C as likely as B or C. See figure 3.2.

The next step in the development introduces a *reference experiment* which enables her to make judgements about probability via comparisons between the events of interest and events in a (hypothetical) experiment for which she 'knows' the probabilities. Imagine, for instance, that she compares an event E of interest – e.g. it will rain tomorrow – with an event A based upon a probability wheel: see figure 3.3. Does she think it more likely that the spinning arrow will stop in the sector A than that it will rain tomorrow?

If these assumptions (1) to (3) above are accepted as sensible criteria that describe the consistency expected of rational beliefs and if she is prepared to make comparisons with the reference experiment, then it can be shown that

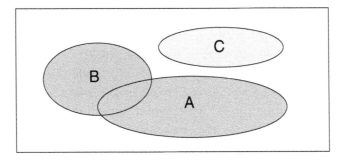

Figure 3.2   Consistency of belief relative to common but disjoint events

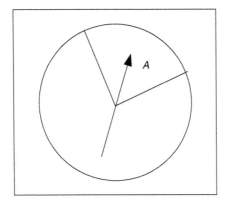

Figure 3.3   A probability wheel

the DM should represent her uncertainty by probabilities (see, *inter alia*, DeGroot, 1970, French, 1986, and French and Ríos Insua, 2000, for full expositions of the argument). Section 8.3 provides a numerical example that essentially illustrates the formal development here.

The reference experiment also provides an operational mechanism for assessing the DM's probability. She can be asked to compare her belief in an external event *E* happening with the event that the spinning arrow stops in sector *A*. The size of the sector *A* can be adjusted until she believes them to be equally likely, thus determining her subjective probability for *E*. Alternatively, if she prefers to choose between gambles than compare her uncertainty about *E* with the sector *A*, she can be asked to choose between two gambles, the first awarding £100 if *E* happens and nothing otherwise, the second awarding £100 if the arrow ends in sector *A* and nothing otherwise. Many people can see little difference between these choices: surely they are the same! The issue here has long been debated in economics and decision theory, however. Do we know our preferences or can we only reveal them through our choices? We tend to subscribe to the view that, after suitable reflection, we do know our preferences; for a discussion of the alternative view, see Savage (1972).

The subjective interpretation of probability gives us a tool for quantifying belief and uncertainty in decision analysis, because it can be applied to *unique* sets of circumstances; we can discuss, for instance, the DM's probability that the stock market increases by more than twenty-five points tomorrow.

Preferences over lotteries

In the world of gambling there are many simple, easily understood examples in which simple decisions with risk have to be made and in which the outcomes are uncertain. We therefore continue our discussion of decisions with risk in this context. Suppose that the DM has to choose between a number of gambles in which the outcomes are determined solely by some simple and fair chance mechanisms. Thus the probability of any outcome is well defined and uncontroversial. We refer to these as *lotteries*.

We lose little by assuming that only a finite number of prizes are possible. Let $C = \{c_1, c_2, \ldots, c_r\}$ be the set of possible prizes. In particular, we assume that one of the prizes is the 'prize' of losing – i.e. of winning nothing. Moreover, we assume that the prizes include the deduction of any stake. Thus, if the DM pays £1 for a lottery ticket and wins a teddy bear, her prize is 'an increase in her possessions of a teddy bear and a decrease in her cash assets of £1'.

A typical lottery is represented by

$$l = \langle p_1, c_1; p_2, c_2; \ldots; p_r, c_r \rangle$$

where $p_i \geq 0$ is the probability of winning c_i ($i = 1, 2, \ldots, r$) and $\Sigma_i p_i = 1$. It is quite possible that several $p_i = 0$, indicating that certain prizes cannot be awarded in a particular lottery. We refer to such lotteries as *simple lotteries*, because, once the chance mechanism is resolved, the prize is determined. We also assume that the DM is prepared to consider *compound lotteries*; here some or all of the 'prizes' may be entries into further lotteries. For instance, the compound lottery

$$\langle q_1, l_1; q_2, l_2; \ldots; q_s, l_s \rangle$$

gives probabilities $q_i \geq 0$ of winning an entry into lottery l_i ($i = 1, 2, \ldots, s$; $\Sigma_i q_i = 1$). Such compound lotteries are often found in real life: raffles in which some of the prizes are premium bonds or national lottery tickets.

We allow lotteries to be compounded several times. Since a lottery may give rise to a prize immediately in C or to an entry into a further lottery, we refer to the *outcomes* of a lottery rather than prizes. A *direct outcome* is one that results from the single randomisation that governs the lottery. The *ultimate prizes* of a lottery are those members of C that may ultimately result from a compound lottery once all the chance mechanisms have been resolved.

We assume that the DM has to choose between lotteries in a set L. These lotteries may be simple or compound. We do assume, however, that all lotteries are finitely compounded. A *finitely compounded lottery* is one that yields prizes from the set C after a finite number of randomisations. We let A be the set of all possible prizes together with a set of simple and finitely compounded lotteries that contains the set L. C and L are thus subsets of A. Note that A contains lotteries that are not members of L; for the present, however, we avoid specifying what these additional lotteries may be.

In considering the DM's preferences between the members of A, we make several reasonable assumptions concerning the consistency of her preferences if she is to be considered rational. We intend to show that these assumptions imply the existence of a utility function $u(.)$ on C such that the DM holds

$$c_i \succcurlyeq c_j \Leftrightarrow u(c_i) \geq u(cj) \text{ for any } c_i, c_j \text{ in } C$$

and

$$\langle p_1, c_1; p_2, c_2; \ldots; p_r, c_r \rangle \succeq \langle p'_1, c_1; p'_2, c_2; \ldots; p'_r, c_r \rangle$$
$$\Leftrightarrow \sum_i p_i u(c_i) \geq \sum_i p'_i u(c_i)$$

for any pair of simple lotteries in A. The first condition shows that $u(.)$ is an ordinal value function on the set of prizes C; the second condition shows that $u(.)$ possesses the *expected utility property* on the set of simple lotteries. The assumptions also justify choosing between compound lotteries according to the expected utility rule.

The first assumption that we make is that the DM's weak preferences, strict preferences and indifferences over A should obey the assumptions that we discussed in section 2; in particular, weak preference between lotteries and prizes should be complete and transitive.

For convenience and without any loss of generality, we label the prizes in the order of her preferences – i.e. such that she holds $c_1 \succcurlyeq c_2 \succcurlyeq \ldots \succcurlyeq c_r$. Since there is little to be gained from discussing a situation in which a DM does not care which prize she receives, we assume that she strictly prefers c_1 to c_r.

Even though we have set our discussion in the context of simple gambling situations, we do not allow our rational DM to enjoy gambling – e.g. from watching a roulette wheel spin or dice being thrown – other than the enjoyment that she gains from any prize she might win. The chance mechanism that gives rise to the probabilities is assumed to be irrelevant.

Our next assumption, which we refer to as the *reduction of compound lotteries*, also denies any value to an aspect of the chance mechanism itself. Consider the compound lottery $l = \langle q_1, l_1; q_2, l_2; \ldots ; q_s, l_s \rangle$, which gives as prizes entries into further simple lotteries $l_1, l_2, \ldots, l_s$, where

$$l_j = \langle p_{j1}, c_1; p_{j2}, c_2; \ldots; p_{js}, c_s \rangle$$

for $j = 1, 2, \ldots, s$. Let l' be the simple lottery $\langle p_1, c_1; p_2, c_2; \ldots; p_r, c_r \rangle$, where

$$p_i = q_1 p_{1i} + q_2 p_{2i} + \ldots + q_s p_{si} \text{ for } i = 1, 2, \ldots, r$$

Then the DM must be indifferent between l and l': namely $l \sim l'$. To understand the import of this assumption, notice that p_i is the probability that the prize c_i will ultimately result from the compound lottery l. Thus, the assumption is simply demanding that the DM's preferences depend only upon the ultimate prizes and the probabilities with which they are obtained; the number of chance mechanisms involved in generating these probabilities is irrelevant.

In the presence of the other assumptions, this reduction of compound lotteries assumption has an implication, which we state now but prove later. Consider the lottery $\langle 0, c_1; 0, c_2; \ldots ; 1, c_i; \ldots ; 0, c_r \rangle$ – i.e. the lottery that gives a 100 per cent chance of receiving c_i and no chance of receiving anything else. It seems reasonable to suppose that the DM is indifferent between simply being given c_i and entering this lottery:

$$c_i \sim \langle 0, c_1; 0, c_2; \ldots; 1, c_i; \ldots; 0, c_r \rangle \text{ for all } i = 1, 2, \ldots, r$$

It might be argued – indeed, many have argued – that, in ignoring the thrill of gambling, our theory loses something. Many people *do* enjoy watching the spin of a roulette wheel to see whether they win, quite independently of the prize that they might win. Visitors to casinos often place imaginary bets just for the pleasure of seeing whether they would have won. Equally, some may have such moral objections to gambling that each spin of the wheel is abhorrent to them. Nevertheless, while these observations are undoubtedly true, they are, we would contend, irrelevant to our present argument. We are not developing a descriptive theory of decision making, and certainly not a descriptive theory of gambling.

Rather, we are developing a normative theory of decision making. How *should* a DM choose in the face of uncertainty? Our ultimate aim is to develop a style of decision analysis that is appropriate to problems such as the siting of nuclear power stations, budgeting decisions in industry, etc. In such contexts we would not think it rational for a DM to allow her enjoyment of watching chance mechanisms being resolved to influence her decision.

Our next assumption, which we call *substitutability*, says that if the DM is indifferent between two objects in A then she does not mind whether she wins one or the other in a lottery. To be precise, let b, c in A be such that the DM holds $b \sim c$. Let l in A be any lottery, simple or compound, such that

$$l = \langle \ldots ; q, b; \ldots \rangle$$

i.e. there is a probability q that b is a direct outcome of l. Let l' be constructed from l by substituting c for b and leaving all other outcomes and all probabilities unchanged – namely

$$l' = \langle \ldots ; q, c; \ldots \rangle$$

Then the DM holds $l \sim l'$. There are a number of points that should be noted about this assumption. First, b, c in A, so each may be a prize or a lottery. Second, q is the probability that b is a *direct* outcome. It is not the probability that b is an *indirect* outcome. Similarly, the only difference between l and l' is that c has been substituted for b as a *direct* outcome. If other outcomes in l are entries into further lotteries that in turn give b as an outcome, then c is *not* substituted for b in these – i.e. c is not substituted for b as an indirect outcome.

At first sight, substitutability seems uncontroversial. If $b \sim c$, how can the DM mind whether she receives b or c as a result of a lottery? Consider the following, however: suppose that b is a prize and c a lottery. Then substituting c for b increases uncertainty, because at least one more chance mechanism may have to be resolved before the ultimate prize of the lottery is determined. Given this extra uncertainty, it is perhaps reasonable for the DM to have a preference between l and l'. Although this argument convinces some, however, it fails to convince us. In holding $b \sim c$ the DM must surely already have allowed for the uncertainty in c. Does the uncertainty inherent in c change in some way when it is substituted into a further lottery? We think not.

The set A contains both the set of prizes C and the set of lotteries L between which the DM must choose. We have also indicated that it contains some further lotteries, and the time has come to explain what these are. We assume that the DM is prepared to consider hypothetical lotteries of the form

$$c_1 p c_r = \langle p, c_1; 0, c_2; 0, c_3; \ldots; 0, c_{r-1}; (1-p), c_r \rangle$$

i.e. a simple lottery that gives rise to c_1, the most preferred prize in C, with probability p, and c_r, the least preferred prize in C, with probability $(1-p)$; any other prize is impossible. Since we need to refer to such lotteries constantly in the next few pages, we use the shortened notation $c_1 p c_r$.

It is easy to see how the DM might visualise such lotteries. She need only imagine a probability wheel with the background divided into two sectors such that the angles θ and $(360° - \theta)$ are in the ratio $p{:}(1-p)$: see figure 3.4. The lottery $c_1 p c_r$ is visualised by imagining that the pointer is spun, and that the prize c_1 is awarded if it stops in the sector with angle θ and the prize c_r awarded if it stops in that with angle $(360° - \theta)$.

We assume that the DM is prepared to imagine and to consider her preferences for such lotteries for all possible values of p, $0 \le p \le 1$. As we shall see, by this assumption we introduce into the problem a reference scale or 'ruler' against which the DM can measure her preference. The set of lotteries $\{c_1 p c_r \mid 0 \le p \le 1\}$ is known as the *reference* or *auxiliary experiment*, and a lottery of the form $c_1 p c_r$ as a *reference lottery*. We assume that all these reference lotteries lie in A – namely

$$c_1 p c_r \text{ is in } A \text{ for all } p, 0 \le p \le 1$$

We are now in a position to state the structure of A. It comprises all the prizes in C, all the lotteries in L and all possible reference lotteries $c_1 p c_r$, together with all finitely compounded lotteries that may be constructed by

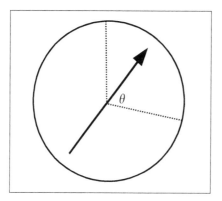

Figure 3.4   A probability wheel with a sector of angle θ

substituting for an outcome of a lottery any prize or reference lottery in A that is indifferent to that outcome. This will become clearer as the discussion progresses.

The introduction of hypothetical reference lotteries is often attacked on the grounds that it requires the DM to consider her preferences between these imaginary objects and the real objects of choice. Why should she have such preferences? It is surely not rational to ask a DM to daydream about what can never be. This argument makes a false and emotive contrast, however, between what is real and what is imaginary. In a sense, all the alternatives in a decision problem are imaginary until one is selected; and, at that point, the decision problem ceases to exist, because the choice has been made. The selected alternative becomes real and the unselected alternatives become not just imaginary but impossible, since the alternatives in a decision problem are mutually exclusive. The true difference between the reference lotteries and the lotteries in L is that circumstances have motivated the DM to consider the objects in L. She may choose one and so affect her future. Thus she is motivated to consider her preferences between the lotteries in L. She is not motivated to think about her preferences between the reference lotteries. Suppose, however, that we provide that motivation. Suppose that we show her that by thinking about the reference lotteries she may clarify her preferences in L and help herself towards a better decision. Then surely that will motivate her sufficiently to consider seriously her preferences over the whole of A and not just over L.

Our next assumption, *monotonicity*, states something that is completely uncontroversial. We assume that the DM's preferences between two reference lotteries are such that she prefers the lottery that gives her the greater probability of winning c_1, the best prize, and, therefore, also the lesser probability of winning c_r, the worst prize – namely

$$c_1 p c_r \succcurlyeq c_1 p' c_r \Leftrightarrow p \geq p'$$

For our final assumption we return to the controversial. To introduce it, we consider an example. Suppose that c_1 is £100, that c_r is £0 and that some prize c_i is £40. Consider reference lotteries $c_1 p c_r$ for different values of p. For large values of p, say $p = 0.9999$, it is likely that the DM prefers the lottery to having £40 for certain – namely

$$£100(0.9999)£0 \succ £40$$

(The parentheses in £100(0.9999)£0 have been introduced to clarify the notation $c_1 p c_r$ when numerical values have been substituted.) Similarly, for small values of p, say $p = 0.0001$, it is likely that the DM prefers having £40 for certain to the lottery – namely

$$£40 \succ £100(0.0001)£0$$

Consider a sequence of reference lotteries as p increases from 0.0 to 1.0. Initially the prize £40 is preferred to the lotteries, but, as p increases, this preference reverses. This argument suggests strongly that there is an intermediate value of p such that the DM is indifferent between the lottery and having £40 for certain. See figure 3.5.

In general, we make the following *continuity* assumption: for all c_i in C there exists u_i, $0 \le u_i \le 1$, such that $c_i \sim c_1 u_i c_r$. We have chosen to use u_i rather than p_i to denote the probability in the reference lottery that gives indifference with c_i, because the utility function, whose existence we shortly show, is such that $u(c_i) = u_i$. Note also that the continuity assumption shows the value of u_i to be unique. Suppose that there were two values, u_i and u_i', such that

$$c_1 u_i c_r \sim c_i \sim c_1 u_i' c_r$$

Then either $u_i > u_i'$, which implies that $c_1 u_i c_r \succ c_1 u_i' c_r$, or $u_i' > u_i$, which implies that $c_1 u_i' c_r \succ c_1 u_i c_r$, both of which contradict the assumed indifference.

There are two important criticisms of continuity. First, many argue that there may be prizes such that for no value of u_i does the DM hold $c_1 u_i c_r \sim c_i$. For instance, suppose that $c_1 = £1$, $c_i = £0$ and c_r is the DM's death. Then surely for any value of $u_i < 1$ the DM would strictly prefer to receive £0 for certain than to take the lottery with its risk of her death; at best, the lottery can make her only £1 better off. If $u_i = 1$, then £1(1)death $\sim$ £1 $\succ$ £0, since preferences clearly increase with monetary value. Thus there is no value of u_i such that £1(u_i)death $\sim$ £0.

Persuasive though this argument is, it hardly bears inspection. Suppose $u_i = (1 - 10^{-20})$; the lottery then gives a 1 in 10^{20} chance of death. The argument above suggests that the DM would not take this risk just for the chance – admittedly very high chance – of making £1. Each day, though, we all take far greater risks for far less substantial gains. For example, crossing the road brings a risk of death far greater than 1 in 10^{20}; and many people cross the road just to be in the sun. There are many things that we would refuse to do if we objected to the slightest risk of death; yet we do them. We allow our rational DM to do them too.

The second criticism accepts that, in principle, a value u_i exists such that $c_1 u_i c_r \sim c_i$, but argues that in practice no DM would ever have the

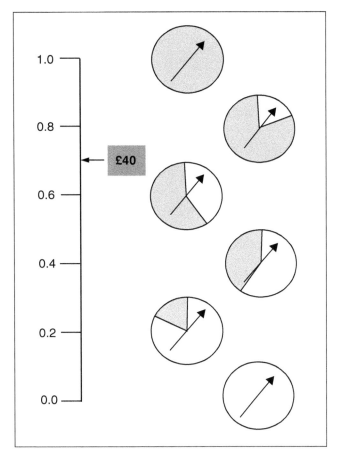

Figure 3.5   Illustration of the idea underlying the continuity assumption
Note: The DM considers her preference for a certain prize of £40 relative to
a sequence of reference lotteries £100(p)£0 as p increases from 0.0 to 1.0.
Probability wheels are shown explicitly for $p = 0.0, 0.2, 0.4, 0.6, 0.8, 1.0$. In each
case the unshaded sector yields £0 and the shaded sector yields £100. For the
sake of example, the DM is assumed to hold £40 $\succ$ £100(p)£0 for $p < 0.7$ and
£100(p)£0 $\succ$ £40 for $p > 0.7$. The indifference point is £40 $\sim$ £100(0.7)£0.

discrimination to give it a precise value. Descriptively this is undoubtedly
true. We are developing a normative theory, however, and in an *ideal*
world the DM should be able to give a precise value of u_i.

In the above we assumed that

$$c_i \sim \langle 0, c_1; 0, c_2; \ldots; 1, c_i; \ldots; 0, c_r \rangle$$

for all $i = 1, 2, \ldots, r$, which we have claimed, but not shown, is
implied by our other assumptions. It is time to rectify that omission.

Consider $\langle 0, c_1; 0, c_2; \ldots; 1, c_i; \ldots; 0, c_t \rangle$. By continuity there is a u_i, $0 \leq u_i \leq 1$, such that $c_i \sim c_1 u_i c_r$. Substitute $c_1 u_i c_r$ for c_i in the lottery. Thus

$$\langle 0, c_1; 0, c_2; \ldots; 1, c_i; \ldots; 0, c_r \rangle \sim \langle 0, c_1; 0, c_2; \ldots; 1, (c_1 u_i c_r); \ldots; 0, c_r \rangle$$

by substitutability

$$\sim \langle u_i, c_1; \ldots; 0, c_2; \ldots; 0, c_i; \ldots; (1 - u_i), c_r \rangle$$

by reducing the compound lottery

$$= c_1 u_i c_r$$

$$\sim c_i$$

Note that this result also ensures the obvious requirements that $u_1 = 1$ and $u_r = 0$.

We are now in a position to justify the existence of a utility function. Consider a simple lottery

$$l = \langle p_1, c_1; p_2, c_2; \ldots; p_r, c_r \rangle$$

By continuity each prize c_i is indifferent to a reference lottery $c_1 u_i c_r$, for $i = 1, 2, \ldots, r$. One prize at a time, substitute $c_1 u_i c_r$ for c_i in the lottery l. Substitutability and transitivity of indifference give

$$l = \langle p_1, c_1; p_2, c_2; \ldots; p_r, c_r \rangle$$
$$\sim \langle p_1, (c_1 u_1 c_r); p_2, c_2; \ldots; p_r, c_r \rangle$$
$$\sim \langle p_1, (c_1 u_1 c_r); p_2, (c_1 u_2 c_r); \ldots; p_r, c_r \rangle$$
$$\sim \langle p_1, (c_1 u_1 c_r); p_2, (c_1 u_2 c_r); \ldots; p_r(c_1 u_r c_r) \rangle$$

Remembering that each reference lottery is a simple lottery,

$$(c_1 u_i c_r) = \langle u_i, c_1; 0, c_2; \ldots; 0, c_{r-1}; (1 - u_i) c_r) \rangle$$

we may reduce the compound lottery, giving

$$l \sim \langle (p_1 u_1 + p_2 u_2 + \ldots + p_r u_r), c_1; 0, c_2; \ldots; 0, c_{r-1}; (p_1(1 - u_1) + p_2(1 - u_2) + \ldots + p_r(1 - u_r)) c_r \rangle$$
$$= x_1 \left(\sum\nolimits_{i=1}^{r} p_i u_i \right) x_r$$

i.e. the simple lottery l is indifferent to a reference lottery that gives a probability of $\Sigma_i p_i u_i$ to the receipt of c_1.

Similarly, if $l' = \langle p_1', c_1; p_2', c_2; \ldots; p_r', c_r \rangle$, $l' \sim c_1 \left(\sum_{i=1}^{r} p_i' u_i \right) c_r$. It follows from our assumptions about weak preference and monotonicity that

$$l \succeq l'$$

$$\Leftrightarrow \quad c_1 \left(\sum_{i=1}^{r} p_i u_i \right) c_r \succeq c_1 \left(\sum_{i=1}^{r} p_i' u_i \right) c_r$$

$$\Leftrightarrow \quad \left(\sum_{i=1}^{r} p_i u_i \right) \geq \left(\sum_{i=1}^{r} p_i' u_i \right)$$

On setting $u(c_i) = u_i$ we obtain the expected utility property.

That $u(.)$ is an ordinal value function over the set of prizes is a straightforward deduction. From continuity and monotonicity we have

$$c_i \succeq c_j$$

$$\Leftrightarrow c_1 u_i c_r \succeq c_1 u_j c_r$$

$$\Leftrightarrow u_i \geq u_j$$

Subjective expected utility

We are now in a position to start pulling things together. Consider a decision table and a decision with risk as introduced in section 1.5. We assumed there that the DM's ranking of the actions would be formed as follows. The DM's beliefs and preferences would be modelled by, respectively,

- a *subjective probability distribution*, $P(.)$, which represents her belief about the unknown state of the world; and
- a *utility function*, $u(.)$, which represents her preferences.

These will be the subjective probability distribution and utility function that we have just developed in this section; *but we have not quite shown that yet.*

In section 1.5 we were discussing a decision formulated as a decision table; here we have been discussing choices between lotteries. To extend our argument in this section to the context of a decision table and justify the SEU model, we need only associate each action, a_i, in the table with the lottery

$$\langle P(\theta_1), c_{i1}; P(\theta_2), c_{i2}; \ldots; P(\theta_n), c_{in} \rangle$$

If we assume that she perceives the real action a_i and this lottery to be equal in value to her, then it is a trivial matter to argue that her preferences between the actions a_i should correspond to the expected utility ranking. Thus we arrive at the SEU model, which asserts that to combine her beliefs and preferences coherently in order to rank the actions in the table the DM should form *expected utilities*:

$$Eu[a_i] = \sum_{j=1}^{n} u(c_{ij}) P(\theta_j)$$

She should then rank a_i above a_k if and only if its expected utility is higher, i.e.

$$Eu[a_i] > Eu[a_k]$$

We should, perhaps, note one further assumption in the above: namely, that decision problems can and should be framed in terms of actions, states and consequences – i.e. as decision tables. This is perhaps one of the least discussed assumptions of SEU theory. It is fundamental to the separation of the modelling of belief from the modelling of preferences: without this separation, neither $P(.)$ nor $u(.)$ could be defined independently of each other. The assumption has been made since the earliest discussions of rational economic man. It is actually implicit in the prospect theory model, which, as we have seen, is a descriptive, not normative, model of choice. Some have questioned its validity, however (Kadane and Winkler, 1988). For further details and discussion of this assumption, see French and Ríos Insua (2000).

3.4 Prescriptive decision analysis and requisite modelling

Man must learn to simplify, but not to the point of falsification. (Aldous Huxley)

Prescriptive decision analysis seeks to guide DMs faced with a real problem of choice towards the rationality encoded in normative theories, mindful that their instinctive judgements may not satisfy the tenets and imperatives of normative decision theory (figure 3.1). The key to 'squaring this circle' is to recognise that DMs are not unchanging beings. They can reflect; they can learn; they can understand. As a result, their preferences and beliefs can change. We often use the word *evolution*. Prescriptive analyses, we argue, guide the evolution of the DMs' perceptions and judgements. During prescriptive analyses these change. Their perceptions and judgements evolve because of the analysis; it is the purpose of the analysis that they should. As we noted in section 2.4, Slovic (1995) has argued that people do not have clearly defined and stable preferences between all possible impacts in all conceivable decision contexts. Rather, they construct them as they consider and deliberate on a particular decision. We see the role of prescriptive decision analysis as helping DMs construct their preferences and also their uncertainties.

It is vital therefore to see the modelling process involved as creative, dynamic and cyclic. The DMs' beliefs and preferences are assessed and modelled. The models are explored, leading to insights and a revision of the DMs' judgements, and thence revision of the models used. As part of this process, we expect the DMs to recognise, for instance, that their initial judgements were intransitive, that this does not seem rational and that, on reflection, they would wish to exhibit transitive preferences. Thus they wish to reflect on and revise their judgements. A major component of prescriptive analysis is the support of this process of reflection and revision towards consistency with the assumptions of the underlying normative model. Because of this it is vital that the assumptions, the axiomatic base, of the normative model are understood. This is why normative theories have such a formal structure: so that the assumptions are clearly exhibited. The DMs and analyst should discuss the assumptions to check that, for the DMs, they do represent canons of rationality. Were it otherwise, the pressure on the DM to revise their judgements in that direction would be quite inappropriate; and another normative model based upon different, more acceptable assumptions should be adopted.

We therefore see prescriptive analysis as an ongoing 'discussion' between the DMs and the model, in which the DMs' judgements are elicited and their implications within the context of the model explored, including their coherence with the axiomatic base of the model. The DMs reflect upon these explorations and in doing so gain insight. These insights lead to evolution in their judgements, and perhaps revisions to the model, and the process repeats. The analyst's role is to mediate and smooth this discussion by handling the technical aspects. The process cycles until no new insights are found. We term this process *requisite modelling* (Phillips, 1984), the final model being requisite or sufficient for the decision faced.

Note here that the modelling process has a different character from that of 'scientific modelling'. Scientists seek to understand the world in all its detail. Thus they examine and model behaviour in as fine detail as they can manage, building in more and more complexity to their models. For many decisions, much more rough and ready models may be sufficient. Suppose that you are travelling tomorrow and need to consider whether to take a raincoat. A meteorologist with access to a supercomputer may be able to be quite precise about the likelihood of rain and its intensity at different times and places on your journey; but, equally, a glance at the latest satellite pictures may tell him or her that it is highly likely to rain on some part of your journey tomorrow. The latter prediction is quite sufficient – requisite – to enable you to take your decision. Conversely, one must be careful not to use too simple a model to support a decision. Checking a barometer at your house and seeing that rain is unlikely locally for the next day is unlikely to be helpful if your journey will take you far from home. Requisite modelling is about using a model that is fit for its purpose: sufficiently detailed to bring understanding to the DMs, but not overly so.

3.5 Value-focused thinking

If you limit your choices only to what seems possible or reasonable, you disconnect yourself from what you truly want, and all that is left is a compromise. (Robert Fritz)

A seminal book on the practice of (prescriptive) decision analysis and support is Keeney's *Value-focused Thinking*. To be honest, in it he says very little that has not been said before, but he does gather together the most coherent and cogent set of arguments to promote the idea that we should think about what we want before we think about how to achieve that end. He begins with the following words (Keeney, 1992):

Values are what we care about. As such, values should be the driving force for our decision making. They should be the basis for the time and effort we spend thinking about decisions. But this is not the way it is. It is not even close to the way it is.

Instead, decision making usually focuses on the choice among alternatives. Indeed, it is common to characterise a decision problem by the alternatives available. It seems as if the alternatives present themselves and the decision problem begins when at least two alternatives have appeared. Descriptively, I think this represents almost all decision situations. Prescriptively, it should be possible to do much better.

He then goes on to argue that we should adopt *value-focused thinking*, namely 'first deciding on what you want and then figuring out how to get it'. In practice, most decision making proceeds in entirely opposite direction. It is *alternative-focused*, in that the options are first identified and only then do the DMs consider their objectives in order to make their choice. Experience has shown that value-focused thinking has two clear advantages.

- Although it may sound paradoxical, value-focused thinking is a more creative way of working. Thinking too much about alternatives seems to constrain the mind, holding its attention on what initially seems possible and what seems to bound the possible. It takes too much as given. Thinking first about the ultimate objectives opens up the mind and allows it think along lines such as 'I wish ... ' or 'Why can't I ... ?' This seems to lead to a more imaginative range of actions from which to choose.

- Value-focused thinking focuses attention on what matters and makes it easier to avoid wasting time on superfluous or irrelevant detail. It directs the resources of the analysis onto the key issues.

Thus, in developing decision analyses we place some emphasis on identifying the DMs' values and objectives very early in the process. In doing so we counter some behavioural evidence – and our own observations in applications – that, left to their own devices, DMs may fail to articulate or even recognise all their objectives within a context (Bond *et al.*, 2008).

3.6 The process of decision analysis and support

An approximate answer to the right problem is worth a good deal more than an exact answer to an approximate problem. (John Tukey)

Supporting a decision can be seen as a consultation process that attempts to focus DMs' attention on the important aspects of a problem. It starts with the definition of a decision problem and it ends with the DMs' commitment to action (Regan and Holtzman, 1995). In order to help the DMs gain insight into the decision problem and clarify their preferences, guidance is given in three stages (figure 3.6).

The first stage is to *formulate* one or more decision models that reflect the decision problem. Note that we see the building of a model as a process that forms a perspective on a set of issues. To understand these issues it may be informative to adopt several perspectives. Hence we should be prepared for a formulation stage that may involve a family of models. Following the tenets of value-focused thinking, the DMs and the analyst should begin by working together to understand the DMs' values and pull these into explicit objectives. Then they should identify

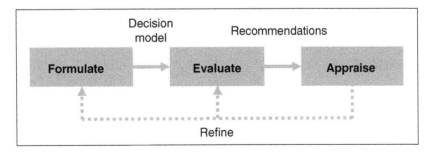

Figure 3.6   The phases of decision analysis
Source: Holtzman (1989).

alternatives and assess the consequences that these may have. They may also need to address and model uncertainties. In the case of instinctive or operational decisions, the effort required to formulate the problem may be relatively small; in the case of strategic decision making, however, problem formulation may require much more thought and effort. Indeed, it may be a very creative process; seldom are all the potential strategies immediately apparent.

The next stage is to *evaluate* the decision models. Essentially, this involves predicting the consequences of each possible alternative and their potential to achieve the DMs' objectives. This process may need to take account of many potential uncertainties in the prediction. The aim of this stage is to guide the DMs towards an alternative that promises to achieve their objectives as well as possible.

The third stage is to *appraise* the recommendation. This involves interpreting the recommended alternative as a real-world action. Remember that the model will be essentially mathematical and that knowing that $x = 2.69$ or whatever may not be meaningful to the DMs. Moreover, since the model is a simplification of the real world, the DMs need to reflect on the recommendation and see if it makes sense once the complexity of reality re-enters their thinking. They need to assess whether the model has brought them enough understanding to make their decision: is the analysis *requisite*? If it is, they can move on and implement the alternative; if not, there is a need to refine the models and analysis. Thus a refinement path loops back in figure 3.6. The decision model is progressively refined until the DMs are confident that the components, structure and values of the decision model accurately represent their decision problem.

We return to the discussion of problem formulation in chapter 9 and the whole process of decision analysis in chapters 7 to 10.

3.7 Decision support software and systems

To err is human, but to really foul things up requires a computer. (Anonymous)

Our discussion so far has focused on decision making and the general process of providing prescriptive support. Prescriptive decision support may be provided via face-to-face discussion between the analyst and DMs, perhaps supported by a few handwritten calculations on a flip chart. More and more, however, the decision support process relies on the use of software and information systems.

There are many definitions of what is meant by a DSS. The classic definition offered by Gorry and Scott Morton (1971) is that they are 'interactive computer-based systems, which help DMs utilise data and models to solve unstructured problems'. Silver (1991) defines a DSS as 'a computer-based information system that affects or is intended to affect how people make decisions'. Lewis (1991) surveys thirty-nine introductory textbooks on information systems and finds that about three-quarters relate the definition of information systems to decision making. The study of DSS would therefore seem to embrace the whole of information systems theory. We intend to be more selective, however, and adopt the following definition.

A *decision support system* is a computer-based system that supports the decision-making process, helping DMs to understand the problem before them and to form and explore the implications of their judgements, and hence to make a decision based upon understanding.

We emphasise support for the evolution of judgement and understanding. In our view, a 'true' DSS is as much about modelling and understanding the perspectives, views, preferences, values and uncertainties of the DMs as exploring and understanding external data. When we wish to emphasise that several DMs interact using a DSS, we call it a group decision support system (GDSS); if we wish to emphasise further that the group may be distributed and the interactions are internet-based, we refer to a web-based group decision support system (wGDSS).

Some categorise DSSs according to whether they are simply driven by data, by being built on a database, or based on a model, such as a linear programme or decision tree (Laudon and Laudon, 2006; Mallach, 2000). We do not follow this route, since all DSSs are built on both data and models, albeit with different emphases. We adopt a different approach, focusing not on the functionality of the DSSs but on the domain of managerial activity they support – namely the corporate strategic domain, the general domain, the operational domain and the hands-on work domain: see section 1.2. Edwards *et al.* (2000) make a similar classification in their discussion of the role of expert systems (ESs) in business decision making (see also Chen and Lee, 2003). Our categorisation also reflects the level of support provided, starting from minimal analytic support to full judgemental support.

Table 3.1 defines four levels of decision support. The first, level 0, refers simply to the presentation of data, or, to be consistent with the distinction between data and information that we make in section 4.3, the presentation

Table 3.1 Levels of decision support

Level 0	Acquisition, checking and presentation of data, directly or with minimal analysis, to DMs.
Level 1	Analysis and forecasting of the current and future environment.
Level 2	Simulation and analysis of the consequences of potential strategies; determination of their feasibility and quantification of their benefits and disadvantages.
Level 3	Evaluation and ranking of alternative strategies in the face of uncertainty by balancing their respective benefits and disadvantages.

of information. At this level the DSS simply extracts the relevant data from databases and presents them to the DMs with minimal analysis. Level 0 DSSs include management information systems (MISs) and executive information systems (EISs), with their graphical and tabular summaries, and geographical information systems (GISs), relating spatial, temporal and factual data. Also included are statistical systems that provide exploratory and inferential analyses,[6] but not forecasting systems.

Level 1 systems take the available data and combine these perhaps with an expert's judgements, either expressed directly or through the use of one or more models, to forecast how the environment will evolve. Such systems predict the future, but stop short of predicting the consequences of the DMs' potential interventions. Thus here we include, *inter alia*, economic forecasting systems, environmental impact forecasts and market share predictions.

Level 0 and 1 systems do not recognise, per se, that DMs face a decision. In terms of our definition of a DSS, they help the DMs' understanding grow only in relation to (their perception of) the external environment, either as it is (level 0) or as it is likely to evolve (level 1). Level 2 systems predict the consequences of the various alternative strategies facing the DMs. Although they may predict the success of alternative actions against a number of performance measures, level 2 systems stop short of prescriptive decision support in our terms. They do not support the process of judgement that DMs must undergo to make the decision. It is at level 3 that we encounter systems that do provide prescriptive support, in that they do help DMs explore, evolve and act upon their judgements. Level 3 decision support helps DMs weigh together conflicting criteria and also balance potential benefits and costs with key uncertainties.

---

[6] Exploratory statistical analyses literally help explore a data set, offering different plots and summary statistics that help the user 'see' patterns and shape in the data. Inferential statistical analyses investigate whether hypotheses or models fit the data, estimating parameters and conducting hypotheses tests.

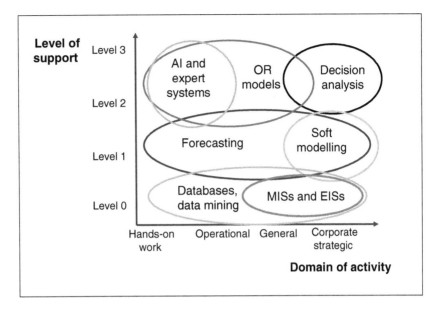

Figure 3.7   Categorisation of a variety of DSSs according to domain and level of support

Figure 3.7 indicates a rough categorisation of a variety of DSSs according to both the domain of managerial activity and the level of support. Databases and data mining can provide level 0 support over the whole range of activities, but are often referred to as management or executive information systems in the case of the higher domains of activity (see section 4.4). ESs, neural nets and other AI techniques again provide level 2 and 3 support (see chapter 5), but are only really suited to the highly structured and repetitive situations found in the hands-on domain (Edwards *et al.*, 2000). OR modelling – e.g. linear programming, inventory models and project planning tools (see chapter 6) – underpins many of the systems used in general operation and hands-on domains at levels 2 and 3, but OR techniques tend to assume too much structure to be used in the corporate domain. For supporting decision making in the highly unstructured contexts of the corporate strategic domain we need the broad range of tools from the discipline known as decision analysis (see chapters 7 to 10).

3.8 Good heuristics

The most important thing in life is not to capitalise on your successes – any fool can do that. The really important thing is to profit from your mistakes. (William Bolitho)

Of course, it does not always require complex processes, detailed calculations and a large computing system to improve decision making.

There are many simple ways of improving our thinking and judgements. Some are 'rational', in the sense that they cohere with a normative theory – at least to a first approximation. Others are heuristics: good rules of thumb and practices that generally are better than our naïve instincts.

For instance, knowing that we are all liable to defensive avoidance or bounded awareness, we can explicitly adopt good habits of continually seeking information and challenging our thinking. Bazerman and Chugh (2006) recommend the following practices.

- See information:
  - know what you are looking for and train yourself to recognise it;
  - develop an external perspective, or bring someone else into to look with you.
- Seek information:
  - challenge the absence of contradictory evidence in reports and recommendations;
  - assume that the information that you need exists;
  - when the risks are high, seek hard.
- Use information:
  - unpack the situation and make sure that you are not just focusing on one aspect while discounting other information and issues.
- Share information:
  - everybody has unique information, so ask for it explicitly;
  - create organisational structures that make sharing information the norm.

In the next chapter we discuss executive information systems and knowledge management systems that help support such good habits: the former seek information to monitor an organisation's operations and strategic process, while the latter encourage information sharing and the comparison of differing perspectives.

In section 2.6 we discussed the issues of overconfidence. Experts who regularly receive feedback enabling them to compare what actually happened with their forecasts tend to become better calibrated. For instance, weather forecasters are necessarily confronted with the actual weather the day after they make a forecast. Any optimism or pessimism in their forecasting is quickly apparent to them and they can adjust their judgemental processes (McClelland and Bolger, 1994; Murphy and Winkler, 1984; Subbotin, 1996). This suggests that we should seek out feedback on the outcome of events on which we have offered judgements and audit our judgements in the light of this feedback. It may be a sanguine experience, but if we reflect we will improve. Russo and Schoemaker discuss a problem of overconfidence in young geologists (overconfident that oil was present at a particular location). This was eliminated by means of a structured training course that required them to make judgements about a series of 'old' cases in which the outcome was already known. Thus, having made a judgement, they received immediate feedback before going on to the next case. This training course eliminated the overconfidence. Such improvements in judgement have considerable impact on organisational effectiveness by, in this case, reducing the number of unnecessary expensive test drillings – 'dry-well dollars' (Russo and Schoemaker, 2002: 106).

Further insight regarding overconfidence and how to reduce it comes from a study by Koriat *et al.* (1980) reviewed earlier in section 2.9. They showed that encouraging people to think about negative evidence is likely to reduce overconfidence. Indeed, in group contexts one may actually appoint a devil's advocate (see chapter 11 for a fuller discussion) whose primary role is to stimulate discussion of arguments that run counter to emerging views.

Again, if we recognise that we may be susceptible to availability, representativeness and other biases, then we can reflect and challenge our thinking and, if we feel it appropriate, we can revise our judgements. Similarly, we can reflect on the framing of the choices before us, look for positive and negative aspects and ensure that we look at the consequences from all directions, appreciating both the losses and the gains so that we can compare alternatives more fairly. Indeed, Russo and Schoemaker (2002) have developed a frame analysis audit that first captures how people currently frame a problem, based on answers given to a series of questions designed to elicit such aspects as the current boundaries they put on the problem, their current reference point, whether they are framing the problems in gains or losses and the metaphors used to make sense of the problem. Then they are asked to reframe the problem by engaging in a variety of activities such as changing reference points and metaphors. The worksheet is designed to ensure that decision problems are framed broadly and not bound by limitations such as the framing bias.

Sometimes a simple drawing or calculation on a scrap of paper can help. Remember the breast-cancer-screening example in section 2.6. We noted that DMs do not instinctively revise their judgements according to Bayes' theorem. Gigerenzer (1994) has shown, however, that, if people think in terms of frequencies and draw a simple *frequency tree*, they see the correct answer quickly. Consider figure 3.8. Of 10,000 women screened, on average

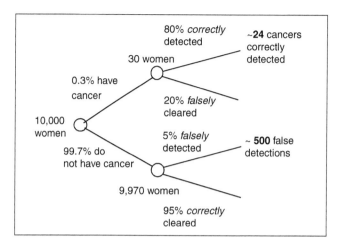

Figure 3.8   Quick frequency calculation for the example in section 2.6

thirty will have cancer and 9,970 will not. Of the thirty, about twenty-four will be detected with a positive screening result, but of the 9,970 roughly 20 per cent, or about 500, will have false positive screening results. So, of the approximately 524 positive results, only twenty-four, or roughly 5 per cent, will actually have cancer.

3.9 Concluding remarks and further reading

For further discussions of the distinctions and interrelationships between descriptive, normative and prescriptive perspectives on decision making, see Bell *et al.* (1988), Brown and Vari (1992), French and Smith (1997) and French and Ríos Insua (2000). You should note, however, that the distinction that we have been making is not honoured widely in the literature. Indeed, one of us in his earlier writings did not explicitly distinguish between normative and prescriptive: see French (1986, 1988).

There is a wide literature on normative decision theory. Accessible introductions for those with some mathematical training are Allingham (2002), Beroggi (1998), Bouyssou, Marchant, Pirlot *et al.* (2000), Bouyssou *et al.* (2006), French (1986), Keeney and Raiffa (1976), Luce and Raiffa (1957) and Roberts (1979). More mathematical introductions or ones that adopt a sophisticated philosophical perspective include Bacharach and Hurley (1991), Edwards (1992), French (1995a), Gardenfors and Sahlin (1988) and McLennen (1990). The development of decision theory was for many years intertwined with the development of statistical methodology. Many texts discuss the foundations of statistical decision theory, including

Bernardo and Smith (1994), DeGroot (1970), Fine (1973), French and Ríos Insua (2000) and Savage (1972). Measurement theory, a branch of mathematics dealing with the relationships between axioms and models, is also relevant (Krantz et al., 1971; Luce et al., 1990; Roberts, 1979; Suppes et al., 1989).

Wenstøp (2005) and his discussants explore the role of emotions in value-focused thinking. Key discussions of prescriptive decision support may be found in Bell et al. (1988), Belton and Stewart (2002), Brown and Vari (1992), Eden and Radford (1990), Keeney (1992), Svenson (1998) and White (1975). Phillips (1982), Phillips (1984) and Raiffa et al. (2003) are seminal works on requisite decision modelling. Lovallo and Sibony (2006) and Edwards and Fasolo (2001) offer further arguments justifying the need to provide prescriptive guidance in strategic decision making.

There are many general texts discussing DSS: see, for example, Klein and Methlie (1995), Mallach (2000), Marakas (2003), Sauter (1997), Silver (1991), Turban et al. (2007) and Watson et al. (1997). Many discuss the software engineering technicalities of designing and building DSSs much more than we do. Our focus is conceptual. We are interested in DSSs purely because of the decision processes that they support. Arnott and Pervan (2005) provide an extensive survey of the DSS literature, which includes an informative and interesting discussion of the history of DSSs. A recent survey of DSS applications is provided by Eom and Kim (2006).

Finally, Baron (2001), Hammond et al. (1998) and Newell et al. (2007) are excellent texts offering suggestions on good heuristics and practices to improve naïve judgements. In addition, Russo and Schoemaker (2002) provide a very practical review of ways of improving judgement.

3.10 Exercises and questions for discussion

(1) Donald Duck is expecting his three nephews to dinner, but he is aware that not all of them might come. He thinks that the probability of no, one, two or three nephews arriving are, respectively, 0.125, 0.250, 0.250 and 0.375. He must decide how many meals to cook. His preferences may be represented by the utility function

$$u(x, y, z) = x - 2y - z^2$$

where x = number of nephews fed, y = number of nephews unfed because he did not cook enough food, and z = number of meals wasted because he cooked too many. No meal can be shared. Each nephew can eat only one meal. How many meals should he cook?

(2)   A man is allergic to fish and chips, loves steak and kidney puddings and will tolerate chicken, although he does not like it very much. He is in a village with two takeaway shops at opposite ends of the main street. One, a fish and chip shop, always sells fish and chips and sometimes steak and kidney puddings. The other only ever sells barbecued chicken. There is only time for the man to reach one of the shops before they close, and he is very hungry. He decides that, *whatever the chance* of the fish and chip shop having steak and kidney puddings, he will go to the chicken barbecue shop. Discuss his choice from the point of view of SEU theory.

(3)   Consider the cynefin categorisation of decision contexts (section 1.2). Why might value-focused thinking assume more prominence in the complex space than in the known or knowable spaces?

(4)   Give some examples of 'decision support systems' that you have seen in use, perhaps on the internet, and classify them according to the scheme in figure 3.7.

(5)   A spreadsheet is the archetypal decision support system. Discuss.

(6)   Consider the following problem. It is estimated that about 3 per cent of school-aged children are physically abused by their parents (American urban figures). It is possible to screen children for evidence of abuse (scars, fractures, etc.) with the intention of follow-up by contact with parents. While allowing abuse to the child to continue causes great damage, falsely suspecting parents is also undesirable. Health officials wish to be very confident of their suspicions before approaching parents. The officials believe that the screening examination is very reliable. They claim that 95 per cent of abused children will be detected, whereas only 10 per cent of non-abused children will be falsely identified by the test. Given that child A has been positively identified by the test, what is the real likelihood that the child is being abused?

   (a)   Without any calculations, use your judgement to give a value between 0 and 100 per cent for the likelihood that child A has been abused.

   (b)   Using the quick frequency calculation introduced in section 3.8 (see figure 3.8), calculate this probability approximately.

   How do your answers compare?

4

Information and knowledge management

[A]ll organisations exist in three tenses as follows:

1. They exist in the flow of time and therefore carry much of their history into their contemporary working methods and practices.
2. They function in the present tense, meeting the needs of clients and customers and solving the operational problems of their daily work.
3. They live in the future, anticipating new developments, planning forward investments, and developing strategies for long-term survival.

(Bob Garvey and Bill Williamson)

4.1 Introduction

Data, information and knowledge are the foundations on which good decision making are built. However rational the analysis that is conducted, however powerful the computations used to support that analysis, without appropriate data, information and knowledge, decision making can at best only be formalised guessing. Of course, that is no more than the cynefin model suggests (section 1.2); without data, information and knowledge, the DM would be operating in the chaotic space. In the known, knowable and complex spaces, the DM is not so ignorant, and we need to consider how various information systems can support her.

To paraphrase the quotation above from Garvey and Williamson (2002), DMs exist in the flow of time, past, present and future: their past history setting the context for their current decisions; operating in the present, making decisions and solving problems; and anticipating future events, planning and developing strategies for the long term. These three functions correspond loosely with the three types of information systems:

- databases – i.e. systems that hold historical data and allow them to be queried and analysed in a variety of ways;
- knowledge management systems (KMSs) – i.e. tools for deploying what has been learnt from the past to address the problems of the present; and

- decision support systems – i.e. systems that help DMs face up to and shape the future.

In this chapter we discuss the first two of these: databases and KMSs. Our discussions in subsequent chapters deal with a range of DSSs. In section 2 we briefly discuss human memory; if it were perfect and unlimited in capacity, we would not need databases and information systems. Then we turn to a consideration of the distinctions and connections between data, information and knowledge and how these relate to decision making. The perceptive reader may have wondered why we have continually used all three terms: data, information and knowledge. Surely this is an overkill of synonyms? Well, not quite: they have different technical meanings that have implications for our understanding of decision analysis and support, as we explain in section 3.

We then turn to a discussion of databases and the tools that are used to query and analyse the data therein. Our discussion is superficial by the standards of most texts on information systems. This is a text on decision making, however, and our purposes are served adequately by a very broad-brush overview. In section 5 we consider knowledge management. Again we are far from detailed, but some understanding of this topic is necessary for an appreciation of the design of decision processes and DSSs. Statistical inference and forecasting are also highly relevant to decision making. In section 6 we relate these disciplines to decision analysis. We close with a discussion and guide to the literature.

In terms of figure 3.7, outlining the different categories of decision support, we intend to consider levels 0 and 1 for all domains of activity. The tools and systems we discuss simply muster information and knowledge for the DMs. There is no attempt to support the DMs' judgements, only to help them understand the external context of the decision. Our objectives in this chapter are thus:

- to understand the limitations of human memory, particularly in relation to its importance for decision making;
- to recognise the differences between data, information and knowledge and how each enters the decision-making process;
- to describe in the very broadest of details how information systems can help in the processes of data, information and knowledge management;
- to consider some generic types of level 0 and level 1 decision support systems; and
- to understand how statistical inference and forecasting methods complement and fit with decision analytic methods.

4.2 Human memory

Time and memory are true artists; they remould reality nearer to the heart's desire.
(John Dewey)

Psychologists have suggested that there are two different types of human memory: *short-term*, more recently referred to as *working memory*, and *long-term*. Working memory is both temporary and short-lived, and in many ways is similar to the main (RAM) memory of a computer. It holds the information that is the focus of our attention, sustains this information by rehearsal and is the workspace where ideas and concepts are registered, transformed and manipulated. A full description of working memory lies outside the scope of this book; see Baddeley (2007) for a recent review. Here we note that a critical feature of this type of memory is that it has limited capacity – that is, only a relatively small amount of information can be held and transformed at the same time. If you doubt this, try the following experiment on your friends.

Ask them to write down the answers to the following three questions (read each question aloud once and allow your friends time to write each answer before giving them the next one!): 'What is 2 + 2?' 'What is 29 + 92?' 'What is 35,986 + 57,989?'

They should have little trouble with the first question, since the answer pops out from long-term memory; after all, everyone knows that two and two make four. The second problem is more difficult, since your friends are unlikely to know the answer in advance. So, in their working memory they need to store the two numbers, taking up some of the available capacity. Then they need to add the units together; adding is a mental activity that takes capacity to implement; and next they need to remember the units total and the carry it into the tens column, requiring further memory capacity! Now they need to add the two digits in the tens column and the carry term, requiring further capacity, to arrive at the final answer. Storage and computations such as adding use up working memory capacity, but the demands of adding two digits are usually within the capacity limitations. The third problem is impossible for most people. Interestingly, you can teach yourself methods for completing this, but most people have not done so. Indeed most people cannot even hold the two numbers in their working memories for any period, because the demands of storing ten digits are beyond their working memory capacity.

If holding ten digits is beyond working memory capacity, one wonders how we cope when we have to make decisions in fast-changing, information-rich environments when large quantities of information have to be registered, evaluated, aggregated, stored and compared – these being the kinds of mental operations that underpin human decision making. The answer is that we simplify our thinking, take account of less information and process it in a less elaborate way, and in doing so reduce the information-processing load. As we argue throughout this chapter, however, these simplifications in thinking can lead to errors and biases in judgements and decision making.

The second type of memory, namely long-term memory, retains large quantities of information over relatively long periods of time. Long-term memory is similar to a hard disk, CD or DVD filing system in a computer. Tulving and Donaldson (1972) distinguished between *episodic memory*, which stores personal experiences (e.g. that I went to the theatre last week), and *semantic memory*, which stores our organised knowledge about the world (e.g. that dogs can bite or that ice cream tastes good). Both these involve *declarative knowledge* – i.e. knowing that something is true or not. In recent years there has been some discussion of *procedural knowledge* – i.e. knowing how to do something, such as riding a bicycle or writing a letter.

While a full description of long-term human memory lies outside the scope of this book (see Baddeley, 2004, for an interesting introductory text), there are some aspects that are important for understanding decision making and how to support it. For example, we remember better those events with high impact, rather than those that are commonplace: see the availability bias (section 2.7).

Second, there is considerable evidence to suggest that long-term memory works by association and reconstruction rather than simple recall. Computers recall precisely what they store, both in terms of the data themselves and their format: what they put away they take out. Human memory is a more reconstructive process. We remember associations between features of an event or fact and then, when we wish to 'recall' it, we reconstruct it from these associations. Moreover, we may not use all the associations, nor in the same order that we stored them (Hogarth, 1980; Klein and Methlie, 1995), so our memories of events may depart significantly from how they actually occurred. In addition, when we retrieve a memory, aspects of the current context may be incorporated into that memory, thereby changing it further. This means that we often have full and rich memories of facts and events that depart in important ways from the objective details.

Finally, the associative nature of memory means that, while retrieving information of a particular type, related memories become temporarily more accessible – a phenomenon often referred to as *priming*. As a result, thinking about a past success makes all other successes temporarily more accessible (and in doing so puts failures into the background). Thus, if we use our past experience to assess the likely success of a new venture, the priming of previous successes may lead us to overestimate this likelihood.

In conclusion, we need to recognise that our memories may be biased, and if we depend too heavily upon them when making judgements and decisions then these activities may also be biased. In this chapter we consider ways in which computers can be used to overcome these biases.

4.3 Data, information and knowledge

His had been an intellectual decision based upon his conviction that if a little knowledge was a dangerous thing, a lot was lethal. (Tom Sharpe)

In everyday language we scarcely distinguish between data, information and knowledge. There is a feeling of increasing value to the user in passing from data to information to knowledge, perhaps, but no clear distinction. We intend to be more precise. Following Boisot (1998), Laudon and Laudon (2006), Marakas (2003) and Turban *et al.* (2006), we define:

- *data* as facts about things, events, transactions, etc. that are not organised for any specific context;
- *information* as data organised and summarised to be meaningful within a specific context, usually a decision, but perhaps an inference or forecast; and
- *knowledge* as generic information – e.g. scientific understanding – that is relevant to several contexts, together with the skills and values that are used in solving problems. Having knowledge implies having understanding, experience and expertise.

So Sherlock Holmes might once have cried out for 'Data, data, data!', but what he really wanted was information to combine with his voluminous knowledge so that he could solve the case. We may also reflect that the common curse of *information overload* is a misnomer. While we may be swamped by data, information – by definition – is a summary of relevant data that supports our decision making. Thus, complaints about information overload indicate that we are not summarising the data sufficiently for our purposes – though, of course, there could be so many data that they overwhelm our cognitive capacity to summarise them.

Table 4.1 From data to knowledge

	Data	→ Information	→ Knowledge
Description	Observations of states and events in the world.	Data endowed with relevance to a context.	General learning and understanding drawing on experience through reflection and synthesis.
Characteristics	Easily captured; easily structured; easily represented; often quantifiable; raw resource.	Needs agreement on meaning; built with analysis; reduces uncertainty within a context.	Transferable between contexts; some knowledge explicit – e.g. science; some tacit and personal – e.g. skills; hard to store and communicate.
Method of acquisition	Observation.	Judgement.	Experience.

Source: Earl

There are many qualifications that we should make to these definitions. Perhaps the most important is that a piece of information for one person in one context may be quite irrelevant to another person in another context, and so simply an item of data to him or her. Indeed, in another context it may also be irrelevant to the first person, and so simply become data again. Knowledge, however, is more long-lasting. It includes *generic* information, such as the theories and models of science, economics and so on. Theories and models are structures that suggest how data should be organised, inferences drawn and predictions made in a range of contexts. Knowledge also includes the generic skills that enable us to form and use information in specific contexts. Information becomes knowledge when the recipient recognises a new 'understanding' derived from it. Table 4.1 provides a summary of several distinctions between data, information and knowledge. We also include skills and values within the general meaning of knowledge. Our skills are an expression of our tacit knowledge (see below); and, while we might question whether our values and preferences per se are part of our knowledge, they are certainly part of our self-knowledge.

Whereas data and information can always be made *explicit* and *codified* – i.e. expressible in some permanent form – not all knowledge can. There is a distinction between a person's unexpressed *tacit* knowledge – e.g. a skill such as riding a bicycle or performing an analysis – and *explicit* knowledge, such as that encoded in an economic model. Philosophy traditionally distinguishes three types of knowledge: 'knowing how' – procedural knowledge that refers to a person's skills and that may be tacit or explicit;

'knowing that' – i.e. propositional or declarative knowledge such as an economic or environmental model, which relates to the generic information used in many contexts; and 'knowing things', which is knowledge of objects, people and systems and which, again, is generic information that may be used in many contexts. These two last forms of knowledge are generally explicit or may be rendered so.

Many have argued that one cannot use explicit knowledge without drawing on some tacit knowledge: knowing how to apply a piece of explicit knowledge is itself a tacit skill. Simply to understand a theory, a supposed piece of explicit knowledge, one must have language skills and much semantic knowledge to decode and know how to apply the theory; and, if one should argue that these language skills and semantic knowledge can, in turn, be codified, then one needs further skills to decode these, thus building an infinite regress. These issues are not easy to resolve; theories of knowledge and language have kept philosophers debating for centuries, with no clear conclusions (Flew, 1971; Polyani, 1962; Ryle, 1949). Even those who believe that, ultimately, all knowledge will be rendered explicit accept that this is not the case today. If it happens, it will happen in the future. Until then, we must accept that any application of knowledge will involve some aspect of tacit knowledge. It is our expectation, therefore, that a DM will need to bring both tacit and explicit knowledge to bear when making a decision.

How is knowledge used in decision making or in the related tasks of making an inference or forecast? We offer an outline in figure 4.1. In the formulation phase the DM will consider the issues that she faces, her objectives in dealing with them and identify what she might do. In the known and knowable domains this will be a relatively well-rehearsed task, drawing on much explicit knowledge; in the complex space she will need to draw on her judgement, experience and creativity to make what sense she can of the situation, thus drawing on much tacit as well as explicit knowledge. She will add further details to her formulation by considering what data she has, selecting those that are relevant and assembling them into information. To do this, she must draw on her existing knowledge to filter the relevant data and then organise these in ways that inform her decision making.

Similarly, making use of the available information to make inferences or forecasts requires the application of knowledge too. Boisot (1998) describes knowledge as providing the perceptual and conceptual filters that the DM uses firstly to select and organise data into information and then to use that information to support an inference, forecast or

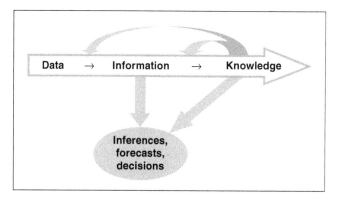

Figure 4.1   (Previously learnt) knowledge must be applied to transform data to information and information to knowledge; and also to make inferences, forecasts or decisions

decision. After doing this a number of times, the DM may recognise regularities in the information that she has used in several contexts, a recognition of a common pattern that she can learn and apply in the future. The ability to recognise such patterns and form new knowledge requires insight and higher-level knowledge of how one learns; some of this will be explicit, but much may be implicit.

We therefore see an inevitable need for tacit knowledge in decision-making, especially in complex contexts. This observation leads us to believe that the ambition within AI to develop truly autonomous decision-making systems will ultimately fail. All the knowledge in a computer system is necessarily codified – i.e. explicit – by virtue of being rendered in an artefact: such a system cannot contain tacit knowledge. Similarly, we see KB-DSS as being confined to the known and knowable domains, unless the interaction between the DM and the DSS is sufficiently sophisticated to allow her to introduce her tacit knowledge into the analysis.

We have explored the relationship between knowledge and decision making in the context of a single decision maker. Much knowledge is created and applied by groups through the social processes of discussion, learning and sharing, however. Nonaka (1991) offers the following perspective on such processes (see also Marwick, 2001, Nonaka, 1999, and Nonaka and Toyama, 2003), postulating these four modes of creating knowledge (illustrated in figure 4.2):

- *socialisation* – sharing experiences and skills in communities, learning from each other, often by collaborating on activities (Wilson *et al.*, 2007);

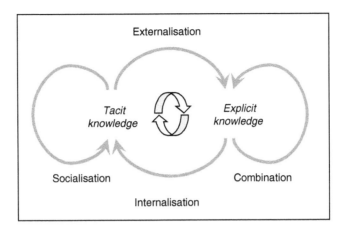

Figure 4.2   Nonaka's perspective on knowledge creation

- *externalisation* – articulating the knowledge explicitly in words, tables, figures, models, etc. (Williams, 2006);
- *combination* – drawing together and systematising explicit knowledge into more generic, simpler and more widely applicable forms; and
- *internalisation* – understanding the implications of generic explicit knowledge and deploying this understanding in our behaviour and decision making.

Tacit knowledge can be shared during socialisation by mechanisms such as showing and copying. For example, think how someone may have *shown* you how to ride a bicycle rather than explaining everything in explicit detail, or how many skilled trades are taught by apprenticeship rather than classroom training. Tacit knowledge therefore circulates on the left-hand side of figure 4.2, while knowledge that can be rendered explicit through externalisation crosses to the right-hand side.

'Information systems' has become the generic term for referring to computer systems in organisations that support their processes and decision making. In the early days of computing the limits to storage and computational power meant that information systems were confined to transaction processing, recording sales, maintaining accounts, paying wages, etc. Later, in the 1970s, when more power was available, *management information systems* were developed that could produce reports organising and summarising the necessary data for management decision making, typically in the general domain (see figure 3.7). During the 1990s systems evolved further, and it was possible to collate and summarise data from many sources to support the corporate strategic domain of decision making: see the discussion of executive information systems below. Currently, the convergence of information and communication technologies (ICT) is supporting more and more subtle means of collaboration, and, as we shall see later, this is the key to building knowledge management systems.

How might we keep data, information and knowledge in computer systems? For data the answer is easy. They are raw facts: they can be kept in a database. For information the answer is in one sense just as easy – and in another almost irrelevant. Since information is data organised and processed to be relevant to a context, we clearly want to keep it while that context is 'live'; and we can do so in reports – i.e. words, tables, figures, etc. When the context is in the past, however the information is information no longer. It decays back to data, unless it becomes relevant for learning or for building further knowledge. In the former case, we need only check that the original data are still in the database, and then we can discard the 'information'. In the latter case, we could argue for keeping all the (ex-) information in case there is something that can be learnt later – though not too much later. Current practice in organisations is to debrief at the end of any analysis, exploring the information used and summarising the parts that may be useful in the future. The value in such debriefing is greatest if conducted very soon after completion, while memories are fresh. Moreover, summarised rather than original documents are more useful to others, particularly if they are summarised and indexed using the language and jargon local to the group sharing the knowledge: see section 5 below for further discussion.

4.4 Databases, data warehouses and data mining

There are three things I always forget. Names, faces, and – the third I can't remember. (Italo Svevo)

Data are 'objective' facts about the world: events, numerical statistics, transactions, etc. While we might argue about whether data can be truly objective, they are by definition context-free, in the sense that they have not been organised, summarised, analysed or presented with a view to supporting a particular activity. When they are so organised and hence meaningful to a user they become information. Data, therefore, form the raw material that information systems hold and use. Within an information system data reside in *databases*. There are many types of database, each with its particular advantages and disadvantages. We do not intend to venture into any technical discussion of databases; for this, see, for example, Laudon and Laudon (2006), Mallach (2000) and Turban *et al.* (2006). Rather, we focus on conceptual issues concerning how databases may enter into the decision support process offering level 0 support.

In section 2 we noted that the limited capacity of human working memory restricts the amount of data that can processed and subsequently stored in long-term memory. In addition, retrieval from long-term memory is founded on reconstructive processes. We remember associations between features of an event or fact and then, when we wish 'recall' it, we reconstruct the memory from these associations. This provides a very rich memory based on the meanings (to us) of facts and events, rather than the objective details. This often introduces bias and inaccuracies into our memories. Thus, we are not good at accurately memorising large quantities of facts and data. Nor can our memory really be termed 'unbiased' (see our discussion of the availability bias in section 2.7). Moreover, recall can be a slow process: how often have we had memories on the 'tip of our tongues', only to wake up during the next night having finally remembered them?

The storing and recall of data in computers is very different. Input is not restricted by the kinds of capacity limitations that are present in working memory. Long-term storage is not founded on associative mechanisms, and retrieval is not reconstructive as it is with human memory; what is stored is retrieved unaltered, therefore. In addition, retrieval processes in computers are often much faster – a matter of microseconds.

The process of interacting with a database is, in rough terms, as follows. Relevant data for a context – i.e. information – are extracted by a *query* at the time they are required. These queries are written in a *query language*, *structured query language* (SQL) being the most common. Many systems allow the user to build queries via an intuitive graphical interface, however. A *report* is generated when the results of a query are formatted and summarised into a document or a screen that can be viewed and used by DMs. A *database management system* (DBMS) is a generic environment in which databases can be built. It allows users to define the formats and characteristics of the data that will be stored, to input and query data, to develop reports and to manipulate databases themselves and maintain their integrity and security, and may allow several users to access and work with the data concurrently in a secure manner.

The use of databases queries to develop management reports is an example of level 0 decision support: see figure 3.7. The query process selects and organises data relevant to the DM's context, quickly and without bias. Sometimes the summaries and simple analyses in the report may forecast how the future might develop, providing some level 1 support, but there is no level 2 or 3 support here. This point should be noted, because in the past some texts on databases and information systems seemed to suggest that all DSSs are essentially database reporting systems. We argue that many DSSs go far beyond this.

Organisations seldom have a single database: they have tens, perhaps hundreds, each built to handle the data relevant to one task or activity. Several databases can exist in the same DBMS. For instance, many of us have two or three simple databases on our PCs, perhaps built within an office suite database application. In such cases it is relatively simple to gather data from two or more of the databases. In many organisations, however, history and geographical dispersion may mean that many of the key databases exist in a variety of DBMSs. The value of the potential information shared between these databases can be immense to a company, for example in comparing customer buying patterns in different regions or countries; gathering data from across these can be difficult, however.

A *data warehouse* is a system in which all the organisations' databases are brought together and archived in one place, together with the software tools to enable detailed querying, more general exploration of the data and the generation of reports (Laudon and Laudon, 2006; Mallach, 2000; Marakas, 2003). Data warehouses seldom archive all the data that has passed through an organisation but, rather, produce snapshots of the data at intervals sufficiently short to capture a useful history of its processes. For a supermarket this might be daily, whereas for a small foundry it might be weekly or monthly. Originally data warehouses were single systems, essentially located in one physical place on one physical system, but technological advances mean that they may be distributed across many systems; indeed, they may be virtual, accessing summaries 'on the fly' from full archives of the original databases.

Using the snapshots of its history contained in a warehouse – often together with current data – an organisation may explore patterns of behaviour and use these to underpin its decision making. To help management explore the volume of data held in data warehouses there are two types of tool, but note that the distinction between them is a subtle one:

- *on-line analytical processing* (OLAP), which allows the user to correlate the highly multidimensional data and to find expected or commonly occurring patterns; and
- *data mining* – i.e. tools that seek to recognise possible *new* patterns.

Case vignette 4.1 Data mining, beer and diapers[1]

An often cited example of an early success of data mining relates to sales of beer and diapers (babies' nappies) in the early evening. A data-mining analysis of the sales within a chain of US supermarkets discovered that sales of diapers and beer were highly correlated in early evening sales, but not in general. An investigation suggested that husbands, returning from work, were being sent out to buy diapers, because the family were running low on them. While in the supermarket, many of the husbands were also picking up a pack of beer, to drink that evening. The supermarket experimented with placing a display of beer beside the diapers to stimulate such behaviour further. Sales of beer increased significantly.

The use of such tools to explore vast amounts of data has allowed organisations, *inter alia*, to:

- increase profits and efficiency by exploiting general trends across their subunits;
- increase profits and efficiency by exploiting local differences between their subunits or between subgroups – segments – of their customers (see case vignette 4.1); and
- personalise their dealings with clients and customers, so building stronger relationships.

For a description of OLAP technologies, see, for example, Laudon and Laudon (2006) or Mallach (2000). Data-mining techniques are many and varied. First, there are the long-established methods of statistical analysis, such as multivariate analysis (Krzanowski and Marriott, 1994, 1998), regression analysis (Gelman *et al.*, 1995) and time series analysis and forecasting (West and Harrison, 1989). Then there are several new methods developed within AI, such as artificial neural networks (ANNs) (see section 5.5), genetic algorithms and fuzzy sets (Mallach, 2000; Marakas, 2003; Turban *et al.*, 2006). A promising research area is the automatic construction of Bayesian belief nets by exploiting the empirical correlations in very large[2] databases (Cheng *et al.*, 2002; Korb and Nicholson, 2004). Because data mining is generally used to explore very large multidimensional databases, there is a need to find intuitively simple methods of presenting the results to DMs. Much effort has therefore been

---

[1] As we complete writing this text, we have heard that this example, taught by many of our colleagues and reported in textbooks, journals and even the *Financial Times*, may be an urban legend (*DSS News*, 2002, volume 3, number 23; http://dssresources.com/newsletters/66.php). It still makes the point, though, and memorably encapsulates the general success of data mining.

[2] The size of the database is very important here. Correlations between many variables are notoriously difficult to estimate even from large data sets. The very large volume of data available in a data warehouse is therefore essential.

put into data visualisation: see, for example, Cleveland (1994), Davis and Keller (1997), Klosgen and Lauer (2002), MacEachren (1992), Marakas (2003) and Tufte (1997).

There are many cognitive issues to be addressed when discussing the use of the automatic pattern discovery algorithms that lie at the heart of data mining. First, the immense volume of the data held in data warehouses means that it is virtually impossible for an unaided human to explore – 'eyeball' – the data and to spot patterns. In addition, the data are typically high-dimensional, whereas the human can see relationships in only two or three dimensions. Thus computer support for discovering patterns is essential. Moreover, people are easily deceived by spurious 'patterns' quite unrelated to any underlying covariation, or they see patterns that they wish to see (Jennings *et al.*, 1982). Unfortunately, automatic pattern recognition algorithms can find spurious patterns too: they are simply looking for conditional or local correlations and relationships within the data, and these can arise by chance. For instance, in case vignette 4.1, the correlation between the sales of beer and diapers was found only in the early evening – a conditional correlation. Statistically based data-mining techniques *might* be able to assess whether any pattern is spurious through appeal to significance level ideas or posterior probabilities. Many data-mining algorithms are not based on formal statistical methods, however. In such cases – indeed, in *all* cases – it is wise for the DMs to look at the patterns discovered and ask themselves whether they make sense.

Consider case vignette 4.1 again: the management investigated the possible link between sales of beer and diapers and identified a plausible explanation of why such a relationship might exist. Had the possible link been between, say, chilli powder and nail clippers, they might well have decided that it was spurious and not rearranged their store. Moreover, in this example there was subsequent empirical verification that the placing of beer near to the diapers led to greater sales.

Data mining is sometimes referred to as a knowledge discovery technique, and, indeed, in our terminology it may be. For instance, the discovery of a link between beer and diapers sales is a piece of generic information that can be used in many design decisions on supermarket layout. Data mining can also discover patterns that are relevant only to a specific context, however, thus finding information rather than knowledge.

Another approach to exploring the data held within an organisation's distributed databases is provided by *executive information systems*, also called *executive support systems*. These 'provide executives with easy access to internal and external information that is relevant to their critical success

Case vignette 4.2 An example of an EIS at a power company

An EIS at a large regional power company with interests in energy, resources and waste management allows executives to monitor regulatory and pricing issues, anticipating their impacts on the overall and individual businesses. They can quickly forecast and summarise production and revenue in the short and long term, enabling them to see the balance of their business and plan accordingly.

Source: Watson *et al.* (1997).

factors' (Watson *et al.*, 1997). EISs are, essentially, very clever querying and reporting software, drawing together and summarising data from many sources across a variety of DBMSs. Using a very intuitive human–computer interface (HCI), they provide simple charts and tabulations to help senior managers explore an organisation's databases: see case vignette 4.2. The technology of EISs is distinguished from that of data mining in that EISs produce broad summaries that allow senior managers continually to review the progress of their organisation against its planned strategy. Data-mining technologies dig down into large data sets, seeking much more detailed, local patterns. Support for such continual reviewing and monitoring of the performance of their strategy is essential if managers are to protect themselves against defensive avoidance (see figure 4.3). EISs provide the opportunity to monitor the success of the current course of action and assess whether there are any serious risks emerging.

It should be admitted, however, that there may be a considerable gap between theory and practice in the use of EISs. Xu *et al.* (2000) found that many executives were disappointed by too great a focus of implemented EISs on operational data and that the systems generally did not provide sufficiently high level summaries to support strategic decision making.

The technologies underpinning EISs are being used more and more throughout organisations, providing support for operational, tactical and strategic decisions. The term *business intelligence tools* is used to describe all these techniques that provide the level 0 support to help guide the DMs through vigilant decision making towards a requisite decision.

Databases are not the only way of storing data. Word processing, spreadsheets and other files, e-mails and, above all, web pages also contain much data. It is because of the wealth of data available on the web that we are now in the *Information Age.*[3] Such data are difficult to extract, however, because they are not stored in a structured form. Within databases, items of data are stored in precise positions both so that they

---

[3] This is a misnomer if we reflect on our distinction between data, information and knowledge.

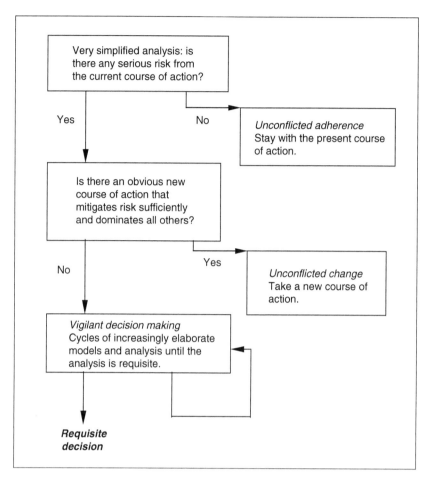

Figure 4.3   The progression through unconflicted adherence, unconflicted change and vigilance towards a requisite decision

can be easily retrieved and so that their meanings are known to the database owner. Other documents are much less structured. Developments such as Extensible Markup Language (XML), tagging and the semantic web, however, mean that it is becoming easier to access the data within unstructured files and web pages.

4.5 Knowledge management

Our knowledge can only be finite, while our ignorance must necessarily be infinite.
(Sir Karl Popper)

In the 1960s commercial and organisational uses of computing were referred to as *data processing*. Then during the 1980s, when there was sufficient computational power to do rather more than store and process data simply, we entered the age of *information systems*, which were able to select and summarise data quickly and flexibly into context-relevant management information. Now there is considerable emphasis on *knowledge management*. Computing has matured into flexible systems that are able to store, retrieve and deploy knowledge.

From our earlier discussion, we know that knowledge management systems (KMSs) need to help us manage both explicit and tacit knowledge. We see KMSs as combining two general families of tools:[4]

- very flexible data and information management systems, to allow storage and access to material stored in a variety of formats and databases distributed across one or more computing systems, together with very flexible querying tools to access such data, ideally using natural language or at least graphical interfaces that make them more accessible to non-technical users; and
- collaborative working tools, to share and work synchronously and asynchronously on materials together with full project, workflow and diary management; such tools are known under the general heading of computer-supported cooperative work (CSCW) tools or groupware (Bannon, 1997; Kraemer and King, 1987; Mallach, 2000; Marakas, 2003).

The former provide the means to manage explicit knowledge, while the latter allow users to share and work with tacit knowledge: see the process of socialisation discussed earlier. Case vignette 4.3 provides an example of a KMS designed to support activities in the hands-on work and operational domains. Note how it involves both a knowledge base and collaboration tools.

Almost everyone who uses the World Wide Web is familiar with search engines. These tools are continually surveying and indexing the web, so that when a user seeks information using a keyword he or she can quickly find a range of relevant pages and sites, usually ranked by some measure of relevance to the keywords sought. Some of these tools accept queries in more natural formats: simple plain questions. Similar tools are now being built into PC operating systems. The data and information management tools in a KMS capitalise on such search tools. They allow individuals in an organisation to search for knowledge and expertise as they need it, by searching all, or at least the majority of, files and databases distributed across their systems. Many organisations debrief and summarise

---

[4] Note that, within the computing literature, there is often undue emphasis on the storage and retrieval of explicit knowledge, with the effect that one might think that KMSs are little more than glorified databases.

Case vignette 4.3 Eureka, a KMS for Xerox field engineers

In 1996 Xerox developed Eureka, a KMS for its field engineers to share repair tips. At this time copiers were complex machines, based upon technologies that were evolving rapidly. To be able to repair the myriad of potential failures of an ever-increasing number of models and product lines, the engineers were continually being confronted with problems that they simply had not seen beforehand. Sorting these out was time-consuming, and the delays did not fit well with a customer service ethos. Eureka sought to share their experiences with all Xerox's field engineers across the world.

It was, essentially, an intranet in which engineers could describe new faults and how they had solved them or ask for help if they had not. They also posted tips and ideas, and generally shared knowledge that would help them all provide a faster service. Because the days of fully mobile computing were still a few years off, Eureka was built so that the knowledge base could be downloaded at the beginning of each day onto a laptop computer. At the end of the day the engineer would upload any tips or 'war stories' arising out of his or her efforts that day, as well as e-mail any outstanding questions. At first Xerox tried financial incentives to persuade the engineers to spend the time contributing their experiences, but they quickly found that peer approval and gratitude provided a better reward. Eureka truly built a community of field engineers, bringing benefits to Xerox of enhanced team spirit, considerable cost savings and much better customer service.

Source: Biren *et al.* (2000).

completed projects on their intranet to increase the information and knowledge available to such searches. This use of KMSs can help share knowledge, either by uncovering appropriate documentation that provides the answer directly or by identifying some related activities and their owners, who may then be contacted for further information.

Such data and information management tools allow the user to retrieve explicit knowledge. As we might expect, there is evidence that they do not provide the broader support needed to work with and deploy tacit knowledge (Lee and Choi, 2003). It is through the use of the collaboration tools in a KMS that tacit knowledge can be shared. The sorts of tools we have in mind here range from simple e-mail and discussion lists through chat rooms, desktop sharing and 'whiteboard' tools to user-configurable websites that provide areas where teams can interact, share documents and manage projects. These tools help teams work together by allowing them to share information and expertise in order to address and solve problems. We would emphasise, however, that, while collaboration tools can support the socialisation process of tacit knowledge management, they may not be able to replace the need for face-to-face meetings and personal contacts (McDermott, 1999; Walsham, 2001).

How might modern approaches to knowledge management affect decision support? Before answering this question, we need to reflect further on figure 4.1 and the interrelationships between data, information and knowledge in decision making. Explicit 'knowing that' and 'knowing things' knowledge will provide contextual information to the decision itself – i.e. one will draw down from the generic to the particular, perhaps looking at the forecasts provided by a well-established economic model. More tacit 'knowing how' knowledge will shape the decision process itself, perhaps by fitting the economic model to current data describing the context. Note here that the 'knowing how' is the *tacit* knowledge of how to fit the model to the problem in question; it is not the *explicit* 'knowing that' knowledge that is embedded in the economic model itself. In the formulation phase the DMs and their analysts will need to 'know how' to bring shape to a mess of issues, particularly in the complex space.

The implications of this for KMSs and DSSs are as follows (see figure 4.4).

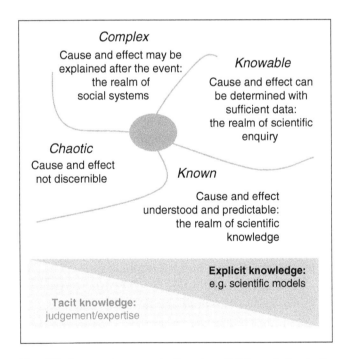

Figure 4.4   The differing emphases on tacit and explicit knowledge in the cynefin domains

- In the known and knowable spaces, explicit knowledge will be deployed through databases, knowledge bases and models. Thus, KMSs and DSSs will be able to draw more on data and information management, along with computational technologies, to perform detailed model-based analyses.
- In the complex and chaotic spaces, where judgement will be needed to a larger extent, we may expect the emphasis with KMSs and DSSs to be more on tools that aid collaboration, share tacit knowledge and build judgement.

4.6 Statistics and decision support

In earlier times, they had no statistics, and so they had to fall back on lies. (Stephen Leacock)

Discussions of level 0 and 1 decision support inevitably draw us into the domain of statistics, the discipline of data analysis. Figure 4.5 suggests how statistical inference and forecasting techniques may be thought of as fitting into the decision support process. In our view, it is essential for DMs to reflect upon any decision problem from two complementary perspectives:

- *science* – what they think might happen; and
- *values* – how much they care if it does.

We have already emphasised the importance of distinguishing between these two perspectives in our discussion of the players in a decision analysis (see section 1.4). The left-hand side of figure 4.5 shows that statistical analysis helps the DMs, their experts and analysts update and refine their understanding of the science. When the statistical analysis is directed at exploring the current decision context, the support provided is at level 0; when the analysis is directed to forecasting the future, the support is at level 1. The right-hand side of the figure reflects the modelling of the DMs' and stakeholders' values. Then both their understanding of the science and their values are drawn together to provide guidance on the evaluation and ranking of the possible actions. Of course, we should admit that the simplifications inherent in figure 4.5 hide as many issues as they elucidate.

In selecting and drawing together data to form information, statistical thinking is vital. Otherwise the DMs may over- or underestimate the importance of patterns in the data – we noted this when discussing data mining. Statistical methods ensure that we do not ignore prior knowledge of base rates. Indeed, without statistical input the DMs risk falling prey to the intuitive, but potentially biased, behaviours discussed in

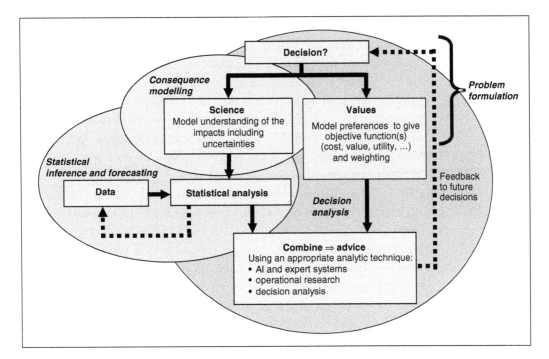

Figure 4.5   How statistical inference and forecasting fit into decision support

chapter 2. In many cases prior knowledge provides the form of appropriate models, and the role of statistics is to fit the models to current data and assess the residual level of uncertainty.

4.7 Concluding remarks and further reading

We began this chapter with a discussion of the distinction between data, information and knowledge. This discussion reflected subtle differences made by academics and not the near-synonymous use of the three words in everyday language. The distinction is vitally important if we are to understand the true power of many management techniques and computing systems, the advertising copy for which includes such phrases as 'information management' (they usually manage *data* and produce information for particular contexts) and 'knowledge-based' (they are *not* based upon *tacit* knowledge). We have also noted that the systems that we have discussed generally provide level 0 decision support, although the collaborative aspects of knowledge management systems do support a whole range of processes for sharing tacit knowledge and expertise that contribute to all levels.

Further discussions of the distinctions and connections between data, information and knowledge, as well as the processes by which one is converted into the other, may be found in the following sources: Boisot (1998), Coakes *et al.* (2002), Earl (2000), Flew (1971), Gourlay (2006), Laudon and Laudon (2006), Nonaka (1991), Polyani (1962), Ruggles and Holtshouse (1999) and Ryle (1949). Beware, however, that, although they discuss the same ideas and concepts, these authors do not all use the terms 'data', 'information' and 'knowledge' in quite the same way. It is also important to remember that the creation of knowledge requires imagination – a point that is sometimes underemphasised (Weick, 1987).

Detailed discussion of databases may be found in Laudon and Laudon (2006), Mallach (2000), Marakas (2003) and Turban *et al.* (2006), and in many other information or decision support system texts. Harry (2001) gives an introduction to databases and information systems that builds on distinctions between data, information and knowledge that are similar to those that we made above. Anisimov (2003) discusses the use of OLAP technologies in providing decision support to management. Watson *et al.* (1997), along with Laudon and Laudon (2006), Mallach (2000) and Marakas (2003), provide discussions of EISs. Singh *et al.* (2002) provide an interesting empirical study of EISs that demonstrates clearly that they provide level 0 and level 1 support, but no higher. Hand *et al.* (2001), Klosgen and Zytkow (2002), Mallach (2000), Marakas (2003) and many others discuss data warehouses and data mining.

Discussion of general issues relating to knowledge management may be found in Boisot (1998), Coakes *et al.* (2002), Courtney (2001), Garvey and Williamson (2002), Lee and Choi (2003), Ruggles and Holtshouse (1999), Williams (2006) and Wilson (2002). Descriptions of KMSs may be found in Laudon and Laudon (2006) and Marakas (2003). More detailed discussion of the technical aspects can be found in Gallupe (2001), Marwick (2001), Sage and Rouse (1999), Santos (2003) and Walsham (2001). Hall and Paradice (2005) discuss the relationships between KMSs and decision support; see also Olson (2001) for a related discussion of the support offered to decision making by information systems. The future of KMSs can, perhaps, be seen in the Kepler scientific workflow project, which uses grid technologies to combine collaboration tools, large databases and scientific computational tools to support large multi-institutional research collaborations (Ludäscher *et al.*, 2006).

The connections between decision analysis and statistical inference are not always fully appreciated. Savage's 1954 text is a seminal work, which laid the foundations of both decision analysis and of Bayesian statistical inference (Savage, 1972). Around the same time Wald and others, influenced by developments in game theory (see section 11.6), were developing more general decision theoretic approaches to statistics (see, for example, Wald, 1945). These approaches argue that, although inference is not necessarily tied to decision making, in many cases we will wish subsequently to use what we learn in support of forecasting the outcomes of our decisions (Berger, 1985; French and Ríos Insua, 2000; Robert, 1994).

Modern statistical methodology is – forgive the gross simplification – divided between two schools: the *frequentist* and the *Bayesian*. Discussions of the distinction may be found, *inter alia*, in Barnett (1999), Feinberg (2006), French (1986) and Migon and Gamerman (1999). Essentially, it relates to whether the analysis limits itself to taking account of uncertainty arising from 'objective' randomness only and represented by frequentist probabilities, or whether it also includes the subjective uncertainty inherent in the DMs' beliefs and prior knowledge, as may be represented by subjective probabilities (see section 8.2 for a discussion of different interpretations of probability). We tend to adopt the latter, the Bayesian approach. Bayesian statistics derives its name from its use of Bayes' theorem to update prior knowledge, represented through a *prior distribution*, to take account of the data to give a *posterior distribution*. Bayesian statistics is far more suited to decision support, since the processes for handling uncertainties fit seamlessly with the processes and techniques for modelling values: see, for example, Bernardo and Smith (1994), Bolstad (2004), DeGroot (1970), French and Ríos Insua (2000), French and Smith (1997), O'Hagan and Forester (2004) and Savage (1972). For Bayesian forecasting methods, see Pole *et al.* (1994) and West and Harrison (1989).

4.8 Exercises and questions for discussion

(1) Give three examples of tacit knowledge that you possess and explain why it is difficult or impossible to render them explicit.

(2) Some writers have suggested that there is a fourth level of understanding beyond data, information and knowledge, which they have called *wisdom*. Investigate this via journals and the web and discuss what it might be.

(3) How many databases do you use in your daily life? List them and discuss how you would manage without them.

(4) Using the web and journals, find and describe three examples of data mining.

(5) Give an example from your own experience of how a group solved a problem by pooling their knowledge in a way that no individual could have done. Relate your description to Nonaka's SECI cycle (figure 4.2).

(6) You are working for a consultancy company. You are preparing a presentation for a client who is considering acquiring another company. How would you use the network of consultants in your company and its knowledge base to prepare your presentation?

Artificial intelligence and expert systems

Technology: the knack of arranging the world so that we need not experience it. (Max Frisch)

5.1 Introduction

When individuals are faced with a decision problem they often attempt to solve it by applying a range of decision rules, such as drawing from past experience or coming up with a solution that satisfies a minimal set of requirements (Janis, 1989). We have already considered recognition-primed decision making in which DMs match current circumstances to similar ones that they have experienced and do what they have learnt works well in such situations: see section 1.2. If they are unfamiliar with the problem, if they perceive it as complex and difficult to solve or if they have to process large amounts of data, then they may seek the help of a friend, colleague or expert. Experts tend to suggest solutions by gathering information on the current situation, holding it in their working memory then matching it to knowledge they already hold in their long-term memory to recognise the kinds of actions normally taken in such situations (Barthélemy et al., 2002). What if help is not available, however, and expertise is scarce or expensive to acquire? How can we support repetitive decision making that is both time- and resource-consuming? Can we build intelligent systems that emulate the performance of, or even outperform, human experts and provide advice in a specific domain?

In this chapter we discuss how we can incorporate intelligence into decision-aiding tools by using AI techniques. AI is a long-established discipline introduced in the 1950s. Despite initial high expectations in the 1960s, and several success stories in the 1970s and 1980s, the discipline went into decline, only to re-emerge in the new information era as an enabler of e-business solutions. AI technologies can be used to support decisions ranging from buying computer equipment to devising a marketing strategy. Were we to take a more philosophical approach we might debate whether machines really can make decisions or whether this is an activity limited to living beings, perhaps just human beings. Interesting though this might be, however, we eschew such a discussion, and occasionally refer to machine or AI decision making, if that seems the most natural form of wording. We also adopt a similar blasé attitude towards metaphysics in occasionally referring to the possibility that a computer might comprehend or understand some behaviour in its environment.

Overall, our objectives in this chapter are:

- to provide an overview of AI technologies as they relate to DSSs; and
- to explore how AI technologies can be used to codify problem-solving strategies, automate decision-making processes and, thereby, extend the capabilities of human DMs.

In the next section we consider the relative strengths and weaknesses of human vis-à-vis artificial intelligence. In section 3 we provide a broad-brush introduction to AI technologies, before discussing expert systems (ESs) in section 4, artificial neural networks in section 5, genetic algorithms in section 6 and fuzzy logic, case-based reasoning and intelligent agents in section 7. We close with a guide to the literature.

5.2 Human versus artificial intelligence

The question of whether computers can think is like the question of whether submarines can swim. (Edsger Dijkstra)

Over the years many definitions of intelligence have emerged. For example, Sternberg (1985) suggests that intelligence is the ability to adapt, shape and select environments, and is based on three facets: analytical, creative and practical thinking. Along the same lines, Turban *et al.* (2005) define intelligence as the degree of reasoning and learned behaviour and argue that it is usually task- or problem-solving-oriented. From this latter standpoint, intelligence is better understood and measured in terms of performance on novel cognitive tasks or in terms of the ability to automate the performance of familiar tasks.

Given that computers can be used to solve problems and for automating performance of familiar tasks, there has been much discussion about whether they can be thought of as acting intelligently and the criteria that should be used to test whether this is indeed the case. A famous test of whether a machine is intelligent was designed by Turing and is widely known as the Turing test[1] (Turing, 1950). According to the test, a machine

---

[1] There is a suggestion that Turing rather had his tongue in his cheek when he designed the test. Be that as it may, it is now a recognised test to identify when AI has been created.

is considered to be intelligent when a third party, who converses with both the machine and a human being without seeing them, cannot conclude which is which based on their responses. ELIZA was an early artificial intelligence programme that appeared in the mid-1960s. It amazed people, because it was able to converse in English about any subject by storing information about the subject (i.e. the interviewee) in data banks and picking up speech patterns. It still failed the Turing test, though! To date no machine has passed the test,[2] suggesting that, on the basis of this criterion, machines do not act intelligently. Despite this limitation, we show in the following sections that 'less than intelligent' machines can nevertheless provide considerable support for human decision making.

To begin, it is important to explain what is meant by artificial or machine intelligence. AI is a broad term, associated with many definitions. Its goal is to develop machines that can mimic human intelligence. There are two main philosophies or schools of thoughts in AI. According to the first philosophy, AI aims to enhance understanding of human intelligence by 'modelling the brain'. The underlying assumption is that if we understand how the human brain works then it may be possible to build machines that can replicate biological functions, especially that of thinking and deploying knowledge. This approach is also known as connectionism, and it is being applied in research domains such as distributed processing and neural networks. The second philosophy aims to 'make a mind', through the representation of processes of human thinking in machines – e.g. computers or robots. Research along these lines has focused on incorporating intelligence into computer-based systems that can undertake tasks such as making predictions and offering recommendations.

There are tangible benefits arising from the use of AI, as opposed to human intelligence, in supporting organisational decision making.

- Codified knowledge is more permanent. Valued employees who have accumulated knowledge and expertise in a domain often leave a company, taking with them skills and experience. AI, however, can codify and permanently store the information used in a decision problem, and note the problem-solving processes and strategies used in its resolution, all for later recall in subsequent problems. A necessary restriction according to our earlier discussion (section 4.2) is that only explicit knowledge can be captured and used in *programmed*

---

[2] It has been suggested, however, that some gentlemen phoning certain chatlines of ill repute have flirted unknowingly with a computer, but maybe their minds were elsewhere and they had suspended disbelief (BBC News, February 2004).

AI systems. It remains a moot point as to whether *tacit* knowledge can either now or at some time in the future, be captured by AI systems that learn, such as ANNs (see section 5).

- Some knowledge becomes more easily accessible. It is not easy to transfer knowledge and experience from one person to another. As we have suggested, KMSs need to involve collaborative techniques to share much knowledge; but AI allows the development of knowledge bases that capture explicit knowledge and are easily accessible, while eliminating the need for data duplication.

- Performance can be improved. Computers, unlike human beings, can work continuously for very long periods, yet be easily switched on and off. They can be transferred to new working environments, including hostile ones (e.g. undersea, space or battlefields). They do not have feelings and are not subject to stress or fatigue, factors that can reduce the effectiveness of human decision making (Flin *et al.*, 1997; Hockey, 1983; Hockey *et al.*, 2000; Mann, 1992; Maule and Edland, 1997). Their performance is therefore consistent and reliable. They can be used to automate those tasks that are boring or unsatisfactory in other ways to people and that often lead to inattention and poor performance.

- The information, perspectives and reasoning behind solutions can be documented, creating an audit trail that can subsequently be used to assess and calibrate the quality of the decision process. A computer can draw a conclusion or take a decision while documenting the rules or facts that contributed to its output. Alternatives that were used in the past to solve problems can be proposed again in similar cases. Human beings often find it difficult to articulate the reasoning behind their decisions and may forget or overlook some of the arguments, reflecting the limitations in human memory outlined in the last chapter. In some cases, they may also misunderstand the importance of the arguments. For example, DMs often report taking a large range of factors into account when making a decision and compliment themselves on embracing so many issues in their deliberations. In reality, people usually place rather more weight than they realise on the last few factors that they considered before committing to a decision (Ross and Anderson, 1982; von Winterfeldt and Edwards, 1986: chap. 10) and actually take account of fewer factors than they think (Slovic and Lichtenstein, 1971).

- Computing technologies almost inevitably increase the efficiency, consistency and effectiveness of processes, although we have to be careful to define what we mean by 'effectiveness'. At the simplest level, AI can often reduce the time needed to perform a task. In many cases, it can also help machines execute tasks better than people at a fraction of the cost required when using human assistants.

AI tools can therefore support and extend the capabilities of DMs, and sometimes even replace them. Systems driven by AI exhibit a range of behaviours that are perceived to be intelligent. They codify rich knowledge about a decision problem as well as problem-solving strategies. They demonstrate reasoning capabilities in problem solving and learn from past experience by analysing historical cases. They cope with uncertainty and missing or erroneous data. They attach significance indicators to pieces of information and make sense of conflicting and ambiguous messages.

Nonetheless, despite the recent progress in AI, many human intelligence characteristics are very difficult to mimic. Human beings are creative; can machines be creative too? AARON is an expert system that creates original paintings using AI techniques. Its creator, Cohen, spent nearly thirty years developing it. AARON generates its drawings autonomously. It takes all the decisions – e.g. how to draw lines, what colour to apply, etc. It is not possible for a human to intervene and change the drawings as they emerge. Whether the machine creates 'art' or whether we, the observers, ascribe the properties of art to its output is a moot point, however.

More importantly, for our discussion, such artistic creativity is not the same as the creativity required in problem solving and decision making. Aside from being creative, humans have instincts, sense their environment and are repositories of vast quantities of tacit knowledge. Behaviours and tasks, such as pattern recognition, that are performed so naturally by humans can be difficult to replicate in machines. Even though AI is very powerful in narrow and well-defined domains it cannot easily adjust to a new environment, respond to a new situation or provide support in a wide range of problems. For these reasons, we argue that DSSs based upon the use of AI methods are confined largely to the hands-on and perhaps operational domains (figure 3.7), in which decision making is highly structured and essentially repetitive. In such domains, AI-based DSSs can be trained and calibrated to perform well. This conclusion is supported empirically; studies by Edwards *et al.* (2000) indicate that ESs that replace experts are quite effective in taking hands-on, operational and perhaps some tactical decisions, but are not so useful at the strategic level.

5.3 AI technologies

Software can recognise speech but cannot understand what is said – a family dog has a better idea of what words mean. (Michael Kenward)

Perhaps the most decision-oriented and, in many ways, the best-known of AI technologies are ESs. These are computer-based systems that assimilate – or are given rule bases that summarise – the reasoning and knowledge used by experts to solve problems. We consider these at greater length in section 4. Here we consider other AI technologies that enable interaction with the DM or take over difficult or repetitive tasks.

Natural-language-processing technologies allow computers to communicate with their users in their native language rather than through menus, forms, commands or graphical user interfaces. There are two sub-fields that concern us in the design of DSSs:

- technologies that seek to enable a computer to *comprehend* or *understand* instructions given by its users in a natural language, such as English; and
- technologies that seek to generate high-quality natural-language text in order to provide easily understood output for the DM (Hovy, 1998).

Together, such technologies promise more effective and accessible HCIs for decision support at all levels and for all domains (for instance, see Bertsch *et al.*, 2009, for a description of the use of natural-language methods in the HCI for a level 3 support DSS).

Neural computing or ANNs emulate the way that neurons work in brains. ANNs are based on studies of the nervous systems and brains of animals, and consist of nodes and connections of varying strength or weight. The weights of the connections are associated with the frequency with which particular patterns have been observed in the past. ANNs form a sub-field of *machine learning*. Machine learning encompasses AI mechanisms that allow a computer to identify patterns in historical data that are important for modelling a problem, and thereby to learn from past experience and examples. The patterns identified can be used for detecting irregularities, making predictions, classifying items or behaviours and providing decision support. We discuss ANNs further in section 5. Other machine learning methods are *data mining* (see section 4.4), *genetic algorithms*, *case-based reasoning*, *inductive learning* and *statistical methods*.

Robotics encompasses methods for controlling the behaviour of a robot. This involves the following.

- *Mechanical motion*, which allows a robot to recognise objects in its environment and move around them. This requires knowledge of statics and dynamics to control the robot's movement, and special forms of knowledge bases have been developed to hold and deploy this (Tracy and Bouthoorn, 1997).

- *Sensory systems*, which give machines the ability to sense their environment and thus provide information for their decision making. Combined with mechanical motion, sensory systems allow robots to undertake repetitive or hazardous activities.
- *Vision* and *pattern recognition*, which allow a robot to interpret patterns by processing the stimuli detected by its sensory systems. This process allows the robot to 'understand' its environment, thus setting the context for its decision making.
- *Planning*, which allows a robot to devise a plan – i.e. a sequence of actions to achieve a goal – often within a limited period of time.

Planning is thus one of the key decision-making activities of a robot. *Theorem proving*, focusing on proving mathematical theorems, is a more conceptual use of AI. It strives to build computers that make inferences and draw conclusions from existing facts. Most AI systems possess the ability to reason, which allows them to deduce facts even in the face of incomplete and erroneous information. One of the disadvantages of theorem provers, however, is their slowness (Tracy and Bouthoorn, 1997). If AI is to develop approaches to undertaking creative decision making that draw on simplified and useful perspectives on complex, unstructured issues and develop strategies for dealing with these, then the technologies of planning and theorem proving may provide the most useful basis. At present, however, they apply well-established rules in fairly tightly defined worlds – i.e. DSSs based upon these would operate in the known and knowable spaces, but not the complex or chaotic spaces of the cynefin model.

Nowadays, AI is considered to be one of the main components of *computer games*. AI can be used to control the behaviour of game opponents such as soldiers, aliens, tanks, armies and monsters. In more sophisticated computer games, AI techniques are used to give characters beliefs, intentions and desires and make them learn from past experience in order to make more effective decisions, albeit in a very stylised world.

5.4 Expert systems

The golden rule is that there are no golden rules. (George Bernard Shaw)

A person is said to have expertise when he or she has a wide range of tacit and explicit knowledge such as skills, experience and domain knowledge of theories and models. Some expertise is general – e.g. meta-knowledge or knowledge about knowledge, such as the reasoning behind a decision. Other expertise is more focused and relates to particular tasks – such as heuristic decision rules – validated by experience, which provide easy ways to solve a problem; for example, if interest rates are expected to rise then a fixed rate mortgage is a good deal. Expertise is gained from study and training and through experience. We should be careful to re-emphasise that, at least in terms of today's ESs, we are not talking about *all* expertise in the following paragraphs, just that which enables commonly occurring problems to be solved. We are considering the expertise involved in recognition-primed and operational decision making.

In many circumstances, DMs either rely on the advice of experts or delegate their decision making to them. Expertise is often a scarce commodity, however, or not available when required. For example, in the modern world of e-commerce, decision making on the creditworthiness of potential customers is needed day and night, and experts need sleep. In such cases, ESs may provide a way forward. They tirelessly replicate aspects of the behaviour of human experts, such as mortgage advisers, loan officers and physicians. Using 'know-how' drawn from knowledge bases in specific domains, they can answer questions, draw conclusions, identify the cause of problems and malfunctions, arrive at a solution, make predictions and, if allowed, automatically make decisions.

The main components of an ES are as follows.

- A *knowledge base*, in which concepts and relationships related to a problem are stored. It emulates short- and long-term memory by codifying elements of decision problems, solutions and problem-solving strategies in a range of forms, including frames and semantic networks. It is the most important element of an ES.

- An *inference engine*, which provides problem-solving skills to a system by determining how and when to apply appropriate knowledge. It is the 'brain' of the ES and uses inference mechanisms that are based on techniques such as rules or algorithms to codify knowledge about problem-solving strategies. Some inference engines are rationalistic in design, drawing on normative theories of inference and decision making; others are more heuristic.

- A *user interface*, to engage users in a dialogue, elicit situational information and users' preferences and communicate the system's results. Special care must be taken to ensure that it is effective – i.e. it enables interactions between the user and the system that achieve the user's intentions – and intuitive – i.e. it displays data and advice in a manner that is truly informative. The results are often displayed in graphical and natural-language forms. In addition to text and graphical displays, speech synthesis can be used to convey the output.

Other components can include *explanation systems*, which justify the reasoning of the ES, and *refining systems*, which evolve the knowledge representations encoded in the ES.

The primary aim of an ES is to transfer expertise from one or more *experts* to a computer system and then to untrained *users*. A *knowledge engineer* interacts with one or more experts to build the (explicit) knowledge base of the ES, facilitating the transfer of expertise to the system. Again, note that knowledge must be or become explicit if it is to be acquired, represented and transferred. The system itself may be built *ab initio* or within a *shell* – i.e. a common framework for building ESs that includes all the major components (user interface, inference engine, etc.) with the exception of the knowledge base. Modern ES shells provide a rule set builder to help users construct rules.

Knowledge engineering involves many skills and processes. These can be grouped around four major activities. *Knowledge acquisition* is the elicitation, transfer and transformation of problem-solving expertise from experts or documented knowledge sources to a computer programme. Sources of expertise include not only human experts but also textbooks, reports, manuals, information available from the World Wide Web and multimedia documents. *Knowledge representation* is the codification of expertise, facts and other information in knowledge representation schemes – e.g. frames, rules and semantic networks. *Knowledge inferencing* is the manipulation of the data structures contained in the knowledge base of an ES using search and pattern-matching methods to draw conclusions, answer questions and perform intelligent tasks.

Finally, *knowledge transfer* involves the transmission of expertise from the ES to the user. Part of the purpose of an ES may be not only to help the user in a particular context, but also to train him or her more generally. ESs often incorporate methods to explain their recommendations. This helps the user learn from the use of the system and acquire expertise him-/herself. For instance, medical ESs may be used by junior doctors when more senior doctors are not available, both to gain guidance on the treatment of a particular patient and to learn in more general terms how to approach and treat patients with particular sets of symptoms. For further details on these issues, see, for example, Klein and Methlie (1995), Marakas (2003), Waterman (1986) and especially Turban *et al.* (2005).

In AI, the *search space* is the set of all potential solutions to a problem. It corresponds to the action space in decision theory and the space of decision variables in OR (see section 6.2). The main aim of many AI tools is to search for a solution. There are some problems for which it might be difficult to identify one solution and other problems in which the search space is very large. AI techniques such as *constraint satisfaction* and *tabu search* can be used to generate all possible solutions and identify those that are *satisfactory* – i.e. satisfy some predefined constraints. Search techniques may be based upon heuristics or they may draw upon optimisation techniques that seek a true optimal solution.

Several issues may arise during the development of an ES.

- *Expertise capture.* Experts may find it difficult to articulate how they reason with regard to problems. Their expertise may be scarce or expensive to acquire. They may have conflicting views and opinions. In some domains, the rules may be vague. It is not always possible to anticipate events or future scenarios and build an ES that provides appropriate advice across a wide range of problems. ESs need to be maintained, and the process of capturing expertise should be continuous.

- *Testing and validation.* A range of software development methodologies, such as prototyping, can be employed to develop an ES. An integral part of such methodologies is to test the system across a range of settings. It may be difficult to verify and validate prototype ESs in some domains, however. For instance, in health care there are ethical issues around the use of real patients for testing purposes, and in design – e.g. building design, factory layout – it is not always possible to test the feasibility of a system's recommendations.

- *Liability.* Imagine that a physician uses an ES to recommend the best course of treatment for a patient. The patient receives the treatment and subsequently dies due to a misdiagnosis or the system's wrong advice. It is not clear who is liable in this case. Is it the expert(s) whose expertise was transferred onto the ES? The knowledge engineer who attempted to capture this expertise? The physician who used ES technology? The support staff who maintained the ES components? The hospital or medical practice management that allowed or encouraged the use of the ES? The system builders who developed the system? Or the vendors and developers of ES solutions?

- *Confidentiality.* Because ESs seek to encode expertise, the competitive edge for many organisations, their development may be shrouded in much secrecy.

Before introducing or developing ESs, businesses should consider a number of criteria for assessing their viability (Hunter, 2000). See figure 5.1 for a list. More details about the development of ESs can be found in Turban *et al.* (2005) and Waterman (1986).

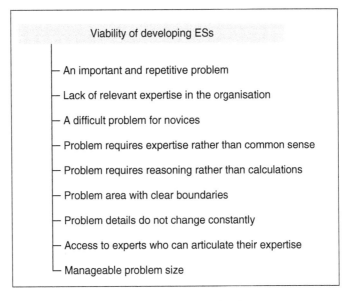

Figure 5.1   Criteria for assessing the viability of ES development

Table 5.1 Three types of expert system

Expert system	End-user
Consultant	Non-expert or novice (e.g. patient, loan applicant) who seeks the advice of an expert.
Associate	Expert (e.g. physician, loan officer) who seeks to validate his or her own judgement or collect more information about a domain.
Tutor	Student or novice (e.g. medical student, loan clerk) who uses the system for training purposes in order to understand a domain or process.

There are several types of ES serving different types of user in different contexts: table 5.1 identifies three of these. Edwards *et al.* (2000) further identify two expert system roles for decision making:

- *advisory*: to support and advise a DM, but not to take the decision for her; and
- *replacement*: to stand in the place of a DM, in that they can take and implement a decision without the need for human approval.

UK businesses mainly use ES technology to undertake tasks such as decision support and routine activities, as well as problem analysis,

Table 5.2 Tasks that may be undertaken by an ES

Interpretation	Make sense of sensory data by drawing inferences – e.g. speech understanding, image analysis, signal interpretation.
Prediction	Forecast based on past and present data – e.g. weather forecasting, marketing and financial forecasting, demographic predictions and traffic forecasting.
Diagnosis	Identify the cause of faults and malfunctions by observing and interpreting data – e.g. medical, electronic, mechanical and software diagnoses.
Prescription	Prescribe solutions for malfunctions or provide recommendations that can help correct a problem.
Planning	Devise plans and actions to achieve given goals – e.g. project management, routing and product development.
Design	Configure specifications of objects to satisfy specific requirements/constraints – e.g. building design and plant layout.
Monitoring	Compare observations to expected outcomes – e.g. air traffic control.
Control	Manage the behaviour of a system – i.e. analyse the current situation, make predictions, identify the causes of anticipated problems, formulate a plan to correct/improve the situation and monitor the execution of the plan.
Instruction	Diagnose, prescribe and guide user behaviour–e.g. build the profile of a student, identify his or her weaknesses and devise a tutorial to address his or her specific needs.

forecasting and fault diagnosis. They adopt ESs to replace human experts, devise strategic IT plans or because their competitors use them (Coakes *et al.*, 1997). Complete lists of tasks that ESs undertake are given Marakas (2003) and Turban *et al.* (2005): a summary is given in table 5.2.

ESs offer improved performance in a number of ways. They can increase efficiency by:

- reducing downtime by working consistently twenty-four hours a day and producing results more quickly than human systems;
- replacing workers, reducing operating costs and operating in hazardous environments; and
- providing a variety of outputs, reducing error rates, coping with uncertainty and solving problems.

In these ways they can reduce costs and, perhaps more importantly, they can improve effectiveness. ESs allow users to gain access to relevant data, tools and other integrated systems. DMs get advice and feedback, which

Case vignette 5.1 XCON, DEC's computer configuration ES

XCON is a very early example of a successful ES implementation. Digital Equipment Corporation (DEC), now taken over by Compaq, in turn taken over by Hewlett Packard, was a major manufacturer of minicomputers with a very distinguished history. It always provided its customers with systems tailored to their needs. Tailoring computer systems is a non-trivial task, however, requiring much knowledge and expertise. Not all the company's sales force were equally and fully endowed with such, so sometimes systems were poorly specified and failed to meet customer needs. To address this issue, DEC developed XCON, an ES that helped its consultants identify configurations that would meet customer requirements. By 1985 all the major VAX systems – i.e. DEC's mainstream minicomputer – were being configured by drawing on the skills and expertise captured within XCON. Both because of the reduction in system misspecification and in the greater availability of its (human) experts for other, less mundane tasks, DEC estimates that it saved $15 million a year.

Sources: Sviokla (1990) and Turban *et al.* (2006).

Case vignette 5.2 MYCIN, an ES shell developed for medical applications but much more widely used

One of the earliest medical experts systems is MYCIN, often considered the forefather of all ESs and still in use in many areas today. Its original purpose was to diagnose certain diseases, prescribe anti-microbial drugs and explain its reasoning in detail to the physician. Its performance equalled that of specialists. MYCIN was developed at Stanford Medical School in the 1970s. It was pioneering in using features now common in most ESs: rule-based knowledge representation, probabilistic rules to deal with uncertain evidence, and an explanation subsystem to explain its reasoning. It was very user-friendly given the technologies available at the time. The ES engine within MYCIN has been developed into a full shell, leading to other medical and non-medical applications – e.g. SACON, an ES to advise structural engineers.

Source: Sauter (1997).

allow them to consider a plethora of information, understand the problem and make better decisions. One should note, though, that the performance of advisory systems is necessarily user-related, and the end-user must be considered part of the 'system'.

Turning to examples of ESs, one of the early and more famous successes was XCON, which was developed at DEC to configure computer orders: see case vignette 5.1. MYCIN (case vignette 5.2) provides another early example.

Building an ES can help a company outperform its competitors and create a substantial competitive advantage (Mattei, 2001). Nowadays ESs are applied in many areas, though sometimes their users and even developers are unaware of this; for example, if–then rules may be encoded into software using programming languages such as C and JAVA without conscious reference to ES methodologies (Hunter, 2000). In the United Kingdom, the financial services sector is the largest user of ESs. It is followed by the consultancy/law, manufacturing and technology sectors. Other sectors that use ESs include public services, energy, sales and marketing, retail and construction (Coakes *et al.*, 1997). Several ES applications are now available on the web (Duan *et al.*, 2005). Some examples of applications are given below.

Financial engineering. Recently introduced international regulations such as Basel II, International Financial Reporting Standards (IFRS) and Sarbanes–Oxley have created a new set of standards for calculating risk and allocating capital. These have generated a lot of interest in exploring the application of ES technology to financial engineering (Baesens *et al.*, 2006). ESs are widely used to support financial decisions related to a wide range of financial tasks, including:

- credit assessment – e.g. a system at American Express assists clerks in reviewing risky accounts and approving credit (Dzierzanowski and Lawson, 1992);
- investment management – e.g. TARA, an intelligent assistant at Hanover Trust, uses historical data to make financial predictions for foreign exchange currency traders (Byrnes *et al.*, 1989);
- fraud detection – e.g. a system at Barclays has reduced credit card fraud by 30 per cent (Young, 2004); and
- other financial activities – e.g. hedging, pricing, trading, asset assessment, risk management and financial planning (Baesens *et al.*, 2006).

Consultancy. There are many applications of AI tools in knowledge-intensive organisations such as consultancy companies. They support a range of knowledge management activities – e.g. knowledge creation, selection and acquisition – by combining knowledge bases with search facilities. Their main function is to codify knowledge (e.g. market reports, information about staff and competitors, articles, project reports, business intelligence) and expertise (e.g. presentations, information about best practices, lessons learnt) and make content available to consultants and clients. Earlier examples of ESs include ExperTax, a tax planning adviser in Coopers & Lybrand (which later merged with Price Waterhouse), and

CONSULTANT, a tool for pricing complex jobs and submitting bids in IBM (Leonard-Barton and Sviokla, 1988).

Depending on how much expertise is codified, some consulting tools may be considered to be knowledge-based systems or business intelligence tools. Strictly speaking, business rules are articulated by experts in ESs. Very few people acknowledge, however, that analytic application tools are increasingly similar to ESs in that they codify human expertise so as to improve business processes (Kestelyn, 2001). These 'new expert systems' often use rules that are not developed from interviews but, rather, from best practice metrics. Examples of data analytic applications that resemble ES technology in consultancy companies are:

- knowledge intelligence – e.g. the Knowledge Cockpit at IBM combines agent[3] and knowledge-based technology to collect information (e.g. customer preferences, competitor analysis) from a wide range of sources, which is then processed and synthesised into knowledge (Huang, 1998);
- benchmarking – e.g. KnowledgeSpace, at Arthur Andersen, combines internal auditing knowledge bases with best practice diagnostics tools that compare a company's performance against that of other companies (Pearson, 1998); and
- online consulting – e.g. Ernie, at Ernst & Young, is an online knowledge-based system that routes business questions (e.g. human resources and sales) to experts, generates customised reports and provides access to answers of frequently asked questions, articles and paper clippings (Makulowich, 1998).

Bioinformatics. ESs can be used to support all phases of a bioinformatics application, including design, integration and codification (Lin and Nord, 2006). The main tasks include collecting, organising and analysing large amounts of biological data with the aim of solving such problems as determining DNA sequences and discovering protein functions. Some examples of applications in bioinformatics are:

- preventative medicine – e.g. computer programmes improved a test for ovarian cancer and identified a sequence of links between a dozen genes and skin cancer melanoma (Winterstein, 2005);

---

[3] 'Agents' are like robots on the web that leave your computer system and visit other computer systems to do your bidding. They can search out websites with specific information that you need – e.g. the cheapest price for an item that you wish to purchase. They can watch for organisations calling for tenders in your area of business. They can, if suitably programmed, negotiate for you and agree a deal with someone else's agent.

- pharmaceutical development – e.g. the Iridescent software scans thousands of medicine papers in minutes to discover new uses for existing drugs (Wren and Garner, 2004); and
- molecular medicine (i.e. understanding the genetic component of a disease so as to develop new drugs) – e.g. a tool at InforMax analyses DNA and proteins to discover new molecules and speed up their creation in the laboratory (Gotschall, 1998).

Further examples.
- *Repair and maintenance*: drilling systems advisers at Elf and BP can diagnose oil rig faults, eliminating the need for experts.
- *Scheduling*: a stand allocation system (SAS) has been designed for Hong Kong International Airport to allocate parking stands to aircrafts and produce towing schedules (Tsang *et al.*, 2000).
- *Patient record management*: LifeCode synthesises patient profiles from hospital records that contain information about a patient's conditions and courses of treatment. The system acknowledges its limitations by prompting for human intervention when necessary (Heinze *et al.*, 2001).
- *Crisis management*: a hospital incident response system is available to 1,800 hospitals from the Amerinet health care group to help them deal with a number of emergencies such as fire, plane crashes and biological and terrorist attacks (Kolbasuk McGee, 2005).

ESs are not without their limitations, however. Some of the more important of these are as follows.
- Explicit domain knowledge may be difficult to elicit from an expert, perhaps because the tacit knowledge of the expert is essential.
- With present technologies, there is only capacity and time to build knowledge bases for relatively narrow domains – e.g. the maintenance of the fuel system of an engine rather than the entire engine.
- ESs, unlike human experts, lack common sense and instincts when solving a problem.
- ESs cannot easily sense their environment and the changes it may be undergoing – e.g. financial expert systems developed in 2006 may be quite unsuited to the circumstances of the 'credit crunch' that arose in money markets in early 2008.
- Experts adapt to new environments and adjust to new situations, whereas ESs need to be updated.
- Systems cannot communicate as effectively as humans. Therefore, users might not trust the advice of ESs and dismiss their results.

- An ES gives advice no better than the expert(s) whose expertise was transferred onto the ES.

Barriers that prevent the implementation and adoption of ESs are mainly concerned with the perceptions of potential users. For example, ESs are believed to be expensive and difficult to build and maintain, they appear to undermine the status of human decision makers and are viewed as inflexible tools (Coakes and Merchant, 1996). Those ESs that change the nature of a decision-making task, improve the performance of the user, increase variety and eliminate the need for monotonous tasks tend to be successful (Gill, 1996).

5.5 Artificial neural networks

Experience teaches slowly. (J. A. Froude)

If expert decision makers make repetitive decisions – e.g. approving loans, devising customer profiles – but have difficulties in reasoning and articulating business rules then ANN technology should be considered (see also Liebowitz, 2001). ANNs are well suited to pattern recognition, classification and prediction problems. They have been applied successfully to many applications, such as risk evaluation for mortgage application, fraud detection in insurance claims and sales forecasting.

Figure 5.2 illustrates an ANN for credit assessment. An ANN consists of nodes, also called process elements or neurons, and connections. The nodes are grouped in layers and may have multiple input and output connections. There are three types of layers: input, intermediate (or hidden) and output. There might be several hidden layers, though usually no more than three, between the input and output layers.

Each input node corresponds to an attribute or characteristic that may be 'sensed'. We can have different types of input – e.g. data, voice, picture. In some cases we might have to process the input data and convert it to a meaningful form. Any time the input connection of a node is stimulated, a computation is performed that produces an output or 'fire'. Connections transfer data from one layer to another. Each connection carries a weight that expresses the importance given to the input data – i.e. the relative importance of each input to another node. This weight indicates how much the input attribute node contributes to an output. The resulting pattern of states in the output layer nodes contains the solution to a problem. For example, in a loan approval example the answer can be 'yes' or 'no'. The ANN assigns a numeric value – e.g. 1 for 'yes' and 0 for 'no'.

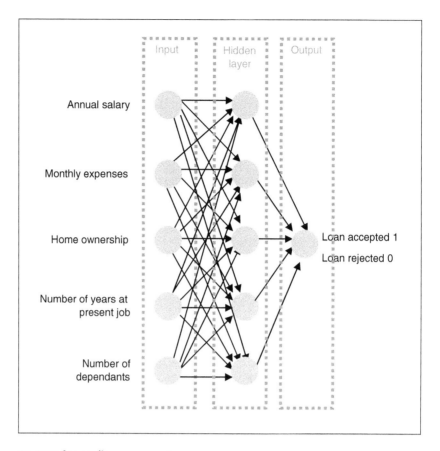

Annual salary

Monthly expenses

Home ownership

Number of years at present job

Number of dependants

Input   Hidden layer   Output

Loan accepted 1

Loan rejected 0

Figure 5.2   An ANN for credit assessment

The output of an ANN is indicative but not always accurate. It depends on the network's structure, the node computations and the weights attached to the links/connections. Training of the ANN is required to adjust the weight values using known examples. These weights represent the importance given to the input data, and training is required to adjust their values using already known examples. Case vignette 5.3 describes an application of an ANN to the prediction of bankrupcies.

ANNs have been criticised chiefly because they require frequent training and large quantities of test data. They act like black boxes that cannot justify their reasoning. The quality of their output – e.g. predictions, classifications – depends on the quality of the data used to train the network. This means that inconsistencies and errors in the training data contribute to inaccurate predictions and classifications.

ANNs can be used in a variety of business applications. They are widely used in financial applications such as buying and selling stock, predicting

Case vignette 5.3 Bankruptcy prediction

This example concerns a neural network that uses financial ratios to predict bankruptcy. It is a three-layer network with five input nodes that correspond to the following well-known financial ratios:
- working capital/total assets;
- retained earnings/total assets;
- earnings before interest and taxes/total assets;
- market value/total debt; and
- sales/total assets.

A single output node classifies a given firm and indicates a potential bankruptcy (0) or non-bankruptcy (1) based on the input financial ratios of the firm. The data source consists of financial ratios calculated for firms (129 in total) that did or did not go bankrupt between 1975 and 1982. The data set was divided into a training set (seventy-four firms; thirty-eight bankrupt, thirty-six not) and a testing set (fifty-five firms; twenty-seven bankrupt, twenty-eight not).

The neural network accurately predicted 81.5 per cent of the bankruptcy cases and 82.1 per cent of the non-bankruptcy cases. An accuracy of about 80 per cent is usually acceptable for applications of neural networks. The performance of a neural network should be compared against the accuracy of other methods and the impact of an erroneous prediction.

Sources: Turban *et al.* (2006) and Wilson and Sharda (1994).

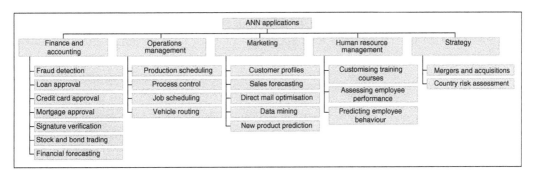

Figure 5.3   Typical applications of ANNs
Source: Turban *et al.* (2005).

bankruptcies and forecasting exchange rates (Turban *et al.*, 2004). Fadlalla and Lin (2001) provide an overview of ANN uses in finance. Other recent applications include filtering web pages, allocating beds in hospitals and tracking intrusions into particular geographic areas (Turban *et al.*, 2005). See figure 5.3 for a list of typical applications.

The process for developing an ANN, such as a credit assessor/ authoriser, is the following (for further details, see, for example, Turban *et al.*, 2005).

Step 1: Collect data from past loan applications – e.g. the applicant's monthly income and expenses (input data) and whether the loan was approved by a human expert (output data).

Step 2: Separate data into a larger training set and a smaller test set that contain both input and output data. The test set is reserved for testing the ANN after it has been trained. The selection of data to be included in each can be done randomly, but it is better if this is based upon a careful experimental design.

Step 3: Transform data into network inputs. For example, the 'Home owner' entries (input data) are converted to '1' if the applicant is a home owner and '0' otherwise. If the loan was approved, the output variable takes a value of 1; otherwise, it takes a value of 0.

Step 4: Select the right network configuration (this impacts on the network's performance and influences the accuracy of its results). Train the network – i.e. feed the network with historical cases whose outputs are known. The network will then seek to identify the relationship between the input and output data. It will make a large number of computations at each node and identify the most important factors – i.e. input nodes – in estimating the output. It will calculate the outputs of the already known loan approval examples until the error – i.e. the difference between the actual output and the output calculated by the neural network – has reached a given level (e.g. the error is less than 5 per cent). The next sub-step will be to test the network and check its predictions using a set of test cases.

Step 5: Deploy the network – i.e. integrate it into the credit approval process – and use a user-friendly interface to allow users to make enquiries and see the results.

Note that step 4, the key step, trains the network. If a suitable (which usually means very extensive) training set is available, and if the system developer is skilled at selecting the appropriate network configuration parameters, then the resulting ANN may well be effective. If not, then it may produce spurious results. Step 1 – i.e. collecting data – is also important. As some researchers point out, drawing on a long tradition of observations on failing, the risk here is a case of 'Garbage in, garbage out'.

5.6 Genetic algorithms

I have called this principle, by which each slight variation, if useful, is preserved, by the term of Natural Selection. (Charles Darwin)

If it is difficult for experts to articulate explicit rules or the quality of the data available is not very good, it is not possible to use ESs and ANNs. In such cases, genetic algorithms may be considered (Holland, 1992). For example, after experimenting with different methodologies, engineers at General Electric used genetic algorithms to design a turbine for the engine that powers the Boeing 777 (Begley and Beals, 1995).

The terminology used to describe genetic algorithms is similar to that used for discussing the concept of evolution. Potential solutions are represented as strings (or chromosomes) of 0 and 1. Algorithms are applied to evolve the strings so as to reproduce better solutions.

The 'knapsack problem' is a typical decision problem that can be solved by genetic algorithms. For example, let us suppose that you want to go on a hike. You can take a number of items from 1, 2, . . . , n (you can take only one of each item) that have a particular benefit – e.g. b_1, b_2, . . . , b_n calculated by a fitness function. The constraint is that the total weight of the items you take should not exceed a fixed amount. The aim is to choose several items so as to maximise the total benefit while satisfying the weight constraint. A solution to the problem may be the 0110 . . . 1 string, which means that you do not take item 1, you take items 2 and 3, you do not take item 4, . . . , you take item n.

In the General Electric example, there were around 100 variables, which could take a range of values, and fifty constraints, which were concerned with the turbulence and velocity of the flow within the engine. Solutions to the problem were those turbine configurations that satisfied all the constraints. All solutions were represented as strings. A fitness function then calculated the efficiency of the solutions in the consumption of fuel. In one approach, the genetic algorithm randomly produced a number of feasible solutions. The fittest solutions – i.e. those with fitness/benefit scores higher than the others – were identified and became parents. Reproduction, crossover and mutation techniques were then applied, by mixing and matching sub-strings or changing digits in the strings, to reproduce children. The fitness function then calculated the scores of the parents and the children to identify the fittest solutions of the generation. These became the parents of the next generation, and the process was iterated until the results – i.e. reproduced solutions – converged satisfactorily.

The idea behind genetic algorithms is that only fit solutions become parents. This increases the probability of reproducing fit solutions in the children. The algorithms have learning capabilities, so as to produce children that are fitter and fitter.

Some business application examples are (Liston, 1993; Marczyk, 2004; Petit, 1998):

- T4, a UK TV channel, applies genetic algorithms to optimise the scheduling of TV commercials and maximise profits;
- United Distilleries and Vintners, a spirits company, uses a genetic algorithm system that codifies blending requirements to provide advice about different types of whisky and manage inventory levels;
- Eli Lilly, a pharmaceutical company, applies genetic algorithms to identify proteins so as to speed up the development of new drugs; and
- Deery and Co., an agricultural manufacturing company, uses genetic algorithms to produce daily schedules for its six factories.

5.7 Other intelligent systems

Fuzzy logic

Fuzzy logic is based on the principle that decision-making methods should resemble the way that people reason about problems. For example, when one makes judgements about someone else's – say Paul's – wealth and height, one does not say that on a scale from 0 to 100 Paul scores 70 in terms of wealth and 20 in terms of height. Rather, one says that Paul is a wealthy and short person. Fuzzy logic methods elicit such qualitative descriptions – e.g. wealthy, short – to estimate the desirability of alternatives.

It can be argued that qualitative judgements are subjective and open to interpretation. Decision making rarely entails a choice between black and white, however. In reality, there is a lot of grey in between, and this fuzziness should be taken into account. Therefore, fuzzy logic is less precise and more flexible.

Fuzzy logic is widely used in consumer products (e.g. washing machines, cameras, microwaves), controls (e.g. anti-lock braking systems in cars) and other applications (e.g. bond investment and real estate appraisal): see Turban *et al.* (2005). It allows users to input qualitative descriptions – e.g. 'low temperature' and 'high humidity'. Any changes to the values of the input variables results in gradual changes in the output variables, which makes the fuzzy logic approach very useful in electronics applications. Fuzzy logic can also be useful when the input variables are themselves fuzzy.[4]

Case-based reasoning

Whilst the aim of developing ESs is to capture and codify the expertise of individuals, case-based reasoning techniques seek to capture and codify collective organisational knowledge that has been accumulated over the years as part of organisational memory. Knowledge is stored in the form of cases − i.e. decision problems with their solutions − that have been modified so as to provide solutions to new problems. When such a new problem arises, similar cases are retrieved from a database. If the number of retrieved cases is large, additional questions are asked to narrow down the number of cases that match the new problem until the closest fit is identified. The solution is then further modified and presented.

Case-based reasoning can be used to support help desk facilities (e.g. call centre tasks). For example, Hilton Hotels Corporation has set up a database of cases that contains the answers to frequently asked questions so as to assist its desk staff in resolving any problems their customers may have (Callaway, 1996). It should be noted, though, that ESs and decision trees are sometimes more suitable approaches; Expert Adviser, for example, replaced an automated help desk case-based reasoning system at Konica Business Machines that was rather slow and did not provide satisfactory call-tracking services. The new system was easy to customise and employed a range of problem resolution techniques to assist technicians (Thé, 1996). Case-based reasoning is more effective, however, in dealing with problems that cannot be solved by applying rules. Successful case-based reasoning applications include software development, air traffic control, online information search, building design and medical diagnosis (Turban *et al.*, 2005).

Intelligent agents

Intelligent agents are autonomous and interactive software programmes that run in the background to undertake specific tasks on behalf of a user (Alonso, 2002). For example, the wizards of MS Word anticipate when the

---

[4] Note that, while fuzzy logic is a useful heuristic for developing AI applications, French has argued that it is not a normative theory and so does not provide a theoretical underpinning for prescriptive applications (French, 1984a, 1986, 1995b).

user requires assistance and offer advice on a range of tasks – e.g. the formatting of texts and graphs. Agent technology at Procter and Gamble has reduced excess inventory levels and transformed their supply chain by modelling their supply network (Anthes, 2003). Software agents have been developed to represent units (e.g. factory, store, truck, driver) and then their behaviour is adapted during simulation exercises by changing rules (e.g. 'produce more soap bars if inventory falls below level X' or 'dispatch this truck only if it is full') so as to optimise the performance of the entire network. Intelligent agents are also used by Ford Motor Company to simulate buyers' preferences and by Southwest Airlines for cargo routing. Another example is Buy.com, which employs agents to collect data from their competitors' websites, which are then used to formulate their pricing strategy (Narahari *et al.*, 2003).

Intelligent agents act as assistants that have learning and decision-making capabilities. In the not so distant future, agents will be able to search for information, for example about holidays, on the web, negotiate prices with other agents from travel agency websites, choose a holiday package based on the preferences of their users and make a booking (Port, 2002).

5.8 Concluding remarks and further reading

In figure 3.7 and at several points in this chapter we have emphasised that AI-based decision support methods are limited to the hands-on and operational domains. We believe this to be the case for two reasons. First, the methodologies currently need to be focused on commonly occurring contexts. Essentially, this is because the rules that the systems use have to be learnt from large data sets representing past experience. In the case of ESs, this learning may be undertaken by experts, who acquire sufficient experience to make their knowledge explicit in the form of a rule base or similar. In the case of ANNs, the learning is accomplished by the system itself. Either way, the resulting system cannot be applied in novel, one-off unstructured contexts that arise in the general and corporate strategic domains. Second, as we shall see in later chapters, unstructured decision making requires a good deal of creativity, and so far AI-based systems have not managed to be creative – at least in the sense required in decision making.

As will be apparent from our frequent citation, Turban *et al.* (2006), a text now in its eighth edition, is a key reference. Other general references include Klein and Methlie (1995), Marakas (2003) and Sauter (1997). Standard texts on information systems, such as Laudon and Laudon (2006), contain chapters on AI technologies with a focus on applications and e-business solutions. Korb and Nicholson (2004) provide a survey of AI methods from a Bayesian perspective.

In section 4 we referred to an explanation function found in some systems and how it can facilitate knowledge transfer – i.e. educate the user. It can also help the user gain confidence in the system's advice. Trust in a computer system comes not only from the quality of its results but also from the assurance that the system's reasoning is sound and appropriate for the task at hand. Even though justifying a system's advice does not improve the quality or accuracy of its results, it helps assure users that the reasoning behind the system is sound (Swartout, 1983, 1990). Bertsch *et al.* (2005) describe an application of an explanation system to a DSS designed to support nuclear emergency management.

5.9 Exercises and questions for discussion

(1) Describe the major benefits and limitations of expert systems.

(2) 'A decision support system can answer a "How?" question whereas an expert system can also answer a "Why?" question.' Discuss.

(3) 'There is little difference between the provision of decision support and an expert system.' Do you agree with this statement? Discuss your view.

(4) Discuss the differences between expert systems and artificial neural networks. What feature of an artificial neural network makes it much easier to maintain than an expert system?

(5) Explain, with reasons, which the most suitable technology is (expert systems or artificial neural networks) for the following tasks:
  (a) filling in a long tax form;
  (b) customer profiling; and
  (c) training new employees.

(6) Can it be said that a neural net captures tacit knowledge?

(7) You are a credit assessor working for a bank.
  (a) What factors would you choose to determine the credit ratings of potential customers who apply for a loan?
  (b) How would you employ an ANN to help you arrive at a decision? Outline and explain the steps that you would follow during the development of an ANN for credit assessment.
  (c) Which of the development steps appear to be more important?
  (d) Produce a diagrammatic representation of what the ANN may look like. Discuss the layers of the network.
  (e) Discuss any problems you may encounter with the use of the ANN.

Operational research and optimisation

The more alternatives, the more difficult the choice. (Abbe' D'Allanival)

6.1 Introduction

We now turn to operational research, or operations research as it is known in American English. OR began just before the Second World War. During the war, both in the United Kingdom and the United States, multi-disciplinary teams of scientists advised military commanders very successfully on how to make operations more effective. In the ensuing peace, OR moved into civilian life and sought to bring the same improvement to industrial operations.

Since OR is sometimes called the science of decision making, it is surprising perhaps that it is not more prominent in this text. There are many reasons for this, not least that to treat the many techniques and processes of OR adequately would take a longer book in itself (see, for example, Hillier and Liebermann, 2004, and Taha, 2006). Moreover, despite the fact that OR scientists support decision making at all levels and in all domains of activity, their focus is largely within the operational domain and generally at levels 2 and 3 (see figure 3.7). Although this focus is due partly to the fact that the initial military applications were on operational issues, there is a more important historical/cultural reason for this focus.

Originally there was a clear intention that the OR process should be scientific. For many years the UK Operational Research Society's definition of OR began:

Operational research is the application of the methods of science to complex problems arising in the direction and management of large systems of men, machines, materials and money in industry, business government and defence. The distinctive approach is to develop a scientific model of the system ...

A defining quality of the scientific method, especially as it was understood in the late 1940s and early 1950s, is that a scientist must be a dispassionate, detached, objective observer of a system. He or she must not interfere. This scientific imperative, pervasive throughout OR until the 1980s, meant that OR professionals were reluctant to work with the perceptions and judgements of DMs and to address rather messy, unstructured strategic issues, which required approaches that draw upon subjective inputs from the DMs. We make this point not to pillory the OR profession but to emphasise that, in our view, supporting DMs is as much about helping them understand their subjective selves as it is about helping them understand the objective issues that they face in the external world.

Since the 1980s the need to support the subjective side of decision making has grown apparent to the majority of the OR profession. This has meant that the methods of decision analysis (chapters 7 and 8) have become a full part of the OR analyst's toolkit. In addition, *soft* OR methods (chapter 9) have been developed, which take a more subjective perspective on helping DMs evolve their understanding.

With this background in mind, our objectives in this chapter are:

- to provide an overview of the OR process;
- to describe the methods of OR in broad terms; and
- to consider how OR methods can be embedded in level 2 and 3 DSSs.

Note that we do not present any OR techniques in great detail – arguably, in *any* detail. Instead, we rely on our references to the literature to do this.

6.2 Optimisation: the heart of OR?

Optimization + objectivity = opt out. (Russell Ackoff)

OR-based decision support techniques focus primarily on decisions in the operational and general domains that are easily structured, usually involving short to medium time spans of discretion and, most particularly, in which clear measures of effectiveness can be defined by the DMs. OR is therefore applied to problem areas such as: inventory and stock control; logistics and routing; repair and maintenance; production planning; queuing; scheduling; and the allocation of scarce resources. In simplistic terms, the usual approach is to build a model of a system and optimise its working with respect to some straightforward objectives – e.g. maximising profits, minimising time from factory to market, etc.

Indeed, since most OR techniques provide solutions to particular optimisation problems, OR has often been falsely characterised as being solely concerned with calculating optimal solutions. In the first paper published by the *European Journal of Operational Research*, Ackoff (1977) focused on the danger of an overemphasis on optimisation, and he did much to lead the subject back to its multidisciplinary origins – that is, to the provision and implementation of broad robust plans of action that lead to improved performance without any claim to achieve optimality (see also Smith and Winkler, 2006). OR gains its subtlety from not taking the optimal solution within a model as a prescription of what to do in the real world. OR analysts are well aware that their models are simplifications of reality, which seek to capture only the *key* factors that affect the decision and which omit many details of lesser importance. Thus the optimal solution in the model provides no more than a guide to a direction for change that may lead to an improvement in the effectiveness of the real system. Moreover, there is a cycle of adjusting the model until it represents the reality of the system *requisitely*. We discuss the full 'OR process' in section 5. Here, trusting to these few words as a protection from misinterpretation, we discuss optimisation that lies at the *computational* heart of OR.

The variety and the details of the many OR models and techniques need not concern us too much. Most OR texts (see references in section 7) have chapters describing some or all of the following:

- mathematical programming including linear, quadratic, non-linear, combinatorial and dynamic programming;
- queuing, reliability, maintenance and other stochastic modelling applications;
- scheduling and project management including critical path analysis (CPA) and programme evaluation and review techniques (PERTs); and
- simulation methods.

All essentially solve the same archetypal constrained optimisation problem, which effectively demands the maximisation of profit, safety or whatever by varying what may be controlled subject to constraints that cannot be surmounted, or the minimisation of cost, time, risk or whatever, again by varying what may be controlled subject to some given constraints (the available manpower, time or whatever).

While this everyday description of a *constrained optimisation problem* or *mathematical programming problem*[1] is relatively transparent, the stark succinctness of its mathematical statement can be more than a little off-putting (though it is worth persevering):

optimise $\pi(\boldsymbol{a})$ with respect to $\boldsymbol{a}$ subject to $\boldsymbol{a}$ being in A, or, yet more succinctly,

$$\underset{a \in A}{\text{optimise}}\ \pi(a)$$

---

[1] 'Programming' refers not to computer programming but to a production programme.

where:

a – is a vector the components of which are the *decision variables* – i.e. those quantities in the model that represent the things the DMs may choose or control in the real world. In many, but far from all, problems the decision variables can take an infinite number of possible values. For instance, in determining the optimal number of tonnes of crude oil to process at a refinery on a particular day, the possibilities range conceptually over any quantity between some lower limit, say ℓ, and some upper limit, say L. Thus the decision variable, a, the quantity to process, is any real number in the interval $\ell \leq a \leq L$.

$\pi(a)$ – is the *objective function* – i.e. the quantity in the model that represents a measure of effectiveness that concerns the DMs in the real system. In the terminology of decision theory, the objective function is a value or expected utility function. Practice in OR sometimes falls short of the ideals of decision theory, however, and, instead of optimising a single function that represents the DMs' preferences, $\pi(a)$ may be vector-valued – i.e. have several components, each of which models a different measure of effectiveness. The imperative 'Optimise' then needs to be interpreted as seeking a solution that performs well against all these measures rather than optimises any single one of them. This leads to a growing body of methods known generally under the headings of multi-objective decision making (MODM) or multi-criteria decision making (MCDM): see section 3.

A – is the *constraint set* (or *feasible region* or *search space*) – i.e. a set limiting the possible values for a, for example as $\ell \leq a \leq L$ above. The set A not only needs to provide specific bounds and ranges, but it may also encode relationships that must hold between different decision variables. The decision variables might be limited to be integers, leading to combinatorial optimisation or integer programming problems.

When all the elements of a mathematical programme are linear functions, we have the familiar structure of a linear programme: see figure 6.1 for a very simple example. While this example may be trivial in the extreme, it does illustrate many of the basic aspects of OR analysis. First the situation is modelled. The important ingredients and the quantities required are encoded in the left-hand sides of inequalities (ii) and (iii). Sid's current stock levels are indicated in the right-hand sides. Inequalities

Sid the butcher makes two types of sausages: standard and premium. Each chain of standard sausages requires 2kg of pork and 3kg of beef, and Sid makes £1 profit on each chain sold. Each chain of premium sausages requires 4kg of pork and 2kg of beef and brings Sid £1.50 profit. Sid has 12kg of pork and 10kg of beef in stock. How many chains should he make of each type to maximise his profit?

Suppose Sid makes x chains of standard sausages and y chains of premium sausages. He would make £$(1x + 1.5y)$ total profit. To do this he would need $(2x + 4y)$kg of pork and $(3x + 2y)$kg of beef. He is constrained by the amounts of pork and beef that he has. His problem therefore is

max: $1x + 1.5y$ (i)

subject to:

$$2x + 4y \leq 12 \quad \text{(ii)}$$
$$3x + 2y \leq 10 \quad \text{(iii)}$$
$$x \geq 0 \quad \text{(iv)}$$
$$y \geq 0 \quad \text{(v)}$$

In this example, the constraint set A is defined by the inequalities (ii) to (v), which the decision variables $\boldsymbol{a} = (x, y)$ must satisfy. The objective function is Sid's profit: $\pi(\boldsymbol{a}) = 1x + 1.5y$.

In the figure, the region defined by $2x + 4y = 12$, $3x + 2y = 10$, $x = 0$, $y = 0$ represents the region A, in this case the quadrilateral OABC; within it, (x, y) satisfy the inequalities. The dotted lines represent $1x + 1.5y = \pi$, for varying values of π. As π increases the lines move towards the upper right. The largest value of π, the profit, occurs therefore at B, which, solving the intersecting lines $2x + 4y = 12$, $3x + 2y = 10$, is (2, 2). Thus, to maximise his profit, Sid should make two chains of each type of sausage. The maximum profit is £$(2 + 1.5 \times 2) = £5$.

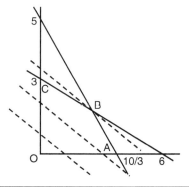

Figure 6.1   A very(!) simple example of a linear programme

(iv) and (v), trivial though they may be, note that only non-negative quantities of the ingredients can be used. The objective function (i) gives the overall profit. Second, the benefits of the modelling process might stimulate Sid to think a little more widely. The OR analyst working with Sid to build this model would inevitably ask questions to check the

Case vignette 6.1 Minimising shipping costs

Incitec is a major supplier of fertiliser products in eastern and southern Australia, distributing its products through major warehousing centres located along Australia's eastern and southern coasts. Each centre is located at a navigable port and comprises warehousing and bagging facilities to supply local and inland customers and dealers. In addition, the centres at Brisbane and Newcastle have some production capabilities. The logistics department is responsible for scheduling the monthly shipments of all products against a rolling twelve-month planning horizon.

From a scheduler's viewpoint, it is extremely difficult to produce *any* schedule manually to meet the expected requirements of the customers while satisfying constraints relating to the current location of ships, their maximum speed, their capacity, minimum discharge tonnages, inventories at warehouses, etc. It becomes virtually impossible if, in addition, the schedulers seek to minimise total transport costs, including shipping and port charges, product value and inventory costs. Experience does generally enable them to achieve satisfactory costs; minimum costs, however, they hardly ever attain. Indeed, even to recognise that they have achieved minimum cost is nearly impossible.

Since the 1960s Incitec has known that the problem could be formulated as a linear programme. Indeed, some attempts were made then to produce schedules that way, but the computing power available relative to the size of the problem meant that the calculations were intractable. In the late 1990s the power of modern PCs and the development of user-friendly modelling and optimisation packages changed that. The firm modelled its scheduling and distribution problem with a linear programme using a standard software package, and the solution saved it several hundred thousand Australian dollars every year. More importantly, the power of the model supported the company's strategic thinking in addition to improving its operational costs. It was able to investigate:

- improving the allocation of its storage facilities between its products;
- the relative advantages of increasing storage capacity; and
- forming joint ventures with other companies to share shipping.

Source: Fox and Herden (1999).

appropriateness of the model. For instance, is Sid free to make any quantities of each type? Maybe he has a regular customer who buys half a chain of premium sausages every day. So he must ensure that $y \geq 0.5$. This would replace inequality (v) in the model, but, while it would raise the bottom, OA, of the region OABC by 0.5 units vertically, it is clear that the optimal solution (2, 2) would not change. Maybe Sid would realise that it takes ten minutes to make a chain of standard sausages and fifteen minutes to make one of premium and that he has only thirty minutes available to prepare sausages. This would introduce a further constraint, $10x + 15y \leq 30$, and, in this case, change the solution.

Case vignette 6.1 indicates a much more realistic problem, which can be and has been addressed by linear programming. The decision variables in this ran to several hundred in number, and there were many more constraints than that. The problem when modelled was huge. Modern computer software solved it, however, and pointed to a solution that was clearly better than the company's current operating practice. More importantly, the process of building and exploring the model, the ability to investigate the value of loosening constraints or changing the number of ships used, etc., helped the management team think strategically and look at further ways of developing the business.

The algorithmic details of optimising $\pi(\boldsymbol{a})$, and the precise specification of $\boldsymbol{a}$ and A, vary according to the class of problem being solved. For instance, logistical problems arising from the supply of several outlets from a few warehouses can often be modelled by a special form of linear programme, called the *transportation problem*. When faced by such a logistical problem the OR analyst will recognise the characteristics of a transportation problem, identify and gather the relevant data, input it into a standard software package for solving transportation problems, run the programme and interpret the results with the DMs to set the operational details of the solution in the context of the original problem. To give another example, in modelling a service process to meet the needs of a random stream of customers, the analyst will work with the DMs to define a queuing model of the system, then, using algebraic, stochastic process or simulation methods, seek a service policy that optimises a performance measure and, finally, working with the DMs, he will interpret this policy into operational details.

In very broad terms, there are two general approaches to solving optimisation problems.

(1) Use mathematics to identify particular defining characteristics of an optimal solution and then find an optimum by solving for these characteristics. Those familiar with calculus will be familiar with the idea of maximising $\pi(a)$ by solving

$$\frac{d\pi}{da} = 0; \ \frac{d^2\pi}{da^2} < 0$$

(Those unfamiliar with calculus will doubtlessly be completely bemused, but do not worry; we do not need such mathematics.) The conditions on the derivatives above apply in the unconstrained unidimensional case. For more general conditions, see Minoux (1986) or Rustem (1998).

(2)   Use an iterative algorithm to search for the optimum – for definiteness, a maximum. First, an arbitrary trial solution $a_0 \in A$ is chosen. Then an improved solution $a_1 \in A$ is generated such that $\pi(a_1) > \pi(a_0)$. Next a second improved solution $a_2 \in A$ is generated such that $\pi(a_2) > \pi(a_1)$. The procedure iterates in a natural way, building a sequence of trial solutions until no (significantly) improved solution can be found.

In practice, and to the complete bewilderment of many students who have struggled heroically with their study of calculus in the mistaken belief that it was directly applicable to optimisation, almost all OR models are optimised via iterative algorithms.

In general, iterative mathematical programming algorithms are distinguished primarily by the mechanism used to generate an improved solution a_1 from the many that are possible. For instance, the standard algorithm for linear programming is the simplex method. The constraint set in figure 6.1 is a quadrilateral. In general, in two-dimensional problems it is a convex polyhedron and in q dimensions a convex polytope. As in the simple example, an optimum always occurs at a vertex of the constraint set. So the simplex algorithm starts from an easily found vertex, often the origin, and moves along the edge that offers the greatest rate of improvement of the objective function. It iterates the process at the vertex at the other end of this edge, and so on, until it arrives at a vertex where no edge offers an improvement – thus finding an optimum for the problem. In contrast to this, the interior-point algorithms for linear programmes take different iterative paths to the simplex, plunging into the centre of the constraint set before homing in on an optimal vertex.

For more general mathematical programmes, in which the objective and constraint may be far from linear, many different algorithms have been developed. Some rely on calculus to find the paths of steepest ascent (or descent), always going in the direction that currently offers the greatest rate of change. Some, such as branch and bound algorithms, continually partition the constraint set and identify in which part of the partition an optimum lies. Using smaller and smaller partitions, they home in on the solution. Others simply search intelligently – or not so intelligently! Monte Carlo methods, for instance, generate solutions at random and pick the largest. In fairness, the random-candidate solutions are often generated according to a distribution that is biased to give a higher chance of improvement than pure randomness. Recent developments in AI have led to more subtle iterative search methods, such as genetic algorithms (section 5.6) and tabu search. Such iterative

Case vignette 6.2 OR helps in the design of an automated warehouse

A steel firm wanted to take advantage of recent technological advances in automated warehouses. To do so it would need to develop new ordering and dispatch processes. An OR team collected and analysed the ordering and demand data from current processes and then developed a simulation model of the new warehouse based upon these data. The team used this to experiment with a range of different operating strategies, and in doing so identified a number of potential bottlenecks, on the one hand, and areas in which the systems could be underutilised, on the other. Using these insights the team modified the design and planned operation of the warehouse and reran the simulations. Again, new insights were acquired into potential problems, and the design was revised further. After a few iterations the team was able to make recommendations that led to an efficient and effective automated warehouse system that achieved the firm's ambitions.

numerical methods are the lifeblood of computation, and there are many software packages available that implement the procedures for particular classes of problem: see section 4.

We have emphasised the iterative nature of optimisation algorithms for two reasons. First, it emphasises again the importance of transitivity in optimisation. As noted in section 3.2, without transitivity one cannot assume that a candidate solution discarded earlier would not dominate a later candidate solution. Second, there are a range of interactive algorithms that require input from the DMs at each iteration. One family of such methods is described in section 3.

Another family of approaches commonly used in OR – simulation – does not formally seek an optimum in the sense used above. Rather, it simulates the system of concern and explores different strategies for managing it. Thus the system is modelled and 'run' according to an agreed control strategy against a random set of inputs. The performance of the system is then assessed and shown to the DMs. The DMs suggest modifications to either the system or the control strategy, or both, and the simulation is run again. The process iterates until the DMs feel that the performance is satisfactory. Simulation therefore does not search for an optimal solution but, rather, a satisfactory one. The process embodies the spirit of satisficing (section 2.2). Case vignette 6.2 describes an OR study that used simulation methods in precisely this exploratory fashion.

The cognitive support provided by the OR methods described above take three forms. First, the ability of DMs to perceive *all* the alternatives in complex problems is limited. The remark by Abbe' D'Allanival that opened this chapter is telling: the more possibilities there are the more difficult it is to choose. By defining the constraint set A on the decision variables, OR analysis helps DMs explore all the production plans, schedules, operating policies or whatever that they might adopt. Without the support of the mathematics, they might miss some possible combinations of the decision variables and, as a result, miss a promising way forward. Second, the optimisation process helps DMs find a good solution. Their cognitive abilities to seek out an optimum from many possibilities are also limited. Thus OR brings analytic and computational support to their search.

A third level of support is more subtle. The OR process is catalytic, helping DMs conceptualise the issues into a succinct problem formulation that encapsulates what matters to them. In the discussion of Sid's sausages, we noted that the process might make him realise more constraints than simply his current stocks of meat; and in case vignette 6.1 we noted that the model helped the company explore several strategic issues beyond the simple optimisation of transport and inventory costs. This element of OR – its ability to catalyse thought – has led to the development of a number of issue and problem formulation tools, known under the heading of soft OR (discussed in chapter 9).

6.3 Interactive multi-objective programming

I'm always thinking of what's wrong with the thing and how it can be improved. (Walt Disney)

In applying mathematical programming methods, it is assumed that the objective function is fully defined at the outset. It is assumed, therefore, that a DM[2] knows her preferences sufficiently well to articulate them in an objective function, before any optimisation or analysis is undertaken. There is a class of algorithms, however, that interlaces elicitation of the DM's preferences with iterations of the optimisation process.

Suppose that the success of a course of action is to be judged against q performance measures, or *attributes*, as we call them: perhaps, for example, measures of profit, safety and reliability. It is convenient to identify a course of action a with its performance as measured on these attributes. Thus we take $a = (a_1, a_2, \ldots, a_q)$ and the constraint set A becomes a subset of q-dimensional space. This may be convenient but in modelling terms it hides a lot of work. Essentially, it means that the consequence of taking a has to be predicted on each of the q attributes. The building of

---

[2] Note that, since we are discussing the elicitation of preference, we explicitly consider a single DM. Group issues are discussed in chapter 11 onwards.

consequence models is discussed further in section 7.3. Here we assume that all the q attributes are real-valued. Moreover, we assume that the DM's preferences are strictly increasing in each attribute. She therefore has q objectives to maximise the performance on each attribute. Each attribute defines an objective, which is why we speak of interactive *multi-objective* programming.

Unfortunately, it is usually the case that there are conflicts between the objectives. Seldom, for example, is it possible to increase reliability and profit simultaneously; increased reliability has costs, which reduces profits. Thus, the DM must trade off greater success on one objective with poorer performance on others. One way forward is to define an objective function $\pi(\boldsymbol{a})$ that incorporates the DM's trade-off between the objectives.[3] This would lead to the problem: maximise $\pi(\boldsymbol{a})$ subject to $\boldsymbol{a}$ remaining in A. We would therefore be back to a mathematical programming problem, as discussed above.

Several criticisms have been levelled, however, against techniques that seek first to assess and then to optimise a function (Goicoechea *et al.*, 1982; Starr and Zeleny, 1977). First, the assessment procedure, which is needed to determine, *inter alia*, the trade-offs between the objectives, can be very time-consuming. Moreover, it almost inevitably involves asking the DM to make hypothetical choices between alternatives that often have no practical reality – e.g. 'How much would you pay to improve a car's fuel consumption by 4 per cent?' even though there may be no car among the alternatives that actually does offer such an improvement. Motivating her to consider and evaluate these choices is difficult; and, indeed, she may see their introduction into the analysis as an unnecessary confusion. Second, once $\pi(\boldsymbol{a})$ has been determined, the decision is implicitly made. All that remains is to optimise $\pi(\boldsymbol{a})$ on a computer. The optimisation process rarely, if ever, involves the DM, yet she often sees this stage as the point where the decision is made. She thus feels excluded from the very part of the analysis that she believes she should be central to. The final and, perhaps, the most important of the criticisms is that the determination of $\pi(\boldsymbol{a})$ is an analytic process. Performance on each of the attributes is determined separately, then combined. Some writers[4] on multi-criteria decision making, however, argue that choice is a gestalt process, in which alternatives are considered holistically – i.e. the value of an object is something more than the sum of its components parts (see, especially, Duckstein *et al.*, 1975, and Goicoechea *et al.*, 1982).

---

[3] Such an objective function would be a multi-attribute value function or the expectation of a multi-attribute utility function, but we leave discussion of these to chapters 7 and 8.

[4] Not us, though, as we indicate in later chapters.

Looking back at the generic iterative optimisation algorithm described in the previous section, notice that the value function $\pi(a)$ is used only in two places: first, in defining an improvement at each iteration, and, second, in checking for convergence. Furthermore, it is possible that much of the information implicit in $\pi(a)$ is not used. Thus, much of the time-consuming introspection and analysis used in determining $\pi(a)$ might be unnecessary.

Suppose, therefore, that we abandon the determination of $\pi(a)$ and instead begin simply with a trial solution, a_0, then ask the DM to determine an 'improvement' a_1 such that she prefers a_1 to a_0. Repeat the process again and again, each time by interaction with the DM determining a point a_n such that she prefers a_n to a_{n-1}. Declare that the process has converged when she feels that a_n is satisfactory.

Naturally, no interactive multi-objective programming method is as simple as this description. Usually much subtlety is used to suggest possible improvements to the DM. Some methods require extensive interaction with the DM, using preference information to check for improvement and also to ensure that the search for the next potential solution is computationally efficient. To avoid placing excessive demands upon the DM's time, many authors (such as Zionts and Wallenius, 1976) build two particular features into their algorithms. First, they limit the search to non-dominated solutions – i.e. a solution such that there is no other solution that is better in at least one attribute and no worse in any other. In doing this, they make use of the assumption that the DM's preferences increase along each attribute, which implies that $\pi(a)$ is monotonic in each of the objectives, a. Second, they assume a particular functional form for the unknown value function. Often they assume that $\pi(a)$ is a known function and that only particular parameters are unknown. Many writers assume a linear value function with unknown coefficients (section 7.4), namely $\pi(a) = \Sigma_i w_i a_i$. The assumption that the form of $\pi(a)$ is known and only some parameters are unknown means that the preference information gained in constructing the sequence of improvements $a_1, \ldots, a_{n-1}$ may be used to place limits on these parameters, and these limits, in turn, may be used to restrict the search for an improvement a_n.

This, in essence, is interactive multi-objective programming. Notice how the criticisms raised above are avoided. The preference information obtained from the DM is precisely sufficient to find a satisfactory solution and no more. No, or little, redundant information on her preferences is obtained. She is not asked hypothetical questions; all her choices are between real alternatives. She is involved throughout the procedure and, indeed, central to it. Lastly, her judgements are made holistically. It is left to her to compare a_n with a_{n-1}; no analysis into component preference

Case vignette 6.3 Interactive methods in vendor selection

This application concerns a major overhaul of the supply network of a manufacturing company, including the identification and selection of new vendors and the allocation of orders between them. The DMs were a group of senior managers, including those responsible for purchasing, engineering and quality, and they were supported by a team of analysts. Globalisation and the resulting increase in competition meant that companies had to reduce their cost base as far as possible without compromising the quality of their products. The development of a cost-effective supply network was therefore of prime importance to a manufacturer. The DMs had to find a strategy that achieved a good balance between a range of criteria such as price, quality, technical service, delivery reliability and lead time and constraints such as the capacity of suppliers, the needs of their own production schedule and the minimum quality requirements of specific components.

The analyst team worked with the DMs using a method known as visual interactive goal (VIG) programming. This allowed the DMs to be involved throughout the analysis once the structure of the model had been built, including clarifying and defining the goals of the analysis, specifying the constraints and allowable ranges for the outputs and, above all, exploring potential solutions and interactively selecting directions for improvement.

The analysis was successful in finding a supply network that was substantially cheaper than the maximum that the DMs were prepared to accept, while performing well in terms of the other criteria. The analyst team observed that 'the application helped overcome the senior managers' mistrust of quantitative techniques. Once the problem had been formulated with the help of the analysis team the managers had the opportunity to maintain control by examining alternative courses of action rather than being presented with a single solution.' The ability of the method to explore alternative solutions helped achieve a solution that robustly met the requirements of just-in-time manufacture.
Source: Karpak *et al.* (1999).

orders is made. We may also note that non-interactive optimisation often 'hides' the constraint set from the DM: she may be involved in defining it implicitly in the process of eliciting the constraints, but she may not appreciate the implications of these constraints. Iterative methods lead her through a structured exploration of the constraint set.

Involving the DMs interactively in the optimisation process does seem to answer some of the concerns that OR supplants DMs. Case vignette 6.3 describes one application in which DMs were reassured of their central role in the process.

Nonetheless, there are significant issues that interactive multi-objective algorithms face and that have yet to be addressed. While many such methods have been proposed, in all but a very few cases the bare skeleton outlined here underlies most of them – and therein lies a problem. In chapter 2 we noted that DMs' unaided judgements are often incompatible with the underlying assumptions of theoretical decision models. We emphasise this further in relation to multi-objective problems in the next chapter. Thus it may happen that the DM offers judgements that do not fit the assumptions necessary for the algorithm to work meaningfully.

- The initial solution a_0 may act as an anchor for her judgements, limiting her ambition and setting low aspirations for the final solution. Anchoring is another bias identified in behavioural studies. People tend to be overly influenced by the first number that they hear or estimate in a given context, and this has too strong a bearing on their final judgement or solution (see, for example, Bazerman, 2006). An analyst should be careful, therefore, not to offer numerical prompts in eliciting values from a DM lest he bias her responses.
- At each stage of the algorithm she is required to compare and choose between two or more candidate solutions. Typically these differ in their performance on many attributes, but not by much on each. Such preference comparisons are precisely the ones that people find the hardest to make consistently. For instance, they may unconsciously use different trade-offs between objectives in different comparisons (von Winterfeldt and Edwards, 1986).
- Her judgements may be intransitive (Tversky, 1969). As we have noted, however, transitivity is a key assumption of any optimisation algorithm, iterative or not.
- We must also bear in mind the issues raised in section 2.4 regarding the compatibility hypothesis – i.e. the form in which people express their preferences focuses them onto some aspects of the available information and leads to the neglect of other aspects.

Thus, interactive multi-objective methods risk building their analyses on inconsistent and inappropriate data (Daellenbach and Buchanan, 1989; French, 1984b; Korhonen and Wallenius, 1996; Loque *et al.*, 2007). Essentially, these methods forget the imperative presented in figure 3.1. Although analyses may aspire to achieve the rationality encoded in a normative decision theory, they need to be mindful of the DM's cognitive characteristics if they are to produce meaningful, informative guidance. There is a need to produce interactive multi-objective methods that encourage the DM to pause and reflect on the consistency of her judgements, perhaps revising ones offered earlier in the light of her thinking about ones she is asked for at later iterations. This still has to be done in

MODM and MCDM, so, for the present, analysts and DMs should take great care in applying the methods and reflect hard on the input judgements at each iteration.

6.4 OR-based DSSs

The integration of OR and AI may proceed from either of two perspectives. First, AI techniques can make the capabilities of OR more accessible to decision makers; that is, they can facilitate the creation of models, automated model building and analysis, evaluation of results, and proper model application. Second, AI techniques can be invoked by OR models. This entails an extension to the traditional thinking of OR, in that an algorithm may include steps that carry out inferences, and may interact with users in the course of its execution. (Committee on the Next Decade in Operations Research [CONDOR])

Early OR developed without the advantage of copious readily available computing power. Slide rules, adding machines, ingenuity and much hard work were used to optimise within models. As computers were developed, however, the OR community took advantage of the new-found ability to solve larger and larger linear programmes and other problems. Nowadays, there are many computational packages available to solve OR problems: see case vignettes 6.1 and 6.4. Textbooks often have discs with suites of OR programmes attached. Spreadsheets have generalised optimisation techniques built in, and a host of add-ins are offered to extend the functionality still further.

There are two points that we should note, however. First, many of the constrained optimisation problems faced are combinatorial – that is, the

Case vignette 6.4 Networked DSSs at United Sugars Corporation

United Sugars Corporation (USC) has implemented a network of decision support systems to solve a range of supply, production, inventory control and distribution problems. USC collaborated with SAS Inc., a software company specialising in operational research, statistical, database and data-mining software, to develop a company-wide system to optimise and manage its supply chain. The system deals with the packaging, storage and distribution of over 250 sugar products at about eighty different plants over a thirteen-month horizon. The system provides essential information relating to production packaging, labour and resource requirements, warehousing and freight expenses, inventory management and order distribution. In total, the system provides the means of planning about 85 per cent of USC's budget. One particularly important feature of the system is that it is managed through web interfaces and therefore can be run anywhere across USC's intranet.

Source: Cohen *et al.* (2001).

constraints require that the solutions are essentially integers, or, equivalently (albeit not obviously so), permutations. Moreover, many of these problems are *NP-complete* (Garey and Johnson, 1979). Essentially, this means that as problems get bigger – i.e. involve more decision variables – there is a combinatorial explosion in the effort required to solve them. Thus, even with modern computers, many large scheduling and allocation models still cannot be solved optimally. Consequently, concepts of heuristic and approximate solution are as important within OR today as they have always been.

Second, notwithstanding the lack of computationally feasible algorithms for solving all optimisation problems, by and large the focus of development of OR DSSs has moved from the solution algorithms themselves to the interface with users. On the input side, modelling tools enable the user either to structure easily very large mathematical programmes or to represent a system in a form ready for simulation. Not only do these tools enable the model structure to be created, often using intuitive graphical interfaces, but they also facilitate the interrogation of databases to populate the models ready for its solution. Such tools use technologies similar to those used in EISs and business intelligence systems, and in time we may expect the development of common interfaces so that managers can monitor aspects of their organisation's performance and then address shortfalls in its operations by running appropriate OR models. On the output side, OR software no longer indicates optimal strategies via enormous arrays of numbers that become intelligible only after close examination. Rather, the strategy is indicated graphically, maybe with a visual simulation of its performance against a typical week (or month, year or whatever) of operation (Fiddy *et al.*, 1991). Visual simulations of performance are extremely valuable as a means of helping a management team understand the details of the strategy, its strengths and, also, the potential weaknesses that they will need to monitor to ensure that it delivers the promised performance.

6.5 The OR process

OR/MS workers have always been conscious that problem solving and analysis should come before the use of techniques. (Mike Pidd)

In section 3.6 we began to discuss the process of decision analysis and support, and we continue this discussion at several points in the book. Here we explore the process of OR, noting parallels with decision analysis.

All problem-solving 'disciplines', such as decision analysis, systems analysis, business process (re-)engineering, information systems engineering, software engineering and OR, recognise a process that cycles through stages in which the problem is identified, solutions are constructed and evaluated, and then they are interpreted into the implementation of some change in the real world. In figure 3.6 we described this as *formulate – evaluate – appraise.* Since the OR profession was perhaps the first to discuss this cycle explicitly, it is appropriate to revisit its broader socio-technical aspects here. Descriptions of the OR process tend to avoid the words 'evaluate' and 'appraise' and use a terminology more appropriate to modelling and optimisation, even though, as we have indicated in section 2, these form only part of the much broader problem-solving process. In figure 6.2 we provide a very schematic overview.

The *monitoring* stage recognises that an OR study arises when there is an acknowledgement that some aspect of a system could be organised and managed better. This requires a monitoring process that continually observes the system and identifies when its current modes of operation begin to perform poorly. Such degradation of performance may arise because of economic changes leading to different demands for the outputs or a different availability of inputs. Technological advances may mean that assumptions on efficiency made when the current system was designed and implemented are no longer valid. Because such changes may occur,

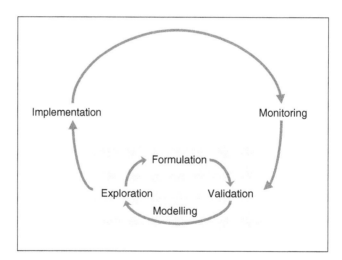

Figure 6.2   The OR process

organisations should continually monitor all aspects of their performance. Remember our discussion of defensive avoidance (section 2.8): only by continual monitoring can organisations defend themselves against such dysfunctional behaviour.

For long periods, of course, monitoring will show that there is no need to seek change, but at some point externalities will have moved on and there will be indications that the system is performing poorly in some sense. The question is: in what sense? At this point an OR study will begin to gather data and model the system. This starts with a *modelling* sub-cycle in which the issues are formulated and a model constructed to represent the system and how it addresses these issues. The model will be validated against available data and experience and then its behaviour will be explored. This exploration will enhance understanding of the issues, and perhaps suggest modifications that will lead to a revised model that better represents the system; and the process cycles. Gradually the model will begin to evolve from the world as it is to how the world might be if the system is operated differently.

The exploration will concentrate increasingly on optimisation to determine how the system's performance might be improved. In the terminology of table 3.1, decision support moves from levels 0 and 1 to level 2. Cycles of modelling and exploration, together with discussions with the managers and workforce, lead to a conception of an improved manner of operating the system. Note that this improvement may be an incremental change in its operating characteristics or something more radical, in which its outputs are achieved via entirely different means. At this point the modelling cycle will change in character, in that the model is explored and used to develop a clear understanding of an improved strategy in sufficient detail for it to be implemented.

The third stage, *implementation*, needs to recognise the social/technical nature of improving a process. For example, the modelling cycle may have identified a better way of working, but this may not be sufficient to motivate the management and workforce to make the change. Improvement means doing things differently, learning new skills, accepting new practices, and so on. The technical solution may not work without sensitivity to these issues, and perhaps some modifications that may reduce its theoretical optimality but increase its acceptability may be necessary for this solution to be implemented. In short, the model informs and gives direction to the implementation stage, but does not dictate it.

6.6 Sequential decision processes

Decisions are seldom taken in isolation: one decision inevitably leads to another. The representation of contingency in decision trees recognises this (see section 8.5). In the case of decision trees, however, although the sequencing of decisions is modelled, the decisions at each stage may have a different structure: a decision to conduct an R&D project, say, may lead to a potential new product and a decision to manufacture and launch it – two interrelated decisions differing considerably in structure, uncertainties and consequences. There are occasions, however, especially in the operational and hands-on domains, when DMs are faced by a sequence of essentially identical decisions. For instance, in maintaining an inventory of parts in a repair shop, a decision to order a particular quantity of a particular part today would set up the circumstances for a further decision in a week's time to consider ordering more of the same part. Order many today and the chances may be that no order will be needed next week, saving the cost of processing another order though incurring costs from holding high inventory levels. Such sequences of decisions are well studied in many areas, from OR to control theory (Berksekas, 1987; Caputo, 2005; DeGroot, 1970; French and Ríos Insua, 2000; Puterman, 1994).

The central result that drives the analysis of sequential decisions is *Bellman's principle of optimality* (Bellman, 1957). This states:

An optimal sequence of decisions has the property that whatever the initial conditions and whatever the initial decision, the remaining decisions must be optimal with respect to the circumstances that arise as a result of the initial decision.

At first sight this seems impenetrable: but once mastered it is a very powerful way of thinking about sequences of decisions. Imagine that we have just the last decision in the sequence to make and that we know how to make this decision for any of the possible circumstances that may have arisen. Now consider the penultimate decision in the sequence. The consequence of taking this will be what we get immediately from taking that decision combined with the consequence of taking the last decision in the sequence. We know how to take the last decision, however, and can calculate what we will get from taking this optimally. So we can work out what the best penultimate decision is. Next consider the decision second from the end of the sequence. Taking this will give us an immediate consequence, and then we shall need to take the penultimate and final decisions. We know how to take these optimally, however, so we can calculate what is optimal for the second decision from the end; and so on. We use this logic in solving decision trees (section 8.5). It is known as (backward) *dynamic programming*.

Dynamic programming ideas have led to some very powerful mathematical algorithms for solving sequential problems, but what is not often realised is that they provide sound qualitative ways of thinking about a sequence of decisions. Essentially, for any decision that you make today, think first about the position this will put you in for any decisions that you make tomorrow. If your brain can cope with building an infinite regress, think also about the position that your decision tomorrow puts you in for the day after that; etc. It is wise to think ahead.

6.7 Concluding remarks and further reading

As figure 3.7 indicates, OR methods are applied in general in the operational and general domains. The focus of the OR community on the operational domain has broadened over the past couple of decades, however, and its work now extends up into the strategic domain as well as down to more detailed aspects in the hands-on domain. For those wishing more detail than is provided here, there are many general introductions to OR available. We mention Daellenbach and McNickle (2005), Denardo (2002), Hillier and Liebermann (2004), Keys (1995), Littlechild and Shutler (1991), Ragsdale (2001) and Taha (2006). There is a very basic, but readable, introduction to some of the ideas in Teale *et al.* (2003). Recently, it has become the fashion with the management literature to refer to many of the skills and techniques of OR under the general title of *analytics* (Davenport, 2006).

The history of OR can be fascinating: see the early chapters of Keys (1995) or Littlechild and Shutler (1991). Most OR texts include introductions to the basics of optimisation; more advanced discussions may be found in Minoux (1986) and Rustem (1998). Silver (2004) provides a recent survey of heuristic and AI optimisation algorithms, including genetic algorithms and tabu search. More general relationships between OR and AI are explored in Kobbacy *et al.* (2007). There are many surveys and discussions of (interactive) multi-objective programming: we mention Climaco (1997), Fandal and Gal (1997), Gardiner and Vanderpooten (1997), Koksalan and Zionts (2001), Loque *et al.* (2007), Pardalos *et al.* (1995) and Trzaskalik and Michnik (2002). For introductions to simulation, see, for example, Evans and Olson (2002) and Pidd (1998). Hollocks

(2006) gives a very readable reflection on the history of simulation, which in many ways also parallels the development of OR itself. Discussions of OR DSSs may be found in Mallach (2000). In addition, the INFORMS (Institute for Operations Research and the Management Sciences) magazine *OR/MS Today* regularly publishes surveys and evaluation of new OR software systems.

White (1985) provides an excellent, if somewhat advanced, introduction to the whole OR process; Keys (1995) offers a much more gentle introduction. Ormerord (2002) provides a relatively recent discussion of the OR process and profession. The 'Viewpoints' section of the *Journal of the Operational Research Society* regularly offers debates about the nature of the OR process. Beware in consulting the literature on the process of OR, however; there is little agreement on terminology, nor, indeed, on the number of stages in the process. Nonetheless, these differences tend to be more differences in description than in perception: read beneath the words and you will discover that there is much more agreement than is immediately apparent.

OR is not the only multidisciplinary activity that supports decision making. Its close cousins *operations management* (Slack *et al.*, 2004) and *management science* (Anderson *et al.*, 1991) are also essentially multidisciplinary. The study of *information systems* (Boddy *et al.*, 2005; Checkland and Howell, 1997; Laudon and Laudon, 2006; Pearlson and Saunders, 2006) and their development (Kendall and Kendall, 2004) requires multidisciplinary perspectives on the impacts and effective use of information and communications technologies. *Systems science* (Pidd, 2004), which seeks to understand how complex systems work and evolve from many perspectives, provides valuable insights for decision making. All these activities and professions are multidisciplinary: they require skills and knowledge associated with a variety of scientific, engineering, human and social science disciplines to achieve their ends. They are closely related to the socio-technical movement, stemming from work at the Tavistock Institute during the 1960s, recognising that the successful implementation of any decision, design or system requires many skills, not just technical correctness (Mumford, 2000). Whether it helps to distinguish between all these multidisciplinary, socio-technical activities is a moot point, but not for us to decide. We simply draw the moral that, in supporting decisions, we must be 'Jacks[5] of all trades'.

---

[5] And Jills!

6.8 Exercises and questions for discussion

(1) In discussing the problem faced by Sid the butcher (figure 6.1), we noted that his limited time to make the sausages could introduce the constraint $10x + 15y \leq 30$. We remarked that this would change the optimal solution. We also remarked, however, that introducing a constraint that at least half a chain of sausages were produced would not change the solution. Confirm these remarks by reanalysing the problem by the graphical method illustrated in figure 6.1.

(2) Most spreadsheets, including Microsoft Excel, have built-in macros to solve mathematical programmes. Using one of these, input and solve Sid the butcher's problem (figure 6.1).

(3) Use a search engine to find the home websites of professional mathematical programming software such as XPRESS-MP or GAMMS. Explore the case studies on such sites that indicate the range of (OR) problems that such software can solve, and has solved.

(4) Currently many companies are referring to *analytics* as a key function in their organisations (Davenport, 2006). Investigate this and discuss the relationship between, on the one hand, analytics and, on the other hand, operational research and statistics.

Decision analysis and multiple objectives

7.1 Introduction

When you can measure what you are speaking of and express it in numbers, you know that on which you are discoursing. But when you cannot measure it and express it in numbers, your knowledge is of a very meagre and unsatisfactory kind. (Lord Kelvin)

In this book we are seeking to provide a very broad overview of decision analysis and support. This makes our book different from most other texts, which tend to concentrate on particular areas, such as OR, DSSs or 'decision analysis'; and therein lies a potential confusion. While we might argue that all the analysis we describe in our book is *decision analysis*, convention has it that *decision analysis* refers primarily to the use of multi-attribute value models, decision trees and influence diagrams to provide prescriptive support for decision making in the general and corporate domains: see figure 3.7. It is to this topic that we turn in the next four chapters.

In this chapter we introduce the basic modelling techniques and forms of quantitative analysis used in circumstances in which uncertainty is not a significant factor, but conflicting objectives are. We contrast these models with some findings from behavioural decision studies and discuss how we should interact with DMs to elicit the judgements that the models need. In the next chapter we do the same for decision contexts with significant uncertainty. In chapter 9 we discuss how we may help DMs explore the complexity, both perceived and hidden, that faces them in unstructured strategic decision making. This exploration helps both to formulate problems and to recognise which decision analytic models may be appropriate. Finally, chapter 10 draws these together into a coherent approach to prescriptive decision analysis, fleshing out the discussion begun in section 3.6.

We should note one general point of terminology. When representing preferences in the context of certainty, we use *value* functions; in cases in which uncertainty is involved, we use *utility* functions. As we shall see in section 8.4, utility functions encode not just preferences for the difference consequences of a decision but also the DM's attitude to risk.

Before turning to a discussion of some of the models used in decision analysis, we need to pause and discuss what we mean by a model, and modelling. A multidisciplinary approach, we believe, gives our perspective a vital richness; but it also introduces ambiguities, because terms such as 'model' have different meanings in different disciplines. To a mathematician, a model is an algebraic formalism that relates inputs to outputs. Essentially, a mathematical model is a mathematical function, allowing the user to calculate the outputs from given inputs. A spreadsheet model is a mathematical model in which the algebra is hidden in the connections between cells and macros; as, for that matter, is a computer programme, or, as it is sometimes termed, a computer model. Such models lie at the heart of the physical, engineering and earth sciences as well as parts of biological and environmental sciences, economic theory, etc. Some of these models are explicit and represented by a function; others are implicit, the outputs being determined by a solution algorithm for, perhaps, a complex differential equation. In contrast, models in management theory, psychology and many social sciences tend to be qualitative, conceptually based and often pictorial. They indicate the range of factors that may influence an outcome, usually specifying the nature of these relations in conceptual rather than mathematical terms – e.g. whether changes in particular factors increase or decrease the magnitude of the outcome: see section 9.6.

Of course, there are many different types of models, ranging between those that are clearly quantitative and those that are clearly qualitative. The cynefin model[1] can provide some insight here. Models can be seen as encoding aspects of explicit knowledge. Mathematical and quantitative models capture knowledge in the known and knowable spaces, but in the complex space our knowledge is too meagre to be modelled quantitatively. Qualitative models thus provide the formalism for capturing what we know in the complex and, occasionally, the chaotic spaces. This is not to say that qualitative models have no place in the known and knowable domains: qualitative representations are vital for enhancing understanding and communicating ideas in all domains. That quantitative models are more common in the known and knowable domains is the nub of the idea that Lord Kelvin was expressing in the quotation at the head of this section. Unfortunately, in drawing on his home discipline of physics he over-emphasised the importance of the quantitative over the qualitative.

---

[1] Or is it a *meta*model, since we are using the qualitative, pictorial cynefin model to discuss aspects of modelling and knowledge?

Models are built through a process of modelling; this is an obvious truism, but there is no single process of modelling, as we have acknowledged in section 3.4. Some models are developed with the intention of representing the world as it is; other models seek to forecast how the world might evolve if left to itself or if we intervene by taking some action. Some models seek to capture our judgements and behaviours as they are; other models explore the implications of revising or evolving these judgements and behaviours. Yet further models consider how the world might be or how we should behave under a range of idealised or just interesting, but perhaps unrealistic, assumptions. The development of different models needs different approaches to elicitation, fitting to data and validation. We argue that it is partly through the interplay between these different processes that decision analysis guides DMs towards a deeper understanding of themselves, the world and the value of potential strategies to them. That is for later, however; here we simply turn to the quantitative models that are used within decision analysis.

Our objectives in this chapter are:

- to introduce findings from behavioural studies that highlight how people make decisions in situations with several, possibly conflicting objectives, draw attention to some of the limitations in how they do this and sketch out what kinds of support might be appropriate to help them make better decisions;
- to consider the modelling of potential consequences of decisions, including their representation in terms of the factors that a DM considers important;
- to provide an introduction to multi-attribute value modelling as a way of balancing conflicting objectives;
- to consider ways of eliciting values and weights in multi-attribute value functions that reduce the discrepancy between the behavioural responses of DMs and the underlying normative theory;
- to present a substantive case study that illustrates the methods introduced in this chapter and supports the discussion in subsequent chapters; and
- to indicate alternative multi-attribute decision analysis methods.

Finally, while there is necessarily some mathematics and some algebra in this chapter, be assured that, in practice, modern software ensures that few of us ever undertake these calculations ourselves. Nevertheless, understanding how we might do so will give us insight into how these models support decision making.

7.2 Choice behaviour in the face of complex alternatives and multi-attribute value analysis

Between two evils, I always pick the one I never tried before. (Mae West)

In this section we review behavioural research explaining how people make decisions in multi-attribute situations in which uncertainty is not a significant factor but conflicting objectives are – i.e. each alternative has its good and its bad points. Such decisions are common but rarely made using formal decision analysis. We explore the different strategies that people use, consider the effectiveness of these and then build on this work to develop a context and justification for using the modelling techniques and forms of quantitative analysis reviewed in later sections of the chapter.

As indicated earlier in chapter 2, Simon (1960) argued that people are unable to make decisions as outlined by the normative model because the mental operations required to do this far exceed their information-processing capacity. He suggested that people *satisfice*, a strategy that involves choosing the first alternative that is reasonable rather than the best. This work has given rise to an important strand of behavioural research showing that people use a broad range of strategies, each varying in terms of the time taken to implement, the cognitive 'cost' to the decision makers of this implementation and the amount/depth of information processing prior to choice. In addition, the strategy adopted has important implications for the accuracy of the decision (see Payne *et al.*, 1993, for a review of these studies.)

Compensatory and non-compensatory strategies

Within this body of research a distinction is made between compensatory and non-compensatory strategies. *Compensatory strategies* allow bad performance by an alternative on one or more attributes to be compensated for by a good performance on others. Put simply: you don't stop evaluating an alternative as soon as you find something bad, because this may be compensated for by something good that you discover later. DMs using this strategy end up using all the available information when making their decisions. Later we argue that one particular compensatory strategy, multi-attribute value analysis (MAVA), provides the normatively appropriate way of making decisions in multi-attribute situations, and develop procedures to assist people to make them in this way. Behavioural research shows that people do occasionally use MAVA (referred to as a *linear strategy* in behavioural studies), but only in an informal and approximate way. Another compensatory approach identified in behavioural studies is the *additive-difference strategy*. This involves a DM computing the difference between alternatives on each attribute. Then a rough summation of these differences across the attributes determines which alternative to choose.

Non-compensatory strategies operate on rules that do not allow a bad rating on one attribute to be balanced out by a good rating on another. Instead, a bad rating usually leads to that option being rejected. Satisficing is non-compensatory, given that an alternative is rejected as soon as it fails to reach an acceptable level on any of the attributes (see chapter 2 for a full description of satisficing). There are many other non-compensatory strategies (see Svenson, 1979). For example, a *conjunctive strategy* is similar to satisficing, with DMs first establishing a minimum standard for each attribute (e.g., when choosing between cars, cost must not exceed a set amount and comfort must be above a particular level) and then choosing the first alternative that meets all standards for all attributes, even if this means that some alternatives are not considered (i.e. the fourth car may meet all standards so selected even though there are many other cars yet to be evaluated). A *disjunctive strategy* is even simpler: it involves selecting the first alternative that meets a standard on any attribute (i.e. choose an alternative that has anything reasonable about it!).

A distinctive group of non-compensatory strategies consists of those that involve the rank ordering of attributes in terms of importance (termed a *lexicographic order*). The lexicographic strategy considers the most important attribute first, and the alternative with the best value on this is selected. If several alternatives are tied for the best value on the most important attribute, then the second most important attribute is considered, with the alternative with the best value on this dimension being selected. The process continues considering attributes, in order of importance, until one alternative is left and consequently chosen. A similar heuristic is the lexicographic semi-order, in which the DM takes the alternative that performs best on the most important attribute unless it betters some of the others only by a small amount, in which case the second most important attribute is considered, and so on (Tversky, 1969). Another example is *elimination by aspects* (EBA) (Payne *et al.*, 1993; Tversky, 1972), which considers the most important attribute first, and all alternatives that do not meet a predetermined standard are eliminated from consideration. The EBA strategy continues to process the attributes

Table 7.1 General characteristics of decision strategies

	Variable search – non-compensatory	Constant search – compensatory
Attribute-based processing	Elimination by aspects (EBA)	Additive-difference
Alternative-based processing	Conjunctive, disjunctive	Linear (MAVA)

in order of importance using the same elimination rule until one alternative remains.

Payne (1976) classifies intuitive decision-making behaviour according to two dimensions.

(1) The degree to which the DM processes information primarily by alternative or by attribute – i.e. evaluating all the attribute information for the first alternative before moving on to the second or evaluating how each alternative performs on the first attribute before moving on to the second.

(2) The degree to which the DM searches for a constant or a variable amount of information for each alternative. Compensatory strategies necessarily involve processing all the attribute information, so the search is constant between alternatives. Non-compensatory strategies involve rejecting an alternative as soon as negative information is discovered, however, so the amount of information accessed about each alternative is variable. Indeed, some alternatives will be neglected altogether if an acceptable alternative has already been found.

Table 7.1 characterises a selection of decision strategies in terms of these two dimensions.

Often DMs use a combination of strategies when making a decision (Montgomery and Svenson, 1976). For instance, when faced with choosing only one alternative from a relatively large set, they often begin their decision process with an initial phase involving the use of quicker or simpler non-compensatory strategies, such as EBA, to reduce the choice set. Then more sophisticated, time-consuming compensatory strategies, such as additive-difference, are used to choose between the alternatives that remain. Payne *et al.* (1993) suggest that DMs select which strategy to use in a particular circumstance by balancing the work needed to decide against the importance they attach to the choice and the resulting need for 'accuracy'. They argue that people are 'cognitive misers', in the sense they do not wish to 'invest' costly mental effort using compensatory strategies when the decision is unimportant or when the complexity of the situation means that the demands will be too great.

Research indicates that DMs are more likely to use non-compensatory strategies in complex situations, since these require less mental effort to implement, so rendering the decision process within the DM's capacity for thinking. These strategies are often suboptimal, however, and can lead DMs to reject or ignore better alternatives than the one selected. In our book we are primarily interested in decisions that lie at the complex rather than the simple end of the spectrum, and so we would expect that DMs rely heavily upon non-compensatory strategies and in doing so expose themselves to the dangers of making suboptimal decisions. In section 3.5 we introduced the arguments of Keeney (1992), which suggest that in prescriptive decision analysis we should follow value-focused thinking. Thus, there is further implicit tension here between our natural decision making and the more structured approach that we are promoting

In response to this one might make an argument that encouraging DMs to use compensatory strategies would be sufficient, but we should recognise that there are limits to human cognitive processing. As indicated in chapter 2, DMs simply cannot keep and compute *all* the relevant information in their minds for complex problems. Instead, we need a structured procedure that breaks down the process into manageable chunks, follows a compensatory process and assists DMs with information storage and the computations necessary to evaluate and compare complex decision alternatives. In later sections of this chapter we present techniques designed to support decision makers in this way. Before this, however, it is necessary briefly to review some more recent behavioural research that challenges the view that using simple non-compensatory strategies are necessarily suboptimal.

Are simple strategies always bad?

In recent years behavioural decision research has identified some situations in which people make better decisions by using simpler rather than complex forms of thinking. In section 3.8 we reviewed some examples of this. More recently, however, there has been a sustained body of research by Gigerenzer and his colleagues (see Gigerenzer *et al.*, 1999) providing some challenging examples of situations in which simplicity is best. In a short but stimulating article, Hertwig and Todd (2003: 216) discuss one such strategy: the *recognition heuristic*. This is a simple non-compensatory decision strategy that says: 'If one of two objects is recognized and the other is not, infer that the recognized object has higher value.' People tend to use this heuristic when their knowledge of an area is limited (if you recognise everything the heuristic fails to distinguish between options, so it cannot be used). Thus, when US students were asked which of a pair of German cities was larger, their performance was better than when they were asked to choose the larger of two US cities. Participants' lack of knowledge about German cities allowed them to use the recognition heuristic in the first task, and this simple strategy was effective. Their greater knowledge about US cities meant that they could not use this heuristic in the second task, however, because they recognised them all. Instead, they used a more complicated decision strategy that took account of their extensive knowledge, but this did not increase decision accuracy. Put simply, knowing less allowed the use of a simpler decision rule that, in turn, led to more accurate decision making. This is one of many studies emerging over the last few years that challenge the idea that decisions are better if they are based on complex compensatory strategies that draw on large quantities of information (Gigerenzer and Goldstein, 1999; Schwartz, 2004).

Recognition is just one of many simple strategies, often referred to as fast-and-frugal heuristics, that can outperform more complicated strategies in situations in which the quality of the decision outcomes can be derived (largely in situations in which there is a correct outcome, such as the German cities examples above). In addition, such strategies have been shown to capture decisions made by professionals – e.g. UK magistrates' bail decisions (Dhami and Ayton, 2001).

Taken at face value, this work challenges a key assumption underpinning many of the ideas presented in this book: that we can help people to make better decisions through the use of structured decision aids that overcome cognitive limitations. Before arriving at this conclusion, however, we need to consider the growing body of evidence suggesting that fast-and-frugal heuristics are not used as frequently as first thought, even when the situation is designed to promote them (see, for example, Broder and Schiffer, 2003), and that there are large individual differences between people in terms of the decision rules that they adopt (Newell and Fernandez, 2006). In addition, much of the research supporting the value of fast-and-frugal heuristics is centred on simple decision tasks with known correct solutions. These are rather different from the tactical and strategic decisions that are our concern, and the primary concern for those developing decision aids.

Overall, we believe that work on the use of fast-and-frugal heuristics provides important insights about decision rules that people use and alerts us to the possibility that simple thinking has the potential to lead to effective decision making. To date, however, there is insufficient evidence from this body of work to suggest that simple strategies are universally better than more elaborate strategies; we believe that this is particularly true in the complex tactical and strategic situations that we focus on in this book. Thus there is still a need to provide support for decision makers confronted by complex multi-attribute decisions, and in the remaining sections of this chapter we provide details of how this can be achieved.

7.3 Consequence and multi-attribute modelling

You can hardly tell where the computer models finish and the dinosaurs begin. (Laura Dern on the film *Jurassic Park*)

In section 1.5 we indicated that at the core of any decision model was the assumed interaction

$$\text{action} \oplus \text{state} \rightarrow \text{consequence}$$
$$a_i \oplus \theta_j \rightarrow c_{ij}$$

i.e. the consequence of a DM's decision will be determined by the interaction between the action and a number of factors beyond her control, which together we refer to as the state of the world. The DMs and their judgements, uncertainties and objectives are not part of this interaction. Later we show how they are overlaid onto the decision model. For the moment we focus on the modelling of the consequence of their action.

We are referring to the 'consequence' of their action in the singular, but perhaps we should emphasise again that there is no assumption that it is unidimensional. As we noted, the c_{ij} should be understood as a description, not a numerical value. Our aim in this section is to introduce methods for deriving this description by means of a vector of q attribute levels that capture the aspects of the consequence that matter to the DMs and stakeholders. Thus c_{ij} will become $(c_{ij1}, c_{ij2}, \ldots, c_{ijq})$, where each c_{ijk} is a representation of a level of achievement against some attribute.[2] We

---

[2] Economists may find a familiar interpretation of such structuring of consequences in terms of *commodity bundles*, $c = (c_1, c_2, \ldots, c_q)$, with c_1 units of commodity 1, c_2 units of commodity 2, etc. Another economic interpretation occurs when $(c_1, c_2, \ldots, c_q)$ represents a time stream of cashflows over q years.

stress, however, that we begin with DMs' holistic perceptions of the possible consequences.

Usually in a decision there are several conflicting objectives, which the DMs must balance in their choice of action. We use the term *attribute* to mean one of the factors that need to be taken into account in a decision. For instance, 'cost' may be an attribute, as may be 'safety' or 'environmental impact'. Other authors sometime use the term *criterion* or, simply, *factor*. The term *objective* or *sub-objective* is used by almost all writers to mean a factor that one wishes to maximise or minimise – i.e. an objective is an attribute plus a direction of preference. For instance, 'minimise cost' is an objective. A *goal* is a target or *aspiration level* on an attribute, but we seldom use these terms.

An *attribute tree* or *hierarchy* essentially provides a pictorial structuring of the attributes into clusters of cognitively similar ones. *Leaf* attributes are those at the bottom of the tree.[3] The tree can help structure an analysis and organise its conclusions in ways that are helpful to DMs' understanding. The structure of the hierarchy adopted in the Chernobyl study, to be discussed in section 8, was instrumental in drawing out the key factors driving the decision making: see, especially, figure 7.16. Using multi-attribute methods can help DMs overcome the cognitive overload brought by the large volume of information that needs to be integrated into the solution of large and complex issues (Brownlow and Watson, 1987). Moreover, taking time to build a tree carefully can help ensure that DMs do not overlook any objectives – a failing that they may fall prey to unless they enter into a structured process (Bond *et al.*, 2008).

Figure 7.1 presents an attribute tree used by Lathrop and Watson (1982) in a study of the risks from nuclear waste management. It was focused purely on the physical health impacts and fatalities that might arise in the event of a radiation leak. This tree does not include any social, political or economic factors that might also be expected to enter into an evaluation: see section 7 for a case in which such factors are introduced. Here only impacts related to the genetic effects on future generations, somatic effects – i.e. cancers – that would result in the present generation, and immediate injuries and fatalities from radiation burns are considered. The somatic and genetic effects are

---

[3] Yes: convention has it that they are leaf, not root, attributes of the tree – and that the tree branches downwards, at least in our case. We represent our attribute hierarchies vertically with the overall attribute at the top, branching downwards to the leaf attributes at the bottom. Some authors and software developers represent the hierarchies from left to right, with the overall attribute at the left and the leaf attributes to the right.

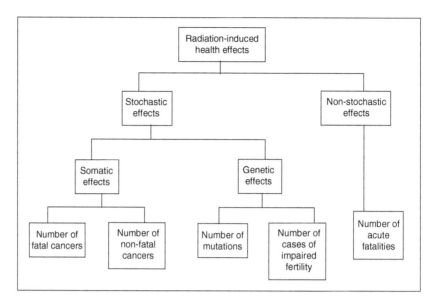

Figure 7.1   An attribute tree for the risks from nuclear waste management

stochastic – i.e. it is impossible to predict who among those exposed to the radiation will develop these impacts.

The lower levels of the attribute tree refer to numbers of effects:

c_{ij1} – number of fatal cancers;
c_{ij2} – number of non-fatal cancers;
c_{ij3} – number of mutations;
c_{ij4} – number of cases of impaired fertility; and
c_{ij5} – number of acute fatalities.

For the purposes of the study, the five numbers (c_{ij1}, c_{ij2}, c_{ij3}, c_{ij4}, c_{ij5}) provided a sufficiently detailed description of the potential consequences of possible waste management policies to evaluate their relative health effects.

The attribute levels (c_{ij1}, c_{ij2}, c_{ij3}, c_{ij4}, c_{ij5}) for a particular strategy a_i and set of circumstances θ_j could be calculated using complex environmental, transport and health impact models. Sometimes the notation $c_k(a_i, \theta_j)$ is used for c_{ijk} to indicate the quantitative modelling relating the prediction of the consequence from knowledge of the action a_i and the state θ_j. Such models may be very complex mathematical models or computer codes. Indeed, they are sometimes a combination of several complex models: see case vignette 7.1. Examples and discussion of such models may be found in, for example, Bäverstam *et al.* (1997), French *et al.* (2007a) and Prado and Bolado (2001).

Case vignette 7.1 Consequence modelling in the RODOS nuclear emergency DSS

The Real-time Online Decision Support system (Ehrhardt and Weiss, 2000; French, Bartzis, Ehrhardt *et al.*, 2000) for nuclear emergencies seeks to model and predict *all* the impacts of an accidental release of radioactivity from a nuclear plant: see case vignette 12.3 for an overview of the full system. Here we just consider the interlinking of the various consequence models. The spread of the release from the plant via a plume and atmospheric dispersion is modelled by an atmospheric dispersion model, itself a chain of near-, meso- and long-range models. This then feeds models that account for deposition from the plume, either gravitationally or via rain, and, in turn, various food chain models. Alternative routes – e.g. via rivers and lakes – and special environments such as forests are modelled separately, as is the spread of tritium. These are drawn together into a dose combination model that predicts the combined impact of all these on human health. Finally, the output from all the models is used to predict the consequences of taking a range of different countermeasures.

Note that each of the component models has been developed and tested by different teams, often working in different institutes. Although the development processes were coordinated through agreement on inputs and outputs, each model was produced and implemented in computer code by teams working relatively independently, using the best available current scientific understanding.

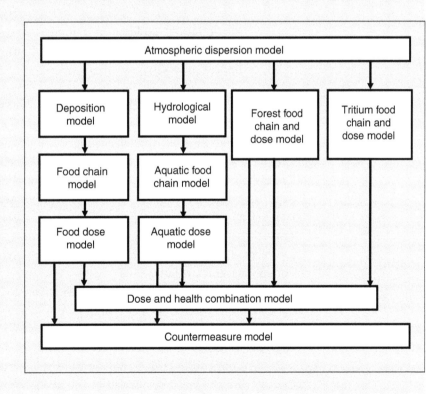

Lathrop and Watson's example is set firmly in the known and knowable spaces of engineering, environmental and medical science. Had they widened their analysis to consider social, political, economic and other impacts they would have quickly found themselves in the complex or chaotic spaces in which they lacked quantitative models to predict the levels of particular attributes. For example, they might have considered the aesthetic impact of the waste management facility on the environment. As we shall discover, there are several ways in which they could proceed in this case. One is to set up a judgemental scale. For instance, they could define a series of contexts in which the aesthetic impacts increased from negligible to severe.

Level n: No noticeable impact. Facility underground with small entrance in pre-existing industrial zone. Traffic routed to site along existing well-used roads.

Level $n-1$:   Substantial parts of the facility above ground in an established industrial zone. Traffic routed to site along existing well-used roads.

                · · ·

Level 0:   Major facility building in national park, visible from a considerable distance. New roads for heavy goods traffic needed to facility.

To use such a judgemental attribute scale DMs would consider each consequence from it and judge it against the scale, identifying, usually after substantial discussion, that they judged a particular waste management facility as, say, 'level 5 in terms of its aesthetic impact'. For similar examples, see French (1988), Keeney (1992) and case vignette 7.2.

Categorising very broadly, there are three types of attributes that we might use in modelling consequences.

- *Natural.* A natural attribute gives a direct measure of the objective involved and the attribute is universally understood. For example, cost is often a natural attribute.
- *Judgemental.* Some attributes are more subjective – e.g. environmental degradation. In general, such attributes involve descriptions of several distinct levels of impact, as in the example of aesthetic impact above. Judgemental attributes are created for a specific decision context.
- *Proxy.* A proxy attribute does not measure achievement against the objective directly, but is (perceived to be) strongly correlated with it. For example, rain acidification could be measured via the amount of

Case vignette 7.2 The marking of paintings in an art examination

Educational assessment may be considered from a decision theoretic perspective (Bouyssou, Marchant, Pirlot et al., 2000; French, 1986). Some assessment areas are clearly very subjective, such as the assessment of paintings in an art examination. At one public examination board the art examiners proceeded as follows. They searched through the canvases submitted, finding a set of paintings that they considered spanned the range from appalling to outstanding. The worst they clustered together and identified two or three that they judged were equally bad and worth no more than 10 per cent. Similarly, they identified a set of outstanding paintings that they judged were each worth 90 per cent. Then they identified two or three they judged midway in quality, awarding each 50 per cent. Continuing to select pictures, they identified groups that they judged were each worth, respectively, 10 per cent, 20 per cent, 30 per cent, 40 per cent, . . . , 80 per cent, 90 per cent. These they laid out along a wall like a ruler. Further paintings were then judged by the examiners walking along this 'ruler' until they identified where they judged their quality lay. Thus they were able to 'measure off' marks for paintings. All paintings were marked independently by two examiners at least and there were seldom differences, and those that occurred were resolved by discussion or an assessment by a third examiner.

sulphur dioxide in the air, ignoring all the other contributors to acidity of rain.

There is no *objectively* correct attribute tree for a problem: just one that is *requisite* for the analysis. It is a subjective choice that needs to be constructed after careful discussion between the DMs. Ideally, one would like to have simple procedures for constructing hierarchies that reflect the views and perceptions of the DMs as they evolve in such discussion; but no such universally applicable procedure exists. Attribute hierarchies are constructed as much by the art of the decision analyst or facilitator as by the application of any procedure. Sometimes the discussion proceeds 'from the top of the hierarchy to the bottom'. Consider the following hypothetical example.

A firm is considering where to site a new warehouse. A list of possible sites and designs has been drawn up. The task is now to represent the consequences of building each by a vector of levels of achievement against a number of attributes; but what attributes? Summarised very briefly, discussion between the decision analyst and the DMs might proceed as follows.

DA: What is the prime consideration in choosing between alternatives?
DMs: Cost-effectiveness.
DA: Yes, but what are the determinants of cost-effectiveness?

DMs: Financial, temporal and social factors.

DA: What financial factors?

DMs: Construction costs and annual running costs.

DA: What temporal factors?

DMs: The time to build the warehouse, because the warehouse is needed to launch a new product; and the working life of the warehouse, because it should last as long as possible.

DA: What social factors?

DMs: The effect on local traffic congestion and the provision of employment opportunities.

The concept of cost-effectiveness is therefore being analysed as in the hierarchy shown in figure 7.2. Indeed, since cost-effectiveness is a fairly meaningless term *in vacuo*, we may say that this discussion is defining the term appropriately for this context. The DMs have some way to go to complete the analysis. First, they must discuss carefully whether they have identified all the attributes that are important in their decision. We assume that they have. Second, they must decide how to measure the level of achievement of each alternative against the six attributes. Possible methods are suggested in figure 7.2. Note that, in traffic congestion, we have an example of a proxy attribute. Since the effect of heavy lorries on traffic congestion is most pronounced when they have to change speed, c_5 is

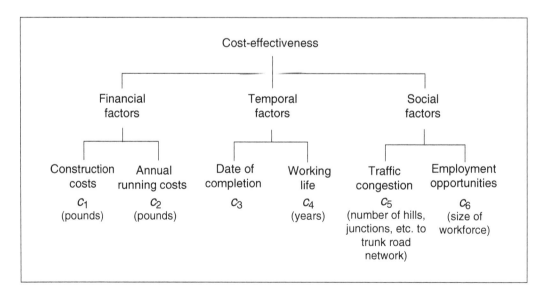

Figure 7.2   The attribute tree for the warehouse example

measured in terms of the number of road junctions, pedestrian crossings and steep hills from the nearest trunk route. Trivial though this example is, it should provide enough of an insight into a general top-down approach. The analyst begins by asking the DMs what they are trying to achieve and then continually challenges them to refine their thinking by asking 'What exactly do you mean by *X*?'.

Another approach is to build the tree bottom-up, first brainstorming (see section 9.2) the attributes that matter to the DMs and then gathering them into clusters (branches) that are cognitively similar. Most often, perhaps, one uses a mixture of the two approaches, building the top half of the tree bottom-up and then analysing some of the lower attributes into further sub-attributes.

There are several requirements that attributes must meet if they are to be useful:

- all attributes must be measurable, either objectively, judgementally or by proxy;
- attributes should not measure the same aspect of the model – i.e. no double counting; and
- attributes should distinguish between consequences, otherwise they are redundant and should not be included in the analysis.

Keeney (1992) provides many examples and illustrates these points further.

In section 3.2 we introduced the concept of a value function that represents DMs' preferential ranking of alternatives or consequences through an increasing set of numbers. Now that we have introduced the idea of the multi-attribute representation of consequences, we should ask how this affects a value function representation of DMs' preferences.

7.4 Multi-attribute value modelling

Rt Revd Host: I am afraid that you've got a bad egg, Mr Jones.
Curate: Oh no, my Lord, I assure you! Parts of it are excellent. (Punch)

Suppose, then, that DMs need to model their preferences between multi-attributed consequences described by vectors of achievement:[4] $c = (c_1, c_2, \ldots, c_q)$. Throughout we assume that each attribute is real-valued; this assumption is not strictly necessary, however. Consider a multi-attribute value function $v(c_1, c_2, \ldots, c_q)$ representing preference over such consequences. What reasonable conditions might hold such that

---

[4] We drop the subscripts '*ij*', taking the dependence on the chosen action and prevailing state as given.

$$v(c_1, c_2, \ldots, c_q) = v_1(c_1) + v_2(c_2) + \ldots + v_q(c_q)$$

i.e. when might the q-dimensional function $v(.)$ be formed as the sum of q one-dimensional functions? We refer to such a representation as an *additive (multi-attribute) value function*. The functions $v_i(c_i)$, known as *marginal value functions*, serve as ordinal value functions on each of the attributes.

Essentially, an additive value function is justified if and only if DMs judge the attributes to be *preferentially independent*. Preferential independence is a technical concept that formalises the very common (but *not* universal) feature of preferences embodied in the following statements.

- All other things being equal, more money is preferred to less
- All other things being equal, greater safety is preferred to less.
- All other things being equal, less environmental impact is preferred to more.

Stated formally: a subset of the attributes is preferentially independent of the remaining attributes if the preference between any pair of alternatives that differ *only* in their levels of achievement on attributes within the subset does not depend on the levels of achievement on the remaining attributes. Note that, because the alternatives differ *only* in terms of their achievement on the subset of attributes, they attain precisely the same levels of achievement on the remaining attributes. If this is true for all subsets, the attributes are said to be (*mutually*) *preferentially independent*.

A little thought shows the importance of preferential independence. Without it, there is no possibility of defining – let alone assessing – the attribute value scales, $v_1(c_1)$. Only when preferential independence holds can one talk of preferences for different levels of achievement on one attribute independently of another. In any decision analysis, therefore, it is imperative that preferential independence assumptions are checked (Keeney, 1992; Keeney and Raiffa, 1976). The analyst will generally do this while the attribute hierarchy is being constructed.

In fact, there is an element of 'chicken and egg' in the process of choosing attributes and checking for preferential independence, since the choice of attributes is closely entwined with the validity of the independence assumption. The folklore among many DAs is that it is usually possible to select appropriate attributes in a problem such that preferential independence holds. Full discussions of preferential independence may be found in, for example, French (1986), Keeney (1992) and Keeney and Raiffa (1976).

A multi-attribute value function is *linear* if

$$v(c_1, c_2, \ldots, c_q) = w_1 c_1 + w_2 c_2 + \ldots + w_q c_q$$

The coefficients $w_1, w_2, \ldots, w_q$ are known as *weighting factors*, or, simply, *weights*. Linear value functions are commonly assumed in many areas of economics, commerce and operational research. For example, comparing time streams of cashflows according to net present value (NPV) assumes a linear value structure in which

$$v(c_1, c_2, \ldots, c_q) = c_1 + \rho c_2 + \rho^2 c_3 + \ldots + \rho^{q-1} c_q$$

where ρ is a discount factor bringing costs and income in different time periods to today's values.

Cost–benefit analysis, a form of decision analysis commonly used by government agencies, assumes a linear value structure – at least, it does in its most naïve form (Bedford *et al.*, 2005). The distinguishing assumption of cost–benefit analysis is that every attribute of an alternative can be given a financial value, positive or negative. Alternatives are compared according to their total financial value, $w_1 c_1 + \ldots + w_q c_q$, in which w_i is the financial value of one unit of the ith attribute.

Clearly, linear value functions are additive. Therefore, an agreeing linear value representation can exist only when the attributes are mutually preferentially independent. We need a further condition, however, namely the existence of constant relative trade-offs between all pairs of attributes.[5] We say that there is a *constant relative trade-off* of γ_{ij} between c_i and c_j if an increase of γ_{ij} on the ith attribute is exactly compensated for by a decrease of one unit on the jth attribute, whatever the levels of achievement on all attributes.

Put formally, there is a constant relative trade-off of γ_{ij} between c_i and c_j if and only if $(c_1, c_2, \ldots, c_i, \ldots, c_j, \ldots, c_q) \sim (c_1, c_2, \ldots, c_i + \gamma_{ij}\varepsilon, \ldots, c_j - \varepsilon, \ldots, c_q)$ for any ε, positive or negative. If $v(\mathbf{c}) = \Sigma_i w_i c_i$, the constant relative trade-off between c_i and c_j is (w_j/w_i). Clearly, the assumption of linearity implies that there are constant relative trade-offs between all pairs of attributes. When the attributes in a problem can be plotted in q-dimensional space, it is informative to consider contours of equal value. An *indifference curve* or *surface* is simply a line or surface joining points that represent consequences between which DMs are indifferent – i.e. they perceive them to be of equal value. The essential

---

[5] In fact, the constant relative trade-offs condition implies mutual preferential independence.

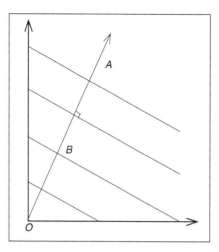

Figure 7.3 The necessity for a monotonicity condition

implication of the constant relative trade-offs condition is that the indifference curves are parallel straight lines or hyperplanes. This is almost, but not quite, sufficient to characterise a linear value function. Consider the two-dimensional case (figure 7.3). OA is the common perpendicular to the indifference curves. A linear value function insists that preference either increases monotonically or decreases monotonically from O to A. It is not possible for, say, B to be the most preferred point on the line OA. Thus it is necessary to assume monotinicity.

So much for the mathematics: what does all this mean? How might we use these ideas in supporting decision making? Value functions apply to circumstances without uncertainty. Thus, for the present we assume that when DMs make a choice the consequence is completely defined – i.e. the consequence and alternative are completely identified.

The simplest form of multi-attribute value analysis seeks to develop and then use an additive value function:

$$v(c_1, c_2, \ldots, c_q) = v_1(c_1) + v_2(c_2) + \ldots + v_q(c_q)$$

Essentially, we assess the marginal value functions and then sum them. To do that, however, we need to ensure that we have developed the marginal value functions $v_k(.)$ *on the same scale* so that we might justifiably add them up. This is not as straightforward as we might hope. We first assess each $v_k(.)$ separately and then bring them to a common scale by the use of weighting factors. Thus we use

$$v(c_1, c_2, \ldots, c_q) = w_1 v_1(c_1) + w_2 v_2(c_2) + \ldots + w_q v_q(c_q)$$

We use this form to produce a set of overall values or scores for the alternatives by:

(i)   scoring[6] each alternative against each of the lowest-level attributes – i.e. assessing the $v_k(c_k)$;

(ii) bringing each set of attribute scores, $v_k(c_k)$, to the same scale by applying weights, w_k; and

(iii) adding up the weighted attribute scores to give an overall score for each alternative.

$$\text{Overall value, } v(c_1, c_2, \ldots, c_q) = \sum_k (\text{weight of } k^{\text{th}} \text{attribute})$$
$$\times (\text{score on } k^{\text{th}} \text{attribute})$$
$$= \sum_k w_k \times v_k(c_k)$$

We illustrate this style of analysis on an extremely simple example, working step by step through the arithmetic and illustrating some of the plots that can be informative in helping to build the DM's understanding of the balance of her preferences for different attributes.

7.5 The 'evening out' example

Who wants to go out and see a bad movie when they can stay at home and see a bad one free on TV? (Sam Goldwyn)

Suppose that a DM has to choose an evening's entertainment and has arrived at the possibilities below and the attribute tree in figure 7.4. She has five options.

TV   Stay in and watch television: there is a good documentary and a couple of soaps that she watches regularly.

Old_Film   Go to the local arts cinema, which is showing a season of Humphrey Bogart movies. She can get to the cinema on foot and it is possible to use the luxury gallery and have a drink while watching the film.

New_Film   Go to the multiplex cinema on the ring road and see the latest Harry Potter blockbuster. She will have to take her car, but parking is easy.

---

[6] A common terminology is to refer to the process of eliciting the marginal value scale on an attribute as 'scoring the attribute'. Similarly, the value of an alternative on a marginal value scale is often referred to as an 'attribute score'.

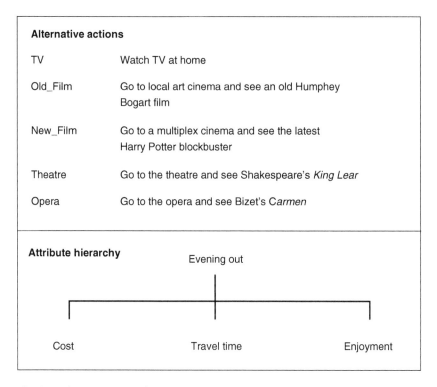

Alternative actions

TV   Watch TV at home

Old_Film   Go to local art cinema and see an old Humphey
                      Bogart film

New_Film   Go to a multiplex cinema and see the latest
                      Harry Potter blockbuster

Theatre   Go to the theatre and see Shakespeare's *King Lear*

Opera   Go to the opera and see Bizet's *Carmen*

Attribute hierarchy   Evening out

Cost   Travel time   Enjoyment

Figure 7.4   The 'evening out' example

Theatre   Go into the city centre and see the current production of *King Lear*, a play she has been intending to see for a long time. This will involve driving, finding a parking space and walking to the theatre.

Opera   Go into the city centre and see the current production of *Carmen*, her favourite opera. Again, this will involve driving, finding a parking space and walking to the opera house.

She has identified three attributes: cost, travel time and enjoyment. The first we take as a natural attribute – i.e. cost itself can be measured objectively. The immediate issue is to represent her preferences for the different costs. Conventionally, attribute scores increase with increasing preference. Suppose that the costs are

TV   £0;
Old_Film £5;
New_Film £8;
Theatre   £15;
Opera   £25.

For small sums of money relative to the total assets of a DM, it is usually satisfactory to take preference to be linear, here with a negative slope, as we are dealing with cost. It is also common to normalise each attribute scale to either 0.00 to 1.00 or 0 to 100. Judgements of preference are not infinitely accurate: perhaps consistent to within 5 per cent, or a little better. The scale need therefore allow only two-figure accuracy. We choose 0 to 100 to avoid decimal points: see figure 7.5.

Suppose that the travel times are

TV   0 minutes;
Old_Film   15 minutes;
New_Film   25 minutes;
Theatre   40 minutes;
Opera   40 minutes.

Moreover, suppose that the DM has a preference not to go out, since the other options involve changing clothes. To her, the difference between travelling for 25 minutes and 40 minutes does not seem too great – certainly not as great as the difference between 0 minutes and 15 minutes. Thus, the DM might value the travel times, as in figure 7.6.

Note that figures 7.5 and 7.6 show plots of the marginal value functions $v_k(.)$ for the two attributes, cost and time. One is linear, the other non-linear. Moreover, while cost is a natural scale, travel time is actually a proxy scale, because it represents not just her preferences for the travelling time but also for avoiding changing clothes. Enjoyment will, of course, be a

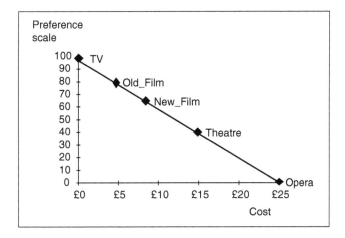

Figure 7.5   The value scale for cost

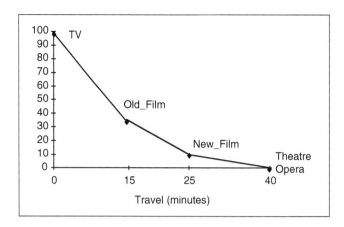

Figure 7.6 The value scale for travel time

judgemental scale. To value her enjoyment of the various options, we do not intend to construct a descriptive scale such as we described in section 4. Rather, we assume that she assesses her preferences directly without going through the intermediary of a marginal value function. Direct assessment of values is a common approach when the number of options is small. This can be done on a 'thermometer' scale: see figure 7.7. The DM begins by asking herself which the best and worst options are in terms of her enjoyment. She is clear that the opera *Carmen* is her most preferred and that seeing an old Humphrey Bogart film is her least preferred. Assigning these 100 and 0, respectively, she then positions the other options relative to these, reflecting that seeing *King Lear* is almost as good as the opera and that seeing the Harry Potter movie is much preferred to the programmes on TV this evening.

We now need to bring these attribute scores onto the same scale so they may be added up. To do this we use *swing weighting*. This takes into account *both* the importance of the attributes in determining her preference *and* the particular difference, remembering that 100 points on each attribute represents the difference between the best and worst of the actual alternatives before her: see figure 7.8. Consider an imaginary alternative that scores 0 on all three scales – i.e. it is as bad as paying £25 and travelling for 40 minutes to watch an old film. If the DM could improve this option up to 100 points on just one of the scales, which would the DM choose? Suppose her answer is cost. Then each point on the cost scale is worth more than a point on the other scales. Suppose, with further consideration, the DM feels that increasing

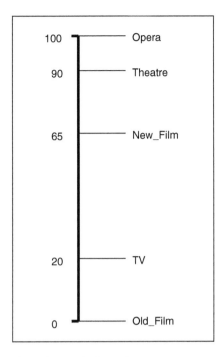

Figure 7.7   The value scale for enjoyment

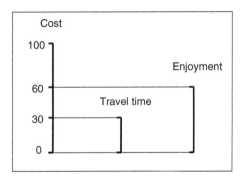

Figure 7.8   Swing weighting

her enjoyment from 0 to 100 points is equivalent to increasing cost from 0 to 60 points – i.e. reducing how much she spends on the evening by £15. By similar introspection, she judges that 100 points on the travel time scale is worth 30 points on the cost scale.

Swing weighting therefore determines the weights w_1, w_2, w_3 as, respectively, 100, 30 and 60. Thus we may calculate overall scores as

TV $100 \times 100 + 30 \times 100 + 60 \times \ 20 = 14{,}200$
Old_Film $100 \times \ \ 80 + 30 \times \ \ 35 + 60 \times \ \ \ 0 = \ 9{,}050$
New_Film $100 \times \ \ 68 + 30 \times \ \ 10 + 60 \times \ \ 65 = 11{,}000$
Theatre $100 \times \ \ 40 + 30 \times \ \ \ 0 + 60 \times \ \ 90 = \ 9{,}400$
Opera $100 \times \ \ \ \ 0 + 30 \times \ \ \ 0 + 60 \times 100 = \ 6{,}000$

Normalising so that the maximum score is 100 – i.e. dividing by $190 = 100 + 30 + 60$, the sum of the weights – gives

TV   75
Old_Film   48
New_Film   58
Theatre   49
Opera   32

It seems that her dislike of travel and her reluctance to spend money on this occasion imply that she will stay at home and watch TV.

Some insights can be drawn from simple *Pareto plots*, in which the success of alternatives against pairs of attributes is plotted. Figure 7.9 illustrates one of the three possible in this example. Note that preference increases towards the top right-hand corner in these plots. It is clear in terms of enjoyment and cost (but ignoring travel time) that the Old_ Film option is dominated – i.e. TV is better than Old_Film in terms of both enjoyment and cost.

Sensitivity analysis is a key component of any analysis that utilises a quantitative model. Since the methods used to assess attribute values and weights are necessarily imprecise, it is important to see how preference ordering changes when different, but in many ways equally plausible,

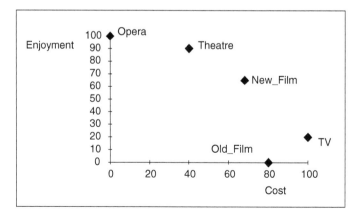

Figure 7.9   A Pareto plot of enjoyment versus cost

assessments are used. If the preference order remain stable across these variations then our solution is robust – i.e. it is likely to hold across all reasonable assessments; if not, then we may have less confidence in our solution (French, 2003b). Here we demonstrate how the DM can investigate the effect of varying the weight on cost.

At present cost contributes $100/190 = 52.6$ per cent of the weight. Thus the overall score for any alternative may be written

$$\text{overall score} = (100/190) \times \text{Cost} + (90/190) \times (30/90 \times \text{Travel Time} + 60/90 \times \text{Enjoyment})$$

or, writing w_{Cost} for the fraction of the weight on cost,

$$\text{overall score} = w_{Cost} \times \text{Cost} + (1 - w_{Cost}) \times (30/90 \times \text{Travel Time} + 60/90 \times \text{Enjoyment})$$

This gives for each alternative

TV	$w_{Cost} \times 100 + (1 - w_{Cost})(30/90 \times 100 + 60/90 \times 20)$
Old_Film	$w_{Cost} \times 80 + (1 - w_{Cost})(30/90 \times 35 + 60/90 \times 0)$
New_Film	$w_{Cost} \times 68 + (1 - w_{Cost})(30/90 \times 10 + 60/90 \times 65)$
Theatre	$w_{Cost} \times 40 + (1 - w_{Cost})(30/90 \times 0 + 60/90 \times 90)$
Opera	$w_{Cost} \times 0 + (1 - w_{Cost})(30/90 \times 0 + 60/90 \times 100)$

In other words,

TV	$w_{Cost} \times 100 + (1 - w_{Cost}) \times 47$
Old_Film	$w_{Cost} \times 80 + (1 - w_{Cost}) \times 12$
New_Film	$w_{Cost} \times 68 + (1 - w_{Cost}) \times 47$
Theatre	$w_{Cost} \times 40 + (1 - w_{Cost}) \times 60$
Opera	$w_{Cost} \times 0 + (1 - w_{Cost}) \times 67$

This leads to the sensitivity plot shown in figure 7.10, in which each of these lines is plotted. Looking at the vertical line at $w_{Cost} = 0.52$, we see that the highest intersection on this is the line for TV followed by that for New_Film, then Old_Film followed closely by Theatre, and the lowest intersection is with the line for Opera, reflecting the overall scores of 75, 58, 49, 48 and 32, respectively. It is also clear that TV will have the highest intersection unless the weight on cost is reduced to 15 per cent or so, when the Theatre and then the Opera will become the most preferred.

The assessment of the marginal value function $v_k(c_k)$ for each attribute transforms the attribute level to a value scale representing the DM's preferences for the different possible consequences in terms of that attribute alone. The weights w_k serve to bring these judgements onto the same

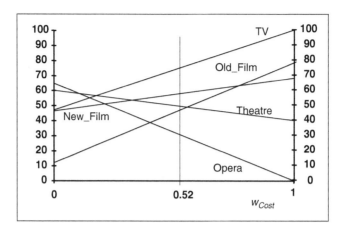

Figure 7.10   The sensitivity analysis on w_{Cost}

scale. We have noted that this requires that the DM's judgements are preferentially independent, but a further condition is needed to ensure that the assessment of the $v_k(c_k)$ and the w_k are consistent. This assumption ensures that value differences on each attribute are well defined in a consistent fashion. Essentially, it is the constant relative trade-offs condition applied to the attribute levels transformed by the $v_k(c_k)$. For further details, see Dyer and Sarin (1979).

7.6 Absolute and relative weights

Excellence, then, is a state concerned with choice, lying in a mean, relative to us, this being determined by reason and in the way in which the man of practical wisdom would determine it. (Aristotle)

Attribute trees can have several levels: figure 7.1 has three; figure 7.2 has two. Forming a weighted sum, as in step 3 of the MAVA procedure, does not acknowledge this. It simply weights and sums the scores at the leaf nodes to form the overall scores.

The existence of attributes at intermediate levels is ignored. We say that the weights developed at the leaf nodes in this way are *absolute weights*. In one sense, we do not need weights at the intermediate nodes; we can simply weight the scores at the leaf attributes and add them up. This would lose some of the opportunities that can be brought by sensitivity calculations, however, and other ways of exploring the reasoning behind the MAVA conclusions. It is possible to capitalise on cognitive understandings implicit in the construction of the tree: we shall see this in the Chernobyl study in section 8.

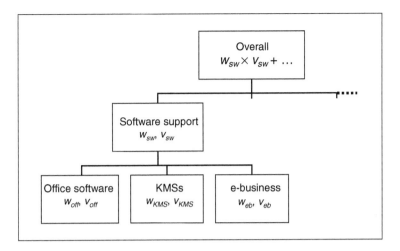

Figure 7.11   Absolute and relative weights

Figure 7.11 shows part of an attribute tree that might arise in choosing a new information system for a company. The DMs would be concerned, *inter alia*, with the support the platform would provide for various types of software: office systems, knowledge management and e-business. The weights and values, w_{off} v_{off} etc., are defined in the figure.

How should the weight w_{sw} and the value v_{sw} be determined? If the weights w_{off}, w_{KMS}, w_{eb} and values v_{off}, v_{KMS}, v_{eb} are assessed without reference to the intermediate nodes, then the contribution that they make to the overall value is

$$w_{off} \times v_{off} + w_{KMS} \times v_{KMS} + w_{eb} + v_{eb}$$

We could therefore define

$$w_{sw} = 1,$$
$$v_{sw} = w_{off} \times v_{off} + w_{KMS} \times v_{KMS} + w_{eb} \times v_{eb}$$

so that $w_{sw} \times v_{sw}$ makes the same contribution. Alternatively, if we adopt the common convention of arranging that all values are assessed on a common scale length, maybe 0 to 1 or 0 to 100, and that the weights all sum to one, then we could renormalise to make

$$w_{sw} = (w_{off} + w_{KMS} + w_{eb}) / \sum_{\text{all leaves}} w$$
$$v_{sw} = \frac{(w_{off} \times v_{off} + w_{KMS} \times v_{KMS} + w_{eb} \times v_{eb})}{(w_{off} + w_{KMS} + w_{eb})}$$

This would ensure that the overall value was on the same value scale length and that all weights summed to one. In either case, we say that we are using *absolute weights*, since the contribution of each leaf attribute is defined relative to the overall value scale.

Alternatively, we could use *relative weights*. In this procedure the weights w_{off}, w_{KMS}, w_{eb} are assessed directly in terms of their contribution to the intermediate software support attribute such that $w_{off} + w_{KMS} + w_{eb} = 1$. The weight w_{sw} is then in turn assessed in terms of the contribution that the software support objective makes to the score at the attribute immediately above in the hierarchy. Thus, in absolute weighting the intermediate weights are constructed from the leaf weights; in relative weighting they are assessed in their own right. It should be noticed that, while in principle swing weighting applies at all levels to assess how much the maximum possible change in one attribute can affect preference at the node immediately above, it becomes progressively harder to do this at higher levels. At leaf nodes, the DM typically has a much clearer understanding of what scores of 0 and 100 *mean*. At the higher levels, she has to synthesise this understanding by considering a possibly hypothetical alternative that achieves 0 on *all* the attributes below, and another possibly hypothetical alternative that achieves 100 on *all* the attributes below.

7.7 Elicitation of weights and values

Decide what you want, decide what you are willing to exchange for it. Establish your priorities and go to work. (H. L. Hunt)

We now turn to a discussion of how values and weights should be elicited in MAVA. If the DM is to evaluate each alternative against each attribute, elicit weights and receive guidance as to her choice by the resulting ranking, what issues may arise? Will she be able to make the judgements involved?

The form of an additive multi-attribute value function is

$$v(c_1, c_2, \ldots, c_q) = w_1 v_1(c_1) + w_2 v_2(c_2) + \ldots + w_q v_q(c_q)$$

As noted in section 4, the first step in MAVA is to assess the marginal value functions $v_k(c_k)$. If the kth attribute is measured on a natural or proxy scale then the task is to assess the function as illustrated in figure 7.12(a). In the case of judgemental attributes, if a scale has been set up by describing different levels of achievement – e.g. the aesthetic impact scale in section 3 – then, again, it is necessary to assess a function. If there are only a few

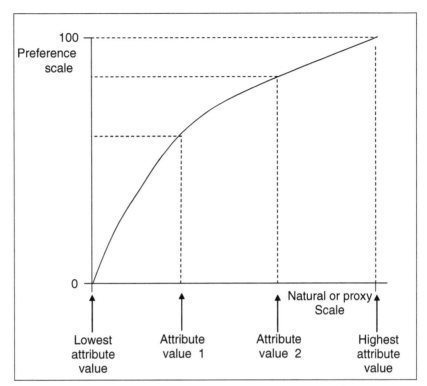

(a) Assessment of value function for natural or proxy attributes

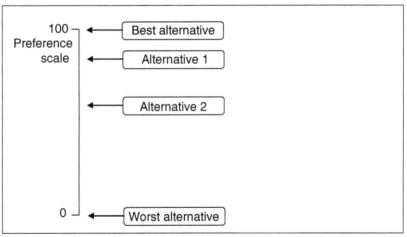

(b) Assessment of value functions for judgemental attributes

Figure 7.12   Assessment of marginal value functions

alternatives, however, then it is common to assess the values directly for each alternative on a thermometer scale, as in figure 7.12(b). In either case, the (preferential) values on the vertical need to be elicited from the DMs.

Typically, the length of the value scale is set as 0.0 to 1.0 or 0 to 100. We have a slight preference for working with 0 to 100, since human judgement can discriminate maybe ten, maybe a few tens of, different levels. Thus, on a scale with 100 levels, there is no need to use fractional numbers. Without decimal points, there is no subliminal pressure on DMs to strive for spurious accuracy. It is also easier to record numbers clearly with little risk of misreading, particularly when working on a flip chart with a group of DMs. When working with a natural or proxy underlying scale for the attribute then the lowest and highest attribute values, which are given the preferential values 0 and 100, should be chosen carefully to span the range needed for the analysis but not too widely. It is useful to use as much of the range of 0 to 100 as possible. For a thermometer scale this can be achieved by setting the least attractive alternative in terms of the kth attribute to have a preferential value 0 and the most attractive 100. If during the analysis further alternatives are introduced that are more or less attractive, the values outside the range 0 to 100 can be used: there is no need to redefine the scale. Such scaling is referred to as *local scaling*, as opposed to *global scaling*, when the minimum and maximum are set without reference to the least and most preferred alternatives.

DMs are often concerned about using a preference value of 0. Surely few alternatives are worth absolutely nothing? One should think of the 0 to 100 scale, however, exactly like a temperature scale. There are colder temperatures than 0°C; and, moreover, 0°C ≠ 0°F. So, aside from the Kelvin scale, temperature scales have arbitrary origins defined purely by convention. The same goes for the unit; the boiling point of water may be 100°C or 212°F. They are measured on what is known as *interval scales*. So it is with marginal value functions: their scale and origin can be chosen to fit with other needs of the analysis (French, 1986; Keeney and Raiffa, 1976; Roberts, 1979). Mental arithmetic with scales 100 units long beginning at 0 is much easier than other conventions; when we get to swing weighting this will be useful.

With the scales for the values defined, the next task for the DM is either to sketch the value curve, as in figure 7.12(a), or fix the scores on the temperature scale, as in figure 7.12(b). In the former case this can be done by considering a few points on the natural scale of the attribute, ranking them in order of preference, then considering how much they 'differ in value'. In figure 7.12(a) we have assumed that preferences increase with the attribute value. The concave nature of the scale implies that the DM perceives decreasing marginal value as the level of the attribute increases. The analyst would work with the DM, exploring different curvatures and confirming that she perceives, for example,

- attribute level 1 to be nearer the maximum attribute level than the minimum in terms of her preferences; and
- the increase in her preference in going from attribute level 1 to attribute level 2 to be greater than that in going from attribute level 2 to the maximum attribute level.

Once a few points are set and the gaps between them ordered then the curve can be sketched in. If the DM's preferences exhibit increasing marginal worth, then the curve would be convex; if they decrease with increasing attribute value, it would slope down not up; and if her most preferred point is in the middle of the attribute range, then it would rise to its maximum and then decrease. For a thermometer scale the process of eliciting the DM's judgements is similar. She is asked to rank the alternatives and then place them on the 0 to 100 scale so that the gaps between them correspond to her assessments of differences in value.

Note that these assessments require the DM to consider value differences. Theoretically, this is a thorny issue. French (1986) is very uncomfortable with this, arguing that, in general, value differences are very difficult to define meaningfully. Dyer and Sarin (1979), however, show how a meaningful definition can be given in the context of additive multiattribute value functions. Moreover, experience has shown that DMs are not uncomfortable in giving these judgements and that the levels of uncertainty introduced by the imprecision of their judgements can easily be explored via sensitivity analysis (see section 10.3). Experience has also shown that it is important to work visually with the DMs, marking points on a graph or using graphical output from decision analytic software.

With the value scales defined, it is now possible to move onto the elicitation of weights from the DM. This is often a difficult task, because the weights in multi-attribute value analysis necessarily confound two issues:

(i) the relative importance of the attributes in determining the DM's preferences; and

(ii) the discrimination provided by the scale in differentiating the alternatives.

Most of us have an intuitive understanding of what we mean by relative importance of an attribute. Few would have difficulty interpreting the sentence 'Safety is a much more important consideration in buying a car than its colour'. It is sometimes confusing to realise, though, that a very important attribute may have little weight in analysis, because all the alternatives are close in terms of that attribute. In buying a car, cost may be such an important attribute that only cars in a small, affordable price range are considered. Cost may therefore be quite unimportant in discriminating between those cars that are included in the MAVA analysis. As a slight aside, remember the evaluability hypothesis (section 2.4): perhaps different evaluations when choices are offered individually or in comparisons is neither irrational nor surprising. One needs context to evaluate options. For this reason, we advocate eliciting weights by swing weighting (Belton and Stewart, 2002; Goodwin and Wright, 2003; Keeney and Raiffa, 1976).

Swing weighting does not refer to the relative importance of the attribute per se but to the relative length of the attribute's preference scale. Initially the DM is asked to imagine an alternative that scores 0 on each and every attribute's preference scale. Then she is asked to consider modifying this very poor alternative in such a way that it increases its score on precisely one attribute preference scale to 100. Which attribute scale would she choose to do this on? Her answer defines the longest attribute value scale in terms of her preferences. Then she is asked to consider the remaining attributes one at a time and scale them off against the longest: 'Imagine an alternative with a preference score of 100 on this attribute and 0 on all others. Now imagine a second alternative with a preference score of x on the attribute with the longest scale and 0 on all others.' What value of x would make you indifferent? If one then sets the weight of the longest attribute scale as 100, then the weight of the shorter scale is given by x. Figure 7.13 illustrates the idea. Subsequently the weights can be renormalised so that they sum to one. An example of swing weighting is also given in figure 7.8.

There are many variants of swing weighting. Attributes may be scaled off against the shortest rather than the longest scale, or against the best-understood scale – e.g. cost. There is no need to swing between the minimum and maximum score; other intervals may be used, particularly if they are more cognitively meaningful.

Swing weighting is not without its difficulty. It requires that the DM imagine alternatives with specific attribute values, all but one of which are 0. Such alternatives may be entirely hypothetical – indeed, physically impossible. With careful discussion, however DMs can provide weights by this method; and no other method addresses the confounding issues of relative importance and contextual discrimination.

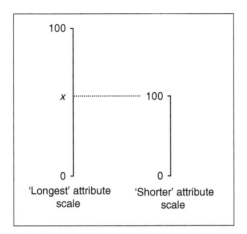

Figure 7.13   Measuring off the scale length – i.e. weight – in swing weighting

Behavioural studies have discovered that the structure and size of the attribute tree can have an effect on the weights elicited from the DM. The splitting bias suggests that presenting an attribute in more detail may increase the weight it receives (see, for example, Jacobi and Hobbs, 2007, and Weber *et al.*, 1988). For instance, if an attribute tree contains a leaf node representing, say, the attribute *environment*, then the weight elicited will tend to be smaller than if the attribute is split into two further attributes, *local environment* and *global environment*. Weights can also vary depending on whether absolute or relative weights are elicited (Stillwell *et al.*, 1987). While there are many such biases, however, there is some evidence that the biases are more prevalent in laboratory experiments. When the DM faces a real problem that matters to her she is better able to 'feel' the importance of the attributes and the discrimination provided between the alternatives (Poyhonen and Hämäläinen, 2000). Nonetheless, to counter this potential bias, an analyst should repeatedly affirm the cognitive meaning of attributes and their position within the hierarchy during an elicitation.

Moreover, it does seem that if the analyst works with the DM, constructively challenging her judgements and reflecting their implications back to her, then these biases can be mitigated. Central to this reflective dialogue is the idea of consistency checking. The analyst should work with the DM to overdetermine her value functions and weights. When inconsistencies in the assessments are found the DM is asked to reflect and revise her judgements. For instance, the analyst might elicit absolute weights and then elicit some relative weights to compare with those constructed from the absolute weights.

7.8 Chernobyl case study

And the name of the star is called Wormwood: and the third part of the waters became wormwood; and many died of the waters, because they were made bitter. (King James Bible, Revelations, 8:11 ['Chernobyl' is the Ukrainian for 'wormwood' . . .])

In this section we describe an application of MAVA within the International Chernobyl Project. Many of the details of the organisation of the workshops will make complete sense only when we have discussed group decision support in later chapters. What should be clear, however, is that this demonstrates the power of a relatively simple multi-attribute structure to articulate complex issues.

Introduction

In 1986 the Chernobyl accident occurred. A nuclear reactor was completely destroyed, releasing radionuclides and radioactive debris for about ten days. Vast tracts of land were contaminated, requiring countermeasures within the Soviet Union and many other countries in the northern hemisphere. Four years later the International Chernobyl Project was initiated at the request of the Soviet authorities. Seven international agencies participated, coordinated by the International Atomic Energy Authority (IAEA). The Soviet request was for

an international experts' assessment of the concept which the USSR [Union of Soviet Socialist Republics] has evolved to enable the population to live safely in areas affected by radioactive contamination following the Chernobyl accident, and an evaluation of the effectiveness of the steps taken in these areas to safeguard the health of the population.

The project tackled the task in a number of ways. Groups of radiation scientists checked the measurements of contamination made by the Russians; doctors looked at the current health of the affected populations and compared them with control populations distant from Chernobyl; agricultural scientists looked at farming methods in the regions; radiation scientists estimated the effect on the population of relocation and other protective measures – e.g. food restrictions – that might be applied. A final task was to identify the key factors that had influenced and were influencing decision making within the Soviet Union. The International Advisory Committee of the project appreciated that it would not be adequate to concentrate on the radiological protection aspects alone; social and political factors, *inter alia*, were also driving the decision making, as a number of preliminary investigations had shown. Accordingly, the outline project description included the use of multi-attribute decision-aiding techniques to investigate and capture these factors. This section reports that study and the models used.

The social and political background

In many ways, the Chernobyl accident could not have happened at a worse place or at a worse time. It happened when the USSR was in the midst of an enormous political and social upheaval. Policies such as 'glasnost' (the greater freedom of information and openness in public debate) and 'perestroika' (the move from a command to a demand economy), economic decline, moves towards democracy and the growing independence on the part of the republics were all taking place.

Information on the accident was first withheld from, and then released, to populations who had yet to gain the experience to assimilate facts and judge open debates on issues that might change their lifestyles for ever. Moreover, some of the information was contradictory. Confusion and misinformation spread among the population. Chernobyl lies in the Ukraine, close to the borders with Belarus (then known as Byelorussia) and the Russian Federation, and the accident affected regions in all three republics, each of which reacted somewhat differently. Before the accident the general level of health in the region was poor in comparison with western European standards, life expectancy being several years shorter. After the accident almost all illnesses were blamed on radiation. Moreover, reports circulated of a general increase in morbidity in the affected areas.

The radiation protection programmes undertaken in the days, months and years after the accident in their way added to the difficulties. Although they protected the populations from the effects of radiation they introduced other problems, many stress-related. Some rural communities were relocated to distant urban locations far from their homeland, their traditions and their lifestyle. Those who were left were not allowed to consume some locally grown foods or to enter certain woodlands and other parts of the countryside. Decontamination procedures involved the movement of much topsoil, leaving permanent reminders of the accident in the community. Far from least in the population's eyes, mushroom picking was banned; fungi naturally leach caesium from the soil. Mushroom picking was – and still is – a national pastime, however; the mushroom soups and stews from the region are magnificent. Banning the picking of mushrooms, an essential part of the radiation protection programmes, came to symbolise the destruction of the peoples' lifestyles brought about by the accident.

While all this was happening the political system was changing dramatically. More and more authority was devolved to the republics and democratic processes grew at both republic and all-Union level. Many more politicians found themselves taking – rather than rubber-stamping – decisions, and thus having to learn many new skills. They might have hoped to cut their teeth on simpler issues than those arising from the Chernobyl accident.

Given this background, those planning the International Chernobyl Project recognised that the decision making concerning countermeasures had not been nor was being driven by radiological protection aspects alone; social and political factors, *inter alia*, were also being taken into account. One of the tasks needed to be the identification of these factors and the assessment of their significance in the decision-making processes. The method employed had to be suited to working with groups, since many ministers and scientists had made important contributions to the decision making that had taken place in the republics and at all-Union level since the accident. Moreover, because of the seniority of those involved in the decision making, the method employed could not require too much of their time. Decision conferencing supported by fairly simple (additive value) decision models seemed to offer the best way forward. Decision conferences are two-day events, designed to stimulate discussion and elicit issues: see section 11.5. The emphasis given by decision conferencing to the creation of a shared understanding made it an ideal technique. In addition, because decision conferences are short, intensive events, they fitted well with the project's tight timescales.

The objectives of the conferences were:

- to enable some of the decision problems related to the Chernobyl accident to be structured efficiently and thus clarify and elucidate issues;
- to summarise for the International Chernobyl Project the key socioeconomic and political factors that, together with the physical, radiological and medical evidence, influenced the relocation and protective measures taken in the republics; and
- to illustrate the use and potential benefits of formal decision analysis methods and the techniques of decision conferencing for the resolution of complex issues.

Note, however, that there was no intention to guide the decision making of the various authorities at republic or all-Union level nor to affect the commitment of any of the parties to the various actions currently being taken. Indeed, the reverse was the case. It would have been quite wrong for the project to plan to affect domestic policy within the Soviet Union. Thus the events were not true decision conferences. They sought to build a shared understanding, but not a commitment to action. Of course, the application of a social science version of the 'Heisenberg principle' would suggest that it is impossible to interact with DMs without changing their perceptions and, hence, their future decision making. Undoubtedly, that is true: but there is a world of difference between planning to achieve such an effect and striving to minimise it. Throughout the conferences care was taken to explore issues and models while avoiding explicit decision making. In this sense, it might be better to refer to the events as structured group interviews (French *et al.*, 1992c). Nonetheless, they are referred to as decision conferences here.

Organisation of the decision conferences

Initially, it had been planned to hold four decision conferences in October 1990, one each in the republics of the Ukraine, Byelorussia and the Russian Federation, and one at all-Union level. Subsequently, however, a fifth decision conference was held in November 1990, at which representatives from the earlier conferences met to build a summary model that represented the main issues and concerns.

The success of any decision conference depends largely on the selection of appropriate participants and their ability to commit their time fully for two days. Ideally, the number of participants should be in the range of ten to fifteen, and only in exceptional circumstances should the number exceed fifteen. Because of the need to explore and capture a wide range of viewpoints on the many issues, however, the numbers taking part in the conference reported here were as high as thirty, not including observers from the project team.

The choice of participants was a matter for the relevant republic or all-Union authorities. They were requested to select participants who had responsibility for the development or formulation of the policy or policies relevant to the remedial measures in contaminated settlements and, in particular, the question of relocation and associated criteria. If possible, they were asked to involve relevant members of the Council of Ministers responsible for dealing with the effects of the Chernobyl accident and similar individuals charged with this responsibility at regional level. It was also desirable for these officials to be accompanied by their main scientific/technical advisers and for there to be some representation from those with the responsibility for the practical implementation of policy or remedial measures.

Representation was also sought from various Soviet academies (e.g. Science, Medical Sciences, etc.). Note that the requested participation included people with timespans of discretion ranging from a few months to many years. We thereby hoped to have, in each event, a useful variety of perspectives on the issues. The same general guidelines were followed for the final conference, at which representatives from each of the earlier conferences took part. It was suggested that between three and five representatives be drawn from each of the earlier events. The selection of participants at all conferences was made successfully and wisely. All the project's requests were met and the participants gave willingly of their time.

Each participant was sent a calling note, which described the objectives of the event and gave some details of the working of decision conferences. It was important that these calling notes set the right atmosphere for the conferences. In particular, emphasis was placed on the informality and the way of working, which differed markedly from the more formal meetings with which they were familiar.

The authorities in the republics and at all-Union level were asked to provide a room large enough to accommodate all the participants comfortably. Seating was to be in a semicircle so that each participant could see each other during discussion. It must be said that, before the events took place, this latter requirement was seen by many to be irrelevant. The success of the decision conferences at stimulating free and wide-ranging discussion with the participants interacting directly with each other rather than through a chairman argues for its relevance, however.

Liquid crystal diode (LCD) panels[7] for overhead projection were used to display multi-attribute value models, which were built using the Hiview[8] and, in one case, VISA[9] software packages (French and Xu, 2004). Flip charts were also used to capture key ideas.

One of us (French) acted as facilitator at all five conferences, supported by a team organised by the European Commission. Simultaneous interpretation was not used. Sequential interpretation gives far more scope for ensuring that all nuances of meaning are faithfully translated. Moreover,

---

[7] A somewhat old-fashioned technology, now supplanted by data projectors.
[8] Current version: www.catalyze.com.
[9] Current version: www.simul8.com

although it slowed one aspect of the proceedings, the pauses gave time for thought and reflection, and it is arguable that the overall effectiveness of the events was improved.

Draft reports on each of the conferences were produced within a few days of the event, in two of the five cases overnight, and sent to the participants for checking. Initially, each of these reports was agreed to be confidential to the participants at the event, save that the reports could be used, but not included verbatim, in writing the overall project report. In 'normal' decision conferences confidentiality is important, because it encourages a free dialogue of ideas and an unfettered discussion of the issues and concerns. The case for confidentiality is perhaps even greater in an *a posteriori* analysis of the reasons behind previously taken decisions, and was further augmented by the changing political circumstances in the Soviet Union. Subsequently, it was agreed with the representatives of the republics and the all-Union authorities that confidentially could be lifted.

Decision modelling

Each of the first four conferences was run as independently of the others as possible. Obviously, since French acted as facilitator to all four, he may have inadvertently carried across some information from one event to another, but his intention was to treat each afresh. Each began with a general discussion of the key issues and concerns as perceived by those present. At each event very similar lists were elicited, albeit with differences in terminology and some differences in priorities. At each a multi-attribute value model was built that allowed ranking of the countermeasure strategies. Again, there was a considerable degree of consensus in the attribute hierarchies used, countermeasures considered and judgements made. It was at this point that the project decided to hold a fifth summary conference, drawing participants from the four conferences already held. The analysis reported here is that of the summary conference. Reports of all five may be found in Lochard *et al.*, 1992.

The fifth conference began with a rehearsal of the key issues and concerns, checking whether any further ones had occurred to the participants since the earlier conferences. None had. The following list is a summary of those considered.

- *Scale of the accident.* This was the world's worst nuclear accident: it would have consequences for decades to come over vast tracts of land.

- *Need for a concept of safe living.* While there was a recognition that the decision making should be based upon some concept of 'acceptable risk', such a concept was not readily understood by the public. They needed to be reassured that they would be 'safe' in their living conditions, particularly since the old Soviet regimes before Chernobyl had always overconfidently assured the public of their safety. This tension ran strongly through all the conferences. Moreover, the identification of a concept of safe living was seen by many of the participants as a problem for scientists alone – one that did not involve any value judgements.
- *Health problems.* The initial countermeasures in the affected regions were judged not to have protected the population's health as had been hoped, possibly because they were implemented either incompletely or after a delay. Moreover, they were generally disliked because of the constraints they placed on lifestyle (see the remarks on the banning of mushroom collection above). An increase in health problems had been reported in the affected regions – e.g. blood disorders, hypothyroidism in children, the severity of chronic illnesses, and risks in pregnancy. Whether this increase was due directly to the Chernobyl accident, a consequence of the increased stress brought about by the accident or simply an artefact of increased medical observation was a matter of some debate.
- *Stress.* According to the best medical estimates available, the risk to an individual of cancer or other health effects was low. The effects of the stress were substantial, however, and were thought to have increased morbidity and mortality.
- *Relocation not a panacea.* Relocation brings socio-political problems, including those of retaining local culture and 'ethnic homogeneity'. Relocation is itself stressful, and is believed to cause increased morbidity and mortality.
- *Lack of trust and understanding.* The population had at first received little information, then suddenly it was given more specialised and often contradictory information. As a consequence, it no longer trusted any information that it received, including that given by doctors. People believed rumour over official channels. There was a speckled pattern of fall-out that people could not properly understand; how could it be unsafe to live and farm in one place, but safe a kilometre away? There was substantial public pressure to adopt a lower criterion for relocation, but this pressure was based more upon mistrust and fear than clear argument.

- *Sarcophagus was still a risk.* After the accident, the damaged reactor unit was sealed in a concrete and steel sarcophagus. The public perceived that the damaged reactor and the continued operation of the other three reactors on the site constituted a continuing danger.
- *Water pollution a risk.* Up to 1990 there had been no significant water pollution, but it remained a possibility, particularly in the event of heavy spring thaws.

Generally, the countermeasure strategies that were evaluated at the conferences took a common form. The population living in the affected region numbered about 700,000. Some, who would otherwise receive a high lifetime dose, could be permanently relocated; some, who would otherwise receive a lower lifetime dose, would remain in their homes, but be protected by countermeasures such as the decontamination of buildings and changes in agricultural practice; and the remaining group, who would receive a very small lifetime dose, would be allowed to remain in their homes with no further countermeasures. The strategies were defined by the numbers falling into each of these three categories.

The attribute hierarchy developed in the fifth summary decision conference is shown in figure 7.14. Those used in the earlier conferences differed in detail, but not in any important respect. The *effect* on *health* provided by a countermeasure strategy was generally seen as having two components: the effect it had in reducing *fatal cancers* and *hereditary* consequences, and the effect it had in terms of increasing or decreasing *stress-related* effects. The *radiation-related* effects could be estimated from the dose averted in the protected and relocated populations. Precise data were not available in a form suitable to estimate quickly the dose saved by

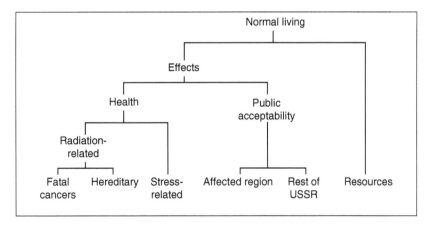

Figure 7.14   The attribute hierarchy used in the fifth decision conference

Table 7.2 Some details on the strategies

Strategy	Number relocated (thousands)	Number protected by other means (thousands)	Estimated number of fatal cancers averted	Estimated number of hereditary effects averted	Cost (billions of roubles)
SL2_2	706	0	3,200	500	28
SL2_10	160	546	1,700	260	17
SL2_20	20	686	650	100	15
SL2_40	3	703	380	60	14

each strategy. Accordingly, approximations and judgement were used. In presenting the success or otherwise of a strategy in reducing *health* effects, attention was paid to the framing issues noted in section 2.4. All outcomes were framed both positively and negatively – e.g. 'Of the population of 700,000, this strategy would be expected to lead to x fatal cancers, leaving $(700,000 - x)$ unaffected.' The average loss in life expectancy over the population was also noted. While this multiple phrasing could not be guaranteed to overcome the framing issue, no biases were detected in the participants' judgements.

The *stress-related* effects were a subject of much debate in all the conferences. The success of strategies in reducing such effects was judged subjectively, using the experience of medical personnel and officials who worked in the regional governments – i.e. the experts were asked to rank the different strategies on a 0 to 100 scale. The process of doing so was very effective in managing the debate about how stress should be interpreted in terms of its effects on the population.

The public acceptability of the strategies was felt to be an important attribute. Many dimensions of this attribute were identified. Two distinct factors stood out, however: the acceptability to the population in the *affected region* and to that in the *rest of the USSR*. These attributes were assessed entirely judgementally. The different *resources* required or costs were clearly an important factor in choosing between strategies. In the final conference, this attribute was expressed simply as the cost in billions of roubles. Other measures related to the difficulty of implementing the countermeasures had been investigated at the earlier conferences, but had led to much the same conclusions.

After exploring many strategies in the earlier conferences, the final conference consider four representative strategies. Table 7.2 provides some

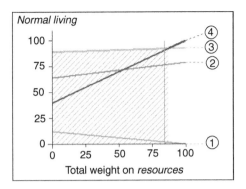

Figure 7.15   Sensitivity analysis of the weight on *resources*

details on these strategies. The *b* in the labelling of the strategies, SL2_*b* (where *b* = 2, 10, 20 or 40), reflects the predicted future lifetime dose value used to separate those relocated from those protected by other means. Note that, in the fifth conference, it was agreed that some protective countermeasures would be applied to all 700,000 or so living in the affected region.

There is space here only to sketch briefly the multi-attribute value analysis; details can be found in Lochard *et al.* (1992). The initial analysis ranked the strategies as follows:

SL2_2   overall score   2;
SL2_10   overall score   76;
SL2_20   overall score   92;
SL2_40   overall score   90.

The weight to be given to *resources* was the most difficult to assess. Within the radiation protection community, the trade-off between economic costs and radiation-related health effects is known as the *alpha value*, α. The weight on *resources* was simply related to α, and this, of course, was a very controversial quantity, because it is in a very real sense the value ascribed to a life. The group had discussed this at length and settled reluctantly on a value that, if anything, they felt was too low. Fortunately, the model showed that the outcome was insensitive to this weight.

Figure 7.15 shows a sensitivity analysis plot of the effect of varying the weight on *resources*. The lines numbered 1 to 4 plot the overall values of the strategies as the weight on *resources* increases from 0 per cent to 100 per cent and the other weights are adjusted proportionally. The analysis initially placed a weight on *resources* equivalent to about 84 per cent of the weight in the model, marked by the vertical line. It can be seen that the third strategy, SL2_20, achieves the highest overall value, just beating the fourth strategy, SL2_40. If the weight on *resources* is decreased, which corresponds to an increase in α, SL2_20 becomes more clearly the highest-scoring strategy. Since none of the group wanted to decrease α and most wanted to increase it, there was no need to argue about the value of α further.

Insight into the reasons for the high score of SL2_20 can be found in figure 7.16, which shows a sequence of Pareto plots of *effects* against the *resources* required (costs) of the strategies. In figure 7.16(a) the *radiation-related* effects are plotted against *resources*. Note first that the *resources* scale is a preference scale – as, indeed, are all the other scales in the model. This means that greater scores correspond to increasing preference and, in this case, decreasing cost. Moreover, conventionally all scales are renormalised to have a range 0 to 100. Thus on the *resources* scale, here the horizontal axis, strategy SL2_40 has a score of 100, since it was the cheapest, whereas SL2_2 has a score of 0, since it was the most expensive. The vertical axis gives the scores for the strategies on the *radiation-related* effects, again renormalised to a 0 to 100 scale with the most preferred strategy, SL2_2, scoring 100.

Figure 7.16(a) corresponds to a cost-effectiveness plot, such as might be used in a conventional cost–benefit analysis. Cost–benefit analyses are commonly used in guiding radiation protection decisions, and, as they are used, take account only of medical factors directly related to the radiation and economic costs – i.e. the *resources* and the *radiation-related* attributes. Before the Chernoloyl International Project, many cost–benefit analyses had shown that SL2_40 should be the preferred strategy.[10] This is perhaps not a surprising result. The costs of the strategies were significant fractions of the gross national products of the republics, yet the highest estimated number of fatal cancers that could be avoided was a few thousand. Moreover, those fatal cancers would be distributed over the next seventy years and, statistically, would be lost in the general mortality figures for the population. This figure simply says that 'hard rational economic arguments' cannot justify adopting anything other than the cheapest strategy when only the *radiation-related* health effects are considered. Nevertheless, there are other factors related to the stress caused in the population by the accident and the subsequent countermeasures and to the acceptability to the public

---

[10] Strictly, they had suggested the optimality of a strategy SL2_35, the so-called '35 REM' strategy, which was very similar to SL2_40.

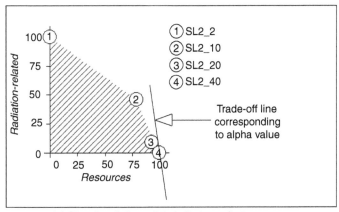

(a) Plot of *radiation-related* effects against *resources*

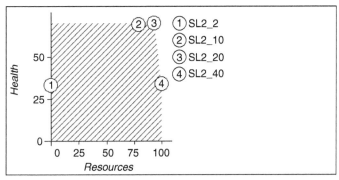

(b) Plot of *health* effects against *resources*

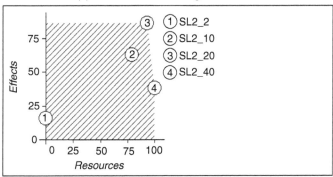

(c) Plot of *effects* against *resources*

Figure 7.16   Plots of different *effects* attributes against *resources*

of the strategies. These factors are introduced, respectively, in figures 7.16(b) and 7.16(c).

Figure 7.16(b) gives a similar plot in which the vertical axis now represents the overall *health* effects, given by combining the *radiation-related* and *stress* scales. Note that, although the *health* scale is normalised so that the maximum and minimum possible scores are 100 and 0, respectively, because no strategy was either best in terms of both *radiation-related* and *stress* scales, or worst in terms of both, the full range of the *health* scale was not used. Figure 7.16(c) again differs in the vertical scale. In this case the attribute *effects*, which arises from combining the *radiation-related*, *stress* and *public acceptability* scales, is plotted. Again, because no single strategy was best, or worst, on all three component scales, the full 0 to 100 range of the *effects* was not used.

As first *stress* and then *public acceptability* were included, as in figure 7.16(b) and figure 7.16(c), respectively, it may be seen that SL2_20 moved towards the top right-hand corner – i.e. in the direction of increasing preference on both horizontal and vertical scales.

From figure 7.16(c), which, in a sense, represents a synthesis of all the preference information, it was clear that SL2_2 and SL2_10 could never be optimal: they were dominated by SL2_20 on both the *effects* and *resources* scales. SL2_40 could be optimal, since it beat SL2_20 on the *resources* scale – i.e. it was cheaper. It could beat SL2_20 overall, however, only if the weight on *resources* was sufficiently high, so that the poorer performance on the *effects* scale was more than compensated for by the financial savings. In fact, no member of the conference felt that it was appropriate to place as high a value on the weight for this to occur. The analysis therefore pointed strongly to the choice of SL2_20.

Without venturing further into the analysis, it can be seen from the sequence of plots in figure 7.16 that the wider issues of *stress-related* health effects and *public acceptability* had a considerable effect on the analysis. Moreover, the sequence of plots provided a vivid and effective report in respect of the second objective of the decision conferences: it summarised the key socio-economic and political factors that, together with the physical, radiological and medical evidence, were influencing the relocation and protective measures.

Concluding remarks

We return to the group dynamic and decision-conferencing aspects of this study in later chapters. For the present, note:
- although simple, the models enabled many insights to be gained on a host of complex issues;
- the analysis was facilitated by the structure of the attribute tree; and
- sensitivity analysis quickly identified that one of the most controversial trade-offs was not a significant determinant of the result.

Further details of this case study may be found in French *et al.* (1992b) and Lochard *et al.* (1992).

7.9 Other schools of decision analysis

In this chapter we have explored how DMs' judgements can be articulated through multi-attribute values to model preferences. We should recognise, however, that there are other schools of decision analysis that seek to support DMs through the use of other forms of models and conceptions of rationality. For instance, we mention the following three families of multi-attribute decision analysis.

The *analytic hierarchy process* (AHP). In 1980 Saaty proposed an approach to multi-criteria decision making that has many similarities with MAVA approaches (Saaty, 1980, 1990). One builds an attribute tree and constructs a ranking using a weighted sum of attribute scores; the process by which DMs' preferences and weights are elicited is quite different, however. One key point is that the elicitation needed requires many pairwise comparisons from DMs; too many to allow the method to be used with more than about a dozen alternatives or criteria. That said, it is one of the most popular methods in the United States for supporting strategic decision making when uncertainties are not a dominating factor.

AHP is not without its critics, and there have been many discussions of its merits and demerits in the literature (Belton and Gear, 1983; Dyer, 1990; French, 1986; Saaty, 1990; Saaty and Vargas, 1984a, 1984b; Salo and Hämäläinen, 1997). One very significant issue concerns the fact that it can exhibit rank reversal – i.e. it does not satisfy the axiom of the irrelevant alternatives. This axiom encapsulates the idea that a rational DM's preference between two alternatives should not be changed if a third alternative is introduced or withdrawn from choice; in other words, if she prefers *a* to *b*, she should do so whether or not she might also have chosen *c* (see discussions in French, 1986, and French and Ríos Insua, 2000). MAVA does not have this flaw. At the heart of the issue is the fact that AHP assumes that all preferences can be represented on *ratio scales* – i.e. there is an absolute zero of preference – whereas MAVA assumes only that preferences are represented on *interval scales*, in which the zero is chosen arbitrarily. A little thought shows that the weights in MAVA are assessed on ratio scales: zero weight means an attribute has no influence on the decision, whatever the scale. This means that MAVA and AHP can be combined in procedures that assess the attribute value scales, as described in section 7, but allow the pairwise comparison method of AHP for assessing weights within the attribute hierarchy (Salo and Hämäläinen, 1997).

The *French school of multi-criteria decision aid* (MCDAid). About thirty years ago Roy suggested an outranking methodology that has become central to approaches to decision analysis in much of the French-speaking world (Roy and Vanderpooten, 1996, 1997). The details of these multi-criteria techniques (Belton and Stewart, 2002; Bouyssou, Marchant, Pirlot *et al.*, 2000; Bouyssou *et al.*, 2006; Roy, 1996) need not concern us here – they would take another chapter or two to present. We will say a few words, however, on general differences between the underlying philosophies of MAVA and MCDAid. These differences are not easy to understand, in part because they relate to differences in the cultural perceptions and under-standings of decision making between the English- and French-speaking worlds. The similarity of the words *decision* and *décision* hides a subtle difference of interpretation. Anglo-American – i.e. English-speaking – understanding emphasises a point of choice at which DMs choose one from a range of alternatives: at the risk of overstatement, the focus is on the moment in time at which the choice is made. Of course, decision analysis is a process extending through a period leading up to that moment of choice, but it is that moment of choice that *is* the decision.

On the other hand, the French understanding of *décision* sees a process that leads to an intentional change from one state of affairs to another as a result of DMs' deliberations, but the emphasis is much more on the process, not on the single moment at which the choice is supposedly made. The result is that, while Anglo-American approaches to decision analysis see their role as helping DMs organise their judgements consistently for that moment of choice, French MCDAid approaches are more concerned with providing information to support the whole process. This they do by identifying partial rankings of the alternatives that may help DMs to recognise some alternatives as clearly better than others. As we say, the difference is subtle, but it is one that ultimately leads to quite distinct techniques. Moreover, along each development one comes across other subtle differences in interpretation of, for example, *weight* and *uncertainty*, and even between the meanings of *subjective* and *objective*.

Fuzzy approaches. In section 5.7 we mentioned fuzzy sets and fuzzy logic. This is essentially an approach to modelling that tries to represent all aspects of uncertainty, particularly those that relate to ambiguity and lack of clarity. French (1984a, 1986, 1995b) offers several criticisms of the methodology when applied in a prescriptive sense to decision analyses in the corporate strategic domain (Bellman and Zadeh, 1970; Roubens,

1997). There are problems with operational definitions of the terms that lead to inconsistencies and difficulties in eliciting judgements from DMs. The methods clearly do have applications in other domains of activity, however. Essentially, they seem to offer DSS tools that are very easy to develop and tailor to repeatable situations such as the application of control to an operational system. The important word here is 'tailor'. If one is developing a controller to run a washing machine in a manner that is sensitive to the load, the temperature of the incoming water, etc. then one can tune parameters in the controller over many, many washing cycles to achieve an excellent overall performance. There is no such opportunity to tailor performance when dealing with highly unstructured decisions. Thus it is important that any decision analyses in these circumstances helps DMs think through the issues. This requires the concepts used to be transparent and operationally defined, as we believe all the methods that we indicate in chapters 7 to 10 are.

There are two points that we should make. First, there are other approaches to handling ambiguity and uncertainty that are closely related to ones dubbed by their authors 'fuzzy': for instance, rough sets (Greco *et al.*, 2001) and possibility theory (Dubois *et al.*, 2001). Second, fuzzy approaches may be overlaid on other decision analytic methodologies. For example, some of the methods of allowing for uncertainty when applying MCDAid techniques involve fuzzy or related concepts. We would remark, however, that in such cases critiques of some of the issues in applying fuzzy decision analysis in strategic decision making may be countered by the structure and process brought by the underlying decision methodology.

7.10 Concluding remarks and further reading

Payne *et al.* (1993) provide a particularly thorough examination of the use of compensatory and non-compensatory strategies and more recent work on fast-and-frugal heuristics is discussed by Gigerenzer *et al.* (1999), Hogarth and Karelaia (2006) and Newell *et al.* (2007: 38–46).

There are many texts that we might recommend on generalities of modelling: we mention Pidd (1996), Ragsdale (2001) and White (1985). Little (1970) has been very influential on the process of OR modelling; see also Little (2004). Multi-attribute modelling is discussed in Brownlow and Watson (1987), Keeney (1992, 2002, 2004), Keeney and Raiffa (1976) and Keeney and Gregory (2005). Waisel *et al.* (2008) provide an interesting descriptive insight into the modelling process. In complex decision problems, such as on environmental issues, we have noted that there is often a need to combine the outputs of consequence models with multi-attribute models (see, for example, Borsuk *et al.*, 2001, Dietz *et al.*, 2004, and French *et al.*, 2007a). Kirkwood (1997) provides guidance on how MAVA may be conducted in a spreadsheet. The decisionarium website (www.decisionarium.tkk.fi) provides an excellent resource of training materials and software (Hämäläinen, 2003).

We have described a general approach to multi-attribute value analysis. Some authors have given names and acronyms to specific forms of such analysis: e.g. simple multi-attribute rating technique (SMART) (Edwards, 1971; Goodwin and Wright, 2003; Watson and Buede, 1987); simple multi-attribute ranking technique exploiting ranks (SMARTER) (Edwards and Barron 1994; Goodwin and Wright, 2003); SMART-Swaps (Hammond *et al.*, 1998). There are several surveys of current software for multi-attribute value analysis: Belton and Hodgkin (1999; French and Xu, 2004; Maxwell, 2006). Finally, there are several texts that discuss the assumptions underlying the multi-attribute value models discussed in this chapter, such as Beroggi (1998), Bouyssou *et al.* (2006), French (1986), Keeney and Raiffa (1976), Krantz *et al.* (1971), Raiffa (1968) and Roberts (1979).

Belton and Stewart (2002), Goodwin and Wright (2003) and Keeney and Raiffa (1976) all provide details of the elicitation processes in multi-attribute value analysis. Keeney (2002) discusses common mistakes and misunderstandings that can arise in assessing trade-offs. We have emphasised constructive approaches for assessing multi-attribute value functions – i.e. ones in which marginal value functions are assessed on each of the attributes separately and then combined into an overall function. There are alternative elicitation procedures that ask the DM for more holistic comparisons and build the multi-attribute value function from these (see, for example, French *et al.*, 1992a, and Krantz *et al.*, 1971). In reading the multi-attribute value literature, one should be particularly careful on the interpretation of the term 'weight'. There are conceptual differences between many writers and schools, notwithstanding any operational differences in the manner in which they are assessed: see Keeney and Raiffa (1976), Roy (1996) and Saaty (1980, 1990).

The International Chernobyl Project and the role of decision conferencing therein is further discussed in French (1996), French *et al.* (1992b, 1992c), IAEA (1991) and Lochard (1992).

The *Journal of Multi-Criteria Decision Analysis* covers the general area of multi-criteria decision analysis, of which MAVA, MCDAid and AHP are but three approaches. The International Society on Multi-Criteria Decision Making (www.terry.uga.edu/mcdm/) organises a regular series of conferences on the topic.

7.11 Exercises and questions for discussion

(1)   Write a short essay on the following: discuss the primary differences between compensatory and non-compensatory decision strategies and explain why managers might adopt one of these types of strategy rather than another and the implication this may have for the effectiveness of their decision making.

(2)   You have been sent a gift voucher for a year's subscription to one of six magazines:

Digital Photo and Multimedia World – a magazine for digital photographers, emphasising computer enhancement of images, etc.;

Student Motoring – a motoring magazine focusing on the needs of the student;

Computers and Software Writing – a computer magazine focused on developing applications with various languages and databases;

Business and IT in Europe – a business and IT magazine focused on the European Union;

Films for an Evening Out – a film critics magazine with an emphasis on entertainment rather than 'art' films; and

Cookery away from Home – a cookery magazine that is aimed at the lifestyles of students and those living away from home for the first time.

You need to choose which magazine to take as your gift. In parts (a) to (c) you should perform the calculations by hand. Part (d) requires you to use software.

(a)   Structure an attribute hierarchy with at least five attributes against which you may represent your preferences. Briefly explain your reasoning and the importance of the attributes to you.

(b)   Score the six magazines and weight the attributes. Explain your calculations, conduct a multi-attribute value analysis.

(c)   Selecting one of the leaf attributes in your attribute hierarchy, construct a sensitivity analysis plot of the form of figure 7.10.

(d)   Using a MAVA software package – e.g. web-hipre at www.decisionarium.tkk.fi – repeat your analysis.

(3)   Imagine that you live about eight miles from the university and are considering various possible means of transport to get in daily for lectures, labs, etc. You have identified a number of options.

Bus: this would involve one change between bus routes, the first bus ride taking about fifteen minutes. and the second about twenty minutes. The frequency on each route is about five buses an hour. Your home is a five-minute walk from the bus stop, and the bus stops outside your department at the university. The cost of the bus fare is £6.00 for a weekly ticket.

Train: the train takes about twenty-five minutes and there is a train every half-hour. A weekly ticket costs £16.00. There is a station that is five minutes walk from your home, and you would arrive at Central Station with a twelve-minute walk to your department.

Bicycle: the journey would take about twenty minutes along major city roads.

Car: the journey would take about thirty-five minutes in rush-hour traffic and car parking costs £3.00 per day.

Conduct a decision analysis to choose your means of transport to the university by following the steps below. You should conduct your calculations by hand and then check your results by using MAVA software.

(a)   Formulate your choice as a multi-attribute problem, including among the attributes cost and travel time plus at least one further attribute of your choice. State whether each of the attributes is natural, proxy or constructed.

(b)   Inventing further data as you require, construct value scales for each of your attributes, explaining how you do so.

(c)   Explaining the process, assess your swing weights for each of the attributes, and thus construct overall scores for each of the alternatives.

(d)   Indicate how a sensitivity analysis might discover the importance of the attribute cost in determining your choice.

(4)   (a)   Please imagine that you are in the job market and then answer the questions in (a) to (c) below. What attributes would you use to guide your choice of job. State which of your attributes are natural, constructed/subjective or proxy. Present them in the form of an attribute tree.

(b)   List the names of four or five different companies that have offered you a job (or from which you expect to get an offer).

Indicate how you would choose between these using multi-attribute value methods, paying particular regard to explaining carefully what is meant by swing weighting.

(c) How might sensitivity analysis be used to increase your confidence in your final choice?

(Note: in this question, you are required to describe in general detail the analysis that you would use. You are *not* required to conduct the analysis in full.)

(5) Benjamin Franklin has suggested a simple method of comparing two alternatives that differ in respect of a number of criteria. In an often quoted letter to Joseph Priestley, he advises:

> In the affair of so much importance to you, wherein you ask my advice, I cannot for want of sufficient premises, advise you what to determine, but if you please I will tell you how. When those difficult cases occur, they are difficult, chiefly because while we have them under consideration, all the reasons pro and con are not present to the mind at the same time, but sometimes one set present themselves, and at other times another, the first being out of sight. Hence the various purposes or inclinations that alternatively prevail, and the uncertainty that perplexes us.
>
> To get over this, my way is to divide half a sheet of paper by a line into two columns; writing over the one Pro, and over the other Con. Then, during three or four days of consideration, I put down under the different heads short hints of the different motives, that at different times occur to me, for or against the measure.
>
> When I have thus got them all together in one view, I endeavor to estimate their respective weights; and where I find two, one on each side, that seem equal, I strike them both out. If I find a reason pro equal to some two reasons con, I strike out the three...and thus proceeding I find at length where the balance lies; and if, after a day or two of further consideration, nothing new that is of importance occurs on either side, I come to a determination accordingly.
>
> And, though the weight of reasons cannot be taken with the precision of algebraic quantities, yet when each is thus considered, separately and comparatively, and the whole lies before me, I think I can judge better, and am less liable to make a rash step, and in fact I have found great advantage from this kind of equation.

Comment on Franklin's advice. What are the good points and bad points of this method? How does it compare, on the one hand, with the unstructured behavioural heuristics described in section 2 and, on the other hand, with MAVA?

(6) Two health trusts, each centred on a relatively large town (town A and town B), have recently merged and are considering a number of

options concerned with the provision of maternity services. They are considering several different options.

Option I   The status quo, with two centres, one in each town, thereby providing local and relatively accessible services for all.

Option II   Focusing all the services in town A, thereby achieving a larger, much better equipped and more specialist single site (a relatively cheap option).

Option III   Focusing all the services in town B, thereby achieving a larger and much better equipped single site (again, a relatively cheap option).

Option IV   Building new services on a new site situated between the two towns, thereby achieving a larger, much better equipped and more specialist single site (an expensive option).

Option V   Focusing most of the services in town A, with a small service available in town B (mid-range in terms of cost).

Option VI   Focusing most of the services in town B, with a small service available in town A (again, mid-range in terms of cost).

It is imperative that they find the best-value solution that can be implemented. The merged health trust has asked you to prepare a report outlining the appropriateness of MAVA to help them make this decision.

The report should include:

- some indication of why decision aids are useful, why MAVA is appropriate and the steps involved in undertaking MAVA, explaining the purpose of each and the activities that would need to be undertaken in this particular situation; and
- some illustration of the likely outputs and how they could and should be used and an appraisal of the strengths and weaknesses of applying MAVA in this situation.

We suggest that you structure your report in the following way.

(a)   A brief introduction outlining the background to the report (including why decision aids are necessary, useful and why MAVA is appropriate in this situation), the aims and objectives of the report and its structure – i.e. the major sections and their purpose.

(b)   A section outlining the steps taken when undertaking a MAVA, how they would be resolved in this situation, their purpose and the kinds of outputs that are generated (illustrate with plausible outputs based on your estimations/guesses of what they are likely to be in this situation).

(c) Some discussion of how the MAVA analysis might be used in this situation – e.g. how stakeholders be kept informed, which aspects would be communicated, etc.

(d) A conclusion outlining the strengths and weaknesses of MAVA in this context and providing some recommendations to the merging hospital trusts.

(7) Suppose a company has to decide which of a number of new products to manufacture and launch. For each product two forecasts are available: the expected net present value (NPV) of cashflows and the expected market share. Both forecasts are subject to error. NPV is more important as a decision criterion to the company than market share. Thus, the company might decide to choose between pairs of products by agreeing to go with the higher NPV unless the difference is less than €50,000. If the difference in NPV is less than €50,000, the choice will be made by going for the higher expected market share. Give an example to show that this rule can exhibit intransitivities. (The rule is known as the *lexicographic semi-order* decision model.)

(8) The management team of Glaxon Inc. (a fictitious company) has expressed interest in acquiring a software company in the area of data mining. The team may have to take two decisions:

Decision 1:   whether to acquire a software company; and

Decision 2:   which software company to acquire.

Explain how

(a) a DSS based on MAVA and

(b) an ES

can be used to support each decision.

Discuss which of the above technologies is more appropriate for each decision.

Decision analysis and uncertainty

But to us, probability is the very guide to life. (Bishop Joseph Butler)

8.1 Introduction

In this chapter we turn to the issue of uncertainty and address how it may be modelled and its impacts allowed for in decision analyses. We work with level 3 methods that apply in the general and corporate strategic domains (figure 3.7). In this chapter we run into strong tensions between behavioural studies and normative theories. As chapter 2 indicated, our instinctive judgements of uncertainty may be very far from that suggested by SEU theory. The simplicity of the SEU model therefore has to be overlaid with subtle approaches to elicitation, sensitivity analysis and interpretation in practice. Here we outline the process of decision analysis using subjective probability and utility and introduce issues related to elicitation: how should the analyst ask DMs to make the judgements that will determine the values, weights, utilities or subjective probabilities needed for the models? We also indicate some approaches to sensitivity analysis; we defer a broader discussion of these, together with the process of decision analysis and the interpretation of its advice, to chapter 10, however.

Our objectives for the chapter are:

- to discuss the ways in which uncertainty may be introduced into a decision analysis and how it may be addressed;
- to introduce the subjective expected utility model and its use in decision analysis;
- to discuss the modelling of decisions using decision trees and influence diagrams;
- to consider ways of eliciting subjective probabilities and utilities that reduce the discrepancy between the behavioural responses of DMs and normative SEU theory; and
- to present a substantive case study that illustrates the methods introduced in this chapter and supports the discussion in subsequent chapters.

In the next section we discuss the modelling of uncertainty, distinguishing in general terms the cases in which it is appropriate to use probability from those in which, rather than model uncertainty, we should investigate and resolve it through discussion and the use of sensitivity analysis. We also briefly discuss the meaning of probability somewhat, a topic that has had a surprisingly controversial history. Then, in section 3, we turn to a simple example of how SEU modelling might be used in the analysis of a very simple decision table. This introduces many of the ideas of elicitation that we explore in greater detail later. Section 4 discusses risk attitude and how the SEU model represents this. We then turn, in section 5, to decision trees and influence diagrams and show how SEU theory integrates with these decision models. Sections 6 and 7 introduce approaches to elicitation that seek to help DMs provide the judgements required by SEU analyses, mindful of their possible behavioural 'biases'. In section 7 we also introduce multi-attribute utility theory, which extends SEU theory to the case in which the consequences are multi-attributed. Finally, we provide a case study in which SEU has been applied to a complex strategic decision. We close, as always, with a guide to the literature.

8.2 Modelling uncertainty

But Uncertainty must be taken in a sense radically distinct from the familiar notion of Risk, from which it has never been properly separated. (Frank Knight)

Uncertainty pervades most decision making. We have seen how value and preference judgements may be modelled. How do we model the other side of the coin, uncertainty? DMs may be uncertain about many things: what is happening in the world, what they want to achieve, what they truly know, etc. Uncertainty may arise in many ways, therefore – or perhaps it would be better to say that DMs may use the word 'uncertainty' in many different ways. Whether they are referring to the same concept each time is a moot point. Knight (1921) first distinguished between uncertainty, ambiguity or lack of clarity, on the one hand, and risk arising from quantifiable randomness on the other. French (1995b), following Berkeley and Humphreys (1982), offered a discussion of how DMs might encounter 'uncertainties' in the decision process and how an analysis should address these.

Broadly, there seem to be three responses to the need to address uncertainty.

(1) The DM may be clear about a range of possible events that might happen, but uncertain about which actually will. These events might happen because of some inherent randomness – e.g. grain prices over the next year will depend upon as yet unknown rainfall and temperatures in various agricultural regions. Alternatively, the events might be determined by the unknown actions of third parties, such as the strategies of competitors. The events might actually have happened, but the DM may not know that they have. In all cases we adopt the terminology of decision tables (table 1.1), saying that there are possible states of the world $\theta_1, \theta_2, \ldots, \theta_n$, and that the DM is uncertain about which of these actually is or will be the case. We model such uncertainty through probability, though in our treatment in this book we do not require any great deal of sophistication in mathematical probability theory. More mathematically sophisticated approaches are reviewed in French and Ríos Insua (2000).

(2) The DM may be uncertain about what factors are important to her and her values and preferences in a particular context. Such uncertainty may occur because of a lack of self-understanding or because the situation is a novel one[1] in which she has not thought through what she wants to achieve. Modelling such uncertainty will not help resolve her lack of understanding. Only careful thought and reflection on her part will do that. The discussion leading to the construction of an attribute tree in section 7.3 provides an idealised example in which such reflection is catalysed. In the next chapter, we describe a wide variety of similar soft modelling techniques that can help DMs develop their perceptions and understanding of aspects of an emerging decision problem.

(3) Any quantitative analysis involves numerical inputs. Some of these may be derived from data; some are set judgementally; occasionally some are fixed by theoretical considerations; but very seldom are any known exactly. Slightly different inputs might lead to significantly different outputs from the analysis. In the case of decision analysis, it would clearly be of concern if the top-ranking action changed as a result of very slight variations in the input data and judgements. Thus, there is a need to check the sensitivity of the outputs to input variation. There are many techniques for doing this. We illustrated one method in the previous chapter, and we illustrate more in this chapter. We defer a general discussion of the use and interpretation of sensitivity analysis to section 10.3, however.

---

[1] The cynefin model would categorise this situation as complex or chaotic.

The first response requires the use of probability. Attaching a meaning to probability is not as trivial as many think. For instance, in the case of gambling, surely everyone would agree that the probability of a die landing 'six' is a sixth – or would they? Suppose it is known that someone has loaded the die; what then is the probability? Alternatively, if that question does not give pause for thought, what about the case in which it is *suggested* that someone might have loaded the die? If we turn from gambling contexts and think about the sorts of problems faced by DMs in government, industry, etc. then we see that the difficulty in identifying probabilities becomes far greater. How, for instance, might the probabilities needed in evaluating investment options on the stock exchange be found? Indeed, how would you define conceptually the probability of the stock market falling over the next year?

Early writers on probability were somewhat pragmatic in their approach, eschewing clear definitions. Their intentions were summarised by Laplace (1952 [1825]). He took the probability of an event to be the ratio of the number of possible outcomes favourable to the event to the total number of possible outcomes, each assumed to be equally likely. Thus, he assumed that it was possible to divide the future into n equally likely primitive events. In considering the throws of a die, he divided the possible future into six events: 'The die lands "one" up', 'The die lands "two" up', etc. Each of these he considered to be 'equally likely' events; and few would disagree with him, until you ask questions such as those above – what happens, for instance, when the die is 'loaded'?

In a very real sense, this *classical definition of probability* is circular. It requires a partition of equally likely events, and surely *equally likely* is synonymous with *equally probable*. To define the probability of one event, therefore, we need to recognise equality of probability in others. This would not be so serious a flaw, however, provided that we could find a method of recognising equally likely events without involving some concept of probability. We may define equally likely events as being those for which there are no grounds for favouring any one *a priori* (i.e. before the throw of the die etc.) – put another way, those for which there is no *relevant* lack of symmetry. Laplace expressed this idea in his famous, or perhaps infamous, *principle of indifference* or *principle of insufficient reason*, which (in modern terminology) asserts: if there is no known reason, no relevant lack of symmetry, for predicting the occurrence of one event rather than another, then relative to such knowledge the events are equally likely.

There are two serious difficulties with this principle. It is seldom applicable: how would you divide the future up into events without relevant lack of symmetry to judge the probability of the FTSE100 index rising by sixty-three points tomorrow? More fundamentally, what does 'no relevant lack of symmetry' mean? Relevant to what? If you answer 'Relevant to judging the events to be of different probability' you enter an infinite regress, since you would have to recognise 'relevance to probability' without having defined what probability is (see, for example, French, 1986, or Barnett, 1999, for further discussion). The classical notion is therefore, at best, inapplicable to the majority of decision-making situations and, at worst, philosophically unsound.

Having discarded the classical interpretation, let us consider the *frequentist* schools of proability. There is no single frequentist approach, but a family of similar ones. The common thread across these approaches is that probability can have a meaning only in the context of an infinitely repeatable experiment. The probability of an event is taken to be its long-run frequency of occurrence in repeated trials of the experiment. Consider repeated throws of a die, a single throw being a trial of the experiment. Suppose that we observe the results of many throws. The results shown in figure 8.1 would not seem unexceptional. The proportion – i.e. the relative frequency – of sixes might well settle down to 0.1666 . . . $= 1/6$; indeed, this is what we would expect of a 'fair die'. If the die were weighted then the proportion might be 0.412, say. Of course, no die can be tossed infinitely often; a frequentist hypothesises that it can, however.

Frequentist concepts of probability underpin much of standard statistical practice, at least as it was developed from the 1930s to the 1970s. Here we note two points that are key to our thinking on frequentist concepts in relation to decision analysis and support. First, it is absolutely essential that the experiment should be repeatable. In many decision contexts the situation is unique and far from repeatable, thus rendering frequentist approaches inappropriate. In terms of the cynefin model, frequentist probability essentially applies to the known and knowable spaces only. In the complex and chaotic spaces, events if not unique are rare enough for it to be inappropriate to embed them conceptually in an infinite sequence of repeatable trials. Second, a frequentist probability is a property of the system being observed; its value is completely independent of the observer of the system.

The *subjective* school of probability is known as such because it associates probability not with the system under observation but with the observer of that system. Different people have different beliefs. Thus different observers, different DMs, may assign different probabilities to the same event. Probability is, therefore, personal: it belongs to the observer. The subjective

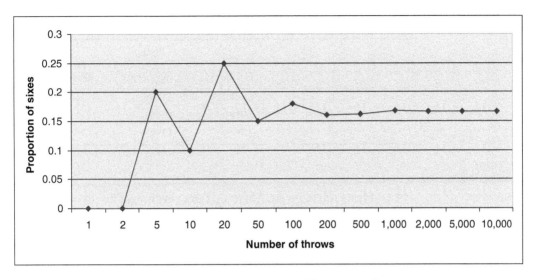

Figure 8.1   The proportion of sixes in repeated throws of a die

school of probability is, like the frequentist, a family of approaches, differentiated mostly in how the meaning of $P(\theta_j)$ is be defined operationally (see, for example, de Finetti, 1974, 1975, and French and Ríos Insua, 2000). Some assume that the DM can articulate a judgement of relative likelihood directly; we indicated one such approach in section 3.3. Others suggest that the DM expresses her uncertainties implicitly in her choices. All demonstrate that subjective probabilities representing a DM's degrees of beliefs behave mathematically according to the normal laws of probability. Since we need to apply probability in unique decision contexts, we adopt a subjective interpretation without further ado, taking $P(\theta)$ to be the DM's degree of belief that θ is the state of the world.

8.3 The subjective expected utility model

If you bet on a horse, that's gambling. If you bet you can make three spades, that's entertainment. If you bet that cotton will go up three points, that's business. See the difference? (Blackie Sherrod)

In section 1.5 we introduced the SEU model[2] in the context of a trivial example of a family meal. Let us look at a more complex example. Instead of a 2×2 decision table we now consider a 3×3 one!

---

[2] Note that, for those of you who followed the development of the SEU model in section 3.3, the approach here is entirely compatible with, and effectively illustrates, the construction of the SEU ranking there.

Table 8.1 The investment problem

		States		
		Fall θ_1	Stay level θ_2	Rise θ_3
Action	a_1	£110	£110	£110
	a_2	£100	£105	£115
	a_3	£90	£100	£120

A DM has £100 to invest. There are three investment bonds open to her. Thus she has three possible actions: a_1, a_2, a_3 – buy the first, second or third, respectively. We assume that she cannot divide her money between two or more bonds and that each must be cashed in one year hence. One of the bonds (a_1) has a fixed return whereas the encashment values of the other two are uncertain, since they depend upon the future performance of the financial market. Suppose that the DM is prepared to categorise the possible state of the market in a year's time into three levels of activity relative to the present: the market might fall, stay level or rise. These are the states of the world for the problem. Suppose further that she predicts the possible consequences of her actions – i.e. the encashment values of the bonds – as being those indicated in table 8.1. We assume that the DM employs a decision analyst to help her think about the problem.

The interview between the DM and DA might go as follows. The probability wheel introduced by the analyst is simply a randomising device in which a pointer is spun and stops completely randomly.

DA: Consider the wheel of fortune or, as I shall call it, probability wheel shown in figure 8.2(a). Which of the following bets would you prefer? I shall spin the pointer and see where it ends.
Bet A: £100 if the pointer ends in the shaded area;
£0 otherwise.
Bet B: £100 if the pointer ends in the unshaded area;
£0 otherwise.
DM: I wouldn't really mind. If I must choose, I'll say bet A.
DA: Would you be unhappy if I made you take bet B?
DM: Not at all. As far as I can see they are the same bet. Look, what is this all about? I have £100 to invest in bonds. Why are you getting me to consider silly gambles?
DA: Investing in the stock exchange is a gamble, isn't it?
DM: Well, yes ...

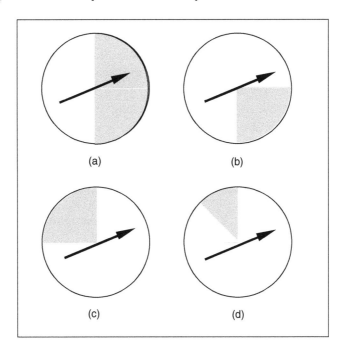

Figure 8.2   Some probability wheels

DA: So what I am going to do to help you decide how to invest your money is to ask you to consider your preferences between a number of simple gambles. These will form a sort of reference scale against which to compare the actual choices available to you. Parts of the investment problem will be represented in each of these; other parts will be forgotten. This will mean that you may concentrate on each particular part of your investment problem in turn without being confused by the other parts. Before I can do this, however, I must ensure that you are thinking 'rationally' about simple gambles. I must ensure that you have a reasonable conception of the probabilities generated by a probability wheel and that you do not believe, say, that the shaded area is 'lucky'. Let me go on. Just one more question about these silly gambles. Consider the probability wheels in figure 8.2(b) and 8.2(c). Do you think it more likely that the spinner will end up in the shaded area of (b) or of (c)?

DM: Both shaded sectors are a quarter of a circle, aren't they?

DA: Yes.

DM: Then they are equally likely.

DA: So you would be indifferent between a bet in which you receive £100 if the pointer ended in the shaded sector of wheel (b) and nothing otherwise, and the same bet based on wheel (c).

DM: Of course.

DA: All right. Let's start looking at some parts of your investment problem. Suppose that you pay me that £100 of yours and as a result I offer you the following choice.

      Bet C: At the end of the year I will spin the pointer on probability wheel (a). You will receive £90 if the pointer ends in the shaded area; £120 otherwise.

      Bet D: £110 for sure (i.e. I guarantee to give you £110 at the end of the year).

      Which bet will you choose?

DM: *Bet D*, the certainty of £110.

DA: OK. Now, what happens if I change bet C so that it is based on probability wheel (d)? Thus you have the choice between

      Bet C: £90 if the pointer ends in the shaded area of wheel (d); £120 otherwise.

      Bet D: £110 for sure.

DM: In this case bet C, but only just.

DA: The shaded sector in wheel (d) is 10 per cent of the area of a circle. How big would it have to be for you to be indifferent between bet C and bet D? You need only give me a rough answer.

DM: About 20 per cent. That gives me odds of four to one on winning £120, doesn't it?

DA: Yes. Now we can start calculating some utilities. Let us set

$$u(\pounds90) = 0$$
$$u(\pounds120) = 1$$

We could choose any other numbers, as long as $u(\pounds120) > u(\pounds90)$. It really doesn't matter. All they do is set the unit of measurement for your preference. From your indifference between the bets we know that

$$u(\pounds110) = 0.8 \times u(\pounds120) + 0.2 \times (\pounds90)$$
$$= 0.8 \times 1 + 0.2 \times 0$$
$$= 0.8$$

DM: But I only said I was indifferent when the shaded sector was *roughly* 20 per cent of the probability wheel. How can we say that my utility is exactly 0.8?

DA: We can't. But it will serve as a working hypothesis. Later we will do a sensitivity analysis to find the significance of this assumption.

Then the DA will go on to question the DM in the same way about her preferences between bets involving the other sums of money of interest, namely £100, £105, £115. He would probably do this by keeping the form of bet C, namely a gamble between £90 and £120, and replacing the certain reward in Bet D by £100, £105 and £115 in turn. Suppose that as a result of this questioning the following utilities are determined:

$$u(£90) = 0.00$$
$$u(£100) = 0.40$$
$$u(£105) = 0.60$$
$$u(£110) = 0.80$$
$$u(£115) = 0.95$$
$$u(£120) = 1.00$$

These values are plotted in figure 8.3.

Notice that the utility function is concave. This is a very common property of utility functions for monetary consequences. Roughly speaking, it means that the DM would be prepared to pay a small premium to reduce the uncertainty associated with each of her possible actions. Having determined the DM's utilities, the DA would check that these values are consistent with some of the DM's other preferences, ones that he had not already elicited. For instance, he might enquire as follows.

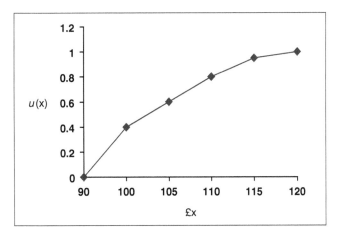

Figure 8.3   The DM's utility curve

DA: Which of the following bets would you prefer? At the end of the year I will spin the pointer on probability wheel (b).

    Bet E: £120 if the pointer ends in the unshaded area;

           £110 otherwise.

    Bet F: £115 for sure.

DM: I don't really mind.

DA: Good. That is comforting; because, if you look at the expected utilities of the bets, you will find they are both 0.95. Thus consistency demands that you should be indifferent.

He would continue questioning the DM until he was satisfied that the utility curve represented her preferences well. If an inconsistency became apparent, he would point it out to her, identifying the points at which her preferences were inconsistent. It would always be left to the DM to revise her preferences to resolve the inconsistency. For instance, if she had preferred bet E to bet F above, it would suggest that the utility function undervalues bet E or overvalues bet F (or both). Since $u(£120)$ takes the conventional value of 1.00, this means that the DM's earlier indifferences, which determined $u(£110)$ and $u(£115)$, are called into question. She would therefore be asked to reconsider these. Typically DMs revise their judgements when an inconsistency is pointed out to them. In the event that they do not, however, the analysis should be halted, because they are, in effect, denying the rationality of SEU analysis: it is not for them.

The next task is to assess the DM's probabilities for the states of the market at the end of the year.

DA: Consider the probability wheel shown in figure 8.2(a). Do you think the event 'that the level of market activity falls over the next year' is more, equally or less likely than the event 'that the spinner ends in the shaded sector of the wheel'?

DM: What do you mean by 'the level of market activity falling'?

DA: Exactly what we meant in the decision table: the state of the world, θ_1.

DM: Oh, I see. I am sure the event on the wheel is more likely.

DA: OK. Now compare the event of the market falling, with the event that the spinner ends in the shaded sector of wheel (d). Which is more likely?

DM: The event of the market falling.

DA: How large would the shaded sector have to be for you to hold the events equally likely?

DM: About twice as big as that on wheel (d).

DA: The shaded area in (d) is about 10 per cent of the wheel. So you would think the events equally likely if it were about 20 per cent?

DM: Yes.

DA: Yes. So we shall provisionally take your subjective probability $P(\theta_1)$ as 0.2.

Note that he asked the DM directly for her feelings of relative likelihood between events. If the DM felt more comfortable discussing preferences, then he might have asked the DM to state her preferences between bets of this form.

Bet A: £100 if the market falls;
        £0 otherwise.

Bet B: £100 if the spinner stops in the shaded sector of wheel (d);
        £0 otherwise.

Varying the area of the shaded sector on wheel (d) until the DM is indifferent would determine her probability for the market falling.

Suppose that the interview continues and that the DM confirms her subjective probabilities as approximately

$$P(\theta_1) = 0.2; P(\theta_2) = 0.4; P(\theta_3) = 0.4$$

Comfortingly, these sum to one, but the DA would not accept this alone as sufficient evidence of consistency in the DM's replies. For instance, he might enquire as follows.

DA: Which do you think more likely:
        event E: market activity does not rise – i.e. it stays level or falls; or
        event F: market activity changes – i.e. it rises or it falls but it does not stay level?

DM: Event E ... I think.

DA: Hm ... now think carefully. Event E occurs if θ_1 or θ_2 happens. Event F occurs if θ_1 or θ_3 happens. By your earlier replies the probability of both events is 0.60. Thus they should both appear equally likely.

DM: Oh, I see what you mean. What should I do?

DA: That is not for me to say, really. I – or, rather, the theory – can tell you where you are being inconsistent. How you change your mind so that you become consistent is up to you. But perhaps I can help a bit. Both events occur if θ_1 happens. So your perception of their relative likelihood should really only depend on whether you think it more, equally or less likely that the market stays level than that it rises. You have said that you consider these equally likely. Do you wish to reconsider your statement?

DM: No, I am happy with that assessment: θ_2 and θ_3 are equally likely.

DA: Then it would appear that you should revise your belief that event E is more likely than event F to the belief that they are equally likely.

DM: Yes, I agree.

DA: But don't worry too much about this. We will remember this conflict later when we do a sensitivity analysis.

The expected utilities of the three investments may now be calculated.

$$Eu[a_1] = 0.2 \times u(£110) + 0.4 \times u(£110) + 0.4 \times u(£110)$$
$$= 0.80$$

$$Eu[a_2] = 0.2 \times u(£100) + 0.4 \times u(£105) + 0.4 \times u(£115)$$
$$= 0.70$$

$$Eu[a_3] = 0.2 \times u(£90) + 0.4 \times u(£100) + 0.4 \times u(£120)$$
$$= 0.56$$

The interview might then continue.

DA: So, a_1 has the highest expected utility.

DM: Which means that I should choose the first investment?

DA: Well, not really. I expect that you will choose that investment, but the analysis is not yet over. Remember that your utilities were determined from replies of the form '*about* 20 per cent'. In a sense, SEU theory assumes that you have infinite discrimination and can discern your preference however similar the bets. But you cannot, er ... can you?

DM: No. I was never sure of my replies to within more than a few per cent.

DA: So we must see how sensitive the expected utility ordering of a_1, a_2 and a_3 is to the values that we have used in the calculations. Now, if we are to consider the possibility that the expected utility of a_1 is less than the expected utility of one of the other actions, we must find a *lower* bound on the expected utility of a_1 and *upper* bounds on the other expected utilities. Let us begin by looking for a lower bound on the expected utility of a_1 – i.e. on $u(£110)$. Which of the following bets would you prefer? At the end of a year I will spin the pointer on wheel (b).

> *Bet G*:   £120 if the pointer ends in the unshaded sector;
>   £90 otherwise.
> *Bet H*:   £110 for sure.

DM: Definitely, bet H.

DA: So we know that

$$u(\text{£}110) > 0.75 \times u(\text{£}120) + 0.25 \times u(\text{£}90)$$

i.e.

$$u(\text{£}110) > 0.75$$

DM: You have assumed that $u(\text{£}120)$ and $u(\text{£}90)$ are exactly 1.0 and 0.0 respectively. Shouldn't we check those values?

DA: No. We can *set* the scale and origin of a utility function arbitrarily. If we varied those values it would be precisely like changing from measuring temperature in centigrade to Fahrenheit. The numbers would be different, but they would place hot and cold objects in the same order. Here the utilities would be different, but the resulting order of your actions would be the same.

Suppose that the DA questions the DM further and determines, similarly, bounds on the other utilities:

$$u(\text{£}100) < 0.45$$
$$u(\text{£}105) < 0.64$$
$$u(\text{£}115) < 0.96$$

Then it follows that, if for the present the DA takes the DM's probabilities as fixed,

$$\begin{aligned}
Eu[a_1] &= u(\text{£}110) \\
&> 0.75
\end{aligned}$$

$$\begin{aligned}
Eu[a_2] &= 0.2 \times u(\text{£}100) + 0.4 \times u(\text{£}105) + 0.4 \times u(\text{£}115) \\
&< 0.2 \times 0.45 + 0.4 \times 0.64 + 0.4 \times 0.96 \\
&= 0.73
\end{aligned}$$

$$\begin{aligned}
Eu[a_3] &= 0.2 \times u(\text{£}90) + 0.4 \times u(\text{£}100) + 0.4 \times u(\text{£}120) \\
&< 0.2 \times 0.0 + 0.4 \times 0.45 + 0.45 + 0.4 \times 1.0 \\
&= 0.58
\end{aligned}$$

Thus the expected utility of a_1 has a *lower* bound of 0.75, which is greater than the *upper* bounds on both the expected utilities of a_2 and a_3. The DM should prefer a_1 to both a_2 and a_3, whatever the numerical values of the utilities within the ranges acceptable to her.

DM: So I should pick a_1?

DA: Yes. It would seem to be your most preferred investment. At least, it does if you believe that your values for the probabilities truly reflect your judgements of the likelihood of events. But we had better check that.

Just as the DA conducted a sensitivity analysis on the DM's utilities, so he must conduct one on her probabilities. Indeed, he should consider variations in *both* her utilities and probabilities simultaneously. He might continue as follows.

DA: Remember that we discovered that you were slightly unsure whether θ_2 and θ_3 were equally likely. Also, remember that your subjective probabilities and utilities were determined from consideration of a probability wheel in which the shaded area was, say, *about* 20 per cent. We must see how sensitive the ordering of the expected utilities is to the values that we have used in the calculations. For this, let

$$P(\theta_2) = p$$
$$P(\theta_3) = q$$

Then, since the probabilities sum to one,

$$P(\theta_1) = 1 - p - q$$

DM: Why have you set $P(\theta_2)$ and $P(\theta_3)$ to be p and q respectively? Why not $P(\theta_1)$ and $P(\theta_2)$?

DA: You have said that θ_2 and θ_3 are equally likely, or, at least, very nearly so. Thus we shall be interested in cases in which $P(\theta_2) = P(\theta_3)$, and such cases will be easy to see, given the assignments that we have made. You'll see.

We shall leave your utilities as they were determined for the time being, and we shall use $Eu[a_i]$ for the expected utility of a_i $(i = 1, 2, 3)$. Then

$$Eu[a_1] > Eu[a_2]$$
$$\Leftrightarrow \quad 0.8 > (1 - p - q) \times 0.40 + p \times 0.60 + q \times 0.95$$
$$8 > 4p + 11q$$

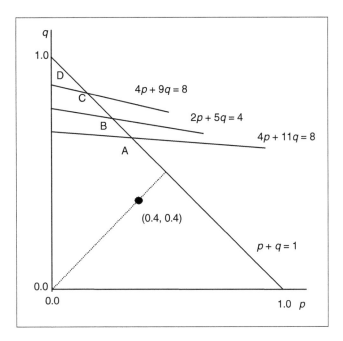

Figure 8.4　　　Plot of the permissible region for p and q

Similarly,

$$\text{Eu}[a_1] > \text{Eu}[a_3]$$
$$\Leftrightarrow \quad 0.8 > (1 - p - q) \times 0.0 + p \times 0.4 + q \times 1.0$$
$$\Leftrightarrow \quad 4 > 2p + 5q$$

And

$$\text{Eu}[a_2] > \text{Eu}[a_3]$$
$$\Leftrightarrow (1 - p - q) \times 0.40 + p \times 0.60 + q \times 0.95$$
$$> (1 - p - q) \times 0.0 + p \times 0.4 + q \times 1.0$$
$$\Leftrightarrow \quad 8 > 4p + 9q$$

Now let us plot these results. In figure 8.4 we have plotted the permissible region for p and q. They are probabilities, so,

$$p \geq 0, \ q \geq 0 \text{ and } p + q \leq 1$$

Hence (p, q) must lie in the triangle running from $(0, 0)$ to $(1, 0)$ to $(0, 1)$ and back to $(0, 0)$. Consider the line $4p + 11q = 8$. Above this, $4p + 11q > 8$, so $\text{Eu}[a_2] > \text{Eu}[a_1]$. Below it, $4p + 11q < 8$, so

$Eu[a_2] < Eu[a_1]$. Similar remarks apply to the regions above and below the other lines. Hence the triangle defining the permissible region for (p, q) is divided into four subregions, A, B, C and D, such that

$$\text{in } A \quad Eu[a_1] > Eu[a_2] > Eu[a_3]$$
$$\text{in } B \quad Eu[a_2] > Eu[a_1] > Eu[a_3]$$
$$\text{in } C \quad Eu[a_2] > Eu[a_3] > Eu[a_1]$$
$$\text{in } D \quad Eu[a_3] > Eu[a_2] > Eu[a_1]$$

In the analysis so far we have modelled your beliefs with probabilities $p = 0.4$ and $q = 0.4$. This is marked by the point • in figure 8.4. Notice that it lies well within region A. Thus, investment a_1 does seem to be your best choice, as we have found already. To confirm this we must check that, if slightly different, but still reasonable, values of p and q were used, then • would still lie in A. Also, we must check that the upper boundary of A does not move down below • if slightly different values are used for your utilities.

DM: Shouldn't we check what happens if the other lines dividing B from C from D are moved slightly?

DA: Theoretically, yes; but practically it is unnecessary. Those lines would have to move a lot further than the upper boundary of A. If that last move seems unreasonable, then so surely will the former. OK let's do the sensitivity analysis. Remember that, when we checked your beliefs for consistency, you initially thought event E was more likely than F.

DM: I did change my mind, on reflection.

DA: True. But, as we can see from the figure, if you changed your mind back again, it would not affect your choice of action. The dotted line goes through • and the origin is the line $p = q$. On it, points represent your belief that a rise in market activity is equally likely as it is to stay level. Below it you think it more likely that the market will stay level. In other words, had you maintained your belief that E was more likely than F, you would have moved further into the region A.

DM: So it seems that I should choose a_1.

DA: Wait a minute! We must consider sensitivity to your utilities again. When we did that before hand, we assumed that the probabilities were exact. We have considered sensitivity to utilities and probabilities independently of the other. Now we must consider sensitivity to both simultaneously. Remember that we obtained the bounds

$$u(\pounds 100) < 0.45$$
$$u(\pounds 105) < 0.64$$
$$u(\pounds 115) < 0.96$$
$$u(\pounds 110) < 0.75$$

With these bounds we know for certain that

$$\mathrm{E}u[a_1] > \mathrm{E}u[a_2]$$
$$\text{if} \quad 0.75 > (1 - p - q) \times 0.45 + p \times 0.64 + q \times 0.96$$
$$\text{namely} \quad 30 > 19p + 51q$$

So let us plot $30 = 19p + 51q$ in the diagram. See figure 8.5. The point • still lies in region A after the upper boundary has been lowered from $4p + 11q = 8$ to $19p + 51q = 30$.

It remains only to see whether you might be prepared to increase your subjective probabilities p and q above the line $19p + 51q = 30$. Are you still content that the possibilities of the market staying level and of it rising are equally likely?

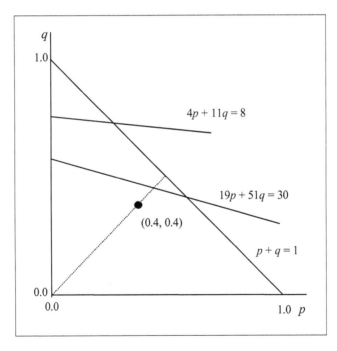

Figure 8.5   The effect of lowering the upper boundary of region A

DM: Yes.

DA: Then we need only consider movement of the point • along the line $p = q$. Now $(1 - p - q)$ is your probability for the market falling. You have said that this is 0.20. Would you be prepared to change this?

DM: I still think 0.20 is about right. I suppose it might be an underestimate.

DA: Well, if $(1 - p - q)$ increases, the point • moves down $p = q$ further into region A. So it does seem that, however we model your beliefs and preferences, the investment a_1 comes out with the highest expected utility.

DM: So I should choose a_1, the first investment.

DA: If you want your beliefs and preferences to be consistent with the principles of rational behaviour assumed by SEU theory: yes. Really, though, you should not ask me or the theory to tell what to do. Rather, I would have hoped that the above analysis helped you think more clearly about your problem and brought you understanding. Now, in the light of that understanding, you must choose for yourself.

DM: I suppose that you are right. I had always favoured investment a_1 but I was afraid that I did so because it was completely without risk. Now I can see that I do not believe that the likelihood of a favourable market is high enough to be worth taking the risk involved in a_2 and a_3. Beforehand, I could not see how to weigh up uncertainties.

8.4 Risk attitude and SEU modelling

Human life is proverbially uncertain; few things are more certain than the solvency of a life-insurance company. (Sir Arthur Stanley Eddington)

In the course of the example above, we noted that the DM's utility function was concave (figure 8.3) and remarked that this reflected risk aversion: she was willing to reduce her expectations of gains to 'insure' against some of the possible losses. Generally, a utility function models a DM's preferences in ways that capture her risk attitude. Because of this we distinguish in our terminology a value function, which models riskless preferences, from a utility function, which models both the DM's preferences and her attitude to risk.

Suppose that the actions have simple monetary outcomes – i.e. each consequence c_{ij} is a sum of money. Associated with any action a_i are two expectations: its expected monetary value $E[c]$ and its expected utility $Eu[a_i]$. The expected monetary value is simply the average pay-off in monetary terms that would result *if* the DM were to take action a_i many, many times. It should be emphasised, however, that in the following she may take the action only once: there is no repetition. Related to the expected utility of an action is its *certainty equivalent*, c_c. This is the monetary value that the DM places on taking a_i once and once only – i.e., if she were offered the choice, she would be indifferent between accepting the monetary sum c_c for certain or taking a_i. Thus $u(c_c) = Eu[a_i]$, i.e. $c_c = u^{-1}(Eu[a_i])$. The *risk premium* of an action is $\pi = E[c] - c_c$. It is the maximum portion of the expected monetary value that she would be prepared to forfeit in order to avoid the risk associated with the action. The risk premium of an action thus indicates a DM's attitude to the risk inherent in *this* action.

A DM is *risk-averse* if for any action her risk premium is non-negative. Equivalently, she is risk-averse for any action if she prefers to receive a sum of money equal to its expected monetary value than to take the action itself. She is *risk-prone* if for any action her risk premium is non-positive. She is *risk-neutral* if for any action her risk premium is zero. Risk attitude is closely related to the shape of the utility function that represents the DM's preferences: see figure 8.6. It may be shown that a concave utility

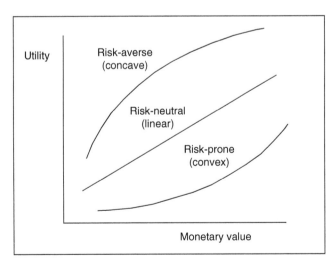

Figure 8.6   Utility modelling of risk attitudes

function corresponds to risk aversion, a convex utility function to risk proneness and a linear utility function to risk neutrality (see, for example, Keeney and Raiffa, 1976).

The utility function $u(c)$ represents the DM's evaluation of the outcome £c and her attitude to risk in the context of her current assets. If her situation changes, then so may her utility function. Behaviourally, it is often observed that the richer a DM becomes the less important moderate losses seem to her; a classic study by Grayson demonstrating this is reported in Keeney and Raiffa (1976). Note also that prospect theory (section 2.5) emphasises the concept of a reference point in evaluating outcomes. Thus, in an ideal world, every time a DM's situation changes we should reassess her utility function. For many purposes, however, the following assumption is both reasonable and sufficient. Suppose that $u_1(c)$ represents the DM's preferences for monetary prizes in the context of a particular set of assets. Suppose also that her monetary assets now change by an amount K, and that her situation changes in no other way. Then her preferences for monetary prizes in the context of her new assets may be taken to be $u_2(c) = u_1(c + K)$. The rationale underlying this assumption is simple. Receiving a prize of £c after the change in her assets is equivalent to receiving a prize of £$(c + K)$ before the change; in either case, her final monetary position is the same.

In the example presented in section 3, the DA developed a discrete utility function in which he elicited the utility values only for the six monetary outcomes that might occur, although values were sketched in by a piecewise linear curve in figure 8.3. Frequently in analyses one goes further and fits a smooth functional form for $u(c)$ that interpolates between the utility values $u(c_i)$ that are actually elicited from the DM. One common form for $u(c)$ is the *exponential*:

$$u(c) = 1 - e^{-(c/\rho)}$$

This function exhibits a constant risk attitude – i.e. the risk premium of any lottery is unchanged if the same quantity is added to all outcomes. When ρ is positive, the utility models constant risk aversion; when ρ is negative, it models constant risk proneness. While we argued earlier that we would expect the preferences of most rational individuals to be decreasingly risk-averse – i.e. their risk aversion to decrease as their assets increase – there are good modelling reasons for using constant risk aversion. First, when the potential change in assets involved in a decision is a moderate fraction of the total, assuming constant risk aversion will provide a reasonable approximation to the DM's preference. Furthermore, the number of parameters that can be introduced and assessed in an analysis is limited by the practical constraints of the time available from the DMs. A single parameter family therefore has attractions.

The quantity ρ is known as the *risk tolerance*. It may be assessed roughly as the sum $£\rho$ for which the DM is indifferent between a gamble

$$£\rho \qquad \text{with probability } 1/2$$
$$£(-\rho/2) \quad \text{with probability } 1/2$$

and a certainty of nothing (Clemen and Reilly, 1996; Keeney and Raiffa, 1976).

8.5 SEU modelling, decision trees and influence diagrams: an example

Developing your plan is actually laying out the sequence of events that have to occur for you to achieve your goal. (George Morrisey)

We developed the SEU model in the context of decision tables. SEU modelling also fits naturally with analyses based upon decision trees and influence diagrams. In this section we work through an example using a decision tree representation.

An airline has been offered the chance of buying a second-hand airliner. Categorising very broadly, such an aircraft may turn out to be very reliable, moderately reliable or very unreliable. A very reliable aircraft will make high operating profits and satisfy customers. A moderately reliable aircraft will break even on operating costs, but will lead to some dissatisfied customers. An unreliable aircraft will cost the company dear, both in terms of operating costs and in terms of customer dissatisfaction. Before making their decision the company may, if they wish, commission a firm of aeronautical engineers to survey the airliner. Of course, the airline will have to pay for the survey. Moreover, the engineers will not make explicit predictions about the aircraft's reliability. All they will do is couch their report in favourable or unfavourable terms. The airline will have to draw its own inferences about future reliability.

The problem represented as a decision tree is displayed in figure 8.7. The first issue facing the airline is the decision whether or not to commission a survey. This is represented by the square to the left of the figure. The upper branch corresponds to the decision to commission a survey and, continuing across to the right, this branch divides according to the possible outcomes of the survey at the chance point representing the assessment of

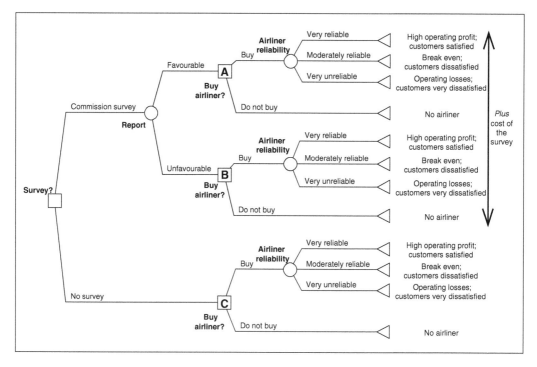

Figure 8.7 The airliner purchasing problem

the airliner's reliability given by the report. The survey may be favourable or unfavourable, and in either case the airline has to decide then whether to buy the airliner. It would be wise to remark, perhaps, that there are decisions to be made at points A and B. While it is usually true that the airline should buy the airliner after a favourable report and should not after an unfavourable one, it is not always so. It depends upon the specific prior beliefs of the airline, its perception of the competence of the aeronautical engineers and its valuation of the possible consequences. The end points describe the consequences that accrue to the airline in the case of each set of decision choices and contingencies.

Note that, despite first appearances, the decisions to be made at points A, B and C are not identical. It is true to say that at each of these points the airline must decide whether to buy the aircraft, but the information that it has to support its decision is different in each case. At A, it knows that the aeronautical engineers have reported favourably on the plane; at B the report is known to be unfavourable; and at C the airline has no report. Thus, the airline's beliefs about the aircraft's reliability will differ at each point.

Suppose that, at the outset, the airline assess the reliability of the aircraft as

$$p(\text{very reliable}) = 0.2$$
$$p(\text{moderately reliable}) = 0.3$$
$$p(\text{very unreliable}) = 0.5$$

It would assess these probabilities on the basis of its knowledge of the average reliability of airliners of the same class as the one it is considering buying, moderated by its knowledge of the particular aircraft's history and ownership.

Next the airline needs to consider how its beliefs would change in the light of the information it may receive from the aeronautical engineers. It could simply assess the probabilities

$$p(\text{very reliable}|\text{favourable report})$$
$$p(\text{moderately reliable}|\text{favourable report})$$
$$p(\text{very unreliable}|\text{favourable report})$$

and a similar set of three probabilities conditional on the receipt of an unfavourable report. Although these are the probabilities that it needs to consider when determining what to do at decision points A and B, they are not straightforward to assess. There is much evidence in the behavioural decision literature to suggest that DMs have difficulty in assessing the effect of evidence on their beliefs: see sections 2.6 and 2.7. For instance, they may forget to include their knowledge of base rates. It is better therefore to help them construct these probabilities from a coherent set of probabilities based upon information available at the *same* time.

The initial or *prior* probabilities were assessed before any report was received from the aeronautical engineers – indeed, before a decision whether or not to consult the engineers had been made. At the same time, the airline will have some knowledge of the engineers – one doesn't consider taking advice of this kind without some background knowledge of the engineers' track record. Thus, the directors of the airline may ask themselves how likely it is that the report will be favourable *if* the airliner is very reliable. Ideally, the answer should be 100 per cent, but no firm of engineers is infallible. Let us therefore assume that they assess

$$p(\text{favourable report}|\text{very reliable}) = 0.9$$
$$p(\text{unfavourable report}|\text{very reliable}) = 0.1$$

Table 8.2 Assessed probabilities of the tone of the report given the airliner's actual reliability

Probability that report is	Conditional on the airliner being		
	Very reliable	Moderately reliable	Very unreliable
Favourable	0.9	0.6	0.1
Unfavourable	0.1	0.4	0.9

along with the two further pairs of probabilities conditional, respectively, on the plane being moderately reliable and very unreliable. Their assessments are given in table 8.2.

Bayes' theorem[3] allows the calculation of the probabilities that are really needed in the analysis: e.g.

$$P(\text{very reliable}|\text{favourable report})$$
$$= \frac{P(\text{favourable report}|\text{very reliable}) \times P(\text{very reliable})}{P(\text{favourable report})}$$

where

$P(\text{favourable report})$

$= P(\text{favourable report}|\text{very reliable}) \times P(\text{very reliable})$

$+ P(\text{favourable report}|\text{moderately reliable}) \times P(\text{moderately reliable})$

$+ P(\text{favourable report}|\text{very unreliable}) \times P(\text{very unreliable})$

$P(\text{very reliable}|\text{favourable report})$

$$= \frac{0.9 \times 0.2}{0.9 \times 0.2 + 0.6 \times 0.3 + 0.1 \times 0.5}$$
$$= \frac{0.18}{0.41}$$
$$= 0.439$$

Similarly,

$P(\text{moderately reliable}|\text{favourable report})$

$$= \frac{0.6 \times 0.3}{0.9 \times 0.2 + 0.6 \times 0.3 + 0.1 \times 0.5}$$
$$= \frac{0.18}{0.41}$$
$$= 0.439$$

---

[3] For a formal statement of Bayes' theorem and details of any of the other probability calculations that we undertake, see almost any introductory book on probability theory.

P(very unreliable|favourable report)

$$= \frac{0.1 \times 0.5}{0.9 \times 0.2 + 0.6 \times 0.3 + 0.1 \times 0.5}$$
$$= \frac{0.05}{0.41}$$
$$= 0.122$$

Note that these numerical calculations can be streamlined considerably. The same denominator, P(favourable report) $= 0.41$, appears in all three cases. Moreover, the three component products in the denominator form in turn each of the numerators.

Next consider the case that the report is unfavourable, and applying Bayes' theorem again:

P(very reliable|unfavourable report)

$$= \frac{0.1 \times 0.2}{0.1 \times 0.2 + 0.4 \times 0.3 + 0.9 \times 0.5}$$
$$= 0.034$$

P(moderately reliable|unfavourable report)

$$= \frac{0.4 \times 0.3}{0.1 \times 0.2 + 0.4 \times 0.3 + 0.9 \times 0.5}$$
$$= 0.203$$

P(very unreliable|unfavourable report)

$$= \frac{0.9 \times 0.5}{0.1 \times 0.2 + 0.4 \times 0.3 + 0.9 \times 0.5}$$
$$= 0.763$$

In this case the common denominator is P(unfavourable report) $= 0.59$.

We have now calculated all the probabilities that we need at the chance events: see figure 8.8. Note how the information in the case of a favourable report shifts the mass of the probabilities towards very reliable, whereas, in the case of an unfavourable report, the shift is towards very unreliable: things are making sense!

Next, the DMs need to consider how they will value the possible outcomes. Initially, let us suppose that the airline simply wishes to think in financial terms – i.e. we assume that the utility of a consequence is purely its monetary value. Assume that the net present value over the next ten years of running a very reliable airliner, having allowed for financing the purchase, is £8.3 million. Suppose that the NPV of operating a moderately reliable airliner is £1.6 million and that the NPV of the losses of operating a

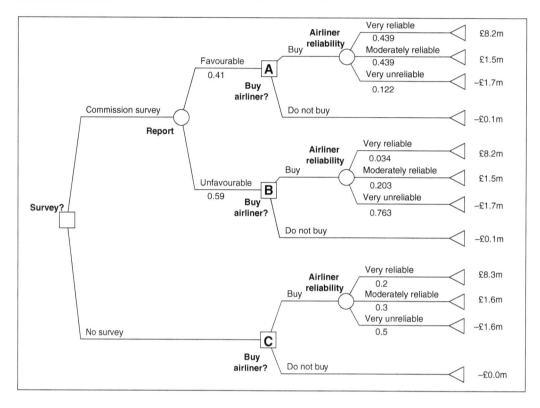

Figure 8.8   The decision tree for the airliner example with the probabilities and NPVs of the outcomes attached

very unreliable airliner is −£1.6 million. Finally, suppose that the survey would cost the airline £100,000 (= £0.1 million). These values have been attached to the end points in figure 8.8.

Consider first the decision at A. Working in millions of pounds here and throughout, if the airline buys the airliner it faces

$$\text{Expected NPV of buying at A}$$
$$= 0.439 \times 8.2 + 0.439 \times 1.5 + 0.122 \times (-1.7)$$
$$= 4.05$$
$$> -0.1$$
$$= \text{Expected NPV of not buying at A}$$

It makes sense therefore for the airline to buy the aircraft *if* it commissions a report and it is favourable. Similarly, consider the decision at B. If the airline buys the airliner it faces

Expected NPV of buying at B
$$= 0.034 \times 8.2 + 0.203 \times 1.5 + 0.763 \times (-1.7)$$
$$= -0.71$$
$$< -0.1$$
$$= \text{Expected NPV of not buying at B}$$

It makes sense for the airline not to buy the aircraft *if* it commissions a report and it is unfavourable. Finally, consider the decision at C. If the airline buys the airliner it faces

Expected NPV of buying at C
$$= 0.2 \times 8.3 + 0.3 \times 1.6 + 0.5 \times (-1.6)$$
$$= 1.34$$
$$> 0.0$$
$$= \text{Expected NPV of not buying at B}$$

If it does not commission a survey, the balance would seem to be in favour of buying the aircraft. Is it worth commissioning the survey? Note that we now know what the airline should do at decision points A and B. Thus we know the expected NPV at these:

Expected NPV at A $= \max\{4.05, -0.1\} = 4.05$
Expected NPV at B $= \max\{-0.71, -0.1\} = -0.1$

It follows that, if a survey is commissioned,

Expected NPV of commissioning a survey
$$= 0.41 \times 4.05 + 0.59 \times (-0.1)$$
$$= 1.60$$

We know the expected NPV if a survey is not commissioned; it is simply the expected NPV of buying at C:

Expected NPV of not commissioning a survey
$$= \max\{1.34, 0.0\}$$
$$= 1.34$$

We can now see that the airline should commission a survey, because the expected NPV of doing so is greater than that of not doing so. The analysis suggests that its optimal strategy is: commission a survey; if the report is favourable, buy the airliner; if not, do not buy it.

Note that the analysis proceeded in reverse chronological order. Later decisions were analysed first, because they determined the consequences of earlier decisions. This procedure is known as *rollback* or *backward dynamic programming*. Thus the analysis is simple:

  (i) take expectations at chance nodes;
 (ii) optimise at decision nodes – i.e. minimise in problems concerning costs and maximise in those concerning profits; and
(iii) calculate from right to left (rollback).

We have assumed that the survey will cost the airline £100,000. In reality, however, the airline would approach the aeronautical engineers, discuss options and be offered a price. The analysis quickly provides them with the most that they should be willing to pay. The expected NPV of commissioning a survey is £1.60 million including the cost of the survey. The expected NPV of not commissioning a survey is £1.34 million. Had the survey cost £(1.60 − 1.34)m = £0.26m more, then the expected NPV for both would have been the same. In other words, the most it is worth paying for a survey is £(0.26 + 0.1)m = £0.36m. The value of the information derived from the survey is £360,000; at least, it is if the decision is to be evaluated in terms of expected NPV.

As we noted in section 1.5, a decision tree displays the different contingencies in a decision well, but does not provide a clear picture of the interrelation and influences between the uncertainties and decisions. Accordingly, figure 8.7 shows the airline that its first decision is whether to commission a survey. Then, in the light of the outcome of the survey, it must decide whether to buy, and only if it does will it discover the plane's reliability. Laying out the chronology of a decision can be very useful; indeed, it may be enough to allow the DMs to see their way through the problem without further analysis (Wells, 1982). The probabilistic dependence of the nature of the survey report on the reliability of the airliner is implicit rather than explicit in the tree, however. An alternative representation of the problem using an influence diagram highlights these dependencies well, but, in doing so, loses the explicit representation of chronological relationships and contingencies. Again, squares are used to indicate decisions and circles or ovals used to indicate uncertainties. The arrows do not indicate a flow of time from left to right, however, nor the range of possibilities that might result from either a decision or by 'chance'. Rather, the arrows indicate dependencies that are reflected by the way the DMs look at the problem.

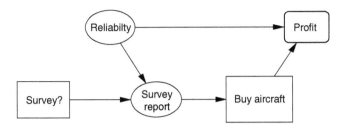

Figure 8.9   An influence diagram representation of the airliner purchasing problem

Figure 8.9 shows an influence diagram representation of the airliner problem. This shows that the survey report depends on the aircraft's reliability and on the decision to commission a survey. The decision to buy the aircraft will be influenced by any survey report; and the profit arising from the decision depends upon both the reliability and on the decision to buy the airliner. So far the interpretation is straightforward; but there are subtleties. Influence diagrams do not show temporal relationships unambiguously. From the tree it is clear that the aircraft's reliability is discovered only after the plane has been bought. This is far from clear in the influence diagram. The influence arc from reliability to the survey indicates that the plane's reliability influences the survey report, *not* that it is known before the report is written. In influencing the profit, however, there is a necessity that the airline observe the actual reliability. There is ambiguity. Some authors resolve this ambiguity by using dotted and solid (or differently coloured) arrows to represent differing temporal relationships. Others (and we prefer this approach) run decision tree and influence diagram representations in parallel, each providing a complementary perspective on the decision problem.

8.6 Elicitation of subjective probabilities

True genius resides in the capacity for evaluation of uncertain, hazardous, and conflicting information. (Winston Churchill)

In section 3 we illustrated the simplest ideas about how an analyst might elicit a DM's probabilities for an unknown state or event. Essentially, he asks her to compare her uncertainty about the state with her uncertainty, on a randomising device such as a probability wheel. He may do this directly or indirectly through the use of simple lotteries. Thus, if θ is the state that is of interest, the analyst may ask the DM to identify a sector on a probability wheel such that she feels that the pointer is as likely to end in the sector on a single spin as θ is to occur. Alternatively, indirectly, he may ask the DM to identify a size of sector such that she is indifferent between the following two bets.

Bet A: £100 if θ occurs; nothing otherwise.
Bet B: £100 if the pointer ends in the sector; nothing otherwise.

While the basic ideas are simple, however, their execution requires much sophistication. We have seen in sections 2.6 and 2.7 that intuitive judgements of uncertainty are subject to many biases. To counter these, a reflective elicitation protocol can be used by the analyst to challenge the DM's judgements gently, helping her construct coherent judgements that represent her beliefs. For instance, because of the anchoring bias, the analyst will try to avoid prompting with a number; or, alternately, prompt with numbers that he is reasonably confident are too high or too low, sandwiching and converging to the DM's judgement. In addition, procedures based on outside rather than inside thinking and on considering the opposite (see section 2.9) can be used.

He will explore her motivation and reasons for entering into the decision analysis. She needs to understand that the process is one that helps *her* think through the problem. She should not see it as a 'black box' process into which she puts numbers and out of which pops the answer. Were she to do that, her motivation would be low and her judgements likely to be poorly thought through. She needs to recognise that the process is designed to help her understand not just her problem but also her perceptions, beliefs and values in the context of that problem. Through this understanding she will make the decision. If she accepts this, she will be motivated to think through her judgements carefully.

Often, if there is time, the analyst will provide some training in uncertainty assessment, explaining potential biases and allowing her to make judgements on some calibration questions for which he knows the answers but she does not. His aim is not just to help her make better judgements but to help her recognise that, without care, her judgements may be flawed.

The next step is to ensure that the DM has a clear understanding of the states or events about which she is being asked. The DA will work with her to ensure that they are clearly defined, with no ambiguities. The states or events should be observable – i.e. it should be possible in due course to determine whether or not they happened. Moreover, the analyst should explore the context of the events with the DM and investigate any dependencies between events: if this happens, is that more likely to? He will also explore different representations of the problem, considering both positive and negative framing of outcomes in order to counter the framing biases predicted by prospect theory (section 2.5).

Then the process turns to the actual elicitation. Here the DA will be sensitive to anchoring, availability and other biases outlined in sections 2.6 and 2.7. He will not prompt the DM with possible values for fear of anchoring her judgements on a value that he has suggested. He will challenge the DM for the evidence on which she is basing her judgements. It is not unusual when working with an expert DM – or an expert reporting to the DM – to ask her to explain in qualitative terms her theoretical understanding of the systems and phenomena that are involved (see, for example, Morgan and Henrion, 1990: chap. 7). Doing so encourages her to use all her knowledge and counter the availability bias. If some further evidence becomes available during the course of the analysis, the analyst will structure the calculations to assimilate this through an explicit application of Bayes' theorem rather than let the DM update her judgements intuitively and risk overweighting the recent data. Above all, the DA will structure the questioning so that he can check the consistency of her judgements, given the strong evidence suggesting that intuitive probability judgements often lack coherence (section 2.6). Do the probabilities add to one? Do marginal, conditional and joint probabilities cohere? And so on. If the DM's judgements are inconsistent he will reflect them back to her, explore the evidence on which she is basing her judgements and help her to revise them in the direction of consistency.

In some cases there will be a need to assess continuous rather than discrete probabilities. Often it will be sufficient to assess a number of quantiles. For instance, if X is the unknown quantity, the DM may be asked to identify a sequence of values $x_5 < x_{25} < x_{50} < x_{75} < x_{95}$ such that

$$P(X \leq x_5) = 5\%$$
$$P(x_5 < X \leq x_{25}) = 20\%$$
$$P(x_{25} < X \leq x_{50}) = 25\%$$
$$P(x_{50} < X \leq x_{75}) = 25\%$$
$$P(x_{75} < X \leq x_{95}) = 20\%$$
$$P(x_{95} < X) = 5\%$$

Alternatively, the analyst may partition the range of X into intervals and elicit the DM's probabilities for each of these. In either case there is a need to consider another potential bias, similar to the splitting bias mentioned in section 7.7. The assessed probabilities may depend on the number of intervals used (Fischhoff et al., 1978; Fox and Clemen, 2005). To guard against this the DA should test and challenge the DM's judgements, asking her for her evidence and helping her reflect on her judgements, perhaps by using consistency checks on probabilities assessed using coarser or finer partitions.

When a parametric continuous distribution is needed, the analyst may work with the DM to assess summary statistics such as mean, median, standard deviation or variance, skewness and so forth and then fit the appropriate distribution. Note that people find it easier to assess some of the summary statistics than others (Garthwaite *et al.*, 2005). Alternatively, the analyst may elicit quantiles as above and fit the distribution to these.

We have presented the elicitation process as being between the DA and DM. If the DM intends experts to be consulted to provide some of the judgements, then the analyst will need to work with the experts in a similar fashion to elicit their judgements. If there are several experts there will be a need to draw together their judgements in some fashion: section 10.4 reviews some methods of doing this.

8.7 Elicitation of utilities

I invest, you bet, he gambles. (Anonymous)

The simplest method of elicitating utilities was illustrated in section 3. It is also the method by which utilities are constructed axiomatically in many of the theoretical developments of SEU theory (section 3.3, French and Ríos Insua, 2000; Luce and Raiffa, 1957). Essentially, the analyst identifies the best and worst possible consequences, c_{best} and c_{worst}, and then asks the DM to compare the other consequences one at a time with a bet of the form

Bet C: c_{best} with probability p
          c_{worst} with probability $(1-p)$

If the DM is comfortable with probabilities and has sufficient experience to have an intuitive feel for events with probability p, then the analyst may state bet C baldly, as above. If the DM is uncomfortable with probabilities, he may construct the bet using sectors on a probability wheel or some similar randomising device. For each consequence c the DM is asked to identify p such that she is indifferent between taking the bet or having c for certain. On setting[4] $u(c_{best}) = 1$ and $u(c_{worst}) = 0$, the SEU model immediately gives $u(c) = p$. Repeating this process for each consequence determines all the necessary utilities.

---

[4] In general, it may be shown that the origin and scale of a utility function can be chosen arbitrarily (French and Ríos Insua, 2000; Keeney and Raiffa, 1976).

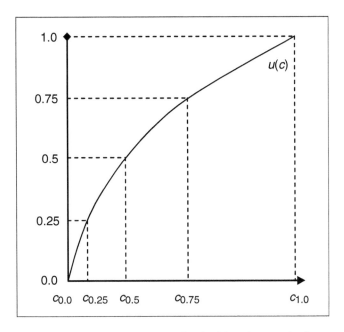

Figure 8.10   Assessment of a utility function by the bisection method

Alternatively, if the consequences are assessed on some continuous natural scale such as money, the DA may begin by asking the DM to identify a consequence value $c_{0.5}$ such that she is indifferent between this and the following bet:

Bet D: c_{best} with probability 0.5
          c_{worst} with probability 0.5

i.e. a fifty-fifty bet between the best and worst consequence values. On setting $u(c_{best}) = 1$ and $u(c_{worst}) = 0$, the SEU model now gives $u(c_{0.5}) = 0.5$. Next the analyst asks the DM to identify two further consequence values, $c_{0.25}$ and $c_{0.75}$, such that she is indifferent respectively between these and the following two bets.

Bet E: $c_{0.5}$ with probability 0.5
          c_{worst} with probability 0.5
Bet F: c_{best} with probability 0.5
          $c_{0.5}$ with probability 0.5

Applying the SEU model now gives $u(c_{0.25}) = 0.25$ and $u(c_{0.75}) = 0.75$. The process continues bisecting the intervals until the DA feels that he has assessed sufficient utilities to sketch in the whole function (see figure 8.10).

The advantage of this second approach to elicitation is that the DM has to consider only fifty-fifty bets and does not have to conceptualise arbitrary probabilities p. The disadvantage is that it works only for consequences measured on a natural scale, so that the DM can imagine any value c between c_{worst} and c_{best}.

In fact, the bets used in the elicitation process can in principle be much more complicated. All that is needed to assess utilities for r consequences is that the DM provides $(r-2)$ indifferences[5] between pairs of bets and/or consequences. Subject to minor conditions, this will enable the analyst to set up a set of simultaneous equations using the SEU model that can then be solved for the unknown utilities (Farquhar, 1984; Keeney and Raiffa, 1976).

So much for the technical details of the elicitation of utilities for uni-dimensional or holistic consequences. Needless to say, the interactions between the DA and the DM require far more subtlety. First, prospect theory suggests that, if the choices between bets are offered to a DM in the simplistic forms above, her responses will not necessary conform to that expected by SEU theory. The analyst needs to explore the DM's framing of the consequences and her assessment of her status quo or reference point, and ensure that she appreciates both the positive and negative aspects of the potential consequences. In addition, he needs to check that she understands the probabilities involved in the bets.

Second, while SEU theory predicts that the DM will answer questions in which a probability is varied consistently with ones in which the values of consequences are varied, in practice there can be systematic biases (see, for example, Hershey and Schoemaker, 1985). Thus, the DA will seldom use only one form of questioning, nor will he simply elicit the minimum number of comparisons to construct the utility function. Instead, he will work with the DM to overdetermine the utility and so create the opportunity for consistency checking. Through a gently challenging discussion the analyst will encourage the DM to reflect on her preferences, think things through and resolve any inconsistencies.

Third, we have seen that the shape of the utility function encodes the DM's attitude to risk. The analyst will explore the DM's feelings about risk, and if she is risk-averse, for instance, ensure that the utility function is concave. Keeney and Raiffa (1976) discuss how such qualitative constraints may be incorporated into the elicitation process. The key point

---

[5] $(r-2)$ arises because two utilities are 'known': $u(c_{best}) = 1$ and $u(c_{worst}) = 0$.

is that, throughout the elicitation, the DA will continually challenge the DM's initial judgements so that she reflects and develops a self-consistent, well-understood set of final judgements within the context of a broad framing of the problem.

The elicitation of unidimensional utility functions is usually only part of the process. The potential consequences in important decision problems are almost inevitably multifaceted, requiring multi-attribute representation. In section 7.4 we introduced multi-attribute value techniques, which provide tools for exploring trade-offs between conflicting objectives under conditions of certainty. How do we approach much more realistic circumstances in which the outcome of any choice has a degree of uncertainty? Earlier we noted that, if an additive value function was to be a suitable representation, then the DM's preferences needed to be preferentially independent. Similar conditions are required for simple forms of multi-attribute utility function to exist. We do not explore these in great depth here, referring instead to the literature (Keeney, 1992; Keeney and Raiffa, 1976). We do indicate their form, however. A key concept is that of *utility independence.*

To motivate utility independence, consider the following example. The prizes in four lotteries involve monetary rewards to be received now and in a year's time: $(£x, £y)$ represents $£x$ received now and $£y$ received a year from now. The four lotteries are illustrated in figure 8.11.

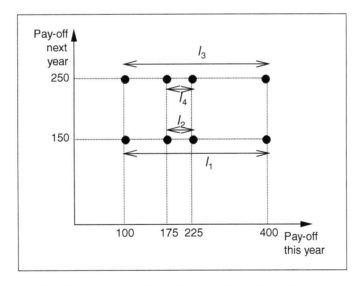

Figure 8.11   The four lotteries in the illustration of utility independence

l_1:   (£100, £150) with probability ½
        (£400, £150) with probability ½
l_2:   (£175, £150) with probability ½
        (£225, £150) with probability ½
l_3:   (£100, £250) with probability ½
        (£400, £250) with probability ½
l_4:   (£175, £250) with probability ½
        (£225, £250) with probability ½

l_1 therefore represents a fifty-fifty bet giving a ½ chance of £100 this year and £150 next and a ½ chance of £400 this year and £150 next. The figure makes it clear that, in the choice between l_1 and l_2, the amount received next year is guaranteed to be £150, whichever lottery is accepted and whatever happens. Similarly, in the choice between l_3 and l_4 the amount received next year is guaranteed to be £250. Moreover, if only this year's pay-off is considered, it is clear that the choice between l_1 and l_2 is identical to that between l_3 and l_4. This suggests very strongly that the DM should prefer l_1 to l_2 if and only if she prefers l_3 to l_4. It should be emphasised, however, that there is only a strong suggestion that this should be so. Suppose that the pay-off next year for l_3 and l_4 is increased to £250,000. Then it might be quite reasonable to prefer l_2 to l_1, since l_2 is less risky, yet to prefer l_3 to l_4, since with income of £250,000 next year the higher risk associated with l_3 is not a significant factor. Despite this reservation, the general tenor of the argument above suggests that the following independence condition might often be reasonable.

An attribute c_1 is said to be *utility independent* of attribute c_2 if preferences between lotteries with varying levels of c_1 and a common, fixed level of c_2 do not depend on the common level of c_2. If the DM is concerned only with two attributes and if c_1 is utility independent of c_2 it is, therefore, possible to assess a utility function for c_1 independently of c_2. Equivalently, the DM's attitude to risk for lotteries over c_1 is independent of c_2. For this reason, some authors use the term *risk independence*.

Consider now the case of q attributes and assume that the DM's preferences between consequences in conditions of certainty may be modelled by an additive multi-attribute *value* function:

$$v(a_1, a_2, \ldots, a_q) = v_1(a_1) + v_2(a_2) + \cdots + v_q(a_q)$$

If, in addition, the DM holds each attribute to be utility independent of all the others, then the *multi-attribute utility* (MAU) function must have one of the following three forms (see exponential utility functions in section 4):

(i) $\quad u(c_1, c_2, \cdots, c_q) = 1 - e^{-\left(v_1(c_1) + v_2(c_2) + \cdots + v_q(c_q)\right)/\rho}$

(ii) $\quad u(c_1, c_2, \cdots, c_q) = v_1(c_1) + v_2(c_2) + \cdots + v_q(c_q)$

(iii) $\quad u(c_1, c_2, \cdots, c_q) = 1 + e^{\left(v_1(c_1) + v_2(c_2) + \cdots + v_q(c_q)\right)/\rho}$

In both cases (i) and (iii), $\rho > 0$.

We emphasise that there are many other types of independence conditions, leading to many different forms of multi-attribute utility function. Here we simply note that this form (and, indeed, many of the others) allows the analyst to elicit marginal value or utility functions on individual attributes and then draw these together into a functional form involving a number of further constants – here ρ, a risk attitude parameter. This very much simplifies the elicitation process. Moreover, with experience it is possible to develop attribute hierarchies such that utility independence holds between all or many pairs of attributes leading to simple forms of multi-attribute utility function similar to those above.

The elicitation process for an MAU function varies according to the precise set of independence conditions that the DM indicates are appropriate, and hence according to its implied functional form. In most cases, however, the elicitation process proceeds roughly as follows.

(1) The analyst explores the formulation of the decision problem and its context in great detail in order to counter potential framing biases, which are all the more likely in such complex circumstances. Throughout the process he will continually challenge the DM on her understanding of the issues and the choices offered her.

(2) He explores the DM's attitude to risk and the independence of her preferences between the attributes. This is achieved by asking general questions, as well as more specific ones based on figures such as that shown in figure 8.11. From these he identifies a suitable form of MAU to represent the DM's preferences and risk attitude. Note that during this process he may revisit the structure of the attribute tree and the definition of the attributes to capture any new insights gained by the DM (Keeney, 1992; Keeney and Gregory, 2005).

(3) Depending on the form of the MAU, he elicits marginal value or utility functions on each attribute. In the simple form given above, it is sufficient to elicit value functions, enabling the DM to consider her preferences in contexts of certainty without the need to confound these judgements with her attitude to risk; for some forms of MAU, however, it is necessary to work with marginal utility functions. Note, though, that, even if the DM has to consider her attitude to risk

and her preferences for differing levels of one attribute, she does not simultaneously have to consider trade-offs between attributes.

(4) Next various weights and scaling factors are assessed that relate to her trade-offs between different attributes and, possibly, her risk attitude.

The process is analytic and constructive, breaking down her preferences into components and then assembling these into an overall prescriptive MAU representation. Many further details are given in Keeney and Raiffa (1976).

8.8 Chemical scrubbers case study

The following example is based upon a real applied study. In the tradition of the best stories, however, the names have been changed to protect the innocent. Similarly, some of the 'facts' have been changed: they would identify the industry concerned. Moreover, some marginal issues have been simplified to focus on the core of the analysis. One of us (French) acted as analyst in the study, working with a manager charged with investigating the issues for the company's board and a small team of experts.

The problem was located in a chemical-processing plant run by a major international company in an EU member state. The plant was relatively modern, one of only a few of its type in the world, and its predicted earnings were substantial over the coming ten to twenty years. The plant was, therefore, important to the company.

All chemical processes have by-products and emit some pollutants. In general terms, the company was socially responsible and wished to reduce polluting emissions. It had had many interactions over the years with the environmental movements, however. Some interactions had been friendly, most not. The culture in the company had become an interesting mixture of genuine concern that it should seek to reduce the pollution of the environment to some 'acceptable' level combined with a deep distrust of environmental pressure groups. The company felt that 'acceptable' levels of pollution could be determined on scientific grounds and that these could be articulated through EU and national regulations.

Another relevant aspect of company culture was that managers genuinely cared for their workers' health and well-being. A cynic might argue that this was simply the result of a concern for shareholder profits in the face of union pressures and liability insurance premiums. It was never explicitly articulated as such, however, and management did seem to want the good health of their workforce for no better reason than simple altruism.

The decision problem related to the emissions of a particular pollutant – call it QZW – at the processing plant. When the plant was built the company had specified the best available scrubbers – i.e. equipment fitted in the chimney stack and vents to remove as much as possible of the pollutant from the emissions. There was now a new technique, however, that could be engineered to build better scrubbers – but the cost would be high. It was expected that this would reduce current emissions of QZW by 80 per cent. There was also the possibility that an even better and cheaper technology would be developed within about five years, and it was known that another company was investigating this. It would be possible to undertake this R&D jointly.

Some background on emission limits is necessary. Generally, regulating authorities set two limits for exposure: that to the public and that to workers. It is presumed that the public cannot choose to avoid the exposure, so the public limits are set as low as reasonably possible. Workers at a plant have chosen to take employment there, however, so they may reasonably be expected to accept the risks – provided, of course, that these have been explained. Thus worker exposure limits are usually set higher, often by one or more orders of magnitude, than public ones when a plant is licensed. The emissions current at the plant at the time of this decision led to public exposures of less than 50 per cent of those licensed. On site the worker exposure was about 30 per cent of worker limits, but the company considered this rather high. Usually they kept worker exposures to any pollutant to less than 10 per cent of those licensed. Currently, an EU study was examining the health effects of QZW. There was a good chance that this might lead the government to lower worker dose limits, perhaps by as much as 50 per cent, and then the current emissions might be unacceptable to the company even if they were still legal. Were this to occur, the company estimated that the new limits would come into force in about five years or so.

The company was concerned not just about the legality of its emissions and the health of its workers but also about the public acceptability of its actions. It wished to be perceived as an environmentally responsible company and it recognised that the public would respond positively if it reduced emissions ahead of legislative changes rather than in response to them. The public relations department was very much in favour of being seen to make an environmentally positive decision proactively, ahead of public opinion and legislation. It emphasised the value of this for the company's general image, particularly in the light of a chemical spill accident that had happened the previous year at a different plant. The accident had led to many adverse comments in the media over several weeks. The company believed, even with hindsight, that it had taken all reasonable precautions beforehand and had implemented emergency clean-up actions quickly and effectively at the time. It had been economical with the truth in its early statements on the incident, however, and had lost public confidence.

Initial discussions with the manager and his team of experts quickly identified the key issues. In particular, it was clear that there were two key uncertainties that needed to be faced: would R&D lead to a cheaper, more effective scrubber technology and would the European Union recommend lower emission levels? This suggested that a decision tree model should be built. Figure 8.12 shows its final form, although many intervening models were built during the analyses. The initial decision was whether to replace the scrubbers now with the current improved but expensive technology. On the upper branch, the decision to install immediately is taken; on the lower branch it is not.

One point of notation: the two chance points are represented by @. At the upper one, the tree continues forward, exploring the options in the event that R&D produces cheaper and better scrubbers within five years. The branch simply finishes at the lower @. Nonetheless, the notation is

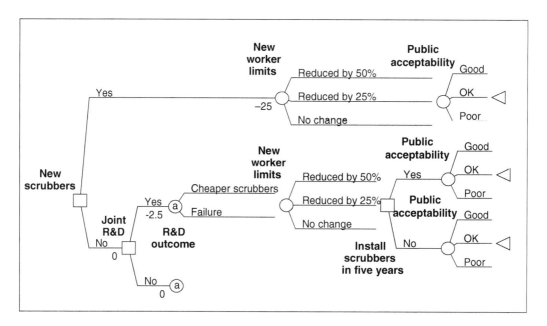

Figure 8.12   The decision to install scrubbers

Table 8.3 Probabilities of R&D outcomes

Probability of	If joint R&D	If no joint R&D
Developing new scrubber technology	0.7	0.4
Failing to develop new technology	0.3	0.6

meant to convey that the tree goes forward, in *structure*, exactly as with the upper one. Of course, there will be differences in the probability and utility values used in the two branches, representing differences between the evolving scenarios.

Some estimated costs at present-day values were immediately available. Installing new scrubbers using the currently available technology would cost £25 million. Were the R&D programme to be successful, installing new scrubbers in five years' time would be cheaper. The estimate was £3 million if the company had joined the R&D programme, but £15 million if it had not. It estimated that it could join the R&D programme for an investment of £2.5 million. The company believed that its investment and expertise would increase the chance of the R&D programme having a successful outcome: see table 8.3.

Talking to the company had identified two attributes other than cost that were driving its thinking: first, the public acceptability of its actions; and, second, its concern for the health and safety of its workforce. The company categorised the public reaction to its business and the management of the plant into three levels: good, OK and poor. The chances of each of these states arising were perceived to depend both on the company's actions – i.e. whether it installed new scrubbers – and also whether new limits were forthcoming. An EU report that reduced discharge limits would shape public opinion one way, whereas one that found no need to recommend any changes would shape it the other. Table 8.4 indicates the probabilities the company assigned to different possible public reactions.

There are several ways that managers' preferences for the outcomes could have been modelled. For a number of reasons, working with equivalent monetary values was chosen, avoiding an explicit multi-attribute analysis. First, the key issue for the company was to understand the structure of the problem: it found great benefit in simply seeing the tree, with its temporal organisation of the decision facing it and the possible consequences. Second, although millions of pounds were at stake, the sums involved were not dramatic in relation to other budgets within the company. Its turnover was many hundreds of millions of pounds annually.

Table 8.4 Probability of different levels of public acceptability conditional on whether new scrubbers are installed and the worker limits set by the European Union

	Worker limits cut to 50%		Worker limits cut to 75%		No change	
	New scrubbers	No new scrubbers	New scrubbers	No new scrubbers	New scrubbers	No new scrubbers
Good	0.4	0.1	0.5	0.3	0.6	0.4
OK	0.3	0.3	0.2	0.3	0.2	0.3
Poor	0.3	0.6	0.3	0.4	0.2	0.3

Thus risk aversion would not be a major factor, and it was acceptable to work with expected monetary values (EMVs) – i.e. to assume risk neutrality. Finally, the manager and others involved found it natural to think in terms of monetary values and there seemed little to be gained in challenging their thinking on this issue, at least for a first analysis.

To value the different levels of public acceptability, the manager considered how much the company would need to save or spend in terms of public relations, setting the following values.

Public acceptability	Equivalent monetary value
Good	+ £20 million
OK	+ £5 million
Poor	− £20 million

It was clear that the manager and his team felt happy with setting these values independently of other aspects of possible consequences, so at least preferential independence held.

The company's attitude to the health safety of its workforce was interesting. At that time it felt that its care of the workforce was commensurate with the risks as they were currently perceived. Were the European Union to lower worker exposure limits the company would not feel that its measures were adequate for the risks, not because of the explicit new limits but because new limits were indicative that health experts had evaluated the risks and found them to be higher than currently understood. On balance the company felt that it would be willing to spend about £40 million to increase worker health and safety if the European Union felt it necessary to cut limits to 50 per cent of the present levels and about £20 million if the limits were reduced to 75 per cent of present levels. If it had already installed new scrubbers, however, these values reduced, perhaps halved. This reduction was debated at some length and was picked up in the sensitivity analysis: see below.

Using the above judgements a baseline analysis was carried out using the DPL decision analysis software package. This simply minimised EMVs, assuming that all the costs and equivalent monetary values could be added, using algorithms equivalent to the rollback used in the airliner example (section 5). The analysis suggested that the company should not invest in new scrubbers now but should join the joint R&D programme. If the R&D was successful then the company should install new scrubbers in five years if worker limits were reduced, but not if they remained the same. If the R&D failed then, whatever happened to the worker limits, the company should not install new scrubbers.

There were many subsequent analyses and discussions as this model was explored. We note just two as illustrative of those that led to understanding on the part of the decision makers.

First, the analysis assumed that the extra expenditure the company might need on worker health and safety would be halved if it had installed new scrubbers. What if it was reduced by 40 per cent or 75 per cent, not simply 50 per cent? To investigate this we performed a simple sensitivity analysis: see figure 8.13. The horizontal axis corresponds to the factor that multiplied the expenditure that the company would be willing to incur on

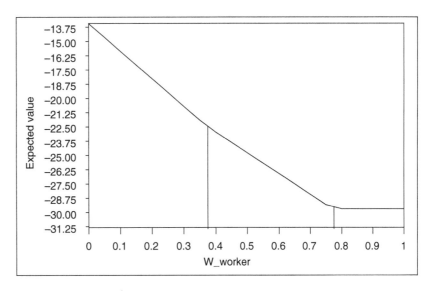

Figure 8.13   Sensitivity plot on the percentage reduction in health and safety attribute if scrubbers had already been installed

health and safety if it had installed scrubbers. The vertical axis is the EMV of the overall strategy. In the baseline analysis, the reduction factor was set at 0.5. The plot indicates that if it were less than 0.37 a different strategy would be recommended: install new scrubbers if R&D were unsuccessful and the worker limits were reduced to 50 per cent of their present value. Similarly, if the value were greater than about 0.79 then a third strategy would be recommended: do not take part in the R&D programme nor install new scrubbers, whatever happens. This exploration helped the manager and his team see that the initial decision whether to seek to take part in the R&D programme depended on their perceptions of whether their attitude to expenditure on worker health and safety would change if the European Union recommended a change in worker limits.

The second analysis concerned the probability that the joint R&D programme would lead to a cheaper technology for scrubbers. Figure 8.14 shows the cumulative distribution of the equivalent monetary outcomes under two circumstances. The first plot (a) applies to baseline analysis. The second plot (b) shows the distribution when joint R&D is certain to lead to an improved technology. Both indicate that the issues faced by the company are essentially loss-bearing: they are about 70 per cent likely to make a loss, at least in equivalent monetary terms. When the joint R&D is certain to be successful, however, the maximum loss is about £45 million (equivalent), whereas in the base case it is about £62 million (equivalent). The reason is obvious: if the joint R&D pays off the cost of new scrubbers falls dramatically. To protect itself, therefore, the company might consider ways of increasing the probability of success of the joint R&D. Maybe it could invest a little more or invite in a third participant with additional

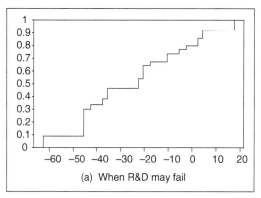

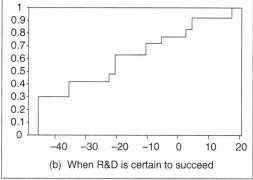

Figure 8.14   Cumulative distributions of monetary equivalent outcomes

skills and knowledge. Here the understanding provided by the analysis helped the manager create new strategies and think more widely.

As indicated earlier, the actual analysis was rather more detailed and involved many more explorations, but the important message is that the decision tree structure helped the DM explore the contingencies in the problem, and it was also possible to articulate the perception that the company's values might change over time. In addition, the analysis helped by facilitating the development of new strategies for dealing with the problem.

8.9 Concluding remarks and further reading

The SEU model has a long and distinguished history within economics; as we have noted, it provides the theoretical basis for the behaviour of rational economic man. A survey of a variety of generally equivalent axiomatisations of this model is given in French and Ríos Insua (2000); see also Beroggi (1998), French (1986), Keeney and Raiffa (1976) and Raiffa (1968).

Decision tree and influence diagram modelling is described in many texts, such as Clemen and Reilly (1996), French (1988), Goodwin and Wright (2003), Smith (1988), Tapiero (2004) and von Winterfeldt and Edwards (1986). Many algorithms and methods have been developed to solve problems represented either as decision trees or influence diagrams. In practice, nowadays, the models are built and solved by using very powerful software, so the need to be able to perform the calculations for oneself is less today than in the past. For descriptions of the algorithms, see, for example, Call and Miller (1990), Clemen (1996), Jensen (2001) and Oliver and Smith (1990). A regular survey of available software is offered in *OR/MS Today*: see Maxwell (2006). Sensitivity analysis for the airliner example in section 5 is explored in French (1992).

The classic text on the elicitation of subjective probabilities is that by Staël von Holstein (1970). More recent surveys are provided by Clemen and Reilly (1996), Garthwaite *et al.* (2005), Merkhofer (1987), O'Hagan, Buck, Daneshkhah *et al.* (2006) and Wright and Ayton (1994). Renooij (2001) specifically considers elicitation of conditional uncertainties in the context of belief nets. Goodwin and Wright (2003) and O'Hagan (2005) describe elicitation protocols for working with DMs and experts. In more complex decision analyses than we are discussing in this text, there is a need to assess multivariate probability distributions. The literature on Bayesian statistics has many suggestions on how this may be undertaken (see, for example, Craig *et al.*, 1998, French and Ríos Insua, 2000, and Garthwaite *et al.*, 2005). There has been some work on using statistical techniques to de-bias expert judgements (see, for example, Clemen and Lichtendahl, 2002, Lindley *et al.*, 1979, and Wiper and French, 1995). One topic that we have not discussed is that of scoring rules. These are a further method of eliciting probabilities, but they are much more important conceptually than practically (see, for example, Bickel, 2007, de Finetti, 1974, 1975, and Lad, 1996).

For the elicitation of utilities, unidimensional and multi-attribute, there is no better text than the classic work of Keeney and Raiffa (1976); but see also Clemen and Reilly (1996), French and Ríos Insua (2000), Keeney (1992) and von Winterfeldt and Edwards (1986). Bleichrodt *et al.* (2001) discuss elicitation processes that take much more explicit account of the behavioural implications of prospect theory. We have emphasised the constructive elicitation of multi-attribute utility functions; more holistic approaches are discussed in Maas and Wakker (1994).

8.10 Exercises and questions for discussion

(1) A builder is offered two adjacent plots of land for house building at £200,000 each. If the land does not suffer from subsidence, he would expect to make £100,000 net profit on each plot. If there is subsidence, however, the land is worth only £20,000 and he could not build on it. He believes that the chance that both plots will suffer from subsidence is 0.2, the probability that one will is 0.3 and the probability that neither will is 0.5. He has to decide whether to buy the two plots outright. Alternatively, he could buy one plot, test for subsidence and then decide whether to buy the other. A test for subsidence costs £2,000. What should he do? Assume that he is risk-neutral and will make the decision based upon expected monetary value.

(2) You are asked to act as an analyst on the following investment problem. There are three possible investments, a_1, a_2 and a_3; and for simplicity it is decided that the future financial market in a year's time can be in one of three possible states: θ_1 – lower; θ_2 – same level; θ_3 – higher. Each investment pays off after one year and the pay-offs are given as follows.

	State of the market		
	θ_1	θ_2	θ_3
a_1	£800	£900	£1,000
a_2	£600	£1,000	£1,000
a_3	£400	£1,000	£1,200

Assume that from your questioning you determine that the DM's probabilities are

$$P(\theta_1) = 0.20; P(\theta_2) = 0.20; P(\theta_3) = 0.60$$

and that these are acceptable to the DM to within ±0.05. Moreover, the DM feels that the market is less likely to fall or stay level than to rise. Further assume that your questioning has determined the following bounds on the DM's utility function:

$u(£1,200) = 1.000$
$0.975 \geq u(£1,000) \geq 0.925$
$0.925 \geq u(£900) \geq 0.875$
$0.850 \geq u(£800) \geq 0.750$
$0.550 \geq u(£600) \geq 0.450$
$u(£400) = 0.000$

Analyse the problem using an SEU model for the DM, including the sensitivity of the recommendation to the possible ranges of her subjective probabilities and utilities.

(3) A DM is required to take part in an unconventional series of bets on three events, E_1, E_2 and E_3, one and only one of which must happen. She must choose three numbers p_1, p_2 and p_3, which she will tell the bookmaker. The bookmaker will then choose three sums of money £s_1, £s_2 and £s_3. The DM's non-returnable stake is £$(p_1s_1 + p_2s_2 + p_3s_3)$ and she will win £s_1 if E_1 occurs £s_2 if E_2 occurs, and £s_3 if E_3 occurs. The DM sets $p_1 = \frac{1}{2}$, $p_2 = p_3 = \frac{1}{3}$. Show how the bookmaker can set s_1, s_2 and s_3 such that the DM must lose £5 whatever happens. (This example lies at the heart of de Finetti's approach to subjective probability. He defined *coherence* as the property that a DM's subjective probabilites must have if the DM cannot under any circumstances be led into a *Dutch bet* – i.e. one in which she is certain to lose money. He showed that this simple requirement leads to all properties of mathematical probability: de Finetti, 1974, 1975; French and Ríos Insua, 2000; Lad, 1996.)

Issue formulation and problem structuring

Everything is vague to a degree you do not realize till you have tried to make it precise.
(Bertrand Russell)

9.1 Introduction

The decision analysis process cycles through stages of divergent and convergent thinking. Initially DMs need to think broadly – *divergently* – about the issues in front of them; indeed, they need to identify a comprehensive list of the issues lest they solve the wrong or a poorly perceived problem. Later they need to *converge* on one or more decision models that capture their understanding of the problem. In this chapter we discuss several tools that can facilitate divergent thinking.

All analysis, problem solving and decision making has to be sensitive to context, both internal and external. For groups and organisations, this has been captured in the concept of *appreciation* – namely that neither a group nor an organisation can understand itself and its context simply through events, its structures and activities; it also needs to understand the ideas, world views and imperatives that shape it; and it must appreciate all these aspects to be able to take appropriate decisions (Lewis, 1991). DMs have to maintain, revise and reflect upon the ideas and notions that shape their and their organisation's understanding of self and their environment. Thus, within the formulation phase of a cycle of decision making (figure 3.6), one of the first things that DMs have to do is to discuss and explore context, setting boundaries for their decision. In this chapter, we explore ways in which such discussion can be catalysed and supported.

We must emphasise at the outset that there is no 'right' way to formulate and solve a problem. School mathematics can leave us with a belief that all problems can be turned into a model and then solved to give a unique, correct answer. In straightforward, repetitive contexts arising in the known domain of the cynefin model, this may often be the case. This is seldom the case, however, for problems arising in the general and corporate strategic domains that lie in the knowable and complex contexts of the model. Rather, DMs bring a plurality of perspectives and objectives on a series of partially appreciated issues. Ackoff (1974) has dubbed this initial confusion before 'problems' are formulated a *mess* – one of the most apt pieces of terminology in management science!

Thus our topic in this chapter is issue formulation and problem structuring. We explore topics such as brainstorming, soft modelling and scenario planning – tools that we regularly use to help DMs make sense of issues and then shape a model to address them. Our objectives are:

- to introduce several different soft modelling techniques;
- to show how these may be used in brainstorming and problem formulation; and
- to emphasise a pragmatic 'mix and match' approach to the use of soft modelling.

We have already used the adjective 'soft' in terminology such as *soft modelling*, *soft OR* and *soft systems*. It is time to be a little clearer on what we mean. A distinction – an unfortunate one to our mind – has grown up over the last few decades between soft and hard methods, the former referring to qualitative methods and the latter to quantitative ones. The juxtaposition of apparent opposites such as soft/hard or qualitative/quantitative has often been seen as suggesting a dichotomy: a simplistic view that one either uses numbers or does not. By the end of this text, we hope that we will have demonstrated that there is no simple dichotomy, but a gradation. In analysis, one begins with the more qualitative and, when there are benefits in doing so, moves to the more quantitative. That is for later, though. In this chapter we focus on soft modelling.

We should also comment on the third of our objectives. Twenty or so years ago, when many of these soft modelling methodologies were being developed, several distinct schools grew up, each seemingly suggesting that its methods were sufficient and that other schools' approaches were in some sense contradictory and unnecessary. Moreover, there were suggestions that soft modelling was all that was necessary to resolve issues and that quantitative models would seldom be needed. Recently, more inclusive and pragmatic views have grown up – and we take this line in the coming pages – but you will find that the old controversies still exist in the literature.

9.2 Brainstorming and soft modelling

Three humble shoemakers brainstorming will make a great statesman. (Chinese proverb)

How does the process of problem formulation begin? The easiest way to begin is simply to ask the open question: what are the issues and concerns that are drawing your attention? As the discussion flows in answer to this question, the key points can be noted down in a list or, perhaps, a number of lists: external factors, opportunities, threats, constraints and any other categories that arise naturally in the discussion. If one is working with a group, it is often useful to write each point on a Post-it and stick it to a board. This allows one to construct lists and groups of related concepts as the discussion continues. Computer software also exists to help; and with technologies such as interactive whiteboards or group decision support rooms, this is becoming more usable.

This process can be made more effective by using formal brainstorming[1] techniques, which seek to generate ideas in a manner that overcomes intra- and interpersonal barriers to creativity (Rickards, 1999). The simplest approaches to brainstorming do little more than we suggested above – ask the participants to list uncritically all the issues that seem relevant to the general problem they face – but there are many variants, all of which introduce more structure to the process to catalyse thinking without biasing perspectives. The key point is to be spontaneous and non-evaluative: no participant is allowed to comment on the contributions of others. The sole aim is to generate ideas for later consideration.

We mentioned computer software. It is instructive to note its potential benefits in the brainstorming processes. In conventional brainstorming, the objective is to produce a stream of ideas. The *ideas* are of value in themselves, because they list the potential components of a model or an analysis. The *stream* of ideas is also of value, however, because it stimulates the thinking of others in the group. As one member suggests something, it may catalyse a thought in another, who then suggests a further idea, which in turn catalyses the thinking of other members. Good brainstorming does not just draw out what is there, it catalyses

---

[1] We debated whether to avoid the term *brainstorming*, which some see as offensive to epilepsy sufferers. It is still used in much mainstream management, however. Our apologies if this does cause offence.

the generation of new ideas. If the activity is conducted within a single group, then all hear the same *stream* of ideas in the same *sequence* at the same *time*. This is why it is often common to use breakout groups, dividing a larger group into several small subgroups that brainstorm the issues independently, before their lists are assembled into a single list of ideas in a plenary session. This way several distinct streams of ideas are developed, hopefully increasing their overall catalytic effect on thinking.

Suppose that the brainstorming exercise is carried out over a network of computers and that the participants do not speak to each other; their only means of communication is via the network. This might be organised in a group decision support room (see section 14.3) or over the internet. As the participants type in their 'top of the head' ideas the software displays the others' ideas on their screens, but not immediately and not in the order that they are entered. Suppose that a brainstorming session is set to last fifteen minutes; then the software gathers the ideas into a global list on the server and sends them out to all the participants at random times during the period, but in a different random order to each. The process is dynamic and adjusts its timings so that by the end of the period everybody has received a complete list. Such a system increases the variety of streams of ideas, which can catalyse further thoughts to a maximum (see Kerr and Murthy, 2004; examples of such systems may be found in, for instance, Nunamaker *et al.*, 1988).

Empirical evidence has shown that brainstorming in groups without software may not be as effective as its proponents suggest. Essentially, although listening to a stream of the ideas of other members of the group may be a good catalyst, it also distracts a member's own thoughts, obviating the advantages of the catalytic process. Without software, moreover, groups experience production blocking (see section 11.2) – i.e. while group members are waiting for their turn to make a contribution they are doing little more than rehearsing what they are going to say rather than listening to others and creating new ideas themselves. Empirical evidence shows that using software may counter these problems, because generally it is used quietly, leaving each member to follow his or her thoughts and make his or her contributions between reading the ideas of others (Kerr and Tindale, 2004). Notwithstanding this evidence, noisy, vocal group brainstorming can have other benefits. As we note in chapter 11, one of the purposes of group decision support is to build a shared understanding of the different perspectives within a group and to contribute to team building and ownership of the final choice. The interactions within the group during an open brainstorming session, when facilitated positively, can help the members see where the others are 'coming from' and begin the process of mutual understanding.

Brainstorming draws out 'top of the head' ideas from DMs, sparking one idea off another; but there is no guarantee that it draws out *all* the ideas they need, and neither does it help organise them. There are a much broader range of techniques of varying degrees of formality that seek to pull out and arrange the issues and concerns informatively. These are the techniques that are known variously as soft-modelling, soft systems or soft OR. We consider six categories:

- checklists;
- simple two-dimensional plots;
- trees and networks;
- management and other models;
- rich pictures; and
- scenario planning.

We include two topics not often considered as methods of soft modelling: management models and scenario planning. In the management literature (ten Have *et al.*, 2003), the term 'model' tends to be used to refer to a graphical aide-memoire that captures the factors and interactions that can be important in determining some economic or organisational behaviour.[2] Not only can these models act as checklists, and so be discussed further in the next section, but they can also introduce other benefits and pointers to good forms of strategy. Scenario planning is important in that it catalyses creative thinking about possible futures.

The key thing to remember when using any of these techniques is not to apply them too rigidly. They are tools to help DMs think – or, rather, to get them thinking. Thus their role is to stimulate, not constrain, discussion. In developing any particular soft representation of the issues, any differences of judgement between DMs will stimulate discussion and enhance understanding. For example, disagreement about the potential influence of a stakeholder can prompt clarification of exactly what options are available to him or her, and what effects these would have. Note further that these discussions should not be thought of in isolation. Thinking about and discussing the roles of stakeholder can, for instance, provide insight into DMs' own objectives or key uncertainties.

---

[2] Might it be that management models tend to be graphical and qualitative because management is mainly concerned with the complex domain in the cynefin model?

9.3 Checklists

You can make a well-considered, well-thought-out decision, but if you have started from the wrong place – with the wrong *decision problem* – you won't have made the smart choice.
(John Hammond, Ralph Keeney and Howard Raiffa)

Checklists are a very simple development of brainstorming in which DMs are prompted with key words focusing on generic aspects of the context of their problem and then asked for their immediate and specific thoughts on these with little evaluation or reflection. There are many checklists suggested in the literature. We give only a few here to illustrate the range of possibilities. Note also that no single list will serve to remind DMs of all the issues they may need to consider. Nor are these checklists mutually exclusive; there are many overlaps. The analyst will need to choose so as to use those that seem most natural for the problem in hand.

PESTEL and 7 S's

A helpful checklist for conceptualising the external context is PESTEL. Having asked a generic question about the issues and concerns that are drawing the attention of DMs, the analyst would introduce more focused but still open questions, such as the following.

- Political: is there anything on current political agendas that may have an effect on these issues?
- Economic: are there any changes in the economy or the financial world that may affect what happens?
- Social: are there any societal issues or changes that should be considered?
- Technical: are there relevant technological issues, including any imminent advances?
- Environmental: should possible environmental impacts be introduced into the discussion?
- Legal: are there any relevant legal issues or potential changes on the government's agenda?

For stimulating discussion of the internal context, 7 S's is a classic list of factors, originally developed by McKinseys, the international consultants (ten Have *et al.*, 2003).

- Strategy: what are the organisation's broad strategic objectives and direction?

- Structure: what is the organisational hierarchy, including responsibilities, accountabilities and authorities?
- Systems: what are the relevant information systems and business processes?
- Style: is there any issue that relates to the way of working and doing business?
- Shared values: what are the organisations's core beliefs, values and expectations?
- Skills: what are the key capabilities and knowledge?
- Staff: how will the organisation's workforce face up to these issues and the response to them?

Prompts to identify uncertainties

In order to build a decision tree or influence diagram, one needs to be clear on the key uncertainties. Some will be obvious, but others may become apparent only after prompting. Browne *et al.* (1997) have identified a series of questions that may catalyse DMs' thinking about uncertainty. Some examples are given in table 9.1.

SWOT

Checklists need not be linear. Perhaps the most common checklist used by managers today has the form of a 2×2 table: SWOT analyses – Strengths, Weaknesses, Opportunities and Threats (table 9.2). This requires DMs to identify these four sets of issues insofar as they, their organisation and their environment are concerned. SWOT analyses help DMs explore the context in which they operate. In particular, the strengths and weaknesses refer to their internal context. Similarly, the opportunities and threats refer to the external context. It is becoming common to see 7 S's, PESTEL and SWOT analyses combined into one, with the strength and weakness row of the SWOT table being subdivided into sub-rows based on the 7 S's and the opportunities and threats row subdivided into sub-rows based on PESTEL.

PROACT and CATWOE

Sometimes the checklists do not refer to the decision context but to the decision-making process itself, reminding DMs and their analyst to engage in well-structured decision making. Two such are PROACT and CATWOE.

Table 9.1 Prompts that may help in identifying uncertainties

Causal-argument-based	Strategy-based
• What do you think might be the cause of this problem or set of issues?	• Can you think of any factors that would make this proposed action fail?
• Can you think of any similar situations that might help in thinking about this matter?	• Under what scenarios would this action work?
• What class of risk issue do you think you are facing and why?	• Under what scenarios would this action *not* work?
• Have you heard anything recently that seems relevant in some way?	• Why do you favour/dislike this action?
• Can you think of any indications that would provide evidence of an event or its absence?	• Why might others disagree with you about the suitability of this action? What eventualities might concern them?

Table 9.2 Format of a SWOT table

Strengths	Weaknesses
• .... 7 S's	• ....
•	• ....
Opportunities	Threats
• .... PESTEL	• ....
•	• ....

PROACT was coined by Hammond *et al.* (1998). It stands for PRoblem, Objectives, Alternatives, Consequences and Trade-offs: sound decision-making processes require DMs to have a clear and deep understanding of all these before they commit to a strategy. Hunink, Glasziou, Siegel *et al.* (2001) modify PROACT to PROACTIVE.

P – define the Problem;
R – Reframe from multiple perspectives;
O – focus on the Objectives;
A – consider all relevant Alternatives;
C – model Consequences; estimate Chances;
T – identify and estimate the value Trade-offs;
I – Integrate the evidence and values;
V – optimise the expected Values; and
E – Explore assumptions and Evaluate uncertainty.

Table 9.3 Checkland's CATWOE

Formulation of root definitions

Consider the following elements

C	customer	who would be the victims/beneficiaries of the purposeful activity?
A	actors	who would do the activities?
T	transformation	what is the purposeful activity expressed as: input $\rightarrow \boxed{T} \rightarrow$ output?
W	weltanschauung	what view of the world makes this meaningful?
O	owner	who could stop this activity?
E	environmental	what constraints in the environment does this system take as given?

Example

An OR team in a manufacturing company, in the light of market forecasts and raw material availability, needs to make detailed production plans for a defined period.

CATWOE analysis

C people in the production function

A professional planners

T need for a production plan $\rightarrow$ need met; or information $\rightarrow$ plan

W rational planning of production is desirable and is a possibility; there is a degree of stability needed to make rational planning feasible

O the company

E staff and line roles; information availability

While Hunink, Glasziou, Siegel *et al.* do cheat a little, making the 'C' serve for both 'consequences' and 'chances', they do make the need to explore uncertainty much more explicit. Moreover, notice that both PROACT and PROACTIVE focus on objectives before alternatives: remember the importance of value-focused thinking (section 3.5).

Another useful checklist is known by the mnemonic CATWOE: see table 9.3 for an explanation. This was developed in the context of Checkland's much more comprehensive *soft systems methodology* (Checkland, 2001; Checkland and Howell, 1997). CATWOE focuses more on the system and context of the decision than on the process itself, but, unless the aspects that are represented by its elements are addressed, the decision making will not be effective.

Checkland defines *Weltanschauung* as 'the stocks of images in our heads, put there by our origins, upbringing and experience of the world, which we use to make sense of the world and which normally go unquestioned'. It is important that an analyst recognises the importance of being 'in tune' with DMs' world views and does not seek to impose his own or some expert's world view on an analysis – at least, not without substantial and open discussion with the DMs. Much of the recent debate in the United Kingdom about health, food and environmental risks has centred around the difference in world views between government scientific advisers and those of the public, often without those concerned realising that there is a difference or the impact this has on the effectiveness of this debate. In many decision-making contexts there is a need to ensure that all the participants' world views are understood and explored. Thus, to support discussion there may need to be several soft models of the same context, each characterised by a different world view. In this way debate of the real issues can be brought into the open.

9.4 Simple two-dimensional plots

What we have to do is to be forever curiously testing new opinions and courting new impressions. (Walter Pater)

Much can be done by drawing two axes with suitable informally defined dimensions and getting DMs to locate aspects of the problem – e.g. stakeholders or uncertainties – against these.

Stakeholder identification

One particularly useful example helps in the identification of stakeholders and their likely roles as circumstances unfold: see figure 9.1. The relevant dimensions are *power* and *stake* – respectively, how much stakeholders can affect what happens and how much they are affected by what happens. *Players* are stakeholders with both high power and high stake. They are the people who DMs either need to work with or identify as competitors. Whatever the case, DMs must be careful to manage and, ideally, try to control the agenda of their interactions with players. *Victims* and *beneficiaries* are those stakeholders with high stake but little power. How DMs react to them depends on their feelings of altruism and the responsibilities they have for these stakeholders. Governments and their agencies may have a legal obligation to be altruistic; others may simply have a moral obligation. *Context setters or loose cannons* have high power but little stake. These stakeholders lack a clear stake in the issues and their actions may be unpredictable, so they can add significantly to the uncertainties facing the DMs. One tactic, therefore, is to try to change the environment and external systems – or influence the loose cannons' perceptions of these – to increase their stake and make them more personally involved. Finally,

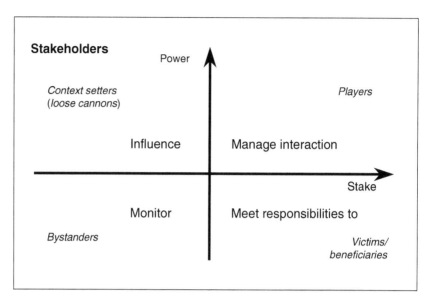

Figure 9.1　Stakeholder identification

there are *bystanders*, who have neither power nor a stake. It should be remembered, however, that they may become more involved in the future, so it might be wise to monitor the bystander groups.

One way of developing such plots and also using the process to structure group discussions is as follows.

(1) The axes are drawn on a blank flip chart. Meanwhile, DMs, working individually, note down their first thoughts on the identity of stakeholders on Post-its, maybe five each.

(2) They then stick the labels in what they think the most appropriate position is on the chart.

(3) The group then examines the resulting plot, noting differences and agreements between the placement of the same stakeholders by different individuals. Discussion of the differences typically leads to revisions of opinion and a growing shared understanding among the group.

Alternatively, instead of asking each DM to work individually and locate a few stakeholders on the plot, the DA may lead a quick brainstorming session to identify stakeholders and then, guided by open discussion and evaluation between the group members, locate each stakeholder on the plot. Either way, the process is catalytic, in that it draws out from the group the identities

Case vignette 9.1 Stakeholder plot developed in a training exercise based around a hypothetical scenario

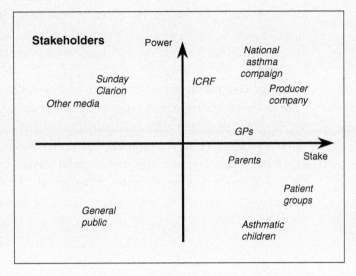

The example of a stakeholder plot shown above is part of one developed in a training exercise within the United Kingdom's Department of Health on health risk management (Bennett *et al.*, 1999). The hypothetical scenario concerned some evidence from an epidemiological study, carried out by the Imperial Cancer Research Fund CICRF), that suggested but did not demonstrate with statistical significance that there was a possible increased risk of laryngeal cancer within groups of asthmatic children who were taking a particular drug for their asthma. The balance of risks was still in favour of maintaining the children's treatment with the drug, since asthma itself is a life-threatening condition if left uncontrolled. Health managers in the Department of Health were considering their possible strategies for advising the public without creating a 'health scare'. A complicating factor was that one Sunday newspaper was known to be aware of the issues and might place the information in the public domain independently of the Department of Health. Hence the actual underlying decision problem concerned the timing and tenor of any government press release.

of potential stakeholders and their importance in the analysis. It is also worth noting that stakeholder involvement and power varies over time, so it is important to revisit the analysis every so often, noting any changes and considering the implications of these for current or future actions. Case vignette 9.1 shows an example of a stakeholder plot that was developed in a training exercise. For further discussion, see Ackermann and Eden (2003) and Bryson (2004).

Uncertainty identification

A similar 2×2 plot of the key uncertainties may also be useful: see figure 9.2. The unknowns can be classified, first, according to their importance either in affecting what may be done or their impacts upon DMs and, second, according to their lack of predictability. Here 'degree of unpredictability' is not a simple probability scale. A certainty arises when one is fairly sure that an event will *not* happen just as much as when one is. Thus, in a very informal sense, the underlying probability scale 'doubles back' on itself. The reasoning behind this classification is to identify important external factors that are currently highly unpredictable and, hence, that may well be worth further investigation. The three-stage process used to identify and classify stakeholders described above can also be used when generating and classifying uncertainties. The resulting plot can be useful in prioritising future information-gathering strategies. For example, efforts to obtain further information should, in the first instance, be focused on uncertainties, which are plotted in the upper right-hand quadrant. Strategies to address less important, more predictable uncertainties involve contingency plans or implementing any strategy flexibly.

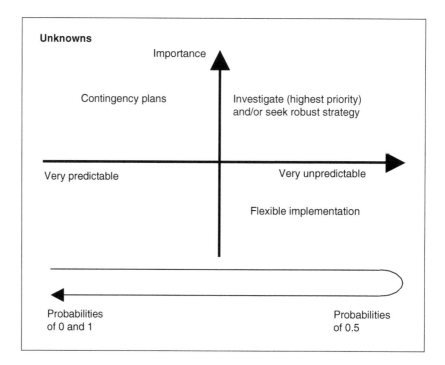

Figure 9.2   Identifying uncertainties

9.5 Trees and networks

[A] model may also represent people's beliefs or opinions, rather than some relatively objective reality. These models, though not objective creations, enable people to explore one another's ideas in a way that is impossible if those concepts remain as mental models. (Mike Pidd)

Trees and networks seek to elicit, display and stimulate discussion of the relationships between concepts. The simplest networks are trees or hierarchies – for instance, attribute hierarchies. This simple structure provides a pictorial breakdown of an overall value into its component factors, connecting higher-level value concepts with sub-values. We discussed how they may be developed in section 7.3, and we do not repeat that discussion here. We simply note that developing an attribute tree is a process that catalyses discussion about values and objectives, and one that helps overcome DMs' tendencies not to articulate or completely overlook their objectives (Bond *et al.*, 2008).

Decision trees provide another example: they show the relationships – in this case, contingencies – between events and potential actions. Textbooks usually introduce decision trees alongside the quantitative analysis of Bayesian modelling (section 8.5). They have great value in exploring and summarising the underlying structure of a decision, however. In fact, Wells (1982) complained that, as an analyst, he seldom got the professional satisfaction of developing a quantitative decision analysis. Once he had worked with DMs to develop a decision tree, the insight they obtained from seeing the contingencies clearly was sufficient for them to proceed to a decision. Carrigan *et al.* (2004) show how structuring medical information in terms of a decision tree increased understanding of the problem and the available treatment options, as well as leading people to feel more informed about their treatment decision. French *et al.* (2005b) also provide an example of decision trees being used qualitatively in problem structuring.

In the same way, drawing an influence diagram without immediately adding and analysing probabilities and utilities is another method of exploring and summarising a problem, this time from the perspective of influence or causality (Daellenbach and McNickle, 2005).

Mindmaps

Mindmaps are among the simplest of plots that connect and associate ideas (Buzan, 2005; Buzan and Buzan, 1994). Their very simplicity makes them transparent and intuitive. Since memory is associative, mindmaps

Case vignette 9.2 Mindmap of information system requirements drawn during a merger

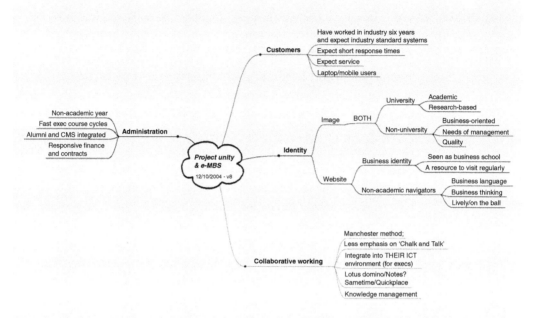

This example of a mindmap identifies some of the issues that arose at Manchester Business School (MBS) in 2003 when we considered the imminent merger between the University of Manchester and UMIST. The business school would grow substantially and become responsible for undergraduate programmes, whereas in the past it had focused on MBA programmes. This mindmap was drawn to support discussions on the character of the current information systems and website used and how it might need to evolve in the course of the merger. Business schools have a different character from other parts of a university, and their customers expect different levels of service. There is a much higher proportion of short courses, requiring faster administrative cycles. Perhaps most importantly, in the case of MBS, our emphasis was on reflective learning from live project work, the Manchester method. This required that we adopt e-learning systems that emphasised collaborative project work rather than ones designed to support more conventional 'chalk and talk' lecturing activities.

provide excellent aide-memoires. Here, however, we focus on their power to help create and organise ideas.

Case vignette 9.2 provides an example of a mindmap. As can be seen, mindmaps do little more than take a major concept or set of issues in a problem and associate this with related concepts, breaking each down to enable DMs to see the issues more clearly. When labelling mindmap branches, one should use key words and phrases, not sentences. Some authors suggest using simple graphics. Whatever the case, the trick is to capture the idea succinctly and memorably. Anything that stands out on the page will stand out in people's memory. Maps can be enhanced by bringing to the fore associations between branches. Simply rearranging the branches so that similar ideas are close on the map can be effective, but using common colours or adding dotted lines to connect branches is perhaps a safer way of emphasising connections.

Cognitive maps

Figure 9.3 shows part of a cognitive map that arose in a study by Belton *et al.* (1997) to develop a strategy for the supplies department in a trust hospital. Without going into the notational conventions used in cognitive mapping – this is a particularly simple example – the picture that this paints of the issues facing the supplies department is intuitively simple to follow (see Eden and Ackermann, 1998, for a full description of cognitive mapping). Issues are related to each other by a network showing the associations in the perceptions of the DMs. More sophisticated cognitive mapping notes the direction of association between concepts – i.e. does the presence of one factor make the other more or less likely? It is also possible to categorise the concepts in a cognitive map into objectives, external factors, key uncertainties, etc. Moreover, software tools allow one to look at a map from a number of viewpoints and to compare the maps of several stakeholders.

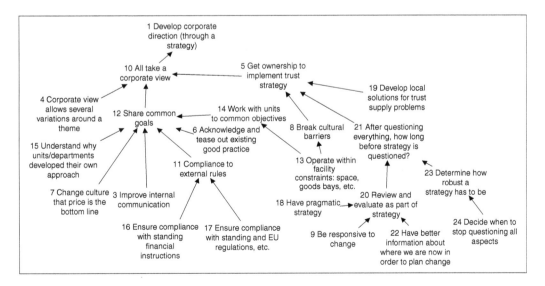

Figure 9.3   Cognitive map of issues arising in defining a supplies strategy for a trust hospital
Source: Belton *et al.* (1997).

Even with such sophistication, however, cognitive maps are intuitive and help capture and convey perceptions. There is an issue of terminology that we should mention. Some reserve the term 'cognitive mapping' for the sophisticated qualitative modelling promoted by Eden and Ackermann, preferring the term 'causal' or 'influence mapping' for more informal applications. In avoiding one clash of terminology, however, they run headlong into others, as such terms may have more quantitative meanings (see, for example, Oliver and Smith, 1990, and Pearl, 2000).

In addition to providing insights into complex issues and facilitating a common understanding of problems among key DMs, cognitive mapping has also been shown to reduce cognitive biases. For example, Hodgkinson *et al.* (1999) show that those senior managers who engaged in cognitive mapping prior to making a strategic decision did not succumb to the framing bias (choosing the safe option when the problem was described in terms of gains but choosing the risky option when the same problem was described in terms of losses). Those who did not engage in cognitive mapping, however, did succumb to this bias (see section 2.5).

9.6 Management models

A manager is responsible for the application and performance of knowledge. (Peter Drucker)

As we noted in section 7.3, many of the qualitative models used in management encode our knowledge of issues and factors that may need to be taken account of in situations that fall into the complex domain of the cynefin model. This makes them ideally suited as 'pictorial checklists', for many management models take the form of simple diagrams suggesting interactions of factors. Furthermore, they may also suggest generic forms of strategy that may help in addressing the issues, just as drawing a stakeholder plot can identify players with whom DMs should interact. Here we give three examples, but there are very many more (ten Have *et al.*, 2003).

Porter's five forces model

Porter's (1988) model is one of the more famous in the management literature, and justifiably so (figure 9.4). It identifies the five factors that need to be considered in assessing a company's competitive position.

- Are there barriers to new entrants – i.e. can new competitors easily join the market?

- To what extent can their buyers bargain?
- Are there alternatives or substitutes for the company's products and to which their customers could switch?
- How much power do their suppliers have?
- How will their current competitors react?

Companies planning their strategy are well advised to use Porter's model to prompt themselves with such questions in order to identify the potential strength of competition vis-à-vis their own.

Simons' levers of control

Simons (1995) notes that, in balancing the need to engender innovation and control risks, a manager has four types of system: see figure 9.5. First, the belief systems and values engendered in an organisation set the levels of innovation and the frameworks within which the organisation's members will respond to opportunities. These will be counterbalanced by systems at its 'boundary' that help manage and protect it from external risks. Internally, there are control systems that set the manner in which the organisation faces up to strategic issues and monitors and reacts to its critical success factors.

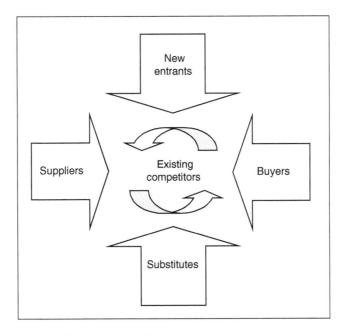

Figure 9.4   Porter's five forces model

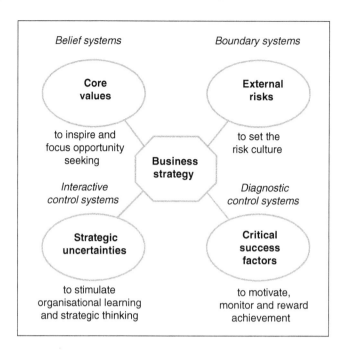

Figure 9.5   Simons' levers of control model

Both Porter's and Simons' models are extremely useful as checklists, ensuring that management teams reflect on key issues when setting strategy and systems. Drawing them on a flip chart can focus discussion on each set of issues in turn, catalysing discussion and drawing out DMs' perspectives. The strategy space model below goes rather further than this, suggesting the form of strategy a company should adopt given its competitive strength in the context of the business environment.

The strategy space model

The strategy space model works by assessing a company's strategic position from four perspectives: two internal, competitive advantage and financial strength; and two external, industry attractiveness and environmental stability. These are used to divide the strategic space into four quadrants, as in figure 9.6. The company's position is assessed, usually judgementally, on each of these scales and the scores joined up to form a quadrilateral. A company operating in an attractive industry (score 3.5) with low environmental stability (score −5.5), good competitive advantage (score −2.0) but poor financial strength (score 2.0) would be plotted as the quadrilateral in figure 9.6. Note that for financial position and industry attractiveness the positive ends of the scales are away from the origin, whereas for

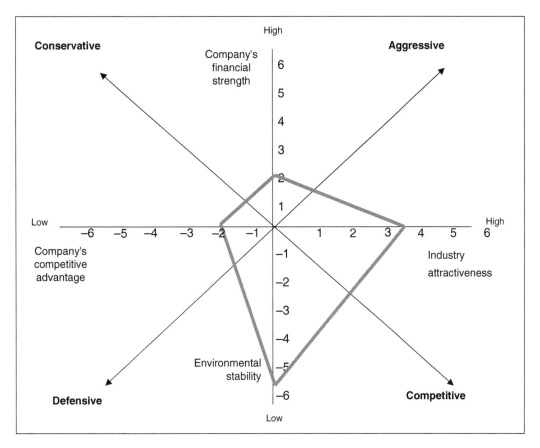

Figure 9.6   The strategy space model

competitive advantage and environmental stability the positive ends are at the origin. Each of the four 'scales' represents a compound judgement taking account of many factors. Although it is possible to devise scoring systems that formalise these judgemental assessments, quick holistic assessments are usually sufficient and invariably stimulate informative discussions among participants.

The quadrilateral may lie predominantly in one of the quadrants, in which case there is a strong suggestion that the company should adopt, respectively, a conservative, aggressive, competitive or defensive strategic stance, as shown in figure 9.6. In more detail, the analysis, strategic imperatives and key issues to be addressed in each of these are as follows.

Conservative stance
- Industry not too attractive but stable environment, reasonable competitiveness and sound financial position.

- Strategic imperatives:
  - develop/focus on more attractive industry areas;
  - if not feasible do not overcommit, but be selective/conservative whilst seeking to maintain competitiveness; and
  - reallocate surplus funds to areas with greater external upside potential.

- Key issues:
  - maintaining financial strength;
  - maintaining competitiveness; and
  - the use of surplus funds.

Aggressive stance
- Both external and internal dimensions favourable.
- Strategic imperatives:
  - aggressively build the business;
  - squeeze competitors, raise the stakes;
  - consider a geographic/product roll-out; and
  - protect the firm's position and avoid complacency.
- Key issues:
  - major structural change;
  - new competitor entry; and
  - the capacity for growth.

Competitive stance
- Competitive advantage in an attractive industry but held back by low financial strength whilst operating in an unstable environment.
- Strategic imperatives:
  - adopt a reactionary stance whilst seeking to protect the competitive advantage;
  - focus on strengthening the financial position; and
  - position to reduce exposure to environmental threats.
- Key issues:
  - how to strengthen the financial position;
  - danger that competitive advantage weakens; and
  - environmental instability may persist/deteriorate.

Defensive stance
- Both external and internal dimensions are unfavourable.
- Strategic imperatives:
  - a radical improvement is required;
  - explore avenues for retreat/exit;

- ask whether the business is worth more to someone else; and
- turnaround.

• Key issues:
  - how feasible is the turnaround?
  - how to stabilise, buy time?

It should be emphasised that the strategy space method does not give definitive prescriptions of strategy. In keeping with the spirit of this chapter, it offers suggestions of issues that strategy should address. It offers another set of prompts to shape thinking.

9.7 Rich picture diagrams

A picture is worth a thousand words. (Anonymous)

Soft systems methodology emphasises the value of *rich pictures*. These seek to explore and summarise issues more pictorially than the methods we have discussed so far. They can be extremely intuitive and can also compress a lot of information into a single picture. Rich pictures can be very useful in forming a backdrop to subsequent analysis, acting as an aide-memoire to allow the group of DMs continually to refer back and check that it is addressing all the relevant issues. Figure 9.7 shows a rich picture diagram that arose during a training programme (French *et al.*, 2005), which was part of a programme to instil better issue formulation skills in crisis management teams (Bennett *et al.*, 1999). During this, a hypothetical[3] scenario was used to help articulate discussions of crisis management and public risk communication. A summary of the scenario is as follows.

The UK FSA has just received information from the Italian authorities about a risk of pesticide contamination in plum tomato products. Three weeks ago routine testing discovered residues of a prohibited pesticide, known as CGB. Subsequent tests identified residues of a number of permitted pesticides that exceed levels currently permitted by a factor of two and found further contamination with CGB. Extensive investigation discovered that, during the drought that had affected much of southern Europe the previous summer, several canning plants reduced the quantity of water used in washing plum tomatoes; and several failed to wash the tomatoes at all. The problem also seems to have been compounded by criminal fraud. Many farmers were approached a

---

[3] The fact that this scenario is hypothetical needs to be emphasised. To our knowledge, no risk event of this kind has ever occurred. For hypothetical scenarios to evoke any realistic thoughts and reactions, they need to have some connection with the real world. Thus we refer to the United Kingdom's Food Standards Agency (FSA) and to Italy.

year ago by a supplier offering pesticides at a quarter of the normal price. The supplier claimed that he was reducing stocks in advance of an impending EU directive, which would reduce the maximum permitted residue levels for many pesticides to such low levels that it would be impossible to use them in future food production. In fact, the pesticides were a very dilute industrial pesticide, CGB, that had never been licensed for agricultural use because of a link with cancer. Fortunately, the dilution was so great that the CGB residue levels in processed plum tomatoes are very slight. Italian police have so far been unable to trace the supplier, who vanished once the pesticides had been distributed in bulk to farmers and cash payments taken. All remaining stocks at farms of the pesticide have been confiscated. The Italian authorities have coordinated an extensive testing programme on canned plum tomatoes and other processed foods incorporating tomatoes over the past two weeks and the scale of the problem has become apparent. Roughly 6 per cent of Italian tomato production has been affected. Much of the production is for domestic use, but a sizeable proportion is exported. Accordingly, the Italian authorities are now notifying EU countries and other countries to which exports are made.

The rich picture diagram in figure 9.7 captures the key aspects of the scenario. Given that the description that we actually gave the participants

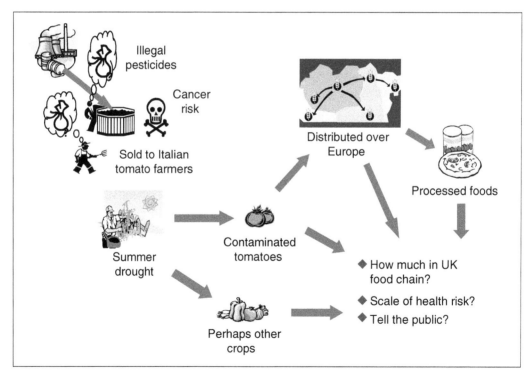

Figure 9.7   Rich picture representing the hypothetical scenario of a tomato health scare
Source: French *et al.* (2005).

was much longer and more detailed than that above, the diagram is a very useful summary, which focused attention on the issues and questions that arose in working through the hypothetical crisis.

Rich picture diagrams can be 'factual', as in figure 9.7, displaying only the key issues of concern. Pictures can also convey emotion and capture feelings and perceptions by drawing on common symbols or icons however. For instance, consider figure 9.8, which shows part of a rich picture diagram developed in 1988 to describe issues relating to the hole in the ozone layer over Antarctica (Daellenbach, 1994). At the time chlorofluorocarbons (CFCs) used in aerosol sprays and refrigeration units were escaping into the upper atmosphere, causing a hole in the ozone layer over the South Pole and allowing harmful ultraviolet (UV) rays to reach the surface. The detail illustrates this by the use of 'creatures' from the then popular Pacman game. In the game these would move around the screen, relentlessly eating anything in sight. By using the same symbols here to represent CFCs, the same negative feeling of relentless consumption is conveyed.

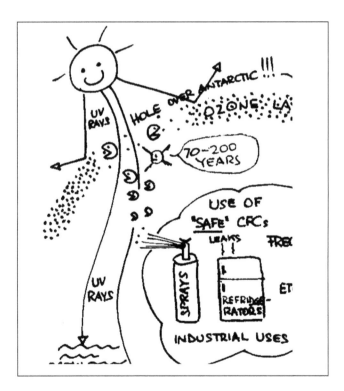

Figure 9.8   Detail from a rich picture diagram of the issues relating to the hole in the ozone layer

Source: Daellenbach (1994).

In the past rich picture diagrams were sketched by hand, as in figure 9.8, and many analysts were reluctant to use them because of poor artistic skills. With modern drawing tools and inventive use of clip art, however, this is now much less of a problem.

9.8 Scenario planning

Forecasts are not always wrong; more often than not, they can be reasonably accurate. And that is what makes them so dangerous. They are usually constructed on the assumption that tomorrow's world will be much like today's. (Pierre Wack)

Another brainstorming technique that can be used to open up DMs' thinking to a range of possible futures is *scenario planning*. This encourages DMs to explore how the world may evolve and how other stakeholders may react to their actions over time. Scenario planning helps DMs think about how things might be rather than how they are, and in doing so stimulates contingent thinking.

Broadly speaking, the approach has eight stages.

(1) Identifying the key variables in the decision. This may be done using some or all of the tools described above. It is important to define the time frame for the decision and the time frame over which each variable is important.

(2) Identifying the key stakeholders in the decision. Again, this may be done by any of the methods above.

(3) Identifying and listing potentially important political, economic, social, technological, environmental and legal (PESTEL) trends that may affect the consequences of the decision – or constrain the choice available.

(4) Identifying the key uncertainties.

(5) Constructing two 'extreme' preliminary scenarios by assuming all good outcomes of the key uncertainties in the first and all the bad outcomes in the second.

(6) Assessing the two scenarios in terms of their self-consistency (there should be a coherent set of events leading from the present to the future envisaged in the scenario) and their plausibility (each scenario should not contain assumptions that are likely to be mutually contradictory). If necessary, the scenarios can be modified to ensure that they are self-consistent and plausible, maintaining as much as possible of the optimism of the first and the pessimism of the second.

(7) Considering the likely response of the stakeholders identified in step 2 to the outcomes in the two scenarios, and, again, modifying the

story in each to make it more plausible and self-consistent, while preserving its essential optimism or pessimism.

(8) Creating a number of less extreme, plausible and self-consistent scenarios.

Note the emphasis on self-consistency, or, in other words, contingent thinking. For example, how might some actions on the part of some players interact with the DMs' own actions. What would their response be?

Usually one builds scenarios by working with a group of DMs, experts and stakeholders. Moreover, rather than the whole group taking part in the development of each scenario, there are advantages in assigning the tasks of building scenarios to subgroups, so that a variety of scenarios are developed in parallel, with a great deal of independent and free thinking.

The essential secret to good scenario planning is to tell a good story – and the greatest risk in scenario planning is to tell too good a story! When used properly, the method opens up DMs' minds to a range of possible futures. It sensitises them to the uncertainties that face them and makes them think about their and other stakeholders' responses to events as they unfold. The danger is that stories can be believed, and psychologists have shown that plausible stories often are (see, for example, Bazerman, 2006, and Kahneman and Tversky, 1982). Earlier we discussed the availability bias: if events have memorable characteristics, their likelihood may be overestimated. Behavioural studies have uncovered a similar bias arising from plausibility: if an event is easily imaginable, it is perceived as more likely. It is vital, therefore, that several scenarios spanning a wide range of possibilities are considered simultaneously to keep DMs aware that there is no claim that any one of these scenarios is *the* future.

Used effectively, scenario planning helps DMs

- understand the impact of key uncertainties;
- think through the responses of key stakeholders;
- devise contingency plans and robust strategies (indeed, it is the ability of scenario planning to help DMs identify and explore contingencies that is arguably its strongest feature); and, generally,
- understand all the issues better.

Scenario planning came to the fore in the early 1970s, when it was used at Royal Dutch Shell to explore potential shocks to the world oil prices. The method was spectacularly successful, in that Shell weathered the oil crisis in 1973 better than most of its competitors. Its managers had thought through the possibilities and identified robust strategies with contingency plans. Its success has perhaps been overemphasised, however, with some consultants seemingly recommending it not as a part of the toolkit of decision analysis but as a complete toolkit for thinking through possible futures and identifying strategy. The interested reader may find discussions in Kleindorfer *et al.* (1993) and Schoemaker (1993). Wright and Goodwin (1999a) discuss the inclusion of scenario planning in the decision analytic process, dubbing the approach *future-focused thinking*, perhaps over-emphasising the contribution of scenario planning relative to other soft approaches to creative problem solving, on the one hand, and under-emphasising the importance of clarity on objectives stemming from value-focused thinking, on the other (see also Montibeller *et al.*, 2006).

9.9 From qualitative to quantitative modelling

Given a particular environment of stimuli, and a particular background of previous knowledge, how will a person organize this complex mass of information into a problem formulation that will facilitate his solution efforts? (Herbert Simon)

There is a large gap between the qualitative soft models that we have discussed in this chapter and the quantitative models introduced in the previous ones. How does an analyst move from the initial brainstorming of DMs' values, uncertainties and key issues through an exploration of how they think that events are evolving developed in, say, a cognitive map and ultimately develop a quantitative consequence model embedded within a value or SEU model of DMs' judgements? The simple, though not particularly helpful, answer is that it is an art. Those of us who regularly attend statistical, environmental, health or economic modelling conferences know that the papers presenting dramatic breakthroughs are often based around modelling insights that allow a difficult interaction to be captured tractably in a quantitative model. Furthermore, with hindsight one is left wondering how such insights have eluded the scientific community for so long. What is it that allows one scientist to see something that so many others have missed until then?

That said, we can be more constructive. It should be clear that the use of checklists and management models should help ensure that issue formulation sessions identify a very high proportion of the events and issues that matter in the context being explored. Stakeholder plots can help DMs, first, think about how other players may behave and, second, identify stakeholder values that they – the DMs – should for altruistic reasons include in their value trees. The use of prompts, such as in table 9.1, can identify further uncertainties. Taken together, one can see that these soft modelling techniques are assembling the components for more quantitative models.

The next step is to identify how these components interact. Mindmaps, cognitive maps and rich picture diagrams clearly move in this direction. So does scenario planning, in that it asks: 'How might we have reached this position? What might have happened in the world and how might other players have reacted?' In the case of consequence models, once one has identified the issues, appropriate experts may be able to provide quantitative models off the shelf. If one is interested in risks from diet, then it may be a relatively easy step to find a previously developed dietary and nutrition model that captures the issues of concern. The use of such models can short-cut the development of a quantitative model, and, moreover, pre-existing models are usually validated to some extent. Care must be taken, though, to ensure that the models address the DMs' real questions and are not simply adopted because of their convenience. Overlaying uncertainty onto such models and updating them in the light of data has long been discussed in the statistical modelling literature (French and Ríos Insua, 2000; French and Smith, 1997). We have indicated how quantitative models of DMs' preferences may be developed and elicited (sections 7.7 and 8.7) (see also Brownlow and Watson, 1987, Keeney, 1992, and Keeney and Gregory, 2005). The final step is to draw all these quantitative models together into an overarching decision model, perhaps an influence diagram. This is not necessarily an easy step, but certainly an easier one than faced the analyst when he originally heard of the DMs' mess of issues and concerns.

9.10 Concluding remarks and further reading

In figure 3.7 we suggested that soft modelling and related methods provided level 1 decision support. They help organise and present information on the current situation and issues faced by DMs. We should note, however, that they provide different qualities of information from that offered by database reports, statistical analyses and forecasts discussed in earlier chapters. The methods here help develop DMs' understanding and capture their perceptions: they are not purely descriptive. They help develop mental models and, indeed, through discussion challenge existing ones. In prescriptive decision support there is a constant need for the process to challenge thinking and shape mental models (see also Chen and Lee, 2003). In section 2.4 we described biases arising from framing and noted that careful and explicit elaboration of the issues before DMs can help them avoid framing baises. Soft modelling tools provide a means of achieving such elaboration (Hodgkinson *et al.*, 1999, 2002; Maule, 1989; Maule and Villejoubert, 2007).

Good general discussions of soft modelling techniques may be found in Belton and Stewart (2002), Daellenbach (1994), Daellenbach and McNickle (2005), Eden and Radford (1990), Falk and Miller (1992), Franco *et al.* (2006), Horlick-Jones *et al.* (2001), Mingers and Rosenhead (2004), O'Brien and Dyson (2007), Pidd (1996, 2004) and Rosenhead and Mingers (2001). The facilitation process that supports soft modelling in workshops is described in Ackermann *et al.* (2004), Eden and Radford (1990) and Papamichail *et al.* (2007). Issue formulation is closely related to Weick's concept of sense making, which, as he points out, requires imagination and creativity (Weick, 1995, 2006).

Our presentation has been cast in terms of decision making – not surprisingly, given the theme of this book. It should be noted, however, that soft modelling techniques have a much wider application. They are valuable in supporting – or, rather, setting the context for – many forms of analysis: from information systems design and implementation to product innovation. In developing an analysis or a design there is a need to be clear on context, on what is being assumed and on what the objectives are. It is worth remembering that many information systems projects flounder because too little attention is paid to the human and organisational aspects of the system. Soft modelling methodologies can identify and focus attention on key issues in these areas, leading to more successful projects (Checkland and Howell, 1997). They also provide very powerful means of developing effective communications to key stakeholders (French *et al.*, 2005).

Our view, as we have said, is that the elicitation of issues and problem formulation is an art. The tools presented here are no more than that: tools. Belton and her co-authors, *inter alia*, have explored how such tools may be deployed in an integrated process from problem formulation through to the completion of a quantitative multi-attribute analysis (Belton *et al.*, 1997; Losa and Belton, 2006; Montibeller *et al.*, 2006); see also Bana e Costa *et al.* (1999). To be effective, they need to be used by a professional analyst or facilitator to draw out DMs' perceptions: see French *et al.* (1998b) and Papamichail *et al.* (2007) for observations of such processes. Therefore we do not believe that they can be fully replaced by software or AI methods that catalyse thinking and structure problems in some algorithmic way. That is not a unanimous view, however. Others, such as Barkhi *et al.* (2005) and Lee and Kim (2002), have developed methods that seek to structure quite complex problems semi-automatically, provided that one has first classified the sort of problem representation – e.g. mathematical programme, influence diagram or decision tree – that one wants.

See also Chen and Lee (2003) for discussion of DSSs that may draw out mental models.

9.11 Exercises and questions for discussion

(1) Imagine that you are on the common room committee of a hall of residence. The committee is investigating the possibility of organising regular party nights in a cellar in the hall that lies close to the hall's boundary with a housing estate and infant school. Draw up an outline attribute tree and stakeholder plot for analysing the issues. You should explain why at least *four* of the attributes might be important to the committee and the reasoning behind the positioning of at least *five* of the stakeholders.

(2) Your son starts senior school next year and you live five miles from the school concerned. There are bus routes to the school that pass close to your house, but require a change at the transport interchange in your town. There is no school bus service per se. Half a mile from your house, on the other side of a major road, there is a tram stop that offers a direct route to the school concerned. Your own route to work passes within a mile and half of the school and would add twenty minutes to your journey in the rush-hour traffic. Your partner also has a car but travels to work in the opposite direction. Several families in your road also have children at the same school, though you are friends with only one of them and they always use public transport for environmental reasons. Formulate the issues facing you in choosing a routing for your child to go to school.

(3) In the following hypothetical scenario, imagine that you are a board member of the confectionary company that produces the chocolate bars concerned.

Two days ago there was an article in the press about a cluster of skin cancers that had been found at an adhesives factory. The adhesive firm is one of your suppliers providing the glue to seal the wrappers of some of your chocolate bars.

The cluster came to light in a general trade union survey of workers' health. The factory was chosen as one of ten from various industries for a ten-year longitudinal study undertaken by a university biostatistics department. The study found that the rate of skin cancer at the factory was significantly raised (p-value 0.015) by a factor of three over normal incidence. The Health and Safety Executive has begun investigations and it is fairly clear that the cause is poor discipline in wearing protective clothing at the plant. The workers seem to have been scrupulous in wearing masks, because they wrongly assumed that the only hazard was the risk from vapours. They have been less careful in wearing gloves all the time, however, and keeping their sleeves rolled down in the hot atmosphere. It is thought that this lack of rigour in the safety culture is the cause.

Yesterday one tabloid newspaper carried an exclusive: 'Choc-Bar Wrappers Cancer Fear!' They have discovered an industrial chemist, Bruce Highman, who used to work at the adhesives factory until a year ago. Dr Highman learnt of the cluster of skin cancers from the press reports the day beforehand. He had been arguing for greater expenditure on safety before he left the firm. Knowing that the adhesives are used in sealing food, including your company's chocolate bars, he is warning of a risk to the public. The carcinogenic power of the adhesive concerned, argues the chemist, is likely to be enhanced in the presence of phenylanaline, which is found in chocolate. Imagine young children licking their chocolate bar with the wrapper rolled down . . . To illustrate the idea the tabloid story had a photo of a cheeky, chubby-faced toddler sucking a well-known chocolate bar.

A lot of public concern has arisen, fanned by a discussion on morning television at which Dr Highman made his claims again. A family doctor, who was doing a medical slot, did argue on air to the chemist that the suggestion was at the very least hypothetical and there was very little likelihood of a risk, and was countered with: 'They said that about mad cow disease.' It should be noted that the chemist's demeanour was calm and persuasive. He did not look like a crank.

Rapid enquiries and calculations, in your company, in industry bodies such as the Food and Drink Federation and at the Department of Health, have discovered the following.

- The carcinogenic risk from exposure to the sort of quantities of adhesive applied to a chocolate bar wrapper is negligible. Over 100,000 wrappers would have to rubbed on a person's arm to create the same exposure as that received by a worker in the adhesives factory.
- The 'phenylanaline' effect of chocolate on the adhesive is thought to be far-fetched, to say the least.
- The chocolate bar used in the newspaper photo does not use the adhesive concerned. Nonetheless, about 40 per cent of the United Kingdom's chocolates and other sweets are wrapped using this adhesive.

Over the past twenty-four hours the media have given a lot of attention to the story. Several eminent food scientists, cancer experts and industrial chemists have been interviewed on radio and TV, and all have discounted any risk to the public.

Unfortunately, late yesterday the media discovered that a further case of skin cancer at the factory had been diagnosed. The person concerned has issued a press release to the effect that the adhesives company had flouted all health and safety regulations in the interests of profit and that he would be taking legal action for compensation. All the morning's press have picked up on this and, although they noted expert opinion that there is no risk to the public, they carried with some emphasis a statement from Dr Highman reasserting his claims.

Use soft modelling techniques to identify key issues, stakeholders, uncertainties and your company's objectives.

(4) A university psychologist has developed a simple algorithm that works with images from a video camera to identify people's emotions. It was developed as part of research into the connection between facial expressions and people's emotions. The research identified a number of simple indicators that discriminate between a wide variety of emotions. It can tell whether a person is cross, happy, distracted, attentive, etc. The algorithm is very quick and works with low-resolution (and hence cheap) video cameras.

You work for a company that develops and markets high-technology items and PC add-ons. You meet the psychologist at a dinner party and learn of the algorithm. You also learn that she has not realised that the algorithm may have any commercial potential. Your instinct is that your company could develop a number of very marketable products from the algorithm. Accordingly, you gather a small group of colleagues to brainstorm possible products before approaching the psychologist formally with a view to exploring a joint venture with the university and her. Identify a number of possible products.

(5) Your company has developed and recently marketed a new toilet cleanser based upon an enzyme component as well as detergents and bleaches. It has been well received in the market place and does produce a genuinely more effective family of lavatory-cleaning and -freshening products.

Three months after its launch, however, several complaints here materialised about a vile smell that occasionally — very occasionally — emanates after WCs have been cleaned with this product. Investigations have shown that this occurs after use of the toilet by a person suffering from epilepsy. It seems that the enzyme reacts with some of the by-products in urine from one of the medications commonly prescribed for epilepsy. In domestic use this is an embarrassment for the user, but a return to normal bleaches solves the problem; and your company has advised this through customer services and a relatively well-handled press release. Unfortunately, the new cleanser has also been marketed very successfully in the industrial cleaner market, and sufferers of epilepsy are being embarrassed in public and workplace conveniences.

In one or two cases patients in family doctors' and hospital outpatient surgeries have been acutely embarrassed, and their lawyers are bringing cases against the doctors and hospital trusts for implicit breach of confidentiality.

What issues would you bring to the management and public relations teams in handling this affair for your company?

Strategic decision analysis

Give no decision till both sides thou'st heard. (Phocylides)

10.1 Introduction

For several chapters we have been discussing the components and context of strategic decision analysis. Our task now is to assemble these into a more complete picture. Even so, we shall take two or three chapters to achieve this. In this chapter we discuss the support of strategic decision making as if there were a single DM. In the next we enlarge the discussion to acknowledge that few major decisions are taken by a single person; they are more often taken by a group. In chapters 12 and 13 we enlarge the discussion to include organisations, societal decisions and democracy.

To recap on our discussion in section 1.2, the context for strategic decisions is that they typically arise in a myriad of unstructured issues and concerns and have impacts that extend long into the future. In terms of the cynefin model, strategic decisions tend to fall into the complex space and, occasionally, the chaotic space. They may require the DMs to face up to many complex uncertainties and address conflicting objectives, and, in doing so, set the framework in which many smaller tactical and operational decisions will be taken. Fortunately, strategy needs to be set relatively infrequently so there is usually time for significant analysis and deliberation before any decision need be made. It is this process of analysis and deliberation that we discuss in this chapter.

We begin with a more detailed discussion of the decision analysis process or cycle. In most strategic decisions experts are called on to give advice. In section 3 we discuss how sensitivity analysis can provide DMs with insights into their problem. We defer discussion of the use of sensitivity analysis in group communication and decision making to later chapters, however. Next we consider how a single DM should incorporate the advice of experts and stakeholders into her deliberation; again, some of this discussion needs to be deferred to later chapters. Decision and risk analyses are natural bedfellows. Some of us see little difference between the disciplines – if either can be considered a true discipline. They do have separate literatures, however, and in section 5 we introduce some of the terminology of risk analysis and reflect on the parallels between the literatures. Finally, in section 6 we conclude with some guidance to the literature.

Our objectives in this chapter are:

- to emphasise that the role of decision analysis is to build understanding, and that it is through this understanding that the decision is taken;
- to demonstrate the interplay between our knowledge of human judgement obtained through behavioural studies and the imperatives of normative decision theory in providing prescriptive decision support;
- to consider how advice from experts and stakeholders may be incorporated into a decision analysis; and
- to reflect on the similarities and differences between decision and risk analyses.

10.2 The decision analysis cycle

Analysis:

1. Create questions.
2. Question questions.
3. Answer questions.
4. Question answers.

(Alistair Carruthers)

In chapter 3 we introduced the general decision analysis process and suggested that it cycled through three phases (figure 3.6):

- problem formulation;
- evaluation of options; and
- appraisal of the recommendation.

Figure 10.1 expands on this outline, indicating some of the activities in each phase. Analysis is seldom purely cyclic. Rather, it moves backwards and forwards between phases. The predominant direction is clockwise, but with many short reversals. The process finishes when the DMs are comfortable with their conclusions – i.e. when they feel that the analysis is *requisite*. We do not claim that our representation of the decision analysis cycle is unique or, indeed, universally accepted. All authors have their own representation, expressed in their own words. In presenting the OR process in section 6.5 we set the cycle in terminology more commonly found in the

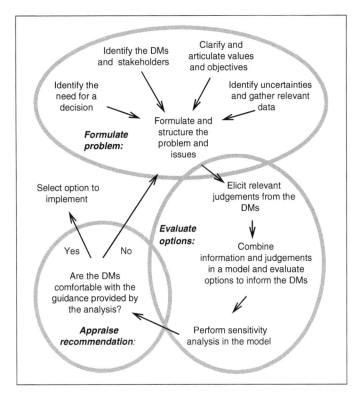

Figure 10.1   Overview of the decision process

OR literature, yet the underlying themes and ideas there are entirely compatible with those we explore here.

Problem formulation

Decision problems seldom arrive fully formulated with a clear set of options and objectives. More often, the DM becomes aware of a set of issues that need to be addressed. Even the issues rarely arrive together; instead, an awareness gradually builds up over a period of time. Eventually, however, that awareness builds to such a level that the DM asks: 'Do I need to take some sort of action here?' The DM moves from a process of unconflicted adherence or unconflicted change to one of vigilant decision making (figure 4.3), and decision analysis begins.

Before any quantitative analysis can begin – indeed, before the problem can be formulated – there is a need to gather data and other material to turn the growing awareness of issues needing to be faced into something more concrete. Lewis (1991) describes this phase as an *intelligence activity*, in which the DM and her team survey 'the economic, technical, political and social environment to identify new conditions which call for new actions' (cf. PESTEL). Business intelligence and EIS tools may well be catalytic here, identifying issues that need be addressed. Once the DM has recognised the need for a decision (and, again, in Lewis's words) she and her team 'invent, design and develop possible courses of action for handling [the] situation'.

Methods of information gathering vary from context to context. There is likely to be a variety of divergent brainstorming sessions during which the bounds of the problem will be explored. Some such sessions may be formal meetings with a facilitator structuring the discussion, but the informal thinking should not be discounted: discussions over cups of coffee or on an organisation's discussion forum, reading reports of related projects and quiet periods of doodling all have a part to play. The soft modelling techniques discussed in chapter 9 are clearly relevant here. Experts may be interviewed or asked for brief reports or reflections on past cases relating to similar issues. Sometimes the interactions with experts might be very formalised; we indicate some methodologies for this in section 4.

Two points should be borne in mind. First, in the very first cycle of a decision analysis, the data and information gathering may be very superficial. Only in later cycles, when models have some substantive structure and much thinking has gone into their construction, will the questions be sufficiently clear that they may be answered with some assurance. Second, as we noted in section 3.5, Keeney (1992) has argued that that the DM should adopt *value-focused thinking*: namely 'first deciding on what you want and then figuring out how to get it'. Thus at an early stage in any decision analysis – long before one starts to identify alternatives – the analyst should work with the DM to explore her values. We do not pretend that value-focused thinking is easy to adopt. There are times when one is presented with a set of alternatives and the DM simply has to choose. In such circumstances the analysis is necessarily led to consider the alternatives first, although we would argue that the question 'What is the DM trying to achieve?' should be addressed as soon as possible.

As we have noted, problem formulation is more an art than a science. There are guidelines that can help construct workmanlike analyses; we introduced many of these in the previous chapter. Sensitivity analysis on simple preliminary models can identify key variables and help refine models: see section 3. Ultimately, however, the most professional analysts draw upon a mix of experience and flair. They need to work with the DM and her team to discover what uncertainties and value judgements will be significant in discriminating between alternative strategies. We emphasise again that it helps to begin by reflecting on the objectives of the decision making. Not only will that help to ensure that preferences are modelled well in the analysis, but it may also help decide on the form of quantitative model needed. If minimising risk is an important objective and several uncertainties are involved, the modelling will usually take the form of a decision tree or influence diagram – or preferably both: analyses gain considerable depth when they are based upon a family of models capturing several complementary perspectives on a problem. Surprisingly, perhaps, in many strategic decisions uncertainties are not the dominant issue; the task is much more about resolving conflicting objectives and setting a strategic direction. In such cases MAVA may be the most appropriate approach.

Whatever the case, the initial model should *not* be over-complex. The art of requisite decision modelling is to begin with a simple model and add complexity as necessary in later cycles of the decision analytic process.

Evaluate alternatives

Once the structure of the model has been developed, the next step is to populate it with numbers. Some will come from data gathered earlier; others will need to be elicited from experts, stakeholders or, of course, the DM herself. In chapters 7 and 8 we indicated, albeit with some simplification, how uncertainty and preference judgements might be elicited. Once the models have been developed and numerical inputs determined, the DA can 'run the analyses', which today usually involves little more than clicking a 'button' in a software package. We emphasise the value of exploring a *series* of models. By looking at a series rather than one complex, all-inclusive model, one can better see the importance of each issue. What does including this or that particular effect do to the analysis?

The exploratory process should also be supported by *sensitivity analyses*. Sensitivity analyses can focus attention on those issues that are key – i.e. that have a significant effect in determining the guidance offered by the analysis. Exploring the sensitivity of the output to different judgemental inputs can identify which ones matter and which have little effect. Sometimes the conclusions of the analysis are unchanged by quite gross changes in inputs, reassuring the DM that any concerns she had about the precise values are unnecessary. We saw one example of this sort of reassurance in the sensitivity of the weight on *resources* in the Chernobyl case study (section 7.8). Of course, there will be judgements that are significant in that small changes may lead to substantially different conclusions. Sensitivity techniques draw the DM's attention to these and focus her efforts on these judgements, the ones that matter. We explore many further roles for sensitivity analysis in the next section.

Review decision models

Decision analyses guide the evolution of the DM's, analyst's and others' perceptions. During an analysis everybody's perceptions evolve – or, at least, have the potential to do so. Their perceptions evolve because of the analysis: indeed, it is the purpose of the analysis that they should. In many cases the analysis helps the DM *construct* her beliefs and preferences (Slovic, 1995). Therefore it is vital to see the modelling process involved in representing their perceptions as creative, dynamic and cyclic, each cycle bringing insight (Phillips, 1984). Eventually, further cycles of analysis provide little more insight, and the DM will have sufficient understanding to make the decision. We have referred to this process as *requisite modelling*, the final model being requisite or sufficient for the decision faced.

Being aware that one needs more analysis is relatively straightforward; but knowing when to stop is harder. Inevitably, the rather vague 'termination condition' of requisite modelling annoys those schooled in the hard sciences. How does one know when there are no new insights to be had? How can it be known for sure that one further round of modelling will not uncover a major new insight? What is an insight, anyway, and what makes an insight significant in terms of keeping the analysis going? These are not easy questions to answer – and certainly they are impossible to answer in any manner that leads to a clear-cut, unambiguous test of when to end an analysis. It is a matter of skill and judgement on the part of the DA and agreement on the part of the DM. That said, we have never been involved in a decision analysis during which it was not clear that the time had come to finish modelling and decide. There are several possible indicators:

- the DM, experts and the analysts cannot find any significant assumption to doubt;
- sensitivity analyses show that the indicated choice is robust to reasonable variations in the inputs;

- everyone concerned is comfortable with the analysis and the DM feels that she has sufficient understanding to decide; or
- the time is up: external factors may demand that a decision *is* made.

In the end the DM needs to accept any remaining uncertainty: based on her current understanding, she simply has to choose and implement a course of action.

10.3 Sensitivity analysis

Uncertainty is the space in which debate takes place. (Andrea Saltelli)

In all quantitative procedures, it is a truism that the output depends upon the input. The significance of this dependence varies from input to input. Moreover, one is generally more confident in some inputs than in others. Thus a wise analyst varies inputs and observes the effect on the outputs: he performs a *sensitivity analysis*. Doing so advances his understanding and that of his client. We noted above that sensitivity analysis has important roles in the process of prescriptive decision analysis.

There are two ways that the inputs may be varied.

- Deterministic variation. In many cases the DA has elicited quantities from the DMs or experts. They may have been able to give him bounds upon these elicited values but little more guidance about their uncertainty. He can then use these bounds to conduct deterministic calculations to investigate the range of outputs that might arise. This is an archetypal example of sensitivity analysis. We have seen examples of such calculations in figures 7.10, 7.15 and 8.13; see also French (1992) for a description of an extended sensitivity analysis of the airliner example.
- Stochastic variation. Here the analyst's confidence in an input value – i.e. data point or parameter – can be encoded by means of a probability distribution. In this case the inputs are varied stochastically in *Monte Carlo* analyses and the resulting distribution of the outputs studied (see, for example, Kurowicka and Cooke, 2006, and Saltelli *et al.*, 2000).

Within decision support, the circumstances for stochastic sensitivity analyses tend to arise in relation to inputs related to physical models, whereas those for deterministic sensitivity analyses tend to arise in relation to judgemental inputs such as preference weights or subjective probabilities. The reason for this is simple. If the DA asks the DM or an expert to capture her confidence in a judgement by means of a subjective – i.e.

a *judgemental* – probability distribution, he enters an infinite regress of eliciting judgemental uncertainty in judgemental uncertainty in judgemental uncertainty …

The remark by Saltelli that opened this section is telling. For us, sensitivity analysis drives the deliberation and debate that underpins decision making. It explores all the uncertainties, allowing the DM to see where the balance of her judgements lies. When we consider groups of DMs in later chapters, we see that sensitivity analysis allows one to explore differences of opinion, usually building consensus, but at worst delimiting disagreement. Danielson *et al.* (2007b) describe three case studies that emphasise the power of sensitivity analysis in articulating the essence of agreements and disagreements in complex situations.

French (2003b) argues that sensitivity techniques support a decision analysis helping the analyst, experts and DM in eight ways.

A *Exploration of consequence models.* In many analyses the consequence models can be very complex, and even the experts may not fully understand their mathematical properties and shape. Varying the inputs and observing the response of the outputs can be very informative in understanding the models mathematically and conceptually.

B *Exploration of the relationship between science and the consequence models.* We have noted (section 7.3) that the consequence models are intended to encode the experts' and DMs' relevant knowledge of the external world. Often the models are built or modified for the specific decision context. There may be a need, therefore, to check that they are valid representation of their knowledge; and there is certainly a need to explore and understand the implications of that knowledge for the decision. Sensitivity analysis can help considerably in both these tasks.

C *Support of the elicitation of judgemental inputs.* Judgemental inputs are necessarily limited in precision. Thus there is considerable potential for the output of the analysis to be ill-determined. The DA, DMs and others need to be sure that the advice provided by the analysis is not determined purely by spurious accuracy on the part of the inputs. Moreover, the time and effort required of experts, who often charge expensive fees, need to be used wisely and effectively. Sensitivity analysis can provide a means of focusing elicitation on the judgemental inputs that matter. For the analyst, sensitivity analysis provides the means of planning the elicitation process. For the DMs, experts and stakeholders, the key benefit of sensitivity analysis is reassurance.

D *Development of efficient computational algorithms.* Despite the advent
   of modern computational power, many decision models, particularly
   in the environmental and engineering arenas, are very, very complex.
   Simply calculating the output for one set of inputs can take many
   hours, and therefore there is a need to build efficient approximations.
   Sensitivity analysis can identify the key variation implicit in the model
   and thus provide important information for this approximation
   process.

E *Design of surveys and experiments to gather relevant data.* Figure 4.5
   indicates how statistical analysis fits into decision analysis, assimilating data to reduce uncertainty. A significant task, but one often
   overlooked by non-statisticians, is designing surveys and experiments
   to collect data. *Experimental design* concerns the choice of the most
   informative points at which to collect data: ones that have the greatest
   potential for reducing the uncertainty. It does this by seeking the
   outputs that are most sensitive to the inputs. In short, sensitivity
   analysis can inform the data collection process.

F *Guidance for inferences, forecasts and decisions.* Many DAs see this as
   the 'true' role of sensitivity analysis. It allows investigation of the
   stability of the model's suggested inference, forecast or decision to
   reasonable input variations. The more stable the output the more
   confidence DMs can have in its guidance.

G *Communication and consensus building.* Sensitivity analysis can help a
   decision-making group reach a mutual understanding of each other's
   position. It can help each member see how far from his or her own
   position others' beliefs and preferences are. Moreover, it can eliminate from debate, often heated debate, those disagreements that have
   no effect on the conclusion by focusing discussion on the differences
   of opinion that matter in terms of the alternative chosen. We discuss
   this further in the following chapters, and see that sensitivity analysis
   provides a medium in which to debate many of the judgements and
   intangibles that enter into group and societal decision making.

H *Development of understanding.* Analyses should not just give a 'number':
   they should inform and bring understanding. Constructing and running
   a model on just one set of inputs brings little understanding. Running
   that model on a range of inputs provides much more information. Case
   studies such as the Chernobyl study (section 7.8), the chemical scrubbers study (section 8.8) and those in Gottlieb and Pauker (1981) and
   Phillips (1982) show how sensitivity analysis can help to build qualitative understanding among DMs. Fundamentally, all the purposes

Table 10.1 The support offered by sensitivity analysis to the different players

	A	B	C	D	E	F	G	H
	Explore models	Explore science	Support elicitation	Design algorithms	Design experiments	Guide inferences, forecasts, decisions	Build consensus	Build understanding
DM		U	**R**			**R**	C	U
Stakeholder		U	R				C	U
Expert	U	U	**R**	U	U		C	U
Analyst	**U**	U	U	U	U	U	U	U

Notes: **Bold** – primary; normal – secondary. U – understanding; C – communication; R – reassurance.
Source: French (2003b).

that we have ascribed to sensitivity analysis are about building understanding in one form or another. If we accept that then we should realise that the development of effective sensitivity analysis requires not just mathematical and analytical skills; it also requires an understanding of the different cognitive abilities of the players so that the results may be conveyed effectively.

While an analyst needs to understand fully the mathematical underpinnings of sensitivity analysis, there is often no need for the DMs or stakeholders, or even the technical experts, to do so. For them, it is sufficient that they understand the broad principles on which the analysis is based and the specific guidance that it provides. There is no need for them to have a sophisticated 'feel' for numerical analyses. Table 10.1 indicates the support offered to the players in terms of bringing understanding and reassurance and in facilitating communication.

10.4 Incorporation of expert and stakeholder opinions

Even when the experts all agree, they may well be mistaken. (Bertrand Russell)

Although we are still focused on the case of a single DM, we should recognise that she will need to interact with experts and stakeholders. In this section we discuss issues relating to the incorporation of expert and stakeholder judgements into her analysis. Remember: experts provide advice on what might happen, and so inform the DM's consequence modelling and subjective probabilities; stakeholders share in the impacts of the decision, and so their preferences may inform the DM's thinking and be incorporated in some way into her value or utility function.

We begin with a discussion of the *expert problem* (French, 1985). In this, a group of experts is asked for advice by a DM, who faces a real, predefined decision problem. The DM is, or can be taken to be, outside the group. Conceptually, it is she alone that has the task of assimilating and aggregating their judgements; therefore, in any decision analysis, it is her subjective probabilities that should be used. How should she form these from the judgements offered by the experts, however? The group of experts may interact together or individually with the DM. For instance, a seriously ill individual may consult several doctors for their assessments of the expected course of her disease. Sometimes a case conference between all the doctors may be held; at other times the DM may simply consult each in turn privately. Whatever the interaction, we assume that the experts articulate their forecasts of future events as probabilities.

If the DM is to assimilate and use a number of probabilities from different individual experts, there is a need, first, to bring all their judgements to the same frame of reference. Experts are human and therefore subject to all the behavioural biases discussed in chapter 2. Thus the DM and her analyst need to calibrate and de-bias each expert's probabilities before they can safely be used. Second, once they have been calibrated, there is a need to combine them into a single probability or probability distribution that can be used in a decision analysis.

There are two quantities that reflect the quality of an expert's forecasts:[1] *calibration* and *refinement*. Suppose that an expert assesses the probability of a number of events. Gather together all the events for which his estimate was, say, 40 per cent. Now look at the occurrence of these events. If the person is well calibrated with reality, one would expect that about 40 per cent of the events would actually happen. Similarly, of those events to which he ascribed a probability of occurrence of 70 per cent, one would expect 70 per cent to occur. As indicated in section 2.6, however, this is not usually the case. Figure 10.2 sketches a typical example of a *calibration curve*. This is a plot of the frequency with which an event occurs against the probability ascribed to it by the expert. Perfect calibration gives the 45° line. When confronted by difficult questions most people depart from this, as illustrated in the sketch. They tend to be overconfident and

---

[1] Of course, one can discuss the calibration and refinement of anyone, expert or not. For reasons of context, here we refer to the person concerned as an expert.

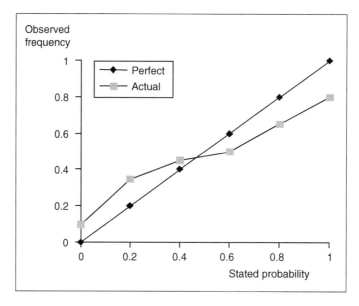

Figure 10.2   A hypothetical calibration curve

ascribe higher probabilities of being correct than justified by their actual performance and show the reverse effect for low probabilities. Of particular importance is the 100 per cent assessment, when people indicate that they are certain they are correct. Findings indicate that, in reality, people are correct on about 85 per cent of these occasions!

When people are certain they are likely to be particularly vulnerable to the negative effects of overconfidence, since they see no need to check the facts or build in any contingency to take account of uncertainty (after all, they are right!). This is nicely summarised in a quote from Will Rogers: 'It's not what we don't know that gives us trouble, it's what we know that ain't so.' When confronted by easy questions, however, the situation reverses and people tend to be underconfident. Thus the difficulty of the situation (e.g. forecasting movements on the London Stock Exchange as compared to forecasting tomorrow's weather) may be critical in determining the nature of this judgemental bias. These effects can also be shown in expert judgement, both in the laboratory (Ayton, 1998) and professional contexts (Goossens and Kelly, 2000), though there is some evidence to suggest that calibration is improved in situations in which experts receive regular feedback on the accuracy of their judgements – e.g. weather forecasters (Murphy and Winkler, 1984) and bridge players (Keren, 1987). For reviews of this work, see Griffin and Brenner (2004) and Lichtenstein *et al.* (1982). Overall, it suggests that we need to be sceptical of our own judgements and those provided by experts, and further supports the need for sensitivity testing.

To understand refinement, sometimes called informativeness, consider an example. Suppose that, for a year, two forecasters are asked to give their probabilities for rain on the next day. Over the year it rains on 40 per cent of the days – i.e. the base rate of rain is 40 per cent. At the end of the year it transpires that one forecaster gave his probability as 40 per cent on each and every day. The other gave probabilities of 0 per cent and 100 per cent, and perfectly forecast the rainy days. Both are well calibrated; but the second forecaster is the more informative. The information that he gave would help listeners discriminate between wet and dry days in advance and thereby help them to make accurate decisions about whether to take an umbrella, go for a picnic or just stay indoors. Obviously, this example points to two extremes of informativeness. There is a continuum of intermediate possibilities.

Many approaches to the expert problem have been developed. Cooke (1991) has developed a particularly straightforward approach, which has received much practical application (Cooke, 2007; Goossens and Kelly, 2000). Essentially, the DA, on behalf of the DM, asks the experts both to give their judgements of uncertainty on the quantities of interest to the DM in her analysis and also their judgements of uncertainty relating to quantities in a *calibration set* of *seed variables*. The analyst is expected to know the actual values of these seed variables, but the experts are not. By comparing the experts' judgements of uncertainty on these seed variables with the actual values, the DA can assess the quality of the experts, giving them scores relating both to their calibration and refinement. He then weights the experts' judgements together using a formula that gives higher weight to better calibration and refinement: for details, see Cooke (1991) and French and Ríos Insua (2000).

The choice of quantities to include in the calibration set is far from easy. Behavioural studies have shown that an individual's ability to encode judgements in probabilistic terms varies according to his or her expertise in that domain. Typically, but far from universally, individuals become better at encoding their uncertainties the more feedback they have had on similar judgements in the past (Cooke, 1991; Lichtenstein *et al.*, 1982; Suantak *et al.*, 1996). This means that they are better at encoding uncertainty in their domain of expertise, because they receive more feedback in areas in which they work regularly. The calibration set therefore has to be chosen to reflect the domain that covers the variables that are important in the real problem. Unfortunately, one tends to call in experts for advice on uncertainty in an analysis in precisely those areas in which there are few past data; otherwise, one would analyse those data statistically and thus construct more 'objective' assessments of the uncertainty. Nonetheless, with care and some subtlety, experience has shown that Cooke's method is applicable (Goossens and Kelly, 2000).

Cooke's method is advanced in that it is one of the few to try and include calibration and refinement in weighting the experts' judgements together. He then suggests combining these weighted judgements in a simple additive form: a *linear opinion pool*. Other methods are available, however, that vary in the complexity of the methods used: see Clemen and Winkler (1999), French (1985) and French and Ríos Insua (2000), for reviews of the advantages and disadvantages of these.

All the approaches outlined above assume that expert judgements should be aggregated by means of a mathematical algorithm of some form. Why? Why not document each expert's estimates and their basis in such detail that the DM can make an informed decision on how to combine the judgements? One reason is that the DM is unlikely to have the necessary skills across all the domains of expertise underpinning a complex analysis to understand the basis of the experts' judgements. In practice the analyst (s) would make the combination.

Equally, one could gather the experts together and let them come to some consensus agreement about the numbers to put into the models. Such behavioural aggregation is commonly used – e.g. the Delphi Technique (section 11.4) – and can be undertaken in group decision support environments (Cooke, 1991; Linstone and Turoff, 1978; Marakas, 2003; Rowe and Wright, 1999). There are many pros and cons to be balanced in choosing between mathematical and behavioural aggregation. Behavioural aggregation can be subject to many group dysfunctional behaviours: see section 11.2. On the other hand, behavioural aggregation can build commitment to the eventual decision and, hence, encourage effective implementation. If decision making within an organisation is the prime objective of the process, this can be a powerful argument in its favour. For a planning or a regulatory decision with a wide variety of stakeholders, mathematical aggregation can be an advantage, both because it is explicit, auditable and, in a sense, objective and also because it leaves all opinions and eventualities in the analysis. Behavioural aggregation can win people over, and thus concerns about hazards held by a small minority of the group of experts may be lost in building a common group view.

There is, of course, the question of whether a group can perform better than its best-performing member. Is there evidence to support this? In behavioural methods, the results are inconclusive. Reagan-Cirincione (1994) reports an experiment in which facilitated groups generally out-performed their best members in forecasting tasks, but also summarises a literature in which the reverse finding seems to be true. An earlier survey of the literature is provided by Hastie (1986). Amongst the mathematical approaches there is evidence that an aggregate forecast can outperform the best component forecast (Cooke, 1991; Wiper and French, 1995). See also section 11.2 for a further discussion of group effectiveness.

In our statement of the expert problem, we have assumed that the experts contribute their advice in the form of probability judgements. Of course, they also contribute their knowledge in advice about the form of the con-sequence models that should be used; and these encode many judgements not of uncertainty but of complete certainty – e.g. that two variables are not related. The DM and her analyst would be well advised to remember that experts are susceptible to overconfidence. Therefore, they should check and perhaps soften the assumptions in the models accordingly. This is much easier to say than to undertake; nonetheless, this point should be addressed in drawing out the main conclusions of the decision analysis.

Turning from uncertainties to value judgements, how should the DM include the views of stakeholders? We discuss this a great deal further in chapter 13; here, however, we note the concept of a *supra decision maker* discussed by Keeney and Raiffa (1976). They were concerned with addressing particular paradoxes in group decision making and suggested constructing an imaginary altruistic DM who simply brought together the value judgements of the DMs and stakeholders. She would have to have the judgement of Solomon, perhaps; but the idea was that attributes on which her value or utility function was constructed would be their preferences. In this chapter we are considering a real DM with sole responsibility and accountability for the decision, but the same idea can be brought into play. The DM can structure her value or utility function so that some or all of the attributes represent the preferences of key stakeholders. The weights would then model the influence that she wishes to give each of them. The literature on supra decision makers suggests many functional forms that may be appropriate, should she do this. There are warnings from the behavioural literature, however, that people find difficulty in making altruistic, empathetic judgements (Faro and Rottenstreich, 2006).

Alternatively, she may take a more informal approach. In the problem formulation stage, particularly in the stakeholder analysis, she should ensure that she builds an attribute tree that includes all the attributes of importance to her stakeholders. Then, through sensitivity analysis, she can investigate how different weightings would affect the decision, and thus understand how far her judgements are from those she perceives of her stakeholders. She can then choose in the light of this and other understandings that evolve during the analysis (see Ackermann and Eden, 2003, and Bryson, 2004).

10.5 Risk analysis

Take calculated risks. That is quite different from being rash. (George S. Patton)

The word 'risk' is part of everybody's vocabulary and currently a buzzword across much of society; it is doubtful, however, whether many really have a clear understanding of the term when they use it. Rather, the word evokes multifaceted impressions of potential events that have unwanted consequences (Adams, 1995; Beck, 1992; Gigerenzer, 2002; Mumford, 1996; Mythen, 2004). Risk analysis and management have become central to organisational and societal processes and have a large and growing literature (Aven, 2003; Bedford and Cooke, 2001; Tapiero, 2004). Our interest arises because there is very little difference between the foundations and practice of risk analysis and those of decision analysis. In figure 10.3 we outline a common presentation of the risk management process. As an aside, it is interesting to compare this with the OR process (figure 6.2) and the decision analytic process (figure 10.1): clearly, but not unsurprisingly, there are many parallels.

The *risk identification* stage concerns identifying risks that threaten a project or strategy. Some estimates suggest that 60 per cent of project failures occur through unforeseen risks, due in part to an overreliance on inside rather than outside thinking (see section 2.9). There is no procedure that is certain to identify all potential risks; but the use of many brainstorming, catalytic and soft modelling methods, such as those discussed in chapter 9 can help identify risks (Horlick-Jones *et al.*, 2001). A very common failing in risk analysis is to ignore correlations and probabilistic dependencies between events. Trivially, if failures in software development or poor labour relations are significant risks of delay on one activity, then they may well be significant risks on others; and the occurrence of a delay through such a cause on one activity will indicate an increased risk on others.

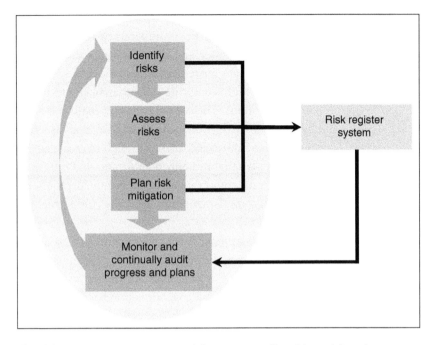

Figure 10.3   The risk management process and the support offered by a risk register

Risk assessment is the process of quantifying the chance of the ultimate consequences, and also the reduction that might be brought by various management strategies. Some of the probabilities will be derived using statistical methods from empirical data, but some will rely on professional judgement based upon experience of similar risks. *Risk analysis* is intended to support the process of balancing the probabilities of the consequences with their (dis)utility in the light of more general uncertainties and unknowns.

Risk mitigation is the implementation of strategies aimed at reducing the identified risks. Developing risk mitigation strategies requires exactly the same qualities of creativity and value-focused thinking that we have been promoting in all our discussion of decision analysis in the strategic and corporate domains. At this stage there is a need to decide upon which risk mitigation strategies to adopt and implement. In the spirit of our approach to decision making under risk, we favour analyses based upon SEU approaches. Again, we do not expect the analysis to be a single-pass calculation in which alternative risk mitigation strategies are ranked. Rather, we expect that the balance of uncertainty and impact will be explored through sensitivity analyses and more qualitative considerations, informing the selection of strategies in a requisite fashion.

A *risk register* is a database that contains information on the identified risks, the strategies being undertaken to mitigate them and the person assigned to monitor and react to events should the risk materialise. The best systems are more than simple databases, monitoring progress much like an EIS and prompting the risk manager to perform scheduled checks and evaluations. The concept of a risk register is something that might be widely emulated within general decision analysis. Often decisions are taken without an immediate follow-through to create an implementation plan – that is, a plan that not only documents what is to be done but also conveys the motivation and reasoning behind the decision, as well as the potential risks to its implementation and how these might be managed (Borges *et al.*, 2005, 2006).

Risk management is the entire process of reducing risks through risk identification and assessment, the appropriate targeting of resources, the maintenance of a risk register, the monitoring of progress and the implementing of risk reduction strategies. It is vital that the latter phases of risk management are not seen as simply the process of implementing a risk mitigation strategy. Risk management must be reflective, always scanning the horizon for unanticipated hazards as well as controlling and avoiding those that have been anticipated. The risk manager should not identify and analyse risk only at the outset of the project and then adopt a management plan without further review. Throughout a project's life he or she should continually scan the horizon for new risks, monitoring whether those already perceived have come to pass and the success of plans to mitigate their consequences should they have done so. There should be a continual audit of the predictions against outcomes to help calibrate the prediction process and learn from experience. For instance, risk management is often based upon expert judgement of three quantiles – say, the 5 per cent, 50 per cent and 95 per cent – of some uncertainties, such as the time to completion of a task within a project. As soon as the outcome is known, the actual quantity should be compared against the quantiles of the prediction. Should a manager continually find, for example, that the outcome exceeds the 95 per cent quantile, his or her experts and management process are hopelessly optimistic, and the forecasting methods need to be revised (remember that in the previous section we showed that expert judgement was better calibrated with feedback).

Case vignette 10.1 describes how an oil company selected potential R&D projects to fund. What should be clear is that balancing the risks with the benefits of success of the different projects could be described as a decision

Case vignette 10.1 Support for the process of selecting R&D projects in an oil company

The R&D division of an oil company wanted to identify and choose between potential research projects in which to invest its limited R&D funds. Anyone in the company with a potential idea that could be developed into a new or improved product would e-mail the system with an outline of the idea. After an initial stage to filter out clear non-runners, the head of R&D would appoint a 'champion' from the R&D group to work up the idea into an implementable development project. He would prepare a report with costings, the resources required, time scales and assessments against a previously agreed attribute hierarchy. He would also assess the risks to the development and outline a project with a clear set of stage gates ('break points').

The reports would be circulated to the R&D management group, and at the same time details of the project would be input into a resource allocation decision model, which provided an evaluation of the project using MAVA subject to resource constraints. Every three months or so the decision model would be used to build portfolios of promising R&D projects that fitted into the available resources across the division. The system would then assemble an implementation schedule and risk register for the chosen projects and distribute these to the R&D teams. The whole process was implemented and monitored through the Lotus Notes collaborative suite. The management group seldom met formally but made their decisions through the system. Data, reports, etc. were passed seamlessly between the team members automatically, as well as being archived into a knowledge base.

problem or a risk assessment. Note also that the system created a risk register to manage each select R&D project.

10.6 Concluding remarks and further reading

Referring back to figure 3.7, remember that we have been discussing decision analysis and support for the corporate strategic domain, in which the key characteristic is that DMs face unstructured complex issues. There are many texts that discuss the process of decision analysis in this context: e.g. Belton and Stewart (2002), Goodwin and Wright (2003), Kleindorfer *et al.* (1993) and Watson and Buede (1987). We would also refer to the discussions in Henig and Buchanan (1996), Lovallo and Sibony (2006), Phillips (1984) and Wright and Goodwin (1999b).

Yim *et al.* (2004) consider the strategic decision-making process and the support that knowledge management and KB-DSSs can provide. There are many software packages designed to support the strategic decision-making process that provide soft modelling support, implement multi-attribute value analysis and produce decision trees and influence diagrams. Regular surveys are provided by the biennial reviews in *OR/MS Today* (Maxwell, 2002, 2004, 2006). The typical simplicity of the models used to elucidate complex issues is often questioned, but is confirmed by the survey undertaken by Corner and Corner (1995). Moreover, the principles of requisite modelling suggest that models will need to be simple if they are to focus on the key understandings necessary to take a decision.

General discussions of sensitivity analysis may be found in Belton and Stewart (2002), French (1995b, 2003b), Ríos Insua (1990; 1999) and Saltelli *et al.* (2000, 2004). A general framework for sensitivity analysis in decision analysis has been proposed by Ríos Insua and French (1991). French (1992) provides a simple application of this framework to the airliner example. There are many different sensitivity techniques and plots that may be used in decision analysis (Belton, 1985; Danielson *et al.*, 2007b; Felli and Hazen, 2004; Hodgkin *et al.*, 2002; Jiménez *et al.*, 2006; Mateos *et al.*, 2003, 2007). We have used the term *sensitivity analysis*; others discuss the same or similar topics under the heading *uncertainty analysis* (Bedford and Cooke, 2001; O'Hagan *et al.*, 1998) or *robustness analysis* (Ríos Insua and Ruggeri, 2000).

There is a large literature on the use of expert judgement, much developed in the context of risk analysis: Bedford and Cooke (2001), Clemen and Winkler (1999), Cooke (1991), French (1985), French and Ríos Insua (2000), Garthwaite *et al.* (2005), Genest and Zidek (1986) and Goossens and Kelly (2000). Mumpower and Stewart (1996) offer a discussion of the reasons behind differences of opinion between experts. A key issue in the incorporation of expert advice into the analysis is the perspective taken on the judgements provided by the experts. Some argue that the experts provide probabilities and thus see their task as providing some sort of average probability derived from the set of elicited judgements. Typically this leads to an approach known as opinion pooling. Alternatively, the experts' judgements can be seen as data that the DM needs to analyse. This typically leads to more Bayesian approaches that seek to update the DM's beliefs in the light of expert opinions. Finally, there is some recent behavioural research on advice taking (Harries and Harvey, 2000).

Risk analysis and management currently constitute a very active area. Stimulated by many societal and corporate failures, most governments have changed the regimes of regulation and governance in both the private and public sectors to ensure that formal comprehensive risk assessments are undertaken before any major commitments are made. Risks need to be assessed in annual company accounts. Aven (2003) and Bedford and

Cooke (2001) provide general introductions to the area, while Tapiero (2004) surveys the area of financial risk management. Covello (1987) provided an early discussion of the links between decision and risk analysis. Griffiths and Newman (1996) provide survey of risk management issues in software development projects. McDaniels and Small (2004) provide an overview of societal risk analysis, a topic that we turn to in chapter 13.

10.7 Exercises and questions for discussion

(1) Compare the decision analysis process with the OR process discussed in section 6.5. Now conduct a short literature review of information systems design processes. How do these compare with the decision analysis and OR processes?

(2) How is the concept of uncertainty used in decision analysis and decision support? When should uncertainty be modelled and analysed and when should it be explored by sensitivity analysis?

(3) How has the discipline of artificial intelligence approached the subject of uncertainty? Are its methods compatible with those used in the decision support literature?

(4) Investigate the functionality of risk register software by exploring software websites. How might such functionality be built into and benefit more general DSS software?

(5) Explain sensitivity analysis and discuss its benefits.

(6) Discuss the phases of the decision analysis cycle – namely problem formulation, the evaluation of alternatives and the appraisal of decision models. Consider a consultancy company that explores whether to open a branch in Asia and list activities that may be undertaken in each phase – i.e. formulation, evaluation and appraisal.

(7) Outline the stages of a risk management process and discuss what risk management activities may be undertaken in the R&D depertment of a large organisaition.

(8) The senior management team of a pharmaceutical company is debating the funding of a new project that may lead to the production of a new drug. The managers are very keen to explore risk management issues. Design the analysis process they should follow and provide a diagram to illustrate your answer. How can they involve experts and stakeholders to inform their decision making? Provide a list of recommendations.

Groups of decision makers

Why do we get so hung up on what we don't agree on, when in fact it's our differences that make life interesting? (Bradley Trevor Grieve)

11.1 Introduction

While we have concentrated on decision making by a single DM, most decisions, at least in organisations and society, are the responsibility of groups rather than individuals. How do the ideas that we have been developing generalise to the context of groups of DMs? Why are groups often preferred to individuals? Do groups always make better decisions? These are important questions, and they are addressed in this chapter.

There is a generally held belief that groups make better decisions than single individuals working alone. This belief has led many to advocate that important decisions should be deferred to groups – e.g. decisions about innocence or guilt made by juries, decisions about national policy made by Cabinets and decisions about corporate strategy made by boards of directors. Among the many reasons why groups might outperform single individuals, four of the more important are that they:

- have a greater amount of knowledge, intelligence and understanding of the problem than any single individual;
- increase members' motivation to work hard and remain task-centred, since their performance is open to the scrutiny of other members of the group;
- facilitate creativity, in that people can often 'spark' off each other and develop new ideas better in group contexts; and
- increase the watchfulness to error and the resolution of ambiguity, given that ideas and assumptions are stated publicly for other members of the group to evaluate, review and challenge when appropriate.

While each of these can lead groups to making better decisions than individuals, there is evidence that these potential advantages are not always realised. For example, Janis (1972) identified a series of high-profile examples in which groups made spectacularly bad decisions – e.g.

the decision by President Johnson and his close advisers to escalate the Vietnam War. This suggests that groups are as much in need of decision support as individuals. Many of the theories we have discussed so far, however, are focused on individual DMs. The SEU model, in particular, is built upon a conception of the beliefs and preferences of a 'rational' individual. Can it be generalised to group decision-making contexts? Unfortunately, no: there have been many explorations of the mathematics of group consensus probability and utility functions, and all have discovered that any formalism for building a single model of group preference is subject to irrational or undemocratic behaviours. Impossibility theorems abound, suggesting that the endeavour is ill-formulated mathematically. A classic impossibility theorem derived by Arrow (section 3) suggests not only that it is impossible to extend SEU to group decision making but that the very idea of democracy may be an ill-defined concept. If this is so, and if most decisions have to be made by groups, why have we been studying the normative formalisms of the previous chapters? How can they help in the majority of real circumstances?

The trick to 'squaring this circle' is to change our perspective and to recognise that group decisions are underpinned by individuals and social processes that translate the judgements and preferences of members into implemented courses of action. This perspective does not contradict the assignment of accountability, authority and responsibility to a group. Groups can have duties and powers. Understanding and facilitating these individual and social processes provides the key to improving group decision making, however. In section 4 we discuss some techniques in this respect, then in section 5 we look at facilitated workshops and decision conferences that bring many of these techniques together into a common framework, often supported by decision analysis techniques. We concentrate on moderately sized groups – e.g., a board of directors, a management team or a Cabinet. In the next chapter we turn to larger organisations, and, in chapter 13, to the largest group of all: society.

Our objectives in this chapter are:
- to identify and evaluate the individual and social processes that underlie group decision making;
- to understand Arrow's impossibility theorem and its implications for group decision making and democracy; and
- to present and evaluate approaches designed to support (small) group decision making.

11.2 Review of research on decision making in groups

Insanity is the exception in individuals. In groups, parties, peoples, and times, it is the rule. (Friedrich Wilhelm Nietzsche)

Reviews of research on group effectiveness show that in judgement tasks in which there is a known solution – e.g. the number of people living in participants' home city – groups generally perform better than the 'average' individual but worse than the 'best' individual (Einhorn *et al.*, 1977; Gigone and Hastie, 1997; Hastie, 1986; Hill, 1982; Kerr and Tindale, 2004). Given our reliance on groups for making important decisions, these findings are rather disappointing. Nonetheless, there is also evidence suggesting that group effectiveness depends in part on the strategy adopted – e.g. groups may adopt an integration strategy that involves combining their individual judgements or an identification strategy that involves establishing the person who is likely to have the greatest knowledge and then using his/her estimate as the primary basis for deriving the group solution (Sniezek and Henry, 1989; Steiner, 1972).

Interestingly, the strategy adopted by the groups in the Sniezek and Henry study depended upon the amount of agreement/disagreement between individuals at the beginning of the task. When there was relatively high initial agreement, the process tended to be based on integration with approximately equal weight given to each individual's judgement, and the overall accuracy was not much higher than the average of the judgements given by individuals before the group discussion. When there was high initial disagreement, averaging did not occur. Instead, identification was more important and the quality of the decision was either much better or much worse than average individual judgement. Thus, the strategy adopted had important implications for the quality of the decision, but was not actually under the direct control of the group.

Overall, these findings suggest that groups do not necessarily make better decisions than individuals; they may not capitalise on their four advantages listed in the introduction to this chapter. It seems that the processes adopted by groups may be critical in determining their effectiveness. Some of the factors that are known to inhibit group decision making are outlined below (for a fuller review, see Baron and Kerr, 2004).

- *Group member characteristics.* Group decisions are often strongly influenced by those individuals who have power, show higher degrees of confidence in the information they present and are more persuasive. This occurs even though these individuals are not necessarily those who know the most. Allowing such individuals too much influence and not listening sufficiently to other group members, who may well be better informed, can reduce the effectiveness of group decisions and reduce the motivation of those members who are unable to make their contribution, thereby further reducing their contribution.

- *Group size*. Larger groups are more likely to have the knowledge and/ or intelligence necessary to make an effective decision. As group size increases, however, it becomes increasingly difficult for each individual to make his/her contribution, given the increased competition for 'airtime'. Therefore, it is less likely that an individual will be able to share his/her knowledge and intelligence with other members of the group, and those who are ignored are also likely to disengage, further reducing their contribution.

- *Conformity*. Individuals often change what they say in group discussions in order to be seen to be consistent with the majority. This occurs out of a fear of being 'different' from everyone else, and may deprive the group of crucial information that challenges emerging views and assumptions that are incorrect.

- *Social loafing*. Individuals are sometimes not sufficiently motivated to make their full contribution to group activities. As indicated above, this is particularly likely to occur when they are unable to make their contribution and this goes unnoticed. They may also disengage if they see the marginal benefit of any of their contributions to be low because it is divided over many contributors. In large groups, social loafing can involve individuals 'sitting out' the meeting by making no contribution at all. Social loafing is lower when each member's contribution to the group output can be identified and evaluated (Comer, 1995).

- *Production blocking*. Individual contributions are sometimes diminished because of the need to wait for an opportunity to share knowledge and experience with other group members. This occurs because group members compete for limited group 'airtime' and so must retain their contribution until they command group attention. Nevertheless, participants who cannot verbalise ideas as soon as they occur may forget them, may suppress them because they seem less relevant later once the discussion has moved on or may be unable to generate further ideas because they are rehearsing their ideas while waiting for their turn (see, for example, Diehl and Stroebe, 1991).

- *Evaluation apprehension*. When individuals feel that they are being judged or evaluated by others in or outside the group they may self-censor their contributions, even though these may be constructive and relevant to group goals. In groups brought together especially for the purpose of making one particular decision, the pressure on individuals to make a positive impression on strangers is likely to increase evaluation apprehension.

- *Biased information pooling.* Groups are more likely to discuss and make use of information that is available to all members – i.e. 'shared' information – but often fail to exchange and discuss information that is available uniquely to a single individual – i.e. 'unshared' information. Thus the unique contribution that individuals can make is often not realised (for a review, see Hinsz *et al.*, 1997).

An emerging theme from the discussion so far is the importance of the process adopted when groups make a decision. Accordingly, we now turn to a brief review of what we know about group processes, beginning with the manner in which they may reach consensus.

A major challenge for groups is to find ways of bringing together their different views to agree a single course of action. Hastie *et al.* (1983) investigated how mock juries reached consensus about guilt or innocence, showing that they followed one of two different strategies. Some groups used a *verdict-driven* strategy, which involved each individual stating his/her initial judgement at the outset – i.e. guilty or innocent – followed by discussion in which individuals became advocates for their position and tried to persuade others to change. Frequent polling of views was undertaken until there was sufficient agreement between the members. Other groups used an *evidence-driven* strategy, which involved members reviewing evidence together to develop a common understanding of what they believed happened – i.e. the most likely sequence of events. Guilt or innocence was derived from this common understanding. Both strategies allow a consensus to be reached, but in radically different ways. In addition, procedures designed to support group decision making may be effective only if they complement the strategy adopted by the group – i.e. we may need different decision support mechanisms for each strategy.

Some groups, such as parliaments, juries and boards of directors, lay down formal rules about how to determine a consensus. For example, juries in the United Kingdom are often instructed to reach a unanimous decision, but later, if this is not possible, then a majority verdict is sought – i.e. agreement between at least ten of the twelve jurors. Thus there is a switch from a unanimity rule to a majority rule. Other groups do not have established rules for consensus and may use less formal procedures. One example is what we like to call a 'mythical majority' rule, in which single individuals periodically claim that their position represents the majority and a lack of strong disagreement from others is sufficient for this to be accepted without further discussion or formal evaluation by voting. In a very insightful article, Miller (1989) suggests that group decision rules can be differentiated in terms of their strictness (i.e. the extent to which all group members must express similar preferences in order for a decision to be reached) and their distribution of power (i.e. whether or not all members have the same amount of power in determining the outcome). He argues that the rule adopted has important implications. For example, the stricter the rule adopted – i.e. consensus rather than majority voting – the greater the likelihood that

- a decision will not be reached;
- members' views will change in direction of the consensus;
- members will not dissent from the decision and express greater satisfaction with it; and
- members will perceive group discussion as uncomfortable, difficult and conflictual but also more thorough and adequate.

This last point identifies a dilemma for those wishing to develop procedures for improving group decision making. Procedures designed to increase the thoroughness of the process by ensuring that group members confront issues that are difficult and conflictual may lead to negative emotions, such as anxiety, apprehension or unpleasantness. This can lead to a diminution in members' desires to be involved with the group in the future and may also reduce the likelihood that they will reuse such procedures.

Groups sometimes exhibit unexpectedly extreme attitudes compared with the views of the individuals making up that group. For example, in his master's thesis, Stoner (1961) reports the results of a study in which he presented individuals with simple everyday scenarios outlining a choice between a risky option – e.g. start a new business – and a safe option – e.g. keep working for the current employer in a secure job. Participants had to report the minimum probability of the small business becoming successful that they would require before choosing this risky option. Having provided this judgement, the research participants formed groups to discuss these same problems in order to agree a group minimum probability judgement. The initial findings were that group judgements were much riskier than the average of the individual judgements, suggesting that coming together as a group had made individuals more prepared to take risks.

Subsequent studies have shown that for some kinds of scenarios the change in risk attitude was reversed in the direction of increased risk aversion in groups (Isenberg, 1986). The direction of the change was dictated by the individual pre-group discussion positions; thus, if the majority favoured risk taking then the shift was towards greater risk taking, and the reverse was true when the majority initially favoured caution. This shift in group risk attitudes, called *group polarisation*, is now very well supported by laboratory and field studies. Indeed, it is a specific example of a more general phenomenon, group-induced attitude polarisation: namely, if individual members of a group hold initial attitudes or opinions in a particular direction (e.g. positive or negative views about a particular option), then this view is enhanced following group discussion (Moscovici and Zavalloni, 1969; Myers and Lamm, 1976). Whether these shifts are in risk attitudes or opinions, they are an unintended outcome of decision making in groups; and one that may have important implications for determining the effectiveness of the decisions taken.

Unsurprisingly, work has shown that the majority view has a stronger influence on the outcomes of group activities than minority views, regardless of whether these activities are agreed by formal rules such as majority voting or by other less informal ways, such as the 'mythical majority' rule described earlier. Minorities can be highly influential, however, when there is a clear set of initial beliefs shared by group members and when the minority position is clearly a better fit to these beliefs (Laughlin and Ellis, 1986). In addition, Kameda *et al.* (1997) introduced the notion of *cognitive centrality*, defined in terms of the amount of knowledge shared with other members. Those with greater centrality have greater influence whether they hold the minority or majority position. Apart from providing insights into some of the factors that allow minorities to influence group decisions, this finding suggests how those holding minority positions might seek to influence majorities.

Perhaps the most influential and in many ways provocative body of research on group failure relates to *groupthink* (Janis, 1972). Having undertaken a detailed analysis of a series of major fiascos, Janis developed the groupthink model in terms of five antecedent conditions, eight symptoms of groupthink and eight symptoms of defective decision making. The antecedent conditions thought necessary for groupthink to occur are

- high levels of cohesiveness between group members, derived from working together often;
- insularity – i.e. little or no inputs or influences from outside the group;
- directed leadership – i.e. a leader who dominates the group;
- a lack of established procedures for searching for and the evaluation of information; and

- a low perceived confidence of finding an alternative solution to that advocated by the leader.

Janis suggested that these antecedent conditions give rise to a distinctive style of decision making that has up to eight negative characteristics or 'symptoms':

- an illusion of invulnerability that induce overly optimistic beliefs that positive outcomes will occur, which can lead to extreme risk taking;
- collective rationalisations that lead the group to ignore warnings that would require a reappraisal of their basic assumptions;
- a belief in the inherent morality of their group that leads members to overlook crucial ethical and moral issues concerning their intended actions;
- a negative stereotyping of opponents that leads them to underestimate the power of opponents and to judge them as too immoral to negotiate with;
- direct pressure on group members to conform that reduces the likelihood that alternative views are presented or considered;
- self-censorship by group members that stops them from expressing doubts or counter-arguments;
- self-appointed 'mind guards' who ensure that contradictory information, doubts and counter-arguments from group members or from outside the group are not considered; and
- an 'illusion of unanimity' derived from the previous points above that leads the group to take what it believes to be the correct decision with confidence given, it seems, that all group members support it; this occurs even if many group members have doubts and concerns – the fact that others have not voiced these leads each individual to suppress voicing them him-/herself.

The eight symptoms of defective decision making may be summarised as deficiencies due to poor information search and biased information processing that lead to an incomplete survey of alternatives and objectives, a failure to examine any risks associated with the preferred choice, a failure to work out contingency plans about how to manage negative outcomes and a failure to reappraise previously rejected alternatives.

The concept of groupthink has had a huge impact on academic research on group decision making (see, for example, Turner and Pratkanis, 1998), but has been criticised by some for being grossly overused as a concept given the lack of strong empirical support for the model (Fuller and Aldag, 1998). The model has also been used extensively by individuals and organisations outside the academic community to describe and explain poor group decision making – for example, in trying to understand how false premises about weapons of mass destruction (WMDs) led to the decision to invade Iraq without any apparent consideration of the risks involved and the failure to develop contingency plans to deal with these risks. The US Senate Intelligence Committee reported:[1]

Conclusion 3: The Intelligence Community suffered from a collective presumption that Iraq had an active and growing WMD program. This 'group think' dynamic led Intelligence Community analysts, collectors and managers to both interpret ambiguous evidence as collectively indicative of a WMD program as well as ignore or minimize evidence that Iraq did not have active and expanding weapons of mass destruction programs. This presumption was so strong and formalized that Intelligence Community mechanisms established to challenge assumptions and group think were not utilized.

Overall, the model does provide some useful insights about the errors that can occur in group decision making and when and why these come about. Over-reliance on the model may be inappropriate, however, in that it highlights only a subset of factors that need to be considered when identifying what causes poor group decision making and how this may be rectified.

We began this chapter by identifying the potential advantages that groups have over individuals when making decisions, and have followed this by a very brief review of theory and research explaining how and why these advantages are not always realised. This body of work not only demonstrates the need for procedures to facilitate group decision making, but also provides important insights about the form these should take given our knowledge of the pitfalls and limitations involved. We now turn to the other side of the coin: formal normative models for group decision making – or the lack of them.

11.3 Arrow's impossibility theorem

Democracy substitutes election by the incompetent many for appointment by the corrupt few. (George Bernard Shaw)

Real group decision-making behaviour is far from perfect, then; but what is 'perfect'? What is the ideal form of group decision making? Sadly, it is non-existent. While we have presented normative models of ideal behaviour for individual decision makers, there is no parallel theory for

[1] See http://intelligence.senate.gov/conclusions.pdf (see also Newell and Lagnado, 2003).

groups of decision makers. Early studies of voting theory (such as that by Marquis de Condorcet, 1785) sounded many warnings that it would be difficult to set up a fair, democratic and rational voting system. For two centuries efforts were directed at finding better ways of voting. In the middle of the last century, however, Arrow showed that several key concepts of democracy were incompatible. To give a flavour of some of the problems, we begin with some examples of the difficulties that can occur with the simplest and most popular of voting procedures: the *simple majority rule*. This rule suggests that a group should, as a whole, strictly prefer *a* to *b* if a majority of its members strictly prefers *a* to *b*. If equal numbers prefer *a* to *b* as prefer *b* to *a*, then the group should be indifferent between *a* and *b*. Members who are indifferent between *a* and *b* are not counted, and so do not affect the group preference.

Consider a problem with three individuals and three alternatives, *a*, *b* and *c*. Suppose that the individuals hold the following strict preferences:

individual 1: $a \succ_1 b \succ_1 c$;
individual 2: $b \succ_2 c \succ_2 a$;
individual 3: $c \succ_3 a \succ_3 b$.

Note that the strict preference relation $\succ$ has been subscripted to indicate the individual. Using $\succ_g$ to indicate strict preference for group, the simple majority rule leads to the following:

$a \succ_g b$, since two out of three prefer *a* to *b*;
$b \succ_g c$, since two out of three prefer *b* to c;
$c \succ_g a$, since two out of three prefer *c* to *b*.

The simple majority rule can lead, therefore, to intransitive group preference. Since the money pump argument (section 3.2) is just as persuasive when money is being pumped from a group as when it is from an individual, this is surely a worrying result.

The example misses a very important point, however. The simple majority rule is seldom, if ever, used to compare all the alternatives simultaneously. Instead, alternatives are considered a pair at a time: *a* might be compared with *b*; the less preferred is discarded; the more preferred is then compared with next alternative, *c*; and so on. For instance, in the passage of a parliamentary bill in the United Kingdom, amendments are voted on one by one; adopted, if passed, and discarded, if not; and, ultimately, the bill itself is voted upon. Thus, in the example, the three individuals might first compare *a* with *b* and then compare the 'winner' with c. The result would be that the group would choose c, since two out of three prefer a to b and then two out of three prefer c to a:

$$\left.\begin{matrix} a \\ b \end{matrix}\right\} \longrightarrow \left.\begin{matrix} a \\ c \end{matrix}\right\} \longrightarrow c$$

Suppose, however, that they had begun by considering the choice between b and c. Then a would have been chosen:

$$\left.\begin{matrix} b \\ c \end{matrix}\right\} \longrightarrow \left.\begin{matrix} b \\ a \end{matrix}\right\} \longrightarrow a$$

Similarly, had they begun with the comparison of a and c, b would have been their ultimate choice:

$$\left.\begin{matrix} a \\ c \end{matrix}\right\} \longrightarrow \left.\begin{matrix} c \\ b \end{matrix}\right\} \longrightarrow b$$

Thus, the alternative selected by this procedure of pairwise comparison would be determined simply by the order in which the alternatives were considered, and not primarily by the group members' preferences. In this example this prospect is not, perhaps, very worrying. The individuals' preferences are clearly substantially and symmetrically opposed, and there is a strong case for arguing that the group as a whole should be indifferent between the three alternatives. The ultimate choice is therefore a matter of little concern. In other cases, however, we might be more concerned. Should the group's choice have any dependence upon the order in which alternatives are considered?

There is another worrying aspect to this problem. Suppose that the first individual knows his/her companion's preferences. If the alternatives are to be compared in the order a and b and then the winner with c, he/she will be able to predict that the ultimate choice will be c. Suppose that he/she lies about his/her true preferences, however, while the others honestly reveal theirs. If he/she says that he/she holds $b \succ_1 a \succ_1 c$, the ultimate choice will be determined as

$$\left.\begin{matrix} a \\ b \end{matrix}\right\} \longrightarrow \left.\begin{matrix} b \\ c \end{matrix}\right\} \longrightarrow b$$

Thus, by lying, he/she will ensure that the group selects b, which he/she prefers to the 'true' group choice c. In these particular circumstances the simple majority rule encourages him/her to lie, or, less pejoratively, to vote tactically. That surely is a little worrying. Arrow sought to characterise the properties that we would expect of a democratic voting system. He framed these as axioms and then showed them to be mutually contradictory. Essentially, no voting system – or *constitution*, as he called it – exists such that in every possible circumstance it satisfies some basic principles of rationality. This argument is summarised in table 11.1.

Since Arrow proved his uncomfortable result many have tried to reframe his axioms slightly to avoid the impossibility, or to argue that one or more of them is irrelevant to democracy and can therefore be dropped. All have, essentially, failed. Worse, it transpires that versions of the impossibility still hold if any one of the properties is abandoned (Kelly, 1978). Arrow has identified a real inconsistency in our hopes and demands for rational democratic decision making. Others have enlarged the debate and shown that any constitution is susceptible to manipulation through strategic voting, the dishonest revelation of preferences or agenda rigging. Perhaps the most hopeful way forward seems to be to allow group members to express not just their preference rankings but also their strength of preference.

While there are a number of mathematical results that offer some hope, all fail because they need interpersonal comparisons of preferences (Bacharach, 1975; French, 1985, 1986; French and Ríos Insua, 2000; Hodge and Klima, 2005; Raiffa *et al.*, 2003; Taylor, 2005). Such comparisons require, for instance, an unambiguous interpretation of 'I prefer coffee to tea more than you prefer a sports car to an mp4 player'. Despite many attempts, no sensible operational meaning has been offered for such statements. However one formulates the issues, there seems to be no way to develop mechanistic algorithms and prescriptions for voting and group decision making that are fair, just, democratic, honest, open … : choose your adjective embodying a good moral imperative!

French *et al.* (2007c) note that over the years several distinct approaches to group decision analysis have been proposed, as follows.

GDM_{GSEU} This assumes that the subjective expected utility model applies at the group level and, moreover, that group probabilities and utilities are constructed from those of its members. Thus, the process is to elicit each group member's subjective probabilities and utilities, and combine these into group probabilities and utilities, respectively. Finally, the corresponding group expected utilities are calculated and the resulting ranking used to recommend choice (Bacharach, 1975).

Table 11.1 Arrow's impossibility theorem

Suppose that there are n individuals who are jointly responsible for choosing an action from a given finite set of possible actions. Let $\succeq_i$ be the weak preference ordering of the ith individual. Similarly, $\succ_i$ will be his/her strict preference. We also refer to the entire preference ordering of the ith individual by $\succeq_i$ (i.e. to the set of alternative actions as ordered by his/her preferences). The preference orders, $\succeq_i$, may be *selfish* and simply reflect what the individual wants him-/herself irrespective of what that may mean for the other group members; or they may be *altruistic* and reflect what the individual wants for the greater good of the group. Given the n individuals and their preferences $\succeq_i$, $i = 1, 2, \ldots$ n, the problem is simply stated. We must prescribe how to combine them into a preference order for the group as a whole. We write $\succeq_g$ for this order and $a \succeq_g b$, $a \succ_g b$ for particular statements of group preference. The voting system or mechanism whereby $\succeq_1, \succeq_2, \ldots, \succeq_n$ are combined to give $\succeq_g$ is called the *constitution* of the group. Arrow (1963) suggests that the following axioms encode the minimum requirements of justice, fairness and rationality that we might ask of a constitution.

Axiom A1: *weak ordering*

$\succeq_1, \succeq_2, \ldots, \succeq_n$ and $\succeq_g$ are all weak orders – i.e. complete and transitive (chapter 3 section 2)

Axiom A2: *non-triviality*

(i) There are at least two members of the group: $n \geq 2$.

(ii) There are at least three alternatives.

Axiom A3: *universal domain*

$\succeq_g$ is defined whatever $\succeq_1, \succeq_2, \ldots, \succeq_n$ may be.

Axiom A4: *binary relevance*

Let $\succeq_1, \succeq_2, \ldots, \succeq_n$ be a set of individual preference orders over a set alternatives, A. Let $\succeq'_1, \succeq'_2, \ldots \succeq'_n$ be another set of individual preference orders over a set of alternatives, A'. Suppose that alternatives a and b lie in both A and A': $\{a, b\} \subset A \cap A'$. Suppose further that $\succeq_1, \succeq_2, \ldots, \succeq_n$ and $\succeq'_1, \succeq'_2, \ldots, \succeq'_n$ are identical on $\{a, b\}$: $\forall i$,

$\quad a \succeq_i b \Leftrightarrow a \succeq'_i b$ and $b \succeq_i a \Leftrightarrow b \succeq'_i a$

Then the constitution should lead to the same group preference between a and b:

$\quad a \succeq_g b \Leftrightarrow a \succeq'_g b$ and $b \succeq_g a \Leftrightarrow b \succeq'_g a$

Axiom A5: *Pareto's principle for strict preferences*

If every individual holds $a \succ_i b$, then the group holds $a \succ_g b$.

Axiom A6: *no dictatorship*

There is no individual whose preferences automatically become the preferences of the group independently of the preferences of the other members.

Axiom A1 is a common requirement for rational preferences, and, while we might well acknowledge that democratic group decision making should encompass the preferences of all, whether 'rational' or 'irrational', we would also surely agree that it should not be permitted to fail just because the group members were rational. Axioms A2 and A3 simply require that the constitution applies to all situations however large the group and however many alternatives. Axiom A4 is a version of the axiom of the irrelevant alternative (French, 1986; French and Ríos Insua, 2000), which requires that the group preference between two alternatives depends only on the members' preferences between those two alternatives and not on their preferences between any others. Axiom A5 is a simple requirement of unanimity. Axiom A6 prohibits the existence of a dictator – even a hidden one, who neither knows that he or she is, nor does any other group member. Unfortunately, Arrow has shown that these requirements are mutually contradictory.

Arrow's impossibility theorem

There is no constitution that allows $\succeq_g$ to be defined from $\succeq_1, \succeq_2, \ldots, \succeq_n$ in a manner that is consistent with axioms A1–A6.

Proof

See, for example, Arrow (1963), French (1986), French and Ríos Insua (2000) and Kelly (1978).

GDM_{vote} An analyst works with each individual and develops a personal decision analysis to guide his/her choice. In the light of this understanding, each individual votes within the group and a group choice is made according to the result. In variants of this, the numerical values of the individuals' expected utilities are used to indicate their strength of preference and this information is incorporated into the voting (Ríos and Ríos Insua, 2008).

$GDM_{SupraDM}$ A *supra decision maker* is imagined to exist. She observes the entire elicitation and decision analysis process for each individual and altruistically uses this knowledge to construct a single decision analysis for the group. The choice is made according to the supra decision maker's analysis (Keeney and Raiffa, 1976).

GDM_{Fac} The group gathers together in a facilitated discussion of issues (we discuss facilitation in section 5). Through discussion between participants, consensual agreement is reached on group probabilities and utilities without formally eliciting individual ones. A group analysis is developed and areas of disagreement explored via sensitivity and robustness analysis. Ultimately, a decision is obtained by consensus without formal voting (Eden and Radford, 1990; French, 2003b).

The many paradoxes and impossibilities stemming from Arrow's and related results have led most decision analysts to doubt the efficacy of GDM_{GSEU} and GDM_{vote}. Note that the generality of these impossibility results means that the difficulties apply not just to SEU approaches but, essentially, to all decision analytic methodologies. Sadly, such a recognition is not common among the designers of some GDSSs. Some systems require individual inputs, manipulate them and ultimately produce a group ranking, inevitably risking an inconsistency, irrationality or injustice or laying themselves open to manipulation.

Approach $GDM_{SupraDM}$ seems more promising, because all interpersonal comparisons are made within the mind of the supra decision maker, and it is the issue of defining valid interpersonal comparisons that tends to cause the paradoxes and inconsistencies. In some cases, the supra decision maker actually exists. There might be an arbiter, formally responsible for recommending a decision that balances all group members' perspectives; or there might be a government agency, which has the responsibility and accountability for making the decision but does want to take into account the views of stakeholders. In most cases, however, the non-existence of a supra decision maker remains a problem: she is a fiction, and that creates a fatal flaw in this approach. She has to be constructed by agreement within the group, and this leads to a further group decision, arguably as hard as the first, and an infinite regress.

Ultimately, we believe that any mechanistic concept of group decision making is flawed and ill-defined. Beliefs, preferences, logical analysis – all reside in each of the individual's minds, not in some disembodied group mind. We look upon groups not as some entity that possesses the power to decide but as a social process, which translates the decisions of the individual members into an implemented action (Dryzek and List, 2003; French, 1985; French and Ríos Insua, 2000). For this reason, we prefer the expression 'groups of decision makers' rather than 'group decision making'. Our approaches thus fall into the approach GDM_{Fac} or perhaps one other. The four approaches discussed so far assume that the group *wants* to cooperate and reach a consensus. It might be that they are more self-serving and wish to negotiate a good end point for themselves.

GDM_{Neg} Bargaining, negotiation analysis or arbitration techniques are deployed to define a process in which the group interacts and discusses a series of solutions, converging through negotiations on a deal or policy that all find acceptable (Raiffa, 1982; Raiffa *et al.*, 2003).

We do not intend to discuss negotiation methods in this text, though we do provide some comments and a guide to the literature in section 14.6.

11.4 Procedures for improving decision making in groups

If you really get the right people, and you've got them working together as team, whether it's in business, whether it's in science, whether it's in politics, you can make a big difference. (Steve Case)

The research reviewed in section 2 provides some important insights about the nature of the social processes that underpin decision making in groups, indicating how and why these may be suboptimal. In this section we briefly review procedures for improving group deliberation that address and in some cases seek to modify the nature of these processes by providing social interaction guidelines, imposing a structure on how members interact and choosing group members appropriately. In section 5 we discuss conferencing and facilitation techniques which can provide further improvements.

Janis (1972) suggested several guidelines by which groups might counter the negative effects of groupthink.

- The leader should encourage each member to air objections and doubts. This requires the leader to be willing to accept criticism.
- The leader should initially remain impartial in discussion, stating his/her own preferences and beliefs only after all the group members have.
- The group should form 'breakout' subgroups to discuss issues independently, then reconvene to compare conclusions and hammer out any difficulties.
- Outside experts should be included occasionally and encouraged to challenge group views.
- At each meeting one member should be appointed to play devil's advocate.

While these seem eminently reasonable and address some of the groupthink limitations, there has been little research to test whether groups can follow these guidelines or, indeed, whether they actually lead to an improvement (see 't Hart, 1998, for other suggestions about protecting against groupthink).

Hall (1971) developed a consensus approach built on a set of rules for inducing a thorough, open and constructive discussion involving all members of a group. These rules, presented in table 11.2, do appear to facilitate behaviour likely to achieve some of the benefits of group decision making identified in the introduction (e.g. rules 4 and 5 encourage a full exchange of information between group members) and to limit damage from some of the factors known to limit the effectiveness of group decision making (e.g. rule 3 limits the damaging effects of conformity). Eils and John (1980) showed that groups that had been trained to use these rules made better decisions – in their experiment, a better prediction of whether lenders would or would not default on loans. Although training groups to follow rules of this kind seems to have great potential, this approach to improving group decision making remains relatively underdeveloped.

A second approach to improving group decision making has been to impose a structure on how groups interact. One such technique, devil's advocacy (Mitroff and Mason, 1981), entails assigning a particular role to an individual or subgroup that involves them critiquing all assumptions and recommendations advocated by the main body of the group in an attempt to show why these should not be accepted or adopted. Proponents

Table 11.2 Hall's group interaction rules

(1) Avoid arguing blindly for your own assumptions and recommendations. Present your position clearly, logically and persuasively, but consider carefully the comments and reactions of other group members. If you present the same points again, take comments and reactions into account.
(2) Avoid making 'win-lose' statements in your discussion. Discard the notion that someone must win and someone lose in the discussion. When impasses occur, look for the next most acceptable solution for all parties.
(3) Avoid changing your mind simply to avoid conflict and reach agreement. Withstand pressures to yield that have no logically sound foundation. Strive for enlightened flexibility; avoid mere capitulation.
(4) Avoid conflict-reducing techniques such as majority voting, tossing a coin, and the like. Differences of opinion indicate an incomplete exchange of relevant information on someone's part; press for additional sharing of task or emotional data when it seems in order.
(5) View differences of opinion as natural and helpful rather than as a hindrance to decision making. Generally, the more assumptions and recommendations expressed the greater the likelihood of conflict, and the richer the resources used in solving the problem at hand.
(6) View all initial agreements as suspect. Explore the reasons for the apparent agreement. Make sure that people have arrived at similar recommendations either for the same reasons or for complementary reasons before incorporating such recommendations into the group's final set.

Source: Schweiger *et al.* (1986).

of this approach believe that appropriate assumptions and recommendations will survive such criticisms but inappropriate ones will not. A related technique, dialectical inquiry, involves splitting the group in two with each subgroup developing a different set of recommendations based on contrary assumptions. Then the two subgroups engage in an in-depth, critical debate about the recommendations and their underlying assumptions. Finally, they agree on those that have survived the scrutiny of debate, and develop recommendations based on them. The detailed scrutiny of decisions and their underlying assumptions is assumed to improve the quality of decision making.

Both techniques have the potential to reduce the chances of groupthink occurring, given the rigorous and critical evaluation of decision options and their underlying assumptions. In addition, these procedures may also reduce the likelihood that groups will be affected by some of the factors known to reduce effectiveness – e.g. social loafing. It is less certain, however, that other factors, such as evaluation apprehension and conformity, are managed effectively by these two techniques.

Direct evidence on the effectiveness of these techniques is mixed (see Schwenk, 1990). Schweiger *et al.* (1986) report a laboratory study that involved giving groups of participants a relatively complex business problem that required a strategic decision. They compared group performance under dialectical inquiry, devil's advocacy and the consensus approach. The findings revealed that dialectical inquiry and devil's advocacy gave rise to higher-quality recommendations and assumptions than the consensus approach, and that dialectical inquiry was better than devil's advocacy with respect to the quality of the assumptions used to make the decision. Despite this, participants in the consensus groups expressed greater satisfaction with their group experience, revealed a greater desire to continue working with their group and were more accepting of their group decisions than participants in the other two groups. This is an important finding, in that is suggests that there may be a tension between improving the quality of the decision, through confrontational approaches such as devil's advocacy and dialectical inquiry, and how pleasant group members find the process and their willingness to continue working together. Both factors need to be considered, and the relative importance of each may vary from situations to situation. In some situations the need to keep a group together may outweigh the quality issues – for example, when there is a group of volunteers running a charity, maintaining the support of these volunteers may be of paramount importance.

A rather different technique for structuring the group process, *Delphi*, was originally developed by Dalkey and his co-workers at the Rand Corporation. It is a procedure designed to 'obtain the most reliable consensus of opinion of a group of experts ... by a series of intensive questionnaires interspersed with controlled opinion feedback' (Dalkey and Helmer, 1963: 458; see also Linstone and Turoff, 1978). The technique does not require that groups meet face to face. Instead, they respond anonymously to a series of questions, and their answers are synthesised and then fed back to members for further comments and the generation of potential solutions; these are again synthesised and sent out for further comment and evaluation, and so on. There may be several such iterations. Thus the group interacts remotely rather than face to face.

Rowe and Wright (1999) argue that the technique maintains many of the positive aspects of group decision making – e.g. increased knowledge and experience as a result of including many individuals and the increased creativity that occurs when people work together – while minimising some of the negative social, personal and political processes – e.g. different power relations are inhibited because contributions are not attributed to particular members, and conformity effects are limited because contributions are made without knowledge of the views of others. In addition, the technique allows a relatively large and geographically dispersed group to work together since there are none of the usual constraints associated with organising a face-to-face meeting. Having reviewed the extant research, Rowe and Wright conclude that the technique is effective in improving group decision making (but see Cooke, 1991).

The Delphi technique has provided the stimulus for a more general discussion about whether it is better for group interactions to be face to face or computer-mediated. The evidence suggests that, for divergent discussion such as the formulation phase of decision analysis, computer-mediated discussion is more effective, perhaps because it allows the members to think along their own lines without constant distraction by the suggestions of other group members. For convergent deliberation in the evaluation and appraisal phases, however, the balance shifts towards face-to-face meetings (Kerr and Murthy, 2004).

Some have argued that group deliberations can be improved by deliberately selecting group members in such a way as to ensure that they have heterogeneous rather than homogeneous views – i.e. initially disagree rather than agree. Choosing members in this way increases the likelihood that groups will debate and discuss assumptions and possible actions. Research has shown that heterogeneous groups show reduced levels of overconfidence (Sniezek, 1992), are less prone to underestimate risks (Williams and Taormina, 1992), reach more accurate judgements (Sniezek and Henry, 1989), generate more hypotheses (Crott *et al.*, 1998) and exchange more information, including unique information (Brodbeck *et al.*, 2002). Indeed, Schulz-Hardt *et al.* (2002) show that selecting group members in this way may be a more effective way of improving group decision making than structured techniques such as devil's advocacy. These findings highlight the importance of recruiting individuals with different backgrounds, beliefs and values if we are to maximise the full potential from working with groups of DMs.

11.5 Facilitated workshops and decision conferencing

When you are a Bear of Very Little Brain and you Think of Things, you find sometimes that a Thing which seemed very thingish inside you is quite different which it gets out into the open and has other people looking at it. (A. A. Milne)

In the previous section we identified guidelines and structured procedures that can counter some of the errors and biases that arise in group deliberations. In this section we discuss facilitated workshops, often known as *decision conferences* (Eden and Radford, 1990; French, 1988; Phillips, 1984). These draws upon three key methodologies:

- facilitation, in which a facilitator, who has no responsibility or accountability for the consequences of the decision, joins the group to structure, smooth and enhance the deliberative processes;
- decision analytic models, to help the DMs understand themselves, the context and the issues before them; and
- interactive software, to explore and display the implications of the models.

We have noted that groups can fall prey to various biases and other dysfunctional behaviours. One of the key roles of a *facilitator* is to counter these. A facilitator is skilled in the process of group discussion, but may have little expertise in the context of the issues at hand. His role is to smooth the group's work, to help the process and make the team more productive and creative. Phillips and Phillips (1993) summarise the key functions of a facilitator as observing, attending, maintaining awareness of feelings and intervening. The content of the discussion, however, comes entirely from the group itself. The group members 'own' the problem, have knowledge of it, have access to relevant data and experts and are responsible for its resolution.

In a sense, a facilitator is no more than an impartial chairperson or group leader, but in practice his 'distance' from the group is far greater (Maier, 1967). Because he does not share in the ownership of the problem, he may concentrate on:

- encouraging members of the group to contribute ideas and listen to those of others;
- assuming responsibility for accurate communication between the members, perhaps cutting through jargon or simply making sure that no one is too shy to say 'I don't understand';
- protecting minority views and ensuring that they are debated fairly;
- being sensitive to people with unexpressed feelings and views and helping them enter the discussion;
- calming conflict by keeping the group task-oriented rather than personality oriented;
- summarising the position at appropriate points in the discussion; and
- generally keeping the discussion moving and focused on the task in hand.

By following these guidelines the facilitator is limiting the extent to which the group falls prey to the factors known to inhibit group decision making discussed earlier in this chapter. Indeed, Ackermann (1996) has surveyed over 100 managers who have taken part in facilitated workshops. She finds that the process was positive for all the reasons given above.

Facilitators concentrate their attention on the *process*, leaving the members of the group free to contribute, explore, shape and understand *content*. Miranda and Bostrom (1999) have suggested that content facilitation can be more effective, however. In truth, both content and process interventions are necessary, but the point that we would make is not that facilitation should concentrate on process or content but that process and content interventions should be explicitly separated so that the group perceives the process facilitation as neutral and unbiased. It is important that group members play the primary role in providing the content of the discussion, identifying opportunities, creating and evaluating the options and generating the action lists to implement their decisions. Through their total involvement in the creation of strategy they become fully committed to its implementation. They 'own' the strategy. Moreover, because of their shared understanding of the reasons behind its adoption, they can explain it to others.

All the above suggests *what* a facilitator should do: *how* he should do it is another matter. How should he intervene to enhance the work of the group? There are some tricks of the trade. Generally, the facilitator should raise issues neutrally, asking open questions – although sometimes, when the group is drawing together behind a single viewpoint, he may play devil's advocate and press an alternative view to test whether groupthink is rearing its ugly head. Ignorance can be a great advantage: a facilitator may often move a group forward by asking a very naïve question and uncovering hidden, perhaps contentious assumptions or misunderstandings. Because he is an outsider, he often questions jargon and so clarifies discussion for the whole group. Not everyone in the group may be au fait with all the jargon used in an organisation, but some may lack the courage to indicate their ignorance.

Not all interventions require the facilitator to distance him calmly from the issues. Occasionally, there may be benefit in his pressing a point forcibly, particularly if a member of the group is trying to take control of the process or if the general level of stress has fallen below that needed for productive activity. Generally, though, a facilitator is wise to hold his temper and intervene gently, catalysing rather than directing or confronting.

The process of decision analysis and its tools can of themselves provide very effective interventions. The prescriptive decision analysis cycle organises the general flow of discussion, moving through issues one by one, concentrating on each in turn. This avoids the confusion that can be caused by simultaneously considering many issues and darting between them. Soft modelling methods can help foster creativity, providing a framework to brainstorm effectively. The model structuring, elicitation, evaluation and sensitivity analysis cycle helps to move the discussion forward productively, focusing on one issue at a time. Sensitivity analysis often defuses heated but irrelevant debates, concentrating attention on the real issues that matter to the problem at hand. Finally, the developing model provides a very effective vehicle for communication.

In a decision conference the DMs responsible for the decision meet together, ideally away from the distractions of their normal working environment, to discuss and explore the issues. The entire group responsible for a decision, including relevant experts and perhaps key stakeholders, should take part in the conference. Ideally, the size of the group should be between seven and fifteen people, so that there are sufficient participants to stimulate wide-ranging discussions yet not so many that it is difficult for each to contribute. The meeting concentrates entirely upon the issues that led to it being called. There are no time-outs to consider peripheral matters 'while the team are together'. The facilitator is usually assisted by one or more decision analysts. The facilitator leads the meeting, guiding the discussion forward in a constructive fashion. The analysts build and run decision models, generating representations of the issues as they arise. The models are projected and the group can look into their implications immediately, modifying the models as they explore different assumptions and inputs, informed by sensitivity analyses of previous models. The analysts also record the development of the debate and the reasoning behind the judgements and decisions made. At the conclusion of the conference the group members are able to take away a record of important conclusions and an action list with them, along with a record of how and why these evolved.

A decision conference is generally a two-day event. Other time scales are possible (see, for example, Hämäläinen and Leikola, 1996), but the inclusion of a night is of considerable advantage. In the evening the group members are able to relax together and reflect on the progress and discussion so far. This reflection, together with the distance from the day's deliberations that a night's sleep brings, helps members acquire a more mature perspective on the issues that concern them. Without the overnight break some may have second thoughts soon after the conference ends, perhaps on the journey home, and much of the value of the event will be dissipated as their commitment to its conclusions evaporates.

Each decision conference is different. It evolves according to the needs of the group and not according to some fixed agenda. There are common themes and patterns, however. The facilitator is always careful to ensure that the opening discussion is as wide-ranging as possible, encouraging divergent thinking. Decision conferences are demanding on the time of busy DMs and so are called only to deal with complex, unstructured strategic issues. During the initial phase the facilitator may simply allow the discussion to develop or he may use soft modelling techniques to add structure to the perspectives being developed. Sometimes the development of such models can occupy the entire event, particularly those dealing with the broad strategic intent and mission of an organisation (Ackermann *et al.*, 2004; Eden and Ackermann, 1998).

With the issues and context defined, the facilitator moves into a decision modelling phase, encouraging convergent thinking on key issues that soft modelling has identified. He generally aims to build an initial 'quick and dirty' model encapsulating the issues and concerns well enough to give a first indication of 'an optimal course of action'. With good scheduling by the facilitator, this will occur just before the overnight break, giving the DMs the opportunity of an extended period to reflect upon the analysis to date. By the next morning they will usually be clear on one thing: whatever the model is doing, it is *not* reflecting an optimal course of action. They will note flaw upon flaw with the analysis – forgotten issues, ill-formed judgements and so on. The associated feelings of frustration – 'Did we waste yesterday entirely?' – will provide added impetus to revitalise their discussions. The facilitator and his team will rebuild the model, adding additional features as necessary, and explore it via sensitivity analysis. The decision analytic cycle continues until the model is requisite.

The final stage of a decision conference is to work with the group members to provide a summary of the conclusions and strategy that they can take with them, along with an action list to implement the decision. One of the reasons for the success of a decision conference is that, because it is *their* model and *their* analysis, the DMs are highly motivated to implement *their* conclusions. There is considerable evidence that, when decisions are implemented by managers who neither own nor fully understand the decision, the outcomes may not be as successful as anticipated (Borges *et al.*, 2005, 2006). This final stage of summarising and allocating tasks ensures that the DMs may return to their usual working environment and colleagues able to communicate the conclusions succinctly. Decision conferences ensure that the participants own the strategy, are committed to its implementation and can communicate their arguments and enthusiasm effectively.

In case vignette 11.1 we reflect on the decision conferences run during the International Chernobyl Project.

Case vignette 11.1 Reflections on the Chernobyl decision conferences

In section 7.8 we described the multi-attribute analysis in the International Chernobyl Project. This analysis was developed over a sequence of five decision conferences.

The conferences were rather large: all had more than thirty participants, not including the support team and observers. This did not cause the anticipated difficulties, however. Having more than thirty people in the room was no less manageable than fifteen. The presence of observers, albeit bound by strict rules of confidentiality, might also have been expected to cause problems, yet no difficulty was encountered. Discussion ebbed and flowed, developing many different perspectives on the issues.

Another standard rule of decision conferences is that no papers or prepared material are allowed on the first morning, so that participants are forced to present their views, composing their words on the spot. This encourages rapid and wide-ranging discussion of the main issues and concerns. It also stops individuals hiding behind prepared data and entrenched positions. Many of the participants, true to their political backgrounds, came prepared to read speeches. They were allowed to: several were ministers of sufficient authority that it would not have been possible to stop them! The facilitator simply sat quietly, politely listening but not reacting to their words, and then let the silence drag out after they had finished, until they had to continue in their own words – and live discussion developed.

Some interesting aspects of working in a different society and culture emerged. For instance, there is no Russian word with a meaning corresponding to 'trade-off'. This made the development of multi-attribute value models difficult, but, since we used swing weighting techniques, not impossible. In fact, explaining the principles of the models without relying on the term 'trade-off' is arguably a very good discipline for decision analysts.

In the past Soviet society hid many value judgements within appeals to scientific objectivity. Moreover, the State had promised the absolute safety of all its projects, denying the need for any risk analysis: if it wasn't safe, the State wouldn't have decided to build it, would it? In dealing with the after-effects of Chernobyl, those involved had to reappraise many of their working assumptions and beliefs, and to tease out and examine many value judgements. Science cannot remove all the contamination from the environment and return it to an absolutely safe condition. Not that it had ever been absolutely safe before the accident: there is always some background radiation and plenty of other non-radiological risks. It is not for science to place a relative social cost on the occurrence of a radiation-induced genetic effect compared with a death from a radiation-induced cancer. That is a value judgement for a society to make through its political and other institutions. The discussion at the conferences time and again returned to and examined such value judgements.

It is often said that people are the same the world over. In a very small sense, these conferences provided some evidence to support this. Once the concerns and issues had been brought to the fore and the discussion had begun in earnest, there was no noticeable difference in the interactions and group behaviour of the participants compared with similar events in the West. This was fortunate, because there had been concern that the interventions that the facilitator might make would have effects other than those intended. They did not. To give one example: on one occasion he was having difficulty getting the group members to 'own' the problem and admit that they had the knowledge to discuss it. Repeatedly a need was expressed to consult others outside the room. It was a hot afternoon, and the doors and windows were open. The facilitator used this to make an intervention to the effect that no one was going to come through the door and windows and 'locked' the team in with their problem. The effect was dramatic. Within minutes the group took responsibility and discussion moved forward rapidly.

11.6 Game theory, negotiation and bargaining

In principle, every social situation involves strategic interaction among the participants. Thus, one might argue that proper understanding of any social situation would require game-theoretic analysis. (John Harsanyi)

In 1944 von Neumann and Morgenstern published their seminal text *Theory of Games and Economic Behavior* (second edition, 1947). It was and is a monumental work, which developed utility theory from a simple set of axioms, essentially completing the definition of rational economic man and, above all, laying the foundations of game theory. Game theory is the study of conflict and cooperation between a number of independent players. It differs from the direction that we have taken earlier in this chapter. There we confined our attention to supporting a group of DMs working together to resolve some set of issues. We recognised that the import of Arrow's theorem was that it was not possible to construct a theory of a democratic group of DMs who together acted as some rational entity. Thus we needed to view the group as a social process and our role as analysts and facilitators was to smooth and support this process.

Game theory takes a quite different tack. It posits several independent players, each with his/her own preferences and each able independently to choose one of a set of actions to take. The combined effect of their individual actions leads to the overall outcome and the 'share' each receives. The purpose of game theory is to investigate what outcomes might arise if one assumes that each plays rationally to achieve his/her own ends. There are variants depending on whether the players compete or cooperate in coalitions and upon the definition that is taken of rationality. Originally von Neumann and Morgenstern suggested that a *maximin* definition of rationality might be adopted. This is a very pessimistic way of taking decisions. For each possible action, the DM identifies what the worst is that could happen and then chooses the action that has the best worst outcome – i.e. maximin = 'maximise the minimum pay-off'. In strictly competitive games, in which all the players are out to maximise their own personal gains whatever the cost to the others, this might be a sensible criterion; for any games with some element of cooperation, however, the rationality of maximin is questionable.

Since von Neumann and Morgenstern's original work, other approaches to rationality have been investigated, notably the Bayesian (Harsanyi, 1977; Smith, 1996). For general reviews of game theory, see, for example, Colman (1995), Osborne (2003) or the classic introductory text by Luce and Raiffa (1957). We would emphasise that, while game theory does provide some guidance for individual players, its primary concern is to explore conflict and cooperation between players. This is a subtle distinction, but it is important. Players looking for advice on their decision making in a game might be better served looking to the general literature on decision analysis rather than game theory itself (French, 1986; Kadane and Larkey, 1983; Kadane *et al.*, 1999; van Binsbergen and Larx, 2007). There have many behavioural studies of the strategies actually adopted by players in games (Camerer, 1997, 2003; Colman, 1995). Finally, we note two game theoretic approaches that can help DMs formulate issues in game-like contexts, hypergames (Bennett, 1977) and metagames (Howard, 1971), which are both related to drama theory (Rosenhead and Mingers, 2001).

Closely related to game theory and its exploration of competition and cooperation between several players is the literature on bargaining and negotiation. Raiffa *et al.* (2003) provide a comprehensive introduction to these topics, exploring normative, descriptive and prescriptive approaches. Two earlier texts by Raiffa are also still very relevant: Luce and Raiffa (1957) and Raiffa (1982). Raiffa *et al.* (2003) adopt an approach that – like ours – explores the normative, prescriptive and descriptive issues. They argue that negotiation is similar to other kinds of decision making: there is a normative theory determining what people should do if they wish to be rational, but this is not descriptive of what people actually do. Instead, people engage in heuristic forms of thinking, which can lead to error and bias; error and bias in this context can include such negative outcomes as not reaching a settlement, or ending up with a settlement that is suboptimal for one or both parties.

Bazerman (2006) devotes a chapter to describing some of these heuristics, many of which we have already met in earlier chapters of this book. For example, he considers framing effects (see section 2.4) that show people are more likely to reach a settlement when the negotiation is framed in gains rather than losses; overconfidence and optimism (see sections 2.6, 2.7 and 3.8) that lead people to believe too strongly that they are right and that their protagonist is wrong; and anchoring effects, whereby possible settlements presented early in a negotiation have a constraining effect upon the discovery of better ones later.

In response to these potential mistakes, Raiffa *et al.* (2003) outline a procedure to follow that, from users' standpoints, is prescriptive for them and descriptive of their protagonists. In particular, the procedure prescribes a series of steps that users should follow to establish their interests, the relative importance of these interests and their bottom line. It then outlines a procedure for developing a description of these same elements from their protagonists' standpoints. They suggest a series of strategies for achieving this – e.g. by building trust so that information is shared, asking questions that are likely to reveal this information and strategically disclosing information as a means of encouraging the protagonist to do the same.

The procedure emphasises the importance of users gathering information to understand better their own objectives and values as well as those of their protagonists. From this standpoint, the process of negotiation is about information gathering rather than influencing. This is an important point to note, since in negotiations it is unlikely that the people involved will change their views. Even when these views are in conflict, however, it is often possible to find a settlement that is of mutual benefit.

Globalisation, the growth of international supply chains and the increasing power of the web have led to much recent work on electronic negotiations to help companies and their suppliers negotiate contracts (Bichler *et al.*, 2003). Modern agent technology means that more and more of these negotiations are being automated (Chen *et al.*, 2005; Macs *et al.*, 1999). Another topical application of negotiation theory is in the arena of public participation (Kersten, 2003; Ríos Insua *et al.*, 2003). Ríos and Ríos Insua (2008) provide an application to the development of a council's budget.

11.7 Concluding remarks and further reading

In this chapter we have continued the discussion of strategic decision making in the corporate strategic and general domains, but begun to acknowledge that such decisions are usually, though not inevitably, taken by groups of DMs. We have not discussed the group context in the operational or hands-on domains. Generally, these problems are better structured and the potential for differing perspectives is less. Organisations have an agreed approach to such decisions, and decision support is usually very similar to that for a single decision maker.

As we have seen, the provision of group decision support has to address the potential for dysfunctional group behaviour, on the one hand, and the nebulous concept of ideal rational and democratic behaviour, on the other. There is much more we could have said on descriptive studies of the behaviour of groups. The classic text is that of Janis and Mann (1977) (see also Argyris, 2001, Baron and Kerr, 2004, Brehmer, 1986, Forsyth, 2006, Hall and Williams, 1970, Kerr and Tindale, 2004, Phillips and Phillips, 1993, and Sudweeks and Allbritton, 1996). Closely related topics on which we were silent are the roles that members play in the group and how, with this knowledge, one can build effective management groups (Belbin, 1991; Naude *et al.*, 2000). Turning to concepts of ideal behaviour, the literature on voting systems, group decision making, social choice and game theory is peppered with discoveries of paradoxes, inconsistencies and impossibility results (Bacharach, 1975; Bacharach and Hurley, 1991; Dryzek and List, 2003; French, 1985, 1986; French and Ríos Insua, 2000; Hodge and Klima, 2005; Kelly, 1978; Luce and Raiffa, 1957; McLean and Urken, 1995; Raiffa *et al.*, 2003; Taylor, 1995, 2005; Tulloch, 1998; von Neumann and Morgenstern, 1947). We have presented Arrow's classic result, but, as we have indicated, there are many other issues, such as the manipulability of systems through tactical voting and agenda rigging (Gibbard, 1973; Hodge and Klima, 2005; Patternaik, 1978).

We have explored various approaches to group decision support that resolved these tensions from the perspective that groups are social processes, not entities that can decide in the same sense that individuals can. This led us to consider facilitated workgroups, also called decision conferences (Eden and Radford, 1990; Hämäläinen and Leikola, 1996; Phillips, 1984). Discussions of the role and effectiveness of facilitation can be found in Ackermann (1996), Antunes and Ho (2001), Eden and Radford (1990), Griffith *et al.* (1998), Macaulay and Alabdulkarim (2005), Ngwenyama *et al.* (1996) and Seifert (2002). A current development is the growth of *collaboration engineering*, a multidisciplinary approach to designing procedures and systems to support specific types of group decisions (Briggs *et al.*, 2003; de Vreede, 2006).

11.8 Exercises and questions for discussion

(1) N & T is a retail organisation of very long standing that has been losing market share every year for each of the last ten years, in contrast to its major competitors, which have increased their market

share. Over this period the personnel on the board have remained largely the same, have worked together very closely to try to rectify the situation, but have had little success. There is now some concern that the quality of decision making of this strategic group may be suboptimal, and they are seeking expert advice from you about possible limitations in their group decision making and how these might be overcome. Write a report for this group outlining some of the potential advantages of group decision making, some of the factors that may inhibit the achievements of these advantages, what can be done to improve this activity and the relevance of these for the situation at N & T.

The report should include:

- a review of theory and research on the potential advantages and disadvantages of group decision making, highlighting the factors that limit the effectiveness of group decision making, and emphasising those that are particularly relevant to the situation at N & T;
- a critical review of the approaches designed to improve group decision making, outlining possible strengths and weaknesses of each, including which aspects of the limitations described above that each approach addresses, and the particular relevance of these for the situation at N & T; and
- some specific recommendations for the group involved.

We suggest that you structure your report in the following way.

- A brief introduction outlining the background to the report (including why these kinds of issues are important and why they come about), the aims and objectives of the report and its structure – i.e. the major sections and their purpose.
- A section reviewing the extant literature on the effectiveness/ineffectiveness of group decision making, highlighting those aspects likely to be particularly relevant to the group in question.
- A section reviewing ways of improving group decision making, pointing out which aspects of poor decision making each addresses and their strengths and weaknesses in the context of their application to the strategic situation at N & T.
- A conclusion outlining some recommendations and limitations in the report.

Organisational decision support

12.1 Introduction

Decision making is an essential – some might say defining – characteristic of human activity.[1] Our thesis is that decision making is the province of the individual, requiring thought, evaluation and a final act of intentionality. Groups, we have suggested, are social processes that provide contexts in which the individual members can coordinate their decisions. Organisations and society provide further levels of context for decision making.

In this chapter we discuss decision analysis and support within organisations. We view organisations as contexts in which decisions and their implementation are coordinated. They exist to further some common, agreed objectives of a group of people. Owners and shareholders may gather together their resources to form a company to manufacture some goods or provide a service. Working together brings advantages of scale, the combining of disparate skills and so on. Communities and nations set up government bodies and agencies to provide common services. For our discussion it is probably best to keep in mind some small company with a board of directors, middle management, shop-floor managers and workers. We emphasise the need for decision making to fit with an organisation's culture and processes, in the general and operational domains particularly.

Our aims in this chapter are:

- to explore briefly how organisational decision making theory has been developed over the years;
- to outline representative organisational decision-making models;
- to discuss current organisational decision-making practices and examples of good practice; and

---

[1] And that of pigs (Orwell, 1945)?

- to explore the need to fit decision support into an organisation's processes and, indeed, to support these processes.

In the next section we explore the development of theories of organisational decision making, seeking to make connections between the different models that have been proposed and to set a context for the later sections of the chapter. In section 3 we discuss the different models of organisational decision making in more detail. With this as background, section 4 considers how decision analysis and support can fit into organisational settings, an issue picked up again in section 6, after a discussion in section 5 of the effectiveness of organisational decision making in practice. We close with a short section on emergency management organisations and a guide to the literature.

12.2 A historical perspective on organisational decision making

[A]n organization is a collection of choices looking for problems, issues and feelings looking for decision situations in which they might be aired, solutions looking for issues to which they might be the answer, and decision makers looking for work. (Michael Cohen, James March and John Olsen)

We do not offer any formal definition of organisations (for a general discussion, see Handy, 1993, and Jacques, 1989). It is difficult to distinguish them precisely from groups, on the one hand, and societies, on the other. Organisations generally have greater permanence than groups, but not always. As we shall see, emergency management organisations are built around a pre-existing skeleton and come into being at the time of an incident so as to resolve that incident, set up recovery and then disband. Organisations often have a legal constitution and many need to be registered, for example as a company or corporation; but small professional partnerships also need legal foundations, though they behave, in our terms at least, more as groups than organisations. The very largest organisations can have the same scale as societies, with the biggest multinationals wielding as much financial power as many small nations and affecting as many lives. There is a much greater degree of commonality in the objectives of those who come together to form an organisation than in society in general. Perhaps the simplest way of indicating what we mean by organisations is to list a few common examples: a company, a professional body, a government agency, a co-operative, an army or a trade union. Some organisations are virtual, with components of their activities serviced by other organisations or individuals.

Organisational decisions are taken by individuals such as managers or organisational units for organisational purposes only (Barnard, 1938). In his book *The Functions of the Executive*, Barnard, a retired telecommunications engineer, sought to interpret the behaviour of individuals who act in the interest of their organisation rather than their own. He was the first to distinguish between individual and organisational decision making. While Barnard is credited with making the distinction and introducing the term 'decision making' into the business world, it is the work of scholars such as Simon, March, Cyert and Mintzberg that established and laid the foundations of managerial decision making (Buchanan and O'Connell, 2006). The 'Carnegie school', in particular, led the efforts to study and interpret organisational decision making. Three of the most representative books of the Carnegie Mellon approach are those of Simon (1957), March and Simon (1958) and Cyert and March (1963).

It was in the beginning of the previous century that Dewey (1910) suggested decision making as a process that can be broken down into phases. Perhaps the most influential process model, however, was developed by Simon (1960), built around a sequence of three stages: intelligence, design and choice (cf. the formulation, analysis and evaluate model in figure 3.6). Other notable developments at the time were those of Simon (1957) and March and Simon (1958), who challenged the economists' view that DMs use accurate and complete information to make choices so as to maximise the utility of their chosen alternative. As Langley *et al.* (1995) remark, however, even though Simon questioned the notion of economic rationality, he advocated 'cerebral rationality', which views decision making as a cognitive process consisting of a number of programmed steps. Simon's *administrative man* (Simon, 1957) seeks to be rational but his rationality is bounded due to cognitive limitations (see 'bounded rationality' in section 2.2). In this sense, administrative man lies between the economists' rational economic man and the psychologists' non-rational man.

Several models of organisational decision making have been proposed, though we do not venture into the details of these. Briefly, following the introduction of Simon's intelligence–design–choice model, Mintzberg *et al.* (1976) proposed a model that involved three major phases of decision making (identification, development and selection), which are not necessarily sequential, and seven decision-making routines, which occur in no particular order and may be repeated. Along these lines, Nutt (1984) identified five types of organisational decision-making processes. Both studies challenge the validity of normative approaches. At the other extreme is the *garbage can model* (Cohen *et al.*, 1972), which seeks to interpret decision making in settings characterised by high levels of ambiguity regarding involvement and participation in decision activities and organisational procedures, and inconsistent preferences. After exploring many organisational decision processes, the 'Bradford group' presented three categories: constricted, sporadic and fluid (Hickson *et al.*, 1989, 2001).

Bazerman (1999) discerns two main research trends since the early efforts of the Carnegie school. First, work on micro-organisational behaviour based on Simon's bounded rationality model that focuses on the psychological aspects of decision making; and, second, research on macro-organisational behaviour based on March's work that focuses on developing organisational decision making research areas. Micro-research focuses on cognitive aspects and judgemental heuristics (see chapter 2) whereas macro-research is concerned with organisational issues such as conflict, rationality and power (see section 3 below).

In an effort to distinguish between organisational decision making and individual decision making, Shapira revisited Barnard (1938). Shapira (1997) argues that individual decision making, particularly as studied in laboratory settings, is different from organisational decision making in the following ways.

- *Ambiguity*. Rather than taking clear-cut decisions, with unambiguous information and probability distributions, there is deep and innate ambiguity over preferences, interpretations and judgements in organisational settings.
- *Longitudinal context*. Organisational decisions involve a number of actors and unfold over a period of time, initiating a myriad of other decisions on the way. Sense making and commitment may be more important elements than accurate judgements.
- *Incentives*. Unlike the meagre rewards in experimental studies, organisational decisions have real incentives and penalties that can have a profound effect on the decisions taken.
- *Repetition*. Organisational decisions at the tactical and operational levels (see section 1.2) tend to be repetitive; decision actors often employ a number of mechanisms, such as developing skills, exercising control and following rules, as opposed to the evaluation of alternatives.
- *Conflict*. Power structures and agenda rigging (section 11.3) often determine the outcome of decisions in organisational contexts.

Shapira (1997) is notable in highlighting a fundamental argument in organisational decision making: whether we need to focus on individual factors to understand organisational decision making or whether we need to study organisational aspects and processes in their own right. The two research streams stem from work by Simon and March, the two co-authors of *Organizations*, who helped to establish the field of organisational decision making. As Payne (1997) points out, if we are to understand the field fully, we need to develop understanding from both perspectives.

12.3 Organisational decision-making models

Intelligent people, when assembled into an organization, will tend toward collective stupidity [Albrecht's law]. (Karl Albrecht)

The main assumption of the Carnegie school approach is that decision making is a central organisational activity (Simon, 1973). This view was later reinforced by Bass (1983), who points out that organisational decision making is the most important facet of organisational life. The centrality of decision making in organisational settings is at the heart of the decision-making paradigm of organisational design (Huber and McDaniel, 1986) that advocates the redesign of organisations so as to enhance and facilitate decision-making processes.

One of the main approaches to studying organisational decision making at the macro-level is to collect a number of cases. Mintzberg *et al.* (1976) discuss twelve distinctive elements, such as phases and routines, in twenty-five cases collected by students. March and Olsen (1976) discuss thirteen cases and Nutt (1984) analyses seventy-eight decision-making cases. One of the most notable research initiatives is that by Hickson *et al.* (1986), later compiled into a book entitled *The Bradford Studies* (Hickson *et al.*, 2001), which explores 150 longitudinal cases of organisational decision-making processes collected from thirty organisations.

Huber (1981) and Eisenhardt and Zbaracki (1992) summarise the work reviewed above by outlining the following organisational decision-making models.

- The rational model assumes that organisational units seek to use information rationally so as to take decisions on behalf of their organisation. The underlying assumption is that actors in a decision have a purpose and pursue goals. They collect information so as to identify a set of alternatives, then determine a range of possible outcomes and choose the optimal alternative depending on organisational objectives. The body of literature on the rational model includes research on the nature of organisational decision making (e.g. March and Simon, 1958; Mintzberg *et al.*, 1976; Simon, 1957); work on rational modelling (e.g. French, 1986; French and Ríos Insua, 2000; Keeney and Raiffa, 1976); research on how to use information in a rational way (e.g. Keen and Scott Morton, 1978); and the application of normative procedures such as OR in organisational settings (e.g. Howard and Matheson, 1984). Several instruments and constructs have been developed to measure rationality (Dean and Sharfman, 1993; Elbanna and Child, 2007; Papadakis *et al.*, 1998). A simple form of the rational model is Simon's three-stage model (Simon, 1960), described in the previous section.

- The political/competitive model focuses on how organisational units develop and apply strategies and tactics to influence organisational decision-making processes in such a way as to benefit themselves. The underlying assumption is that organisations are political systems that can be viewed as coalitions of individuals with conflicting objectives (March, 1962) shaped by status, ambitions, biases and the way they perceive the future (Allison, 1971). There are four research threads: studies on how power is enacted (e.g. Pettigrew, 1972); field studies to interpret the relationship between decision processes and outcomes from a political perspective (e.g. Dean and Sharfman, 1993; Pfeffer and Salancik, 1974); representative case studies (e.g. Baldridge, 1971); and studies exploring the role of politics (e.g. March, 1962; Pettigrew, 1973).

- The garbage can model views organisations as 'organised anarchies'. In such organisational settings, events occur by chance, decisions are complex and fuzzy and decision actors with different perspectives come in and out of the process depending on their schedules, energy and interests. DMs make choices whenever they are faced with a problem, take advantage of opportunities or have solutions and seek to identify what problems these solutions can address. Small changes in circumstances can change the decision outcome substantially. Unlike the previous two models, it is not clear what the beginning and end of a decision process are. The name 'garbage can model' may suggest that it is rather superficial, but it can be used to describe decision processes in ambiguous, complex and volatile settings. The two most representative publications on the model are those by Cohen *et al.* (1972) and March and Olsen (1976).

- The process/programme model was introduced to fill the gap created when rationality, political behaviour or anarchy are not viewed as the drivers of a decision process. It is in line with Simon's bounded rationality model, which allows for the presence of cognitive and other kinds of resource limitations in decision making. The model is based on three assumptions. First, that 'programmes' such as procedures and financial considerations place constraints and affect decision making. Second, that decision behaviour can be influenced by 'programming' in the form of training schemes and initiatives to motivate staff. Third, that decision-making behaviour is predictable. As Huber (1981:4) points out, the essence of the process/programme model is that 'organisational decisions are consequences of the programming and programs of the units involved'.

The above models are representative in the sense that there is some evidence in the literature to support them all. Other models have been developed to interpret decision behaviour in particular settings, such as a crisis (e.g. Snyder and Paige, 1958). The four models are complementary; all of them can be used to interpret different aspects of the same decision process, with the possibility that some models are more relevant than others (see, for example, Allison 1971). In other words, in every decision we may be able to identify political traits, rational elements, choices made by chance and process-predictable behaviour.

12.4 The internal and external contexts of organisations

[A]nyone who has spent time with any variety of organisations, or worked in more than two or three, will have been struck by the differing atmospheres, the differing ways of doing things, the differing levels of energy, of individual freedom, of kinds of personality. (Charles Hardy)

To consider how and where decision analysis and support fit into organisational structures and processes, we need to reflect a little on the many different aspects of the context[2] in which an organisation undertakes its work: see figure 12.1.

Its work. The work of an organisation, by which it achieves its objectives, takes inputs from the external world and processes these into its outputs. The inputs may include, for example, raw materials, customer orders and requests, finance, consultancy or knowledge; and its outputs may include goods, services, reputation or environmental impacts.

Structure. Organisations come in many shapes and sizes and have many structural forms. Many are structured hierarchically within divisions, but over the past two decades there has been a growth in matrix organisations and organisational structures built around its key processes (Hammer and Champy, 1993; Jacques, 1989; Scott Morton, 1991; Warboys *et al.*, 1999).

---

[2] Cf. 7 S's and PESTEL (section 9.3).

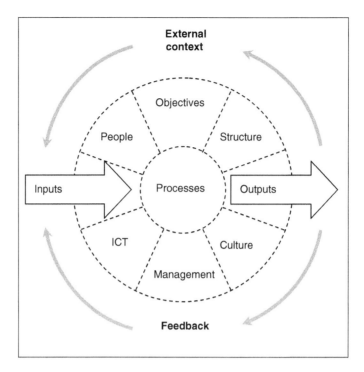

Figure 12.1   The internal and external contexts of organisations

Culture. Organisational cultures differ in a myriad of ways, relating to norms, attitudes, beliefs and underlying values. Some organisations are consensual in their decision making while others are more hierarchical and directive. In some, team working is the norm and there is a supportive culture between its members; in others, individuals work more on their own. In addition, of course, there are issues of national culture (Hofstede, 1984, 1994), which are of growing importance with globalisation: see case vignette 12.1.

Management. In addition to scheduling the workflows and strategically developing the organisation to meet its objectives, the management group ensures that all the necessary infrastructure and resources are in place to conduct the organisation's work. It has the responsibility for ensuring that the organisation conforms to regulations and for monitoring its performance.

Information and communications technology. While ICT is only one part of the infrastructure that supports an organisation, it is a key part in relation to our discussion of DSSs. It is also the major driver of many of the current developments in the ways that organisations do business. Information systems are becoming more and more aligned with an organisation's

Case vignette 12.1 Cultural issues in the use of GISs

Walsham and Sahay (1998) described the use – or, rather, lack of use – of geographical information systems in Indian district administrations. An American aid programme had provided many district councils in India with GISs, but subsequently found that they were seldom used. Walsham and Sahay found that Indian cultures have different spatial understandings and metaphors from Western cultures, so that the HCIs of the systems were literally foreign to them and difficult to use.

processes and less divided into servicing divisional needs separately (Laudon and Laudon, 2006; Warboys *et al.*, 1999). Moreover, as automation and workflow systems grow and supply chains are coordinated via the web and e-business technologies, ICT is becoming the integrator of all organisational activities.

People. Since we hold that decision making is the province of individuals, the people within an organisation are central to our study of decision analysis and support. Their knowledge and perspectives shape the decision making.

External context. No organisation exists in a vacuum. It interacts with its external context in many ways, not the least of which is in servicing some societal needs. For many of an organisation's decisions, some of its stakeholders are external to it.

Feedback. The outputs of an organisation's processes do not simply disappear; they are used outside the organisation, and this inevitably leads to feedback, which the organisation should take in and react to as one of its inputs.

Objectives. To reiterate: from our decision-making perspective the key drivers of an organisation's activities should be its objectives (see value-focused thinking: section 3.5). The objectives will evolve in discussions within the organisation and between it and its stakeholders, but for its day-to-day activities its objectives should be the determining factor. Note the word 'should'; many organisations do not have such a clear focus.

12.5 Organisational decision-making practices

An organization's ability to learn, and translate that learning into action rapidly, is the ultimate competitive advantage. (Jack Welch)

The ability of an organisation to take efficient and effective decisions can have a major impact on business sustainability and agility (Metcalfe, 2003). Understanding decision practices and the way that decisions are taken can help us understand decision choices and outcomes (Sutcliffe and McNamara, 2001).

Surveys on organisational decision-making practices have revealed some important limitations that have had a very negative impact. Capgemini (2004) reported that UK executives take approximately nineteen critical decisions every year. The report showed that the average decision failure is 24 per cent and that wrong or delayed decisions cost UK businesses £800,000 per executive. A similar study (Metcalfe, 2003) estimated the number and cost of all decisions in a typical business with dozens of executives, hundreds of middle managers and thousands of employees. The research suggested that in such an organisation there would be five strategic decisions (valued at €10 million each), fifty tactical decisions (valued at €1 million each) and 500,000 operational decisions (valued at €200 each). The report concluded that the total revenue impact of decisions is €200 million per year; see also Teradata (2004).

These studies show that poor decision making significantly affects company productivity and profits. Nevertheless, a more recent report indicates that customer loyalty and company reputation are the top two casualties of poor decision making (Teradata, 2006), and that these can have a long-term effect on a company's viability. The emphasis in organisational decision making research has now shifted from finding the 'right answer' to developing the necessary capabilities that are needed to develop systematic and effective methods for solving complex decision problems (Papamichail and Rajaram, 2007). Besides, there is clearly a demand for real-time data as well as a vertical and horizontal distribution of critical decision making across the organisation (Teradata, 2006).

As the importance of a decision increases, DMs feel obliged to demonstrate competence in decision making, and in doing so they are more likely to adhere to organisational procedures (Sutcliffe and McNamara, 2001). Therefore, if we identify and promote examples of good decision making, we may be able to improve decision performance.

Research on decision performance often focuses on organisational outputs rather than decision effectiveness and outputs (Elbanna and Child, 2007). Papamichail and Rajaram (2007) outline studies that specifically focus on decision outcomes such as success (Rodrigues and Hickson, 1995), achievement (Miller *et al.*, 2004) and quality (Roberto, 2005). Ireland and Miller (2004) summarise notable findings on decision performance taken from the strategic decision-making literature (cf. section 11.4).

- Organisational decisions tend to be effective when DMs apply their knowledge about an industry or a market place in which their organisation operates and they use real-time information about competitors and environmental conditions.

- The composition of groups of DMs, the assumptions they make and the extent to which their views are divergent are all important factors in the making of decisions.
- Divergent views and diversity in a group encourage thorough consideration of alternatives as long as diverse views are handled carefully.
- Conflict and differences on judgements can be constructive.
- Devil's advocacy and dialectical inquiry (involving the development of an anti-thesis and a counter-plan) are both useful in promoting healthy debate.

These findings overlap with recommendations on how to improve group decision making discussed in section 11.4. Further insights are outlined by Spetzler (2007) with suggestions that an organisation exhibits high-level decision competence when it meets the following criteria (see figure 12.2):

- making high-quality decisions on a regular basis;
- having decision-making procedures in place and highly skilled staff with access to a toolbox of decision analytic techniques;
- having DMs who clearly understand their roles and how they can contribute to decision-making processes;
- having a decision-making vision that is shared amongst all DMs; and
- being a learning-oriented organisation that strives to learn and improve its decision capabilities.

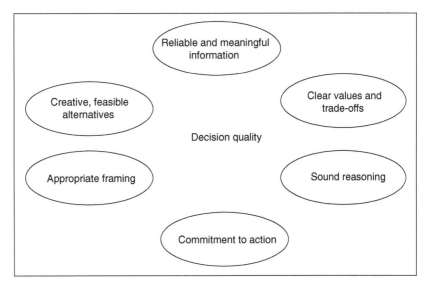

Figure 12.2   Decision quality elements
Source: Spetzler (2007).

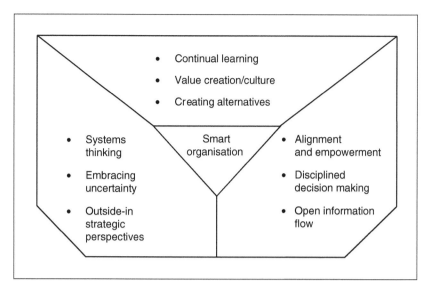

Figure 12.3   The nine characteristics of a smart organisation
Source: Matheson and Matheson (2007).

Matheson and Matheson (1998) reported a study of R&D strategic decisions in hundreds of companies and identified forty-five best practices,
such as understanding drivers of industry change, focusing on those factors that generate value and attracting and retaining the best. They found
that some organisations are more successful in adopting these practices
than others (Matheson and Matheson, 2007). Such smart organisations
tend to conform to 'nine principles' or characteristics: see figure 12.3.
Their 'organisational IQ' is much higher and they have a much higher
chance of performing well financially.

Sound judgement, high-quality data, empowering employees to take
decisions, giving them access to tools and training are all elements of good
decision making (EIU [Economist Intelligence Unit], 2007). Papamichail
and Rajaram (2007) identified a number of criteria for assessing decision
making practices: see figure 12.4. They present several examples of good-
practice organisations.

- Organisations in which it is easy to allocate authority and implement
  decisions and in which a trusting culture is fostered and an equal
  access to information is ensured.
- Having active learners and creative problem solvers who use and share
  information and seek to adopt best-practice examples.
- Companies that use ICT to compile and disseminate information in a
  thorough and timely manner.

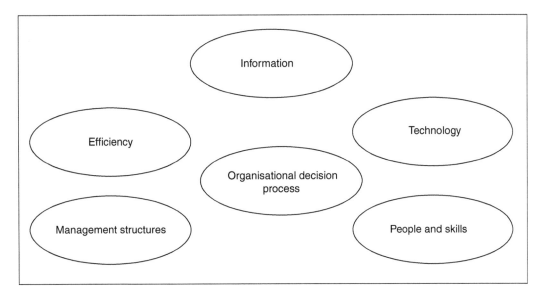

Figure 12.4   Criteria for assessing organisational decision-making practices
Source: Papamichail and Rajaram (2007).

- Organisations that provide an immediate response to a decision stimulus, have no delays/interruptions in the process and provide the right level of resources.
- Determining the composition of the decision-making body, involving experts and deciding how to decide.

12.6 Organisational decision analysis and support

[A]ny DSS of genuine significance is usually an integral part of a work system and often cannot be separated out easily. (Steven Alter)

Decisions seldom happen in isolation; usually one decision leads to another. Although organisations coordinate this process, the garbage can model suggests that they may not do this as well as they might hope. Good use of information systems and DSSs can, if introduced sensibly, reduce the tendency to muddle through, however.

For example, a decision to enter a new market brings decisions about which products to introduce, then where to manufacture these and how to distribute them to retailers, along with decisions on marketing and advertising. There may be a need to modify the products to conform with new regulations or simply a new language. How should such decisions be coordinated?

We believe that a key coordinating factor should be the development and use of clear and consistent objectives: see case vignettes 10.1 and 12.2. Of course, for some decisions the objectives will be more detailed than others; but there should be consistency.

In addition, ICT can also provide a key coordinating role through the use of enterprise resource planning, e-business and workflow systems. Papamichail and Robertson (2005) point out, however, that much still remains to be done to realise the full potential of these techniques. They propose a system, D2P (decisioning for decision support), to integrate all

Case vignette 12.2 Cascaded budgeting processes in organisations

Traditional budgeting techniques can lead to dysfunctional behaviour, with managers overestimating costs and underestimating growth in an implicit plea for easier funding. Financial objectives are overemphasised, with many of an organisation's less tangible objectives being underweighted. One approach to making the process more rational, open and inclusive involves the use of the multi-attribute value approach to resource allocation (Goodwin and Wright, 2003). The method uses a linked series of decision conferences. In the first conference the board of directors meet and agree the objectives for the budget allocation. They set up the attribute tree that will be used in all the subsequent analyses, agreeing the meanings of the attributes and defining the scales to be used to measure success against these. Each director then holds a decision conference with his or her support team, in which they consider what they would do in their division with different levels of funding.

Recognising that small changes in the budget would not change what they did in any significant way, the different levels are defined by their answers to questions of the form 'How much would the budget need to increase/decrease before we could do something qualitatively different?'. All costs and benefits are assessed against the attribute tree. The results from the directors' decision conferences are then brought together in a final decision conference attended by all directors. At this they draw together the results into an overall view across the organisation. Because they have well-argued cases of what each directorate would do with more or less funding, they can trade off increased activity in some areas with decreased activities in others, thereby building a portfolio that addresses the organisation's objectives.

Weaver and Morgan (1993) describe an application of this process in local government. The council concerned had in previous years spent many weeks in deciding how to divide its overall budget between areas such as housing, education, roads and recreation. The process had been far from easy, and often it had been heated. Using the process described here they developed a budget more acceptable to the various parties with less overall effort, and, above all, the method provided an audit trail that explained how and why the budgetary decisions had been made.

decision making – i.e. from that in the corporate strategic domain through the general and operational domains down to the hands-on domain. In many ways they take forward some of the imperatives that have been driving the evolution of OR. As we noted in chapter 6, OR began with a focus on operational problems but, over time, has developed approaches that deal with more strategic problems. Initially, OR addressed individual decisions, but, with the advent of much greater computational power, it now provides an integrated approach to many interrelated purchasing, production, inventory and distribution decisions: see case vignette 6.1. Papamichail and Robertson's work addresses how less structured strategic decisions, which set the parameters for decisions in other domains, can be integrated into such systems and, moreover, how to use workflow technologies to coordinate DMs, their inputs and the process.

Papamichail and Robertson present a vision of a fully integrated organisation with coherent decision making running alongside its other processes, all supported by enterprise-level workflow and information systems. The reality is generally quite different, however, albeit rapidly improving. Consider our categorisation in figure 3.7. The vision of an organisation's data being held in a single coherent database promoted in the 1970s may still be a pipe dream for the majority. The advent of data warehouses and business intelligence tools, howevers, means that in many cases data can be accessed, and thus consistent level 0 and level 1 support can be provided in all domains of activity. Forecasting OR models can be built upon these data, providing level 2 and 3 support in the operational and general domains. The advent of enterprise resource planning systems has facilitated this. In some businesses, AI and expert systems have been integrated into level 2 and 3 support in the hands-on domain. For instance, in online banking or call centre sales credit assessment, DSSs are fully integrated into the overall systems. That said, there are many stand-alone DSSs dotted around organisations offering staff level 2 and level 3 support, based upon small local databases and ways of working. In addition, within the corporate strategic domain, soft modelling and decision analytic tools are rarely used. In organisations in which the senior management has more authoritative styles, the use of such tools can be seen as usurping their roles: see section 6.3. Sadly, many executives believe that they are naturally good DMs, despite or in ignorance of many behavioural studies: see chapter 2.

Implementing DSSs within an organisation is far from easy. It has long been recognised that general information systems seldom bring all the benefits that were promised, and the ones that are achieved arrive more slowly than expected: the so-called productivity paradox (Galliers *et al.*, 1999). Implementing DSSs, KMSs and general CSCW systems is far more difficult. Decision support, we have argued, is a process designed to help users' cognitive perspective evolve, often by challenging their perceptions and assumptions. It is possible to design collaborative tools that require users to demonstrate team spirit and commit their efforts to save those of others: see the challenges proposed by Grudin (1994) (section 14.5). In short, such systems require not just the evolution of an organisation's processes but the evolution of its culture and continual learning and knowledge sharing on the part of its members. Implementing the methods we are promoting requires a subtle change to the management programme – one that acknowledges all the socio-technical aspects (Mumford, 1995, 2003). Few organisations allocate sufficient resources for this aspect of the implementation process, so reducing the impact that systems have on improving their decision making.

12.7 Emergency management support

'Yes, sir,' answered the victorious subordinate, 'it is a great thing to know exactly what to do in an emergency. When in doubt whether to attack or retreat I never hesitate a moment – I toss us a copper.'
   'Do you mean to say that's what you did this time?'
   'Yes, general, but for Heaven's sake don't reprimand me: I disobeyed the coin.'
(Ambrose Bierre)

Much of our discussion in this chapter has assumed the permanence of the organisation concerned. Some organisations form for a specific purpose, however, and then disband – e.g. organising a conference or a campaign. All three of us have been heavily involved in helping public authorities handle emergencies and incidents. In such cases one can argue that, technically, the emergency management organisation exists: indeed, its structure and existence are usually laid down in statute. In practice, however, emergency management organisations are usually skeletons onto which, during an emergency, many groups from other government agencies and departments are grafted to help deal with the issue and facilitate recovery. Experience in past emergencies has shown that it is vital to ensure coherent information management and consistent decision making in order both to handle the emergency in a technical sense and to ensure that the concerns of all those affected are addressed effectively and sensitively (French *et al.*, 2007a; French and Niculae,

2005). DSSs and KMSs both have a major role to play in achieving this: see case vignette 12.3 for a brief description of the RODOS system for nuclear emergency management.

Case vignette 12.3 The RODOS system for supporting the management of nuclear accidents

A key lesson drawn from the Chernobyl accident was the importance of a coherent, harmonised and sensitive response to nuclear emergencies. To assist this, a comprehensive DSS has been developed. The Real-time Online DecisiOn Support (RODOS) system is now deployed in several countries to provide support from the earliest threat to the longer-term clean-up and restoration of normal living. RODOS has a modular design, reflecting its objective of meeting the needs of many users in many countries. For instance, while it includes an atmospheric dispersion module to predict the spread of a plume, the precise meteorology and dispersion physics needed will vary from county to country according to the prevailing terrain and meteorology. Each country can thus integrate consequence models appropriate to its environment.

The architecture of RODOS is split conceptually into three distinct families of modules: see figure on next page.
- *Analysing subsystem* (ASY) modules process incoming data and forecast the spread of contamination. These modules embody meteorological, dispersion, deposition and absorption, health effect and other models. ASY modules provide support at levels 0 and 1.
- *Countermeasure subsystem* (CSY) modules suggest possible countermeasures, check them for feasibility and predict their effects in ameliorating the consequences in terms of a number of attributes. CSY modules provide level 2 support.
- *Evaluation Subsystem* (ESY) modules rank countermeasure strategies using MAVA. ESY modules provide the level 3 support of the system.

The interconnection of all programme modules, the input, transfer and exchange of data, and interactive and automatic modes of operation are controlled by the RODOS Operating System (OSY), a layer built upon the network operating system. Interaction with users and display of data takes place via a graphical subsystem (GSY), which includes a purpose-built geographical information system (RoGIS). RODOS is designed to be used on local- and wide-area networks with different functionality and interfaces appropriate to the needs and skills of particular users.

The content of the modules and the databases vary depending on the nature and characteristics of the accident. The timing of decisions has considerable influence on what information is available and how information can be aggregated. RODOS recognises this temporal context; as the situation evolves, RODOS will arrive at different decision points, at which it must select three modules to form an ASY–CSY– ESY chain appropriate to the context.

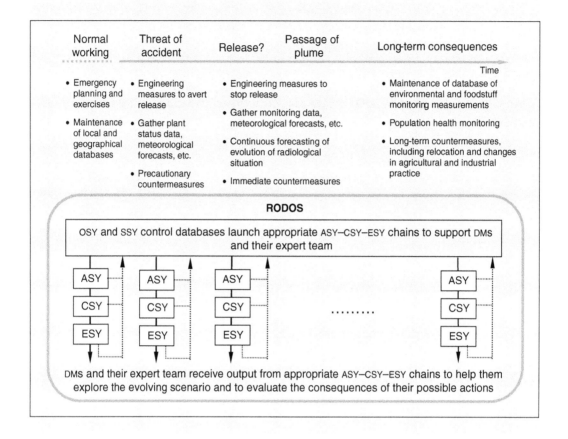

12.8 Concluding remarks and further reading

Our discussion of organisational decision making has barely touched on many key issues and omitted many more. For more general discussions, we refer to the literature (Handy, 1993; Jacques, 1989). Kleindorfer *et al.* (1993) provide a longer discussion of decision making within organisations, while Boddy *et al.* (2005) take an organisational perspective on the whole subject of information systems. The volume edited by Hodgkinson and Stasbuck (2008) explores organisational decision making at different levels, including those of individuals and inter-organisational activities. Courtney (2001) discusses the need for more collaborative paradigms for DSSs and KMSs in the context of learning organisations. In our discussion of decision making in organisations we recognised that many decisions are interrelated. There is a substantial literature on the theory of sequential and interrelated decisions: see section 6.6.

There have been notable readings that have shaped our understanding of organisational decision making from several perspectives, including sense making (Weick, 1995), information processing (Salancik and Pfeffer, 1978), intuition (Khatri and Alvin, 2000; Simon, 1987) and contextual factors (Papadakis *et al.*, 1998). Decision making has been studied in a variety of settings, including naturalistic settings (Klein, 1998) and high-velocity environments (Eisenhardt, 1989). There has been extensive research on cognitive limitations (e.g. Anderson, 1983; Cyert and March, 1963; Pinfield, 1986) and decision processes (e.g. Rajagopalan *et al.*, 1993). The Cuban Missile Crisis is an example of a well-documented organisational decision process that has been thoroughly explored from different perspectives (e.g. Allison, 1971; Anderson, 1983; Roberto, 2005). Decision making phases, such as the initial stage (e.g. Mintzberg *et al.*, 1976) and the formulation phase (e.g. Nutt, 1993), have also been investigated.

In case vignette 12.3 we briefly described the RODOS DSS for nuclear emergency management (Ehrhardt and Weiss, 2000; French *et al.*, 1998a, 2000; Papamichail and French, 2005). Several other similar systems exist (Bäverstam *et al.*, 1997; French *et al.*, 2007a; Hohenberg and Kelly, 2004; Papazoglou and Christou, 1997). More general issues relating to DSSs for emergency management may be found in the *International Journal of Risk Assessment and Management*, volume 2, issue 3–4 (2001). Carter and French (2006) look at the processes of nuclear emergency management and ask whether the current ones are adequate. A closely related literature is that of high-reliability organisations (Bigley and Roberts, 2001; Roberts, 1990; Weick, 1987).

12.9 Exercises and questions for discussion

(1) 'Herbert Simon's "cerebral man" can be placed in the middle between the economists' "rational man" and the psychologists' "non-rational man".' Discuss.

(2) What are the differences between individual and organisational decision making?

(3) Discuss the two approaches to interpreting and studying organisational decision making (i.e. micro- versus macro-organisational behaviour).

(4) Outline and discuss the four models of organisational decision making.

(5) What is 'good practice in organisational decision making'? Illustrate your answer with examples.

(6) How can we *support* organisational decision processes?

Societal decision making

I know of no safe depository of the ultimate powers of the society but the people themselves; and if we think of them as not enlightened enough to exercise their control with a wholesome discretion, the remedy is not to take it from them, but to inform their discretion. (Thomas Jefferson)

13.1 Introduction

Many decisions are taken by the whole or significant parts of a society. In Western countries, they are generally made through systems of representative democracy, though after our discussion in section 11.3 we might wonder how democratic they actually are. In representative democracies, politicians are elected to run the state, perhaps informed by occasional referendums. In many cases they delegate much societal decision making to regulators and planning agencies, such as the US Food and Drug Administration or the British Health and Safety Executive. There are also tiers of democracy, national, regional and local governments with a complex weave of powers and authorities flowing between them. Sometimes an independent judiciary oversees the political process, providing checks and balances against misused authority. In addition, of course, any description of a political system is an ideal: in politics 'political' behaviour is rife, and decision making can sidestep some of the formal procedures, driven by other agendas and horse-trading. Against this background there is an overwhelming need for analytic methodologies that document explicitly the reasoning behind a decision, indicating the evidence and how it was weighed. The methods of decision analysis that we have been promoting can, we argue, provide such documentation and audit trails.

We do not intend to discuss political constitutions and general structures of representative democracies here. Rather, we focus on some of the processes and analyses that may support societal decision making on particular issues: for instance, the siting of major facilities such as hospitals or airports, the regulation of risks associated with food hygiene or industrial discharges, environmental management and major changes to the law in which moral judgements may be key – e.g. the licensing of human stem cell research. In fact, the history of decision analysis is closely linked with such decisions. As the opening paragraph indicates, major public decisions need to be open to scrutiny. Formal analytic processes that document all the pros and cons of various alternatives are attractive, therefore, and have long been adopted in the public sector.

In the next section we look back briefly at the development of cost–benefit analysis (CBA), which, coming from economic and social welfare theory, had its origins in very different imperatives from those of decision analysis. We contrast the two approaches, noting that nowadays their differences are more imagined than real: they have converged to become essentially parallel methodologies. In section 3 we turn to public risk perception and communication. If society is, in some sense, to make a decision then society needs to understand the issues upon which it is deliberating. In many cases these involve uncertainty and risk, and it is a common observation that individuals understand and relate to risks in many different ways, offering potential for misunderstanding and mis-communication in the debates and deliberations that precede societal decision making. Major societal decisions have impacts on many stake-holders apart from those who are responsible for the decision and those who directly benefit from it. To reach such decisions in an inclusive, democratic way, there is a need for debate between all the stakeholders as to the merits and disadvantages of various policies and on the uncertainties involved. In section 4 we discuss modern approaches to deliberative democracy and public participation – e.g. stakeholder workshops and citizens' juries. Recognising the pervasiveness of the internet and the web in support of the workings of society, we then turn to e-participation and e-democracy, asking if these are as transparent and effective as their proponents suggest. Finally, we provide a brief overview of the literature and suggest further reading.

Our objectives in this chapter are:

- to understand the differences between cost–benefit and decision analytic approaches to societal decision making;
- to explore communication issues, particularly risk communication ones, across very large groups and societies;
- to discuss public participation in modern societal decision making; and
- to recognise that web-based deliberation and decision support, e-participation and e-democracy may not the panacea for the global networked world of the twenty-first century that is sometimes assumed.

13.2 A brief look at cost–benefit analysis

Surely there comes a time when counting the cost and paying the price aren't things to think about any more. All that matters is value – the ultimate value of what one does. (James Hilton)

For many years the most common analytical tool used in government was cost–benefit analysis (BA): see, for example, Layard and Glaister (1994) or Pearce and Nash (1981). This methodology[1] has its roots in economic theory and social welfare functions. A social welfare function seeks to represent the overall value to society of different scenarios or options – an objective that Arrow's theorem warns is a trifle optimistic! CBA articulates this idea by trying to make a quantitative evaluation of the benefits and disbenefits of any decision, expressing these in terms of their monetary value. Since monetary value was presumed to be objective, CBA was seen as supporting societal decision making in terms of objective analyses. Nonetheless, the 'objectivity' of a CBA study depends on the extent to which *all* relevant consequences and their 'objective' monetary values can be unambiguously determined – a situation unlikely to occur in reality.

In the need to identify *all* the relevant consequences, the problem faced by CBA is no different from that faced by decision analysis or any other analytic process. One can never be sure that one has identified all the possibilities. Between thirty and fifty years ago, however, when CBA was in its heyday, it was uncommon to involve many stakeholders in the analysis, so many important perspectives on potential consequences went unremarked and unanalysed. This led to much criticism of CBA, some of which was not entirely justified. In its claim to provide an *objective* monetary evaluation of the consequences that it did identify, however, CBA can justifiably be criticised. One can, as CBA's proponents did, appeal to market economics to claim that the 'market' determines monetary value; but there is seldom, if ever, a clear choice of market on which all stakeholders can agree; and different markets may value the possible consequences differently. Even if one could identify unambiguous monetary values for all aspects of all consequences, the idea of evaluating alternatives according to their net expected benefits minus net expected costs is suspect. The resulting evaluation ignores who pays and who benefits. It is rare for the same people or legal entity to both receive the benefits and pay the costs.

---

[1] We should perhaps note that there never was a single CBA methodology but, rather, a family of methods sharing a common philosophical origin: namely that the value of a decision equals the net expected benefits expressed in monetary terms minus the net expected costs, again expressed monetarily.

For example, consider the costs of pollution. Despite the current political imperative to make the polluter pay, it is uncommon for the full cost of dealing with pollution to fall entirely and only on those creating the pollution. Thus other parts of society pay without sharing in the polluter's profits. Hence, CBA proponents take recourse to the Kaldor–Hicks or 'mutual gains' principle, arguing that those gaining *could* in principle compensate those losing. In practice, compensation rarely happens, although some possible mechanisms do exist to do this – for example, power utilities could reduce prices to compensate those members of public at risk from living near the generation plants. A further criticism derives from work on the compatability and evaluability hypotheses reviewed earlier in section 2.4. These hypotheses and the research that underpins them show that the actual values derived from any public consultation vary significantly according to the methods and scales used in evaluation. This makes it extremely difficult to establish what the public's 'true' values are. Indeed, Slovic (1995) has argued that there are no true values; rather, people construct them 'on the spot', and varying the ways in which the questions are asked changes their expressed values. More general critiques of CBA may be found in Adams (1995), Bedford *et al.* (2005) and Layard (1972).

The aims of CBA are laudable. It seeks to analyse and evaluate alternative future scenarios according to their monetary worth to a (large) group of people, ideally society in general. The imperative to do so is based upon the hope that such an evaluation will be objective and so diffuse potentially bitter debate between the proponents of the alternatives. The difficulty is that values, whether expressed monetarily or otherwise, are essentially subjective judgements. They are necessarily made by individuals, and there need be little agreement. Thus, in seeking to present a single, objective valuation of any course of action, CBA places at its heart an ill-defined concept. It begs controversy in assuming agreement and unanimity when it is virtually certain that there is none. It is *not* an objective methodology; it simply fails to acknowledge its subjectivity. Decision analysis, as described in the previous chapters, is explicitly subjective. It renders the subjective judgements explicit and open for exploration and debate. It is based upon a model of an idealised DM, actually the self-same rational economic man who underpins much of the market theory underlying CBA. Instead of looking at an idealised model of several rational economic men involved in buying and selling, however, decision analysis considers an individual rational DM who faces the same problem as the organisation, stakeholder groups and society as a whole does. Subject to consistency conditions, the model can express the beliefs and value judgements of any individual in society. Usually, differences between individuals in society are reflected in the weights that they place upon different factors or in the perceived likelihood of some event. By careful use of sensitivity techniques, an analysis can identify which differences are critical and thus focus debate on the issues that matter. It can often be shown that, despite differences in judgements, many elements of society agree on the course of action to be taken, so diffusing sterile debate. Note that we are arguing that disagreements between groups are addressed via sensitivity analysis and debate, not via some mathematical formula that combines judgements in some 'democratic' way and prescribes a consensus decision. We do not forget the import of Arrow's theorem.

Despite these remarks, nowadays CBA and decision analysis are not so different. Many years ago the proponents of each were locked in controversy, given that they saw the world from very different perspectives. Today there has been a convergence: both are seen as analytical tools for supporting public debate by supplying interesting and useful perspectives on the issues. The differences in the two approaches are well understood and in practice the methods have often adopted techniques and perspectives of the other – for instance, a 'market value' of an impact may be used as a point of reference in a decision analysis and the region around it explored via sensitivity analysis. Just such an example occurred in the Chernobyl study of section 7.8. In the analysis, the value on a life was given by the so-called α value, which in fact derives from cost–benefit analyses of human lives in different societies. How much would be paid by insurance firms or society to compensate families and others for the loss of a life? How much might a law court award in damages? Various bodies, such as the International Atomic Energy Agency, had surveyed such values across various countries and provided a range of values for α. In figure 7.15 the initial weight was determined from a knowledge of this range (Lochard *et al.*, 1992). This example illustrates one way in which an interplay between the two approaches can inform the same analysis. The convergence of CBA and decision analytic approaches is further charted in Fischhoff (1977).

We close this section by turning to a difficulty that faces both CBA and decision analysis: how to value the impacts that occur over time, particularly those that may not occur until long into the future. Strictly, this is not an issue for societal decision making alone; it is potentially relevant in all decision-making contexts. Because societal decisions may have more long-lasting impacts and because there is a greater imperative for any analysis to be explicit and auditable, however, debate on methodologies for valuing time streams has occurred extensively in this arena. We have already encountered NPV approaches, in which time streams of cashflows are discounted to the present day using a constant discount rate: see section 7.4. Since CBA determines a monetary equivalent of each benefit and disbenefit in a decision problem, it is natural to apply NPV to bring the monetary values of different impacts to the present day.[2] The preferences between different time streams are determined substantially by the choice of discount rate. Unfortunately, discount rates have the property of reducing large impacts in the distant future to almost negligible present values. Indeed, discounting can give outcomes that often seem unreasonable, and in contradiction with other legal requirements. Consider, for instance, the case of nuclear waste disposal, for which Western governments have typically specified requirements for safety over periods of several thousand years, despite the fact that any discounting implies that health effects that occur far into the future have negligible NPV. Of course, another problem with NPV is that actual discount rates are non-constant and highly uncertain.

Decision analysis can suffer from the same problems. First, decision analysis may adopt expected NPV as a criterion: if the DMs are risk-neutral in a particular context, then working with expected monetary values and expected NPV is equivalent to working with SEU (section 8.3). Second, there are many axiomatic developments of SEU models for time streams of impacts that show that discounted utility models can be a reasonable representation of temporal preferences (Keeney and Raiffa, 1976: chap. 9). Harvey (1995) suggests a varying discount rate that would 'devalue the future' at a much slower rate. Loewenstein (1987) proposes another modification to discounting based on a modified utility function that takes account of the 'pleasures of expectation'. This has the effect of giving a higher weight to assets received in later years. Although one might imagine that this model is applicable only to positive benefits (given that it is concerned with pleasure), it can also apply to negative benefits when there may be negative anticipation (fear, etc.). For example, in some studies research participants will accept an early negative consequence rather than wait for a later (inevitable) less negative consequence. Presumably, the anticipated worry and anxiety that will occur while waiting for later negative consequence is taken into account and makes these consequences even more negative.

---

[2] Actually, more than being a natural approach, it is the logically coherent one: CBA and NPV share a common basis in economic theory.

Table 13.1 How a DM might perceive different time eras

Now–25 years	Affects the DM and her children	Very important
25–50 years	Affects DM's children and grandchildren	
50–100 years	Affects grandchildren and great-grandchildren	Important
100–500 years	Some distant descendants	
500–1,000 years	World will have changed dramatically	
1,000 years plus	Will human race still be around?	Not that important

Atherton and French (1998) suggest that any model that applies discount factors, constant or varying, to a regular series of time periods may miss something crucial in the way that DMs perceive long periods into the future. They argue that people tend to section future plans into distinct eras with differing importance. Thus, a DM may evaluate outcomes broadly as lying in eras, as illustrated in table 13.1. Of course, the precise number, definition and perception of the eras are likely to differ from individual to individual and would need to be elicited for the particular context. Atherton and French illustrate how this idea might be applied to the selection of a radioactive waste strategy.

13.3 Public perception and risk communication

A nuclear power plant is infinitely safer than eating, because 300 people choke to death on food every year. (Dixy Lee Ray)

Very many societal decisions, especially those that engage the public's attention, relate to risk issues: food and drug safety, the adoption of nuclear energy, the siting of a pedestrian crossing, etc. Over the past decades it has been made clear time and again that communication between the authorities and various stakeholders has been wanting in many respects. Since a necessary prerequisite for deliberation and decision making is communication between the parties concerned, we now discuss some studies of risk perception, and their implication for public risk communication.

Risk communication is 'the label used to refer both to the content of any message concerning a hazard and the means of delivering that message' (Breakwell, 2000). It is an activity that takes place against a background of investigations and actions on the part of the authorities, and many other players, designed to reduce the likelihood of the hazard and/or the scale of its impact. Indeed, the communication is usually designed to inform the actions of the recipients, thus mitigating the risk upon them. We should recognise that communication itself is an action and therefore results from a decision process (French and Maule, 1999). The intended consequence of the action is to change behaviour, often through informing the recipients' decision making: see language games (Searle, 1969; Wittgenstein, 1953). Thus we frame our discussion in decision analytic and behavioural terms. We also note that, while communication ideally should be two-way, risk communications are often one-way broadcasts by the authorities – e.g. through the media, advice leaflets, websites or labelling.

There are many reasons why risks are difficult to communicate and discuss across a wide audience. As outlined in chapter 2, intuitive behaviour in the face of uncertainty can be diverse and at odds with normative models. The authorities' presentation of their advice based on careful scientific analysis is inevitably cast in rational terms yet it is heard through the ears of an intuitive public. It is not surprising, therefore, that misunderstanding and poor communication can result. In particular, we have seen the importance of framing in understanding issues. There can be considerable difference between the framing adopted by the scientific experts advising the authorities, the authorities' interpretation of this advice and the public's intuitive framing of the issues. Moreover, the public's understanding of the process of science can be very different from actual practice, as witnessed by the recent debates in the United Kingdom on the risks from the triple measles, mumps and rubella vaccination (Bellaby, 2003).

Science (and here we mean physics, chemistry, biology, etc.) is more than the knowledge accumulated through experience. It is knowledge accumulated by auditable, explicit methods in which the evidence, empirical or otherwise, and the arguments built thereon are displayed to a community of peers for review, debate and – if they are convinced – adoption within the current working body of knowledge. Each science has its own *scientific method* appropriate to the type of data available, whereby this process of accumulation of knowledge is articulated. Until sufficient data are gathered to identify a theory that demonstrably explains and predicts the world, science is vibrant and full of controversy. At the boundaries of research, science is not a stable body of unquestioned, universally accepted knowledge. Scientists live with this uncertainty and the lack of knowledge, and are comfortable doing so – which, of course, is a problem when communicating with the public, business, politicians and other stakeholders, all of whom tend to be desperately uncomfortable when faced with uncertainty.

In a series of very influential studies Slovic and his co-workers (Slovic, 1986, 1997, 2001) have identified a set of factors that the public takes

Table 13.2 Examples of hazard classification for two primary factors in risk perception

	Low 'dread'	High 'dread'
High 'unknown'	E.g. medical technology, solar power	E.g. nuclear power, genetic engineering
Low 'unknown'	E.g. driving, smoking, alcohol	E.g. crime, handguns

account of when assessing risk but that are often thought to be irrelevant by risk analysts. These researchers identify two primary factors: dread and the unknown. Dread is associated with a lack of control, the inequitable distribution of the benefits among those at risk, threats to future generations, irreversible effects, risk increasing over time and the potential for catastrophe (e.g. a very large number of fatalities). The unknown is characterised as unfamiliarity, that which is unobservable and that which is unknown to science – hence the public's discomfort with relating to scientific uncertainty. Thus, to the extent that a particular hazard is perceived to incorporate these factors, it will be perceived to be more risky and less acceptable. This shows that characteristics of a hazard that are normally not considered relevant by experts influence how the general public judge the risk. The public are particularly sensitive to risks that they dread or perceive as having unknown causes and consequences.

Table 13.2 illustrates some examples of risks classified in these terms. Research suggests that people do indeed underestimate those in the bottom left quadrant and overestimate those in the top right quadrant, as predicted (Lichtenstein *et al.*, 1978). In the United Kingdom, the Department of Health (1998) has translated the dread and unknown factors into a series of *fright factors* that help their risk managers and communicators predict situations in which the public are likely to perceive risks in ways that are different from the scientific estimates (see table 13.3). If a risk situation has several fright factors present and/or each is strongly characteristic of that situation then the public are likely to judge the risks as being higher than formal risk estimates based on scientific and statistical procedures. This is a useful and easy to use checklist to predict how the public are likely to respond to risk information.

Thus, public perceptions of risk do not always tally with the opinions of scientific and technical experts. This has led some to make a distinction between 'expert' and 'lay' perspectives. Traditionally, the two perspectives have been conceived as opposite. On the one hand, the public is accredited with forming 'subjective' and intuitive interpretations of risk, and, on the

Table 13.3 'Fright factors'

- Exposure to the hazard is seen as involuntary (e.g. exposure to pollution) rather than voluntary (e.g. drinking alcohol).
- Inequitable distribution of the potential impacts.
- Individuals cannot influence their risk by taking personal precautions.
- The risk is perceived to be man-made rather than natural.
- The source of danger is unfamiliar/novel.
- The underlying issues appear poorly understood by science.
- Contradictory statements emerge from responsible sources.
- The effects of the impacts may be delayed.
- The risk concerns children, pregnant women or, more generally, future generations.
- The form of death, illness or injury involved arouses particular fear.
- Those exposed to the hazard are identifiable rather than anonymous.

Source: Department of Health, (1998).

Table 13.4 Languages of risk communication

Two languages of risk	
Expert	*Public*
Scientific	Intuitive
Probabilistic	Yes/no
Acceptable risk	Safety
Changing knowledge	Is it, or isn't it?
Comparative risk	Discrete events
Population averages	Personal consequences
'A death is a death'	'It matters how we die'

other, experts are accredited with the 'objectivity' provided by scientific investigation and statistical principles. Indeed, some have argued that there are two languages of risk (see table 13.4):

- an expert language, which is grounded in scientific, specialised and statistical knowledge; and
- a lay language, which is grounded in social and intuitive knowledge.

Unfortunately, some risk managers have taken it that the expert language is 'right' and the public language is 'wrong', and so have assumed that the primary function of risk communication is to address this deficit in thinking by focusing on scientific arguments. This has led to an over-emphasis on public misperceptions, with risk communication being conceived as a one-way process, flowing from experts to the public, with the expert trying to convey information in ways that encourage the public to assess risk as they do and to draw similar conclusions. Such an approach sees the public as pliable receivers of risk information and overlooks the fact that the public are concerned with the everyday environments in which risk communications are 'made real'. Now there is a growing realisation that this conclusion is wrong and that it is more appropriate to view both languages as valid ways of conceptualising risk. An important implication of this conclusion is that we need both to understand and take account of the lay conceptions of risk when communicating and working with the public.

To understand fully the public response to risk, we need to go beyond how individuals, in general, respond to risk and focus more on social and cultural factors. Three complementary perspectives are informative: culture and social groups, social amplification and trust.

A social groups perspective highlights the fact that perceptions and attitudes to hazards are shaped by the culture and world views shared by the social groups to which individuals belong (Douglas, 1992; Thompson *et al.*, 1990). Society is assumed to be composed of different groups, each with different world views, which, in turn, lead to different risk perceptions and assessments. For instance, research on nuclear power shows that pro-nuclear respondents see economic aspects as most salient, whereas the anti-group see accidents and consequences for the environment as most salient. Thus different stakeholders may hold different world views, leading them to focus on different aspects of the available information/facts that, in turn, may lead to different perceptions and attitudes to risk. One way of distinguishing between groups is in terms of simple categorisations around age and gender – e.g. people are assumed to become more cautious with age, and there is some evidence to suggest that women are more cautious than men (Harris *et al.*, 2006).

An influential approach, *cultural theory* (Douglas, 1992), characterises four cultural groups, each having a distinctive attitude towards risk and a predisposition to accept some hazards and not others. Note that the theory does not suggest that every individual belongs to one of these groups: far from it. Any coarse categorisation of social groups would, clearly, be naïve. In any case, an individual's risk attitude varies over time in response to many aspects of his or her life. In society at any particular time, however, and in relation to a given debate about a societal risk, one can discern behaviours that may be characterised as one of the following:

- *individualists/entrepreneurs* see risks as presenting opportunities, save those that threaten freedom of choice and action within free markets;

- *hierarchists* fear threats to social order and believe that technological and environmental risks can be regulated and managed within set limits;
- *fatalists* do not knowingly accept risks but accept what is in store for them; and
- *egalitarians* fear risks to the environment, the collective good and future generations.

Cultural theory is important in highlighting the importance of differences in world views for the different stakeholders in relation to different risks. The theory also suggests that trying to find a single metric for risk assessment is futile, since it is determined by social and cultural factors. Most importantly, the effectiveness of risk communication strategies will depend crucially upon the relevance of the message for the different groups involved.

Social amplification theory (Kasperson *et al.*, 2003; Kasperson, 1992) provides another perspective on communication issues. This model suggests that hazards and their objective characteristics (e.g. deaths, injuries, damage and social disruption) interact with a wide range of psychological, social and cultural factors in ways that intensify or attenuate perceptions and responses to risk. When information about the risk associated with a hazard is put into the public domain the effect on the public is similar to dropping a stone in a pool: there are ripples; and these can be amplified by any of three mechanisms:

- media coverage – e.g. whether it 'hits the front page';
- the fit with the agenda of a particular social group – e.g. a pressure group – that may 'take up the cause' and engage in a campaign; or
- a sign of inadequacy in the current risk management process, particularly when the risk concerned has high 'dread' or 'unknown'.

Table 13.5 summarises some characteristics of a situation, so-called 'media triggers', that may increase media coverage and possibly 'sensationalise' the issues, making risk communication harder. Similar to the fright factors, if one or more of these triggers is present then there is likely to be more media coverage, and this is likely to be negative since most triggers reflect negative aspects of the situation. This, in turn, makes discussion of the risk less objective and effective communication more difficult.

A third factor known to affect risk perception is *social trust* (Cvetkovich and Lofstedt, 1999). Research indicates that how people perceive and act in the face of risk information is crucially affected by the levels of trust associated with the communicator. Indeed, trust may well influence how people conceptualise the dread and unknown aspects thought to underpin

Table 13.5 'Media triggers'

The media may show increased interest or possibly sensationalise discussions of risk if there are associated:

- questions of blame
- alleged secrets and cover-ups
- human interest through heroes, villains, victims, etc.
- links with existing high-profile issues or personalities
- conflict
- signal value – the story as a portent of future ills
- many people exposed to the risk: 'It could be you!'
- strong visual impact
- links to sex or crime

Source: Department of Health (1998).

risk perception. Accepting what trusted individuals are saying provides a way of simplifying complex hazard situations and may be preferable to trying to work through all the information for oneself: see the discussion in section 4.2 on the problem of limited cognitive capacity. The widely recognised decline of trust in government and regulatory authorities suggests that this is an important factor when considering how to improve risk communications. There are many attributes contributing to trust – e.g. the technical competence of the communicator, his/her 'independence' from the other parties and players in the situation, his/her fairness in acknowledging other points of view and the consistency of his/her statements and behaviour over time. Research suggests that communicators should be addressing these attributes, trying to improve how the public rate them on each. This will almost certainly require a wide range of continuing activities, not simply developing an appropriate form of words whenever a problem occurs.

Where does this discussion lead us in relation to developing good communication strategies? First, the issue of trust means that authorities and regulators would be wise to maintain a general, ongoing dialogue with as many potential stakeholders as possible, building mutual trust and understanding of each other's perspectives. When there is a decision to be made, early consultation before suggesting ways forward can build trust further. When it comes to framing risk communications, press statements, information booklets, websites, etc., social amplification theory suggests that one needs to be sensitive to fright factors (table 13.3) and media triggers (table 13.5) in anticipating responses from the public and stakeholders. One can draw on cultural theory to frame one's words in relation to the likely reactions of the different caricatures of members of society, testing possible wordings in one's mind against each: 'How would they react if I said . . . ?' Finally, Fischhoff and colleagues have developed the *mental models approach* to risk communication (Morgan *et al.*, 2002). The approach involves eliciting and comparing how experts and the public conceptualise a risk situation – i.e. their mental models, capturing their understanding, assumptions, beliefs and values. Comparisons between the two groups is undertaken so as to reveal misunderstandings and errors in lay mental models. Once discovered, communications are developed to rectify these shortcomings. This approach has the advantage of being underpinned by a systematic and clearly articulated methodology, though it is in danger of overemphasising deficits in public understanding and underemphasising the legitimacy of the lay public's view of the world.

The soft modelling methods discussed in chapter 9 can also help in shaping risk communication. Three obvious ways in which they can provide guidance are as follows.

- Initially they can help to identify stakeholders and how they may be affected, and thus establish with whom it is important to communicate.
- They can help structure the communication. PESTEL and 7 S's, for instance, give a useful set of subheadings or issues that need to be covered in a press statement or a fuller report.
- They can provide the form of the communication itself: a well-drawn diagram or figure can communicate better that words (see French *et al.*, 2005b, for a fuller discussion).

Finally, we note that, until recently, communication was seldom integral to the societal decision-making process. Rather, it was a final step, only thought about once a way forward had been decided, and often it simply reported what had happened and what was being done. We believe that communication, and hence consideration of communication issues, should permeate the entire societal decision-making process. We argue this more broadly in the next section.

13.4 Deliberative democracy and public participation

Whenever the people are well informed, they can be trusted with their own government. (Thomas Jefferson)

A few decades ago all societal decisions were taken by the authorities – i.e. governments or their agencies. Many still are, though things are changing. The public were sometimes consulted via a call for comments on a 'Green

Paper' outlining the issues and options, but, essentially, the decision making was internal to government processes. A typical planning process, for instance, might have begun with an electricity utility company wishing to build a new generating plant. The company would have screened several possibilities, focused on a very few and analysed the advantages and disadvantages of each from its own viewpoint, finally deciding on one and developing a case to present to the regulatory body or regional government. These authorities would have examined the case to see if it fitted or came close to fitting legal requirements, and then and only then would the discussion become more open and inclusive. The result was often, in social and political terms, a process that almost inevitably became confrontational, because of what had gone on already 'behind closed doors'. In prescriptive decision-making terms, the process almost certainly lacked in creativity and breadth of attributes considered, because only one perspective, the company's, entered at the problem formulation phase. By the time that more varied and potentially catalytic views could come into play, entrenched positions were likely to have been taken.

Over the years disillusionment has grown as the public, various stakeholders and, in particular, pressure and single-issue protest groups complained both at the decisions and the seeming exclusion of key issues from consideration within the decision-making process. This has led to mechanisms for greater inclusion of the public and stakeholders from the earliest deliberations on the issues. In many countries there have been small steps back from full representative democracies, in which governments analysed and decided with little or no interaction with anyone else, towards more inclusive deliberation and public participation. Politicians' motives in encouraging this movement probably relate to gaining greater public acceptance of the ultimate decision than to reducing the democratic deficit per se (Steffek and Kissling, 2007); whatever the cause, though, there is undoubtedly wider use of participatory methods nowadays in societal decision making (French *et al.*, 2005; Renn *et al.*, 1995; Slovic, 1993; Susskind and Field, 1996).

Fischhoff (1995) argues eloquently for a greater 'partnership' between the authorities, stakeholders and the public, recognising eight stages in growth towards full partnership: see table 13.6. Note that stages 1 to 4 relate to the 'science' – e.g. the numerical probability that the risk will occur – whereas stages 5 to 8 relate to value issues. So how might a more inclusive and sensitive societal decision process be established? How can disparate stakeholder perspectives be brought together in ways that ensure that all concerns are addressed? What type of process allows issues to be

Table 13.6 Eight stages towards partnership

1. All we have to do is get the numbers right.
2. All we have to do is tell them the numbers.
3. All we have to do is explain what we mean by the numbers.
4. All we have to do is show them that they've accepted similar risks, values and costs in the past.
5. All we have to do is show them that it's a good deal for them.
6. All we have to do is treat them nicely.
7. All we have to do is make them partners.
8. All of the above.

Note: The 'we' are the government authorities and the 'they' the public.
Source: Fischhoff (1995).

explored in a variety of languages and conceptualisations so that the ideas are communicated as clearly and widely across society as possible? In ancient Athens its citizens used to gather together to discuss and decide the way forward on major issues. Can such deliberative democratic procedures, sometimes called substantive or direct democracies, be recreated for the twenty-first century?

In fact, such a simplistic view of Athenian politics is a myth; it was far from inclusive, being exclusively male and almost completely dominated by the rich, who had slaves to do their work while they deliberated (Crick, 2002). Nonetheless, to many it serves as a model for societal decision making. Its imperatives are leading to ways in which the public and stakeholders can be better engaged in a societal decision. Today, from the outset of the decision process it is common to find a range of activities designed to build dialogue with stakeholders: information leaflets, broadcasts on local and national media, websites, public meetings, focus groups, electronic discussion forums, surveys, stakeholder workshops, citizens' juries and perhaps even referendums (see Rowe and Frewer, 2005, for a fuller list and definitions). Some of these instruments relate to the better provision of information and canvassing of opinion; some to debate and interchange of ideas; some to involvement in the analysis; some, such as referendums, to shared responsibility and accountability for the decision. Case vignette 13.1 illustrates some of these ideas in relation to deciding a policy for managing forests in British Columbia.

There are many variants of public participation processes. At one extreme, participation is part of a direct democracy and concludes with a binding vote between all citizens on what should be done. At the other, the authority and responsibility for the decision remains firmly within a

Case vignette 13.1 Stakeholder involvement in sustainable forest management planning

Sheppard and Meitner (2005) describe how MAVA helped support stakeholder discussions in developing a policy for sustainable forest management. In this environmental area, as in many others, there is growing demand for active public involvement in such policy making. Moreover, stakeholder positions can be quite polarised, and there is a considerable need for consensus building. Their paper describes how a new approach to public participation in the Arrow Forest District of British Columbia was developed by means of a pilot study using MAVA of forest management scenarios. Broadly, the process, which involved a wide range of stakeholders as well as technical experts, was as follows.

(1) Identification of stakeholders, public, governmental, commercial, interest groups, etc., to take part in the process.

(2) Identification of attributes and criteria to reflect the issues of concern to stakeholders and technical experts in forest management.

(3) Stakeholder prioritisation of attributes and criteria – i.e. weightings.

(4) Development of future alternative forest management scenarios by the experts for a selected area within the Arrow Forest District, using spatio-temporal forecasting of ecological and operational conditions.

(5) Technical evaluation by the experts of the impacts of alternative scenarios on attributes and criteria, based on output modelling and professional evaluation.

(6) Comparison of scenarios based on the expert evaluations and stakeholder weightings.

Steps 3 and 6 were conducted in a series of focus groups and workshops. These stakeholder interactions also helped orientate participants and obtain their feedback. The alternative forest management scenarios were presented using realistic 3D landscape visualisations (see case vignette 13.2). Essentially, either the modelling or the experts provided scores for the alternative scenarios on each of the technical criteria, and then these were weighted according to input from the stakeholder groups. There was considerable commonality of results among groups, with general agreement between experts and stakeholder groups on the overall scenario preferences. In the study, the results were presented back to the participants including government agencies, but were not directly used in the formal decision-making process. Nevertheless, Sheppard and Meitner conclude that approaches such as this 'can play a vital role in developing a more comprehensive, engaging, open and accountable process to support informed and socially acceptable decision-making for sustainable forest management'.

government agency. Before making its decision, however, it interacts with citizens and stakeholders. For many reasons, we expect this latter model of citizens interacting with a government body to dominate in the coming years. It is not clear that all citizens within the appropriate constituency will have the skills, cognitive abilities, time and motivation to participate fully. The representation of views may therefore be biased in some sense. Leaving the ultimate responsibility for the decision with a government agency is a pragmatic way of leaving routes open to debiasing the conclusion of unrepresentative participation exercises, albeit one that is hostage to many questions of democratic ideals, trust and legitimacy. It is interesting to reflect that agencies may need to act as an altruistic supra decision maker in such cases.

We should be clear on terminology: we need to distinguish a *participatory process* from a *participatory instrument, mechanism* and *technique*. We use the latter three terms interchangeably for a specific activity to engage the public or selected stakeholders in some aspect of a decision process. The overall participatory process is the combination of these into a sequence of activities interacting with the public and stakeholders leading to a decision. In figure 3.6 we indicated that a decision process can be divided roughly into three phases: formulation, analysis and appraisal. Such a perspective is helpful in thinking about participatory processes. Different participatory instruments have different advantages and disadvantages at each stage. For instance, a discussion board open to all may be very effective in widening the discussion and encouraging divergent thinking during the formulation phase, but quite unsuitable during the appraisal phase because its openness would allow anyone to participate in the actual decision whether or not they belonged to the appropriate constituency.

In designing a participatory process one needs to build a sequence of instruments across the three phases to meet a range of objectives. Bayley and French (2008) suggest that the following need to be considered when setting these.

- *Information sharing.* A vital purpose of public participation processes is the exchange of information in order to educate participants and explore issues thoroughly. Some of this will relate to factual information and forecasts. Decisions and risk management are not based solely on the science of the situation, however; there is also a need to consider values. Hence the information sharing may involve understanding the public's and specific stakeholder groups' values and objectives. For both these reasons, there is a need to consider the directionality required of the information flow: should it be one- or two-way, and, if two-way, a genuine dialogue?

- *Democratic ideals.* There is a wide range of democratic imperatives that need to be considered in designing a participatory process. Indeed, is it intended to be democratic? The handling of some issues may require too much urgency to allow debate with the public and involve them in the ultimate decisions. Participation in such cases is much more likely to be focused on explaining what is being done and why.

- *Community cohesion.* A well-designed participatory process may contribute to social cohesion both in the small and the large. In the small it can smooth tensions between those closely involved in the issues and who may have conflicting objectives and, in the large, it can create a more general feeling of community involvement.
- *Practicability.* The process must be practicable. Full participation can be very costly and time-consuming, requiring complex logistics. One may need to consider not just the direct costs but the opportunity costs as well. Could the effort be better used in developing participation on some other set of issues?
- *Decision quality.* Participation can increase the quality of the decision process, essentially because it brings more minds to bear on the issues. Stakeholder and public perceptions of the issues can widen and enrich the perceptions that may have been driving the authorities' thinking. More debate can lead to greater clarity on the issues and the process can become more innovative, with a broader framing. Assumptions will be more widely challenged and tested. Equally importantly, because the decision process becomes more visible it may also become more structured and auditable: stages will not be skipped or dealt with perfunctorily.

To date, most participatory processes that have been run have involved information-sharing and discussion instruments, on the one hand, or referendums and straw polling instruments, on the other. Thus, in terms of the three phases of decision analysis, the focus has tended to be confined to the formulation and appraisal phases. Recently, however, there have been moves to use participatory instruments that involve stakeholders and the public in the more analytical evaluation phase (Gregory *et al.*, 2005; Renn, 1999; Winn and Keller, 2001). Typically these have involved stakeholder workshops, which, roughly, have the structure of a decision conference with participation from a wide range of stakeholder groups. The workshops in case vignettes 13.1 and 13.3 take this form – as, in a sense, do the workshops in the Chernobyl study (section 7.8). Supporting such events through MAVA has proved to be very successful. In many societal decisions, although there may be uncertainties about the potential impacts, the key contentious issues are more usually concerned with values, and exploring trade-offs though sensitivity analysis can focus discussion and build consensus (see, for example, Danielson *et al.*, 2007b).

13.5 E-participation and e-democracy: a panacea?

The neutral communications medium is essential to our society. It is the basis of a fair competitive market economy. It is the basis of democracy, by which a community should decide what to do. It is the basis of science, by which humankind should decide what is true. Let us protect the neutrality of the net. (Tim Berners Lee)

To date, public participation exercises that have involved the public and stakeholders in the analysis and appraisal phases have seldom used the internet significantly other than in providing the means for voting. Case vignette 13.2 describes an application of a geographic information system over the internet that helped formulate, but not analyse and resolve, issues. By and large, most of the current moves towards e-government have focused mainly on using web techologies to automate the administrative tasks of government. Nevertheless, all the signs are that the next development will be to engage the public and stakeholders via the internet, using Web 2.0 and social computing tools. In particular, wGDSSs will form the basis of e-participation tools that allow stakeholders and the public to explore and contribute to the decision analysis. Many exploratory studies and experiments are already under way (Danielson *et al.*, 2007a; French, 2003a; 2007a; Gronlund, 2003; Ríos Insua, 2008).

In this section we discuss web-based interactions to support participation and deliberative democracy, which we call e-participation and e-democracy, respectively. We indicate that, while the idea of using the internet in this way is undoubtedly attractive and may do much to address the growing democratic deficit in many countries, it is not without its

Case vignette 13.2 Virtual Slaithwaite: the use of a GIS in formulation and discussion

Carver *et al.* (2001) describe how they developed a geographic information system to support deliberation among the residents of Slaithwaite in West Yorkshire, United Kingdom, about future improvements to their village. Initially the tool allowed villagers to attach 'flags' to particular areas or features of Slaithwaite. They could annotate the flag with any concern or thought – e.g. 'crime', 'difficult path' or 'lovely view'. The flags were colour-coded to indicate the sort of concern. The system was launched at terminals at a 'Shaping Slaithwaite' event organised by the local authority and subsequently made available over the web. At first comments were kept confidential, to encourage candour and imaginative responses. At the end of the consultation period, however, the system was updated to allow the public to query a map containing all the comments made. All the comments and ideas were fed into and informed the regional 'Planning for Real' initiative.

problems. As in the previous section, we assume that in many cases the ultimate responsibility for the decision remains with a government agency or regulator. First, we should remind ourselves that the import of Arrow's theorem (section 11.3) is, of course, just as strong in the context of e-participation as in any other group activity. There can be no simple algorithmic system that draws together citizen's views, judgements or votes across the web to produce a rational and bias-free societal decision. Just as in meetings and other interactions, e-participation systems will need to focus on supporting a social process of decision making, fostering good communication and building a shared understanding and recognition of different perspectives.

Furthermore, in the context of society, this will be a much harder task than in organisations and small groups. Organisations that adopt wGDSSs to support distributed decision making may reasonably assume that their DMs share the common goals of the organisation and a common culture. The organisation can train and work with the group so that they 'understand' the GDSS and its purpose. This will not be the case for e-democracy and e-participation. Societies are multicultural and often multilingual; their citizens span a vast range of abilities and backgrounds, subscribe to many different world views and, above all, hold many different values. This means that there are many hurdles to be overcome if citizens are to participate in societal decisions effectively. French *et al.* (2007b) point, *inter alia*, to the following issues.

- *Possible lack of common values.* If two or more participants involved in the deliberation have diametrically opposed views, then it is possible that, no matter how sensitive the facilitation and no matter how wide-ranging the debate, there will be no ultimate agreement. Within organisations there is usually sufficient commonality in objectives, and perhaps sufficient deference to a higher authority external to the group who demands a conclusion that some agreement can be reached. Is it the same in modern multicultural societies, however? Diametrically opposed views are more common; and thus convergence to consensus will be that much harder.

- *Some groups may be disenfranchised.* The process itself may exclude certain groups, perhaps because of the digital divide – i.e. some may lack either access to the web or the skills to interact sufficiently. Then again, some may reject the decision analytic methodology. Whereas an organisation can adopt and insist that a single analytic paradigm is used consistently in all its decision making, society cannot. There is a need to recognise that not all citizens share the ideals behind the SEU or any other normative model, and so different decision paradigms will need to coexist within any e-participation or e-democracy system.

- *Diversity of the population.* While no one would suggest that organisations are unicultural, there are shared understandings of the world, shared languages and shared histories that make deliberation and debate easier to manage. Communication is easier and more likely to be accurate than in a more hetrerogeneous population. All the issues that we raised in the discussion of risk communication will apply to building effective e-participation systems that truly inform and communicate with all the public and different stakeholder groups. Cognitive abilities may span the entire spectrum of intelligence. This makes the task of facilitating the process much harder; it will be more difficult to keep all participants moving forward with their deliberations.

- *More parallel discussion.* In a two-hour face-to-face meeting there are two hours of deliberation to listen to and participate in, and, for the majority of the time at least, only one person will be speaking. On the web many more can participate, and usually they can contribute to the discussion in parallel, so two hours of interaction could take several hundred hours to scan, assimilate and organise. This raises problems for the participants, the facilitators and the analysts building decision models. Have they the time to achieve the potential that this greater volume of input might be seen as promising? Indeed, is there a legal issue? Might the process lack legitimacy if the facilitators and analysts do not read each and every interaction?

- *Legitimacy and trust.* To overcome the democratic deficit, citizens need to believe that the system will allow them to express their views fairly and securely. In simple e-voting systems this is difficult enough, because the recording and counting are not as open to scrutiny as counting crosses on paper; nor are there systems as convincing of their anonymity as simply placing a vote in a ballot box behind a screen. There is the problem too of defining the appropriate constituency. Building trust in and acceptance of a much more complex e-participation system in which the citizens' judgements are explored in a decision analysis is not easy. First, in-depth understanding of the process itself will stretch the cognitive abilities of many, and, second, there is the need to trust the software and the analysts to implement and conduct the process accurately and fairly.

We do not claim that these nor several other issues in French *et al.* (2007b) are insurmountable, but we are concerned that they are seemingly unrecognised by many of the proponents of e-participation and e-democracy. How developers of such tools rise to these and other challenges will do much to shape the democratic nature of our society in the twenty-first century.

We close with a further case vignette, one in which citizens could explore a full MAVA implemented in the web-based software Web-Hipre.

13.6 Concluding remarks and further reading

For discussions of societal decision making, see Beroggi (1998), Carley (1980), Keeney (1992), Keeney and Raiffa (1976), Kleindorfer *et al.* (1993) and McDaniels and Small (2004). Since the 1970s there has been a steady growth in decision analytic studies supporting societal decisions: see Keefer *et al.* (2004) for an extensive survey. Hobbs and Meier (2000) focus on energy and environmental decisions, Rasmussen *et al.* (2007) discuss the necessity for transparency and sound risk communication in the regulation of societal risks. We should not be surprised, perhaps, that so many of the reported applications of decision analysis are in societal context. As we have noted, there is a need for openness in the public sector; conversely, there is often a need to respect commercial confidentiality in the private sector.

Cost–benefit analysis took centre stage in societal decisions for much of the second half of the twentieth century (see Layard, 1972, Layard and Glaister, 1994, and Pearce and Nash, 1981, for reviews). Section 2 rehearsed many of the arguments in Bedford *et al.* (2005). The theory of temporal decision making is discussed further in Atherton (2000), Atherton and French (1997), Harvey (1995) and Keeney and Raiffa (1976), while Loewenstein and his co-workers have explored behavioural aspects of intertemporal choice (Loewenstein, 1987, 1988; Loewenstein and Prelec, 1991). A further normative perspective is provided by discussions of intergenerational equity (Atherton, 2000; Portney and Weyant, 1999).

There is a wide literature on risk communication and a related literature on public engagement with science (Bennett and Calman, 1999; Berry, 2004; Breakwell, 2000; French *et al.*, 2005b; Langford *et al.*, 1999; Leach *et al.*, 2005; Maule, 2004, 2008; Petts *et al.*, 2002; Poortinga *et al.*, 2004; Renn, 1998a; Renn and Levine, 1991). Slovic *et al.* (2004) discuss the effects of emotion on the ability to frame, communicate and comprehend risk. Oughton and Bay (2002) discuss ethical issues in the development of communication strategies. There are many case studies – or should the word be *post-mortems*? – of the risk communication surrounding various

Case vignette 13.3 A case of lake regulation policy

Hämäläinen and his co-workers at Helsinki University of Technology are one of the leading groups on the application of decision analysis in Europe. In Mustajoki *et al.* (2004) they report on the application of such techniques within the context of public (e-)participation in the regulation of Lake Päijänne in Finland. This is Finland's second largest lake, which has been regulated for over thirty years in order to increase hydro-electric power generation and to decrease flooding of agricultural land. The lake is also important for its recreational use, and there are many houses on its shores.

When the study started there was growing public concern both that the recreational uses needed more prominence in the regulatory framework and that wider environmental issues needed to be considered. During the period 1995 to 1999 an extensive project was undertaken to explore the issues with a wide range of stakeholders. Interviews and workshops were held, leading to a MAVA of the issues, supported by the Web-Hipre software (Hämäläinen, 2003). The majority of these evaluations were carried out in workshops, with the software facilitating the discussion between the stakeholders and building consensus on the key issues. Nevertheless, use was made of the fact that Web-Hipre, as its name suggests, is web-enabled, so that stakeholders could explore the analysis outside the interviews and workshops in their own time. An online survey tool was also used to maintain their involvement as discussions continued. The whole approach enabled consensus to be reached in circumstances in which the stakeholders, particularly the fishermen, had begun the process distrusting the authorities.

crises (see, for example, Drottz-Sjöberg and Persson, 1990, Phillips, 2000, and Rubin, Page, Morgan *et al.*, 2007).

Academic studies of deliberative democracy and public (e-)participation covering such issues as the philosophical underpinnings, the categorisation of different types of activity and case studies are legion (Arnstein, 1969; Arvai, 2003; Asaro, 2000; Beierle, 1999, 2002; Beierle and Cayford, 2002; Beierle and Konisky, 2000; Chappelet and Kilchenmann, 2005; Chess and Purcell, 1999; Fischhoff, 1995; French, 2003a, 2007a; Irvin and Stansbury, 2004; Mustajoki *et al.*, 2004; Regan and Holtzman, 1995; Renn, 1998a, 1999; Renn *et al.*, 1995; Ríos Insua, 2008; Rowe and Frewer, 2000, 2005; Sheppard and Meitner, 2005; Slovic, 1993; Susskind and Field, 1996; Webler, 1995, 1999; Webler *et al.*, 2001). One point that should be noted is the lack of agreement on terminology in this literature: what is a stakeholder workshop to one writer is nearer a citizens' jury to another (Bayley and French, 2008; Rowe and Frewer, 2005). Moreover, there is remarkably little discussion on how to design a participatory process; nor, indeed, are there the comparative studies available on which to base such design decisions (Abelson, Forest, Eyles *et al.*, 2003; Atherton, Hicks, Hunt *et al.*, 2003; Bayley and French, 2005; Rowe *et al.*, 2005). Critical reviews of the current state of the art in the use of decision analytic methods in public participation and e-participation are provided by French *et al.* (2007b) and Gregory *et al.* (2005).

13.7 Exercises and questions for discussion

(1) Consider the scenario in question 3 of section 9.11. What risk communication issues does this raise?

(2) Dizzy Fizzy, a company that produces a broad range of fizzy drinks for children, has contacted you for advice. The production manager has reported a problem with the fizzy drink bottling process for a short period of time last week. This has allowed some fluid, used to lubricate the machinery, into the product. This problem occurred for just a short period and the amount of fluid was very small. The concentration in the contaminated drinks discovered so far, although much higher than normal, did not exceed the permitted levels as specified by the European Union, and from this standpoint does not represent any risk to consumers. It will give the product a slightly bitter taste that should be detectable by most adults, but it is not clear whether it would be detectable by children There is some evidence to suggest, however, that this fluid is carcinogenic if consumed at higher concentrations over long periods of time. The company is pretty sure that it has the batch numbers. The batch was sent to a central distributor, however, who is likely to have split the batch across a number of different stores countrywide. The company is not sure how the public are likely to react to any information, and has asked you to prepare a report on how the public perceive and act in the face of risk.

The report should include the following.

- A review of theory and research on how the public perceive and act in the face of risk, including some of the reasons why the public's response can be different from those predicted by formal risk analyses, some ideas about the different languages of risk and a review of the individual and social processes involved.

- A review of procedures that the organisations might take to improve the situation (e.g. building trust, increased public participation), assessing each critically for this problem and the broader context.

We suggest that you structure your report in the following way.

- A brief introduction outlining the background to the report (including why these kinds of issues are important and why they come about), the aims and objectives of the report and its structure – i.e. the major sections and their purpose.
- A section reviewing the extant literature on how the public perceive and act in the face of risk and the relevance of these for managing the situation at Dizzy Fizzy. In this section all aspects should be properly referenced, as in a formal academic essay.
- A section reviewing ways of improving risk communication in general, their strengths and weaknesses and the relevance, if any, of all of this for the current situation at Dizzy Fizzy.
- A conclusion outlining some recommendations and limitations in the report.

(3) Investigate a controversial decision currently being taken in your community – e.g. on the licensing of a waste-processing plant, the closure of a school, or changing traffic access to part of a town. Who is responsible for and has authority to make the decision? How are they interacting with stakeholders and exploring public opinion? Are data available publicly to undertake an analysis of the issues and explore the relative advantages and disadvantages of various alternatives? Indeed, are different alternatives being explored or is the choice to approve or not approve a single option? Provide a critique of the current process.

(4) Investigate the 'Virtual Slaithwaite' process (Carver *et al.*, 2001), sketched in case vignette 13.2. The web-based GIS tool did not allow individual residents to view, comment on or discuss the issues and concerns raised by others. The intention was to encourage all to input their ideas without being shy or fearful of future discussion. It was believed that this would make the process more creative and capture a wider range of ideas. Do you agree with this? What are potential balancing arguments that might favour more openness for discussion?

Decision support systems

[W]e cannot solve present-day major political and organisational problems simply by grinding through a mathematical model or computer algorithm. What we require besides is the design of better deliberation and judgement. (C. W. Churchman and H. B. Eisenberg)

14.1 Introduction

In chapters 4, 5 and 6 we discussed how information and knowledge management, artificial intelligence, OR systems and tools can be used to support decision making, mainly at the operational and tactical levels. Having explored a wide range of decision analysis and behavioural topics, including multi-attribute decision analysis, uncertainty and groups of decision makers we can now revisit the area of decision support with an informed view that will allow us to explore the topic in greater depth and suggest future directions.

Throughout this book we have explored decision support issues taking into account the domain of managerial activity involved (see figure 3.7). In this chapter, we seek to include both the main research strands from the DSS field and to step into the literature that predominately discusses DSSs according to their functionalities. Our aims in this chapter are:

- to present taxonomies of DSSs;
- to discuss representative types of DSSs;
- to explore human–computer interface issues in the design of DSSs;
- to introduce a methodology for evaluating DSSs; and
- to discuss the latest trends in the area of decision support.

14.2 Decision support systems

The data-processing and management information systems introduced in the 1950s and 1960s were used largely to provide managers with periodic reports, mostly addressing accounting issues. These evolved over time, with a new type of system emerging in the late 1960s that was designed to support decision-making activities by generating ad hoc managerial documents. The role of these DSSs was to support individual managers rather than organisational departments (Arnott and Pervan, 2005), and they were viewed as successful (Alter, 1980).

Two lines of research shaped the early phases of DSSs: work on organisational decision making at the Carnegie school (see section 12.2) and work on interactive computer systems at the Massachusetts Institute of Technology (Keen and Scott Morton, 1978). The concept of managerial decision support, in particular, was first articulated and explored in Scott Morton's PhD thesis in 1967. This was later compiled into a book on management decision systems (Scott Morton, 1971). The term 'DSS' was then formally introduced (in an article by Gorry and Scott Morton, 1971).

As we mentioned in section 1.1, Simon (1960) suggested that decision-making processes fall along a continuum ranging from highly structured (often called 'programmed') to highly unstructured (called 'non-programmed'), with semi-structured processes lying halfway between. Anthony (1965) then presented a taxonomy for managerial activity consisting of the following categories: strategic, tactical and operational. Gorry and Scott Morton combined these classifications to produce a matrix with decision types – i.e. structured, semi-structured and unstructured – as rows and types of organisational control and planning – i.e. operational control, tactical control and strategic planning – as columns (Gorry and Scott Morton, 1971). Each cell of the framework identifies the need for particular kinds of computer-based systems to provide decision support. Even though the framework was introduced in the early 1970s it remains one of the most cited frameworks in the DSS field.

Alter (1977) offered another well-cited taxonomy, which classifies DSSs into seven categories:

- *file-drawer systems*, for immediate access to data;
- *data analysis systems*, such as statistical and financial analysis tools;
- *analysis information systems*, providing access to several databases and models;
- *accounting models*, for forecasting the consequences of planned actions in terms of standard accounting quantities;
- *representational models*, for forecasting the non-financial consequences of planned actions;
- *optimisation models*, for providing guidelines for action by generating optimal solutions consistent with constraints on inputs; and
- *suggestion models*, for the rule-based generation of decisions in well-structured, repetitive contexts.

Power (2002) argued that DSS taxonomies help give a better under-standing of the DSS subject. Depending on the component that provides the main focus of the DSS design, Power's classification includes data-driven DSSs, model-driven DSSs, knowledge-driven DSSs, document-driven DSSs, communications-driven and group DSSs and web-based DSSs. This is in line with the categorisation provided by the DSS special interest group of the Association for Information Systems (AIS SIGDSS).

Arnott and Pervan (2005, 2008) identified seven areas of intensive research in the DSS field (see figure 14.1). Some of these have been dis-cussed in earlier parts of the book and others are discussed in more detail in this chapter. This arrangement reflects the spiral approach followed in the writing of this book: some tools, such as knowledge management systems, did not require any particular background knowledge, and so were presented in the introductory chapters of decision support (chapters 4 and 5); it was not until later, however, that other systems, such as group DSSs, could be presented, following the discussion of group decision making.

The main DSS sub-fields are described briefly below.

- *Personal DSSs* are designed to assist individual managers in their decision-making tasks (see discussion below).
- *Group DSSs* are designed to support groups or teams of decision makers (see GDSSs in section 14.3).
- *Negotiation support systems* facilitate negotiation processes involving opposing parties (negotiation processes were briefly discussed in section 11.6).
- *Intelligent DSSs* combine artificial intelligence and decision analytical techniques to enhance decision-making capabilities (see intelligent DSSs in section 14.4).
- *Knowledge management DSSs* aid decision making by augmenting organisational memory and facilitating knowledge storage, access, retrieval and dissemination (see KMSs in section 4.5).
- *Data warehousing* provides access to large-scale data sets and historical data collected from internal and external sources (see section 4.4).
- *Enterprise reporting and analysis systems* are dedicated to aiding enterprise decision making. They include EISs and business intelli-gence tools (see section 4.4) and corporate performance measurement systems (Neely *et al.*, 2005; Simons, 2000). Performance measurement tools aid managers in the implementation of strategy by helping them to measure the efficiency and effectiveness of strategic actions through the systematic application of performance methods such as

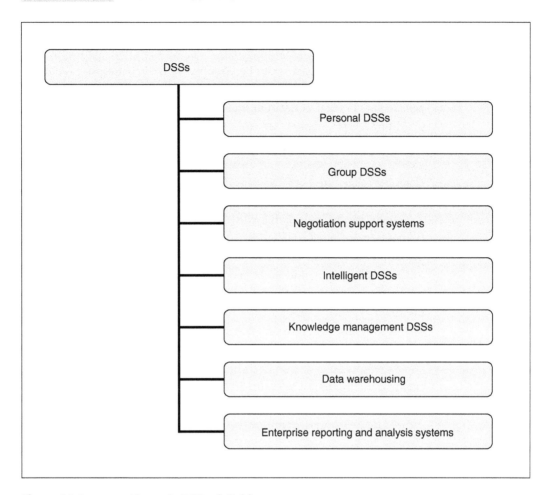

Figure 14.1   The main DSS sub-fields
Source: Arnott and Pervan (2005).

the *balanced scorecard* (Kaplan and Norton, 1996), the *performance prism* (Neely *et al.*, 2002) and the *framework of results and determinants* (Fitzgerald *et al.*, 1991).

The ideas expressed in this chapter are broadly in line with the views of Turban *et al.* (2007) – namely that 'DSS' is an umbrella term that encompasses any computer-based system that supports decision-making activities. In that sense, a data warehouse assisting a group of managers in devising their sales strategy is a DSS, as is an expert system helping a couple to choose appropriate fertility treatment. Management information systems (see section 4.3) that automate business processes such as compiling reports and processing transactions cannot be classified as DSSs, however. Power (2002), in particular, argued that transaction-processing tools and enterprise resource planning systems that support information flows cannot be viewed as DSSs; interactive tools, however, that analyse the data generated by such systems can be classified as DSSs (enterprise reporting and analysis systems). Our view is that any computer-based system that generates data used in decision making activities can be classed as a DSS providing level 0 support (see table 3.1). Similarly, if a KMS that supports knowledge management functions aids decision making then it can also be viewed as a DSS. Another grey area is that of ESs and ANNs (discussed in chapter 5) that automate decision-making activities and replace DMs. For example, a loan authoriser that approves/rejects loan applications or a fraud detector that suspends credit cards without any human intervention cannot be considered a DSS. If the outputs of these systems inform human decision making then these can be classed as a DSS.

The findings of Arnott and Pervan's (2005) bibliometric study of DSS publications indicate that personal DSSs, GDSSs and intelligent DSSs are the main types of DSS and have received the most attention in the literature. We discuss personal DSSs in this section, and the other two are discussed in the next two sections. In a later study, Arnott and Pervan (2008) reported the outcomes from a content analysis of DSS articles and explored their practical relevance in terms of the gap between research and practice. They demonstrated that personal DSS and intelligent DSS papers showed a significant improvement in practical relevance during the period 1990 to 2004.

Personal DSSs tend to be small-scale systems designed for use by one manager or a limited number of managers for a significant decision activity (Arnott, 2008). It is the most widespread type of DSS, particularly the spreadsheet-based system. It is also the oldest form of DSS, introduced in the 1960s to replace MISs, and it was the only type available for about a decade. Rather than supporting organisational functions, personal DSSs empower individuals in taking decisions. They are different from MISs, and the differences between MISs and personal DSSs have been identified by other readings (see, for example, Watson and Hill, 1983)

The architecture of a personal DSS comprises a database for accessing data about the decision problem and context, a model base that contains models with analytical capabilities, the user interface, which is highly interactive with reporting and graphical facilities, and the user who interacts with the system. Personal DSS users are senior or middle managers who tend to be easy learners, choose whether they wish to have decision support and have to deal with urgent decision problems (Arnott, 2008). A central theme in the area of personal DSS development is that of evolution. The design of a personal DSS evolves in continuous development cycles (see, for example, Keen, 1980, Silver, 1991, and Sprague and Carlson, 1982).

The field of personal DSSs is informed by a range of disciplines, including computer-based information systems, OR, optimisation and simulation models, report systems and behavioural decision research (Arnott and Pervan, 2005). Another term often used for a personal DSS is that of analytical DSS or analytics (Arnott, 2008). Such a DSS could be combined with large-scale data warehouses and business intelligence tools to obtain input data and process it by highly analytical models. There is a wide range of personal DSS applications, such as a cognitive aiding tool to assist in strategy implementation (Singh, 1998), a workflow-based geographic information system (Seffino *et al.*, 1999) and a DSS for production planning (Mallya *et al.*, 2001).

14.3 Group decision support systems

I not only use all of the brains I have, but all I can borrow. (Woodrow Wilson)

In section 11.5 we introduced facilitated workshops and decision conferences. These are far from the only way of supporting groups of decision makers, however. In this section, we turn to GDSSs and the use of groupware as an alternative way of supporting groups. GDSSs encompass computer, communication and decision support systems that help DMs in all decision-making phases – e.g. formulation, evaluation, etc. – during group meetings (DeSanctis and Gallupe, 1987). 'Groupware' or 'computer-supported cooperative work' are used as generic terms for such systems.

Groupware may be distinguished by whether the group 'meets'

- at the same time in the same place;
- at the same time, but in different places; or
- at different times.

In chapters 10 and 11 we outlined five contexts for using decision analytic software to support a group of DMs. These, together with a setting of personal decision support which we use as a reference point (context A), are outlined below.

(A) A single-user context in which a single DM analyses the problem for herself on her own computer: a self-help or DIY context (Belton and Hodgkin, 1999). Note that individuals can conduct their own individual analyses to explore and understand their own position even if a group is responsible for the decision.

(B)   A consultancy role in which an analyst meets with the DMs – perhaps as a group, perhaps one to one – and then analyses the issues 'offline', reporting back to the DMs with recommendations in due course.

(C)   A facilitated workshop or decision conference in which the DMs work with an analyst and discuss the issues in plenary sessions; the analyst runs the software, and the results are projected for the group to see together.

(D)   The group uses a group decision support room and networked GDSS to conduct a range of analyses, some individually and some in plenary or in subgroups (i.e. the archetypal model, discussed by Nunamaker *et al.*, 1988, 1991).

(E)   The group does not meet, formally at least, to discuss the problem but uses web-based GDSSs to resolve the issues. The activity may take place at the same time but at different places, taking the form of a net meeting; or it may be conducted over a period of time, with participants joining and leaving the deliberations as their other responsibilities allow.

Nowadays, it is possible to discuss issues, debate objectives, formulate problems, access data, analyse models, conduct sensitivity analyses, vote and decide and implement actions all without the group meeting, other than virtually. The advent of web technologies has brought the possibility of supporting geographically and temporally dispersed decision-making teams. Thus sometimes we talk of wGDSSs. They can interact with the same decision analytic model through distributed software. Video techniques mean that members of the group may see each other's reactions at the same time as hearing their comments. It is possible to use large-scale monitors or wall projection to create the impression that members of the group are 'in the same room'. It is also possible to meet in virtual space using avatars, although we are unclear how that might help decision making (other than in the context of game playing!).

Technology can also record members' comments on and interactions with a model for transmission to other members at a later time, and, in turn, record their reactions to transmit to the former members at a yet later time. Whether this 'stop-go' meeting takes place at the same place or in different locations is, essentially, irrelevant. Generally, such temporally separated interactions will not be as effective as same-time interactions, but, if a simultaneous meeting is impossible, the technology does now provide an improvement over postal communication.

Whatever the temporal and spatial relationship of the participants, one advantage of groupware is that some interactions may be anonymous.

In such activities as brainstorming, general discussion and the elicitation of judgements, it is often hard for some members to dissociate the status of the member offering a comment from its content. If the interaction takes place via a keyboard and screen, it is possible to enforce anonymity, thereby addressing the group characteristics, conformity and evaluation apprehension issues that can inhibit effective groups of DMs (see section 11.2). Others have questioned whether anonymity is valuable, however (see, for example, Cooke, 1991, and French, 1981). All the same, the potential to ensure anonymity *when* it is appropriate is one of the strengths of groupware. Nunamaker and his co-workers make much use of this in their software systems (Nunamaker *et al.*, 1988). In addition, groupware has the potential to limit the negative effects of other factors known to limit the effectiveness of group decision making: for example, allowing members to respond simultaneously overcomes production blocking, and logging members' contributions may help to overcome social loafing.

A more worrying concern with some groupware is that it automates the evaluation stage, for instance by providing group members with a simple voting scheme. If the group is aware of the voting paradoxes discussed in section 11.3 then, perhaps, there is no harm in this. The voting can be taken as an informative summary of the current thinking within the group. Indeed, some GDSSs provide statistical summaries of the voting patterns alongside or in place of the ranking that results from the vote. Nonetheless, it seems wiser to include a process of facilitation in order to help the group reach a consensus based upon a shared understanding. An additional advantage of facilitation is that it can use disagreement constructively to encourage discussion and information sharing, whereas GDSSs may overly focus on determining the majority view. Facilitation may therefore be better for achieving the potential advantages of group decision making outlined in section 11.1.

For the corporate strategic and general domains, decision support is often provided in purpose-built group decision support rooms, also called electronic meeting rooms. Figure 14.2 shows two layouts for group decision support rooms. In figure 14.2(a) the participants sit in a semicircular arc. This arrangement means that they can see each other during discussions, and also a screen, flip charts and whiteboards at the end of the room. The facilitator would operate in the space in the middle, sometimes sitting down when he or she does not wish to dominate the proceedings. At the end of the room the support team and recorder sit. Under these arrangements, all the discussion is conducted in open plenary form. The soft OR and decision models are built in front of the whole group, either

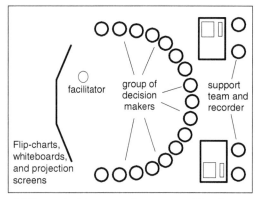 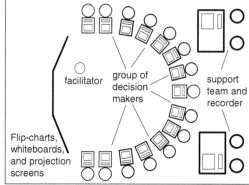

(a) Group decision support arrangement for plenary projection of common model

(b) Group decision support in which each participant has access to own decision model

Figure 14.2   Group decision support environments

with pen on the whiteboards and flip charts or projected on the screen from the support team's computer(s). Whatever the case, model building is done by the whole group with continuous plenary discussion.

In figure 14.2(b) the set-up is different, in that each member of the group has his or her own computer, in addition to those used by the support team. All the computers are networked together. Thus, each group member can either build his or her own personal decision model that captures his or her understanding of the problem, or the group member can work jointly on a communal model.

Although the differences between the two formats may seem less than their similarities, the two environments represent quite distinct approaches to group decision support. Facilitators who favour the arrangement illustrated in figure 14.2(a) feel that it is vitally important to maintain group discussion at plenary level, building a common model in their midst. There are no machines in front of people, so that each can see the others' body language and maintain eye contact. All this builds shared understanding and a common commitment to the developing strategy. On the other hand, facilitators who prefer the arrangement in figure 14.2(b) feel that much is gained by allowing periods when the individual members can explore the models on their own so as to understand things for themselves (Morton *et al.*, 2003; Nunamaker *et al.*, 1991; Phillips and Phillips, 1993). At present, although the debate is strong between the proponents of these two approaches, there is little empirical evidence to suggest whether one approach supports DMs better than the other. Both arrangements have been used successfully on many occasions to support groups of clients, who subsequently reported themselves well satisfied with the arrangement and methods used.

One point in common between the two views is that there is a distinct advantage in a semicircular arrangement with a space in the middle. Apart from allowing the facilitator to move around among the group, the presence of such a space seems more conducive to calmer, non-confrontational meetings than sitting around a large table.

The schematic arrangements in figures 14.2(a) and (b) are no more than that: schematic. Real arrangements differ in many details. Some group decision support rooms have oak tables, oil paintings and plush carpets 'to make boards of directors feel at home'; others are high-tech 'pods', which surround the participants with technology; most often, however, hotel conference suites are used in which portable computers and networks have been installed.

Finally, perhaps the most traditional way of supporting a group of decision makers is consultancy. In many cases the DMs call in a decision analyst, outline the problem to him and ask him to formulate the issues and conduct a decision analysis, returning with a report. The analyst will then meet individually with the DMs, their experts and key stakeholders to elicit their views and judgements. With this information, the analyst will then build a model or series of models, write a report and return to the DMs to present them with the results; ideally, he will work with them in a short workshop to allow them to explore sensitivity analyses and the underlying assumptions so that they truly understand the import of the analysis and the solution.

14.4 Intelligent decision support systems

An individual understands a concept, skill, theory, or domain of knowledge to the extent that he or she can apply it appropriately in a new situation. (Howard Gardner)

Intelligent DSSs are interactive computer-based systems that use data, expert knowledge and models to help DMs in organisations solve semi-structured problems by incorporating AI techniques (Sarma, 1994; Turban, Aronson and Liang, 2005). Intelligent DSSs differ from ESs in principle, although in practice the difference may be hard to discern. The emphasis in intelligent DSSs is on enhancing the DMs' capabilities by focusing on their strengths while compensating for their weaknesses.

Silverman (1995) reviews intelligent decision systems that combine mathematical modelling with ESs. These systems use a variety of techniques, such as influence diagrams, Bayesian belief nets, risk and reliability analysis and knowledge-based systems, for forecasting and model-based reasoning in decision making. Intelligent DSSs have been applied in a variety of applications, such as design, forecasting, risk management, operations planning, network routing, legal reasoning and the estimation of software development work effort.

Goul, Henderson and Tonge (1992) argue that AI can increase the impact of DSSs on organisations by incorporating machine-based expertise, and they make the following three observations. First, the focus of research on DSSs at the time had shifted from highlighting the differences between the disciplines of AI and DSSs to promoting a synergy. Second, a user interacting with an ES-based DSS is automatically placed in a group decision setting with machine-based decision counterparts. Third, adding knowledge into organisational DSSs has the potential to eliminate bureaucratic procedures by giving the personnel wider access to organisational knowledge. This reduces the time it takes for DMs to respond to situations while lowering the cost and simplifying their interactions.

Hollnagel (1987) stresses that the main purpose of an intelligent DSS should be to improve the quality of the information conveyed to the user. This involves determining the meaning and content of the information ('what'), the framing of the information ('how') and the timing of displaying information ('when'), as well as whether the display should be user-driven or automatic ('how'). Holsapple and Whinston (1996) point out that intelligent DSSs have the ability to acquire, maintain, select and generate different types of knowledge as well as interact with users in an intelligent manner. DSS capabilities are mainly concerned with information/knowledge representation, processing and the user interface (Phillips-Wren *et al.*, 2006)

An intelligent DSS can take three different roles depending on the type of information provided (Hollinagel, 1987):

- a constant guard, preventing any fallacies occurring when the users have to deal with incomplete information (Reason, 1987);
- an intelligent assistant, anticipating the user's needs and carrying out all the necessary computations when there is sufficient information; or
- an information filter, removing any redundant or superfluous data when information overflow occurs.

Turban *et al.* (1993) illustrate how DSSs whose architecture comprises a database, a model base, a user interface and user(s) can be combined with ESs (or other intelligent systems, such as ANNs and intelligent agents) to produce intelligent DSSs. They present three approaches to designing intelligent DSSs.

The first approach is to develop a multi-purpose ES that supports several aspects of the decision-making process, such as problem formulation and criteria modelling, and make it a central component of the DSS.

The second approach is to develop an ES as a separate DSS component. The ES can be used to integrate the database and a model base in an intelligent manner; provide input to the DSS, such as determining the most important factors to consider, classifying the problem and generating alternatives; and interpret the results of the DSS when it is faster and cheaper to obtain explanations from an ES than from a human expert or when the quality of the explanations provided is superior.

The third approach is to develop several ESs to support the functionalities of DSS components and the interaction between the DSS and the DM. In this architecture, an ES can undertake one of the following roles:

- an intelligent agent for managing the database;
- an intelligent agent for managing the model base;
- the management and customisation of the user interface;
- an adviser or consultant to the users – e.g. describing the decision problem and the feasibility of the alternatives under consideration, as well as how to use the DSS and how to interpret its results; or
- an adviser or consultant to the DSS developers – e.g. giving advice on how to structure the DSS and assemble the various parts together.

14.5 Design of DSSs

Take advantage of every opportunity to practice your communication skills so that when important occasions arise, you will have the gift, the style, the sharpness, the clarity, and the emotions to affect other people. (Jim Rohn)

We have emphasised that prescriptive decision support seeks to guide DMs towards the ideals of behaviour encoded in normative models, mindful of their cognitive capabilities. The models (MAVA, SEU, etc.) embedded in DSSs encode the normative ideals; their calculations ensure that their output is compatible with the canons of rationality that the DMs would like to adopt. The decision analytic process as we have described it ensures a reflective use of these software tools that is sympathetic to DMs' cognitive capabilities. In addition, the design of the interface should recognise potential pitfalls and biases in DMs' perceptions.

For instance, the input screens of a DSS in eliciting the DMs', experts' and stakeholders' judgements should

- check for and guide the users away from biases, such as
  - anchoring (see section 6.3),
  - availability (see section 2.7),
  - overconfidence (see section 3.8) and
  - loss–gain framing effects (see section 3.4);
- ask questions that are cognitively meaningful to the users, using, if possible, *their* language – e.g. it is inappropriate to use technical language such as decision theoretic, statistical or economic concepts in seeking judgemental values;
- ask about real observable quantities rather than modelling constructs so that the users can relate their responses to their experience;
- use relatively simple scales, since measures of human judgement become less reliable when there are too many points along the scale;
- use sensitivity analysis techniques to focus the users' efforts and reassure them that greater accuracy is not necessary; and
- recognise that the unfamiliarity of the tool and judgemental effort required may exhaust the users.

Above all, the elicitation tasks should be cognitively meaningful and behaviourally possible for the DMs, experts and stakeholders. Consider the elicitation of probabilities, utilities and weights. There are many ways in which this may be achieved, and most decision analytic software incorporates some visualisation of these quantities to help, first, in their elicitation and, subsequently, in their presentation. Figure 14.3 shows two representations of probabilities. Behavioural studies suggest that different people may perceive the relative likelihoods conveyed by these differently, although the numbers are precisely the same. There are similar difficulties

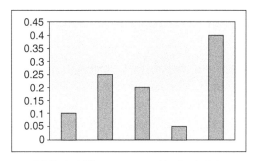
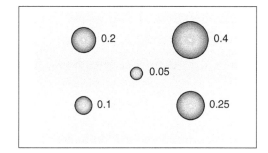

(a) Probabilities represented by bar height   (b) Probabilities represented by area

Figure 14.3   Two representations of the same set of probabilities

if the software tries to define uncertainty in natural language: people seldom agree on the interpretation of words such as 'likely' (Hunink, Glasziou, Siegel *et al.*, 2001; Lichtenstein and Newman, 1967; Theil, 2002).

Similarly, the output screens that guide DMs' choice of action should

- use the DMs' language;
- use the DMs' metaphors, not those of the analysts or experts;
- beware of misleading DMs by poor framing of the output;
- avoid over-cluttering the screen, as too much detail can hide or distract from the key points;
- give numeric output to appropriate and usable precision;
- watch wording for undesired associations; and
- watch colour for associations – e.g. red for danger.

Let us now consider the five contexts for using decision analytic tools discussed in section 3. As noted by Belton and Hodgkin (1999), different contexts lead to different requirements on the functionality and HCI of decision analytic software. In the single-user context (case A), the DM may be a non-expert user and will need more support in the form of help and other explanation features than an expert analyst. In case B, the software may offer advanced, complex functions to an expert analyst, but should also offer report-writing features and simple plots to enable the insights gained from its use to be conveyed to a wider audience. For decision conferences (case C), the software should project well, offer the audience clear, uncluttered screens without distracting information and include options that would be of use only to an expert user. Nevertheless, since DMs do not operate the software nor interpret the analysis themselves, there is less need for help and explanation. Software designed for use in a group decision support room (case D) will be controlled by the facilitator and analysts, who will 'release' functionality to DMs at the appropriate time, when the users can be quickly trained in its use. Thus help and explanation facilities will be less important, and, while the full software suite may contain some very advanced functionality, only the analysts need to have comprehensive access to this. Thus the DMs will need context-sensitive menus, so that they can focus on the current group task.

Case E, i.e. wGDSS, has – or can have – parallels with all the other four cases. Sometimes the users can be left to work the software themselves, as in case A; at other times an analyst or facilitator can be involved, running either an online decision conference (case C) or activities similar to those in case D; in yet other circumstances the analysis may be developed and run, as in case B, by an analyst, who continually consults the group over the web to keep in abreast of developments and involves it in the assessment of some of the key judgements. If we consider problem formulation, the software may need to help non-expert DMs structure the problem quickly and effectively in case A, whereas, in the other cases, the analyst may use his expertise to structure the problem before inputting it into the model format assumed by the software. The need to support the decision analysis process also varies with the level of involvement of analysts or a facilitator.

As we noted in figure 1.3, strategic decision making tends to fall in the complex domain of the cynefin model. Following figure 4.4 and the discussion of KMSs in section 4.5, therefore, we would expect GDSSs for strategic decision making to emphasise the sharing of tacit knowledge. This requires many collaborative and communication tools to be integrated into such GDSSs. At present this is not entirely the case, especially in web-based GDSSs – i.e. case E (see French, 2007b).

Designing or adopting an appropriate GDSS is only a first step towards its implementation. The effective use of GDSSs – or, indeed, any DSS – in an organisation requires it to be tailored and embedded into the organisation's processes and culture. Grudin (1994) lists eight challenges for the successful implementation of GDSSs, and, more generally, KMS and CSCW systems.

- *Disparity in work and benefits.* Groupware applications often require input from users who do not themselves receive any immediate benefit from the system.
- *Critical mass.* Some systems simply cannot work until sufficient members of the organisation adopt them fully.
- *Disruption of social processes.* At the very least, effective use of the system usually requires changes in working practices and relationships; sometimes it can create social divisions – e.g. between those important enough to attend a decision conference and those not.
- *Exception handling.* Inevitably there will be issues that cannot be handled effectively by the system. Groupware should not apply a straightjacket that stops the use of other kinds of decision processes when this occurs.
- *Unobtrusive accessibility.* The HCI should emphasise more frequently used functions without hiding less used ones.
- *Difficulty of evaluation.* Information systems are notoriously difficult to evaluate, and this is no less true of GDSSs.
- *Failure of individual intuition.* Each user understands what helps him or her and how the information provided by the system affects his/her

perceptions, but may lack the intuition to understand how his/her colleagues use the system and what they gain from it.

- *The adoption process.* One cannot train users of the system one at a time. Groupware requires that the group use it in their work as a team. Thus all have to be trained and helped to adopt the system simultaneously.

In addition, of course, any system should adopt the best HCI practice for all information systems (see, for example, Laudon and Laudon, 2006, and Sankar *et al.*, 1995). It is a sad comment that very few software packages make much attempt to meet these requirements. Several allow the user to set the basic terminology – e.g. whether one uses the terms 'attributes', 'objectives' or 'criteria' to define the verbal input of value scales (Bana e Costa and Vansnick, 2000) – but, beyond that, the implementation of best HCI practice in strategic decision support interfaces is somewhat rudimentary. In a sense this is surprising, because MAUD, one of the earliest and now defunct MAVA packages, took a lot of care to manage the interaction with the DM in a very sensitive manner (Humphreys and McFadden, 1980). Other authors have investigated the importance of natural language interfaces and the provision of context-sensitive explanations of the analysis, but the methods have not found their way into off-the-shelf software (Bertsch, French, Geldermann *et al.*, 2009; Klein, 1994; Papamichail and French, 2003). Most of the available decision analytic software simply implements algorithmic solutions of multi-attribute value models, decision trees and influence diagrams and provides a number of fairly standard plots of the solution and its sensitivity.

What we would really like to see is software support for the whole decision analytic process. Software should offer support for problem formulation, linking the early exploration of issues to the construction of the decision model: see Belton *et al.* (1997). Some software does allow one to brainstorm words, then gather them together into an attribute tree (French and Xu, 2005), but, at best, the support is at the level of providing graphical functionality, not supporting the *process* of problem formulation. In the evaluation phase, there should be support to ensure that numbers are processed through meaningful, appropriate calculations. Modern object-oriented programming methods can enable this to be policed effectively (Liu and Stewart, 2003). Lastly, there is little support for the implementation of the decision – or, rather, outside risk management there is little. In section 10.5 we mentioned the risk register software. This is, essentially, a database that regularly prompts the risk manager to check and audit a strategy against the potential risks. The idea could and should be extended to support all aspects of the implementation of the chosen strategy in any decision analysis (see, for example, case vignette 11.1).

14.6 Evaluation of decision support systems

[T]here is the still poorly understood shifting boundary between what computers can do well and what humans can do well. This has major implications for the relevant application set for DSS are therefore their successful use in organizations. (Michael Scott Morton)

Evaluation is one of the important activities in the development of a DSS. It either takes place at the end of the development process, however, or is not carried out at all (Adelman, 1992). If a DSS is evaluated in the early stages of its development it will be easier and less expensive to resolve any problems (Borenstein, 1998). A thorough examination of a DSS would allow DSS developers to establish how accurate the output is, how well the system and the users perform and whether the DSS addresses the needs of its users.

The main aim of the evaluation process is to verify and validate a DSS. 'Verification' and 'validation' are two terms that often overlap in the literature (Miser and Quade, 1988). According to O'Keefe *et al.* (1987), 'verification is building the system right, validation is building the right system'. 'Verification is part of validation; a system that has not been built right is unlikely to be the right system' (O'Keefe and Preece, 1996).

Based on Adelman's (1992) evaluation framework, Papamichail and French (2005) have devised a methodology for assessing an intelligent DSS for nuclear emergencies. The methodology can be applied for the evaluation of any DSS. It comprises three evaluation levels.

Technical verification. Check the technical aspects of the DSS to find out how well it has been built. Establish the appropriateness of the approaches and techniques used to develop the system. Use programming methods to test how well the code is written. Invite domain experts to inspect the completeness and accuracy of the codified knowledge and models that have been employed. Compare the DSS against other systems in the same domain. Compile a set of documents and manuals to describe the operations and interfaces of the system.

Performance validation. Demonstrate the DSS to different groups of users. Invite potential users to interact with the system. Explore how well the system performs its tasks, how complete the DSS components are and

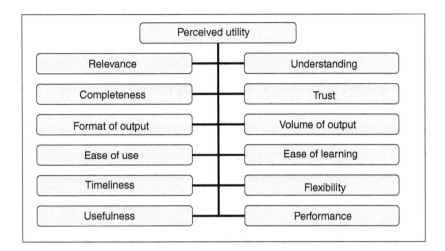

Figure 14.4   An attribute tree for assessing DSSs

whether its advice is sound. Examine whether the DSS can improve users' performance in executing decision-making tasks. Establish the link between the system's outputs and the decisions taken – i.e. whether the use of the system increases the quality of the decisions.

Subjective assessment. Measure the utility of the DSS to find out how users perceive it, whether the system fits the users' needs and how well its interface is designed. Identify evaluation criteria, such as the usefulness, relevance and completeness of the output. These can be structured into an attribute tree (an example is given in figure 14.4). Devise a questionnaire to measure how well the system rates over the evaluation criteria used. Include open-ended questions to establish the strengths and limitations of the system.

Other steps that could be added include that of reflection (i.e. review the results of the DSS evaluation), choice (i.e. devise an action plan to improve the DSS) and development (i.e. develop an improved version of the DSS).

There are several technical challenges and cultural issues to consider during the evaluation of a DSS (Papamichail and French, 2005). DSS developers should take into account the feasibility of conducting validation tests (Finlay and Wilson, 2000) and assess the suitability of the methods used to review their system (Adelman, 1992). Two of the most challenging evaluation tasks are assessing whether a DSS improves the performance of its users and devising a complete evaluation framework and set of criteria like the attribute tree of figure 14.4 (Papamichail and French, 2005). The following two readings are particularly helpful: Adelman (1992), who provides a comprehensive discussion of evaluation frameworks, and Phillips-Wren *et al.* (2006), who have drawn from the DSS literature to present a wide range of evaluation criteria.

14.7 Latest trends in decision support

Oh, so they have internet on computers now! (Homer Simpson)

There is a wide range of DSS applications in such domains as production/operations, marketing, logistics and transportation (Eom and Kim, 2006). With twenty new DSS publications per day in 2004 (compared to fewer than three publications in 1980, based on Google Scholar results), the DSS field is getting stronger (Burstein and Holsapple, 2008).

One of the most cited DSS articles is that by Shim *et al.* (2002), in which there is a discussion of the agenda for future DSS design and development; data warehouses, collaborative support systems and virtual teams are highlighted as being particularly important. New topics, such as stakeholders' perspectives, digital media and emotion in decision making, are emerging (Paradice, 2007). Formulating mental models using DSS output and accuracy of information are two further topics of particular importance (Papamichail and Maridakis, 2006).

Web-based applications are transforming the way that DSSs are designed and developed (Bhargava *et al.*, 2007). Recent applications of DSSs include mobile decision making (i.e. decision making on the move: Cowie and Burstein, 2007), decision support for extreme events (e.g. terrorist attacks: Mendonça, 2007) and predicting final prices on eBay (van Heijst *et al.*, 2008).

When the concept of DSSs was introduced by Scott Morton (1971) the assumption was that they would have analytical capabilities that would be combined with the intelligent abilities of a user. DSSs were later augmented with AI so as to build machines with human-like abilities – e.g. seeing, hearing and thinking (Leonard-Barton and Sviokla, 1988). Despite the advent of AI techniques, however, there are currently no organisational DSSs that can take strategic decisions without some contribution from executives (McCosh and Correa-Pérez, 2006). Even though there are several examples of new forms of DSS architectures incorporating AI techniques (see, for example, Bolloju *et al.*, 2002), we have seen very few implemented frameworks.

Papamichail and Maridakis (2006) discuss four concepts that are important in the design of DSSs: sense making (Choo, 1996; Weick, 1995), knowledge management (Boisot, 1998; Bolloju *et al.*, 2002), organisational learning (Antonacopoulou and Papamichail, 2004; Hall and Paradice, 2005) and intuition (Kuo, 1998; Sauter, 1999). In particular, the next generation of DSSs should

- help DMs make sense of changes in their environment so as to discern their meaning and come up with a shared interpretation;
- facilitate knowledge management processes so as to enable DMs to create and evolve organisational knowledge assets;
- enhance DMs' learning capabilities to ensure that assumptions are thoroughly tested and that biases in beliefs and perceptions are reduced; and
- support the intuitive and creative aspects of human decision making.

Using DSSs should lead to better decision processes and better decisions (Pick, 2008). DSS projects may fail, however, due to a lack of executive sponsorship, a lack of appropriate skills in the DSS development team and other factors (Arnott and Dodson, 2008). Conducting a larger number of case studies, obtaining more funding for DSS projects and shifting the DSS research focus onto the development of data warehousing and business intelligence systems are further ways for improving DSS research (Arnott and Pervan, 2008).

14.8 Further reading

The two edited volumes of the *Handbook on Decision Suppport Systems* (Burstein and Holsapple, 2008) provide a comprehensive review of the field, while Gupta *et al.* (2006) provide a similarly comprehensive review of intelligent DSSs. Alavi and Tiwana (2003) discuss how a range of DSSs, such as ESs and data warehousing, support KM functions.

Methods for developing DSSs have been proposed by Sprague and Carlson (1982). Gachet and Haettenschwiler (2006) review the DSS development literature. A discussion of DSS history is given by Power (2002) and McCosh and Correa-Pérez (2006).

14.9 Exercises and questions for discussion

(1) Outline and discuss the main types of DSSs.
(2) 'Business intelligence tools are not DSSs.' Do you agree with this statement? Explain your answer.
(3) Discuss the HCI aspects of DSSs. Do you think that knowledge of behavioural decision making is important in designing DSSs that provide prescriptive decision support?

(4)   Discuss the five contexts for using decision analytic software in a group of DMs. What are the HCI and functionality requirements for using the decision analytic software?

(5)   (a)   What specific group behavioural issues need to be addressed in designing group decision support systems? Would you expect the importance of these behavioural issues to vary between the corporate strategic, general, operational and hands-on work domains of activity? If so, how and why?

(b)   Describe the following two styles of providing group decision support:
- decision conferencing; and
- networked GDSS rooms with little central facilitation.

How do these address the issues that you identified in part (a) of the question? Are they equally well suited to all domains of activity?

(c)   The internet can provide decision support to groups distributed around the world, possibly working on the issues at different times. Can such distributed GDSSs address the behavioural issues that you identified? What others might arise? Does the domain of activity affect your response?

(6)   Discuss whether there are parallels between knowledge management systems and group decision support systems, particularly in relation to strategic decision contexts.

(7)   Discuss the need for evaluating DSSs. What are the main issues to consider?

(8)   How can we improve the use of DSSs in organisations? Provide recommendations.

(9)   What are the latest trends in decision support?

15

Conclusions

It is good to have an end to journey toward; but it is the journey that matters in the end.
(Ursula LeGuin)

15.1 The key messages

We have covered a lot of material in the previous fourteen chapters and discussed decision making from many perspectives. Indeed, if you take only one message from this book, make it that an understanding of decision making and how to improve it requires a multidisciplinary approach. Without this, our understanding of decision making is necessarily naïve and partial. This is true regardless of whether one is primarily interested in normative approaches designed to identify the principles underpinning rational decision making, descriptive approaches that seek to explain how decisions are actually taken or prescriptive approaches that are concerned with developing ways of improving decision making. As we have shown throughout the book, these approaches not only draw on common concepts, but also demonstrate that their use in one context can be considerably enhanced by reflecting on how they are used in other contexts.

For example, some of the concepts drawn from normative theory, such as utility, risk and probability, maximisation and alternatives, have been investigated and clarified by descriptive approaches, often revealing that people understand and use these in ways that depart from normative assumptions. Such departures not only challenge the notion that human beings are rational decision makers, but also pinpoint issues and problems that prescriptive approaches should address, and in many cases have addressed. Despite these common concepts and similar historical roots, however, the three approaches have tended to develop separately without taking full advantage of the insights and ideas from each other. We hope that our book has provided convincing arguments for the need to take a multidisciplinary approach and, in some small way, shown both how to do this and the value of doing so.

415

In the next section we expand on the value of taking a multidisciplinary approach, highlighting in more specific terms some of the advantages of combining prescriptive and descriptive approaches (focusing on these two because they have been the primary focus of the book).

15.2 Linking prescriptive and behavioural approaches

One of the primary objectives of the book has been to explore the interrelationships between prescriptive and descriptive approaches to decision making, in particular to consider procedures designed to help people make better decisions in the light of our knowledge of what people actually do and some of the limitations and biases inherent in how they do it. Exploring these interrelationships is important for the following four reasons.

How description can benefit prescription

First, knowing what people actually do and some of the problems inherent in this process provide a sound basis for justifying and explaining to others why prescriptive techniques are necessary. For example, in chapter 4 we showed how known limitations in human memory can reduce the effectiveness of human decision making. In particular, retrieval from long-term memory favours high-impact, positive events, leading DMs to draw more heavily on these aspects of their experience rather than equally important events that have less impact or are negative. We noted that this was a major reason for people being overly optimistic in their predictions and forecasts. We argued that information and knowledge management systems can provide ways of overcoming these biases. Thus, known limitations in human memory can provide a powerful justification for the use of information support systems.

Similarly, in chapter 7 we presented research showing that people depend upon a range of different decision strategies, some of which are quite simple and use only a small proportion of the relevant information. In addition, this research showed that simple strategies can, on occasions, lead to suboptimal decision making. On this occasion, we argued that decision analysis overcomes these problems by means of a series of techniques designed to help DMs execute complex strategies that use more of the relevant information and do so in a more balanced way. Again, a recognition of limitations in how people actually make decisions, in this case in terms of the strategies they use, can provide powerful justifications for the use of prescriptive techniques, in this case decision analysis. Finally, in chapter 11 we identified a broad range of factors that limit the effectiveness of group decision making, such as conformity, the common knowledge effect and groupthink. Demonstrating the presence of these effects in groups provides powerful arguments in support of the use of structured techniques such as devil's advocacy, Delphi and decision conferencing or through GDSSs. These are a few of many examples in which the use of prescriptive procedures can be justified in terms of their propensity to address known problems in human decision making.

Second, knowing the errors and biases in human decision making can help to target prescriptive approaches more effectively. The examples outlined in the two paragraphs above also serve to support this point, since each shows how prescriptive techniques have been used to target known problems. We believe that the full potential of this possibility has not been fully realised, however. Prescriptive and descriptive approaches are founded on rather different academic traditions, and this has led to each developing independently of the other. In general, books and articles tend to be written from one or other standpoint, thereby reducing the interplay between the two. We believe that this lack of communication between the two strands can lead to serious problems. For example, in sections 2.9 and 8.6 we showed that DMs are generally overconfident about the accuracy of their judgements, and that this comes about, in part, because of a strong tendency to focus on information that supports initial views and to neglect information that does not. Therefore, simply making more information available, by using information systems and KMSs, may simply exacerbate this bias in information processing, leading to even higher levels of overconfidence.

This illustrates the importance of taking account of behavioural decision research in the design of systems and training. For example, in the context of information and knowledge management support systems, it would be appropriate to provide training to encourage 'consider the opposite' thinking (section 2.9) for developing a more balanced information acquisition strategy. A further example can be drawn from work by Yates *et al.* (2003) on definitions of good and bad decision making. They show that, in retrospect, bad decisions never seem quite as bad as they actually were, thereby leading people to hold an overly optimistic view of the efficacy of their decision making. Unless people recognise this optimism they may see little need for decision support techniques. These are just two examples showing that a closer working relationship between prescriptive and descriptive approaches would be beneficial.

Third, it is important to recognise that there has been some discussion of prescriptive issues among those who work in the behavioural decision-making area. For example, in section 2.9 we identified two examples in which behavioural decision researchers have suggested procedures to improve thinking. While this is a positive development, the full impact of this work may not be realised until descriptive researchers have a broader understanding of prescriptive approaches and how their procedures can be used in the context of existing decision analysis and support techniques. The separation between the two strands of work is in danger of leading to these kinds of thinking aids being neglected by those working in prescriptive decision theory.

Finally, each approach can provide useful pointers for identifying future research priorities in the other. We begin by presenting three examples in which the descriptive approach highlights future priorities for decision analysis and support; we hope you may have thought of many others as you have read the book.

(1) While the primary focus of the prescriptive approach has been on developing effective processes as a means of achieving good outcomes, Yates *et al.* (2003) show that there are other factors that people use for distinguishing good from bad decisions – e.g. feeling good about the decision. This suggests that prescriptive approaches should develop a broader view of those aspects that are important to decision makers and then develop techniques that support them. Otherwise, DMs may be disappointed, because the techniques fail to address factors that are important to them.

(2) In section 2.8 we reviewed research showing that DMs' emotional state can affect how they make decisions. The pressures of organisational life mean that DMs experience a broad range of emotions – e.g. happiness when a project goes well, anger when a colleague has let them down, anxiety about whether a new product launch will be successful. Research indicates that changes in emotional state can change the nature of human thinking and, thereby, the basis upon which a decisions is taken. Despite this, we know virtually nothing about the effects that emotions have when people are using decision analysis and support techniques, and whether these effects are stronger or weaker with some techniques rather than others. Such information would be useful when choosing which techniques to use in a particular situation or context. A further intriguing possibility is that we may be able to build techniques or training to help DMs manage their emotions, nullifying biases such as the tendency to provide more optimistic predictions when experiencing positive as compared with negative emotions.

Perhaps the most intriguing possibility of all, however, is that we may deliberately induce moods to facilitate particular kinds of thinking. For example, we already know that people engage in more creative and wide-ranging thinking under positive emotions and more focused and analytical thinking under negative emotions. Therefore, why not induce emotions to support the kinds of thinking appropriate to the decision task in hand (e.g. whether convergent or divergent thinking is appropriate)? If you think this is far-fetched then reflect on the following true story. Some time ago one of us (Maule) was offered a lift to work by a neighbour. Usually this neighbour wears a smart suit and tie, but on this occasion he wore jeans and a casual shirt. Maule remarked, 'Well, obviously a brainstorm and nice hotel today, then.' The neighbour was flabbergasted, because both were true! This prediction was founded on research showing that, under positive emotions, people are more creative. Accordingly, making people feel good by treating them nicely, allowing them to dress casually and pampering them in an expensive hotel is likely to induce positive emotions that facilitate creative thinking. It may be more difficult to justify inducing negative emotions when wishing to facilitate more convergent thinking, but we believe that some senior managers do this anyway (though perhaps not always with the intention of inducing more analytical thinking!).

(3) In section 7.1 we reviewed research on fast-and-frugal heuristics that demonstrated that there are some occasions when simpler strategies are better than complex ones. These findings challenge some of the fundamental assumptions underpinning much of decision analysis and support – namely improving decision making involves helping people to use more elaborate forms of thinking. There is an urgent need for future research to identify those decision contexts in which fast-and-frugal heuristics are effective, since trying to induce DMs to use decision analysis and support techniques is likely to be inappropriate in these situations – i.e. it may disrupt existing efficient ways of working. Indeed, it may be the case that we will be able to develop techniques that can support fast-and-frugal decision making. At present we believe that some tactical and perhaps all strategic decisions will benefit from decision support and that the fast-and-frugal approaches are likely to be beneficial for some tactical and operational decisions. The provision of requisite decision analysis and support may vary more with context than previously appreciated. Further work is needed to test these suggestions, however.

How prescription can benefit description

Since the review and evaluation of prescriptive approaches is the primary objective of this book, we have necessarily said much less about descriptive approaches in earlier chapters, so there is less to cover in this section. We present two examples, however, and once again we hope that you have thought of others while reading the book.

First, prescriptive techniques can provide new and highly relevant contexts in which to evaluate existing descriptive theories. To exemplify further, consider a situation in which a prescriptive technique has been developed to support a particular aspect of decision making that descriptive research has shown to be subject to error and bias. Testing participants' decision-making behaviour with and without the prescriptive technique can provide an appropriate context for assessing the underlying behavioural theory. Hodgkinson *et al.* (1999) provide an example of just such a study. They wanted to test a prediction, based on existing descriptive research, that the framing bias disappears when people engage more elaborate thinking. They reasoned that cognitive mapping (which was briefly outlined in section 9.5) would support this kind of thinking, and so should lead to a reduction in the bias. Their predictions were supported in an experimental study that involved giving a complex strategic decision problem to senior managers. This is an example of how prescriptive techniques can be used to develop descriptive theory, though in reality there have been very few studies that have actually realised the potential of this approach.

Second, prescriptive approaches put decision makers into very distinctive contexts in terms of the amounts, type and format of available information and the procedures and strategies that are implemented to resolve choice. As such, these contexts provide new and interesting environments in which to make predictions and to test theories of how people make decisions. One of the criticisms of descriptive approaches is that they have been overly dependent upon laboratory studies (cf. Fischhoff, 1996), so investigating in situations in which prescriptive procedures are in operation opens up new possibilities of undertaking research in more everyday and work-related situations. Indeed, since the research process necessarily involves recording decision-relevant behaviours (including but not exclusively final choices), it may be relatively straightforward to add this to existing computer-based prescriptive approaches.

There is the possibility of a further fruitful link between decision analysis and support, on the one hand, and the field of cognitive psychology, on the other. Although much behavioural decision research has been developed from a cognitive perspective (and, hopefully, we have already shown the value of this), there are other aspects of cognitive psychology that may provide useful insights into possible future developments. In section 4.2 we showed how relatively simple concepts drawn from theory and research on human memory support the need for and usefulness of information and knowledge management. The field of human memory is very well developed, however, and provides a good deal of understanding about how people store and retrieve information (see, for example, Baddeley, 2004). Thus, a better understanding of the factors that aid the retrieval of information from long-term memory may provide useful insights into how to design knowledge management interfaces so as to complement natural ways of thinking and stimulate more detailed search for relevant information.

15.3 The challenges to decision support brought by Web 2.0

In 2004 O'Reilly coined the term 'Web 2.0' and heralded a new era of social networking and collaboration on the internet (O'Reilly, 2005). Whether one can really talk of a 'second release of the web' or whether it is just that the original vision of Berners Lee is at last being implemented may be moot. What is unarguable, however, is that the web is clearly developing as a platform for collaboration. We noted this in chapters 13 and 14, recognising the development of wGDSSs and e-participation based upon the potential for distributed collaboration now offered by web-based tools. The implications for decision analysis and support are many.

More and more management interactions in organisations are being conducted via the web. Globalisation means that organisations are becoming geographically – and temporally – dispersed, so face-to-face meetings to explore and resolve issues are often difficult and costly to arrange. Even for organisations working from just one location, diary management issues encourage management teams to interact by electronic means. We noted in chapter 13 that the involvement of citizens in addressing societal issues was also leading to greater use of the internet in communication and deliberation. There are strong pressures, therefore, to take advantage of the opportunities that Web 2.0 technologies bring to communication and distributed collaboration. We can only wonder what new developments there will be in the future and the implications that these will have for decision analysis and support.

As we have argued throughout this book, however, decision making is seldom as straightforward as it might seem. There are many different types of decisions, and the support that might be offered can vary across a number of levels. Our instincts and behaviours can be at odds with more 'rational' approaches to decision making. Culture and other causes of miscommunication can lead to poor decision-making performance in groups, organisations and society. We recognise and understand these problems in face-to-face and other traditional forms of interaction. Our knowledge of the forms these problems may take in web interactions is much more sketchy. The designers of some of the Web 2.0 technologies, keen to sell their systems, sometimes seem oblivious to these issues, however. So too do public and private sector managers anxious to cut the internal costs of management processes. Adoption of the technologies may outstrip our ability to use them and may bring new forms of heuristic thinking with hitherto unrecognised errors and biases. Thus, while the end of the twentieth century saw huge leaps forward in our understanding of how to support and improve decision making, the impact of Web 2.0 may be to introduce further issues, obviating some of these advances.

In our opinion, multidisciplinarity is essential if we are to tackle these fundamental challenges to the development of decision support. The many complementary themes and approaches that we have attempted to convey in the preceding pages will be needed more than ever as a foundation for our decision making in the coming years. Moreover, as we have tried to indicate, all will need to be developed further if we are to meet the challenges that the twenty-first century brings.

References

Abelson, J., P. G. Forest, J. Eyles, P. Smith, E. Martin and F. P. Gauvin (2003). 'Deliberations about deliberative methods: issues in the design and evaluation of public participation processes.' *Social Science and Medicine* 57(2), 239–51.

Ackermann, F. (1996). 'Participants' perceptions on the role of facilitators using group decision support systems.' *Group Decision and Negotiation* 5(1), 93–112.

Ackermann, F., and C. Eden (2003). *Powerful and Interested Stakeholders Matter: Their Identification and Management.* Working Paper no. 2. Business School, University of Strathclyde.

Ackermann, F., C. Eden and I. Brown (2004). *The Practice of Making Strategy.* London, Sage.

Ackoff, R. L. (1974). *Redesigning the Future: A Systems Approach to Societal Planning.* New York, John Wiley and Sons.

(1977). 'Optimization + objectivity = opt out.' *European Journal of Operational Research* 1(1), 1–7.

Adams, J. (1995). *Risk.* London, UCL Press.

Adelman, L. (1992). *Evaluating Decision Support and Expert Systems.* New York, Wiley-Interscience.

Alavi, M., and A. Tiwana (2003). 'Knowledge management: the information technology dimension.' In M. Easterby-Smith and M. A. Lyles (eds.), *Handbook of Organizational Learning and Knowledge Management.* Oxford, Basil Blackwell, 104–21.

Allais, M. (1953). 'Le comportement de l'homme rationnel devant le risqué: critique des postulats et axioms de l'école américaine.' *Econometrica* 21(4), 503–46.

Allais, M., and O. Hagen (eds.) (1979). *Expected Utility Hypothesis and the Allais Paradox.* Dordrecht, D. Reidel.

Allingham, M. (2002). *Choice Theory: A Very Short Introduction.* Oxford, Oxford University Press.

Allison, G. T. (1971). *Essence of Decision: Explaining the Cuban Missile Crisis.* Boston, Little Brown.

Alonso, E. (2002). 'AI and agents: state of the art.' *AI Magazine* 23(3), 25–30.

Alter, S. (1977). 'A taxonomy of decision support systems.' *Sloan Management Review* 19(1), 39–56.

(1980). *Decision Support Systems: Current Practice and Continuing Challenges.* Reading, MA, Addison-Wesley.

Anderson, D. R., D. J. Sweeney and T. Williams (1991). *An Introduction to Management Science*. St Paul, MN, West.

Anderson, P. A. (1983). 'Decision making by objection and the Cuban Missile Crisis.' *Administrative Science Quarterly* 28(2), 201–22.

Anisimov, A. (2003). 'Decision support in the absence of necessary information and models by means of OLAP-systems: organisational and managerial perspectives.' *International Journal of Technology, Policy and Management* 3(3–4), 285–300.

Anthes, G. H. (2003). 'Agents of change.' *ComputerWorld* 37(4), 26–7.

Anthony, R. N. (1965). *Planning and Control Systems: A Framework for Analysis*. Boston, Harvard University Press.

Antonacopoulou, E. P., and K. N. Papamichail (2004). 'Learning-supported decision making: ICTs as feedback systems.' In G. Doukidis, N. Mylonopoulos and N. Pouloudi (eds.), *Social and Economic Transformation in the Digital Era*. London, Idea Group, 271–88.

Antunes, P., and T. Ho (2001). 'The design of a GDSS meeting preparation tool.' *Group Decision and Negotiation* 10(1), 5–27.

Argyris, C. (2001). 'Interpersonal barriers to decision making.' In *Harvard Business Review on Decision Making*. Boston, Harvard Business School Press, 59–95.

Arkes, H. R. (1991). 'Costs and benefits of judgment errors: implications for debiasing.' *Psychological Bulletin*, 110(3), 486–98.

Arkes, H. R., and K. R. Hammond (eds.) (1986). *Judgement and Decision Making*. Cambridge, Cambridge University Press.

Arnott, D. (2008). 'Personal decision support systems.' In F. Burstein and C. W. Holsapple (eds.), *Handbook on Decision Support Systems 2*. Berlin, Springer, 127–50.

Arnott, D., and G. Dodson (2008). 'Decision support systems failure.' In F. Burstein and C. W. Holsapple (eds.), *Handbook on Decision Support Systems 2*. Berlin, Springer, 763–90.

Arnott, D., and G. Pervan (2005). 'A critical analysis of decision support systems research.' *Journal of Information Technology* 20(2), 67–87.

(2008). 'Eight key issues for the decision support systems discipline.' *Decision Support Systems* 44(3), 657–72.

Arnstein, S. R. (1969). 'A ladder of citizen participation.' *American Institute of Planners Journal* 35(4), 216–24.

Arrow, K. J. (1963). *Social Choice and Individual Values*, 2nd edn. New York, John Wiley and Sons.

(1982). 'Risk perception in psychology and economics.' *Economic Inquiry* 20(1), 1–9.

Arvai, J. L. (2003). 'Using risk communication to disclose the outcome of participatory decision making process: effects on the perceived acceptability of risk-policy decisions.' *Risk Analysis* 23(2), 281–9.

Asaro, P. M. (2000). 'Transforming society by transforming technology: the science and politics of participatory design.' *Accounting, Management and Information Technologies* 10(4), 257–90.

Atherton, E. (2000). 'From discounting to incorporating decisions' long-term impacts.' *Risk: Health, Safety and Environment* 11(2), 125–50.

Atherton, E., and S. French (1997). 'Issues in supporting intertemporal choice.' In M. H. Karwan, J. Spronk and J. Wallenius (eds.), *Essays in Decision Making*. Berlin, Springer-Verlag, 135–56.

(1998). 'Valuing the future: a MADA example involving nuclear waste storage.' *Journal of Multi-Criteria Decision Analysis* 7(6), 304–21.

Atherton, E., T. Hicks, J. Hunt, A. Littleboy, W. Thompson and R. Yearsley (2003). *RISKOM II: Dialogue Processes – Summary Report*. Brussels, European Commission.

Aven, T. (2003). *Foundations of Risk Analysis: A Knowledge and Decision-oriented Perspective*. Chichester, John Wiley and Sons.

Ayton, P. (1998). 'How bad is human judgement.' In G. Wright and P. Goodwin (eds.), *Forecasting with Judgement*. Chichester, John Wiley and Sons, 237–67.

Bacharach, M. (1975). 'Group decisions in the face of differences of opinion.' *Management Science* 22(2), 182–91.

Bacharach, M., and S. Hurley (eds.) (1991). *Foundations of Decision Theory*. Oxford, Basil Blackwell.

Baddeley, A. D. (2004). *Your Memory: A User's Guide*. London, Carlton Books.

(2007). *Working Memory, Thought, and Action*. Oxford, Oxford University Press.

Baesens, B., C. Mues, T. Van Gestel and J. Vanthienen (2006). 'Special issue on intelligent information systems for financial engineering – preface.' *Expert Systems with Applications* 30(3), 413–4.

Baldridge, J. V. (1971). *Power and Conflict in the University: Research in the Sociology of Complex Organizations*. New York, John Wiley and Sons.

Bana e Costa, C. A., L. Ensslin, E. C. Corrêa and J.-C. Vansnick (1999). 'Decision support systems in action: integrated application in a multicriteria decision aid process.' *European Journal of Operational Research* 113(2), 315–35.

Bana e Costa, C. A., and J.-C. Vansnick (2000). 'Cardinal value measurement with Macbeth.' In S. H. Zanakis, G. Doukidis and C. Zopounidis (eds.), *Decision Making: Recent Developments and Worldwide Applications*. Dordrecht, Kluwer, 317–29.

Bannon, L. J. (1997). 'CSCW – a challenge to certain G(DSS) perspectives on the role of decisions, information, and technology in organizations.' In P. C. Humphreys, S. Ayestaran, A. McCosh and B. Manyon-White (eds.), *Decision Support in Organizational Transformation*. London, Chapman and Hall, 92–121.

Barber, B. M., and T. Odean (2000). 'Trading is hazardous to your wealth: the common stock investment performance of individual investors.' *Journal of Finance* 55(2), 773–806.

Barkhi, R., E. Rolland, J. Butler and W. Fan (2005). 'Decision support system induced guidance for model formulation and solution.' *Decision Support Systems* 40(2), 269–81.

Barnard, C. (1938). *The Functions of the Executive*. Cambridge, MA, Harvard University Press.

Barnett, V. (1999). *Comparative Statistical Inference*, 3rd edn. Chichester, John Wiley and Sons.

Baron, J. (2001). *Thinking and Deciding*, 3rd edn. Cambridge, Cambridge University Press.

Baron, R., and N. Kerr (2004). *Group Process, Group Decision, Group Action*, 2nd edn. Milton Keynes, Open University Press.

Barthélemy, J. P., R. Bisdorff and G. Coppin (2002). 'Human centered processes and decision support systems' *European Journal of Operational Research* 136(2), 233–52.

Bass, B. M. (1983). *Organizational Decision Making*. Chicago, R. D. Irwin.

Bäverstam, U., G. Fraser and G. N. Kelly (1997). Editorial: 'Decision making support for off-site emergency management.' *Radiation Protection Dosimetry* 73(1), xiii.

Bayley, C., and S. French (2008). 'Designing a participatory process for stakeholder involvement in a societal decision.' *Group Decision and Negotiation* 17(3), 195–210.

Bazerman, M. H. (1999). 'Reviews on decision making.' *Administrative Science Quarterly* 44(1), 176–80.

(2006). *Managerial Decision Making*, 6th edn. New York, John Wiley and Sons.

Bazerman, M. H., and D. Chugh (2006). 'Decisions without blinders.' *Harvard Business Review* 84(1), 88–97.

Beach, L. R., and T. Connolly (2005). *The Psychology of Decision Making: People in Organizations*. Thousand Oaks, CA, Sage.

Beck, U. (1992). *Risk Society: Towards a New Modernity*. London, Sage.

Bedford, T., and R. M. Cooke (2001). *Probabilistic Risk Analysis: Foundations and Methods*. Cambridge, Cambridge University Press.

Bedford, T., S. French and E. Atherton (2005). 'Supporting ALARP decision-making by cost benefit analysis and multi-attribute utility theory.' *Journal of Risk Research*, 8(3), 207–23.

Begley, S., and G. Beals (1995). 'Software au naturel.' *Newsweek* 8 May, 70.

Beierle, T. (1999). 'Using social goals to evaluate public participation in environmental decisions.' *Policy Studies Review* 16(3–4), 75–103.

(2002). *Democracy On-line: An Evaluation of the National Dialogue on Public Involvement in EPA Decisions*. Washington, DC, Resources for the Future.

Beierle, T., and J. Cayford (2002). *Democracy in Practice: Public Participation in Environmental Decisions*. Washington, DC, Resources for the Future.

Beierle, T., and D. M. Konisky (2000). 'Values, conflict, and trust in participatory environmental planning.' *Journal of Policy Analysis and Management* 19(4), 587–602.

Belbin, R. M. (1991). *Management Teams: Why They Succeed or Fail*. Oxford, ButterworthHeinemann.

Bell, D. E., H. Raiffa and A. Tversky (1988). *Decision Making*. Cambridge, Cambridge University Press.

Bellaby, P. (2003). 'Communication and miscommunication of risk: understanding UK parents' attitudes to combined MMR vaccination.' *British Medical Journal* 327, 725–8.

Bellman, R. E. (1957). *Dynamic Programming*. Princeton, NJ, Princeton University Press.

Bellman, R. E., and L. A. Zadeh (1970). 'Decision making in a fuzzy environment.' *Management Science* 17(4), B141–B164.

Belton, V. (1985). 'The use of a simple multi-criteria model to assist in selection from a short-list.' *Journal of the Operational Research Society* 36(4), 265–74.

Belton, V., F. Ackermann and I. Shepherd (1997). 'Integrated support from problem structuring through to alternative evaluation using COPE and VISA.' *Journal of Multi-Criteria Decision Analysis* 6(3), 115–30.

Belton, V., and A. E. Gear (1983). 'On a shortcoming of Saaty's method of analytical hierarchies.' *Omega* 11(3), 227–30.

Belton, V., and J. Hodgkin (1999). 'Facilitators, decision makers, D.I.Y. users: is intelligent multi-criteria decision support for all feasible or desirable?' *European Journal of Operational Research* 113(2), 247–60.

Belton, V., and T. J. Stewart (2002). *Multiple Criteria Decision Analysis: An Integrated Approach*. Boston, Kluwer Academic.

Bennett, P. G. (1977). 'Towards a theory of hypergames.' *Omega* 5(6), 749–51.

Bennett, P. G., and K. C. Calman (eds.) (1999). *Risk Communication and Public Health: Policy Science and Participation*. Oxford, Oxford University Press.

Bennett, P. G., S. French, A. J. Maule, D. G. Coles and A. McDonald (1999). 'Improving risk communication: a programme of work in the Department of Health.' *Risk, Decision and Policy* 4(1), 47–56.

Berger, J. O. (1985). *Statistical Decision Theory and Bayesian Analysis*, 2nd edn. New York, Springer Verlag.

Berkeley, D., and P. C. Humphreys (1982). 'Structuring decision problems and the "bias heuristic".' *Acta Psychologica* 50(3), 201–52.

Berksekas, D. P. (1987). *Dynamic Programming: Deterministic and Stochastic Models*. Engelwood Cliffs, NJ, Prentice Hall.

Bernardo, J. M., and A. F. M. Smith (1994). *Bayesian Theory*. Chichester, John Wiley and Sons.

Beroggi, G. (1998). *Decision Modelling in Policy Management: An Introduction to the Analytic Concepts*. Dordrecht, Kluwer Academic.

Berry, D. C. (2004). *Risk Communication and Health Psychology*. Maidenhead, Open University Press.

Bertsch, V., S. French, J. Geldermann, R. P. Hämäläinen, K. N. Papamichail and O. Rentz (2009). 'Multi-criteria decision support and evaluation of strategies for nuclear remediation management.' *Omega* 37(1), 238–51.

Bhargava, H. K., D. J. Power and D. Sun (2007). 'Progress in Web-based decision support technologies.' *Decision Support Systems* 43(4), 1083–95.

Bichler, M., G. Kersten and S. Strecker (2003). 'Towards a structured design of electronic negotiations.' *Group Decision and Negotiation* 12(4), 311–35.

Bickel, J. E. (2007). 'Some comparisons among quadratic, spherical and logarithmic scoring rules.' *Decision Analysis* 4(2), 49–65.

Bigley, G. A., and K. H. Roberts (2001). 'The incident command system: high reliability organising for complex and volatile task environments.' *Academy of Management Journal* 44(6), 1281–99.

Biren, B., S. Dutta and L. Van Wassenhove (2000). *Xerox: Building a Corporate Focus on Knowledge*. Fontainebleau, INSEAD.

Bleichrodt, H., J. L. Pinto and P. Wakker (2001). 'Making descriptive use of prospect theory to improve the prescriptive use of expected utility.' *Management Science* 47(11), 1498–514.

Boddy, D., A. Boonstra and G. Kennedy (2005). *Managing Information Systems: an Organisational Perspective*, 2nd edn. Harlow, FT Prentice Hall.

Boisot, M. (1998). *Knowledge Assets: Securing Competitive Advantage in the Information Economy*. Oxford, Oxford University Press.

Bolloju, N., M. Khalifa and E. Turban (2002). 'Integrating knowledge management into enterprise environments for the next generation decision support.' *Decision Support Systems* 33(2), 163–76.

Bolstad, W. M. (2004). *Introduction to Bayesian Statistics*. Hoboken, NJ, John Wiley and Sons.

Bond, S. D., K. Carlson and R. L. Keeney (2008). 'Generating objectives: can decision makers articulate what they want?' *Management Science* 54(1), 56–70.

Bordley, R. F., and G. B. Hazen (1992). 'Non-linear utility models arising from unmodelled small world intercorrelations.' *Management Science* 38(7), 1010–7.

Borenstein, D. (1998). 'Towards a practical method to validate decision support systems.' *Decision Support Systems* 23(3), 227–39.

Borges, M. R. S., J. A. Pino and R. M. Araujo (2006). 'Common context for decisions and their implementation.' *Group Decision and Negotiation* 15(3), 224–42.

Borges, M. R. S., J. A. Pino and C. Valle (2005). 'Support for decision implementation and follow-up.' *European Journal of Operational Research* 160(2), 336–52.

Borsuk, M., R. T. Clemen, L. Maguire and K. Reckhow (2001). 'Stakeholder values and scientific modeling in the Neuse River valley watershed.' *Group Decision and Negotiation* 10(4), 355–73.

Bouyssou, D., T. Marchant, M. Pirlot, P. Perny, A. Tsoukias and P. Vincke (2000). *Evaluation and Decision Models: A Critical Perspective*. Dordrecht, Kluwer Academic.

Bouyssou, D., T. Marchant, M. Pirlot, A. Tsoukias and P. Vincke (2006). *Evaluation and Decision Models with Multiple Criteria: Stepping Stones for the Analyst*. New York, Springer.

Breakwell, G. (2000). 'Risk communication: factors affecting impact.' *British Medical Journal* 56(1), 110–20.

Brehmer, B. (1986). 'The role of judgement in small-group conflict and decision making.' In H. R. Arkes and K. R. Hammond (eds.), *Judgement and Decision Making*. Cambridge, Cambridge University Press, 293–310.

Briggs, R. O., G.-J. de Vreede and J. F. Nunamaker (2003). 'Collaboration engineering with thinklets to pursue sustained success with GSS.' *Journal of Management Information Systems* 19(4), 31–64.

Brodbeck, F. C., R. Kerschreiter, A. Mojzisch, D. Frey and S. Schulz-Hardt (2002). 'The dissemination of critical, unshared information in decision-making groups: the effects of pre-discussion dissent.' *European Journal of Social Psychology* 32(1), 35–56.

Broder, A., and S. Schiffer (2003). '"Take-the-best" versus simultaneous feature matching: probabilistic inferences from memory and the effects of representation format.' *Journal of Experimental Psychology: General* 132(2), 277–93.

Brown, R. V., and A. Vari (1992). 'Towards a research agenda for prescriptive decision science: the normative tempered by the descriptive.' *Acta Psychologica* 80(1–3), 33–47.

Browne, G. J., S. P. Curley and P. G. Benson (1997). 'Evoking information in probability assessment: knowledge maps and reasoning-based directed questions.' *Management Science* 43(1), 1–14.

Brownlow, S., and S. R. Watson (1987). 'Structuring multi-attribute value hierarchies.' *Journal of the Operational Research Society* 38(4), 309–17.

Bryson, J. M. (2004). 'What to do when stakeholders matter: a public management guide to stakeholder identification, analysis and influence techniques.' *Public Management Review* 6(1), 21–53.

Buchanan, L., and A. O'Connell (2006). 'A brief history of decision making.' *Harvard Business Review* 84(1), 32–41.

Burstein, F., and C. W. Holsapple (eds.) (2008). *Handbook on Decision Support Systems*, 2 vols. Berlin, Springer.

Buzan, T. (2005). *Mindmap Handbook*. London, Thorsons.

Buzan, T., and B. Buzan (1994). *The Mind Map Book: How to Use Radiant Thinking to Maximize Your Brain's Untapped Potential*. New York, Plume.

Byrnes, E., T. Campfield and B. Connor (1989). 'Innovation and AI in the World of Financial Trading.' In M. Schorr and A. Rappaport (eds.), *Innovative Applications of Artificial Intelligence*. Menlo Park, CA, AAAI Press, 71–80.

Call, H. J., and W. A. Miller (1990). 'A comparison of approaches and implementations for automating decision analyses.' *Reliability Engineering and System Safety* 30(1–3), 115–62.

Callaway, E. (1996). 'Mind meld.' *PC Week* 13(15), 15–16.

Camerer, C. (1997). 'Progress in behavioral game theory.' *Journal of Economic Perspectives* 11(4), 167–88.

(2003). *Behavioral Game Theory: Experiments in Strategic Interaction*. Princeton, NJ, Princeton University Press.

Camerer, C., and M. Weber (1992). 'Recent developments in modeling preferences: uncertainty and ambiguity.' *Journal of Risk and Uncertainty* 5(4), 325–70.

Capgemini (2004). *Business Decisiveness Report*. Paris, Capgemini.

Caputo, M. R. (2005). *Foundations of Dynamic Economic Analysis: Optimal Control Theory and Applications*. Cambridge, Cambridge University Press.

Carley, M. (1980). *Rational Techniques in Policy Analysis*. London, Heinemann Educational.

Carrigan, N., P. H. Cardner, M. Conner and A. J. Maule (2004). 'The impact of structuring information in a patient decision aid.' *Psychology and Health* 19(4), 457–77.

Carter, E., and S. French (2006). 'Are current processes for nuclear emergency management in Europe adequate?' *Journal of Radiation Protection* 26(4), 405–14.

Carver, S., A. Evans, R. Kingston and I. Turton (2001). 'Public participation, GIS, and cyberdemocracy: evaluating online spatial decision support systems.' *Environment and Planning B: Planning and Design* 28(6), 907–21.

Casscells, W., A. Schoenberger and T. Grayboys (1978). 'Interpretation by physicians of clinical laboratory results.' *New England Journal of Medicine* 299(18), 999–1000.

Chappelet, J.-L., and P. Kilchenmann (2005). 'Interactive tools for e-democracy: examples from Switzerland.' In M. Boehlen, J. Gamper, W. Polasek and M. Wimmer (eds.), *E-Government: Towards Electronic Democracy*. Berlin, Springer-Verlag, 36–47.

Checkland, P. (2001). 'Soft systems methodology.' In J. Rosenhead, and J. Mingers (eds.), *Rational Analysis for a Problematic World Revisited*. Chichester, John Wiley and Sons, 61–89.

Checkland, P., and S. Howell (1997). *Information, Systems and Information Systems: Making Sense of the Field*. Chichester, John Wiley and Sons.

Chen, E., R. Vahidov and G. Kersten (2005). 'Agent-supported negotiations in the e-marketplace.' *International Journal of Electronic Business* 3(1), 28–49

Chen, J. Q., and S. M. Lee (2003). 'An exploratory cognitive DSS for strategic decision making.' *Decision Support Systems* 36(2), 147–60.

Cheng, J., R. Greiner, J. Kelly, D. Bell and W. Liu (2002). 'Learning Bayesian networks from data: an information-theory based approach.' *Artificial Intelligence* 137(1–2), 43–90.

Chess, C., and K. Purcell (1999). 'Public participation and the environment: do we know what works?' *Environmental Science and Technology* 33(16), 2685–92.

Choo, C. W. (1996). 'The knowing organization: how organizations use information to construct meaning, create knowledge and make decisions.' *International Journal of Information Management* 16(5), 329–40.

Christensen-Szalanski, J. J., and J. B. Bushyhead (1981). 'Physician's use of probabilistic information in a real clinical setting.' *Journal of Experimental Psychology: Human Perception and Performance* 7(4), 928–35.

Clarke, S. (2007). *Information Systems Strategic Management: An Integrated Approach*, 2nd edn. Abingdon, Routledge.

Clemen, R. T., and K. C. Lichtendahl (2002). *Debiasing Expert Overconfidence: A Bayesian Calibration Model*, working paper. Duke University, Durham, NC.

Clemen, R. T., and T. Reilly (1996). *Making Hard Decisions with Decision Tools*, 2nd edn. Pacific Grove, CA, Duxbury, Thomson Learning.

Clemen, R. T., and R. L. Winkler (1999). 'Combining probability distributions from experts in risk analysis.' *Risk Analysis* 19(2), 187–203.

Cleveland, W. S. (1994). *The Elements of Graphing Data*. Summit, NJ, Hobart Press.

Climaco, J., (ed.) (1997). *Multicriteria Analysis*. Berlin, Springer Verlag.

Coakes, E., and K. Merchant (1996). 'Expert systems: a survey of their use in UK business.' *Information & Management* 30(5), 223–30.

Coakes, E., K. Merchant and B. Lehaney (1997). 'The use of expert systems in business transformation.' *Management Decision* 35(1), 53–7.

Coakes, E., D. Willis and S. Clarke (eds.) (2002). *Knowledge Management in the SocioTechnical World*. London, Springer Verlag.

Cohen, M.-D., C. B. Kelly and A. L. Medaglia (2001). 'Decision support with Web-enabled software.' *Interfaces* 31(2), 109–29.

Cohen, M. D., J. G. March and J. P. Olsen (1972). 'A garbage can model of organizational choice.' *Administrative Science Quarterly* 17(1), 1–25.

Colman, A. M. (1995). *Game Theory and Its Applications in the Social and Biological Sciences*. Oxford, Butterworth-Heinemann.

Comer, D. R. (1995). 'A model of social loafing in real work groups.' *Human Relations* 48(6), 647–67.

Condorcet, Marquis de (1785). 'Essai sur l'application de l'analyse à la probabilité des décisions rendues à pluralité des voix.' In Marquis de Condorcet, *Oeuvres Complètes*. Paris, Harmattan.

Cooke, R. M. (1991). *Experts in Uncertainty*. Oxford, Oxford University Press.

Corner, J. L., and P. D. Corner (1995). 'Characteristics of decisions in decision analysis practice.' *Journal of the Operational Research Society* 46(3), 304–14.

Courtney, J. F. (2001). 'Decision making and knowledge management in inquiring organizations: toward a new decision-making paradigm for DSS.' *Decision Support Systems* 31(1), 17–38.

Covello, V. T. (1987). 'Decision analysis and risk management decision making: issues and methods.' *Risk Analysis* 7(2), 131–9.

Cowie, J., and F. Burstein (2007). 'Quality of data model for supporting mobile decision making.' *Decision Support Systems* 43(4), 1675–83.

Craig, P. S., M. Goldstein, A. H. Seheult and J. A. Smith (1998). 'Constructing partial prior specifications for models of complex physical systems.' *The Statistician* 47 (1), 37–53.

Crick, B. (2002). *Democracy: A Very Short Introduction*. Oxford, Oxford University Press.

Crott, H. W., M. Giesel and C. Hoffmann (1998). 'The process of inductive inference in groups: the use of positive and negative hypothesis and target testing in sequential rule-discovery tasks.' *Journal of Personality and Social Psychology*, 75(4), 938–52.

Cvetkovich, G., and R. E. Lofstedt (1999). *Social Trust and the Management of Risk*. London, Earthscan.

Cyert, R. M., and J. G. March (1963). *A Behavioral Theory of the Firm*. Englewood Cliffs, NJ, Prentice-Hall.

Daellenbach, H. G. (1994). *Systems and Decision Making.* Chichester, John Wiley and Sons.

Daellenbach, H. G., and J. T. Buchanan (1989). 'Desirable properties of interactive multi-objective programming methods.' In A. G. Lockett and G. Islei (eds.), *Improving Decision Making in Organisations.* Berlin, Spinger Verlag, 212–23.

Daellenbach, H. G., and D. C. McNickle (2005). *Management Science: Decision Making through Systems Thinking.* Basingstoke, Palgrave Macmillan.

Dalkey, N., and O. Helmer (1963). 'An experimental application of the Delphi method to the use of experts.' *Management Science* 9(3), 458–67.

Damasio, A. R. (2000). *The Feeling of What Happens: Body, Emotion and the Making of Consciousness.* London, Vintage.

Danielson M., L. Ekenberg, A. Ekengren, T. Hökby and J. Lidén (2007a). 'Decision process support for participatory democracy.' *Journal of Multi-Criteria Decision Analysis*, available at www3.interscience.wiley.com/journal/117345498/abstract?CRETRY=1&SRETRY=.

Danielson, M., L. Ekenberg, J. Idefeldt and A. Larsson (2007b). 'Using a software tool for public decision analysis: the case of Nacka municipality.' *Decision Analysis* 4(2), 76–90.

Davenport, T. H. (2006). 'Competing on analytics.' *Harvard Business Review* 84(1), 98–107.

Davis, T. J., and C. P. Keller (1997). 'Modelling and visualizing multiple spatial uncertainties.' *Computers and Geosciences* 23(4), 397–408.

Dawid, A. P. (2002). 'Influence diagrams for causal modelling and inference.' *International Statistical Review* 70(2), 161–89.

De, Finetti, B. (1974). *Theory of Probability*, vol. I. Chichester, John Wiley and Sons. (1975). *Theory of Probability*, vol. II. Chichester, John Wiley and Sons.

De Vreede, G.-J. (2006). 'Collaboration engineering: current directions and future opportunities.' In S. Seifert and C. Weinharat (eds.), *Proceedings: Group Decision and Negotiation (GDN) 2006*, Karlsruhe, Universitatsverlag Karlsruhe, 15–19.

Dean, J. W., and M. P. Sharfman (1993). 'Procedural rationality in the strategic decision-making process.' *Journal of Management Studies* 30(4), 587–610.

DeGroot, M. H. (1970). *Optimal Statistical Decisions.* New York, McGraw-Hill.

Denardo, E. V. (2002). *The Science of Decision Making.* New York, John Wiley and Sons.

Department of Health (1998). *Communicating about Risks to Public Health: Pointers to Good Practice.* London, HMSO.

DeSanctis, G., and R. B. Gallupe (1987). 'A foundation for the study of group decision support systems.' *Management Science* 33(5), 589–609.

Dewey, J. (1910). *How We Think.* Boston, D. C. Heath.

Dhami, M., and P. Ayton (2001). 'Bailing and jailing the fast and frugal way.' *Journal of Behavioral Decision Making* 14(2), 141–68.

Diecidue, E., U. Schmidt and P. Wakker (2004). 'The utility of gambling reconsidered.' *Journal of Risk and Uncertainty* 29(3), 241–59.

Diehl, M., and W. Stroebe (1991). 'Productivity loss in idea-generating groups: tracking down the blocking effect.' *Journal of Personality and Social Psychology* 61(3), 392–403.

Dietz, T., J. Tanguay, S. Tuler and T. Webler (2004). 'Making computer models useful: an exploration of the expectations by experts and local officials.' *Coastal Management* 32(3), 307–18.

Douglas, M. (1992). *Risk and Blame: Essays in Cultural Theory*. London, Routledge.

Dowie, J., (ed.) (1988). *Professional Judgment: A Reader in Clinical Decision Making*. Cambridge, Cambridge University Press.

Drottz-Sjöberg, B.-M., and L. Persson (1990). 'Risk perception and worries after the Chernobyl accident.' *Journal of Environmental Psychology* 10(2), 135–49.

Dryzek, J. S., and C. List (2003). 'Social choice theory and deliberative democracy: a reconciliation.' *British Journal of Political Science* 33(1), 1–28.

Duan, Y., J. S. Edwards and X. M. Xu (2005). 'Web-based expert systems: benefits and challenges.' *Information & Management* 42(6), 799–811.

Dubois, D., H. Prade and R. Sabbadin (2001). 'Decision-theoretic foundations of qualitative possibility theory.' *European Journal of Operational Research* 128(3), 459–78.

Duckstein, L., C. C. Kisiel and D. Monarchi (1975). 'Interactive multi-objective decision making under uncertainty.' In D. J. White and K. C. Bowen (eds.), *The Role and Effectiveness of Decision Theories in Practice*. London, Hodder and Stoughton, 128–47.

Dyer, J. S. (1990). 'Some remarks on the analytic hierarchy process.' *Management Science* 36(3), 249–58.

Dyer, J. S., and R. K. Sarin (1979). 'Measurable multi-attribute value functions.' *Operations Research* 27(4), 810–22.

Dzierzanowski, J., and S. Lawson (1992). 'The credit assistant: the second leg in the knowledge highway for American Express.' In C. Scott and P. Klahr (eds.), *Innovative Applications of Artificial Intelligence*, Menlo Park, CA, AAAI Press, 127–34.

Earl, M. J. (2000). ''Every business is an information business.' In D. A. Marchand, T. H. Davenport and T. Dickson (eds.), *Mastering Information Management*. London, Prentice Hall, 16–22.

Eden, C., and F. Ackermann (1998). *Making Strategy: The Journey of Strategic Management*. London, Sage.

Eden, C., and J. Radford (eds.) (1990). *Tackling Strategic Problems: The Role of Group Decision Support*. London, Sage.

Edwards, J. S., Y. Duan and P. C. Robins (2000). 'An analysis of expert systems for business decision making at different levels and in different roles.' *European Journal of Information Systems* 9(1), 36–46.

Edwards, K. D. (1996). 'Prospect theory: a literature review.' *International Review of Financial Analysis* 5(1), 19–38.

Edwards, W. (1971). 'Social utilities.' *Engineering Economist, Summer Symposium Series* 6, 119–29.

   (ed.) (1992). *Utility Theories: Measurements and Applications.* Boston, Kluwer Academic.

Edwards, W., and F. H. Barron (1994). 'SMARTs and SMARTER: improved simple methods for multi-attribute utility measurement.' *Organizational Behavior and Human Decision Processes* 60(3), 306–25.

Edwards, W., and B. Fasolo (2001). 'Decison technology.' *Annual Review of Psychology* 52(1), 581–606.

Ehrhardt, J., and A. Weiss (eds.) (2000). *RODOS: Decision Support system for Off-Site Nuclear Emergency Management in Europe*, EUR19144EN. Luxembourg, European Commission.

Eils, L. C., and R. S. John (1980). 'A criterion validation of multiattribute utility analysis and of group communication.' *Organizational Behavior and Human Performance* 25(2), 268–88.

Einhorn, H. J., R. M. Hogarth and E. Klempner (1977). 'Quality of group judgment.' *Psychological Bulletin* 84(1), 158–72.

Eisenhardt, K. M. (1989). 'Making fast strategic decisions in high-velocity environments.' *Academy of Management Journal* 32(3), 543–76.

Eisenhardt, K. M., and M. J. Zbaracki (1992). 'Strategic decision making.' *Strategic Management Journal* 13(S2), 17–37.

EIU (2007). *In Search of Clarity: Unravelling the Complexities of Executive Decision-making.* London, Economist Intelligence Unit.

Elbanna, S., and J. Child (2007). The influence of decision, environmental and firm characteristics on the rationality of strategic decision-making.' *Journal of Management Studies* 44(4), 561–91.

Ellsberg, D. (1961). 'Risk, ambiguity and the Savage axioms.' *Quarterly Journal of Economics* 75(4), 643–69.

Elsbach, K. D., and P. S. Barr (1999). 'The effects of mood on individuals' use of structured decision protocols.' *Organization Science* 10(2), 181–98.

Eom, S., and E. Kim (2006). 'A survey of decision support applications (1995–2001).' *Journal of the Operational Research Society* 57(11), 1264–78.

Evans, J. R., and D. L. Olson (2002). *Introduction to Simulation and Risk Analysis.* Upper Saddle River, NJ, Prentice Hall.

Fadlalla, A., and C.-H. Lin (2001). 'An analysis of the applications of neural networks in finance.' *Interfaces* 31(4), 112–22.

Falk, R. F., and N. B. Miller (1992). *A Primer for Soft Modeling.* Akron, OH, University of Akron Press.

Fandal, G., and T. Gal (eds.) (1997). *Multiple Criteria Decision Making.* Berlin, Springer-Verlag.

Faro, D., and Y. Rottenstreich (2006). 'Affect, empathy and regressive mispredictions of others' preferences under risk.' *Management Science* 52(4), 529–41.

Farquhar, P. H. (1984). 'Utility assessment methods.' *Management Science* 30(1), 1283–300.

Feinberg, S. E. (2006). 'When did Bayesian inference become "Bayesian"?' *Bayesian Analysis* 1(1), 1–40.

Felli, J. C., and G. B. Hazen (2004). 'Javelin diagrams: a graphical tool for probabilistic sensitivity analysis.' *Decision Analysis* 1(2), 93–107.

Fiddy, E., J. G. Bright and K. J. Johnson (1991). 'Visual interactive modelling.' In S. C. Littlechild and M. F. Shutler (eds.), *Operations Research in Management*. New York, Prentice Hall, 222–35.

Fine, T. L. (1973). *Theories of Probability*. New York, Academic Press.

Finlay, P. N., and J. M. Wilson (2000). 'A survey of contingency factors affecting the validation of end-user spreadsheet-based decision support systems.' *Journal of the Operational Research Society* 51(8), 949–58.

Finucane, M. L., E. Peters and P. Slovic (2003). 'Judgment and decision making: the dance of affect and reason.' In S. L. Schneider and J. Shanteau (eds.), *Emerging Perspectives on Judgment and Decision Research*. Cambridge, Cambridge University Press, 327–64.

Fischhoff, B. (1977). 'Cost–benefit analysis and the art of motorcycle maintenance.' *Policy Science* 8(2), 177–202.

 (1995). 'Risk perception and communication unplugged: twenty years of process.' *Risk Analysis* 15(2), 137–45.

 (1996). 'The real world: what good is it?' *Organizational Behavior and Human Decision Processes* 65(3), 232–48.

Fischhoff, B., P. Slovic and S. Lichtenstein (1977). 'Knowing with certainty: the appropriateness of extreme confidence.' *Journal of Experimental Psychology: Human Perception and Performance* 3(4), 552–64.

 (1978). 'Fault trees: sensitivity of estimated failure probabilities to problem representation.' *Journal of Experimental Psychology: Human Perception Performance* 4(2), 330–44.

Fishburn, P. C. (1980). 'A simple model for the utility of gambling.' *Psychometrika* 45(4), 435–48.

 (1988). *Non-linear Preference and Utility Theory*. Brighton, Wheatsheaf Books.

Fitzgerald, L., R. Johnston, S. Brignall, R. Silvestro and C. Voss (1991). *Performance Measurement in Service Business*. London, Chartered Institute of Management Accountants.

Flew, A. (1971). *An Introduction to Western Philosophy: Ideas and Arguments from Plato to Sartre*. London, Thames and Hudson.

Flin, R., E. Salas, M. Strub and L. Martin (1997). *Decision Making under Stress*. Aldershot, Ashgate.

Forsyth, D. R. (2006). *Group Dynamics*, 4th edn. Belmont, CA, Thomas Wadsworth.

Fox, C. R., and R. T. Clemen (2005). 'Subjective probability assessment in decision analysis: partition dependence and bias towards the ignorance prior.' *Management Science* 51(9), 1417–32.

Fox, C. R., and K. E. See (2003). 'Belief and preference in decision under uncertainty.' In D. Hardman and L. Macchi (eds.), *Thinking: Psychological Perspectives on*

Reasoning, Judgment and Decision Making. New York, John Wiley and Sons, 273–314.

Fox, M., and R. Herden (1999). 'Ship scheduling of fertilizer products.' *OR Insight* 12(2), 21–8.

Franco, A., D. Shaw and M. Westcombe (2006). 'Problem structuring methods: new directions in a problematic world.' *Journal of the Operational Research Society*. 57(7), 757–8.

French, S. (1981). 'Consensus of opinion.' *European Journal of Operational Research* 7(4), 332–40.

(1984a). 'Fuzzy decision analysis: some criticisms.' In H. J. Zimmermann, L. A. Zadeh and B. R. Gaines (eds.), *Fuzzy Sets and Decision Analysis*. Amsterdam, North Holland, 29–44.

(1984b). 'Interactive multi-objective programming: its aims, applications and demands.' *Journal of the Operational Research Society* 35(9), 827–34.

(1985). 'Group consensus probability distributions: a critical survey.' In J. M. Bernardo, M. H. DeGroot, D. V. Lindley and A. F. M. Smith (eds.), *Bayesian Statistics 2*. Amsterdam, North-Holland, 183–201.

(1986). *Decision Theory: An Introduction to the Mathematics of Rationality*. Chichester, Ellis Horwood.

(ed.) (1988). *Readings in Decision Analysis*. London, Chapman and Hall.

(1992). 'Mathematical programming approaches to sensitivity calculations in decision analysis.' *Journal of the Operational Research Society* 43(5), 813–19.

(1995a). 'An introduction to decision theory and prescriptive decision analysis.' *IMA Journal of Mathematics Applied in Business and Industry* 6(2), 239–47.

(1995b). 'Uncertainty and imprecision: modelling and analysis.' *Journal of the Operational Research Society* 46(1), 70–9.

(1996). 'Multi-attribute decision support in the event of a nuclear accident.' *Journal of Multi-Criteria Decision Analysis* 5(1), 39–57.

(ed.) (2003a). Special edition: 'The challenges in extending the MCDA paradigm to e-democracy.' *Journal of Multi-Criteria Decision Analysis* 12(2–3).

(2003b). 'Modelling, making inferences and making decisions: the roles of sensitivity analysis.' *Top* 11(2), 229–52.

(ed.) (2007a). Special edition: 'Interface issues in e-democracy.' *International Journal in Technology and Policy Management* 7(2).

(2007b). 'Web-enabled strategic GDSS, e-democracy and Arrow's theorem: a Bayesian perspective.' *Decision Support Systems* 47(4), 1476–84.

French, S., P. Allatt, J. B. Slater, M. Vassiloglou and A. S. Willmott (1992a). 'Implementation of a decision analytic aid to support examiners judgements in aggregating components.' *British Journal of Mathematical and Statistical Psychology* 45(11), 75–91.

French, S., J. Bartzis, J. Ehrhardt, J. Lochard, M. Morrey, K. N. Papamichail, K. Sinkko, and A. Sohier (2000). 'RODOS: decision support for nuclear emergencies.' In S. H. Zanakis, G. Doukidis and G. Zopounidis (eds.), *Recent Developments and Applications in Decision Making*. Dordrecht, Kluwer Academic, 379–94.

French, S., E. Carter and C. Niculae (2007a). 'Decision support in nuclear and radiological emergency situations: are we too focused on models and technology?' *International Journal of Emergency Management* 4(3), 421–41.

French, S., and J. Geldermann (2005). 'The varied contexts of environmental decision problems and their implications for decision support.' *Environmental Science and Policy* 8(4), 378–91.

French, S., M. T. Harrison and D. C. Ranyard (1997). 'Event conditional attribute modelling in decision making when there is a threat of a nuclear accident.' In S. French and J. Q. Smith (eds.), *The Practice of Bayesian Analysis*. London, Hodder Arnold, 131–50.

French, S., G. N. Kelly and M. Morrey (1992b). 'Decision conferencing and the International Chernobyl Project.' *Radiation Protection Dosimetry* 12(1), 17–28.
 (1992c). 'Decision conferencing as a group interview technique in the International Chernobyl Project.' *Insight* 5(4), 23–7.

French, S., and A. J. Maule (1999). 'Improving risk communication: scenario-based workshops.' In P. G. Bennett and K. C. Calman (eds.), *Risk Communication and Public Health: Policy Science and Participation*. Oxford, Oxford University Press, 241–53.

French, S., A. J. Maule and G. Mythen (2005). 'Soft modelling in risk communication and management: examples in handling food risk.' *Journal of the Operational Research Society* 56(8), 879–88.

French, S., and C. Niculae (2005). 'Believe in the model: mishandle the emergency.' *Journal of Homeland Security and Emergency Management* 2(1), 1–18.

French, S., K. N. Papamichail, D. C. Ranyard and J. Q. Smith (1998a). 'Design of a decision support system for use in the event of a nuclear emergency.' In F. J. Giron (ed.), *Applied Decision Analysis*. Dordrecht, Kluwer, 3–18.

French, S., and D. Ríos Insua (2000). *Statistical Decision Theory*. London, Hodder Arnold.

French, S., D. Ríos Insua and F. Ruggeri (2007b). 'e-participation and decision analysis.' *Decision Analysis* 4(4), 211–26.

French, S., L. Simpson, E. Atherton, V. Belton, R. Dawes, W. Edwards, R. P. Hämäläinen, O. Larichev, F. A. Lootsma, A. D. Pearman and C. Vlek (1998b). 'Problem formulation for multi-criteria decision analysis: report of a workshop.' *Journal of Multi-Criteria Decision Analysis* 7(5), 242–62.

French, S., and J. Q. Smith (eds.) (1997). *The Practice of Bayesian Analysis*. London, Hodder Arnold.

French, S., and Z. Xie (1994). 'A perspective on recent developments in utility theory.' In S. Ríos (ed.), *Decision Theory and Decision Analysis: Trends and Challenges*. Dordrecht, Kluwer Academic, 15–31.

French, S., and D.-L. Xu (2005). 'Comparison study of multi-attribute decision analytic software.' *Journal of Multi-Criteria Decision Analysis* 13(2–3), 65–80.

Fuller, S. R., and R. J. Aldag (1998). 'Organizational tonypandy: lessons from a quarter-century of the groupthink phenomenon.' *Organizational Behavior and Human Decision Process* 73(2–3), 163–84.

Gachet, A., and P. Haettenschwiler (2006). 'Development processes of intelligent decision-making support systems: review and perspective.' In J. N. D. Gupta, G. A. Forgionne and M. Mora (eds.), *Intelligent Decision-making Support Systems*. London, Springer, 97–121.

Galliers, R. D., D. E. Leidner and B. S. H. Baker (eds.) (1999). *Strategic Information Management: Challenges and Strategies in Managing Information Systems*. Oxford, Butterworth-Heinemann.

Gallupe, B. (2001). 'Knowledge management systems: surveying the landscape.' *International Journal of Management Reviews* 3(1), 61–77.

Gardenfors, P., and N.-E. Sahlin (eds.) (1988). *Decision, Probability and Utility*. Cambridge, Cambridge University Press.

Gardiner, L., and D. Vanderpooten (1997). 'Interactive multiple criteria procedures: some reflections.' In J. Climaco (ed.), *Multicriteria Analysis*. Berlin, Springer verlag, 290–301.

Garey, M. R., and D. S. Johnson (1979). *Computers and Intractability: A Guide to the Theory of NP-completeness*. San Francisco, W H Freeman.

Garthwaite, P. H., J. B. Kadane and A. O'Hagan (2005). 'Statistical methods for eliciting probability distributions.' *Journal of the American Statistical Association* 100, 680–701.

Garvey, B., and B. Williamson (2002). *Beyond Knowledge Management: Dialogue, Creativity and the Corporate Curriculum*. Harlow, Prentice Hall.

Gelman, A., J. B. Carlin, H. S. Stern and D. B. Rubin (1995). *Bayesian Data Analysis*. London, Chapman and Hall.

Genest, C., and J. V. Zidek (1986). 'Combining probability distributions: a critique and annotated bibliography.' *Statistical Science* 1(1), 114–48.

Gibbard, A. (1973), 'Manipulation of voting schemes: a general result.' *Econometrica* 41(4), 587–601.

Gigerenzer, G. (1994). 'Why the distinction between single event probabilities and frequencies is important for psychology and vice versa.' In G. Wright and P. Ayton (eds.), *Subjective Probability*. Chichester, John Wiley and Sons, 129–61.

(2002). *Reckoning with Risk: Learning to Live with Uncertainty*. Harmondsworth, Penguin Books.

Gigerenzer, G., and D. G. Goldstein (1999). 'Betting on one good reason: the take the best heuristic.' In G Gigerenzer, P. M. Todd and ABC Research Group (eds.), *Simple Heuristics that Make Us Smart*. New York, Oxford University Press, 75–95.

Gigerenzer, G., P. M. Todd and ABC Research Group (eds.) (1999). *Simple Heuristics that Make Us Smart*. New York, Oxford University Press.

Gigone, D., and R. Hastie (1997). 'The impact of information on small group choice.' *Journal of Personality and Social Psychology* 72(1), 132–40.

Gill, T. (1996). 'Expert systems usage: task change and intrinsic motivation.' *MIS Quarterly* 20(3), 301–29.

Gilovich, T., D. Griffin and D. Kahneman (eds.) (2002). *Heuristics and Biases: The Psychology of Intuitive Judgment*. Cambridge, Cambridge University Press.

Glaser, M., T. Langer and M. Weber (2007). 'On the trend recognition and forecasting ability of professional traders.' *Decision Analysis* 4(4), 176–93.

Goicoechea, A., D. R. Hansen and L. Duckstein (1982). *Multi-objective Decision Analysis with Engineering and Business Applications.* New York, John Wiley and Sons.

Goodwin, P., and G. Wright (2003). *Decision Analysis for Management Judgement,* 3rd edn. Chichester, John Wiley and Sons.

Goossens, L. H. J., and G. N. Kelly (2000). Special issue: 'Expert judgement and accident consequence uncertainty analysis.' *Radiation Protection Dosimetry* 90 (3), 293–381.

Gorry, G. A., and M. S. Scott Morton (1971). 'A framework for management information systems.' *Sloan Management Review* 13(1), 55–70.

Gotschall, M. G. (1998). 'InforMax riding crest of bioinformatics wave.' *Washington Business Journal* 31 July, www.bizjournals.com/washington/stories/1998/08/03/focus3.html (accessed 24 March 2006).

Gottlieb, J. E., and S. G. Pauker (1981). 'Whether or not to administer to an immunosuppressed patient with hematologic malignancy and undiagnosed fever.' *Medical Decision Making* 1(1), 75–93.

Goul, M., J. C. Henderson and F. M. Tonge (1992). 'The emergence of artificial intelligence as a reference discipline for decision support systems research.' *Decision Sciences* 23(6), 1263–76.

Gourlay, S. (2006). 'Towards conceptual clarity for tacit knowledge: a review of empirical studies.' *Knowledge Management Research and Practice* 4(1), 60–9.

Greco, S., B. Matarazzo and R. Slowinski (2001). 'Rough sets theory for multicriteria decision analysis' *European Journal of Operational Research* 129(1), 1–47.

Gregory, R. S., B. Fischhoff and T. McDaniels (2005). 'Acceptable input: using decision analysis to guide public policy deliberations.' *Decision Analysis* 2(1), 4–16.

Griffin, D., and L. Brenner (2004). 'Perspectives on probability judgement calibration.' In D. Koehler and N. Harvey (eds.), *Blackwell Handbook of Judgment and Decision Making.* Oxford, Blackwell, 177–99.

Griffith, T. L., M. A. Fuller and G. B. Northcraft (1998). 'Facilitator influence in group support systems: intended and unintended effects.' *Information Systems Research* 9(1), 20–36.

Griffiths, C., and M. Newman (1996). 'Risk management.' *Journal of Information Technology* 11(4), 273–378.

Gronlund, A. (2003). 'e-democracy: in search of tools and methods for effective participation.' *Journal of Multi-Criteria Decision Analysis* 12(2–3), 93–100.

Grudin, J. (1994). 'Groupware and social dynamics: eight challenges for developers.' *Communications of ACM* 37(1), 92–105.

Gupta, J. N. D., G. A. Forgionne and M. Mora (2006). *Intelligent Decision-making Support Systems.* London, Springer.

Hall, D. J., and D. Paradice (2005). 'Philosophical foundations for a learning-oriented knowledge management system for decision support.' *Decision Support Systems* 39(3), 445–61.

Hall, J. (1971). 'Decisions, decisions, decisions.' *Psychology Today* 5(6), 51–4, 86–8.

Hall, J., and M. S. Williams (1970). 'Group dynamics training and improved decision making.' *Journal of Applied Behavioral Science* 6(1), 39–68.

Hämäläinen, R. P. (2003). 'Decisionarium: aiding decisions, negotiating and collecting opinions.' *Journal of Multi-Criteria Decision Analysis* 12(2–3), 101–10.

Hämäläinen, R. P., and O. Leikola (1996). 'Spontaneous decision conferencing with top-level politicians.' *OR Insight* 9(1), 24–8.

Hammer, M., and J. Champy (1993). *Reengineering the Corporation*. London, Nicholas Brearley.

Hammond, J. S., R. L. Keeney and H. Raiffa (1998). *Smart Choices: A Practical Guide to Making Better Decisions*. Boston, Harvard Business School Press.

Hammond, K. R. (1996). 'How convergence of research paradigms can improve research on diagnositic judgement.' *Medical Decision Making* 16(3), 281–7.

Hand, D., H. Mannila and P. Smyth (2001). *Data Mining*. Cambridge, MA, MIT Press.

Handy, C. (1993). *Understanding Organisations*. Harmondsworth, Penguin Books.

Harries, C., and N. Harvey (2000). 'Taking advice, using information and knowing what you are doing.' *Acta Psychologica* 104(3), 399–416.

Harris, C. R., M. Jenkins and D. Glaser (2006). 'Gender differences in risk assessment: why do women take fewer risks than men?' *Judgement and Decision Making* 1(1), 48–63.

Harry, M. (2001). *Business Information: A Systems Approach*. Harlow, Pearson Education.

Harsanyi, J. C. (1977). *Rational Behaviour and Bargaining Equilibrium in Games and Social Situations*. Cambridge, Cambridge University Press.

Harvard Business Review (2001). *Harvard Business Review on Decision Making*. Harvard Business School Press.

Harvey, C. (1995). 'Proportional discounting of future benefits and costs.' *Mathematics of Operational Research* 20(2), 381–99.

Hastie, R. (1986). 'Experimental evidence of group accuracy.' In B. Grofman and G. Owen (eds.), *Information Pooling and Group Decision Making*. Greenwich, CT, JAI Press, 129–57.

Hastie, R., S. D. Penrod and N. Pennington (1983). *Inside the Jury*. Cambridge, MA, Harvard University Press.

Heinze, D. T., M. Morsch, R. Sheffer, M. Jimmink, M. Jennings, W. Morris and A. Morsch (2001). 'LifeCode: a deployed application for automated medical coding.' *AI Magazine* 22(2), 76–88.

Henig, M. I., and J. T. Buchanan (1996). 'Solving MCDM problems: process concepts (with discussion).' *Journal of Multi-Criteria Decision Analysis* 5(1), 3–21.

Hershey, J. C., and P. Schoemaker (1985). 'Probability versus certainty equivalence methods in utility measurement: are they equivalent?' *Management Science* 31(10), 1213–31.

Hertwig, R., and P. M. Todd (2003). 'More is not always better: the benefits of cognitive limits.' In D. Hardman and L. Macchi (eds.), *Thinking: Psychological*

Perspectives on Reasoning, Judgment and Decision Making. Chichester, John Wiley and Sons, 213–31.

Hickson, D. J., R. J. Butler, D. Cray, G. R. Mallory and D. C. Wilson (1986). *Top Decisions: Strategic Decision-making in Organizations*. San-Francisco, Jossey-Bass.

(1989). 'Decision and organization: processes of strategic decision making and their explanation.' *Public Administration* 67(4), 373–90.

Hickson, D. J., R. J. Butler and D. C. Wilson (2001). *The Bradford Studies of Strategic Decision Making*. London, Ashgate.

Hilary, G., and L. Menzly (2006). 'Does past success lead analysts to become overconfident?' *Management Science* 52(4), 489–500.

Hill, G. W. (1982). 'Group versus individual performance: are $N + 1$ heads better than one?' *Psychological Bulletin* 91(3), 517–39.

Hillier, F. S., and G. J. Liebermann (2004). *Introduction to Operations Research*, 8th edn. New York, McGraw-Hill.

Hinsz, V. B., R. S. Tindale and D. A. Vollrath (1997). 'The emerging conceptualization of groups as information processors.' *Psychological Bulletin* 121(1), 43–64.

Hobbs, B. F., and P. Meier (2000). *Energy Decisions and the Environment: A Guide to the Use of Multi-criteria Methods*. Dordrecht, Kluwer Academic.

Hockey, G. R. J. (ed.) (1983). *Stress and Fatigue in Human Performance*. Chichester, John Wiley and Sons.

Hockey, G. R. J., A. J. Maule, P. J. Clough and L. Bdzola (2000). 'Effects of negative mood on risk in everyday decision making.' *Cognition and Emotion* 14(6), 823–55.

Hodge, J. K., and R. E. Klima (2005). *The Mathematics of Voting and Elections: A Hands-on Approach*. Providence, RI, American Mathematical Society.

Hodgkin, J., V. Belton and A. Koulouri (2002). *Intelligent User Support for MCDA: A Case Study*, Working Paper no. 9. Business School, University of Strathclyde.

Hodgkinson, G.P., N. J. Bown, A. J. Maule, K. W. Glaister and A. D. Pearman (1999). 'Breaking the frame: an analysis of strategic choice and decision making under uncertainty.' *Strategic Management Journal* 20(10), 977–85.

Hodgkinson, G. P., A. J. Maule, N. J. Bown, A. D. Pearman and K. W. Glaister (2002). 'Further reflections on the limitation of framing bias in strategic decision making.' *Strategic Management Journal* 23(11), 1069–76.

Hodgkinson, G. P., and W. H. Starbuck (eds.) (2008). *The Oxford Handbook of Organizational Decision Making*. New York, Oxford University Press.

Hofstede, G. (1984). *Cultural Consequences*. Beverley Hills, Sage.

(1994). 'Management scientists are human.' *Management Science* 40(1), 4–13.

Hogarth, R. M. (1980). *Judgement and Choice*. Chichester, John Wiley and Sons.

Hogarth, R. M., and N. Karelaia (2006). 'Regions of rationality; maps for bounded agents.' *Decision Analysis* 3(3), 124–44.

Hohenberg, J.-K., and G. N. Kelly (eds.) (2004). Introduction: 'Off-site nuclear emergency management: capabilities and challenges.' *Radiation Protection Dosimetry* 109(1–2), 1.

Holland, J. H. (1992). 'Genetic Algorithms.' *Scientific American* 267(1), 66–73.

Hollnagel, E. (1987). 'Information and reasoning in intelligent decision support systems.' *International Journal of Man–Machine Studies* 27(5–6), 665–78.

Hollocks, B. W. (2006). 'Forty years of discrete event simulation: a personal reflection.' *Journal of the Operational Research Society* 57(12), 1383–99.

Holsapple, C. W., and A. B. Whinston (1996). *Decision Support Systems: A Knowledge-based Approach.* St Paul, MN, West.

Holtzman, S. (1989). *Intelligent Decision Systems.* Reading, MA, Addison-Wesley.

Horlick-Jones, T., J. Rosenhead, I. Georgiou, J. R. Ravetz and R. Lofstedt (2001). 'Decision support for organisational risk management by problem structuring.' *Health, Risk and Society* 3(2), 141–65.

Hovy, E. (1998). 'Language generation: overview.' In R. A. Cole, J. Mariani, H. Uszkoreit, G. Battista Varile, A. Zaenen, A. Zampolli and V. Zue (eds.), *Survey of the State of the Art in Human Language Technology.* Cambridge, Cambridge University Press, 139–46.

Howard, N. (1971). *Paradoxes of Rationality: Theory of Metagames and Political behavior.* Cambridge, MA, MIT Press.

Howard, R. A. (1990). 'From influence to relevance to knowledge.' In R. M. Oliver and J. Q. Smith (eds.), *Influence Diagrams, Belief Nets and Decision Analysis.* Chichester, John Wiley and Sons, 3–23.

  (2004). 'Precise decision language (with discussion).' *Decision Analysis* 1(2), 71–92.

Howard, R. A., and J. E. Matheson (1984). *Readings on the Principles and Applications of Decision Analysis,* 2 vols. Menlo Park, CA, Strategic Decisions Group.

  (2005a). 'Influence diagrams.' *Decision Analysis* 2(3), 127–43.

  (2005b). 'Influence diagrams retrospective.' *Decision Analysis* 2(3) pp. 144–7.

Hsee, C. K. (1996). 'The evaluability hypothesis: an explanation for preference reversals between joint and separate evaluations of alternatives.' *Organizational Behavior and Human Decision Processes* 67(3), 247–57.

  (2000). 'Attribute evaluability and its implications for joint–separate evaluation reversals and beyond.' In D. Kahneman and A. Tversky (eds.), *Choices, Values and Frames.* Cambridge, Cambridge University Press, 543–63.

Huang, K.-T. (1998). 'Capitalizing on intellectual assets' *IBM Systems Journal* 37(4), 570–83.

Huber, G. P. (1981). 'The nature of organizational decision making and the design of decision support systems.' *MIS Quarterly* 5(2), 1–10.

Huber, G. P., and R. R. McDaniel (1986). 'The decision-making paradigm of organizational design.' *Management Science* 32(5), 572–89.

Humphreys, P. C., and W. McFadden (1980). 'Experiences with MAUD: aiding decision structuring versus bootstrapping the decision maker.' *Acta Psychologica* 45(1), 51–69.

Hunink, M., P. Glasziou, J. Siegel, J. Weeks, J. Pliskin, A. Elstein and M. Weinstein (2001). *Decision Making in Health and Medicine: Integrating Evidence and Values.* Cambridge, Cambridge University Press.

Hunter, A. (2000). 'Expert systems.' www.cs.ucl.ac.uk/staff/a.hunter/tradepress/expert. html (accessed 23 March 2006).

IAEA (1991). *The International Chernobyl Project: Technical Report.* Vienna, International Atomic Energy Agency.

Ireland, R. D., and C. Miller (2004). 'Decision-making and firm success.' *Academy of Management Executive* 18(4), 8–12.

Irvin, R. A., and J. Stansbury (2004). 'Citizen participation in decision making: is it worth the effort?' *Public Administration Review* 64(1), 55–66.

Isen, A., and R. Patrick (1983). 'The effect of positive feelings on risk-taking: when the chips are down.' *Organizational Behavior and Human Performance* 31(2), 194–202.

Isenberg, D. J. (1986). 'Group polarization: a critical review and meta-analysis.' *Journal of Personality and Social Psychology* 50(6), 1141–51.

Jacobi, S. K., and B. F. Hobbs (2007). 'Quantifying and mitigating the splitting bias and other value tree induced weighting biases.' *Decision Analysis* 4(4), 194–210.

Jacques, E. (1989). *Requisite Organization.* Arlington, VA, Cason Hall.

Janis, I. L. (1972). *Victims of Groupthink: A Psychological Study of Foreign Policy Decisions and Fiascos.* Boston, Houghton-Mifflin.

  (1989). *Crucial Decisions: Leadership in Policy Making and Crisis Management.* New York, The Free Press.

Janis, I. L., and L. Mann (1977). *Decision Making: A Psychological Analysis of Conflict, Choice and Commitment.* New York, Free Press.

Jennings, D. L., T. M. Amabile and L. Ross (1982). 'Informal covariation assessment: data-based versus theory-based judgements.' In D. Kahneman, P. Slovic and A. Tversky (eds.), *Judgement under Uncertainty.* Cambridge, Cambridge University Press, 211–30.

Jensen, F. V. (1996). *An Introduction to Bayesian Networks.* London, UCL Press.

  (2001). *Bayesian Networks and Decision Graphs.* New York, Springer.

Jiminez, A., S. Ríos Insua and A. Mateos (2006). 'A generic multi-attribute analysis system.' *Computers and Operations Research* 33(4), 1081–101.

Johnson, E. J., and A. Tversky (1983). 'Affect, generalization, and the perception of risk.' *Journal of Personality and Social Psychology* 45(1) 20–31.

Kadane, J. B., and P. D. Larkey (1983). 'The confusion of is and ought in game theoretic contexts.' *Management Science* 29(12), 1365–79.

Kadane, J. B., M. J. Schervish and T. Seidenfeld (1999). *Rethinking the Foundations of Statistics.* Cambridge, Cambridge University Press.

Kadane, J. B., and R. Winkler (1988). 'Separating probability elicitation from utilities.' *Journal of the American Statistical Association* 83, 357–63.

Kahneman, D., and S. Fredrick (2002). 'Representativeness revisited: attribute substitution in intuitive judgment.' In T. D. Gilovich, D. W. Griffin and D. Kahneman (eds.), *Heuristics and Biases: The Psychology of Intuitive Judgment.* Cambridge, Cambridge University Press, 49–81.

Kahneman, D., P. Slovic and A. Tversky (eds.) (1982). *Judgement under Uncertainty.* Cambridge, Cambridge University Press.

Kahneman, D., and A. Tversky (1979). 'Prospect theory: an analysis of decisions under risk.' *Econometrica* 47(2), 263–91.

Kahneman, D., and A. Tversky (1982). 'Causal schemas in judgements under uncertainty.' In D. Kahneman, P. Slovic and A. Tversky (eds.), *Judgement under Uncertainty.* Cambridge, Cambridge University Press, 117–28.

Kahneman, D., and A. Tversky (eds.) (2000). *Choices, Values and Frames.* Cambridge, Cambridge University Press.

Kameda, T., Y. Ohtsubo and M. Takezawa (1997). 'Centrality in socio-cognitive networks and social influence: an illustration in a group decision making context.' *Journal of Personality and Social Psychology* 73(2), 296–309.

Kaplan, R. S., and D. P. Norton (1996). *The Balanced Scorecard: Translating Strategy into Action.* Cambridge, MA, Harvard Business School Press.

Karpak, B., E. Kumcu and R. Kasuganti (1999). 'An application of visual interactive goal programming: a case in vendor selection decisions.' *Journal of Multi-Criteria Decision Analysis* 8(2), 93–105.

Kasperson, J. X., R. E. Kasperson, N. Pidgeon and P. Slovic (2003). 'The social amplification of risk: assessing fifteen years of risk and theory.' In N. Pidgeon, R. E. Kasperson and P. Slovic (eds.), *The Social Amplification of Risk.* Cambridge, Cambridge University Press, 13–46.

Kasperson, R. E. (1992). 'The social amplification of risk: progress in developing an integrative framework.' In S. Krimsky and S. Golding (eds.), *Social Theories of Risk.* New York, Praeger, 153–78.

Keefer, D. L., C. W. Kirkwood and J. L. Corner (2004). 'Perspective on decsion analysis applications, 1990–2001 (with discussion).' *Decision Analysis* 1(1), 4–34.

Keen, P. G. W. (1980). 'Decision support systems: a research perspective.' In G. Fick and R. M. Sprague (eds.), *Decision Support Systems: Issues and Challenges.* Oxford, Pergamon Press, 23–44.

Keen, P. G. W., and M. S. Scott Morton (1978). *Decision Support Systems: An Organizational Perspective.* Reading, MA, Addison-Wesley.

Keeney, R. L. (1992). *Value-focused Thinking: A Path to Creative Decision Making.* Harvard, MA, Harvard University Press.

(2002). 'Common mistakes in making value trade-offs.' *Operations Research* 50(6), 935–45.

(2004). 'Framing policy decisions.' *International Journal of Technology, Policy and Management* 4(2), 95–155.

Keeney, R. L., and R. S. Gregory (2005). 'Selecting attributes to measure the achievement of objectives.' *Operations Research* 53(1), 1–11.

Keeney, R. L., and H. Raiffa (1976). *Decisions with Multiple Objectives: Preferences and Value Trade-offs.* New York, John Wiley and Sons.

Kelly, F. S. (1978). *Arrow Impossibility Theorems.* New York, Academic Press.

Kendall, K. E., and J. E. Kendall (2004). *Systems Analysis and Design.* Upper Saddle River, NJ, Prentice Hall.

Keren, G. (1987). 'Facing uncertainty in the game of bridge: a calibration study.' *Organizational Behavior and Human Decision Processes* 39(1), 98–114.

Kerr, D. S., and U. S. Murthy (2004). 'Divergent and convergent idea generation in teams: a comparison of computer-mediated and face-to-face communication.' *Group Decision and Negotiation* 13(4), 381–99.

Kerr, N. L., and R. S. Tindale (2004). 'Group performance and decision making.' *Annual Review of Psychology* 55, 623–55.

Kersten, G. (2003). 'e-democracy and participatory decision processes: lessons from e-negotiation experiments.' *Journal of Multi-Criteria Decision Analysis* 12(2–3), 127–44.

Kestelyn, J. (2001). 'The new expert systems.' *Intelligent Enterprise*, 18 September, 6.

Keys, P. (ed.) (1995). *Understanding the Process of Operational Research.* Chichester, John Wiley and Sons.

Khatri, N., and H. Alvin (2000). 'The role of intuition in strategic decision making.' *Human Relations* 53(1), 57–86.

Kirkwood, C. W. (1997). *Strategic Decision Making: Multiobjective Decision Analysis with Spreadsheets.* Belmont, CA, Duxbury Press.

Klein, D. A. (1994). *Decision-Analytic Intelligent Systems: Automated Explanation and Knowledge Acquisition.* Mahwah, NJ, Lawrence Erlbaum Associates.

Klein, G. A. (1993). 'A recognition-primed decision (RPD) model of rapid decision making. In G. A. Klein, J. Orasanu, R. Calderwood and C. E. Zsambok (eds.), *Decision Making in Action: Models and Method.* Norwood, NJ, Ablex, 138–47.

Klein, G. A. (1998). *Source of Power: How People Make Decisions.* Cambridge, MA, MIT Press.

Klein, M. R., and L. B. Methlie (1995). *Knowledge-based Decision Support Systems.* Chichester, John Wiley and Sons.

Kleindorfer, P. R., H. C. Kunreuther and P. Schoemaker (1993). *Decision Sciences: An Integrative Perspective.* Cambridge, Cambridge University Press.

Klosgen, W., and S. R. W. Lauer (2002). 'Visualization of data mining results.' In W. Klosgen and J. M. Zytkow (eds.), *Handbook of Data Mining and Knowledge Discovery.* Oxford, Oxford University Press, 509–15.

Klosgen, W., and J. M. Zytkow (eds.) (2002). *Handbook of Data Mining and Knowledge Discovery.* Oxford, Oxford University Press.

Knight, F. H. (1921). *Risk, Uncertainty and Profit.* Boston, Houghton Mifflin.

Kobbacy, K. H., S. Vadera and M. H. Rasmy (2007). 'AI and OR in the management of operations: history and trends.' *Journal of the Operational Research Society* 58(1), 10–28.

Koksalan, M., and S. Zionts (eds.) (2001). *Multiple Criteria Decision Making in the New Millennium.* Berlin, Springer Verlag.

Kolbasuk McGee, M. (2005). 'New tools help hospitals handle terror attacks and other disasters.' *InformationWeek* 14 April http://informationweek.com/story/showArticle.jhtml?article ID=160900664 (accessed 24 March 2006).

Korb, K. B., and A. E. Nicholson (2004). *Bayesian Artificial Intelligence.* Boca Raton, FL, Chapman and Hall/CRC.

Korhonen, P., and J. Wallenius (1996). 'Behavioural issues in MCDM: neglected research questions.' *Journal of Multi-Criteria Decision Analysis* 5(3), 178–82.

Koriat, A., S. Lichtenstein and B. Fischhoff (1980). 'Reasons for overconfidence.' *Journal of Experimental Psychology: Human Learning and Memory* 6(2), 107–18.

Kraemer, K. L., and L. K. King (1987). 'Computer-based systems for co-operative work and group decision making.' *ACM Computing Surveys* 20(2), 115–46.

Krantz, D. H., R. D. Luce, P. Suppes and A. Tversky (1971). *Foundations of Measurement Theory*, vol. I: *Additive and Polynomial Representations*. New York, Academic Press.

Krzanowski, W. J., and F. H. C. Marriott (1994). *Multivariate Analysis*, vol I: *Distributions, Ordination and Inference*. London, Hodder Arnold.

   (1998). *Multivariate Analysis*, vol. II: *Classification, Covariance Structures and Repeated Measurements*. London, Hodder Arnold.

Kühberger, A. (1998). 'The influence of framing on risky decision making.' *Organizational Behavior and Human Decision Processes* 75(1), 23–55.

Kühberger, A., M. Schulte-Mecklenbeck and J. Perner (2002). 'Framing decisions: hypothetical and real.' *Organizational Behavior and Human Decision Processes* 89(2), 1162–75.

Kuo, F. Y. (1998). 'Managerial intuition and the development of executive support systems.' *Decision Support Systems* 24(2), 89–103.

Kurowicka, D., and R. M. Cooke (2006). *Uncertainty Analysis with High Dimensional Modelling*. Chichester, John Wiley and Sons.

Lad, F. (1996). *Operational Subjective Statistical Methods*. New York, John Wiley and Sons.

Langford, I., C. Marris and T. O'Riordan (1999). 'Public reactions to risk: social structures, images of science and the role of trust.' In P. G. Bennett and K. C. Calman (eds.), *Risk Communication and Public Health: Policy, Science and Participation*. Oxford, Oxford University Press, 33–50.

Langley, A., H. Mintzberg, P. Pitcher, E. Posada and J. Saint-Macary (1995). 'Opening up decision making: rhe view from the black stool.' *Organization Science* 6(3), 260–79.

Laplace, P. S. (1952 [1825]). *Essai Philosophique sur les Probabilités*, 5th edn. New York, Dover.

Larrick, R. P. (2004). Debiasing. In D. Koehler and N. Harvey (eds.), *The Blackwell Handbook of Judgment and Decision Making*. New York, Basil Blackwell, 316–37.

Lathrop, J. W., and S. R. Watson (1982). 'Decision analysis for the evaluation of risk in nuclear waste management.' *Journal of the Operational Research Society* 33(5), 407–18.

Laudon, K. C., and J. P. Laudon (2006). *Management Information Systems: Managing the Digital Firm*. 9th edn. Upper Saddle River, NJ, Prentice Hall.

Laughlin, P. R., and A. L. Ellis (1986). 'Demonstrability and social combination processes on mathematical intellective tasks.' *Journal of Experimental Social Psychology* 22(3), 177–89.

Lauritzen, S. (2004). 'Discussion on causality.' *Scandinavian Journal of Statistics* 31(2), 189–93.

Layard, R. (1972). *Cost–Benefit Analysis.* Harmondsworth, Penguin Books.

Layard, R., and S. Glaister (1994). *Cost–Benefit Analysis.* Cambridge, Cambridge University Press.

Leach, M., I. Scoones and B. Wynne (eds.) (2005). *Science and Citizens.* London, Zed Books.

Lee, H., and B. Choi (2003). 'Knowledge management enablers, processes and organisational performance: an integrative view and empirical examination.' *Journal of Management Information Systems* 20(1), 179–228.

Lee, J. K., and J. K. Kim (2002). 'A case based reasoning for building a decision model.' *Expert Systems* 19(3), 123–35.

Lee-Jones, M. W., G. Loomes and P. R. Phillips (1995). 'Valuing the prevention of non-fatal road injuries: contingent valuation vs standard gambles.' *Oxford Economic Papers* 47(4) 676–95.

Leonard-Barton, D., and J. J. Sviokla (1988). 'Putting expert systems to work.' *Harvard Business Review* 66(2), 91–8.

Levin, I. P., S. L. Schneider and G. J. Gaeth (1998). 'All frames are not created equal: a typology and critical analysis of framing effects.' *Organizational Behavior and Human Decision Processes* 76(2), 149–88.

Levy, J. S. (2003). 'Applications of prospect theory to political science.' *Synthese* 135(2), 215–41.

Lewis, P. J. (1991). 'The decision making basis for information systems: the contribution of Vickers' concept of appreciation to a soft systems perspective.' *European Journal of Information Systems* 1(1), 33–43.

Lichtenstein, S., B. Fischhoff and L. D. Phillips (1982). 'Calibration of probabilities: the state of the art to 1980.' In D. Kahneman, P. Slovic and A. Tversky (eds.), *Judgement under Uncertainty.* Cambridge, Cambridge University Press, 306–34.

Lichtenstein, S., and J. R. Newman (1967). 'Empirical scaling of common verbal phrases associated with numerical probabilities.' *Psychonomic Science* 9(10), 563–4.

Lichtenstein, S., and P. Slovic (1971). 'Reversals of preference between bids and choices in gambling decisions.' *Journal of Experimental Psychology* 89(1), 46–55.

Lichtenstein, S., P. Slovic, B. Fischhoff, M. Layman and B. Coombs (1978). 'Judged frequency of lethal events.' *Journal of Experimental Psychology: Human Learning and Memory* 4(6), 551–78.

Liebowitz, J. (2001). 'If you are a dog lover, build expert systems; if you are a cat lover, build neural networks.' *Expert Systems with Applications* 21(1), 63.

Lin, B. S., and G. D. Nord (2006). 'Special issue on intelligent bioinformatics systems.' *Expert Systems with Applications* 30(1), 1.

Lindley, D. V., A. Tversky and R. V. Brown (1979). 'On the reconciliation of probability judgements (with discussion).' *Journal of the Royal Statistical Society Series* A 142(2), 146–80.

Linstone, H. A., and M. Turoff (1978). *The Delphi Method: Techniques and Applications*. London, Addison-Wesley.

Liston, G. (1993). 'Channel 4 Television are using advanced optimization technology based on genetic algorithms.' www.attar.com/pages/case_c4.htm (accessed 6 March 2006).

Little, J. D. C. (1970). 'Models and managers: the concept of a decision calculus.' *Management Science* 16(8), B466–B485.

(2004). 'Comments on "Models and managers: the concept of a decision calculus": managerial models for practice.' *Management Science Commemorative CD*, 1–7.

Littlechild, S. C., and M. F. Shutler (eds.) (1991). *Operations Research in Management*. New York, Prentice Hall.

Liu, D., and T. J. Stewart (2003). 'Integrated object-oriented framework for MCDM and DSS modelling.' *Decision Support Systems* 38(3), 421–34.

Lochard, J., T. Schneider and S. French (1992). *International Chernobyl Project: Summary Report of Decision Conferences held in the USSR, October–November 1990*. Luxembourg City, European Commission.

Loewenstein, G. (1987). 'Anticipation and the valuation of delayed consumption.' *Economic Journal* 97, 666–84.

(1988). 'Frames of mind in intertemporal choice.' *Management Science* 34(2), 200–14.

Loewenstein, G., and D. Prelec (1991). 'Decision making over time and under uncertainty: a common approach.' *Management Science* 37(7), 770–86.

Loomes, G., and R. Sugden (1982). 'Regret theory: an alternative theory of rational choice under uncertainty.' *Economic Journal* 92, 805–24.

Lopes, L. L. (1981). 'Decision making in the short run.' *Journal of Experimental Psychology: Human Learning and Memory* 7(5), 377–85.

Loque, M., R. Caballero, J. Molina and F. Ruiz (2007). 'Equivalent information for multi-objective procedures.' *Management Science* 53(3), 125–34.

Losa, F. B., and V. Belton (2006). 'Combining MCDA and conflict analysis: an exploratory application of an integrated approach.' *Journal of the Operational Research Society* 57(5), 510–25.

Lovallo, D. P., and D. Kahneman (2003). 'Delusion of success.' *Harvard Business Review* 81(7), 57–63.

Lovallo, D. P., and O. Sibony (2006). 'Distortions and deceptions in strategic decisions.' *McKinsey Quarterly* 2006(1), 18–29.

Luce, M. F., J. R. Bettman and J. W. Payne (1997). 'Choice processing in emotionally difficult decisions.' *Journal Experimental Psychology: Learning, Memory, and Cognition* 23(2), 384–405.

Luce, R. D., D. H. Krantz, P. Suppes and A. Tversky (1990). *Foundations of Measurement Theory*, vol. III: *Representation, Axiomatisiation and Invariance*. San Diego, Academic Press.

Luce, R. D., and H. Raiffa (1957). *Games and Decisions*. New York, John Wiley and Sons.

Ludäscher, B., I. Altintas, C. Berkley, D. Higgins, E. Jaeger-Frank, M. Jones, E. A. Lee, J. Tao and Y. Zhao (2006). 'Scientific workflow management and the

Kepler system.' *Concurrency and Computation: Practice & Experience* 18(10), 1039–65.

Maas A., and P. Wakker (1994). 'Additive conjoint measurement for multi-attribute utility.' *Journal of Mathematical Psychology* 38(1), 86–101.

Macaulay, L., and A. Alabdulkarim (2005). 'Facilitation of e-meetings: state-of-the-art review.' In *Proceedings of the 2005 IEEE International conference on e-Technology, e-Commerce and e-Service.* Washington, DC, IEEE Computer Society, 728–35.

MacCrimmon, K. R. (1968). 'Descriptive and normative implications of the decision theory postulates.' In K. H. Borch and J. Mossin (eds.), *Risk and Uncertainty.* London, Macmillan, 3–23.

MacEachren, A. M. (1992). 'Visualizing uncertain information.' *Cartographic Perspectives* 13, 10–19.

Machina, M. J. (1991). 'Dynamic consistency and non-expected utility.' In M. Bacharach and S. Hurley (eds.), *Foundations of Decision Theory.* Oxford, Basil Blackwell, 39–91.

Maes, P., R. H. Guttman and A. G. Moukas (1999). 'Agents that buy and sell.' *Communications of ACM* 42(3), 81–91.

Maier, N. R. F. (1967). 'Assets and liabilities in group problem solving: the need for an integrative function.' *Psychological Review* 74(4), 239–49.

Makulowich, J. (1998). 'Ernst & Young Web service takes off.' *Washington Technology* 3 May, www.washingtontechnology.com/news/12_23/news/13811-1. html (accessed 22 March 2006).

Mallach, E. G. (2000). *Decision Support and Data Warehouse Systems.* Boston, McGraw-Hill.

Mallya, S., S. Banerjee and W. G. Bistline (2001). 'A decision support system for production/ distribution planning in continuous manufacturing.' *Decision Sciences* 32(3), 545–56.

Mann, L. (1992). 'Stress, affect and decision making.' In J. F. Yates (ed.), *Risk-taking Behaviour.* Chichester, John Wiley and Sons, 201–30.

Marakas, G. M. (2003). *Decision Support Systems in the 21st Century,* 2nd edn. Upper Saddle River, NJ, Prentice Hall.

March, J. G. (1962). 'The business firm as a political coalition.' *Journal of Politics* 24(4), 662–78.

March, J. G., and J. P. Olsen (1976). *Ambiguity and Choice in Organizations.* Bergen, Universitetsforlaget.

March, J. G., and H. A. Simon (1958). *Organizations.* New York, John Wiley and Sons.

Marczyk, A. (2004). 'Genetic algorithms and evolutionary computation.' www. talkorigins.org/faqs/genalg/genalg.html (accessed 6 April 2006).

Marwick, A. D. (2001). 'Knowledge management technology.' *IBM Systems Journal* 40(4), 814–30.

Mateos, A., A. Jiménez and S. Ríos-Insua (2003). 'Modelling individual and global comparisons for multi-attribute preferences.' *Journal of Multi-Criteria Decision Analysis* 12(2–3), 177–90.

Mateos, A., S. Ríos-Insua and A. Jiménez (2007). 'Dominance, potential optimality and alternative ranking in imprecise multi-attribute decision making.' *Journal of the Operational Research Society* 58(3), 326–36.

Matheson, D., and J. E. Matheson (1998). *The Smart Organization: Creating Value through Strategic R&D*. Boston, Harvard Business School Press.

Matheson, J. E., and D. Matheson (2007). 'From decision analysis to the decision organization.' In W. Edwards, R. F. Miles and D. von Winterfeldt (eds.), *Advances in Decision Analysis: From Foundations to Applications*. Cambridge, Cambridge University Press, 419–50.

Mattei, M. D. (2001). 'Using "expert systems" for competitive advantage.' *Business and Economic Review* 47(3), 17–20.

Maule, A. J. (1989). 'Positive and negative decision frames: a verbal protocol analysis of the Asian disease problem of Kahneman and Tversky.' In O. Svenson and H. Montgomery (eds.), *Process and Structure in Human Decision Making*. Chichester, John Wiley and Sons, 163–80.

Maule, A. J. (2004). 'Translating risk management knowledge: the lessons to be learned from research on the perception and communication of risk.' *Risk Management* 6(2), 15–27.

  (2008). 'Risk communications in organizations.' In G. P. Hodgkinson and W. Starbuck (eds.), *The Oxford Handbook of Organizational Decision Making*. Oxford, Oxford University Press, 517–33.

Maule, A. J., and A. C. Edland (1997). 'The effects of time pressure on judgement and decision making.' In R. Ranyard, W. R. Crozier and O. Svenson (eds.), *Decision Making: Cognitive Models and Explanation*. London, Routledge, 189–204.

Maule, A. J., and G. Villejoubert (2007). 'What lies beneath: reframing framing effects.' *Thinking and Reasoning* 13(1), 25–44.

Maxwell, D. (2002). 'Aiding insight VI.' *OR/MS Today* 29(3), 44–51.

  (2004). 'Aiding Insight VII.' *OR/MS Today* 31(3), 44–55.

  (2006). 'Improving hard decisions.' *OR/MS Today* 33(6), 51–61.

McClelland, A. G. R., and F. Bolger (1994). 'The calibration of subjective probabilities: theories and models 1940–94.' In G. Wright and P. Ayton (eds.), *Subjective Probability*. Chichester, John Wiley and Sons, 453–81.

McCosh, A. M., and B. A. Correa-Pérez (2006). 'The optimization of what?' In J. N. D. Gupta, G. A. Forgionne and M. Mora (eds.), *Intelligent Decision-making Support Systems*. London, Springer, 463–81.

McDaniels, T., and M. J. Small (eds.) (2004). *Risk Analysis and Society: An Interdisciplinary Characterisation of the Field*. Cambridge, Cambridge University Press.

McDermott, R. (1999). 'Why information technology inspired but cannot deliver knowledge management.' *California Management Review* 41(4), 103–17.

McLean, I., and A. B. Urken (eds.) (1995). *Classics of Social Choice*. Ann Arbor, University of Michigan Press.

McLennen, E. F. (1990). *Rationality and Dynamic Choice: Foundational Explorations*. Cambridge, Cambridge University Press.

McNeil, B. J., S. G. Pauker, H. C. Sox and A. Tversky (1982). 'On the elicitation of preferences for alternative therapies.' *New England Journal of Medicine* 306(21), 1259–62.

Mendonfa, D. (2007). 'Decision support for improvisation in response to extreme events: learning from the response to the 2001 World Trade Center attack.' *Decision Support Systems* 43(3), 952–67.

Mercer, J. (2005). 'Prospect theory and political science.' *Annual Review of Political Science* 8, 1–21.

Merkhofer, M. W. (1987). 'Quantifying judgemental uncertainty: methodology, experiences and insights.' *IEEE Transactions on Systems, Man and Cybernetics* 17(5), 741–52.

Metcalfe, D. (2003). *Enterprise Visibility Makes Decisions Profitable.* Cambridge, MA, Forrester Research.

Migon, H. S., and D. Gamerman (1999). *Statistical Inference: An Integrated Approach.* London, Hodder Arnold.

Miller, C. E. (1989). 'The social psychological effects of group decision rules.' In P. B. Paulus (ed.), *Psychology of Group Influence.* Hillsdale, NJ, Lawrence Erlbaum Associates, 327–55.

Miller, J. S., D. C. Wilson and D. J. Hickson (2004). 'Beyond planning: strategies for successfully implementing strategic decisions.' *Long Range Planning* 37(3), 201–18.

Milnor, J. (1954). 'Games against Nature.' In R. Thrall, C. Coombs and R. Davis (eds.), *Decision Processes.* New York, John Wiley and Sons, 49–59.

Mingers, J., and J. Rosenhead (2004). 'Problem structuring methods in action.' *European Journal of Operational Research* 152(3), 530–54.

Minoux, M. (1986). *Mathematical Programming: Theory and Algorithms.* Chichester, John Wiley and Sons.

Mintzberg, H. (1987). 'Crafting strategy.' *Harvard Business Review* 65(4), 66–75.
    (1992). 'Five Ps for strategy.' In H. Mintzberg and J. B. Quinn (eds.), *The Strategy Process.* Englewood Cliffs, NJ, Prentice Hall, 12–19.

Mintzberg, H., D. Raisinghani and A. Théoret (1976). 'The structure of "unstructured" decision processes.' *Administrative Science Quarterly* 21(2), 246–75.

Miranda, S. M., and R. P. Bostrom (1999). 'Meeting facilitation: process vs content interventions.' *Journal of Management Information Systems* 15(4), 89–114.

Miser, H. J., and E. S. Quade (1988). *Handbook of Systems Analysis: Craft Issues and Procedural Choices.* Chichester, John Wiley and Sons.

Mitroff, I. I., and R. O. Mason (1981). 'The metaphysics of policy and planning: a reply to Cosier.' *Academy of Management Review* 6(4), 649–51.

Montgomery, H., and O. Svenson (1976). 'On decision rules and information processing strategies in multiattribute decision making.' *Scandinavian Journal of Psychology* 17(1), 283–91.

Montibeller, G., H. Gummer and D. Tumidei (2006). 'Combining scenario planning and multi-criteria decision analysis in practice.' *Journal of Multi-Criteria Decision Analysis* 14(1–3), 5–20.

Moore, P. G. (1983). *The Business of Risk*. Cambridge, Cambridge University Press.

Morgan, G., B. Fischhoff, A. Bostrom and C. Atman (2002). *Risk Communication: A Mental Models Approach*. Cambridge, Cambridge Universtiy Press.

Morgan, M. G., and M. Henrion (1990). *Uncertainty: A Guide to Dealing with Uncertainty in Qualitative Risk and Policy Analysis*. Cambridge, Cambridge University Press.

Morse, G. (2006). 'Decisions and desire.' *Harvard Business Review* 84(1), 24–51.

Morton, A., F. Ackermann and V. Belton (2003). 'Technology-driven and model-driven approaches to group decision support: focus, research philosophy, and key concepts.' *European Journal of Information Systems* 12(2), 110–26.

Moscovici, S., and M. Zavalloni (1969). 'The group as a polarizer of attitudes.' *Journal of Personality and Social Psychology* 12(2), 125–35.

Mumford, E. (1995). *Effective Systems Design and Requirements Analysis: the ETHICS Method*. London, Macmillan.

(1996). 'Risky ideas in the risk society.' *Journal of Information Technology* 11(4), 321–31.

(2000). 'A socio-technical approach to systems design.' *Requirements Engineering* 5(2), 125–33.

(2003). *Redesigning Human Systems*. Hershey, PA, IRM Press.

Mumpower, J. L., and T. R. Stewart (1996). 'Expert judgement and expert disagreement.' *Thinking and Reasoning* 2(2–3), 191–211.

Murphy, A. H., and R. L. Winkler (1984). 'Probability forecasting in meteorology.' *Journal of the American Statistical Society* 79, 489–500.

Mussweiler, T. F., and T. Pfeiffer (2000). 'Overcoming the inevitable anchoring effect: considering the opposite compensates for selective accessibility.' *Personality and Social Psychology Bulletin* 26(9), 1142–50.

Mustajoki, J., R. P. Hämäläinen and M. Marttunen (2004). 'Participatory multi-criteria decision analysis with Web-Hipre: a case of lake regulation policy.' *Environmental Modelling and Software* 19(6), 537–47.

Myers, D. G., and H. Lamm (1976). 'The group polarization phenomenon.' *Psychological Bulletin* 83(4), 602–27.

Mythen, G. (2004). *Ulrich Beck: A Critical Introduction to the Risk Society*. London, Pluto Press.

Nadkarni, S., and P. P. Shenoy (2004). 'A causal mapping approach to constructing Bayesian networks.' *Decision Support Systems* 38(2), 259–81.

Narahari, Y., C. V. L. Raju, K. Ravikumar and S. Shah (2005). 'Dynamic pricing models for electronic business.' *Sādhanā* 30(2–3), 231–56.

Naude, P., A. G. Lockett, G. Islei and P. Drinkwater (2000). 'An exploration into the influence of psychological profiles upon group decision making.' *Journal of the Operational Research Society* 51(2), 168–75.

Neely, A. D., C. Adams and M. Kennerley (2002). *The Performance Prism*. London, Financial Times/Prentice Hall.

Neely, A. D., M. Gregory and K. Platts (2005). 'Performance measurement system design A literature review and research agenda.' *International Journal of Operations & Production Management* 25(12), 1228–63.

Newell, B. R., and D. Lagnado (2003). 'Think-tanks, or think tanks.' *The Psychologist* 16(4), 176.

Newell, B. R., and D. Fernandez (2006). 'On the binary quality of recognition and the inconsequentiality of further knowledge: two critical tests of the recognition heuristic.' *Journal of Behavioral Decision Making* 19(4), 333–46.

Newell, B. R., D. A. Lagnado and D. R. Shanks (2007). *Straight Choices: The Psychology of Decision Making*. Hove, Psychology Press.

Ngwenyama, O. K., N. Bryson and A. Mobolurin (1996). 'Supporting facilitation in group support systems: techniques for analyzing consensus relevant data.' *Decision Support Systems* 16(2), 155–68.

Nonaka, I. (1991). 'The knowledge- creating company.' *Harvard Business Review* 6(8), 96–104.

(1999). 'The dynamics of knowledge creation.' In R. Ruggles and D. Holtshouse (eds.), *The Knowledge Advantage*. Dover, NH, Capstone, 63–87.

Nonaka, I., and R. Toyama (2003). 'The knowledge-creating theory revisited: knowledge creation as a synthesising process.' *Knowledge Management Research and Practice* 1(1), 2–10.

Nunamaker, J. F., L. M. Applegate and B. R. Konsynski (1988). 'Computer-aided deliberation: model management and group decision support.' *Operations Research* 36(6), 826–48.

Nunamaker, J. F., A. R. Dennis, J. E. George, J. S. Valacich and D. R. Vogel (1991). 'Electronic meeting systems to support group work: theory and practice at Arizona.' *Communications of ACM* 34(7), 40–61.

Nutt, P. C. (1984). 'Types of organizational decision processes.' *Administrative Science Quarterly* 29(3), 414–50.

(1993). 'The formulation processes and tactics used in organizational decision making.' *Organization Science* 4(2), 226.

O'Brien, F. A., and R. G. Dyson (eds.) (2007). *Supporting Strategy: Frameworks, Methods and Models*. Chichester, John Wiley and Sons.

O'Hagan, A. (2005). 'Elicitation.' *Significance* 2(2), 84–6.

O'Hagan, A., C. E. Buck, A. Daneshkhah, R. Eiser, P. H. Garthwaite, D. Jenkinson, J. E. Oakley and T. Rakow (2006). *Uncertain Judgements: Eliciting Experts' Probabilities*. Chichester, John Wiley and Sons.

O'Hagan, A., and J. Forester (2004). *Bayesian Statistics*. London, Hodder Arnold.

O'Hagan, A., M. C. Kennedy and J. E. Oakley (1998). 'Uncertainty analysis and other inference tools for complex computer codes.' In J. M. Bernardo, J. O. Berger, A. P. Dawid and A. F. M. Smith (eds.), *Bayesian Statistics 6*. Oxford, Oxford University Press, 503–24.

O'Keefe, R. M., O. Balci and E. P. Smith (1987). 'Validating expert system performance.' *IEEE Expert* 2(4), 81–90.

O'Keefe, R. M., and A. D. Preece (1996). 'The development, validation and implementation of knowledge-based systems.' *European Journal of Operational Research* 92(3), 458–73.

O'Reilly, T. (2005). 'What is Web 2.0? Design patterns and business models for the next generation of software.' www.oreillynet.com/pub/a/oreilly/tim/news/2005/09/30/what-is-web-20.html (accessed 19 March 2008).

Oliver, R. M., and J. Q. Smith (eds.) (1990). *Influence Diagrams, Belief Nets and Decision Analysis.* Chichester, John Wiley and Sons.

Olson, D. L. (2001). 'Rationality in information systems support to decision making.' *Information Systems Frontiers* 3(2), 239–48.

Ormerod, R. J. (2002). 'On the nature of OR: taking stock.' *Journal of the Operational Research Society* 53(8), 475–91.

Orwell, G. (1945). *Animal Farm.* London, Secker and Warburg.

Osborne, M. J. (2003). *An Introduction to Game Theory.* Oxford, Oxford University Press.

Oughton, D., and I. Bay (2002). *Ethical Considerations for Communication Strategies.* Ås, Agricultural University of Norway.

Papadakis, V. M., S. Lioukas and D. Chambers (1998). 'Strategic decision-making processes: the role of management and context.' *Strategic Management Journal* 19(2), 115–47.

Papamichail, K. N., G. Alves, S., French, J.-B. Yang and R. Snowdon (2007). 'Facilitation practices in decision workshops.' *Journal of the Operational Research Society* 58(5), 614–32.

Papamichail, K. N., and S. French (2003). 'Explaining and justifying the advice of a decision support system: a natural language generation approach.' *Expert Systems with Applications* 24(1) 35–48.

Papamichail, K. N., and S. French (2005). 'Design and evaluation of an intelligent decision support system for nuclear emergencies.' *Decision Support Systems* 41(1), 84–111.

Papamichail, K. N., and S. M. Maridakis (2006). 'Developing the next generation of decision support systems: a human-centered approach.' Paper presented at the sixty-sixth annual meeting of the Academy of Management, Atlanta, 16 August.

Papamichail, K. N., and V. Rajaram (2007). *A Framework for Assessing Best Practice in Decision Making.* Paper presented at the ninth International Decision Sciences Institute conference, Bangkok, 12 July.

Papamichail, K. N., and I. Robertson (2005). 'Integrating decision making and regulation in the management control process.' *Omega* 33(4), 319–32.

Papazoglou, I. A., and M. D. Christou (1997). 'A decision support system for emergency response to major nuclear accidents.' *Nuclear Technology* 118(2), 97–122.

Paradice, D. (2007). 'Expanding the boundaries of DSS.' *Decision Support Systems* 43(4), 1549–52.

Pardalos, P. M., Y. Siskos and C. Zopounidis (eds.) (1995). *Advances in Multi-Criteria Analysis.* Dordrecht, Kluwer.

Patternaik, P. K. (1978). *Strategy and Group Choice.* Amsterdam, North-Holland.

Payne, J. W. (1976). 'Task complexity and contingent processing in decision making: an information search and protocol analysis.' *Organizational Behavior and Human Performance* 16(2), 366–87.

(1997). 'The scarecrow's search: a cognitive psychologist's perspective on organizational decision making.' In Z. Shapira (ed.), *Organizational Decision Making*. Cambridge University Press, 353–74.

Payne, J. W., J. R. Bettman and E. J. Johnson (1993). *The Adaptive Decision Maker*. Cambridge, Cambridge University Press.

Pearce, D. W., and C. A. Nash (1981). *The Social Appraisal of Projects: A Text in Cost–Benefit Analysis*. London, Macmillan.

Pearl, J. (2000). *Causality, Models, Reasoning and Inference*. Cambridge, Cambridge University Press.

Pearlson, K. E., and C. S. Saunders (2006). *Manageing and Using Information Systems*, 3rd edn. New York, John Wiley and Sons.

Pearson, D. (1998). 'Arthur Andersen KnowledgeSpace: Where are they now?' *CIO Magazine* 15 May, www.cio.com/archives/051598/revisit.html (accessed 22 March 2006).

Petit, C. W. (1998). 'Touched by nature: putting evolution to work on the assembly line.' www.genetic-programming.com/published/usnwr072798.html (accessed 6 April 2006).

Pettigrew, A. M. (1972). 'Information control as a power resource.' *Sociology* 6(2), 187–204.

Pettigrew, A. M. (1973). *The Politics of Organisational Decision-making*, London, Tavistock.

Petts, J., A.-J. Gray and S. Pollard (2002). *Participatory Risk Assessment: Characterising Environmental Agency Decisions on Risk*, Technical Report E2-043/TR/02. Bristol, Enviroment Agency.

Pfeffer, J., and G. R. Salancik (1974). 'Organizational decision making as a political process: the case of a university budget.' *Administrative Science Quarterly* 19(2), 135–51.

Phillips, L. D. (1982). 'Requisite decision making: a case study.' *Journal of the Operational Research Society* 33(4), 303–11.

(1984). 'A theory of requisite decision models.' *Acta Psychologica* 56(1–3), 29–48.

Phillips, L. D., and M. C. Phillips (1993). 'Facilitated work groups – theory and practice.' *Journal of the Operational Research Society* 44(6), 533–49.

Phillips, N. (2000). *The Phillips Report on the BSE Crisis*. London, HMSO.

Phillips-Wren, G., M. Mora, G. A. Forgionne, L. Garrido and J. N. D. Gupta (2006). 'A multicriteria model for the evaluation of intelligent decision-making support systems (i-DMSS).' In J. N. D. Gupta, G. A. Forgionne and M. Mora (eds.), *Intelligent Decision-making Support Systems*. London, Springer, 3–24.

Pick, R. A. (2008). 'Benefits of decision support systems'. In F. Burstein and C. W. Holsapple (eds.), *Handbook on Decision Support Systems 2*. Berlin, Springer, 719–30.

Pidd, M. (1996). *Tools for Thinking: Modelling in Management Science.* Chichester, John Wiley and Sons.

(1998). *Computer Simulation in Management Science,* 4th edn. Chichester, John Wiley and Sons.

(ed.) (2004). *Systems Modelling: Theory and Practice.* Chichester, John Wiley and Sons.

Pinfield, L. T. (1986). 'A field evaluation of perspectives on organizational decision making.' *Administrative Science Quarterly* 31(3), 365–88.

Pole, A., M. West and J. Harrison (1994). *Applied Bayesian Forecasting and Time Series Analysis.* London, Chapman and Hall.

Polyani, M. (1962). *Personal Knowledge.* New York, Anchor Day Books.

Poortinga, W., K. Bickerstaff, I. Langford, J. Niewohner and N. Pidgeon (2004). 'The British 2001 foot and mouth crisis: a comparative study of public risk perceptions, trust and beliefs about government policy in two communities.' *Journal of Risk Research* 7(1), 73–90.

Port, O. (2002). 'The next Web.' *BusinessWeek* 4 March, www.businessweek.com/magazine/content/02_09/b3772108.htm (accessed 23 March 2006).

Porter, M. E. (1988). *Competitive Strategy: Techniques for Analysing Industries and Competitors.* New York, Free Press.

Portney, P. R., and J. P. Weyant (1999). *Discounting and Intergenerational Equity.* Washington, DC, Resources for the Future.

Power, D. J. (2002). *Decision Support Systems: Concepts and Resources for Managers.* Westport, CO, Quorum Books.

Poyhonen, M., and R. P. Hämäläinen (2000). 'There is hope in attribute weighting.' *Journal of Information Systems and Operational Research* 38(3), 272–82.

Prado, P., and R. Bolado (eds.) (2001). *SAMO 2001: Third Intrnational Symposium on Sensitivity Analysis of Model Output.* Madrid, Ciemat.

Puterman, M. L. (1994). *Markov Decision Processes.* New York, John Wiley and Sons.

Ragsdale, C. T. (2001). *Spreadsheet Modelling and Decision Analysis.* Cincinnati, South Western College Publishing.

Raiffa, H. (1968). *Decision Analysis: Introductory Lectures on Choice under Uncertainty.* Reading, MA, Addison Wesley.

(1982). *The Art and Science of Negotiation: How to Resolve Conflicts and Get the Best out of Bargaining.* Cambridge MA, Belknap Press.

Raiffa, H., J. Richardson and D. Metcalfe (2003). *Negotiation Analysis: The Science and Art of Collaborative Decision Making.* Cambridge, MA, Harvard University Press.

Rajagopalan, N., A. M. A. Rasheed and D. K. Datta (1993). 'Strategic decision processes: critical review and future directions.' *Journal of Management* 19(2), 349.

Rasmussen, B., K. K. Jensen and P. Sandoe (2007). 'Transparency in decision-making processes governing hazardous activities.' *International Journal of Technology, Policy and Management* 7(4), 422–38.

Reagan-Cirincione, P. (1994). 'Improving the accuracy of group judgment: a process intervention combining group facilitation, social judgment analysis, and information technology.' *Organizational Behavior and Human Decision Processes* 58(2), 246–70.

Reason, J. (1987). 'Cognitive aids in process environments: prostheses or tools?' *International Journal of Man–Machine Studies* 27(5–6), 463–70.

Rees, N. (1978). *Quote . . . Unquote*. London, George Allen & Unwin.

Regan, P. J., and S. Holtzman (1995). 'R&D advisor: an interactive approach to normative decision system model construction.' *European Journal of Operational Research* 84(1), 116–33.

Renn, O. (1998a). 'The role of risk communication and public dialogue for improving risk management.' *Risk, Decision and Policy* 3(1) 5–30.

  (1998b). 'Three decades of risk research: accomplishments and new challenges.' *Journal of Risk Research* 1(1), 49–72.

  (1999). 'A model for an analytic-deliberative process in risk management.' *Environmental Science and Technology* 33(18), 3049–55.

Renn, O., and D. Levine (1991). 'Credibility and trust in risk communication.' In R. E. Kasperson and P. J. M. Stallen (eds.), *Communicating Risks to the Public in the Netherlands*. The Hague, Kluwer Academic, 175–218.

Renn, O., T. Webler and P. Wiedermann (eds.) (1995). *Fairness and Competence in Citizen Participation: Evaluating Models and Environmental Discourse*. Dordrecht, Kluwer.

Renooij, S. (2001). 'Probability elicitation for belief networks: issues to consider.' *Knowledge Engineering Review* 16(3), 255–69.

Rickards, T. (1999). 'Brainstorming.' In M. A. Runco and S. R. Pritzker (eds.), *Encyclopaedia of Creativity*, vol. I. New York, Academic Press, 219–27.

Ríos, J., and D. Ríos Insua (2008). 'A framework for participatory budget elaboration support.' *Journal of the Operational Research Society* 59(2), 203–12.

Ríos Insua, D. (1990). *Sensitivity Analysis in Multi-Objective Decision Making*. Berlin, Springer-Verlag.

  (ed.) (1999). 'Sensitivity analysis in MCDA.' *Journal of Multi-Criteria Decision Analysis* 8(3), 117–87.

  (ed.) (2008). Special issue: 'e-democracy.' *Group Decision and Negotiation* 17(3).

Ríos Insua, D., and S. French (1991). 'A framework for sensitivity analysis in discrete multi-objective decision making.' *European Journal of Operational Research* 54(2), 176–90.

Ríos Insua, D., J. Holgado and R. Moreno (2003). 'Multicriteria e-negotiation systems for e-democracy.' *Journal of Multi-Criteria Decision Analysis* 12(2–3), 213–18.

Ríos Insua, D., and F. Ruggeri (2000). *Robust Bayesian Analysis*. New York, Springer-Verlag.

Robert, C. P. (1994). *The Bayesian Choice: A Decison-Theoretic Motivation*. New York, Springer Verlag.

Roberto, M. A. (2005). 'Why making the decisions the right way is more important than making the right decisions.' *Ivey Business Journal* 70(1), 1–7.

Roberts, F. S. (1979). *Measurement Theory*. New York, Academic Press.

Roberts, K. H. (1990). 'Some characterisitics of one type of high reliability organisation.' *Organization Science* 1(2), 160–76.

Rodrigues, B. S., and D. J. Hickson (1995). 'Success in decision making: different organizations, differing reasons for success.' *Journal of Management Studies* 32(5), 655–78.

Rosenhead, J., and J. Mingers (eds.) (2001). *Rational Analysis for a Problematic World Revisited*. Chichester, John Wiley and Sons.

Ross, L., and C. A. Anderson (1982). 'Shortcomings in the attribution process: on the origins and maintenance of erroneous social assessments.' In D. Kahneman, P. Slovic and A. Tversky (eds.), *Judgement under Uncertainty: Heuristics and Biases*. Cambridge, Cambridge University Press, 129–52.

Roubens, M. (1997). 'Fuzzy sets and decision analysis.' *Fuzzy Sets and Systems* 90(2), 199–206.

Rowe, G., and L. J. Frewer (2000). 'Public participation methods: a framework for evaluation.' *Science, Technology, and Human Values* 25(1), 3–29.

   (2005). 'A typology of public engagement methods.' *Science, Technology, and Human Values* 30(2), 251–90.

Rowe, G., T. Horlick-Jones, J. Walls and N. Pidgeon (2005). 'Difficulties in evaluating public engagement initiatives: reflections on an evaluation of the UK *GM Nation?* public debate.' *Public Understanding of Science* 14(4), 331–52.

Rowe, G., and G. Wright (1999). 'The Delphi technique as a forecasting tool: issues and analysis.' *International Journal of Forecasting* 15(4), 353–75.

Roxburgh, C. (2003). 'Hidden flaws in strategy.' *McKinsey Quarterly* 2003(2), 26–39.

Roy, B. (1996). *Multicriteria Methodology for Decision Aiding*. Dordrecht, Kluwer Academic.

Roy, B., and D. Vanderpooten (1996). 'The European school of MCDA: emergence, basic features, and current works.' *Journal of Multi-Criteria Decision Analysis* 5(1), 22–36.

   (eds.) (1997). Special edition: '20th anniversary of the European Working Group 'Multicriteria Aid for Decisions.' *Journal of Multi-Criteria Decision Analysis* 6(2).

Rubin, G. J., L. Page, O. Morgan, R. J. Pinder, P. Riley, S. Hatch, H. Maguire, M. Catchpole, J. Simpson and S. Wessely (2007). 'Public information needs after the poisoning of Alexander Litvinenko with polonium-210 in London: cross-sectional telephone survey and qualitative analysis.' *British Medical Journal* 335, 1143–6.

Ruggles, R., and D. Holtshouse (eds.) (1999). *The Knowledge Advantage*. Dover, NH, Capstone.

Russo, J. E., and P. Schoemaker (2002). *Winning Decisions: Getting It Right the First Time*. New York, Currency/Doubleday.

Rustem, B. (1998). *Algorithms for Nonlinear Programming and Multiple-objective Decisions*. Chichester, John Wiley and Sons.

Ryle, G. (1949). *The Concept of Mind*. London, Hutchinson.

Saaty, T. L. (1980). *The Analytical Hierarchy Process*. New York, McGraw-Hill.

(1990). 'An exposition of the AHP in reply to the paper "Remarks on the analytic hierarchy process".' *Management Science* 36(3), 259–68.

Saaty, T. L., and L. G. Vargas (1984a). 'Inconsistency and rank preservation.' *Journal of Mathematical Psychology* 28(2), 205–14.

(1984b). 'The legitimacy of rank reversal.' *Omega* 12(5), 513–16.

Sage, A. P., and W. B. Rouse (1999). 'Information systems frontiers in knowledge management.' *Information Systems Frontiers* 1(3), 205–19.

Salancik, G. R., and J. Pfeffer (1978). 'A social information processing approach to job attitudes and task design.' *Administrative Science Quarterly* 23(2), 224–53.

Salo, A., and R. P. Hämäläinen (1997). 'On the measurement of preferences in the analytical hierarchy process (with discussion).' *Journal of Multi-Criteria Decision Analysis* 6(6), 309–43.

Saltelli, A., K. Chan and E. M. Scott (eds.) (2000). *Sensitivity Analysis.* Chichester, John Wiley and Sons.

Saltelli, A., S. Tarantola, F. Campolongo and M. Ratto (2004). *Sensitivity Analysis in Practice: A Guide to Assessing Scientific Models.* Chichester, John Wiley and Sons.

Sankar, C. S., F. N. Ford and M. Bauer (1995). 'A DSS user interface model to provide consistency and adaptability.' *Decision Support Systems* 13(1), 93–104.

Santos, F. M. (2003). 'The role of information technologies for knowledge management in firms.' *International Journal of Technology, Policy and Management* 3(2), 194–203.

Sarma, V. V. S. (1994). 'Decision making in complex systems.' *Systems Practice* 7(4), 399–407.

Sauter, V. L. (1997). *Decision Support Systems.* New York, John Wiley and Sons.

(1999). 'Intuitive decision-making.' *Communications of the ACM* 42(6), 109–15.

Savage, L. J. (1972). *The Foundations of Statistics*, 2nd edn. New York, Dover.

Schoemaker, P. (1993). 'Multiple scenario development: its conceptual and behavioural foundation.' *Strategic Management Journal* 14(3), 193–213.

Schultz-Hardt, S., M. Jochims and D. Frey (2002). 'Productive conflict in group decision making: genuine and contrived dissent as strategies to counteract biased information seeking.' *Organizational Behavior and Human Decision Processes* 88(2), 563–86.

Schwartz, B. (2004). *The Paradox of Choice: Why More Is Less.* New York, HarperCollins.

Schwarz, N. (2000). 'Emotion, cognition, and decision making.' *Cognition and Emotion* 14(4), 433–40.

Schwarz, N., and G. L. Clore (1996). 'Feelings and phenomenal experiences.' In E. T. Higgins and A. Kruglanski (eds.), *Social Psychology: Handbook of Basic Principles.* New York, Guilford, 433–65.

Schweiger, D. M., W. R. Sandberg and J. W. Ragan (1986). 'Group approaches for improving strategic decision making: a comparative analysis of dialectical inquiry, devil's advocacy, and consensus.' *Academy of Management Journal* 29(1), 51–71.

Schwenk, C. R. (1985). 'Management illusions and biases: their impact on strategic decisions.' *Long Range Planning* 18(5), 74–80.

(1990). 'Effects of devil's advocacy and dialectical inquiry on decision making: a meta-analysis.' *Organizational Behavior and Human Decision Processes* 47(1), 161–76.

Scott Morton, M. S. (1971). *Management Decision Systems: Computer-based Support for Decision Making*. Cambridge, MA, Harvard University Press.

(ed.) (1991). *The Corporation of the 1990s: Information Technology and Organisational Transformation*. Oxford, Oxford University Press.

Searle, J. R. (1969). *Speech Acts*. Cambridge, Cambridge University Press.

Seffino, L. A., C. B. Medeiros, J. V. Rocha and B. Yi (1999). 'Woodss: a spatial decision support system based on workflows.' *Decision Support Systems* 27(1–2), 105–23.

Seifert, J. W. (2002). *Visualization, Presentation, Moderation: A Practical Guide to Successful Presentation and Facilitation of Business Processes*, 2nd edn. Weinheim, Germany, Wiley-VCH Verlag.

Shapira, Z. (ed.) (1997). *Organizational Decision Making*. Cambridge, Cambridge University Press.

Sheppard, S. R. J., and M. Meitner (2005). 'Using multi-criteria analysis and visualisation for sustainable forest management planning with stakeholder groups.' *Forest Ecology and Management* 207(1–2), 171–87.

Shim, J. P., M. Warkentin, J. F. Courtney, D. J. Power, R. Sharda and C. Carlsson (2002). 'Past, present, and future of decision support technology.' *Decision Support Systems* 33(2), 111–26.

Sieck, W., and J. F. Yates (1997). 'Exposition effects on decision making: choice and confidence in choice.' *Organizational Behavior and Human Decision Processes* 70(3), 207–19.

Silver, E. A. (2004). 'An overview of heuristic solution methods.' *Journal of the Operational Research Society* 55(9), 936–56.

Silver, M. S. (1991). *Systems that Support Decision Makers: Description and Analysis*. Chichester, John Wiley and Sons.

Silverman, B. G. (1995). 'Knowledge-based systems and the decision sciences.' *Interfaces* 25(6), 67–82.

Simon, H. A. (1957). *Administrative Behavior*. New York, Free Press.

(1960). *The New Science of Management Decision*. New York, Harper and Row.

(1973). 'Applying information technology to organization design.' *Public Administration Review* 33(3), 268–78.

(1978). 'Rationality as a process and as a product of thought.' *American Economic Review* 68(2), 1–16.

(1986). *Decision Making and Problem Solving*. Washington, DC, National Academy Press.

(1987). 'Making management decisions: the role of intuition and emotion.' *Academy of Management Executive* 1(1), 57–64.

Simons, R. (1995). *Levers of Control: How Managers Can Use Innovative Control Systems to Drive Strategic Renewal*. Boston, Harvard University Press.

Simons, R. (2000). *Performance Measurement and Control Systems for Implementing Strategy: Text and Cases.* Upper Saddle River, NJ, Prentice Hall.

Singh, D. T. (1998). 'Incorporating cognitive aids into decision support systems: the case of the strategy execution process.' *Decision Support Systems* 24(2), 145–63.

Singh, K. S., H. J. Watson and R. T. Watson (2002). 'EIS support for the strategic management process.' *Decision Support Systems* 33(1), 71–85.

Slack, N., S. Chambers and R. Johnston (2004). *Operations Management*, 4th edn. Harlow, FT Prentice Hall.

Slovic, P. (1986). 'Informing and educating the public about risk.' *Risk Analysis* 6(4), 403–15.

(1993). 'Perceived risk, trust and democracy.' *Risk Analysis* 13(6) 675–82.

(1995). 'The construction of preference.' *American Psychologist* 50(5), 364–71.

(1997). 'Trust, emotion, sex, politics and science: surveying the risk-assessment battlefield.' In M. Bazerman, D. Messick, A. Tenbrunsel and K. Wade-Benzoni (eds.), *Environment, Ethics and Behaviour.* San Francisco, New Lexington Press, 277–313.

(2001). *Perceptions of Risk.* London, Earthscan Library.

Slovic, P., M. L. Finucane, E. Peters and D. G. MacGregor (2004). 'Risk as analysis and risk as feelings: some thoughts about affect, reason, risk and rationality.' *Risk Analysis* 24(2), 311–22.

Slovic, P., and S. Lichtenstein (1971). 'Comparison of Bayesian and regression approaches to the study of information processing in judgment.' *Organizational Behavior and Human Performance* 6(6) 649–744.

Slovic, P., and A. Tversky (1974). 'Who accepts Savage's axioms?' *Behavioral Science* 19, 368–73.

Smith, J. E., and R. Winkler (2006). 'The optimizer's curse: skepticism and post-decision surprise in decision analysis.' *Management Science* 52(3), 311–22.

Smith, J. Q. (1988). *Decision Analysis: A Bayesian Approach.* London, Chapman and Hall.

(1996). 'Plausible Bayesian games.' In J. M. Bernardo, J. O. Berger, A. P. Dawid and A. F. M. Smith (eds.), *Bayesian Statistics 5.* Oxford, Oxford University Press, 387–406.

Sniezek, J. A. (1992). 'Groups under uncertainty: an examination of confidence in group decision making.' *Organizational Behavior and Human Decision Processes* 52(1), 124–55.

Sniezek, J. A., and R. A. Henry (1989). 'Accuracy and confidence in group judgment.' *Organizational Behavior and Human Decision Processes* 43(1), 1–28.

Snowden, D. (2002). 'Complex acts of knowing: paradox and descriptive self-awareness.' *Journal of Knowledge Management* 6(2), 100–11.

Snowden, D., and M. Boone (2007). 'A leader's framework for decision making.' *Harvard Business Review* 85(11), 68–76.

Snyder, R. C., and G. D. Paige (1958). 'The United States' decision to resist aggression in Korea: the application of an analytical scheme.' *Administrative Science Quarterly* 3(3), 341–78.

Soll, J. B., and J. Klayman (2004). 'Overconfidence in interval estimates.' *Journal of Experimental Psychology: Learning, Memory and Cognition* 30(2), 299–314.

Spetzler, C. S. (2007). 'Building decision competency in organizations.' In W. Edwards, R. F. Miles and D. von Winterfeldt (eds.), *Advances in Decision Analysis: From Foundations to Applications.* Cambridge, Cambridge University Press, 451–68.

Sprague, R. H., and E. D. Carlson (1982). *Building Effective Decision Support Systems.* Upper Saddle River, NJ, Prentice Hall.

Staël von Holstein, C.-A. S. (1970). *Assessment and Evaluation of Subjective Probability Distributions.* Stockholm, Economic Research Institute, Stockholm School of Economics.

Starr, M. K., and M. Zeleny (1977). 'MCDM: state and future of the art.' In M. K. Starr and M. Zeleny (eds.), *Multi-criteria Decision Making.* Dordrecht, North Holland, 5–29.

Steffek, J., and C. Kissling (2007). *Civil Society Participation in European and Global Governance: A Cure for the Democratic Deficit?* New York, Palgrave Macmillan.

Steiner, I. D. (1972). *Group Processes and Productivity.* New York, Academic Press.

Sternberg, R. J. (1985). *Beyond IQ: A Triarchic Theory of Human Intelligence.* New York, Cambridge University Press.

Stewart, T. A. (ed.) (2006). Special edition: 'Decision making'. *Harvard Business Review* 84(1), 12–134.

Stillwell, W. G., D. von Winterfeldt and R. S. John (1987). 'Comparing hierarchical and non-hierarchical weighting methods for eliciting multi-attribute value models.' *Management Science* 33(4) 442–50.

Stoner, J. (1961). *A Comparison of Individual and Group Decisions Involving Risk*, MA thesis. School of Industrial Management, Massachusetts Institute of Technology, Cambridge, MA.

Suantak, L., F. Bolger and W. R. Ferrell (1996). 'The hard–easy effect in subjective probability calibration.' *Organizational Behavior and Human Decision Processes* 67(2), 201–21.

Subbotin, V. (1996). 'Outcome feedback effects on under- and over-confident judgements (general knowledge tasks).' *Organizational Behavior and Human Decision Processes* 66(3) 268–76.

Sudweeks, F., and M. Allbritton (1996). 'Working together apart: communication and collaboration in a networked group.' In C. D. Keen, C. Urquhart and J. Lamp (eds.), *Proceedings of the 7th Australasian Conference of Information Systems (ACIS96)*, vol. II. Hobart, Department of Computer Science, University of Tasmania, 701–12.

Suppes, P., D. H. Krantz, R. D. Luce and A. Tversky (1989). *Foundations of Measurement Theory*, vol. II: *Geometrical, Threshold and Probabilistic Representations.* San Diego, Academic Press.

Susskind, L., and P. Field (1996). *Dealing with an Angry Public: The Mutual Gains Approach.* New York, Free Press.

Sutcliffe, K. M., and G. McNamara. (2001). 'Controlling decision-making practice in organizations.' *Organization Science* 12(4), 484–501.

Svenson, O. (1979). 'Process descriptions of decision making.' *Organizational Behavior and Human Performance* 23(1), 86–112.

(1998). 'Multi-criteria decision aids and human decision making: two worlds?' *Journal of Multi-Criteria Decision Analysis* 7(6), 353–4.

Sviokla, J. J. (1990). 'An examination of the impact of expert systems on the firm: the case of XCON.' *MIS Quarterly* 4(2), 127–42.

Swartout, W. R. (1983). 'XPLAIN: a system for creating and explaining expert consulting systems.' *Artificial Intelligence* 21(3), 285–325.

(1990). 'Explanation.' In S. C. Shapiro (ed.), *Encyclopedia of Artificial Intelligence.* Chichester, John Wiley and Sons, 298–300.

'T Hart, P. (1998). 'Preventing groupthink revisited: evaluating and reforming groups in government.' *Organizational Behavior and Human Decision Processes* 73(2–3), 306–26.

Taha, H. A. (2006). *Operations Research*, 8th edn. Englewood Cliffs, NJ Prentice Hall.

Tapiero, C. (2004). *Risk and Financial Management.* Chichester, John Wiley and Sons.

Taylor, A. D. (1995). *Mathematics and Politics.* New York, Springer-Verlag.

(2005). *Social Choice and the Mathematics of Manipulation.* Cambridge, Cambridge University Press.

Teale, M., V. Dispenza, J. Flynn and D. Currie (2003). *Management Decision Making: Towards an Integrative Approach.* London, FT Prentice Hall.

ten Have, S., W. ten Have, F. Stevens and M. van der Elst (2003). *Key Management Models.* London, FT Prentice Hall.

Teradata (2004). *Enterprise Decision Making 2004–2005.* Miamisburg, OH, Teradata.

(2006). *Enterprise Decision-Making 2006–2007.* Miamisburg, OH, Teradata.

Thé, L. (1996). 'AI automates a help desk.' *Datamation* 42(2), 54–8.

Theil, M. (2002). 'The role of translations of verbal into numerical probability expressions in risk management: a meta-analysis.' *Journal of Risk Research* 5(2), 177–86.

Thompson, M., R. Ellis and A. Wildavsky (1990). *Cultural Theory.* Boulder, CO, Westview.

Tracy, K. W., and K. Bouthoorn (1997). *Object-Oriented Artificial Intelligence Using C++.* Basingstoke, Computer Science Press.

Trzaskalik, T., and J. Michnik (eds.) (2002). *Multiple Objective and Goal Programming.* Heidelberg, Physica-Verlag.

Tsang, F. M. F., D. W. M. Yeung, A. H. W. Chun and S. H. C. Chan (2000). 'Stand-allocation system (SAS): a constraint-based system developed with software components.' *AI Magazine* 21(4), 63–74.

Tufte, E. R. (1997). *Visual Explanations.* Connecticut, Graphics Press.

Tulloch, G. (1998). *On Voting: A Public Choice Approach.* Cheltenham, Edward Elgar.

Tulving, E., and W. Donaldson (eds.) (1972). *Organization of Memory.* New York, Academic Press.

Turban, E., and J. E. Aronson (2001). *Decision Support Systems and Intelligent Systems*, 6th edn. Upper Saddle River, NJ, Prentice Hall.

Turban, E., J. E. Aronson and T.-P. Liang (2005). *Decision Support Systems and Intelligent Systems*, 7th edn. Upper Saddle River, NJ, Prentice Hall.

Turban, E., J. E. Aronson, T.-P. Liang and R. Sharda (2006). *Decision Support and Business Intelligence Systems*, 8th edn. Upper Saddle River NJ, Prentice Hall.

Turban, E., E. McLean and J. Wetherbe (2004). *Information Technology for Management: Transforming Organizations in the Digital Economy*. Hoboken, NJ, John Wiley and Sons.

Turing, A. M. (1950). 'Computing, machinery and intelligence.' *Mind* 59, 433–60.

Turner, M. E., and A. R. Pratkanis (eds.) (1998). Special edition: 'Twenty-five years of groupthink theory and research.' *Organizational Behavior and Human Decision Processes* 73(2–3), 103–376.

Tversky, A. (1967). 'Utility theory and additivity analysis of risky choices.' *Journal of Experimental Psychology* 75(1), 27–36.

  (1969). 'Intransitivity of preferences.' *Psychological Review* 76(1), 31–48.

  (1972). 'Elimination by aspects: a theory of choice.' *Psychological Review* 79(4), pp. 281–99.

Tversky, A., and D. Kahneman (1981). 'The framing of decisions and the psychology of choice.' *Science* 211, 453–8.

  (1983). 'Extensional versus intuitive reasoning: the conjunction fallacy in probability judgment.' *Psychological Review* 90(4), 293–315.

Van Binsbergen, J. H., and L. M. Larx (2007). 'Exploring relations between decision analysis and game theory.' *Decision Analysis* 4(1), 32–40.

Van Heijst, D., R. Potharst and M. van Wezel, (2008). 'A support system for predicting eBay end prices.' *Decision Support Systems* 44(4), 970–82.

Vlek, C. (1996). 'A multi-level, multi-stage and multi-attribute perspective on risk assessment, decision making and control.' *Risk Decision and Policy* 1(1), 9–31.

Von Neumann, J., and O. Morgenstern (1947). *Theory of Games and Economic Behavior*, 2nd edn. Princeton, NJ, Princeton University Press.

Von Winterfeldt, D., and W. Edwards (1986). *Decision Analysis and Behavioural Research*. Cambridge, Cambridge University Press.

Waisel, L. B., W. A. Wallace and T. R. Willemain (2008). 'Visualizaton and model formulation: an analysis of sketches of expert modellers.' *Journal of the Operational Research Society* 59(3), 353–61.

Wakker, P. (2004). 'On the composition of risk preference and belief.' *Psychological Review* 111(1), 236–41.

Wald, A. (1945). 'Statistical decision functions which minimise the maximum risk.' *Annals of Mathematics* 46(2), 265–80.

Walsham, G. (2001). 'Knowledge management: the benefits and limitations of computer systems.' *European Management Journal* 19(6), 599–608.

Walsham, G., and S. Sahay (1999). 'GIS for district-level administration in India: problems and opportunities.' *Management information Systems Quarterly* 23(1), 39–66.

Warboys, B., P. Kawalek, I. Robertson and M. Greenwood (1999). *Business Information Systems: A Process Approach.* London, McGraw-Hill.

Waterman, D. A. (1986). *A Guide to Expert Systems.* New York, Addison-Wesley.

Watson, H. J., and M. M. Hill (1983). 'Decision support systems or what didn't happen with MIS.' *Interfaces* 13(5), 81–8.

Watson, H. J., G. Houdeshel and R. K. Rainer, Jr. (1997). *Building Executive Information Systems and Other Decision Support Applications.* New York, John Wiley and Sons.

Watson, S. R., and D. M. Buede (1987). *Decision Synthesis: The Principles and Practice of Decision Analysis.* Cambridge, Cambridge University Press.

Weaver, M., and T. Morgan (1993). 'Budget making: is there a better way?' *Public Finance and Accountancy* 11 June, 51–6.

Weber, M., F. Eisenfuhr and D. von Winterfeldt (1988). 'The effects of splitting attributes on weights in multiattribute utility measurement.' *Management Science* 34(4), 431–45.

Webler, T. (1995). '"Right" discourse in citizen participation: an evaluative yardstick.' In O. Renn, T. Webler and P. M. Wiedemann (eds.), *Fairness and Competence in Citizen Participation: Evaluating Models for Environmental Discourse.* Dordrecht, Kluwer Academic, 35–86.

   (1999). 'The craft and theory of public participation: a dialectical process.' *Journal of Risk Research* 2(1), 55–71.

Webler, T., S. Tuler and R. Kruger (2001). 'What is a good public participatory process? Five perspectives from the public.' *Environmental Management* 27(3), 435–50.

Wedell, D. H., and U. Bockeholt (1998). 'Moderation of preference reversals in the long run.' *Journal of Experimental Psychology: Human Perception and Performance* 16(2), 429–38.

Weick, K. E. (1987). 'Organizational culture as a source of high reliability.' *California Management Review* 29(2), 112–27.

   (1995). *Sensemaking in Organizations.* Thousand Oaks, CA, Sage.

   (2006). 'The role of imagination in the organising of knowledge.' *European Journal of Information Systems* 15(5), 446–52.

Wells, G. E. (1982). 'The use of decision analysis in Imperial Group.' *Journal of the Operational Research Society* 33(4), 313–18.

Wenstøp, F. (2005). 'Mindsets, rationality and emotion in multi-criteria decision analysis (with discussion).' *Journal of Multi-Criteria Decision Analysis* 13(4), 161–90.

West, M., and J. Harrison (1989). *Bayesian Forecasting and Dynamic Models.* New York, Springer Verlag.

White, D. J. (1975). *Decision Methodology.* Chichester, John Wiley and Sons.

   (1985). *Operational Research.* Chichester, John Wiley and Sons.

Williams, R. (2006). 'Narratives of knowledge and intelligence . . . beyond the tacit and explicit.' *Journal of Knowledge Management* 10(4), 81–99.

Williams, S., and R. J. Taormina (1992). 'Group polarization on business decisions in Singapore.' *Journal of Social Psychology* 132(2), 265–7.

Wilson, J. M., P. S. Goodman and M. A. Cronin (2007). 'Group learning.' *Academy of Management Review* 32(4), 1041–59.

Wilson, R. L., and R. Sharda (1994). 'Bankruptcy prediction using neural networks.' *Decision Support Systems* 11(5), 545–57.

Wilson, T. D. (2002). 'The nonsense of knowledge management.' *Information Research* 8(1), 1–54.

Winn, M. I., and L. R. Keller (2001). 'A modelling methodology for multi-objective multi-stakeholder decisions: implications for research.' *Journal of Management Inquiry* 10(2), 166–81.

Winterstein, D. (2005) 'Brains, cancer and computers: studying the machines that will study us.' *The Register*, 16 August, www.theregister.co.uk/2005/08/16/ bioinformatics_2005_report (accessed 2 March 2006).

Wiper, M. W., and S. French (1995). 'Combining experts' opinions using a normal-Wishart model.' *Journal of Forecasting* 14(1), 25–34.

Wittgenstein, L. (1953). *Philosophical Investigations*. Oxford, Basil Blackwell.

Wren, J. D., and H. R. Garner (2004). 'Shared relationship analysis: ranking set cohesion and commonalities within a literature-derived relationship network.' *Bioinformatics* 20(2), 191–8.

Wright, G. (1984). *Behavioural Decision Theory: An Introduction*. Harmondsworth, Penguin Books.

Wright, G., and P. Ayton (eds.) (1994). *Subjective Probability*. Chichester, John Wiley and Sons.

Wright, G., and P. Goodwin (eds.) (1998). *Forecasting with Judgement*. Chichester, John Wiley and Sons.

(1999a). 'Future-focused thinking: combining scenario planning with decision analysis.' *Journal of Multi-Criteria Decision Analysis* 8(6), 311–21.

(1999b). 'Rethinking value elicitation for personal consequential decisions (with discussion).' *Journal of Multi-Criteria Decision Analysis* 8(1), 3–30.

Xu, X. M., B. Lehaney and S. Clarke (2000). 'Doing it right: a survey of the use of executive information systems in practice.' *OR Insight* 13(2), 3–9.

Yates, J. F., E. S. Veinott and A. L. Palatino (2003). 'Hard decisions, bad decisions: on decision quality and decision aiding'. In S. L. Schneider and J. Shanteau (eds.), *Emerging Perspectives on Judgement and Decision Research*. Cambridge, Cambridge University Press, 13–63.

Yim, N.-H., S.-H. Kim, H.-W. Kim and K.-Y. Kwahk (2004). 'Knowledge-based decision making on higher level strategic concerns: system dynamics approach.' *Expert Systems with Applications* 27(1), 143–58.

Young, K. (2004). 'Mimicking fraudsters.' *The Guardian*, 9 September.

Zajonc, R. B. (1980). 'Feeling and thinking: preferences need no inferences.' *American Psychologist* 35(2), 151–75.

Zionts, S., and J. Wallenius (1976). 'An interactive programming method for solving the multiple criteria problem.' *Management Science* 22(6), 652–63.

Index

For EU product safety concerns, contact us at Calle de José Abascal, 56–1°,
28003 Madrid, Spain or eugpsr@cambridge.org.

www.ingramcontent.com/pod-product-compliance
Ingram Content Group UK Ltd.
Pitfield, Milton Keynes, MK11 3LW, UK
UKHW012201180425
457623UK00020B/347